Arthur Collins

THE
PEERAGE
OF
ENGLAND

Containing
a Genealogical and Historical Account
of All the
Peers of that Kingdom

Volume 4

Elibron Classics
www.elibron.com

Elibron Classics series.

© 2005 Adamant Media Corporation.

ISBN 1-4021-7424-1 (paperback)
ISBN 1-4212-8510-X (hardcover)

This Elibron Classics Replica Edition is an unabridged facsimile of the edition published in 1768 by H. Woodfall, etc., London.

Elibron and Elibron Classics are trademarks of Adamant Media Corporation. All rights reserved.

This book is an accurate reproduction of the original. Any marks, names, colophons, imprints, logos or other symbols or identifiers that appear on or in this book, except for those of Adamant Media Corporation and BookSurge, LLC, are used only for historical reference and accuracy and are not meant to designate origin or imply any sponsorship by or license from any third party.

Mr. COLLINS's PEERAGE OF ENGLAND.

THE PEERAGE OF ENGLAND;

CONTAINING

A Genealogical and Historical ACCOUNT OF ALL THE PEERS of that KINGDOM,

Now exifting, either by Tenure, Summons, or Creation:

Their DESCENTS and COLLATERAL LINES:

Their BIRTHS, MARRIAGES, and ISSUE:

Famous ACTIONS both in WAR and PEACE:

Religious and Charitable DONATIONS:

DEATHS, PLACES of BURIAL, MONUMENTS, EPITAPHS:

And many valuable Memoirs never before printed.

ALSO

Their Paternal COATS of ARMS, CRESTS, SUPPORTERS and MOTTOES, Curioufly engraved on 200 COPPER-PLATES.

Collected from Records, Old Wills, Authentic Manufcripts, our moft approved Hiftorians, and other Authorities, which are cited.

By ARTHUR COLLINS, Efq;

IN SEVEN VOLUMES.

The FOURTH EDITION, carefully Corrected, and continued to the prefent Time.

VOL. IV.

LONDON:

Printed for H. WOODFALL, J. BEECROFT, W. STRAHAN, J. RIVINGTON, W. SANDBY, J. FULLER, R. BALDWIN, L. HAWES, W. CLARKE and R. COLLINS, R. HORSFIELD, W. JOHNSTON, T. CASLON, S. CROWDER, T. LONGMAN, C. RIVINGTON, W. GRIFFIN, M. and J. SHUCKBURGH, W. NICOLL, S. BLADON, M. FOLINGSBY, T. PAYNE, J. ROBSON, T. DAVIES, R. DAVIS, J. ALMON, and H. GARDNER.

MDCCLXVIII.

THE PEERAGE OF ENGLAND.

D'ARCY, Earl of Holdernesse.

AS such, who served the Conqueror in his victorious expedition, were rewarded with lands and possessions; it is highly probable, that Norman de Arecy (as then wrote) the ancestor of the present Earl of Holdernesse, was in the battle of Hastings, Oct. 14, 1066, whereby William Duke of Normandy obtained this kingdom: For the name [a] occurs in the roll of Battel-abbey, and in the list of those who landed with that monarch. And at the time of the general survey, [b] the said Norman de Arecy held no less than thirty-three lordships in Lincolnshire, by the immediate gift of the Conqueror, of which Noctone was one, where he and his descendants had their chief seat for divers generations [c].

This Norman, in 6 William Rufus, being with the King then dangerously ill at Gloucester, when those about him, thinking his case desperate, advis'd a council to be call'd; and the King, repenting him of his sins, promised, if he recovered, to mend his life. Thereupon, as an instance of his contrition, he [d] confirmed to the monks of St. Mary's-abbey, at York, their possessions; to which this Norman de Areci (as he then wrote his name) subscribed as one of the witnesses, and [e] gave at that time to the said abbey three carucates of lands in Brunnum. He was also a [f] witness to the grant made by Billcheld,

[a] Ex tab. ol. m in abb. de bello. Hollinshed, p. 4. [b] Lib. doomsd. in Com' Linc. in scacc regis. [c] Hollinsh. p. 20. [d] Mon. Angl. tom. 1. p. 386. [e] Ibidem. p. 387. [f] Ibid. p. 201.

D'Arcy, Earl of Holderneſſe.

wife of Baldrick of Pecfortun (now Pickton) in Cheſhire, to the convent of St. Werberg in Cheſter.

Robert de Areci (as the name was alſo then wrote) his ſon and heir, gave to the religious at [g] Santoft in Com' Lincoln (a cell to St. Mary's-abbey) the churches of Noƈton and Duneſton, as alſo two parts of the tythes of Fiſceburre, and founded a [h] priory for canons regular of the order of St. Auguſtine, at Nokton before-mentioned, giving them the ſite of the ſaid convent, a meſſuage, and a carucate of land in Nokton. He gave alſo to the monks of [i] Kirkeſtede in Lincolnſhire, certain lands in Duneſton and Nockſton aforeſaid, extending from the great road weſtward, which leadeth through Mere to Scapewiche; and left iſſue [k] Thomas his ſon and heir, alſo [l] Robert a younger ſon.

Which Thomas, anno 1163 (9 Hen. II.) confirm'd that [m] grant made by his father to the monks of Kirkſtede: and being wrote Thomas de Arcy, ſon of Robert de Arcy, confirm'd the [n] gifts of his father and grandfather, to the abbey of St. Mary, York. And on aſſeſſment of the aid, for marrying Maud the king's eldeſt daughter, in 12 Hen. II. it was [o] certified, that he held twenty Knights fees, according to the old acception, with half a Knight's fee, and a fourth part, according to the new; for which, anno 14 Hen. II. he paid [p] thirteen pounds, ſix ſhillings and eight-pence.

He became a peculiar benefaƈtor to the canons of Noƈton afore-mentioned, for having (as it ſeems) by ſome compoſition with the abbot and convent of St. Mary, York, regained the churches of Noƈton, and Duneſton, beſtowed on them by his father (as hath been before obſerv'd) he [q] granted them to that religious houſe, with the church of [r] Cankewell (now Cawkwell in that county) and certain lands, meadows, and woods in and near Noƈton, particularly abutted and bounded. He died on July 15, the feaſt of St. Swithin, 1181, 27 Hen. II. (as appeareth by the [s] preſentment made before the juſtices in eyre, 32 Hen. II.) leaving Thomas his ſon and heir, then 18 years of age; whereupon William Baſſet (then ſheriff of Lincolnſhire) [t] ſeized his whole barony for the King's uſe, and [u] committed it, with the whole ſtock thereon, to Michael d'Arcie. After which [x] Alice his widow, daughter of Ralph Lord D'eincourt, of Granby, in Nottinghamſhire, [y] founder

---

[g] Ibidem, p. 405. [h] Ibid. tom. 2. p. 211. [i] Ibid. tom. 1. p. 309. [k] Ibid. tom. 1. p. 405. [l] Ibid. p. 406. [m] Ibid. p. 809. [n] Ibid. p. 405. [o] Lib. rub. in ſacc. titl. Linc. [p] Rot. pip. anno 14 Hen. II. Linc. [q] Mon. Angl. tom. 2. p. 211. [r] Ibid. [s t u] Rot. de dominab. pueris & puellis penes remem. reg. in ſacc. ſub. tit. Linc. [x] Thoreſby's antiq. of Leeds, p. 226. [y] Jekyl's baron. extinƈt. mſ. f. 71. b.

of Thurgarton convent, obtain'd the [z] poffeffion thereof, with the cuftody of her children; for which fhe paid, as a fine, two hundred pounds.

This Thomas had [a] alfo two younger fons, and four daughters, one of which, while he was living, was [b] married to ———— de Munbegon, and two other (at the time of the aforefaid prefentment) were [c] marriageable, and the youngeft but eight years of age; being defcended of Barons, faith the record; and [d] that he held twenty Knights fees of the King, and of the fee of William de Perci.

His eldeft fon, Thomas, was with King Richard I. in that expedition into Normandy, A. D. 1195, the 6th of his reign, when the [e] King went to raife the [f] fiege of Verneuil, which he effected the night before Whitfunday, and forced the enemy to depart. In 1204, 5 John, he was retain'd to [g] ferve the King in his wars in Normandy againft the French, who had taken the [h] towns of Couches, le Val de Raeil, and Lifle-Dandele (the fecond being furrendered without any great oppofition by two noblemen, who had the charge of them, viz. Robert Fitz-Walter, and Saier de Quincie) with three Knights, for one whole year, beginning on Wednefday before Midfummer-day; in confideration whereof the King [i] remitted him a debt of two hundred twenty-five marks which he then owed to the Jews; but befides this retainer he was to perform the like [k] fervice for his barony, as others did.

To him fucceeded Norman de Areci his fon and [l] heir, who in 7 John, paying [m] 500 marks, with fix palfries, and one horfe for the great faddle, and doing his homage, had livery [n] of all the lands defcended to him by the death of his father. In 13 John, he had a fpecial difcharge [o] from his fcutage, due upon the expedition made that year into Scotland.

In 15 John, Robert d'Arci [p] attended the King on that expedition againft the French into Poictou; but whether he was uncle or brother to this Norman, does not appear.

The faid Norman being one of the Barons in the rebellion againft King John, in the 17th year of his reign, had his lands [q] feized by [r] John le Marefchall, a Baron, fheriff of Lincolnfhire, and marfhal of Ireland, and by the King's command they were [s] difpofed of to Peter de Warcop. But in 1216, 1 Hen. III. he had livery of them again, the King and his Ba-

z Rot. pip. anno 28 Hen. II.   a b c d Rot. de dominab. pueris & puellis ut fupra.   e Rot. pip. anno 6 Rich. I. Linc.   f Hollinfh. p. 144. g Oblat. anno 5 John.   h Hollinfhed, p. 166.   i k Oblat. anno 5 John.   l m n Rot. fin. anno 7 Joh. m. 7.   o Rot. pip. anno 13 Joh. Linc.   p Rot. clauf. anno 15 Joh. d. m. r.   q Rot. clauf. anno 17. Joh. m. 10.   r Fuller's worthies in Linc.   s Rot. clauf. anno 17 Joh. m. 10.

rons coming to a peaceable accord, by the industry and good council of [t] William Marshall, Earl of Pembroke, who, to win the good will of the subjects to the young King (to whom he was governor) offered pardon to all those Barons who should take part with the King. And this Norman embracing the opportunity, and giving good [u] pledges for his future fidelity, had his lands [x] restored to him; as had also the before-mentioned Robert Darci his [y] lands in Hantshire.

In 3 Hen. III. the said Norman gave [z] to the King a foregoshawke of Norway, to have a market at his lordship of Noctone; and in 1245, 29 Hen. III. [a] answered twenty pounds (for the Knights fees he held) on an assessment of the aid for marrying Margaret, the King's eldest daughter, to Alexander III. King of Scotland, whose marriage was celebrated on Dec. 26, 1251, at York; as also 40 l. anno 38 Hen. III. on [b] collection of the aid for making Prince Edward, the King's eldest son, a Knight. In which year the King, in regard to his great age and infirmities, granted the custody of his lands, so long as he should live, unto Philip d'Arci his son and heir.

Which Philip, adhering to the interest of the crown in those turbulent times, about the latter end of King John's reign, had, anno 1 Hen. III. a [c] grant of the lands of Robert le Camberleng, or Chamberlayne.

After which I find no mention of him till 27 Hen. III. in which year he had an assignation [d] of 23 l. 13 s. then in arrear to those soldiers who served under his command in the wars of France; and of 20 marks due to himself.

In 34 Hen. III. he is said to have been the accuser [e] of Sir Henry de Bath, Knt. one [f] of the judges of the court of common-pleas, for his unfaithfulness and corruption in point of judicature.

In 37 Hen. III. the King, on displeasure [g] conceived against Henry Plantagenet Duke of Lancaster, Earl of Leicester, lord high steward of England, oblig'd him to resign the office of warden of Gascony, for that the Gascoigners had charged him with too much severity. And they continuing in rebellion, the King went over, and this Philip de Arci being ready to attend him according to the service he owed, having [h] information, that his father designed to alienate certain lands, which were part of his inheritance, and complaining thereof to the King; he obtained a precept to the [i] sheriff, commanding him not to admit any one to enter on them during his continuance

[t] Hollinshed, p. 197.   [u] [x] Rot. clauf. anno 1 Hen. III. m. 10.   [y] Ibid. m. 19.   [z] Rot. pip. anno 3 Hen. III. Linc.   [a] Ibid. anno 29 Hen. III. Linc.   [b] Rot. pip. anno 38 Hen. III Linc.   [c] Rot. clauf. 1 Hen. III. m. 12.   [d] Vascon. 27 Hen. III. m. 5.   [e] Mat. Paris, in ann. 1250. p. 811. n. 40.   [f] Dug. orig. jurisd. in chron. series.   [g] Hollinshed, p. 247.   [h] Clauf. 37 Hen. III. m. 10.   [i] Ibid.

D'Arcy, Earl of Holdernesse.

in that service. And the King also sent his commands to the Queen and Richard Earl of Cornwal, that so long as he should continue beyond the seas, he should not be sued.

In 38 Hen. III. being in the [l] camp with the King at Lupiel in Gascoigne, he was made governor of the castle at Millans, and captain of those forces then remaining there. And the [m] next year, having contracted great debts by his large expences in the King's service beyond the seas, he procured certain letters [n] hortatory to all his tenants by military service, and other; earnestly moving them to grant him such reasonable aid, towards easing him of that burthen, as that they might be worthy of the King's thanks for the same. And paying in that year his relief, [o] had livery of his lands.

In 1260, 44 Hen. III. he was [p] summoned to be at Shrewsbury on Sept. 8, the nativity of the Virgin Mary, with horse and arms, ready to march against Llewellin, and the Welsh his accomplices; and [q] died, anno 48 Hen. III. leaving issue by [r] Isabel his wife, second daughter of Ralph de Bertram, Baron of Mitford (and sister and one of the coheirs of Roger de Bertram, who died anno 4 Ed. II.) four sons, viz. 1. Norman, 2. Sir Thomas. 3. Roger, and 4. Ralph.

Which Norman, at the decease of his father, was [s] 28 years of age and more; and doing his [t] homage, and giving security for the payment of his relief as a baron, had livery of his lands. Nevertheless, the next year, 1265, being among the rebellious Lords, who were vanquished in the battle fought at [u] Evesham in Com' Worc. August 6, his [x] lands were seized by the King.

Roger [y], the third brother of the said Norman, and Thomas their [z] uncle, were also engaged in that [a] rebellion; but there being a peaceable composure afterwards betwixt the King and the transgressors (by that memorable decree call'd dictum de Kenilworth) both this Norman, his brother Roger, and uncle [b] Thomas (taken prisoner at the siege of Northampton, in 48 Hen. III.) were in 51 Hen. III. admitted to [c] favour, John de Burgh of Kent, Adam de Newmarch of Yorkshire, and Robert de Ufford of Norfolk (all Barons) being sureties for their future loyalty and quiet demeanor.

In 1277, 5 Edw. I the [d] King signifies that Llewellin Prince of Wales had rebelled, and therefore sent his mandate to this

---

l Rot. vasc. 38 Hen. III. m. 20. m n Pat. 39 Hen. III. m. 1. o Rot. p'p. 39 Hen. III. Linc. p Reymer, tom. 1. p. 707. q Esc. 48 Hen. III. n. 15. Linc. r Jekyl's baron. extinct. præd. p. 62. b. s Esc. 48 Hen. III. n. 15. Linc. t Rot. fin. 48 Hen. III. m. 3. u Hollinsh. p. 270. x Esc. 50 Hen. III. n. 3. y z a Rot. pat. 51 Hen. III. m. 14. b MS. in bodl. Oxon. 8 V. 8. th. f. 138. b. c Rot. pat. 51 Hen. III. m. 14. d Rymer, tom. 2. p. 74.

Norman Darcy, to be at Worcester in the octaves of St. John Baptist next, with horse and arms, and his whole service, to go against him. In 9 Edw. I. John de Vaux, William de Saham, and others, being ᵉ appointed justices in eyre for the county of Lincoln, they summon'd this Norman to shew by ᶠ what authority he held his lands in Nocton, Doneston, and elsewhere, in Lincolnshire, and what services and privileges he claim'd in that county: Whereunto he reply'd, that he held his lands in chief of the King, by the service of two Knights fees only, or of one Knight and two Esquires, in the King's army for forty days, at his own charges; and that he claim'd in Nocton, and Doneston, free warren, gallows, and infangthef, with a market at Nocton upon the Tuesday, and assize of bread and beer, and a fair upon the eve and feast-day of St. Mary Magdalen; and that he claim'd free warren and a gallows in Conyngsby; and in his manor of Stalinburgh, wreck of sea, weyth, and gallows.

In 1282, 10 Edw. l. the Welsh having taken Roger Clifford, sen. and imprisoned him, and kill'd and taken several of the King's subjects, he had ᵍ orders to be at Worcester on the day of Pentecost, with horse and arms, ready, if occasion requir'd, to march against them. And another mandate, dated at Hertelbyrough, May 24, the same year, was ʰ sent to him to be at Rothelan on Sunday, the morrow after Aug. 1, to go against the Welsh. Also on June 28, 10 Edw. I. the King, at Rotheland, ⁱ gave him notice in what manner the Welsh had taken up arms, killed his nobles, and other subjects, both men, women, and children, and of having David, the last of the race, in custody; and therefore desires to consult with him and others, as to the disposal of him, requiring him to be at Shrewsbury on the morrow after the feast of St. Michael.

In the 11 Edw. I. so well did he behave, and such great ᵏ service did he perform for the King, in the expedition then made into Wales against ˡ Prince Llewellin (who had committed great hostilities in those parts about the mountains of Snowdone, and ᵐ in Montgomeryshire) that in recompence thereof he had an assignation ⁿ of 50 l. per ann. for five years to come; and also a discharge ᵒ for 100 l. due at the exchequer for his relief. In 22 Edw. I. ᵖ he was summoned to attend the King immediately, and to give his opinion in those great and difficult points relating to a war with France: the French in that year having taken two English men of war, sailing by the Norman coast; as also four others, sent by the King for the safe-guard of

e Dug. orig. in chron. ser. f Plac. de quo warrant. in octab. trin. ann. 9 Edw. I. Rot. 13 d. g Rymer, tom. 2. p. 196. h Ibid. p. 207. i Hollinsh. p. 290. k Rymer, ibid. p. 248. l Clauf. ann. 11 Edw. I. m. 10. m Hollinsh. p. 281. n Stowe, p. 202. o Clauf. anno 11 Edw. I. m. 10. p Commun. term. ann. 12 Edw. I. Rot. 3.

D'Arcy, Earl of Holdernesse.

Bordeaux. And thereupon q had another summons to be at Portsmouth on Sept. 1 following, ready with horse and arms, and his whole service, to sail with the King into France. And on the same occasion, he had in that year orders to summon all abbots, priors, knights, and others within his bailiwick, who held in chief, or by Knight's service, or serjeantry, to be at Portsmouth on Sept. 1 next, with horse and arms, and their whole service, ready to go beyond sea. But after this he lived not long; for in 24 Edw. I. Sir Philip his son and heir, doing his homage, r had livery of all his lands, whereof he died seized. He also left two other sons, Sir John, of whom hereafter; and Robert.

Which Sir Philip, in 25 Edw. I. s attended the King in that expedition into Gascony, where the English were worsted, going to relieve Bellegard, besieged by the Earl of Artois. But before I treat further of him, I shall give some account of Robert, his third brother.

Which Robert d'Arci was also in 25 Edw. I. in that expedition into Gascony t; likewise that year, an insurrection beginning in Scotland, at the instigation of Sir William Wallace, on account of the Scots refusing to do homage, u he was then sent into those wars, in which x the English forces suffered not a little. And in 27 Edw. I. being lord of the manors of Stallingburgh and Doneston in Com' Linc. y he had a grant of free warren in all his demesne lands there z. In 1306, 34 Edw. I. the King sending an army into Scotland, against Robert Bruce, who had caused himself, on Lady-day, to be crowned at Scone, this Robert d'Arci leaving the King there, without licence, a the sheriff of Lincolnshire had command to seize all his lands and possessions in that county b. But this breach of trust was afterwards forgiven; for in 4 Edw. II. c the custody of the castle and honour of Striguil d in Scotland, was committed to him. And in 15 Edw. II. he was made governor of Sleford castle in Lincolnshire, which for some reasons was then taken into the King's hands. Also in 18 Edw. II. he was constituted one of the arrayers in the parts of Lindsey in com' Linc. In 1 Edw. III. he had a e grant of free warren in all his demesne lands in Clipston in com' Northampt. and in Pachensham in com' Sussex f; and the next year obtained a patent of view of frank-pledge in his manor of Lethered (Leatherhead) in Surrey, to himself and Joan g his wife, and the heirs of their bodies. In 5 Edw. III. he had a grant of a mar-

q Rot. Vascon. 22 Edw. I. m. 8. d.   r Rot. ibid. m. 7. d.   s Rot. fin. 24 Edw. I. m. 16.   t Rot. vas. 25 Edw. I. m. 1.   u Hollinsh. p. 303. x Rot. scoc. 25 Edw. I. m. 1.   y Hollinsh. p. 303.   z Cart. 27 Edw. I. n. 30. a Hollinsh. p. 314.   b Rot. fin. 34 Edw. I. m. 2.   c Pat. 4 Edw. II. p. 1. m. 21.   d Pat. 15 Edw. II. p. 1. m. 21.   e Rymer, vol. 4. p. 80.   f Cart. 1 Edw. III. n. 42.   g Cart. 2 Edw. III. n. 20.

ket every week on the Friday, with a fair yearly on Lammas-day, at Lethered aforesaid [h]. This Robert d'Arci was one of the Knights in parliament for Lincolnshire, 12 Edw. II.

But now I return to Sir Philip, who, in 26 Edw. I. [i] was summoned to be at Carlisle on Whitsun-eve, with horse and arms, ready to march against the Scotch then in rebellion; and in 27 Edw. I. Sir Thomas his uncle dying without issue, [k] the manor of Scotelthorpe escheated to him as his next heir, being then forty years of age. In 31 Edw. I. he [l] was with the Lord Segrave, and others, in that expedition into Scotland, where the English, [m] after a sharp and doubtful fight for a time, were overcome, and the said Lord taken; who (as my author says) had more courage than foresight. In 34 Edw. I. the King having an intention to make Edward Prince of Wales, his fourth son (but then the only surviving one by his first Queen) a Knight, [n] summoned this Sir Philip to be at Westminster on the morrow of the Holy Trinity, to fix with other counsellors the aid to be granted for that purpose.

In 4 Edw. II. [o] he was in the wars of Scotland; and in 5 Edw. II. doing his homage, as cousin and heir to Roger Bertram of Mitford in Com' Northumb. had livery of such lands as on that account descended to him. And having been, in 1312, concerned in the apprehending and murder of Piers de Gaveston, Earl of Cornwal, he [p] had with Thomas Earl of Lancaster, and others, in 1314, 7 Edw. II. his pardon on that account, or of any other misdeed whatever.

The same year he [q] was in Scotland with the King, who with a great power intending to raise the siege of Strivelling (Stirling) castle, [r] a bloody battle ensued, June 24, wherein the English were vanquish'd, and many slain and taken prisoners.

The year after, 8 Edw. II. [s] he was again in the wars of Scotland; as also in 9 Edw. II. in which year arrived in England two cardinals [t], who brought bulls from the pope, to excommunicate the Scots, if they refused agreeing to a treaty of peace with England. What I have found further of him is, that he was [u] one of those who were with Thomas Plantagenet, Earl of Lancaster, in the insurrection made in the North, in 15 Edw. II. But on security given for his future loyalty, and good behaviour, had the year following restitution of his lands, which had been seized by the King for that transgression. He had

h Cart. 5 Edw. III. n. 47.   i Rymer's fœd. vol. 2, p. 829.   k Esc. 27 Edw. I. n. 12.   l Rot. scot. 31 Edw. I. m. 12.   m Hollinsh. p. 311. n Rymer, vol. 2. p. 987.   o Rot. scoc. 4 Edw. II. m. 8.   p Rymer's fœd. vol. 3. p. 442, 443, & seq.   q Rot. scoc. 7 Edw. II. m. 3.   r Stow's annals, p. 216.   s Rot. scoc. 8 Edw. II. m. 9.   t Stow, p. 218.   u Hollinsh. p. 128.

summons

D'Arcy, Earl of Holderneſſe.

ſummons to parliament ˣ among the Barons, from the 25th to the 34th of Edw. I. incluſive.

He had iſſue by Eleanor his wife three ſons, 1. Norman, 2. Robert, and, 3. John; whereof the two laſt died without iſſue male.

Norman d'Arcy, his eldeſt ſon and heir, was in the wars of Scotland, ʸ in 7 and 9 Edw. II. and adhering to Thomas Earl of Lancaſter, had his lands in Kalkwell ſeized, ᶻ but was afterwards reſtored to his eſtate.

In 12 Edw III. he ᵃ was with the King in that deſcent then made into Flanders, ᵇ likewiſe in the following year; and died on March 25, 1340, 14 Edw. III. ᶜ leaving iſſue, by Iſabel his wife, Philip his ſon and heir, ten years of age, ᵈ who dying in 24 Edw. III. Sir Philip de Limbury, Knt. ſon of Julian, the eldeſt of the two ſiſters and coheirs to the ſaid Norman, and Agnes (the wife of Sir Roger de Pedwardine, of Burton-Pedwardine in Lincolnſhire, Knt.) the other ſiſter and coheir, were found his heirs; Sir Philip de Limbury being then (viz. in 24 Edw. III.) thirty years of age, and Agnes fifty.

Thus the male line failing, I am now come to Sir John, ſecond brother to Philip, father of the laſt mentioned Norman d'Arci.

Which Sir John (frequently ſtiled of Park, as owner of Conyngſby-park) was of great courage and eminent abilities, as evident by the many offices he bore in the reigns of Edw. I. II. and III. In ᵉ 25 Edw. I. he was in that ᶠ expedition made into Scotland againſt ᵍ Wallace, ʰ and his adherents then in arms. Alſo in 31 Edw. I. when Sir John Segrave Knt. was ſent thither with an army, the Scots being in arms, on account ⁱ of the truce expiring on All-ſaints day. And ᵏ in 1306, 34 Edw. I. he was again there on Robert Bruce's ˡ aſſuming the ſovereignty, and cauſing himſelf to be ſolemnly crown'd on March 25, at the abbey of Scone, by the biſhops of St. Andrew's and Glaſgow. In 3 Edw. II. ᵐ he was likewiſe there when the King fortified Berwick with a ſtrong wall and deep ditch, and thence with his army march'd into Scotland to ſeek his adverſary Robert Bruce, who ⁿ refuſing him battle, the King came back to Berwick. In 1313, 6 Edw. II. (May 3.) he had ᵒ the King's protection to hold in force till Aug. 1 following; he at

---

x Clauſ. 16 Edw. II. m. 15. y Rot. ſcot. 7 Edw. II. m. 3. & 9 Edw. II. m. 6. z Clauſ. 16 Edw. II. m. 23. a Rot. aleman, 12 Edw. III. p. 1. m. 3. b Rot. alem. 13 Edw. III. m. 19. c Eſc. 15 Edw. III. n. 21. d Eſc. 24 Edw. III. n. 100. Linc. e Rot. ſcot. 25 Edw. I. m. 1. f Stow, p. 207. g Rot. ſcot. 31 Edw. I. m. 6. h Hollinſh. p. 311. i Rot. ſcot. 4 Edw. I. m. 13. k Stow, p. 209. l Hollinſh. p. 320. m Rot. ſcot. 3 Edw. II. m. 5. n Hollinſh. p. 321. o Rymer's fœd, tom. 3. p. 406.

D'Arcy, Earl of Holdernesse.

that time being P appointed to go with the King and Queen into France, to the coronation of Lewis X. son of Philip IV. King of France and Navarre; and the same year q was commissioned to treat at Newcastle with Sir Robert de Loweden, Knt. and others, deputed by the Scots, on such matters as should be offer'd by them.

In 7 Edw. II. having been concern'd, with Thomas Earl of Lancaster, in the death of Piers Gaviston, r he had a pardon of all manner of accusations on that account.

In 7 Edw. II. Robert Bruce having recover'd the greatest part of Scotland, and won from the English those castles they held there, and conquer'd those Scots which were in the English service; the King, to be reveng'd on them, marched with a powerful army, and entering Scotland, this John Lord Darcy was then with him, and meeting with the enemy near s Bannockburn, were entirely defeated on June 24, King Edward himself hardly escaping. Robert Paston, a Carmelite friar, being present, he in heroical verse sadly bewails the sorrowful disaster. The first night (saith he) the English bathed themselves in wine, with other rioting far above measure; whereas the Scots lay close and quiet, fasting the evening before the battle, and had made trenches three feet deep, and the like in breadth, from the right wing of their army to the left, covering them with turf and grass laid on twigs, not of strength to bear horsemen, so that the English horse, advancing thereon, founder'd in the trenches, which occasioned the loss of the battle.

In 10 Edw. II. the King stiles him t John d'Arci, le cosyn, appointing him governor of the castle of Norhan in Northumberland; and in 13 Edw. II. he was sheriff of the u counties of Derby and Nottingham; as also in 14 and 15 of that King's reign; and sheriff x of Lancashire in 16 Edw. II. In 17 Edw. II. y he was constituted lord justice of Ireland, z and arrived at Dublin, February 2. During his abode in that kingdom, excellent ordinances, for the government thereof, were assented to by the King and his council, which are at large in Prynne's animadversions on the fourth institutes; and the annals of those times make no mention of any disturbance there during that reign, other than was occasion'd by private murders. In 18 Edw. II. being then in that kingdom, a he had commands, from the King, to seize, in his jurisdiction, all persons of Agenois, Pierregort, Xaintonge, and

---

p Hollinsh. p. 321. q Rymer, vol. 4. p. 535. r Hollinsh. p. 322.
s Rot. scot. 8 Edw. II. m. 2. t Stow's annals, p. 316. u Pat. 2 Edw.
II. p. 2. m. 29. x Fuller's worthies in com' Derb. p. 241. y Rot. fin.
16 Edw. II. m. 13. z Pat. 17 Edw. II. p. 1. m. 4. a Borlace's reduct.
of Ireland. p. 45.

D'Arcy, Earl of Holdernesse. 11

other places, then in rebellion against the King, and them safe to keep with their goods and effects, and to certify their names, goods, &c. in writing.

In 20 Edw. II. when the King, for the defence of his kingdom against the invasion of foreigners, and others, who adhered to Queen Isabel and Prince Edward, ordered in council, that all ships of or above the burden of thirty ton, from the mouth of the Thames riding northward, should be at Orewell in Suffolk, on St. Matthew's-day, well arm'd, double mann'd, and a month's provision on board each vessel; [b] he appointed this John Darcy (then call'd the uncle) to see that the royal mandate be duly executed in the ports and towns of Saltfletby, Waynfleet, and Grymsby, in Lincolnshire.

In 1327, 1 Edw. III. he was some part of it sheriff of Yorkshire; and was that year again sent lord justice into Ireland; [c] and the same year, having the title of John d'Arci le frere, obtained [d] a grant of free warren in all his demesne lands in Conyngsby-park, Flixborough, and Winterton, in Com' Lincoln; also the next year in those at Wranby in that county. In 2 Edw. III. being called John d'Arci le neveu, he had [e] an assignation of certain sums of money due to him for his services in Ireland the preceding year; also for other services during his abode in Yorkshire, in October, November, and December, that year, for the defence of those parts. On August 21, the same year, [f] he was made justice of Ireland, and governor of that country; also had his patent renew'd, in the year [g] following; in which time Macoghegan of Meath, and other Irish men of Leinster, broke out into rebellion; [h] yet this common calamity could not unite the English, altho' taught by experience, that they never suffered any great damage but from civil dissentions among themselves. And the enemy, thro' the many small victories they obtained, so weakened the English, that the lord justice was obliged [i] to invite Maurice (afterwards Earl of Desmond) to take the field, which he did with success, with an army of near ten thousand. That year the king ordered him to pay to William Earl of Juliers 300 l. due at Michaelmas, in part of 600 l. per ann. granted in fee to him; and in consideration of his many good services, had from the King a grant of [k] the manor of Werk in Tindale in Com' Northumb.

In 4 Edw. III. he was [l] sent by the King into Aquitain, to treat about certain affairs relating to that dutchy, and with

---

b Rymer's fœd. tom 4. p. 225, & seq.   c Orig. 1 Edw. III. Rot. 11.
d Cart. 1 Edw. III. n. 24.   e Clauf. 2 Edw. III. m. 15.   f Pat. 2 Edw. III. p. 1. m. 24.   g Pat. 3 Edw. III. p. 1. m. 28.   h Cox's hist. Ireland, p. 108.   i Ibid. p. 109.   k Cart. 3 Edw. III. n. 40.   l Rymer, vol. 4. p. 432.

any

any persons who were willing to serve the King for life, or term of years, at such wages as should be agreed on. And [m] the same year obtained a charter for a market every week on the Saturday; as also a fair yearly on the eve and day of St. Barnabas the apostle, and four days following, at his manor of Knaith in Com' Linc. and free warren in all his demesne lands at Kettesby and Upton in the same county. This year also he was in Guienne, when the King gave him to understand, that the French would no longer abide by the treaty; [a] and in case they should bring forces to take possession of that province, he had orders to oppose them; and to promise the people there, that for the damages they should sustain, reparation should be made.

In 1331, 5 Edw. III. July 15, [o] he with Sir William Truffel, Knt. were sent ambassadors to Philip VI. King of France, to treat about a marriage between Edward Prince of Wales, and the daughter of the said King of France, in order to prevent a war; but it had no effect. In 6 Edw. III. he [p] with William de Denum were commissioned to treat at Newcastle with Sir Robert de Loweden Knt. and others, deputed by the Scotch, on such matters as then shall be offered by them.

In 7 Edw. III. being still justice of Ireland, he left Aquitain to revenge [q] the death of William de Burgh, Earl of Ulster, who had been slain by the Irish; and on his landing in that nation, call'd a parliament, by whose advice he went by sea to Carigfergus, on July 1, and by help of the country people, he destroyed the murderers and their abettors. After which, he appointed Sir Thomas Burgh his deputy, as lieutenant of Ireland, and made directly for Scotland; whither, as Barnes in his history of Edw. III. observes, he came just in time to give a specimen both of his loyalty and valour. The King of England was then return'd to the siege before Berwick, with a resolution not to stir, till he had taken the place, or that David King of Scotland should raise the siege by a battle. And at this juncture of the Lord Darcy's arrival, the Scots having muster'd a considerable army, resolved to force King Edward to retire; whereupon the memorable battle of Hallidown near Berwick ensued June 8, 1333, wherein the Scots are said to have lost 8 Earls, 90 Knights, 400 Esquires, and 35000 common soldiers, according to our historians; but their own writers mention only 14000 to be slain. In this engagement, the Lord John Darcy, with his Irish troops on the one side, made a great slaughter; while the King with a choice brigade of men

[m] Pat. 4 Edw. III. p. 1. m. 17. [n] Rymer, tom. 4. p. 450. [o] Pat. 5 Edw. III. p. 2. m. 28. [p] Rymer, tom. 4. p. 53. [q] MS. in bibl. bodl. Oxon de Rebus hibernicis, tom. 3.

of arms, and archers on horfeback, fo encompaffed them on the other fide, that very few could efcape, except thofe who firft of all began the flight.

On this victory King Edward entered into Berwick with great folemnity, and advanced Edward Baliol to the crown of Scotland; and then the Lord John Darcy, as [r] is obferved, having obtained much honour in this war, return'd now with all his forces to his province of Ireland, where all along he exercifed much wifdom and integrity in that his government; and upon his return, prefently deliver'd Walter Bermingham, primate of Armagh, out of the caftle of Dublin.

In 9 Edw. III. continuing ftill Juftice of Ireland, [s] he again failed into Scotland, with fix and thirty fhips, the chief of the Irifh nobles accompanying him; and having wafted the ifles of Arran and Bute, return'd with great prey and glory. For which memorable fervices, Edward III. [t] granted to him the manors of Louth and Ballionany, in Ireland, which Simon Earl of Eue had forfeited by adhering to the French King; as alfo to him, and to Joan, then his wife, and to the heirs-male of their two bodies lawfully begotten, the manors of Rathwer and Kildalk lying in that realm.

In 11 Edw. III. he with others [u] were commiffioned by the King, to declare to the people in the counties of Nottingham and Derby, certain matters contain'd in a fchedule fent to them: and in that year, being [x] fteward of the King's houfhold, he was fent ambaffador (together with William de Bohun Earl of Northampton, and Robert de Ufford Earl of Suffolk) into Scotland, to treat of peace with David de Brus, who then affumed there the title of King. After which, he was alfo fent [y] ambaffador into France (with thofe Earls) to treat with Philip VI. King of France, or his commiffioners, touching the right of King Edward to the crown of that realm [z]. But being arrived at Boulogne, they there received command from the King not to proceed, conceiving their journey might be hazardous, and expofe them to the fury of a paffionate Prince, who had before threatened the negociators with death, if ever they came again; when, before his coronation, they were pleading the King of England's right to that crown in the chamber of France. Whereupon they had another commiffion [a] to treat with Lewis Earl of Flanders, about a marriage between the faid Earl's eldeft Son, and Joan the King's fecond daughter: Alfo by [b] another, to fettle with the faid Earl and

---

[r] Barnes's hift. Ed. III. p. 80.   [s] MS. in bibl. bodl. Oxon, tom. 3. f. 99. & tom. 4. p. 64.   [t] Pat. 18 Edw. III. p. 2. m. 3. per infpect.   [u] Rymer, tom. 4. p. 205.   [x] Rot. fcot. 11 Edw. III. m. 7.   [y] Barnes's hift. Edw. III. p. 15.   [z] Rymer, tom. 4. p. 814.   [a] Ibid.   [b] Ibid. p. 815, 816.

his subjects, and with the burgo-masters, consuls, scabins, and good men of the towns of Bruges, Ghent, and Ypres, all manner of differences: And by several other separate commissions [c] to treat with all persons and powers about an alliance, and particularly with Lewis Emperor of the Romans; and to dispose of and grant any honours, lordships, castles, towns, manors, lands, tenements, possessions, rents, jurisdictions, &c. belonging to the King in the kingdom of France, dutchy of Aquitain, or elsewhere beyond the seas, as well as in the kingdoms of England, Ireland, or Scotland, in fee for such a term of years, and to such persons, as to them shall seem best. Further, they were impowered to borrow money of such people as should be willing to advance any sum, or sums, on the security of any of the King's dominions. They were also [d] on October 7, 11 Edw. III. sent to several of the cardinals with credentials.

Before he began his journey into France, [e] he was constituted constable of the Tower of London; and on his return from his embassies, he had a special assignation of such wages as had been allowed for his support in those services: And moreover obtained the King's grant [f] of the manors of Temple-Newsome, and Temple-Hyrst, in Com' Ebor. as also of the manor of Torksey in Com' Linc. to himself and the heirs male of his body; and in default to revert to the crown.

In 12 Edw. III. he [g] was in that expedition then made into Flanders; and the same year being at Antwerp [h] with Henry Burghersh bishop of Lincoln, William de Bohun Earl of Northampton, and Robert de Ufford Earl of Suffolk, on a treaty relating to trade with Flanders, 'twas agreed by them, that all persons, going from England into Holland or Zealand, should be safe both in their persons, as well as goods, and that the Flemings might have a free trade in England; which the King [i] afterwards confirmed. Moreover, he in conjunction with the aforesaid bishop of Lincoln, Reginald Earl of Gelderland and Zutphen, William de Montacute Earl of Salisbury, Henry de Ferrers the King's chamberlain, William de la Pole, and Paul de Flearmont, [k] entered into a recognizance to pay to the archbishop of Triers 55,000 florins, and for the due payment thereof, they were by the King impowered to pledge his crown of England.

In 13 Edw. III. the King having borrowed of Nicholas Bartholomæi of Antwerp, 140,000 florins of gold, [l] this John Lord Darcy (then steward of the King's houshold) together

---

[c] Rymer, tom. 5. p. 821.   [d] Clauf. 11 Edw. III. m. 34.   [e] Cart. 11 Edw. III. n. 15.   [f] Rot. Aleman, 12 Edw. III. p. 2. m. 5.   [g] Rymer, tom. 5. p. 53.   [h] Ibid. p. 59.   [i] Ib. p. 101.   [k] Ib. p. 110.   [l] Ib. p. 113.

D'Arcy, Earl of Holdernesse.

with John Stratford archbishop of Canterbury, and others, were bound for the re-payment thereof on the feast of All-faints that year. This year also the King, at Bruffels on Midsummer-day, agreeing with the Duke of Brabant, that his son Edward should marry Margaret the said Duke's daughter, and that he would settle a dower on her equal to Queen Isabel's, provided the said Duke give her 50,000 l. for her portion; he also, [m] with others of the prime nobility, were bound for the King's performance of his part. And the King having borrowed, at Antwerp, of John Richier, 54,000 florins of gold, he [n] likewise with others, were bound for the King's re-payment of that sum. And [o] he with others advised the King to give the title of an English Earl to William Marquis of Juliers, which the King promised to do as soon as the said Marquis returned from the Emperor; and in performance of that promise, he created him Earl of Cambridge the year after.

On March 1, 1340, the King, at his palace of Weftminfter, delivering the great seal to John de St Paul. [p] this John Darcy, being entitled le cosyn to the King, and steward of his household, was then present. He was also the same year [q] constituted justice of Ireland for life, yet never after went into that kingdom; but, in May following, sent over Sir John Morris, his deputy. And that year having been with the King at the siege of Tournay, [r] return'd with him on November 30; when landing at the Tower early in the morning, he found there no guard, and his children only waited on by three servants. Whereupon the King in great anger discharged most of his great officers the day following, when this John Lord Darcy was present.

In 15 Edw. III. tho' the King revoked his grants of all lands in Ireland, [s] yet in consideration of his good services (and then call'd John d'Arci the elder) by his constant attendance on his person, and employments, those granted to him were excepted. And on the meeting of the parliament at Weftminfter on Easter-Monday, when John Stratford archbishop of Canterbury (who had been accused by the King of breach of duty to him) with a great company of clergymen, was coming to take his place among the peers, this John Lord Darcy, the King's steward, met him on his entrance into the house, and in the King's name forbad him to enter the parliament, until in the King's exchequer he had undergone a trial concerning crimes laid to his charge; and is said to be the archbishop's open enemy. In the same year, being then the King's cham-

m Ib. p. 138.   n Ib. p. 139.   o Ib. p. 175.   p Pat. 14 Edw. III. p. 1. m. 32.   q Rymer, tom. 5. p. 216.   r Clauf. 15 Edw. III. p. 3. m. 91.   s Rymer, tom. 5. p. 289.

berlain.

D'Arcy, Earl of Holderneſſe.

berlain, he was preſent [t] when Sir Robert de Bourchier, Knt. chancellor of England, delivered up the ſeals to the King in the palace at Weſtminſter, on the eve of St. Simon and Jude; and thereupon had them committed to his care, till the evening following, when the King gave them to Sir Robert Parnyng. He was [u] alſo this year in that expedition then made into Scotland; and being juſticier of Ireland, [x] the King, on November 20, ordered him to take care, that neither arms or proviſions be ſent out of Ireland to the Scotch.

In 16 Edw. III. [y] he was ſent into Britanny, together with William de Bohun Earl of Northampton, and other Engliſh nobles, to aid the Counteſs of Montfort (whoſe Lord was a priſoner at the Louvre) [z] againſt the Lord Charles of Blois; where, after relieving Henebond, the Counteſs being reſident therein, and on the point of yielding, they attacked don Lewis and the Spaniards, who had come to the aſſiſtance of the French, and ſo entirely routed them, that of ſix thouſand, there eſcaped ſcarce three hundred.

In 18 Edw. III. (being call'd John d'Arci le piere, [a] and made conſtable of Nottingham-caſtle for life) he obtained a charter for free warren [b] in his lordſhips of Temple-Newſome, and Temple-Hyrſt in Com' Ebor. Torkſey in Com' Linc. Ekington in Com' Derb. and Kirby in Aſhfield in Com' Nott. In 19 Edw. III. [c] he was in that expedition made into France, when ſeveral towns were taken, and the French army, under the Lord Charles of Blois, defeated near Morlaix. In the ſame year he [d] obtained a grant for two markets every week at Torkſey, viz. one on the Monday, and the other on the Wedneſday, with a fair yearly, to begin on the eve of the tranſlation of St. Thomas the martyr, and to continue for that day, and ſix days following.

In 1346, 20 Edw. III. [e] he was again in the wars of France; at which time the famous battle of Crecy was fought Auguſt 26; and was [f] alſo at the ſiege of Calais, having in his retinue, 12 Knights, 68 Eſquires, and 80 archers. And in conſideration [g] of his laudable ſervices for many years, and 1000 marks in money given to the King, he had a grant of the marriage of James the ſon and heir to James le Bottiller; alſo was [h] made conſtable of the Tower of London for life. And the King, near Calais, commiſſion'd him, [i] September 8, 1346 (being

[t] Ib p. 292. [u] Rot. ſcot. 15 Edw. III. m. 1. [x] H. Knighton, 2581. n. 60. & Rot. franc. 16 Edw. III. m. 24. [y] Barnes's hiſt. Edw. III. p. 256. [z] Pat. 18 Edw. III. m. 35. [a] Cart. 18 Edw. III. n. 1. [b] Rot. franc. 19 Edw. III. m. 4. [c] Cart. 19 Edw. III. n. 17. [d] Rot. franc. 20 Edw. III. p. 1. m. 5. [e] Rot. fin. 20 Edw. III. m. 23. [f] MS. in bibl. harley, not. 125. [g] Pat. 20 Edw. III. p. 1. m. 16. [h] Rymer, tom. 5. p. 526. [i] Ib. p. 535.

then

D'Arcy, Earl of Holdernesse.

then the King's Chamberlain) with Bartholomew de Burgherſh, John de Thorſeby keeper of the privy-ſeal, and John de Carleton, to declare to the parliament (which was to meet at Weſtminſter, on Monday after the feaſt of the Nativity) the King's intention relating to the poſture of his affairs; and was afterwards ſent into the north, [k] to take care of David Bruce King of Scotland, and others, taken priſoners in that great battle near Durham, October 17.

On December 16, that year, [l] the King directed his warrant to the Treaſurer and Chamberlains of the Exchequer to pay him 50 l. for his journey into the north for the cuſtody of the ſaid priſoners. Alſo the King ſent to him to ſtay there till Sir Thomas de Rokeby, ſheriff of York, delivered to him the ſaid King David, &c. and then to accompany them to London. And accordingly by indenture, dated January 2, [m] being ſtiled John Darcy le Piere conſtable of the Tower, he received the ſaid King at the Tower of London, from Sir Thomas de Rokeby, who received him from Ralph de Nevil at York. Moreover, the King ſignified to his Treaſurer, &c. that whereas he ſent John Darcy le Piere [n] from London, towards the caſtles of Rockeſburgh, Werk, and Bamburgh, for David Bruys, Malcolm Flemyng, and others, taken in the battle of Durham, he commands them to pay to him toward his expences after the rate of 20 s. a day.

Whilſt he was thus employed in the north, and being with the Lord Burwaſh, &c. (as before obſerved) to deliver from the King a meſſage to the parliament, which was to meet on the Monday next after Chriſtmas-day; and not arriving till the Tueſday, and the houſe being then informed, that they could not be ready to make their appearance, the parliament was prorogued till the Wedneſday ſeven-night following, when they declared, ' the good ſucceſs of the King, ſince his arrival
' at la Hogue in Normandy; as in ſurpriſing and taking of
' many towns and caſtles of war, as well at Caen as elſe-
' where; as alſo of the great victory obtained at Crecy,
' where the whole power of France was diſcomfited; and
' how the King was now come before Calais, from whence
' he intended not to depart, till by the help of God he had
' won the ſame. After which, he intended to purſue the enemy
' without return, till the war ſhould be fully ended, &c.'

He had ſummons to [o] parliament among the Barons, from 28 Edw. I. unto the 16 Edw. III. incluſive, and departed [p] this life full of honour, on May 30, 1347, 21 Edw. III. leaving

k Rymer, p. 537.   l Ibid. p. 535.   m Clauſ. 20 Edw. III. m. 1. dorſ. 1.
n Rymer, p. 551, & Barnes's hiſt. Edw. III. p. 387.   o Clauſ. de iiſdem, anno in Dorſ.   p Eſc. 21 Edw. III. n. 54. Ebor.

D'Arcy, Earl of Holderneſſe.

Sir John d'Arcy Knt. his ſon q and heir, at that time thirty years of age. He married two wives; firſt, Emeline, the daughter r and heir to Walter ſon and heir to William Heron, Baron of Hedeſton in com' Northumb. and afterwards Joan daughter s to Richard Burgh Earl of Ulſter, Lord of Connaught, widow t of Thomas Earl of Kildare, whom he married July 3, 1329, 3 Edw. III. at Maynoth in Ireland. By which firſt wife he had iſſue u John Lord d'Arcy, Roger, and Eleanor; and by the ſecond, William born x in Ireland, in 1330, 4 Edw. III. who was ſeated at Palatine in com' Meath, in that kingdom; alſo a daughter, Elizabeth, married to James Butler ſecond Earl of Ormond.

Which William, in conſideration y of the many good ſervices performed by his father, as alſo z for the good ſervices of him the ſaid William, had a grant from the king of the caſtle of Markynegan in Ireland, to hold for life; and had to wife Catherine, daughter to Sir Robert Fitz-Gerald of the county of Kildare, Knt.

His ſecond ſon, Sir Roger Darcy, was made a Lord Juſtice of Ireland, in 1346, 21 Edw. III. from whom the Darcys of the county of Eſſex deſcended; whereof Thomas Darcy, of Chiche in the ſaid county, was a perſon of great note in the reigns of Hen. VIII. and Edw. VI. who in the 5th year of his reign called him up to the houſe of Peers, by the title of Lord Darcy of Chiche, being then Chamberlain of his houſhold; and at a chapter *, held at Hampton-court, Sept. 28, the ſame year, he was elected Knight of the Garter, and by eſpecial commiſſion inſtalled at Windſor on October 9 following.

The eldeſt ſon, John Lord Darcy, in 9 Edw. III. his father then living, being called Johannes d'Arci le Fitz, was b in the wars of Scotland; and having, for his eſpecial ſervices, deſerved very well from the King, he in 15 Edw. III. obtained a grant c of an annuity of 40 l. per ann. to himſelf and his heirs for ever, which is enjoyed at this day.

In 16 Edw. III. he obtained d licence, that Alice, the widow of Nicholas Menill, might marry to whom ſhe pleaſed, being the King's loyal ſubject. In which year he was e in that expedition then made into France. In 19 Edw. III. he was f preſent in the Archbiſhop's palace at Lambeth, when John de Montfort Duke of Britanny did homage to the King.

q Eſc. 21 Edw. III. n. 54. Ebor.   r DD. f. 69.   s Annal. Hibern. per Camd.   t Clauſ. 20 Edw. III. m. 18.   u Fin. levat. 6 Edw. III.   x Annal. Hibern. ut ſupra.   y z Pat. 21 Edw. III. p. 2. m. 29.   a Borlace's reduction of Ireland, p. 49.   * Anſtis's regiſt. Garter, p. 448.   b Rot. Scot. 9 Edw. III. m. 52.   c Orig. 1 Hen. IV. Bund. Rot. 4.   d Clauſ. 16 Edw. III. p. 1. m. 15.   e Rot. Franc. 16 Edw. III. m. 18.   f Rymer, tom. 5. p. 452.

In 20 Edw. III. having had the custody of the King's liberty of Holderness in com' Ebor. as also,[h] of the manor of Bruftwycke, with its members, and the manor of Bareweck in com' Linc. likewife granted to him, he was, in confideration [i] of his many fervices done and to be done, difcharged [k] from rendering accompt to the King for them, or any of them: In which year King Edward, landing with a great army at La Hogue in Normandy, made him a Banneret, and gave him 200 l. per ann. out of the exchequer, during life, for his better fupport [l] of that honour, as by his patent [m] there dated July 15 appeareth. So that it is not to be doubted, but being there at that time, he was one of thofe, who, on Auguft 26 following, behaved themfelves fo bravely in that memorable battle of Crecy, where the Englifh obtained such lafting fame, as all our hiftorians do amply declare. And at the fiege of Calais, [n] in the fame year, it appears he had, in his retinue, 1 Banneret, 13 Knights, and 35 Archers on horfeback.

In 1347, 21 Edw. III. he found fuch favour [o] from the King, that upon doing his homage, being then of full age, he had livery of his lands before the inquifitions, taken after his father's death, which were, according to cuftom, returned into the chancery. In which year (September 25) he was conftituted [p] one of the three commiffioners to treat and conclude of peace between King Edward and the King of France; and was likewife conftituted [q] conftable of the Tower of London for life.

About this time he gave [r] the advowfon of the church of Knayth to the nuns of Hevenings. Soon after which, being again employed by the King in his wars with France, he had [s] 120 great horfes fent over to him at Calais. In 28 Edw. III. he was [t] one of the Peers who appointed Richard de Wymondefwold and others, their proctors, to affent to fuch things as fhall be agreed on between the King's ambaffadors, and thofe of France, before the Pope, not judicially, but as a private perfon.

This John Lord Darcy had fummons,[u] to parliament, amongft the Barons of this realm, from 22 until 28 Edw. III. but after that time, I have not feen any more of him till his death; which happened at [x] Nocton on Saturday next after March 2, the feaft of St. Chad, 1356-7, 30 Edw. III. and was buried in the priory of Gifborough in Yorkfhire. He died feized [y] of the manors of Ekynton in com' Derb. Kirby and Stretton, in com' Nott. Haddefton in com' Northumb. as alfo of the moiety of the manors of Wollore and Belforth, and moiety of the ham-

h i˙ k Rot. fin. 20 Edw. III. m. 27.   l m Rot. Franc. 20 Edw. III. m. 21.
n MS. Not. 125. in bibl. Harley.   o Rot. fin. 21 Edw. III. m. 20.   p Carf.
& Pat. 21 Edw. III. m. 4.   q Ibid. m. 17.   r Efc. 21 Edw. III. n 19.   s Rot.
Franc. 21 Edw. III. p. 1. m. 10.   t Rymer, tom. 5. p. 798.   u Clauf. de iifd.
ann. in Dorf.   x y Efc. 30 Edw. III. n. 33.   & Clauf. 47 Edw. III. m. 2.

let of Yefington in the fame county ; likewife of the manor of Knayth in com' Linc. Nocton and Silkfton in com' Ebor. and of the reverfion of the manors of Temple-Hurft and Temple-Newfom, after the death of Mary de St. Paul Countefs of Pembroke; as alfo of the caftle and manor of Whorlton, the manor of Aldwerk with its members, and of the manor of Yarum in the faid county of York: leaving [b] John his fon and heir not much above five years of age; and Philip fecond fon, with a daughter Ifabel: Elizabeth his wife, daughter [c] and heir to Nicholas Lord Menill, of Wharlton-caftle, then furviving him; who foon afterwards was remarried [d] to Peter de Mauley the fixth Baron of Mulgrave, and died 42 Edw. III.

Which John, who was thus within age at his father's death, died [e] in minority upon Auguft 26, 1362, 36 Edw. III. being feized [f] of the manor of Weftbroke in com' Hertf. Ekynton in com' Derb. Kirby and Stretton in the Clay in com' Nottingh. Knayth and Southorpe in com' Linc. Haddefton in com' Northumb. as alfo of Nocton and Silkfton in com' Ebor. He then alfo died feized of an annuity of 9 l. 16 s. 2 d. iffuing out of the farm of Newcaftle upon Tyne: Which annuity was granted [g] to John his father, in compenfation for his office of Juftice of Chefter, leaving Philip his brother and heir, then 11 years of age.

Which Philip, Lord Darcy and Meynell, making proof of his age, in 1373, 14 Edw. III. and doing his homage, had livery [h] of his lands. In 1377, 1 Rich. II. on the King's coronation, July 13, [i] he attended at that folemnity, and together with other Lords and great men did him homage. In 3 and 4 Rich. II. he was [k] in that expedition made into France, with Thomas of Woodftock Earl of Buckingham; and [l] arriving at Calais, three days before Maudlin-tide, July 22, rode with his banner difplayed: and became an active [m] perfon in the wars of France; having a command [n] of divers men at arms, and archers, for the recovery of the King's rights there. In the 5th of Rich. II. he with others of Lincolnfhire, were [o] ordered to proclaim, in that county, how the King expected all perfons, tenants there, fhould do their accuftomed fervices, as they ufed to perform before the late difturbances. And in confideration of his fignal fervices in the wars of France [p], in 6 Rich. II. he was fpecially excufed [q] from repairing into Ireland, as all perfons having lands there by an act of parliament made in 3 Rich. II. were then obliged unto, for the de-

[b] Clauf. 47 Edw. III. m. 2. [c] d Efc. 42 Edw. III. n. 44. [e] Ibid.
[f] Ibid. [g] [h] Clauf. 47 Edw. III. m. 2. [i] Rymer, tom. 7. p. 159.
[k] [l] m Froiffard, f. 237. a. [n] Rot. Franc. 3 Rich. II. m. 3. [o] Rymer, tom. 7. p. 316. [p] Clauf. 6 Rich. II. p. 21 m. 6. [q] Rot. Franc. 6 Rich. II. m. 1.

fence of that realm againſt the Iriſh rebels then in arms. And in the ſame year, with others, was ʳ commiſſioned to receive the homage of the Earl of Flanders, and thoſe of that province due to the King, as true ſovereign of France. In 7 Rich. II. for the like conſideration, ˢ and in regard of his great ᵗ charge, in ſupporting himſelf in thoſe wars; as alſo ᵘ for that he was then marching towards Scotland againſt the King's enemies there, he had a grant ˣ of all the iſſues and revenues of his own lands in Ireland, for the aid and defence of the country. And the Scots having taken Berwick-caſtle, the King on June 13, in the 18th year of his reign, ʸ commanded this Philip to be at Newcaſtle upon Tyne July 14 following, with horſe and arms, and his whole ſervice, or more if poſſible, in order to march againſt them, and ſuppreſs their rebellion; adding, that his loyalty and probity ſhall be not only acknowledged, but alſo commended.

Moreover, in 9 Rich. II. being conſtituted ᶻ Admiral of all the King's fleet, from the river of Thames northwards, he took certain prizes at ſea from the enemy; which, being brought ᵃ into the port of Sandwich, were, by the King's command, in conſideration of his ſervices, re-delivered ᵇ to him for his own uſe; and in 16 Rich. II. was ᶜ in that expedition then made into Ireland.

In 21 Rich. II. he had the King's licence ᵈ to go into Ireland on his own occaſions; and having been ſummoned ᵉ to parliament, from 1 Rich. II. until 21ſt of that King's reign incluſive, he by his ᶠ teſtament, bearing date April 16, 1399, 22 Rich. II. bequeathed his body to be buried in the priory of Giſborough in com' Ebor. near to his father's grave, appointing that five wax lights (each weighing eight pounds) and twenty-four torches ſhould burn about it, on the day of his ſepulture; of which torches (after the ſolemnity of his exequies) two to be diſpoſed of to the chapel of the bleſſed Virgin at Giſborough, two to the church of Rudby, two to the chapel at Querlton, two to the chapel of Hyrſt, two to the chapel of Newton, two to the chapel of Noƈton, two to the chapel of Aldwerk, two to the chapel of Kirkby, two to the church of Ekynton, two to the church of Knayth, and two to the church of Henyngs. And to the frabrick of the church of Querlton (without the caſtle) he bequeathed 40 s. and for covering the church of Torkſey 40 s. to the nuns of Foſſe 40 s. and to the rector of the church of Knayth 26 s. 8 d. to his ſon Philip, a coat of mail of Mylain; and to his ſon Thomas, of Newſted, a gilt

r Rymer, tom. 7. p. 396   s t u x Pat. 7 Rich. II. p. 2. m. 20.   y Rymer, tom. 7. p. 475.   z Rot. Franc. 9 Rich. II. m. 25   a b Clauſ. 10. Rich. II. m. 11.   c Pat. 16 Rich. II. p. 2. m. 22.   d Pat 21 Rich. II. p. 3. m. 7.   e Clauſ. de iiſdem ann. in Dorſ.   f Regiſt. Beaufort, Linc. Epiſcop.

cup with a cover, and crowns, which he had of King Edward's gift. He likewise ordered that 20 s. should be bestowed on an image of St. Anne, made of alabaster, to be placed at the altar of the blessed Virgin at Henyngs; appointing that his executors shall be at the charge of ten pounds for a marble stone to be laid on his grave, with the image of himself, and Elizabeth his wife, fixed thereon, who was daughter to Sir Thomas Grey of Heton in Northumberland, and died 13 Hen. IV. He soon after departed [g] this life, viz. on the morrow after St. George's day, being seized [h] of the manor of Ekington in com' Derb. Kirkby in com' Notting. Wollore, Hethpole, Hodereſtaw, Beiford, Yeſington, Lowyk, Haddeſton, and of that great waſte, called the foreſt of Cheviot; as alſo of the advowſon of the hoſpital of Wollore, all in the county of Northumberland; likewiſe of the manors of Temple-Hyrſt, Temple-Newſom, Yarum, Aſelby, Aldewerk, and Noéton in com' Ebor. as alſo of Torkſey and Knayth in com' Linc. leaving John, his ſon and heir, then [i] 22 years of age.

Which John [k], doing his homage [l] the ſame year, had livery [m] of all thoſe lands before-mentioned; excepting [n] ſuch, whereof Elizabeth, the widow of the ſaid Philip, was endowed. And in 8 Hen. IV. was [o] one of thoſe Lords who conſented to the act of parliament, then made, for ſettling the ſucceſſion to the crown of England on Henry Prince of Wales, and the heirs of his body, with remainder to his brothers, Thomas, John and Humphry, and the heirs of their bodies. To which all the Lords preſent ſet their hands and ſeals. And having had ſummons to [p] parliament, from 23 Rich. II. until 12 Hen. IV. incluſive, departed [q] this life Decem. 9, 1411, 13 Hen. IV. leaving Philip, [r] his ſon and heir, 14 years of age; and Sir John, of whom hereafter. Margaret [s] his widow, daughter [t] to Henry Lord Grey of Wilton, ſurviving, was afterwards married to Sir Thomas Swinford, Knt.

Which laſt-mentioned Philip, being to [u] go with Henry Prince of Wales, appointed governor of Calais, had the King's protection for one year, and died [x] Auguſt 2, 1418, 6 Hen. V. before he accompliſhed his full age, leaving Eleanor his wife (daughter [y] of Henry Lord Fitz-Hugh) ſurviving, and Elizabeth and Margery, his two daughters and heirs; the one two years of age, and upwards; and the other not much more than one. Of which [a] Elizabeth became the wife of Sir James Strangeways the younger, of Weſt-Hartſey caſtle,

g h Eſc. 22 Rich. II. n. 17. i Eſc. ibid. k l m n Rot. fin. 22 Rich. II. m. 12. o Rymer, tom. 8. p. 463. p Clauſ. de iiſdem ann. in Dorſ. q r Eſc. 13 Hen. IV. n. 36. s Clauſ. 14 Hen. IV. m. 8. t Eſc. 36 Hen. VI. n. 30. Derb. u Rymer, tom. 8. p. 705. x Eſc. 7 Hen. V. n. 78. Ebor. y Eſc. 13 Hen. IV. n. 36. z Eſc. 7 Hen. V. præd. & Clauſ. 10 Hen. VI. m. 15. a Rot. fin. 33 Hen. VI. m. 9.

Ebor.

D'Arcy, Earl of Holderneſſe.

Ebor. Knt. and Margery of Sir John Conyers, of Hornby-caſtle, Ebor. Knt. And in 36 Hen. VI. were likewiſe by [b] inquiſition found to be couſins and heirs to John d'Arci le Fitz, viz. daughters of Philip, ſon of John, ſon of the ſaid John.

Which Margery, ſo married to Conyers, made proof [c] of her age at Maſham in com' Ebor. on April 29, 1433, 11 Hen. VI. where it was found, that ſhe was born at Ravenſwath in com' Ebor. upon Sept. 1, the feaſt-day of St. Gyles the Abbot, 1418, 6 Hen. V. and baptized in the church of Kirkby on the hill; ſo that ſhe was at the time of taking that inquiſition, 14 years of age and upwards.

But Sir John, the brother [d] of the before-mentioned Philip Lord d'Arcy, was his next [e] heir male and then 15 years old, and upwards, and was of Torkſey in Lincolnſhire. Which Sir John [f], during the time of his minority, whilſt he was in ward [g] to the King, taking to wife [h] Joan the daughter of John Lord Greyſtock, without licence; for pardon [i] of that tranſgreſſion, afterwards paid 200 marks. And making proof [k] of his age in 6 Hen. VI. had reſpite [l] for doing his homage, as alſo livery [m] of his lands: But on Saturday next, after the feaſt of the Aſcenſion of our Lord, in 1454, 32 Hen. VI. he departed [n] this life, leaving Sir William d'Arcy his grandſon [o] and heir (viz. ſon of Richard, who died in his life-time) then four [p] years of age; and had alſo a daughter Joan, wife of John Beaumont, of Cole-Orton, in com' Leiceſter, Eſq; Which Richard had to wife Eleanor daughter of John Lord Scroop of Upſal, by whom he had iſſue Sir William before-mentioned.

Which Sir William [q] married Eufemia, daughter of Sir John Langton of Farnely in com' Ebor. Knt. and died [r] in 3 Hen. VII. leaving Thomas his ſon and heir, 21 years of age, and upwards.

This Thomas, in 12 Hen. VII. was [s] one of the northern Lords that marched with Thomas Earl of Surrey, towards Norham-Caſtle, unto which James IV. King of Scotland had then laid ſiege. And on his retreat, following him, after ſome plunder of the borders, returned.

In 13 Hen. VII. on the defeat of Perkin Warbeck, and the Corniſh traitors, he was [t] impowered with Sir Amias Paulet, Knt. and Robert Sherborne dean of Paul's, to enquire into their crimes, and to puniſh them by fine or otherwiſe, according to their deſerts. And the ſame year being [u] a Knight for

---

b Eſc. 36 Hen. VI. n. 30. Derb.   c Eſc. 11 Hen. VI. n. 43.   d e Eſc. 7 Hen. V. n. 78. Ebor.   f g h Pat. 6 Hen. VI. p. 1. m. 1.   i k l m Clauſ. 6 Hen. VI. m. 3.   n o Lib. Cedul. p. 648. Linc.   p Eſc. 32 Hen. VI. n. 15. p. 5. q Ex ſtemmate.   r Eſc. 3 Hen. VII. Linc.   s Polyd. Virg. p. 602. 603. t Hall's chron. fol. 48.   u Pat. 1 Hen. VII. p. 1. m. 18.

the King's body, he was made constable [x] of Bamburgh-castle in Northumberland. In 14 Hen. VII. he was constituted captain [y] of the town and castle of Berwick, as also warden [z] of the east and middle Marches towards Scotland. In 15 Hen. VII. he had special commission [a] to exercise the office of constable and marshal of England, in all points, against certain rebels; and was the same year made constable [b] of Sheriff-Hutton castle in com' Ebor. as also steward of that lordship.

In 17 Hen. VII. being still [c] captain of Berwick, he was made [d] treasurer and chamberlain there, as also customer [e] of that port. In 18 Hen. VII. the King confiding in his loyalty, industry, and foresight, commissioned him and Henry Babyngton, D. D. to go to James King of Scotland, to tender him the oath he was obliged to take, to observe the peace lately concluded; and were also [f] impowered to exchange with the ambassadors of Scotland the ratification of the peace, as also of the articles of marriage between the said King of Scotland, and Margaret, eldest daughter of King Henry.

In 21 Hen. VII. being [g] then one of the King's privy-council, he was made [h] general warden of the Marches towards Scotland. And in 23 Hen. VII. a treaty of marriage [i] being set on foot between Charles Prince of Spain, Archduke of Austria, and Mary the King's third but second surviving daughter; for the performance of which marriage-articles the King was bound in a recognizance of 250,000 crowns; and this Thomas Lord d'Arcy, and other Lords, each in the sum of 50,000 crowns. After which he was [k] present in the palace of Richmond on Decemb. 7, 24 Hen. VII. at the solemnizing of their nuptials, which, however, were not consummated.

On the accession of Hen. VIII. to the throne, April 22, 1509, he was [l] one of the eleven counsellors elected by his grandmother the Countess of Richmond, out of those his father most trusted, for the government of the kingdom: and was again made general warden of the Marches towards Scotland [m] (Sir Thomas d'Arcy Knt. being joined with him;) in which year also the title and dignity of a Baron was revived to him, through the special favour of that King, by writ [n] of summons to parliament. Which title of honour, enjoyed by many of his ancestors, ceased in the daughters and heirs of Philip Lord d'Arcy, married to Strangeways, and Conyers, as hath been already observed. In

x Ibid.　y Privat. sigil. 14 Hen. VII.　z Ibid.　a Pat. 15 Hen. VII. p. 2.　b Ibid. m. 17.　c d Orig. 17 Hen. VII. Rot. 39.　e Rymer, tom. 13, p. 33.　f Ibid. p. 51.　g h Pat. 21 Hen. VII. p. 1. m. 33. i Rymer, tom. 13. p. 177.　k Ibid. p. 238.　l Herbert's life of Hen. VIII. in hist. of Eng. vol. 2. p. 2.　m Pat, 1 Hen, VIII, p, 2, in Dorf, m, 22, n Clauf. de eodem, ann. in Dorf,

In this first year of Henry VIII. his commission ᵒ for the office of treasurer and chamberlain of Berwick, and customer there being also renewed, he was made steward and surveyor of all the King's lands beyond Trent, during the minority of the Earl of Westmoreland; as also surveyor-general of the castles and lordships of Sheriff-Hutton, Middleham, Richmond, Cottingham, Sandall, Wakefield, Hatfield, and Coningsburgh; and likewise chief warden and justice of all the King's forests in those parts; and was ᵖ also elected, May 18, 1 Hen. VIII. Knight of the most noble order of the Garter, and was installed on the 21st following at Windsor.

In 2 Hen. VIII. ᑫ Ferdinand, King of Castile and Aragon, having sent ambassadors to the King, to require 1500 archers to be sent in aid to him against the Moors; and this Thomas Lord d'Arcy (then a Knight of ʳ the Garter, and governor of the town and castle of Berwick) requiring to command those forces, the King in confidence ˢ of his loyalty, valour, and industry, granted his desire, with power of conferring the honour of knighthood, rewarding the meritorious, and punishing of delinquents, by letters patent, bearing date March 11, 1511. And accordingly, on Monday in Rogation week, he sailed from Plymouth with four royal ships, and on ᵗ June 1, arriving at Cadiz, sent to the King of Aragon notice of his arrival. On the 8th of that month, ᵘ that King's council, waiting on the Lord d'Arcy on ship-board, informed him that a peace was made, and that the King gave him and his followers thanks for their great pains and travail, but had then no occasion for their service. And inviting the Lord d'Arcy, in the King's name, to come to court, he replied, ' That is not ' my desire; for my men shall not say that I brought them ' out of their country, and, to do myself pleasure, leave them ' without an head, as men of me forsaken. Nay, nay, my ' Lords, the King's banquet is not my desire.' Whereupon the next morning he and his soldiers were liberally rewarded, and dismissed; but the same day a fray happening between some of the English and Spaniards, the Lords of Spain came to the Lord d'Arcy, saying, ' Sir, we pray you, since ' you know the King's pleasure, and have your wages, that ' you, with all your people, will go with your ships away, ' for we perceive you owe us some displeasure.' Whereunto he nobly answered, ' That he would all the world knew that ' he was as able to conduct his men homewards, as he was to ' bring them out of their country, without the King of Ara-

ᵒ Orig. 1 Hen. VIII. Rot. 62.   ᵖ Anstis's regist. of the garter, p. 272.
ᑫ Hollinshed, p. 808.   ʳ Ashmole's order of the gart. p. 713.   ˢ Rymer, tom. 13. p. 294.   ᵗ Hall's chren. fol. 12, a & b.   ᵘ Ibid. fol. 13. a.

' gon's

' gen's wages (saving his honour;) and as for the fray it was
' against his will, and without his knowledge.' And that
night he and all his men embarked, and arriving at Plymouth,
went to the King at Windsor.

In 1513, 5 Hen. VIII. he was at the siege of Teroven, [y] and
commanded the left wing in the battle that ensued, called by our
historians, The Battle of Spurs, from the swiftness of the
French in running away, Aug. 16. In 14 Hen. VIII. he was
[z] in that expedition against the Scots under the Duke of Albany,
who had invaded the English borders, and came near to Carlisle. Also in the year following he [a] commanded against the
Scots, and forced them to retreat.

In 21 Hen. VIII. he was [b] one of the Lords which exhibited
the articles against Cardinal Wolsey; and in 22 Hen. VIII.
subscribed [c] that letter to Pope Clement VII. intimating to
him the loss of his supremacy here, in case he did not comply
in that cause of King Henry's divorce.

In 26 Hen. VIII. in regard [d] of his age, and debility of
body, he procured a special licence [e] to be absent from parliament: Which was thought rather to proceed from his un-
willingness to be there, foreseeing the ruin of the religious
houses near approaching; wherein he had no mind to give his
vote (the contrivance, in order thereto, having been laid long
before, tho' the work was not fully perfected until the following year, viz. 27 Hen. VIII.) and that this was the real cause
of such his deserting the parliament, is evident enough from
his after-actings: For [f] in 28 Hen. VIII. the next year ensuing the dissolution of the lesser houses (it being then dis-
cernible enough what was like to become of all the rest) sundry persons being employed, by the most subtle practices, to
accomplish the work, it caused an insurrection, [g] under the
command of Robert Aske, and by them called [h] The Pilgrimage of Grace; when this Thomas Lord d'Arcy, being [i] with
the Archbishop of York in Pontefract-castle, delivered it up
to the rebels, and took [k] the oath, viz.

' To enter into the pilgrimage of grace, for the love of God,
' the preservation of the King's person and issue, the purifying
' of the nobility, expulsing all villain blood and evil counsel-
' lors; for no particular profit to themselves, nor to do dis-
' pleasure to any, nor to slay nor murder any for envy, but to
' put away all fears, and to take afore them the cross of Christ,
' his faith, the restitution of the church, and the suppression
' of heretics, and their opinions.'

y z Hall's chron. fol. 26 & 32. and, a Ibidem, fol. 115.   b Herbert's
life of Hen. VIII. in hist. of Engl. p. 129.   c Rymer, tom. 14. p. 486.
d Pat. 26 Hen. VIII. p. 2.   e Herbert's life, præd. p. 206.   f g h i Ibid.
k Ibid.

D'Arcy, Earl of Holderneſſe.

Certain it is, that though this Lord d'Arcy, and the Archbiſhop, pretended [1] want of proviſion to hold out the caſtle; yet were they ſuſpected [m] to render it in favour of the rebels; for on that treaty, afterwards had betwixt the Duke of Norfolk, and others truſted by the King, he was, with Aſke himſelf, and ſome of that party, employed to treat for them. And notwithſtanding, he afterwards excuſed [n] it to the Lord Cromwell, ſaying, ' [o] That what he did was merely for retaining ' ſo much credit with the Commons, as might better enable ' him to do the King ſervice;' it did not ſatisfy: for, together with Aſke, and ſome others, being brought [p] priſoner to London, he was arraigned [q] at Weſtminſter; and being found guilty [r] of high treaſon, was beheaded [s] on Tower-hill, June 20, 30 Hen. VIII. and buried in the church of St. Botolph without Aldgate; where, in the eaſt end of the chancel, was a handſome alabaſter monument, of curious workmanſhip, with the following [t] inſcription, ſet up in memory of him, and of Sir Arthur Darcy his ſon.

' Here lyeth Thomas Lord Darcy of the north, and ſome-
' time of the garter, Lady Elizabeth Carew, daughter to
' Sir Francis Brian, Knight; and Sir Arthur Darcy Knight,
' younger ſonne to the above-named Lord Darcy and Lady
' Mary his deare wife, daughter to Sir Nicholas Carew Knight,
' who had tenne ſonnes and five daughters. Here lye Charles,
' William and Philip, Mary and Urſula, ſons and daughters
' to the ſaid Sir Arthur, and Mary his wife, whoſe ſouls God
' take to his infinite mercy, amen.'

He married two wives; [u] firſt, Edith, daughter of Sir John Sands, and ſiſter of William the firſt Lord Sands, who, dying on Aug. 22, 1529, was buried at the Friars Minors in Greenwich, in Kent; leaving iſſue an only daughter Elizabeth, married to Sir Marmaduke Conſtable, of Flamborough in com' Ebor. Knt. His ſecond wife was, [x] Douſabella, daughter and heireſs of Sir Richard Tempeſt, of Ridleſdale in com' Northumb. Knt. by whom he had iſſue three ſons and a daughter, George Lord Darcy, Sir Arthur Darcy Knt. from whom the preſent Earl of Holderneſſe is deſcended; Richard, third ſon, and Mabilla, who died without iſſue.

The ſaid Thomas Lord Darcy had ſummons [y] to the parliaments of 1, 6, 21, and 28 Hen. VIII.

George his eldeſt ſon, in 5 Hen. VIII. had [z] a command in the rear of that army which encountered with the Scots at Braunſton, or Flodden, where a great victory was obtained

---

l Ibid. m Ibid. n o Ibid. p. 211. p Ibid. q r s Herbert's life, præd. p. 212. t Stowe's ſurvey of Lond. p. 119. u Ex ſtemmate. x MS. J. 3 in offic. arm, fol. 71. b. y Clauſ. de iiſdem, ann. in Dorſ. z Hollinſh. p. 828.

Sept.

Sept. 9, 1513, and James IV. King of Scots flain. And afterwards waiting on Hen. VIII. who a little before had taken the town of Teroven, and was befieging of Tournay, he had the honour [a] of knighthood conferred on him at Lifle, Oct. 14 following. He was [b] fheriff of Yorkfhire, in 27 Hen. VIII. And in 2 Edw. VI. was reftored [c] in blood, with the title [d] of Lord d'Arcy of Afton, to himfelf, and the heirs male of his body.

In the year 1556, he [e] had a letter from Queen Mary to be in a readinefs, with what forces he could raife, an invafion being feared from the Scots, and a rebellion in the north parts of the kingdom. And by his laft will and teftament [f] bequeathed his body to be buried in the choir at Brayton, near to this wife, appointing, that a convenient tomb fhould be made and fet over them both, according to his eftate and degree. He bequeaths to Agnes Fairfax, his daughter, an hundred marks, and his beft-wrought filk carpet, bordered with crimfon velvet, which fhe had made; to Mary, his daughter, an hundred marks; to his daughter Dawney, his beft cup; and to Elizabeth, with his other daughters, certain annual rents out of part of his lands for divers years. He departed this life [g] Aug. 28, 4 & 5 Phil. & Mar. and had iffue by Dorothy his wife, daughter and heirefs of Sir John Melton, of Afton in com' Ebor. five fons, William, Thomas, another William, who died all young; John Lord Darcy his heir, and George: [h] and fix daughters, Edith, wife of Sir Thomas Dawney, of Cowick, Knt. Agnes (or Anne according to fome) firft wife to Sir William Fairfax, of Walton, Knt. and died without iffue; Dorothy, wife to Sir Thomas Metham of Metham, Knt. all in Yorkfhire; Clara, who died unmarried; Mary, 2d wife to Henry, fon and heir of Thomas Babington, of Dethick in Derbyfhire, Efq; and Elizabeth, to Sir Brian Stapleton, of Carlton, in com' Ebor. Knt.

His fucceffor John Lord Darcy married Agnes, daughter of Thomas Babington of Dethick in com' Derb. Efq; and in 1573, 16 Eliz. [i] accompanied Walter Earl of Effex in his expedition againft the rebels in Ulfter, in Ireland. He died in the year 1587, leaving John his grandfon and heir to fucceed him in honour and eftate; Michael Darcy, Efq; his eldeft fon dying in his life-time, on Dec. 13, 1580, having married Margaret, daughter of Thomas Wentworth of Wentworth-Woodhoufe in com' Ebor. Efq; and leaving by her (who

---

a Nom. equit. MS. in bibl. cotton. not. Claudius. c. 3.   b Fuller's worthies, p. 220.   c d Journal of parliam. de 2 Edw. VI.   e Strype's memorials, vol. 3. p. 353.]   f Ex regift. Heath, fol. 291.   g Glover's vifit. Yorkfh. m. 84. MS. p. 42, 43.   h Efc. de eodem ann.   i Camden's ann. of Q. Eliz. in hift. of Eng. vol. 2. p. 450.

D'Arcy, Earl of Holdernesse.

wedded 2dly Jasper Blythman, of New-Lathes, Esq; but sine prole) the said John, successor to his grandfather John Lord Darcy, as also two daughters, Margaret, who died unmarried, and Anne, who was heir to her brother, and married to Henry Saville of Copley, in com' Ebor. Esq; from whom Sir John Saville, of Copley, Bart. whose daughter and heir, Mary-Elizabeth, was the wife of Lord Thomas Howard, father of Edward, the present and ninth Duke of Norfolk.

This John Lord Darcy was [k] one of the Peers, who, in 32 Eliz. was summoned to attend the trial of Philip Howard, Earl of Arundel. His Lordship had four wives, 1. Rosamond, daughter of Sir Peter Frechevile of Stavely, in the county of Derby, Knt. and by her had John, his only son, and two daughters, Rosamond and Elizabeth, who all three died young, in the life-time of their father. His second was Isabel, daughter to Sir Christopher Wray, of Glentworth in Leicestershire, Knt. Lord Chief Justice; but by her, who had been successively the relict of Godfrey Foljambe, of Walton in Derbyshire, Esq; and of Sir William Bowes, Knt. had no progeny. He wedded, 3dly, Mary, daughter of Thomas Bellasyse, Lord Viscount Fauconberg, and had no issue by her; nor by his fourth wife, Elizabeth, daughter to William West, of Firbeck in Yorkshire, Esq. His Lordship departed this life in July, 1635, when Anne, his sister before-mentioned, became his heir: but the honour ceased in this family, till Charles I. by his letters patent, bearing date Aug. 10, the 17th year of his reign, 1641, declared, restored, and confirmed, unto Sir Conyers d'Arcy, Knt. grandson of Sir Arthur Darcy, second son to Thomas Lord Darcy, and to the heirs male of his body, lawfully begotten, the stile, title, and dignity of Lord d'Arcy.

I am now therefore to treat of the said Sir Arthur and his descendants. In 13 Hen. VIII. (before which time he had the honour of knighthood conferred on him) he, [l] together with the Marquess of Dorset, on April 2, entering into Teviotdale and Galloway, after burning several towns and villages, returned with 4000 head of cattle and other booty. And having, in several other encounters with the Scots, shewed his conduct and courage, the King, in 23 Hen. VIII. being to pass over sea, and considering that the Scots had robbed his subjects, both by sea and land, and imagining that in his absence they would attempt some outrageous enterprize, he sent Sir Arthur Darcy, Knt. with 300 men to Berwick, to preserve the borders from their invasions. Of whose proceed-

[k] Ibid. p. 551.   [l] Hall's chron. fol. 106.

ings my author [1] gives this account: 'The Scottes hearyng of his commyng into Northumberlande to the Middle Marches, and came to a place called Fowbery, and in the journey fired certain villages and returned. Sir Arthur Darcy hearyng of this adventure, was nothyng contente. Nowe at this feafon there laie at Berwick, Archibald Duglas Erle of Angus, whiche had maried the Quene of Scottes, the Kynges fifter, and was banifhed Scotlande, and fhe was from hym divorfed, and maried to another. The Scottes bragged of their enterprife, and faied that Sir Arthur had brought them good lucke, and faid, that he and the Erle of Angus, flepte well in Barwicke: Thei hearyng of this bragge, made a roade with 400 men into Scotlande, and fet a village on fire: then fhortly affembled together 800 Scottes. When thenglifhemen perceived the Scottes, thei caufed their trompet to blowe a retreate, and the Erle and 20 with hym fhewed himfelf on a hill, even at the face of the Scottes, and the trumpette blewe at their backes fo that the Scottes thought that there had been 2 compaignies, whiche caufed the Scottes to flie, and the Englifhmen folowed, and flewe a great nomber and toke many prifoners, and brought them to Berwicke, the twentie daie of October.'

In 25 Hen. VIII. on information given to the King, that the Emperor (Charles V.) had threatened war againft England, and treated fecretly with James V. King of Scotland, for his aid therein; [m] he was (on expiration of the then five years truce) permitted to enter the borders, and to forage that country, which he did, burning divers towns, and carrying away much booty. And for his fervices, in September following, he was made Captain [n] of the Ifle of Jerfey: which government he [o] fold, by leave of the King, two years after, to Thomas Lord Vaux of Harrowden.

In 5 Edw. VI. he was conftituted Lieutenant [p] of the Tower of London; and in the firft year of Queen Mary was [q] commiffioned to infpect into the ordnance and ftores of the kingdom; he was alfo fteward of the foreft of Galtries, and land within the faid foreft, [r] and mafter of the wild beafts therein, and all the herbage, pannage, and wood called wyndfalne and brofyng therein. And departed this life [s] on April 3, 1561, 3 Eliz. was buried by his father Thomas Lord Darcy, in the church of St. Botolph without Aldgate.

[1] Hall, fol. 209. m Herbert's life of Hen. VIII. in hift. of Engl. p. 166. n Pat. 25 Hen. VIII. p. 1. o Fall's account of Jerfey, p. 91, 93. p Hift. of Edw. VI. by Sir J Haywood, p. 132. q Strype's memoirs, vol. 3. p. 33. r Rymer, vol. 15. p. 441. s Ex ftemmate.

D'Arcy, Earl of Holderneſſe. 31

He married Mary, daughter of Sir Nicholas Carew of Bedington, in com' Surr. Knight of the Garter, and coheir to her brother Sir Francis Carew, by [t] whom he had ten ſons and five daughters, whereof Charles, William, and Philip, Mary and Urſula, died in their infancies, and were buried by him in the church of St. Botolph before-mentioned. His other ſons were, 1. Sir Henry; 2. Thomas, anceſtor to the preſent Earl of Holderneſſe; 3. Sir Edward; 4. Arthur Darcy, of Alderton, in Northamptonſhire, Eſq; 5. Nicholas; 6. John; and 7. Francis.—Sir Henry Darcy, Sir Arthur's eldeſt ſon, was of Brimham, in Yorkſhire, and alſo of Leighton-Bromewould in Huntingdonſhire; for which county, and that of Cambridge, he ſerved ſheriff in the 5th and 26th of Elizabeth: and had two wives. His firſt was Catherine, daughter of Sir John Fermor, of Eaſton-Neſton in Northamptonſhire, Knt. and relict of Michael Pulteney of Miſterton, in the county of Leiceſter, Eſq; His ſecond was Catherine, daughter and heir of Sir Robert Tirwhytt, of Leighton beforementioned, by whom he had a daughter, named Catherine, wedded to Gervaſe Lord Clifton.—Sir Edward Darcy, the third ſon of Sir Arthur, was of the privy chamber to Queen Elizabeth; and dying at his houſe called Dartford-place in Kent, on Oct. 28, 1612, aged 69 (having been knighted on May 11 preceding, at the Charter-houſe) was interred with his anceſtors in St. Botolph's church aforeſaid. He married Elizabeth, daughter of Thomas Aſtely, of Writtle in Eſſex, Eſq; and by her, beſides two younger ſons, Chriſtopher and Cary, and a daughter, Catherine, wedded to William Weſt, of Firbeck in com' Ebor. had Sir Robert Darcy, Knt. his heir, who married Grace, daughter and coheir of Alexander Redyſhe, of Redyſhe in Lancaſhire, Eſq; and by her was father of Edward Darcy, of Dartford-place before-mentioned, and of Newhall in Derbyſhire, Eſq; who, by Lady Elizabeth, his wife, daughter of Philip Stanhope, firſt Earl of Cheſterfield, left four daughters his coheirs, viz. Catherine, wedded to Sir Eraſmus Phillips, of Picton-caſtle in Pembrokſhire, Bart. ——— to Capt. Barnes; ——— to Sir ——— Rokeby; and Anne, to Thomas Milward, of Stanton in Derbyſhire, Eſq; Of three other daughters of Sir Arthur Darcy, Elizabeth was married to Lewis Lord Mordaunt.

I now return to Thomas Darcy, Eſq; ſecond ſon beforementioned, who, by the death of his brother Sir Henry Darcy, Knt. without male iſſue, became the chief heir male of the family, and deceaſed on Nov. 6, 1605, the 3d of King James I. He married Elizabeth, ſecond daughter and

[t] Inſcriptio tumuli.

cohei

coheir of John Lord Conyers, by the Lady Maud his wife, daughter of Henry Percy, Earl of Northumberland, and Knight of the Garter. Which Lord Conyers died in 3d and 4th of Philip and Mary, leaving issue three daughters his coheirs, but of them only the said Elizabeth left issue, viz. Conyers Darcy, her son and heir.

Which Conyers received the honour of knighthood, in the life-time of his father, [u] viz. at Whitehall, July 23, 1603. And being seated at Hornby-castle (which came by his mother) in com' Ebor. and setting forth, by his petition to King Charles I. in that parliament begun at Westminster, Nov. 3, 1640, That after the attainder of Thomas Lord d'Arcy, his great grandfather, in 29 Hen. VIII. Sir George d'Arcy, Knt. eldest son to the said Thomas, being restored in blood by King Edward the sixth, obtained a grant of the title and dignity of Lord d'Arcy to himself and the heirs male of his body; and that by the death of John Lord d'Arcy, late of Aston in com' Ebor. without issue male in the eleventh of his reign) the title and dignity of Lord d'Arcy was utterly extinct, did humbly desire, that, being grandchild and heir male to the beforespecified Sir Arthur d'Arcy, Knt. and likewise son and heir of Elizabeth, daughter and coheir of John Lord Conyers, lineal heir to Margery, daughter and coheir to Philip Lord d'Arcy, son of John Lord d'Arcy, one of the Barons of this realm in the time of King Henry the fourth, his majesty would be pleased to declare, restore, and confirm, to him the said Sir Conyers d'Arcy, and to the heirs male of his body, the stile, title, and dignity of Lord d'Arcy, with such place, pre-eminence, and precedency, as the said John Lord d'Arcy had; and by right from his ancestors then enjoyed.

And his said Majesty, graciously condescending, did, by his letters patents, bearing date at Westminster Aug. 10, 1641, the 17th year of his reign, declare, restore, and confirm to him the said Sir Conyers d'Arcy, Knt. and to the heirs male of his body lawfully begotten, the stile, title, and dignity of Lord d'Arcy, so enjoyed by his ancestor John Lord d'Arcy, as aforesaid; whereupon he had summons to parliament accordingly. And departing this life March 3, anno 1653, left issue by Dorothy his wife, daughter of Sir Henry Belasyse of Newborough, in com' Ebor. Knt. and Bart. six sons, viz. 1 Conyers Darcy his son and heir, created Earl of Holdernesse: 2. Sir William Darcy, of Witton-castle, in the county-palatine of Durham, Knt. who was sequestered for his loyalty to Charles I. being obliged to compound with the usurping powers for 1000 l. and 40 l. per annum to the teachers of those times. By ———

[u] Philpot's cat. of Knights.

his

his wife, he had several sons, of whom, Thomas, the third, was a captain in the army; and a daughter, Margaret, wedded to Sir Metcalfe Robinson, of Newby-park, in Yorkshire, Bart. but without issue. 3. Henry Darcy, of Newpark and Colborne, in com' Ebor. Esq; who, by Mary his wife, daughter and heir of William Scrope, of Highley, in the bishopric of Durham, Esq; had Philip Darcy, Esq; his heir, and nine other children; and dying on April 28, 1662, aged 57, was buried in the church of St. Olave, in York. 4. Thomas Darcy, of Winkburne, in com' Nott. Esq; 5. Marmaduke Darcy, born 1615, a gallant gentleman (as my Lord Clarendon [y] writes) who was sent by the Earl of Rochester into the north, to prepare the way for the restoration of Charles II. where he brought many who would have rose for the King, had not the Earl, who came there, discouraged them. He was Gentleman-usher of the Privy-chamber to Charles II. and dying unmarried on July 3, 1687, aged 72, was buried at Windsor, having been member for Richmond part of the long parliament called in 1661. 6. James Darcy, of Sedbury-Park near Richmond, in com' Ebor. who, by Isabel his wife, daughter of Sir Marmaduke Wyvill, of Constable-Burton in com' Ebor. Knt. and Bart. had issue James, aged 15, 1665, who took to wife Mary, daughter of Sir William Hickes, of Ruckholts in Essex, Bart. and was succeeded by Henry Darcy, Esq; who was Sheriff of Yorkshire in 1742, and left Maria-Catherine, his daughter and heir, wife to Sir Robert Hildeyard, of Wynstead in com' Ebor. Bart.—This Conyers Lord Darcy had also seven daughters, viz. Barbara, married to Matthew Hutton, of Marke in com' Ebor. Esq; Ursula, to John Stillington, of Kelfield, Esq; Margaret, to Sir Thomas Harrison, of Allerthorpe, Knt. Dorothy, to John Dalton, of Hawkeswell, Esq; all in the same county; and Anne, to Thomas Metcalfe, of Routh-Park in com' Linc. Esq; Grace, first married to George Best, of Middleton, Esq; and secondly, to Francis Molineux, of Mansfield in com' Nott. Esq; second son of Sir Francis Molineux, of Teversall in the same county, Bart. and Mary, to Acton Burnell, of Winkburne, in the said county of Nottingham, Esq;

To the said Conyers Lord Darcy succeeded Conyers Darcy, his son and heir, who most loyally taking arms on the behalf of Charles I. against his rebellious subjects, in the time of that insurrection raised and carried on by the greatest number of the members of that unhappy long parliament, begun at Westminster on Nov. 3, 1640, behaved himself most valiantly in di-

[y] In hist. of rebellion, vol. 3. book 14. p. 556, 560.

vers sharp and bloody fights; and was obliged to compound for his estate [z] with the sequestrators for 1337 l. 6 d. with 120 l. per ann. settled on the teachers of those times. And living to see the happy restoration of Charles II. he was, in consideration thereof, and his father's eminent merits, by his said Majesty, advanced to the dignity of an Earl of this realm, by the title of Earl of Holdernesse, by letters patent dated at Westminster, Dec. 5, in the 34th year of his reign.

This Earl [a] died in the year 1688; and having married Grace, sole daughter and heir to Sir Thomas Rokeby, of Skyers, in the said county of York, Bart. had issue Conyers Darcy, his only son, and five daughters, viz. Ursula, married to Sir Christopher Wyvill, of Constable-Burton in com' Ebor. Bart. Elizabeth, to Sir Henry Stapleton, of Myton in the said county, Bart. Grace, to Sir John Legard, of Ganton in the said county, Bart. Margaret, to Sir Henry Marwood, of Little Buskby in the said county, Bart. without issue; and Anne.

Which Conyers (his only son) in consideration of his singular loyalty and merit, being summoned to parliament among the Barons of this realm, by the title of Lord Conyers, by writ dated Nov. 1, anno 32 Car. II. took his place as Lord Conyers, next below the Lord Stourton, and next above the Lord Sands. And in the year 1688, succeeding his father, was second Earl of Holdernesse. He married to his first wife the Lady Catherine, daughter to Francis Fane, Earl of Westmorland, and she dying without issue, he took to wife, secondly, the Lady Frances, daughter to Thomas Howard Earl of Berkshire, by whom he had issue three sons, John, Philip, and Charles, which last died unmarried, anno 1615; thirdly, the Lady Frances, daughter to William Seymour Duke of Somerset, widow to Thomas Wriothesley Earl of Southampton, Lord High Treasurer of England, by whom he had no issue. And lastly, on June 7, 1684, he married to his fourth wife, Elizabeth, second daughter and coheir of John Lord Frecheville, and widow of Philip Warwick, Esq; He departed this life, anno 1692-3, and was succeeded by Robert his grandson, John his eldest son and heir dying on Jan. 7, 1688-9, in his life-time.

The said John, who was three times elected member for Richmond in Yorkshire, had sepulture in Westminster abbey; and having married Bridget, the only surviving daughter of Robert Sutton, first Lord Lexington, and sister to Robert, last Lord, had issue by her (who died on July 18, 1736) two sons;

---

[z] List of compounders, edit. 1655, in lett. d. p. 350.   [a] Heylin's help to hist.

D'Arcy, Earl of Holderneſſe.

Robert, third Earl of Holderneſſe, and Conyers; and alſo two daughters, Elizabeth, married to Sir Ralph Milbank, of Halnaby in the county of York, Bart. to whom ſhe bore an only child, Bridget; and Charlotte, married to Wardel-George Weſtby, of Ranfield in Yorkſhire, Eſq; one of the Commiſſioners of his Majeſty's cuſtoms in the port of London.

Conyers, the youngeſt ſon, ſeated at Aſke in Yorkſhire, was, in the reign of Queen Anne, Cornet-Major in the firſt troop of life-guards, and on July 18, 1712, made Gentleman of the Horſe, and firſt Commiſſioner for executing the office of Maſter of the Horſe to her Majeſty. On the acceſſion of George I. he was, December, 23, 1715, again made firſt Commiſſioner for executing the office of Maſter of the Horſe; and in January $17\frac{19}{20}$, was appointed Maſter of the Houſhold to his Majeſty; alſo on May 27, 1725, was choſen a Knight-companion of the moſt honourable order of the Bath; and made Comptroller of the Houſhold to his late majeſty, May 11, 1730; and on June 11 following was ſworn of the Privy Council. He was likewiſe on Nov. 10, 1727, conſtituted Lord Lieutenant of the North-riding in Yorkſhire, during the minority of his nephew the preſent Earl of Holderneſſe. In 1707, he was choſe one of the Knights for Yorkſhire; as alſo in the parliaments ſummoned on 1747, and 1754; and for the borough of Richmond in that county, in the four preceding parliaments, and in part of that ſummoned in 1705. He firſt married, in the year 1714, Mary relict of Algernon Earl of Eſſex, grandmother of the preſent Earl, by whom he had no iſſue; and 2dly, on September 12, 1728, Elizabeth, daughter to John Rotherham of Much-Waltham in the county of Eſſex, Eſq; widow firſt of Sir Theophilus Napier of Luton-Hoo in the county of Bedford, Bart. and 2dly, of Thomas Lord Howard of Effingham: but had no iſſue by either, and died at Aſke, December 1, 1758.

His elder brother Robert [b], late Earl of Holderneſſe, took his ſeat in the houſe of Peers, Dec. 22, 1702. On the acceſſion of George I. to the crown of theſe realms, he was conſtituted Lord Lieutenant of the North-Riding of Yorkſhire; alſo on Jan. 31, $17\frac{17}{18}$, his Lordſhip was made Firſt Lord Commiſſioner for inſpecting into trade and the plantations, and ſworn of his Majeſty's moſt honourable Privy Council at St. James's, Feb. 13 following; and on May 9, 1719, he was appointed one of the Lords of the Bed-chamber to his Majeſty. He took to wife the Lady Frederica, eldeſt of

[b] Journal Dom. procer.

the two daughters and coheirs to Meinhardt Schonbergh, third Duke of Schonbergh in England, Duke of Leinster in Ireland, Count of the Roman Empire, and Knight of the most Noble Order of the Garter, by the Lady Charlotte his wife, eldest daughter to Charles Lewis, Elector Palatine; and died at the Bath after a long illness, on Saturday Jan. 20, 1721-2, leaving issue a son and a daughter, viz. Robert, the present and fourth Earl of Holderness, and the Lady Louisa Carolina, married to William Earl of Ancrum, son and heir apparent of William Marquis of Lothian, in Scotland.

Which Robert, fourth Earl of Holderness, having been constituted Lord Lieutenant of the North-Riding in Yorkshire, and Vice-Admiral of the same, took the oaths of qualification, before his Majesty in Council, Nov. 21, 1740; and in April, 1741, was appointed one of the Lords of his Majesty's Bed-chamber. In 1743, his Lordship attended the King when he was abroad that year, and was present with his Majesty at the battle of Dettengen, on June 16. In 1744, he was appointed his Majesty's Ambassador Extraordinary to the Republic of Venice; where having resided about two years, he took his leave of the Doge and Senate, and Aug. 23, N. S. 1746, set out on his return for England. In May, 1749, his Lordship was appointed Minister Plenipotentiary to the States General, and presented his credentials in June following; and resided there till May 1, 1751. On July 12 that year, he was sworn of his Majesty's Privy Council, and one of his Principal Secretaries of State. On October 15 following, he set out for the Hague, with his Majesty's compliments of condolence, on the deceafe of William-Charles-Henry Friso, Prince of Orange, and Stadtholder of the United Provinces. On March 30, 1752, he was appointed by his Majesty, one of the Lords Justices, for the administration of the government during his absence that year. Sir Thomas Robinson, Knight of the Bath, and now Lord Grantham, having resigned, in Nov. 1755, the seals of the office of one of his Majesty's Principal Secretaries of State, his Majesty was pleased to appoint his Lordship to succeed him, as Secretary of State for the Northern department. On the demise of his late Majesty, Oct. 25, 1760, he was one of the persons of distinction, who signed the order for proclaiming the present King, and was one of the members of the Privy Council, present the same day at his Majesty's taking and subscribing the oath relating to the security of the church of Scotland. His Majesty, in consideration of his Lordship's faithful services, was pleased to continue him at the Council-Board, and as Secretary of State, and in the places of Lord Lieutenant and Vice-Admiral of the North-Riding

Darcy Earl of Holderness

D'Arcy, Earl of Holdernesse.

Riding of Yorkshire, together with those of Keeper of the Liberty and Forest of Richmond, and Constable of Middleham-castle, all which he enjoyed in the preceding reign: but he resigned the seals belonging to his office as Secretary, in March, 1761, which his Majesty was pleased to give to the Earl of Bute.

His Lordship, who is also one of the Governors of the Charter-House, married, at the Hague, Mary, daughter of the Sieur Doublet, one of the Nobles of Holland, and niece to the Greffier Fagel, by whom he had issue two sons, 1st, George, who was born in Sept. 1745, and died Sept. 27, 1747; 2d, Thomas, who was born at the Hague, May 7, 1750, and deceased July 27, 1750: Also a daughter, Lady Amelia, born Oct. 12, 1754.

TITLES.] Robert D'Arcy Earl of Holdernesse, Baron D'Arcy, Menill, and Conyers.

CREATIONS.] Baron D'Arcy, and Conyers, August 10, (1641) 17 Car. I. but summoned to Parliament by writ, as Baron D'Arcy, June 8 (1294) 22 Edw. I. summoned as Baron Conyers in 1506, 22 Henry VII. and Earl of Holdernesse in the county of York, Dec. 3 (1682) 34 Car. II.

ARMS.] Quarterly, 1st. Azure, three Cinquefoils and Semée of Cross Crosslets Argent, for D'Arcy: 2d. Azure three Bars Gemel, and a Chief Or, for Menill: 3d. Azure, a Maunch Or, for Conyers: 4th. Gules, a Saltire Argent, thereon a Mullet, for Nevile.

CREST.] On a Wreath, a Spear broken in three pieces, Or, headed Argent, and banded together at the middle by a Ribban, Gules.

SUPPORTERS.] On the Dexter, a Tyger Argent, collared, rayant rayonnée, and chained Azure, and maned and unguled, Or. On the Sinister, a Bull Sable, spotted with Mullets, Argent, with a like Collar and Chain, and armed, Or.

MOTTO.] Un Dieu, un Roy.

CHIEF-SEATS.] At Hornby-Castle in the county of York, 5 miles from Richmond, and 174 from London; and at Aston, Hurdwick, and Patrick-Brampton, in the same county.

WINDSOR, Earl of Plymouth.

II. THE learned Camden [a] and other of our antiquaries agree, that variations in furnames were ufual; and an evident proof of the alteration thereof appears in this family of Windfor.

Othoere, Other, or Otho (as fometimes wrote) is faid, in fome pedigrees of this family, to be defcended from the Dukes of Tufcany, and, coming from Florence into Normandy, paffed from thence into England: But Othoere is mentioned, in the appendix [b] to the life of King Alfred, to be living in his reign, a rich and powerful Lord, and to derive his defcent from anceftors in the kingdom of Norway.

It alfo appears, that Other, as wrote in Doomfday Book [c], was living in England in the reign of Edward the Confeffor; and in the pedigrees is made to be the fon of Othoere.

The moft ancient record in this kingdom is that furvey made by William the Conqueror, which is kept in the Exchequer at Weftminfter, and entitled, Liber Judiciarius, or Doomfday Book, begun in the 14th of that monarch, but not perfected till the 20th, as the book itfelf declareth. By this furvey it appears [d], that Walter Fitz Other (i. e. Walter the fon of Other) was found to be poffeffed, in Godelmin hundred, in the county of Surry, of fourteen hides of land in Contone; and that Tezelin held Hormer of this Walter for fifteen hides; and Gerald held of him Piperherge for five hides. In Kingeftone hundred, he had a man of the foke of Kingeftone, to whom he gave in charge the keeping of the King's mares in the forefts [being warden of all the forefts in Berkfhire, and caftellan of Windfor] and that man held two hides there, but had no right in the fame. In Wachinges hundred, he held Horfeley, which was rated at ten hides.

In Hamtefcire, in Noteham hundred, he held Wildehel for one hide; and Gerlei, in Cillei hundred, for three hides. In Berecfcire, in Riplefmer hundred, he held Ortone for one hide and a half. In Nachededorne hundred, he held Ciltone for five hides, and Borcheldeberie for one hide, which a man of his held of him, lying in the foreft, and never was taxed, as the Seyre fays. In Theneteberie, he held half a hide, which King Edward gave his anceftor out of his farm, free from all dues (for the cuftody or keeping of the forefts) except forfeitures to the King, fuch as Larcenary, Manflaughter, Hamfare, and Breach of Peace. In Blithberie hundred, he held Hacheburne for ten hides; but it was rated only at fix hides and an half;

[a] Vide his remains, in loco furnames, p. 110, 111. [b] Vide p. 205.
[c] Ex lib. vocat. Doomfday.   [d] Ibid. in iifd. commitat.

Windsor-Hickman, Earl of Plymouth.

and of this land Robert held of him one hide and an half. In Redinges hundred, he held Offelle, which a certain Knight held of him for one hide and an half. In the county of Middlesex, in Spelethorn hundred, he held of the King the manor and lordship of Stanwell for fifteen hides. In Bedefunde, were held of him, by Richard, ten hides; and, of this manor, Azor also held of him eight hides and an half, which was then a village in Stanwell. In Westbedefunt, Walter de Muchedent held of him eight hides for one manor; and also held of him in Haitone one hide, three yard lands, and the third part of one yard land. In Bochinghamscire, in Stoches hundred, he held Hortone, rated at ten hides; and, in Burneham hundred, he held Eatone for twelve hides; also, in Burneham, eighteen hides: And, in Moselaie hundred, he held four hides. All which [a] lordships, manors, and lands, Sir Other (his father) held in the reign of Edward the Confessor.

The said Sir Other had, as may be presumed, a brother named Gerold (also living in the reign of Edward the Confessor) whose son, Robert Fitz Gerold, in the 15th of William I. 1082, [b] was one of the witnesses to the Conqueror's charter granted to the monks of Durham. And at the time of the general survey [c], he held two lordships in Berkshire, nine in Wiltshire, three in Dorsetshire, one in Somersetshire, and ten in Hantshire. His son, Henry Fitz Gerold, was Chamberlain to Henry II. by which title [d], he was one of the Barons, witnesses to that agreement made at Dover, 14. Cal. Apr. (i. e. March 19) 1163, 9 Hen. II. whereby Theodore, Earl of Flanders, obliged himself to furnish the King (when required) with 1000 Knights, to be transported at the King's expence; and, for the said aid, 500 marks were to be paid, viz. 400 to the Earl, and 100 to the Countess of Flanders; the said Henry Fitz Gerold being also bound for the due performance thereof by the King. He was succeeded by his son Warine Fitz Gerold [e], Chamberlain and Treasurer to Henry II. but this line, in the reign of Henry III. terminated in daughters and heirs [f] : Margery, married to Falcase de Breant; Joan, [g] to Hugh de Nevil; and Alice, [h] to Robert Baron Lisle; from all which there are descendants.

Walter Fitz Other, before-mentioned, was warden of all the forests in Berkshire, and castellan of Windsor, in the reign

a Doomsday, ut antea. b Monast. Angl. vol. 1. p. 44. l. 10. c Doomsday, in iisd. comitat. d Rymer's fœdera, vol. 1. p. 23 to 27. e Monast. Ang. vol. 1. p. 691, a. f Clauf. 2 Hen. III. m. 5. g Ib. 9 Hen. III. m. 24. h Plac. cor. rege T. Trin. 3 Edw. II. pro maner. de Heyford-Warine.

of William the Conqueror. He bore [i] for his arms, gules, a saltier argent; and is said, in the Earl of Kerry's pedigree (a descendant from him) attested by Sir William Seager (Garter King of Arms) 1615, to marry Gladys, daughter of Rygwallon ap Convyn, Prince of North-Wales: But by Vincent (who was a learned and laborious Herald) Beatrix is made to be his wife, and that he had issue by her three sons, William, Robert, and Gerald. Of these sons, there have been disputes concerning the priority of their births. In the Earl of Kildare's genealogy, drawn in 1662, Gerald is said to be the eldest son; but the before-mentioned Sir William Seager, Garter, Sir William Dugdale, Garter, John Anstis, Esq; late Garter, and other of our English Heralds, versed in records, assert, that William was the eldest son, Robert the second son, and Gerald the youngest son. It is also a presumptive evidence that William was the eldest, as he inherited the capital seat and possessions of his father; whereas Gerald raised himself by his services in Wales, in manner following:

King Henry II. being at variance with Rhese, Prince of South Wales, sent the said Gerald, as Captain-General, with a chosen band of men, to reduce him to submission; which being performed by him, he was [k] constituted castellan or governor of Pembroke-castle, which he fortified and defended with great courage against the Welch; and, having slain Owen, son of Cadugan ap Blethyn, chief Lord of Cardiganshire, was made president of the county of Pembroke; and was also Chamberlain to the King, as Vincent [l] asserts; and that he married Nesta, daughter of Rhese, and sister of Griffith, Princes of South-Wales, and concubine to King Henry I. who had issue by her Henry, whose son, Robert Fitz Henry, was slain in the isle of Anglesey 1197. The said Nesta, by her husband Gerald, had issue four sons, according to Vincent, viz. William, Maurice Fitz Gerald, Mauger Fitz Gerald (who had two sons, Melier and Robert) and David, who was Archdeacon of Cardiagn, and, by the name of David Fitz Gerald [m], consecrated Bishop of St. David's, December 19, 1147, 13 Steph.

Some dispute has also been about the priority of the births of William, and Maurice Fitz Gerald; but Vincent, and our English antiquaries, as likewise the Earl of Kerry's pedigree, agree in making William the eldest, which may well be presumed, as he was possessed of the castle of Karria, or Carrio

[i] Ex stemmate penes Edw. Rowe Moore. [k] Vincent's Baronage, MS. n. 20. p. 239, & seq. in offic. arm. [l] Vincent's Baron. MS. [m] Le Neve's fasti ecclef. Ang. p. 511.

Windsor-Hickman, Earl of Plymouth.

(being written both ways) in South-Wales, the inheritance of his mother, and [n] was Governor of the castle of Pembroke. From this said William de Carrio, descended the Carews of Devonshire and Cornwall; the family of Gerard, Earls of Macclesfield, which terminated in Fitton Gerard, who died on December 26, 1702: Likewise the families of the Lords Gerard of Bromley, the Gerards of Bryn, in Lancashire, and others of the name of Gerard. And Raimond Crassus (le Gross) Lord of Lereton, in Ireland, is, by Vincent, [o] said to be the third son of William, and that he married Basilia, daughter of Gilbert (de Clare) and sister to Richard, commonly called Strongbow, Earls of Strigul and Pembroke.

Maurice Fitz Gerald, son of Gerald and Nesta, beforementioned (and younger brother of the said William de Carrio) was the principal person [p] by whose assistance in the reign of Henry II. the conquest of Ireland was obtained, and was engaged in most of the considerable actions in reducing the Irish. Thereupon he had a grant of large possessions, in reward of his services, as [q] the town of Wexford, &c. And from him the noble family of the Fitz Geralds in that kingdom derive their origin; of whom the present Marquis of Kildare, the extinct Fitz Geralds, Earls of Desmond, and Francis-Thomas Fitz Maurice, now Earl of Kerry, with other families of great eminence, descended.

It now only remains to shew the descendants from William the eldest son, and Robert the second son of Walter Fitz Other. Which Robert had the lordship of Eston [r], now called Estains, in Essex, and bore his coat of arms differenced from the chief branch, adding a border engrailed argent, and charging the saltier with a crescent. He was succeeded by his son William, to whom Henry II. confirmed the lordship of Estains, with all his other lands [s]. And, leaving an only daughter and heir, Delicia, she became the wife of Robert de Hastings, who also left an only daughter and heir, Delicia, married to Henry de Cornhill, who, in her right, was Lord of Estains; and his only child and heir Delicia (as Vincent attests) was married to Godfrey de Lovain [t], a younger son of Henry IV. Duke of Brabant, by Maud, daughter of Matthew, Earl of Flanders. From which Godfrey, descended the Barons de Lovain, of Estains, in Essex; whereof John de Lovain, dying in 24 Edw. III. [u] left issue Eleanor, his only daughter

n Vincent's Baronage, MS. n. 20. p. 239, & seq. in offic. arm.   o Ibid. p. 241.   p Dr. Keating's general hist. of Ireland, p. 531, & seq.   q Hollinshed's conquest of Ireland, p. 4.   r Vincent's Baronage, MS. præd.   s Ibid. t MS. inter collect. Harbin.   u Descent of nobility, MS. per Henry Chiting, Cester. Fecial, Not, B. 20, in bibl. Joh. Anstis, arm nup. gart, reg. armor.

and

42 Windsor-Hickman, Earl of Plymouth.

and heir, married to William Bourchier; and she dying in 21 Rich. II. left issue William Bourchier, created Earl of Ewe, in Normandy (in 7 Hen. V.) who married Anne, daughter of Thomas Woodstock, Duke of Gloucester, seventh and youngest son of Edward III. and by her had Henry, Earl of Essex, William, Lord Fitz Warrin (grandfather of John Bourchier, created Earl of Bath July 9, 1536, 28 Hen. VIII.) Thomas, Archbishop of Canterbury, 1454; and John, Lord Berners; from whom are descendants now living.

I now return to William, the eldest son and heir of Walter Fitz Other. He bore the name of Windsor, as also Fitz Walter (i. e. son of Walter) by which name Camden stiles him [x], mentioning, that Henry I. granted to him the lordship and manor of Molesford, in Berkshire, and that the Carews, as well of England as Ireland, descended from him. He succeeded his father Walter Fitz Other, in his offices of warden of the forests in Berkshire, and castellan of Windsor, and was a Baron of great possessions. Maud the Empress, at Oxford [y], confirmed to him all the grants made to his ancestors of the custody of Windsor-castle, and of all his lands, in as full a manner as they enjoyed them in the reign of her father Henry I. He took the surname of Windsor from his office, and left issue [z] two sons, William; and Hugh de Windsor, Lord of the manor of West Horsely, in com' Surry, held by him as one [a] knight's fee of the new feofment, in the reign of Henry II. which by heirs female, devolved on the Barons de Berners. Which [b] Hugh de Windsor was a witness to the charter of John, Earl of Warren and Surry, son of William, Earl of Warren and Surry, whereby he confirmed to the abbey of Letleyn, in the county of Southampton, the manor and church of Schyre, in com' Surry, dated on August 15 (the assumption of the blessed Mary) 1243 [c]: Also to the ratification of the said Earl's charter on the day of the Epiphany, 1252.

William de Windsor, eldest son and heir of the last William, was also a powerful Baron in the reign of Henry II. [d] and certified that he held, of the old feoffment (that is, in the reign of Hen. I.) sixteen knights fees, and an half: And of the new feoffment, viz. since the beginning of the reign of Henry II. that Hugh de Windsor, beforementioned. held of him, at Horseley, one knight's fee; William de Hasting, at Suainton, half a knight's fee; Alexander de Windsor, in the same town, a

---

[x] Vide Britannia in com. Berks.   [y] Ex stemmate in genealog. nobil. Angl. in bibl. Archiep. apud Lambeth.   [z] Ibid.   [a] Lib. rub. de feod. Mil. Temp. Hen. II. in scac.   [b] Monast. Ang. vol. 1. p. 592.   [c] Ibid. p. 933, 934.   [d] Lib. rub. de feod. Mil. Temp. Hen. II. in scac.

Windsor-Hickman, Earl of Plymouth.

third part of a knight's fee; and that there remained, upon his demesne, two knights fees, except the third part of a knight's fee.

The said William de Windesore [a], by his charter, without date (as was customary in those times) released and quitted claim, for himself and his heirs for ever, to Robert Fitz-Piers, of Horton, the fourth part of a knight's fee, of the ward of the castle of Windsor, the which neither he, or his father, ever acknowledged of him, or his predecessors. And King Henry II. confirmed, to this William de Wyndsore [b], the inheritance he enjoyed, from William Fitz Walter, his father, and Walter Fitz Other, his grandfather, to hold the same to him and his heirs, as well in war as in peace, honourably, freely, quietly, and justly, as his father and grandfather held the same, in the reign of King Henry, his grandfather, and his ancestors, &c. And to the King's charter were witnesses, William the King's brother, Earl Reginald, and Jocelin de Bailliol, &c.

In 1165, 12 Hen. II. this William de Windesore, on the assessment of the aid then levied, for marrying the King's daughter [c], certified, that he had sixteen knights fees and a half, de veteri feoffamento, and three and a half de novo; for which, in 14 Hen. II. [d] he paid twelve pounds two shillings and eleven pence.

In 18 Hen. II. on the [e] collection of the scutage of those who were not in the expedition that year into Ireland, he was rated at eighteen pounds three shilling and four pence.

In 1194, 6 Rich. I. he [f] attended the King in his expedition into Normandy [g], when he crossed the seas from Portsmouth, and raised the siege of Vernuel; and also vanquished the French in several skirmishes. The next year, and the year after, the King, continuing abroad, with those who went over with him, obtained three victories over the French; in [h] the last of which, between Curseles and Gysors, Philip II. King of France fell into the river of Ethe, the bridge breaking under him, with the throng of his army, flying to save their lives from the English; and, before he could be drawn out of the river, he was very near being suffocated with the water.

This William de Windsor was either slain, or died in the said expedition, as may be presumed; for, in 7 Rich. I.

---

a Ex stemmate penes Edward. Rowe Moore.   b Ex. lib. rub. in scacc.
c Ibid. sub. tit. Buckingh.   d Rot. pip. 14 Hen. II. Buckingh. and Bedf.
e Rot. pip. 18 Hen. II. Buckingh.   f Rot. pip. 6 Rich. I. Buckingh.
g Speed's chron. p. 489, 490.   h Ibid. p. 491.

Walter,

44   *Windsor-Hickman, Earl of Plymouth.*

Walter, his son and heir, was possessed of the inheritance, who had a brother named William de Windsor, as will hereafter appear.

The said Walter de Windsor [a], accompanied his father, in 6 Rich. I. in the expedition into France. And, having no issue male, he, in 9 Rich. I. by a fine levied in Easter term, divided, in conjunction with his brother William, the whole barony of William de Windsor, their father [b] : the said Walter and his heirs, by the partition, having the town of Burnham, and the advowson of the church of Burnham; the town of Beconsfield, with the advowson of the church; Eton, with the advowson of the church; and Ortone, with the members and appurtenances; also, half of the town of Horseley in Surry. He likewise held [c] a knight's fee, in Essex, of Richard de Montfichet, that was in the King's hands, and for which he paid escuage, or knight's service to Richard I.

He had issue only two daughters his heirs, whereof Christian [d], in the 5th of King John, gave a fine of 220 marks, that it might be tried, whether she was his next heir or not, and to have livery of the land, whereof Walter de Windsor, her father, died seized: And, three years after, this Christian [e], with Duncan de Lascells, her husband, as also Ralph de Hodseng, who had married Gunnora, her sister, gave a fine to the King of 240 marks, for livery of those lands.

Having before recited, that, by a fine levied in 1197, 9 Rich. I. Walter de Windsor (father of the aforementioned Christian and Gunnora) and William de Windsor, his brother, made a partition of the Barony of Windsor, I shall now treat of the said William, the sole heir male of the family.

This William de Windsor [f] had allotted, for his share, the lordships of Hakeburn with the appurtenances, Stanwell, and the Meres, with the appurtenances, and the advowson of the church of Stanwell; the whole town of Horton, with the advowson of the church; half the town of Horseley, and advowson of the church, yielding and paying, yearly, a pair of gilt spurs, for all services. The knights fees of the barony were likewise divided, viz. of Walter de Windsor's part, this William de Windsor had assigned him four knights fees, to hold to him and his heirs, by homage and service;

a Rot. pip. 6 Rich. I. Buckingh. & Bedf.   b Ped. fin. levat. Westminst.
c Rich. 1.   c Nom. Baron. & milit. qui scutag. solver. Rich. I. in bibl. Joh. Anstis, nup. gart. reg. arm. not. B. 5.   d Rot. pip. 5 Joh. Essex & Hertf.
e Rot. pip. 8 Joh. Buckingh. & Bedf.   f Ped. fin. levat. Westminst.
9 Rich. I.

whereof

Windsor-Hickman, Earl of Plymouth. 45

whereof Miles, fon of Thorold, held two knights fees, in Chilton and Wokefield; John Vautort owed the fervice of one knight's fee, in Willehale; and Henry de Bedefunt owed the fervice of one knight's fee in Bedefunt. Of the faid four knights fees, William, and his heirs, were to do fervice to Walter de Windfore, and to his heirs. And whatfoever accrued to the faid barony, by common cuftom, was to be fhared between them.

This William de Windlefore (as the name was then wrote) was [a] one of the witneffes to the foundation charter of Richard King of the Romans, of the abbey of Burnham, in the county of Buckingham, dated at Cippeham, April 18, 1197, 9 Rich. I. In 1212, 14 King John, he [b] paid into the exchequer one hundred pounds for livery of fome part of the lands that were Walter de Windfor's, his brother, and were fometime poffeffed by his daughters, beforementioned. And, in 16 John, on collection of the fcutage of Poictou [c], he was found to hold nine knights fees, and an eighth part, being the moiety of the honour of William de Windfore, as the record fpecifieth, for which he paid eighteen pounds five fhillings. The year following, 17 John, the Barons entering into recognizances to ferve the King as long as he lived, and to aid and affift his heirs, begotten on the body of Ifabel his wife, this William de Windfor [d] was bound for Gilbert Fitz Reynfrid's performance on his part, whofe niece he had married. He was fucceeded in his eftate by William, his fon and heir.

Which William de Windfor, by his deed [e] without date (as cuftomary in that age) granted to William Fitz Alured, of Grove, that half yard land in Stanwell, which Jordan, the fon of the faid William Fitz Alured held of him and his heirs, paying to him and his heirs, for all fervices, three fhillings at Lady-day and Michaelmas, yearly; referving to the King fuch fervice as is due for an half yard of free land; and, in confideration thereof, the faid William Fitz Alured paid as a fine, to the faid William de Windfore, three marks and a half of filver, and to Agnes, his wife, a bezant. And, in 31 Hen. III. he had [f] a grant from the King of 100l. owing to the exchequer from William, his father. In 38 Hen. III. when all thofe, who held lands of the value of twenty pounds, were fummoned by the fheriff of every county, to be at London with horfe and arms, from thence to go to Portfmouth,

a Monaft. Angl. vol. 1. p. 535, b. b Rot. pip. 14 Joh. Lond. & Middlefex.
c Rot. pip. 16 Joh. Buckingh. & Bedf. d Rymer's fœdera, vol. 1. p. 206.
e Ex ftemmate penes Edw. Rowe Moore, f Lib. geneal. not. 257. p. 68, 69, in bibl. Lambeth.

46 *Windfor-Hickman, Earl of Plymouth.*

to be tranfported into Gafcoin, to ferve againft the King of Caftile, who had entered on the King's lands and committed hoftilities [a], this William de Windfor was certified to hold twenty pounds in lands, and more, in the county of Middlefex, as alfo twenty pounds in lands in Berkfhire. And, in 45 Hen. III. he [b] was certified to hold the manor of Stanwell, in the county of Middlefex, of the value of twenty pounds and more, and thereupon was called to receive the honour of Knighthood. He died about 1275, [c] 3 Edward I. as appears by an exemplification in the exchequer, of affize of bread and beer in Stanwell; and by Agnes, his wife [d], left iffue two fons, William de Windfor, and Hugh de Windfor; alfo a daughter, Joan, married to Richard de Dray, Knt. who had with her the manor of Horton, and the advowfon of the church fettled, by her father, on them and their iffue.

Hugh de Windfor, the youngeft fon [e], died in 11 Edw. I.

Of William de Windfor, the eldeft fon, I find no further mention, than that he was feated at Stanwell, whereof he died poffeffed in 7 Edw. I. [f] held by the ward of Windforcaftle for 40 days; and that by Margaret, his wife, daughter of John Drokensford, and fifter of Sir John Drokensford, Knt. [g] he left iffue Richard, his eldeft fon; and Walter, fecond fon; alfo a daughter Margaret, who was a nun in Ankerwyke monaftry, in com' Buckingh.

His eldeft fon, Richard de Windfor, being of full age in 13 Edw. I. [h] had livery of the manor of Stanwell in Middlefex, and Weft-Hakeburne in Berkfhire. In 23 and 25 Edw. I. [i] he was returned one of the Knights for Berkfhire in the parliaments then held. And in 1297, 25 Edw. I. when the King by writ, dated May 20, commanded the fheriffs of every county, to require all who held lands to the value of twenty pounds, or more, to be at London on Sunday next following the Octave of St. John Baptift, with horfe and arms, apparalled according to their degree, in order to go beyond the feas with the King, to their own honour, and the welfare and common profit of the realm [k], this Richard de Windfor appeared accordingly. And the King (as our hiftorians recite [l]) fent over his army into Gafcoiny, under the command of his brother Edmund, Earl of Lancafter, with divers Lords, Knights &c.

a MS. Not. B. 5. p. 42 & 46. in bibl. Joh. Anftis, arm.   b Nom. Millit. ib.
c Exempl. de fcac. de affiza pent de man. de Stanwell.   d Ex ftemmate penea Moore præd.   e Efc. 11 Edw. I. No. 22.   f Efc. 7 Edw. I. N. 23.
g Ex ftemmate præd. in bibl. Lambeth.   h Efc. 13 Edw. I. N. 202.   i Willis's notit. parliam. vol. 1. p. 23.   k MS. Claudius, C. 2, in bibl. Cotton.
l Fabian's chron. fol. 83. b.

In 26 Edw. I. he attended in parliament, being returned one [a] of the Knights for the county of Middlesex. And, on May 20, 28 Edw. I. when the King (to satisfy his Earls [b] and Nobles) impowered the principal persons in each county, to punish all offences against the articles of Magna Charta, the charter of the forests, and the statute of Winton, not punishable by the common laws of the realm, he [c] appointed this Richard de Windsor to officiate, for that purpose, in Berkshire. The year after, 29 Edw. I. he was summoned [d], with other great men, to attend the King at Berwick upon Tweed, on the feast of St. John Baptist's nativity, well appointed with horse and arms, to march against the Scots. In 33 Edw. I. he [e] was again returned one of the Knights for Berkshire; in which parliament King Edward having assented [f] that ten persons might be elected in Scotland to repair to his parliament in London, pro tota communitate terræ Scotiæ, they accordingly attended. In 34 Edw. I. he [g] was summoned to be at London at a great council, called by the King on special affairs; and that year a fine was levied at Westminster, beween [h] John de Drokensford, clerk (soon after bishop of Bath and Wells, and treasurer of England) plaintiff, and Sir Richard de Windsor, Knt. deforciant, of the manor of Stanwell in com' Middlesex, and of Hakeborn in Berkshire; whereby, after the decease of the said Richard and Joan, his wife, the said manors were entailed on Richard, son of the aforesaid Sir Richard, and the heirs of his body, remainder to William his brother, remainder to the right heirs of Sir Richard the father.

In 2 Edw. II. he [i] served again in parliament, as one of the Knights for Middlesex; as also in the following parliaments, in [k] 5 and 6 Edw. II. In 17 Edw. II. [l] on an inquisition in every county, returned into Chancery of such who bore arms from their ancestors, Sir Richard de Windsor was named among those of the county of Middlesex, and of Berkshire. He died in 19 Edw. II. [m] seized of the manors of Stanwell in Middlesex, and West Hakeburn in Berkshire; also the ward of the castle of Windsor, wherein he was succeeded by Richard, his son and heir, then 27 years of age, by his first wife [n], Julian, daughter of Sir Nicholas Stapleton, of Hachilsay, in com' Ebor. Knt. by whom he had also issue William de Windsor, rector of the church of Stanwell. But by his second wife, Joan, he had no issue.

a Pryn's brevia parliament. p. 120.   b Pryn's hist. of Edw. I. p. 850, & seq.
c Pat. 28 Edw. I. m. 14.   d Clauf. 29 Edw. I. m. 13. & Ryley's palacit. parl.
p. 491.   e Willis's not. parl. p. 23.   f Pryn's 4th part of a brief register, p. 22, 23.   g Willis ut antea.   h Ped. fin. levat. 34 Edw. I.   i Pryn's brevia parl. p. 1. p. 55.   k Ibid. p. 56.   l MS. Claudius, C. 2. in bibl. Cotton.
m Esc. 19 Edw. II. n. 54.   n Lib. de geneal. nob. in bibl. Lambeth. &c.

48 *Windsor-Hickman, Earl of Plymouth.*

The said Richard de Windsor, his eldest son, in 4 Edw. III. as also in 12 Edw. III. [a] served in parliament for the county of Middlesex; and for Berkshire [b] in the parliament held at Westminster in 14 Edw. III. He had three wives, 1st, Joan, by whom he had issue a daughter Joan [c]; and by his 2d wife, Julian, daughter and coheir of James Molyns, of the county of Southampton, and of his wife Margaret, daughter and coheir of William de Bintworth, had James, his son and heir, and Sir William, 2d son, who raised himself to great honours. Claricia was his 3d wife, daughter of John Drokensford, and relict of . . . . . Yorke [d], who survived him, and died on March 21, 1403-4, 5 Hen. IV. He deceased in 1367, 41 Edw. III. and was succeeded in his estate by James, his eldest son and heir.

Which James de Windsor was seated at Stanwell, and had the honour of Knighthood conferred on him by Edward III. and departed this life [e] on October 2, in the 44th year of that King's reign, leaving [f], by Elizabeth, his wife, daughter of Sir John Streeche, Knt. Sir Miles de Windsor, his only son and heir, sixteen years of age, and more; from whom the present Earl of Plymouth is descended, and of whom more fully hereafter.

But I shall first treat of Sir William de Windsor, second son of Richard de Windsor, last mentioned. The said Sir William entered early into a martial life. He was knighted before 35 Edw. III. for, on April 4, 1360, by that title [g], he, with Sir William Sutton, were witnesses to the will of Bartholomew Lord Burgherst, then dated. And in 35 Edw. III. on March 15, 1360-1, the King, finding the incursions of his enemies in Ireland [h], appointed Lionel Earl of Ulster, his son, Lord Lieutenant, forthwith to repair thither, and, bringing from England 1500 men, this Sir William de Windsor was retained by him [i] at two shillings per diem; also, for two Knights in his retinue, two shillings each; for forty-nine Esquires, twelve pence each, and ten archers on horseback, six-pence each. The Earl, having subdued Obryan, and done many other good acts, to the satisfaction of that nation [k], returned to England on April 22, 1363, 37 Edw. III. yet, whether Sir William de Windsor was left behind, does not appear. But, in 1367, 41 Edw. III. on the French surprizing Ponthieu, he was appointed, with all expedition, to go [l]

---

a Pryn ut antea, p. 56.   b Willis ut antea, p. 24.   c Ex stemmate præd.
d Ashmole's Berkshire, vol. 1. p. 55.   e Esc. 44 Edw. III. n. 67.   f Ex stemmate ut antea.   g Register Witlesey apud Lambeth, p. 98.   h Rymer's fœdera, vol. 6. p. 318.   i Cox's hist. of Ireland, p. 126.   k Ibid. p. 127.
l Barnes's hist. of Edw. III. p. 739.

with

Windsor-Hickman, Earl of Plymouth.

with the forces, then at Dover, ready to cross the seas for the defence thereof, when news came, that the French King, Charles V. had taken the country. Whereupon [a], King Edward hearing that the Scots had also engaged with the French King, and designed to invade his dominions, he, on Sept. 4, the same year [b], appointed this Sir William Windsor, with the Bishop of Carlisle, and the Lord Clifford, Wardens of the West Marches, towards Scotland. After which, on intelligence that the French King had set forth a great navy to invade Ireland, he was constituted, in 43 Edw. III. [c] Lieutenant of Ireland; and for his better support in the King's service, had a grant of a thousand marks per annum, to be paid out of the King's Exchequer, until such time as the King should grant lands and rents of that value to himself and his heirs for ever. And, immediately thereupon [d], he had a grant of the manor and castle of Dungarvan, also of the castle called Bluck-castle, to him and the heirs of his body. And with him went, on this expedition [e], the Lord Thomas Faulconbergh, and others of rank and conduct. He landed in Ireland [f] on July 12, 1369, and called a parliament at Kilkenny [g], and soon after another at Ballydoil. He vigorously prosecuted the war against the rebels in Leinster, but was interrupted by O Connor and O Bryan, who got the better of the English in the county of Limerick, so that he was obliged to march to the defence of Munster, where he behaved so well, that John Macnamara (a great man in Thomond) submitted, and gave hostages to keep the peace, especially towards the Bishops of Limerick and Killalow, nor annoy the city and castle of Limerick, &c. He was sent for to England, and, thereupon, on March 21, 1370, he deputed Maurice Earl of Kildare Custos of Ireland, who was sworn the next day.

In 49 Edw. III. he returned again to Ireland [h], landing at Waterford, April 18, 1374, and was sworn at Kilkenny, on May 4. The King being fully satisfied (as the patent [i] recites) of the fidelity and circumspection of his beloved and faithful William de Windsore, he constitutes him his Lord Lieutenant in Ireland, with full power to admit the rebels, as well English as Irish, to their allegiance, and to pardon them of all rebellions, manslaughters, robberies, felonies, sedition, larcenary, and combinations, whatsoever, in the said realm by them committed, and to receive their fines and redemptions.

a Barnes's hist. of Edw. III. p. 740.   b Rymer, ibid. p. 569.   c Pat. 43 Edw. III. p. 1. m. 27.   d Pat. ibid.   e Pat. 43 Edw. III. p. 1. m. 32.   f Borlase's reduction of Ireland, p. 56.   g Cox, p. 128, 129.   h Ibid. p. 131.   i Pat. 49 Edw. III.

Windsor-Hickman, Earl of Plymouth.

Also to recover, to the King's use, all forfeited lands and tenements, and to farm-let them, by the advice and assent of the Chancellor and Treasurer of that nation. And to inspect into the behaviour and administration of all who are in office there, and such as shall be found unprofitable to displace, and put in others (the Chancellor and Treasurer excepted) more proper to administer justice, according to the laws of the nation. He undertook the custody of Ireland, for eleven thousand two hundred and thirteen pounds six shillings and eight pence per annum, and obtained an order, from the King and Council, that all, who had lands in Ireland, should repair thither, or send sufficient men in their room, to defend the country, on penalty of forfeiting their estates [a]. Nevertheless, finding the Irish stubborn, he left James Earl of Ormond Lord Justice, July 24, 1376.

The year following, 51 Edw. III. the French threatening an invasion, he had orders from the [b] King, to fortify such towns and forts as were under his government. The next year, or soon after, he took to wife the famous Allice Perrers, of whom I shall recite some account from Mr. Barnes, who, in his elaborate history of the reign of King Edward III. examined all facts asserted by other authors. He says [c], ' That,
' being a person of extraordinary beauty, she was, in 48 Edw.
' III. made Lady of the Sun, and rode from the Tower of
' London through Cheapside, accompanied with many Lords,
' Knights, and Ladies; every Lady leading a Lord or a
' Knight, by his horse's bridle, till they came into West-
' Smithfield; where presently began solemn justs, which held
' for seven days together. That she had been constantly mis-
' represented by most of our writers (one taking it from an-
' other) as being King Edward's concubine, but that it was
' improbable, from the reputation she had of being taken in
' marriage by so considerable a person as the Lord William
' Windsor; and that King Edward, who never else is said
' to have gone astray, even in the flower of his age, should,
' within five years of his Queen's death, when he was very
' impotent, burn in flames. That the records wherein she is
' mentioned, are not severe on her reputation, as appears
' from the charge against her, brought into parliament in
' 1 Rich. II. in these words [d]:

' Dame Allice Perrers was introduced before the Lords, and
' by Sir Richard le Scrope, Knt. Steward of the King's house-

[a] Cox, p. 131.   [b] Rymer, vol. 7. p. 142, 143.   [c] Vide his hist. p. 872.
[d] Ibid. p. 873. and Sir Rob. Cotton's abridgment of records, p. 158.

'hold, charged for purfuing of matters, contrary to orders
'taken two years before; namely, that no woman fhould,
'for any advantage, prefent any caufe in the King's court, on
'pain of lofing all they had, and being banifhed the realm for
'ever. That, particularly, fhe had procured Sir Nicholas
'Dagworth to be called from Ireland, whither he was fent;
'and that fhe alfo procured, from the King, reftitution of
'lands and goods, to Richard Lyon, merchant, of London,
'whereas the fame lands, having been forfeited by him, had
'been given to the King's own fons. To all which the faid
'Dame Allice replied, that fhe had not purfued any fuch
'thing for any advantage of her own: whereupon divers
'officers, counfellors, and fervants to King Edward the third,
'being examined, proved, that fhe made fuch purfuit; and
'that, in their conceits, for her own private gain. Then
'judgment was given by the Lords againft the faid Dame,
'that, according to the order aforefaid, fhe fhould be banifh-
'ed, and forfeit all her goods and lands whatfoever.' But
Sir Robert Cotton makes this remark on it: ' To fay truth
'of the devil is counted commendable, and therefore furely
'the record againft the faid Lady, being very long, proves
'no fuch heinous matter againft her; only it fheweth, that
'the fame Dame was in fuch credit with Edward the third,
'as fhe fat at his bed's head, when all of the council, and
'of the privy-chamber, ftood waiting without doors; and
'that fhe moved thofe fuits that they dared not; and thefe
'two fuits, whereof fhe was condemned, feemed very ho-
'neft; her mifhap was, that fhe was friendly to many, but
'all were not fo to her.'

By the faid record, being ftiled Allice Perrers, it fhould
feem, that fhe was not then the wife of Sir William Windfor, and that he married her afterwards: for the next year,
2 Rich. II. in the records of parliament, it is thus fpecified [a]:
' Sir William of Windfor, and Alice his wife, late Dame
' Allice Perrers, pray the revocation of a judgment made in
' the laft parliament, tit. 41, 42, 43, againft the faid Allice,
' for errors therein contained. The record was brought
' forth, and errors affigned. But the King's learned council
' adjudged, that they could not fue in fuch wife, but that
' by attorney they might fue. Whereupon the faid William,
' and Allice, his wife, late called Dame Allice Perrers, by a
' new bill required, that they, by Edmund Clay and Ro-
' bert Brown, their attornies, might purfue the reverfal of

a Cotton's records, p. 177.

' the

'the said judgment. The King committed the matter to the
'Lords, who licensed them by the King's favour to pursue
'the same.'

In 3 Rich. II. the King, by his letters patent bearing date at Westminster, 15 Martii, reciting [a], that Allice Perrers, whilst she was single, having purchased the third part of the manor of Compton-Murdak, in Warwickshire, and two parts thereof in reversion, after the death of Allice, the widow of Sir John Murdak, Knt. grants it to Sir William Windsor, and his heirs, for ever, out of the singular respects (as in the patent) that he bore towards the said Sir William, for his many notable services; and, especially, for his being at that time retained by indenture to serve him in his wars, with two hundred men at arms, and two hundred archers, under the conduct of Thomas de Wodstoke, Earl of Buckingham (the King's uncle) for the expedition into Britany, in which the said Earl was to be general. They landed at Calais [b], June 4, and from thence marched through France, being (as Stowe writes [c]) approved and tried Knights, who, in their way, spoiled the French, and entered Britany without opposition. And Sir William Windsor was appointed [d] Governor of Cherburgh, in the room of Sir John de Harleston, Knt. who was recalled.

On March 24, 1380-1, 4 Rich. II. he [e] had the King's writ of summons, among the Barons of the realm, to the parliament holden at Northampton, the Monday after the feast of All Saints. Also [f] to the parliaments in 5 and 6 Rich. II. and 7 Rich. II. held at Westminster, the Monday before the feast of All Saints [g]; likewise at Salisbury, on the Friday after St. Mark the Evangelist. On Feb. 8, 1383-4, 7 Rich. II. the King constituting conservators of the truce between him and the French King [h], Charles VI. this Sir William de Windsor was appointed for the King's dominions in Normandy, being then Governor of Cherburgh. He died before Nov. 28 ensuing, when the King constituting Thomas de Holland, Earl of Kent, Governor of the town and castle of Cherburgh for three years [i], a mandate was sent to the Lieutenant of Sir William de Windsor, to surrender the same to him, with all ammunition, stores, &c. Also, on Feb. 25 following, the King reciting, that whereas [k] he had committed to William

---

a Pat. 3 Rich. II. p. 3. m. 5.   b Life of K. Rich. II. in compleat hist. of Eng. vol. 1. p. 243.   c Annals, p. 282.   d Walsingham, p. 243. e Cotton's records, p. 187, 188.   f Claus. de iisd. an. in dorso.   g Cotton, p. 282, 297.   h Rymer, vol. 7. p. 421.   i Ibid. p. 450. k Ibid. p. 464.

de Wyndefore and Sir Thomas Morwell, Knts. the cuftody of the county of Richmond, from Michaelmas, in the fifth year of his reign, to the ufe of Johanna, his [uterene] fifter, fecond wife of John de Montfort, Duke of Britany and Earl of Richmond, during her abode in England, allowing her one thoufand pounds per annum, for her fupport; and, fhe being now deceafed, he conftitutes John de Holland, Thomas de Percy, John Fitz Nicol, and Thomas Talbot, receivers of the arrears from the time of her death.

On the inquifition taken after his deceafe, before Nicholas Brembre, Mayor of London, Oct. 4, 1384, 8 Rich. II. [a] the jury found that he died poffeffed of the manor of Bourneball, and lands in Bufhy, in the county of Hertford: the manor of Weft-Newland, the manor of Lalling, and two parts of the hundred of Dantfey, in the county of Effex: two meffuages in Oxford: the manors of Poreftock, and hundred; Lucton and Chywton, in Dorfetfhire: the manors of Ludford, Church Fodington, Cherleton, and Knolle, in the county of Somerfet: the manor of Manerbyr, and Penaly-caftle and manor, in the county of Pembroke, in Wales: and that he died on Sept. 15, 8 Rich. II. leaving his three fifters heirs to his eftate; Iffabel Windfor, of the age of 38; Chriftian, wife of Sir William Morleux, Knt. of the age of 34; and Margery, wife of John Duket, of the age of 32; and other inquifitions in feveral counties confirm it.

By his laft will and teftament, nuncupative [b], bearing date at Everfham, in the diocefe of Lincoln, Sept. 10, 1384, William de Cawood, Rector of the church of Bolefby, and the reverend Sir John Bakon, Archdeacon of Richmond, being prefent, he bequeathed all his goods, chattels, &c. to Sir William de Melton, Sir James de Pykerynge, Sir Walter de Strykland, Knts. and John de Wyndefor, fen. ordering them to pay his debts, and to provide for his foul. The probat is dated on October 22 following, when adminiftration was granted to Sir William de Melton, Sir James de Pykerynge, and John de Wyndefor, fen. And dying without iffue male [c], his daughters, fays Sir William Dugdale, became his heirs, whereof Joan, the elder, married to Robert Skerne, of Kingfton upon Thames, was, in her right, poffeffed of Compton-Murdak, in com' Warwick: but it is apparent, that Joan was the daughter of Allice, his wife, who had children by another hufband, as appears by her will.

a Efc. 8 Rich. II. N. 38.   b Ex regift. Rouf. p. 8. in cur. prærog. Cantuar.   c Dugd. Warwickfhire, p. 435.

Which Allice, writing herself relict of Sir William Wynd-fore, Knt. [d] made her last will and testament, dated at Vpmynstre, on the Assumption of the Virgin Mary (Aug. 15) 1400, 1 Hen. IV. wherein she ordered her body to be buried in the parish church of Vpmynstre, before the altar of St. Mary the Virgin; and bequeathed ten marks for ornaments to the church, and forty shillings for the repairing thereof; and that ten marks be distributed to the poor the day of her sepulture, six marks to the chaplain, and to John Pelham, sacrist of the church, three shillings and four pence. She bequeaths to John, her younger son, her manor of Gaynes, in Vpmynstre; and the residue of her goods, chattels, &c. to John and Joan, her children. And appoints Joan, her youngest daughter, with John Kent, merchant, of London, her executors: and Sir John Curson, Knt. and Robert de Litton, Esq; supervisors of her will.

I now return to Sir Miles Windsor, before-mentioned, eldest son of Sir James Windsor [e], elder brother to the said William Lord Windsor. Which Sir Miles was only 16 years of age on the death of his father, as said before. He was knighted before 1383, the 5th year of Rich. II. when he appeared [f] on that great trial at Chester, on Sept. 30, before John of Gaunt, King of Castile, and Duke of Lancaster, in relation to the bearing of the coat of arms then in contest between Richard le Scrope Lord Scrope, of Bolton, and Sir Robert Grosvenor, Knt. certifying, that the said Richard Lord Scrope had a right to the arms, Azure, a Bend Or, which was confirmed to him, the said Lord Scrope.

In 9 Rich. II. this Sir Miles Wyndesore, Knt. [g] (as the name is wrote in the record) going in the King's service into Spain, under the command of John, King of Castile and Leon, and Duke of Lancaster, had the King's letters of protection for one year, from March 6, 1386, when they were granted: and probably he died there; for, in 10 Rich. II. [h] an inquisition was taken after his decease that year, when the jury found, that he died seized of the manors of Stanwell, Warnersland, Gullays, and Gardons, in the county of Middlesex: the manors of Huntercombe, and Burnham, in Buckinghamshire, with the ward of the castle of Windsor: the manor of West-Hakeburn, in Berkshire: the manors of West-Horsley, Piperharewe, Hurtmere, Bagshute, Estbury in Compton,

[d] Ex regist. Arundel, p. 188. a, in offic. principal. Cantuar.   [e] Ex lib. Geneal. bibl. Lambeth. præd.   [f] MS. in bibl. Ashmole, Oxon. Dorf. 1120. [g] Rymer, vol. 7. p. 499.   [h] Esc. 10 Rich. II. N. 46.

Donne

Donne in Compton, Longditton, Aulton, and lands in La-Muil, in the county of Surry: alfo lands in Froile, Bromlegh, Bere, Bynteworth, and twenty fhillings chief rent in Gretham, in the county of Southampton. And that he died March 31, that year, leaving Brian de Windfor his fon and heir, of the age of 15 years, and more, by his wife [i] Allice, daughter of Adam de Wymondham, of Wymondham, in the county of Norfolk, who furvived him, and deceafed in 1394, 18 Rich. II.

The faid Brian de Windfor had to wife [k] Allice, daughter of Thomas Drew, Efq; who furvived him, and died in 1405, 7 Hen. IV. He deceafed in 22 Rich. II. [l] poffeffed of the manor of Bynteworth, in the hamlet of Afheley, and lands called le Bol and Con, parcel of the manor aforefaid: the manor of Mulle, in Beneftede, the manor of Efington, the manor of Bromleye, with one meffuage, and forty acres of land, called Little Bynteworth, and lands in Gretham: the manor of Bere juxta Warneford: the fee and manor of Wynhale, held by Thomas Bromflete, by one Knight's fee; and Malefhangre, in Yerdlegh manor, by William Hornby, by one Knight's fee; all in the county of Southampton: the manor of Stanwell, with the advowfon of the church, by one Knight's fee, and the ward of Windfor-caftle: the manor of Weft-Bedefont, parcel of the priory of New Place, by one Knight's fee: the manor of Shepcote, by John de Ticheborne, for one Knight's fee; all in the county of Middlefex: the manor of Weft-Hakeburn, with fixty fhillings rent, parcel of the manor there: the manor of Chilton, by one Knight's fee: the manor of Wokefield, by half a Knight's fee: the manor of Colrugge, by half a Knight's fee, in Berkfhire: the manor of Weft-Horfley, held by Sir James Berners, for a Knight's fee: the manor of Piperharewe, held by Sir Bernard Brocas, Knt. for a Knight's fee: the manor of Hartmere, held by the prior of New Place, for a Knight's fee: the manor of Bagfhutt, held by the Duke of Surry, for half a Knight's fee: the manor of Eftbury, in Compton, and the manor of Donne, in Compton: the manor of Berewe; all in the county of Surry. By the inquifitions taken at Winchefter, in com' Southamp. May 26, and at Stanwell, June 9, 1399, 22 Rich. II. it appears, that he died on April 30, that year, and that Miles de Windfor was fon and heir of the faid Brian, and Allice, his wife; and, at his deceafe, of the age of thirteen years and an half, and one quarter, and more.

i Lib. gen. præd. in bibl. Lambeth.   k Ibid.   l Efc. 22 Rich. II. N. 52.

Miles the eldeſt ſon [a] dying unmarried, Richard [b], his brother, ſucceeded to his eſtate. The ſaid Richard de Windſor married Chriſtian, daughter of Richard Faulkner, of the county of Southampton, Eſq; [c] and dying at London in 6 Hen. VI. was buried at Stanwell, leaving iſſue Miles de Windſor, his only ſon and heir.

This Miles had to wife [d] Joan, daughter of Walter Green, of Bridgenorth, in com' Salop, Eſq; and is ſaid, in ſeveral pedigrees, to have died in parts beyond the ſeas, near Ferrara, in Italy. The inquiſition [e] taken after his deceaſe, at Colbrook, in com' Buck. Jan. 21, 1451-2, 30 Hen. VI. ſhews that he died on Sept. 30 preceding, leaving Thomas de Windſor, his ſon and heir, then of the age of eleven years.

Which Thomas married Elizabeth, eldeſt of the two daughters and coheirs of John Andrews, of Baylham, in com' Suff. Eſq; and of Elizabeth, his wife, daughter and coheir of John Stratton, Eſq; which Elizabeth Andrews ſurvived her huſband, John Andrews, as is evident from her laſt will and teſtament, which being remarkable, and ſhe ſo nearly allied to the family, I ſhall give ſome account of it, before I proceed to treat further of the ſaid Thomas Windſor, Eſq;

In the name of God, amen [f]. So be it. I dame Elizabeth Andrewes, widow, in the feaſt of St. Luke the Evangeliſt, the year of our Lord Jhu Chriſt, MccccLxxiiii [15 Edw. IV.] being in whole Mynde, and to God only diſpoſed, make my teſtament, and alſo my laſt will, in the manner and form following: Firſt, I bequeath my ſoul to Almighty God, our Lady St. Mary, and all the holy company of Heaven, and my body to be buried in the chancel of the church of St. Denys Bakchurch, in London, by the lycence of the parſon of the ſaid church. Item, I will that all my debts be paid. Item, I bequeath to the parſon of Baileham, for my Tyths forgotten, xx s. Item, I bequeath, to the uſe of the ſame church, an howſeling towell of diaper, and an altar cloath of diaper, there to remain. Item, I will that my two rings with diamonds, the one to be ſent to our Lady of Walſingham, and the other to our Lady of Wolpit. Item, I bequeath to the uſe of the church of Stoke, beſide Epiſwiche, a towel and an altar cloath of diaper, and a doſen ſheepe, to the uſe of the ſame church. Item, I bequeath to the high altar of the ſaid church of St. Dennys, in neceſſary things to be bought for the ſame, xx s. and alſo to the parſon of the ſaid church, xx s.

a Lib. geneal. in bibl. Lambeth. præd.   b Ibid.   c Ibid.   d ibid.
e Eſc. 30 Hen. VI. N. 11.   f Ex regiſtr. vocat. Wattis, N. 6. Qu. 11. in cur. prærog. Cant.

Item,

Item, I will that Bailham church shall have a surplice and rochet. And, also, that Stoke church shall have a surplice made of a piece of linnen cloath, containing twenty-six yards. Also, I bequeath to the church of Weston, in Norfolk, a Chalice, and twenty yards of linnen cloath, to make a surplice, and a towel of diaper, and a towel of cotton. Item, I bequeath to Dermesdon church a towel and an altar cloath. Item, I bequeath to the church of Blakenham a towel and an altar cloath. Item, I will, that as soon as God sendeth for me to his blifs out of this world, costs be done of my burying, by the advice and discretion of my surveyor, and mine executors; and, that great part of the host be done to poor bedrede people, most need having, to the honour and pleasure of God. Item, I will, that my houshold and servants be kept eight weeks after my departing, with wages, and other necessarys. Item, I bequeath to my Lady Wyche, my sister, for a remembrance to think of me, a goblet of silver, and gilt cover. Item, I give to my daughter, Elizabeth, a blew gown furred with white. Item, I give to my daughter, Anne, a cremesine gown single, and a furre of grey, and a single gown of violet, and furre of white. Item, I bequeath to Andrew Suliard, a pair of beeds of gold. Item, I bequeath to Anne Suliard, my daughter's daughter, a girdle of green, harnesed with silver. Item, I bequeath to Bridget Wyndefore, my daughter Elizabeth's daughter, my white bed, with all the hangings of the same. Item, I bequeath to William Wyndefore, a red bed of worsted, with all the hangings. Item, I bequeath to Elizabeth Wyndefore, and Allice Wyndfore, my daughter's daughters, two pieces of silver with coverings, and fifteen spoons of silver. Item, I bequeath to my daughter Elizabeth a powder-box of silver. Item, I will, that ten pair of sheets of the best be divided between my two daughters.

After which, she leaves legacies to her servants, and orders John Milles, one of them, to deliver a doublet of defence, that was her husband's, to remain in the manor of Bailham; and the residue of her goods, &c. after her debts paid, and bequests performed, she bequeaths to her two daughters, Elizabeth, the wife of Thomas Wyndefore, and Anne, the wife of John Suliarde. Item, I make and ordeyn mine executors, John Suliarde, Thomas Wyndefore, Elizabeth and Anne, their wives; and my Lady Wyche, my sister, mine overseer. In witness whereof I have put my seal, given at the feast and year aforesaid. And by a codicil, she bequeaths her two coverlids, one of cotton, the other of silk, the one to the church of Bailham, the other to the church of Stoke, and to remain

in

in the manor of Bailham. Item, I will, that the new great brafs pot remain in the faid manor of Bailham, to the intent that, when the brethren of the guild of the church of Darmefdon make their dinner they to occupy the fame pot for the time, and to deliver it again in the faid manor of Bailham. Item, I will, that all the women fervants of my Lady Wyche's houfe be rewarded by the difcretion of my overfeer, and executors. She died the fame year, the probat bearing date December 11 after.

Her fifter, Lady Wyche, aforefaid, died the fame year, [a] writing herfelf in her will dame Allice Wyche, of London, widow, late the wife of Sir Hugh Wyche, Knt. late alderman and merchant of London, and dated June 16, 1474, 15 Edw. IV. fhe therein orders her body to be buried in the fouth fide of the quire of the parifh church of St. Denys Bakchurch, London, by the fepulture of William Holt, her late hufband; and bequeathing feveral torches and tapers, to contain, in weight, fixteen pounds, orders four to each church there named, and the refidue to the church of Stanwell, in Middlefex, to have her faid hufband's foul and her's prayed for. She bequeaths to her cozen Elizabeth, wife of Thomas Wyndfore, one hundred pounds in plate and houfehold, of the beft; and to Andrews Wyndfore, their fon, xxl. and to her god-daughter Allice, his fifter, twenty pounds, and one of her beft ftanding cups of filver and gilt covered, and twelve filver fpoons; to Elizabeth, her fifter, and William, their brother, xl. each. She wills to Henry Wyche all her lands, &c. in the parifh of St. Michael, in Bafingfhaw, London, to him and his heirs, in default, to be fold by her executors. And her other lands and tenements, in London and in Effex, to be fold by her executors, and to be difpofed by them in manner following: Firft, to poor hufbands, plowmen in the country, fuch as have wives and children, and poor widows, and other fuch poor diligent labourers, in poor villages, two hundred pounds, whereof one hundred pounds to be difpofed of in Lewes and Haftings, and thereabouts, in Suffex, to pray efpecially for the foul of William Holt, her hufband, who was born at Lewes. Item, to one hundred poor houfeholders, to have every of them a milch cow, and thirteen fhillings and four pence, and three ewes, price fixteen pence a piece. Item, in marriage of poor maidens, of good converfation in the country, and in mending the highways, two hundred pounds; and the remnant of the faid money coming of fuch fale, I will, that my executors fhall difpofe for my foul, and other fouls, as aforefaid, as they fhall feem

[a] Ex regift. Wattis, præd. p. 136.

Windsor-Hickman, Earl of Plymouth. 59

best to be done. The residue of her estate, goods, chattles, &c. her will fulfilled, she bequeaths to her executors, her cosin Thomas Wyndesor, Esq; Humphry Starky, Esq; Recorder of London, and Henry Wellys, priest, and to have for their labour, Thomas, forty pounds; Humphry, forty marks, and Henry, twenty marks. And ordeins overseer of her will, John Catesby, serjeant of the law, and to have ten pounds for his labour. The probat is dated November 16, 1474, which shews that she died about three months after the making of her will.

The said Thomas Windsor, Esq; was summoned [a] on June, 5, 1483, 1 Edward V. to prepare and furnish himself to receive the noble Order of Knighthood at his coronation, intended to be solemnized on the 22d of that month, at Westminster. But Richard Duke of Gloucester, causing the young King his nephew to be murthered, that degree of Knighthood of the Bath was not conferred on him and the others recommended, as Mr. Anstis recites in his observations on Knighthood of the Bath. It may justly be said, that he was a person of piety, good morals, and of a sound judgment, with a tender care for his wife and children; evident from his last will and testament, part of which I have taken literatim, and an extract of the most memorable parts of the rest.

'In the name of God, amen [b]. The xiii day of the
'month of August, the yer of our Lord God MccccLxxix,
'and the xix yere of the reigne of King Edward the IIIIth, I
'Thomas Wyndesor, Esquyr, of the parish of Stanwell, in
'the countie of Middlesex, beying in hole mind and good
'memory, thankid be Almyghty God, make, ordeyn, and
'dispose this my present testament and last will in manner and
'forme following: That is to sey, first, I bequeath and re-
'commend my soule to Almyghty God my Maker and Sa-
'vyor, and to the blessid Vyrgyn our Lady Saint Mary, his
'glorious moder, and to all the holy company of Hevyn;
'and my body to be buried in the north side of the quer of
'the church of our Lady of Stanwell, afor the Ymage of our
'Lady, wher the sepultur of our Lord stondith. Wherupon
'I will ther be made a playn tombe of marble of a compe-
'tent height, to thentent that yt may ber the blessid body
'of our Lord, and the sepulture at the tyme of Estre, to
'stond upon the same, and with myne Armes and a Scriptur
'convenient to be sett about the same tombe, by thadvice of
'myne executors and overseers underwretyn. Item, I will

[a] Rymer's fœdera, vol. 2. p. 185. MS. in bibl. Harley, b. 18.   [b] Ex regist. Logge, N. 7. p. 100, in cur. prærog. Cantuar.

'that

'that I have brennyng, at my burying and funeral service, iiii tapers and xxii torches of wax, every taper to conteyn the weight of x pounds, and every torch xvi pounds, which I will that xxiiii very poor men, and weldifpofed, fhall hold afwell at the tyme of my burying, as at my monethes mynde; and that every of the feid xxiiii poor men fhall have for his labour for both tymes viii pence, and a gown of frife ; the poor men of the parifh of Stanwell to be thereto preferrid before all other parifhes. Item, I will, that, after my monethes mynd doone, the faid iiii tapers be delivered to the church wardens of the faid church of Stanwell, ii of them to burne yerely, as long as they will endure, about the fepultur of our bleffed Lord at the tyme of Eftre, and the other ii to help the light that ftondeth upon the branch afore the Ymage of our Lady in the quer there, as long as the fame wax will endur; to thentent that the v candlefticks may bren at the antem of our Lady in the quer, and at all other tymes convenient, as aforetyme, hath been ufed.' Thus far I have taken literatim.

He further wills, that there be three priefts and three clerks, after the difcretion of his executors, to fing by note, in the church of Stanwell, Placebo and Diridge, and mafs of Requiem, every day, during thirty days next enfuing his deceafe, and to pray for his foul, and all Chriftians foules. And of the faid xx torches, after his funeral fervice, he bequeathes four of them to the church of Stanwell, and the other fixteen, to be given to fixteen churches within the countie of Middlefex, next adjoyning to the faid church of Stanwell. Willing, that the chapells of Woxbridge, and Houndeflow, have each of them one. And that there be one hundred children each, within the age of fixteen years, to be at his month's mind, to fay for his foul, in the church of Stanwell, our Lady Pfalter, and each of them to have for his labour four pence; and that againft his month's mind, the candles burn afore the rude in the faid church, with all other lights, afore our Lady, the Trinity, or any other faints in the faid church, to be renewed and made at his coft. Alfo, that at his month's mind, his executors provide xx priefts, befides the clerks that cometh, to fing Placebo, Diridge, and mafs of Requiem, on the morrow, and be rewarded after the difcretion of his executors, becaufe fome of them may come further than fome. And that there be provided a convenient dinner, to the pleafure of God, and the comfort of his lovers and friends, which fhall like them to be there at that tyme, with all other his tenants at Stanwell.

He further wills, that ten pounds be distributed amongst his poor tenants that are householders in Stanwell, and other towns adjoining, viz. every poor householder of Stanwell, one shilling and eight pence, and of the other towns twelve pence, as farr as it will go. He also charges his executors to content and pay all such debts and duties, as of right he ought to pay to any person or persons at the time of his decease. And wills, that they provide an honest and well disposed priest to sing and say divine service in the said church of Stanwell, or in his chapel at his manor of Stanwell, during the term of xx years next after his decease; and to have for his wages vi l. 13 s. 4 d. and find himself; or else his wife or his heir to give him meat and drink, and 35 s. 4 d. in money, and a gown; to the intent to pray for his soul, the souls of his father and mother, the soul of dame Alice Wich, and all Christian souls.

He wills that his servants, such as dwell with him, be kept together at Stanwell, where his wife is, with meat, drink, and wages, during a year next ensuing his decease; and bequeaths legacys to several of them.

His will also is, that Elizabeth, his wife, or Andrews his son, or who shall be his next heir after his decease, ordein and keep solemnly his obiit by note (the day and time of year he shall happen to decease on) with vi priests and 3 clerks, in the said church of Stanwell yearly, during the space of 40 years next after his decease, to pray for his soul, his father and mother's souls, John Andrews, and Elizabeth his wife's soules, and the soul of dame Alice Wiche, his friends souls and all christians souls. The said priests to be found out of the issues and profits of his purchased lands.

It appears further by his will, that he was a most affectionate father, and a very prudent person in providing for his children in the disposition of his estate, which he settled in trust; and wills that his feoffees stand seized thereof, till Anthony Windsor, the youngest of his sons, come to the age of twenty-one years, if he so long lives. Provided that, if his son Andrews, or other of his sons that shall happen to be lord of Stanwell, and next heir of all his lands, find his priest and his obite, that then his feoffees suffer his heir to receive the profits thereof, and make estate of the said manors and lands to the said Andrews, his son, or to him of his said sons, that shall be alive after twenty-one years. That Elizabeth, his wife, should have the rule and oversight of his lordship and manor of Bailham, in the county of Suffolk, during the nonage of William Windsor, his son, if God fortune she lives so long after his decease. And, if she dye, that John Catesby, serjeant at law,

and

and John Holgrave, and his executors, have the rule of the said manor, praying them to be assisting to his said son William therein. Also, that, after twenty years past, every one of his said sons shall, beside their bequests to them, have xxl. To Anne, his daughter, a hundred marks towards her marriage. Also, that, his daughters, Elizabeth and Allice, hold them content with such goods, as he had delivered to their marriages. And to his children not named in his will, that his executors give and deliver to them part of the issues of his purchased lands to their marriages, according to their discretion.

He also wills, that there be paid one hundred pounds in performing of such articles as be not finished in the last will of dame Allice Wiche, which appeareth in the great leadger, of such debts as be due to her, as soon as they can be recovered; and all such dues as he owed to the Lady Fowler, and to William Puttenham, by his daughters marriages, that such lands, as he have of them for their jointures, shall rest in their hands, till they be content and paid. Likewise, that the Lady Abbefs, and convent of Burnham, have xx marks, in contentation of what she claimeth of him, if it be her due; and, if not, that she and her convent pray for his soul, and all christian souls.

The residue of all his goods, &c. not bequeathed, he leaves to Elizabeth, his wife, whom he ordeyns executor, and Sir John Tokett, priest, and Edward Cheesman, executors with her, and to have xxl. each. And appoints overseers, his cosin, John Catesby, and John Holgrave, and they to have ten pounds each for their labour and advice.

The probat bears date Feb. 15, 1485, and administration was granted to Elizabeth, his relict, who afterwards married Sir Robert Litton, Knight. He died, as the probat shews, in 1 Hen. VII. and was buried, according to the directions in his will, at Stanwell, where is yet remaining, under a cornice, a raised tomb, on which were the figures of a Gentleman and his Lady, inlaid in brass, with an escutcheon of their arms; but are now torn off, as also the inscription.

Sir Andrews Windsor, his eldest son, succeeded him in his estate, at Stanwell, &c. and was made one of the Knights of the Bath in the Tower of London [a] June 23, 1509, the day before the coronation of Henry VIII. In the summons sent to him to take that degree, the King recites [b], 'That he 'hath appointed twenty-six of the most able persons, and of 'honourable blood, and ancient houses coming, being no

---

[a] Anstis's observat. of Knighthood of the Bath, p. 47, 48. [b] Ibid.

'Knights

Windsor-Hickman, Earl of Plymouth.

'Knights of this his realm, to take the order of Knighthood,
'and to repair to the Tower of London, the 22d day of June,
'and that day to serve the King at his dinner, and they that
'shall be made Knights, to bear dishes unto the King that
'said day, in token that they shall never bear none after that
'day, and to be Knights of the Bath in the Tower of Lon-
'don, the 23d day of June next coming, called the even of
'his coronation, &c.' And, in the number of the said
twenty-six, seven were Lords, and Sir Andrews Windsor the
third Knight.

In June 1513, 5 Hen. VIII. he embarked with the King in the expedition into France, and [c] was treasurer of the King's middle ward of battle; and having been at the siege of Terroven, and the battle which ensued, August 16, called, by our historians, the battle of Spurs, from the swiftness of the French in running away; he was, for his valiant behaviour therein, the [d] fourth of those who were advanced to the honour of Knights Bannerets. And afterwards [e], the King, with his army, set down before Tournay, which they also took.

In 1514, 6 Hen. VIII. he [f] was one of the Knights Bannerets, that, on the marriage of the Princess Mary, sister to Henry VIII. with Lewis XII. King of France, attended on her into that kingdom, having, in his retinue, twenty horse, and was allowed by the King, for his expences, twenty-six shillings and eight pence per day. The King, with the Queen, and the whole Court, accompanied her to Dover, in the month of September, and [g] there stayed some time, the wind being so high, that one of the King's ships, called the Lubeck, was driven ashore before Sandgate, and there wrecked, whereby, of six hundred men, scarcely three hundred escaped. On October 2, at four in the morning, the Princess took her ship, with all her noble company, and, when they were about a quarter over the sea, the wind rose and severed the fleet; some reached Calais; some were forced on the shore of Flanders, and the ship she was in, was with great difficulty brought to Boulogne, with such danger, that the master run the ship on shore, and Sir Christopher Garnyshe stood in the water, receiving her in his arms, and carried her to land. She was received by the Duke of Vendosme, and a Cardinal, with a great retinue, who welcomed the Queen, and all her train. And, within three miles of Abbeville, King Lewis met her on a great courser, and she would have

---

c Jekyl's nom. milit. MS. & Claudius, c. 3. in bibl. Cotton.　　　d Ibid.
e Hall's chron. fol. 23, 24.　　f MS. in bibl. Joh. Anstis, garter, reg. armor. not. G. 11. p. 197.　　g Hall's chron. fol. 48.

alighted

64 Windsor-Hickman, Earl of Plymouth.

alighted, but the King would not suffer her; but complimented her on coming, and after a little conversation returned to Abbeville by a secret way; and she, with great triumph, procession, and pageants, was received in the town of Abbeville, October 8, by the Dauphin, with all demonstrations of honour. The next day they were married in the church there, and a great banquet was prepared for her attendants, who were highly entertained. On Tuesday, October 10, all her train of English, except a few officers were discharged, the French King willing them to take no longer pain in attending; and giving them rewards, they took leave of the Queen and returned to England.

In 10 Hen. VIII. he was [h] charged with providing ten men for the King's service in his wars, according to the tenure of lands he held in Berkshire. And in 1520, 12 Hen. VIII. was summoned to attend the King and Queen to Canterbury, and so to Calais and Gysnes, to the meeting of Francis I. the French King [i], with eleven servants and eight horses in his retinue. They landed at Calais, on May 31, and, on June 4, removed, with their whole train, to Guisnes; and a particular relation of the grand interview, and expensive entertainment, with their rich apparel, is recited in Hall's Chronicle, from folio 73, to 84. The King, and the Queen, with the whole court, returned to Calais, June 25; and having there concluded on an interview with the Emperor, new provisions were made for that triumph; but the King, considering the charge of those who attended on him [k], caused Cardinal Wolsey to call them all before him, when the Cardinal, in the King's name, gave them thanks with great commendations, and, for eschewing of cost, licensed them to send home the half of their number of servants; and bid them, after their long charges, to live warely, which term warely, was (says my author) amongst the most part of them taken for barely, and sore disdained by them. On July 10, the King rode to the town of Graveling, in Flanders, waited on by his Nobles, Knights, and Gentlemen; and, at a place called Waell, the Emperor Charles V. met the King, and shewed such affection to him, and affability to all his court, that he won the love of all the English; and at Graveling the Nobles, Knights, and Gentlemen, were feasted with such chearfulness, that they much praised the Emperor's court. And they were also welcomed by the Emperor's aunt, Margaret, the particulars whereof are recited by Hall, and the masks on that oc-

[h] MS. sub effig. Otho. E. 11. in bibl. Cotton. Antis, not. b. 5. p. 380. [k] Hall, fol. 84.   [i]. MS. in bibl. Joh.

casion,

casion. The Emperor, and his aunt, the said Margaret, Dutchess dowager of Savoy, and governess of the Netherlands, came with the King to Calais, and were royally entertained there [l]; and when they took leave of the King and Queen, were accompanied by them part of the way, and friendly embraced. On their departure, the King, with his train, returned to Calais, and immediately embarked for England, safely landing the latter end of July.

In 14 Hen. VIII. the merchants of England, that had factors at Bourdeaux, complaining [m], that the French King, contrary to his league, had taken their goods, and imprisoned their factors and friends; also, restrained their ships in every port in France, rifling their goods on board them; the King, and his council, thereupon sent for the French Ambassador, who denying the matter as they had reported, the Cardinal said to him, If you note the council of England so light, as to tell fables, you be misadvised, &c. Whereon four French hostages in England, that lay for the payment of the money for the surrender of Tournay, were delivered to the Lord St. John's, this Sir Andrews Windsor, Sir Thomas Lovell, and Sir Thomas Nevil [n], each of them safely to keep one of the said hostages, and not permit any of their nation to speak privately to them; and the ambassador was commanded to keep his house, till he was sent for; and all the goods belonging to the French were attached, &c.

In 15 Hen. VIII. the parliament advising the King to a war with France, the Duke of Suffolk was appointed with a royal army, as Captain-General, to pass into France [o], and this Sir Andrews Windsor was one of the commanders of those forces. They arrived at Calais, on August 24, and, there being a great mortality in the town, they encamped on a fair green near St. Peter's church. On September 8, the Duke, with the chief officers of his army, rode to Graveling, to meet Christian the deposed King of Denmark, and the Lord Isilsten, Captain-General of Flanders, who amicably entertained them; and, having concerted measures with that King for invading France in several places, returned again to the army without Calais. Hall gives an account of their several marches into France [p], till they came to a strong town well fortified, called Bray, on the river Somme, garrisoned by 1600 veteran soldiers; and, the ordnance being brought to play on it, October 20, it was taken by assault the same day, by the valour of the English nobles (as my author writes) who comforted and encouraged their men. After which they took the town of Roye, and

l Hall, fol. 85. m Ibid. fol. 92. n Ibid. fol. 93. o Ibid. fol. 113, 114. p Ibid. fol. 117.

coming, October 25, before the ftrong town of Montdedier, laid fiege to it; when the Duke taking it into confideration, that in it were two thoufand foot, and one thoufand horfe, he therefore q fent for the chief officers of his army, and praifing them for their hardinefs, and the noble courage he faw in them, faid it did much encourage his fetting forward in the fiege, the praife whereof fhould be to them, and not to him, and requefted them to continue in their valiant doings, for with God's grace he intended to bring his ordnance before the town the next morning; which was accordingly done, and on the 28th the town capitulated, and the Englifh took poffeffion thereof. On November 13, they came r before the caftle of Boghan (now Bouchain) thought to be impregnable, and though great rains had fallen, and after came a fevere froft, whereby many foldiers died of cold, yet they befieged it, and it was delivered by capitulation. But, the froft continuing very fervent, whereby many died, the Duke of Suffolk difpatched the Lord Sandes to declare the neceffity of retiring into winter quarters. And that Lord coming to the King at Windfor s, declaring that his army was in great mifery, the ways deep, long nights and fhort days, great journeys and little victuals, had caufed the foldiers daily to die: 'Well, fays the King, ' all this we knew before your coming; wherefore we have ' appointed the Lord Montjoy, with 6000 men, for the relief ' of our army.' And, in all hafte, Sir Robert Jernyngham was difpatched to the Duke; but before he arrived there, his ordnance was laid up in the city of Valenciennes in Hainault, and meeting Sir Robert at Bruges, who making known to him the King's commands, he did what he cóuld to bring his forces together. But many had took fhipping at Antwerp, Sluys, Newport, and other havens. And finding he could not bring the fourth part of his army together, he licenced thofe who were at Calais to depart. Of this breaking up of the army, letters were fent to the King, who ftopped the Lord Montjoy, and his forces, from going over-fea, and was much concerned at it, of which Hall gives a particular account.

In a chapter of the Knights of the Garter, held at Greenwich, on April 23, 1525, 17 Hen. VIII. the Duke of Suffolk, and the Duke of Norfolk t, named this Sir Andrews Windfor, in their lifts, for to be elected one of the Knights of that moft noble fociety. And, on June 7, following u, he was named by the all the Knights then prefent, except Sir Thomas Boleyne. He was likewife nominated in the chapters held in 18 Hen. VIII. and in 19 Hen. VIII. he was w nominated by the

q Hall, fol. 118. r Ibid. fol. 120. s Ibid. fol. 121. t Anftis's regift. of the garter, vol. 1. p. 367, 368. u Ibid. p. 370, 371. w Ibid. p. 380, 381.

Dukes

Dukes of Norfolk and Suffolk, the Marquis of Exeter, the Earl of Arundel, the Lord Lifle, the Lord Abergavenny, and the Lord Rochford, which were all the Knights prefent, except three. In 1529, 21 Hen. VIII. he was fummoned among the Peers of the realm [x], to that parliament which began at Weftminfter, on November 3; and was admitted into that houfe on December 1, the fame year, as Baron Windfor, of Bradenham in Bucks. And this parliament, on the reprefentation of the vices and enormities of the priefts, reduced the leffer monafteries, and thereby open the way to the furrender of all the reft, which foon after happened.

The next enfuing year, 22 Hen. VIII. [y] he was one of the temporal Lords, who fubfcribed that letter to Pope Clement VII. intimating to him, that unlefs he complied with King Henry in his divorce from Queen Catherine, which our own univerfities, the univerfity of Paris, as well as many others in France; and what almoft all men of learning, knowledge, and integrity, both at home and abroad, have determined to be true and juft; defiring him to take it into his ferious confideration, and conform, by pronouncing fentence to that truth, which has been examined, approved, and, after much deliberation, confirmed by the moft learned men of all nations. And that, if they have not, by his Holinefs's authority, a confirmation of what is juft, righteous, and true, they fhould therein reft fatisfied, and feek to attain this end by other means.

In 23 Hen. VIII. on St. George's day at Windfor, at a chapter then held, this Andrews Lord Windfor [z] was nominated for one of the Knights of the Garter, by the Duke of Suffolk, the Marquis of Exeter, the Earl of Suffex, the Earl of Rutland, the Earl of Ormond, the Lord Montjoy, and the Lord Fitz William; who were all the Knights prefent, except two. And in another chapter, in 26 Hen. VIII. [a] by all the Knights except one. But, new Knights of the Garter having been elected, he had not afterwards that intereft in them; and though he had votes in the feveral chapters of that diftinguifhed order, he was not unanimoufly named, whereby he was not elected.

In 35 Hen. VIII. he was keeper of the King's great wardrobe [b], as appears by a warrant directed to him, on February 13, to provide robes of the Garter, for Sir John Wallop, then elected. Alfo had a warrant on April 27, 36 Hen. VIII. to provide robes for Henry Fitz Allan Earl of Arundel, and Sir Anthony St. Leger, deputy of Ireland, then elected.

That which I find further of this Lord Windfor is, the information Sir William Dugdale had from Thomas Lord

[x] H. 13. in Offic. Armor. f. 398. [y] Rymer's fœdera, vol. 14. p. 405, 406.
[z] Anftis's regift. of the garter, p 386, 387. [a] Ibid. p. 394, 395. [b] ibid. p. 426.

Windsor, viz. 'That after the dissolution of the greater mo-
'nasteries, in 31 Hen. VIII. the King being informed by
'Cromwell, and others who had been his chiefest agents in
'the work, that the most likely means to secure them, from
'ever returning again to those uses, would be to dispose of
'most of them, into the hands of the nobility and gentry, by
'free gift, easy purchases, or advantageous exchanges. The
'project so wrought with the King, as he soon assented to put
'it in practice; and in order thereunto thought fit (among
'others) to engage this Andrews Lord Windsor, to be a par-
'taker. To which end, in 34 Hen. VIII. he sent him a mes-
'sage, that he would dine with him at Stanwell, on a certain
'day, and accordingly came; where he was magnificently
'entertained. Whereupon the King told him, he liked that
'place so well that he was resolved to have it; yet not with-
'out a more beneficial exchange. And the Lord Windsor
'answering, he hoped his Highness was not in earnest; it hav-
'ing been the seat of his ancestors for many ages, and hum-
'bly begging he would not take it from him. The King
'with a stern countenance replied, 'It must be,' command-
'ing him, on his allegiance, to go speedily to his Attorney-
'General, who would more fully acquaint him with his rea-
'sons for it. Being therefore afraid of his displeasure, he ac-
'cordingly repaired to the Attorney-General, who shewed
'him a draught, ready made, of an exchange of his lordship
'and manor of Stanwell, with its appurtunances, lying, as
'the [c] patent sets forth, in the counties of Middlesex, Surry,
'Buckinghamshire, Berkshire, and Southampton (by which
'the greatness of it may, in some sort, be discerned) in lieu
'of Bordsley-Abby with the lands and appurtenances there-
'unto belonging, in Worcestershire. Whereof being con-
'strained to accept of this exchange, he was commanded
'to quit Stanwell, though he had then laid in his Christ-
'mas provisions for the keeping of his wonted hospitality
'there. All which he left in the house; saying, 'They
'should not find it bare Stanwell:' Yet the King, in recompence, made him keeper of his great wardrobe, as afore-
mentioned.

He made his last will and testament, whilst he resided at
Stanwell [d], bearing date March 26, 1543, 34 Hen. VIII.
writing himself Andrews Windsor of Stanwell, in the county
of Middlesex, Knight, Lord Windsor. And orders his body
to be buried in the quire of the church of the holy Trinity of

[c] Pat. 34 Hen. VIII. p. 10. Prærog. Cant.   [d] Ex regist. Spert. N. 29. quire 23. in cur.

Hounsflow

Houndflow, in the said county of Middlesex, whether he deceases within the realm of England or without, if by any reasonable means he could be conveyed thither; and to be placed between the pillars where his entire well beloved wife, Elizabeth Lady Wyndsore, lieth buried; and that there be made a convenient tomb of freestone, with such arms, images, and scriptures, as shall be thought best, by the discretion of his executors; likewise, that his son George's tomb be also finished. And further directs, that his said burial be conveniently done according to his degree, with such cloathing to his houshold servants, and such mourners as shall be appointed by his executors, and to none others. And that, at the day of his interment, there be 24 torches, and four great tapers about his hearse, to be holden by 28 poor men, every torch weighing 16 lb. and every taper containing 12 lb. and every of the poor men (which he desires may be of the parish of Stanwell) to have 6 d. and a gown of frize.

He also by his will directs, that, during one month after his decease, Placebo and Dirige, with Masse of Requiem, should be said daily for him in the said church, and that 10 l. be given to poor tenants, in Stanwell and Horton. Also, that his executour or next heir keep solemnly an obite yearly, in the church of Stanwell, or in such church or parish as he shall hereafter happen to dwell in, for him, his wife, his father, mother, ancestors and friends, and all Christian soules, on the day of the decease of his loving father, Thomas Wyndesore, Esq; or within 14 days of the same, for the space of 14 years, next after his decease, with as many priests and clerks, as by his said father's will is directed; to be paid out of such part of the revenues and profits, as shall come and grow of his manor of March Baldyngton, otherwise called Baldyngton Wyndsore, within the county of Oxford; over and above such sumes of money, as he had assigned for two chauntries to be founded in the churches of Stanwell and Dorney. For the which obite, he wills, that the vicar of Stanwell shall have xx d. and every priest assisting at Dirige and Mass, x d. and, for Masse only, 6 d. every clerk, for Dirige and Mass, 8 d. and for Mass only, 4 d, except the clerk of Stanwell, to whom he wills 20 d. and to the bell-ringers, 16 d. Also, that there be bestowed on the poor people of the parish, at every obite, one quarter of wheat; two kilderkins of beer, and malmesye, and compfitts, for the quire, as heretofore has been used.

He wills, that all such plate and houshould goods, as he had of his Lady his mother, be left with Sir William Windsor, Knt. his son and heir apparent, or such other as shall happen to be his next heir, for the occupation of his heirs and their wifes,

Windsor-Hickman, Earl of Plymouth.

wifes, during their lives, finding sufficient security for delivery thereof to the same heirs, when they may come to it. To his son Edmund, all his houshold goods, &c. in his house of Bonvorden, in Stoke-Poges, in Bucks. To his son Thomas, all in his chamber at London, and in his own chamber at Stanwell. Also legacies to his daughters, dame Elizabeth, wife of Sir Peter Vavasor, of Spaldington in York; Anne, wife of Roger Corbet, of Morton Corbet in Shropsh. Esq; Edith, wife of George Ludlow, of Hill-Deverell, in Wilts, Esq; every of which he married in his life time, and well provided for, desiring them to pray for his soule. To his sister Margaret Windsor, late prioress of the late monastery of Sion, an annuity of 8l. vi s. viii d. out of his manor of Crainford, in com' Middlesex, to pray for his soul, his father and mother's soules, &c. To Sir William Windsor, his son, his chayne of gold, with a cross of diamonds and perles; his cupp of silver gilt, called the helmet; a bason and ewer of silver, with the Lady Bedyll's arms in it, and other plate; to remain to his heirs males, and to the heirs males of his brother, Sir Anthony Windsor, who had a son Anthony, and daughter Edith, to whom he left 100 marks.

It further appears by his will, that he was a kind master and benefactor to his servants, who were many. And so just was he, that he directs, if he has wronged any man, or is indebted to any, if it can be proved, that his executors recompense them. And that the will of his loving mother, dame Elizabeth Litton, and the will of his Lady his wife, and of his son George Windsor, be fulfilled. He bequeaths to Agnes Windsor, and Ursula, daughters of his son Thomas Windsor, 100 marks on their marriages, and, on their decease without issue, to Peter Windsor, Miles Windsor, and Andrew Windsor; and, in default, to his son Thomas, younger brother of Edmund. The residue of his goods, chattels, &c. his debts and legacys paid, he bequeaths to his son and heir, Sir William Windsor, Knight. And appoints executors, Sir Thomas Audley, Knight, Lord Audley of Walden, and Lord Chancellor; Sir John Baker, Knight, Chancellor of the Tenths; Sir William Windsor, his son and heir, and his son Edmund Windsor, Esquire; and overseers of his will, Thomas, Duke of Norfolk, and his brother, Sir Anthony Windsor, Knight. And for their labour, to the Lord Chancellor, fifty pounds: to Sir John Baker, thirty pounds, six shillings, and eight pence: to Thomas, Duke of Norfolk, forty pounds: to his brother, Sir Anthony Windsor, ten pounds: praying them to be aiding and assisting in the execution of this his will and testament.

The probat bears date July 31, 1543 (35 Hen. VIII.) and adminiftration was granted to Sir William Windfor, Lord Windfor, and his brother Edmund Windfor, executors.

He had to wife Elizabeth [e], daughter and coheir of William Blount, Lord Montjoy, and fifter and coheir of Edward Blount, Lord Montjoy, by whom he had iffue four fons, and four daughters.

1ft, George Windfor, who married Urfula, daughter [f] of Sir George Vere, Knt. and fifter and coheir of John Vere, the fourteenth Earl of Oxford, but died without iffue by her, in the life-time of his father; and, fhe was 2dly married to Sir Edmund Knightley, of Falvefley, in com' Northamp. The faid George had fepulture in the chapel at Hounflow, which belonged fometime to the friery adjoining; but being by Hen. VIII. given in exchange to Andrews, Lord Windfor [g], he made it a chapel of eafe for the inhabitants of two parifhes adjoining, Hefton, and Thiftleworth, and erected there a monument, whereof there are no remains; but Mr. Weaver, in 1630, took this fragment of the infcription:

Orate pro animabus Georgij Windfore, filij Andree Windfore de Stanwell, Militis : Et Vrfule uxoris ejus . . . . fuorum & heredis apparentis, Johannis Comitis Oxonie . . . .

2d, William, fecond Lord Windfor, of whom I fhall hereafter treat.

3d, Edmund Windfor, of Stoke Poges, in Buckinghamfhire, who was made [h] one of the Knights of the Carpet, Oct. 2, 1553, the day after Queen Mary's coronation, at the palace of Weftminfter, before her, in the chamber of prefence, under the cloth of ftate, by the Earl of Arundel, Lord Steward, who had her command to execute the fame. This Sir Edmund died unmarried.

4th, Thomas Windfor, Efq; who married Mary, daughter and heir of Thomas Bokenham, of Berkfhire [i], by whom he had iffue three fons and two daughters; but no iffue is remaining from them.

His four daughters were, 1ft, Elizabeth, married to Sir Peter Vavafor, of Spaldington, in com' Ebor. who had iffue by her [k] : 2d, Anne, the wife of Roger Corbet, of Morton, in com' Salop, who had iffue by her Andrew, and other fons, alfo four daughters : 3d, Edith, wedded to George Ludlow, of Hill-Deverell, in com' Wilts, Efq; 4th, Eleanor, mar-

[e] Ex ejufdem familiæ ftemmate. and hift. collect. of the fam. of Vere, p. 259. [f] Vincent's Baronage in offic. amor. [g] Weaver's fun. monuments, p. 529. [h] Strype's memorials, vol. 3. in appendix, p. 11. [i] Ex ftemmate, per Glover Somerf. MS. penes Tho. Wotton, de com' Surr. [k] Ex ftemmate, per Glover Somerf. MS. præd.

Windsor-Hickman, Earl of Plymouth.

ried first to Ralph Lord Scrope, of Upsall, who died without issue by her; and, 2dly, to Edward Nevill, second son of George Lord Abergavenny [l], who had issue by her Edward Nevill Lord Abergavenny, ancestor to the present Lord [m], and Sir Henry Nevill, of Billingbeare, in com' Berks, Knt. with other children.

I now return to William, second Lord Windsor, beforementioned. In 1533, 25 Hen. VIII. he was made one of the Knights of the Bath, against the coronation of Queen Anne Boleyne, with the [n] Marquis of Dorset, the Earl of Derby, and other Peers; and the King being in the Tower of London, May 30, all such, as were appointed to be Knights of the Bath, served the King and Queen at dinner, and after were brought to their chambers, and that night bathed and shriven, according to the old usage of England; and the next day, in the morning, they were knighted with the ceremonies thereto belonging. The day after, being Whitsunday, June 1, the King and Queen came from the Tower in great state to Westminster, where her coronation [o] was performed with great solemnity, the Knights of the Bath being in the procession.

In 1 Edw. VI. he was in commission [p] with Edward, Duke of Somerset, the Protector, Thomas, Archbishop of Canterbury, and eight temporal Peers, to prorogue the Parliament, that was adjourned to Jan. 20, to March 2 following. And at the decease of that King, he was one [q] of the twelve Peers, chief mourners, who, on Aug. 8, 1553, attended his funeral at Westminster.

On Queen Mary's claiming the crown, he [r] was one of the first that raised the commons, and proclaimed her title in Buckinghamshire; and afterwards marched into Norfolk [s] to the Queen, many joining them in their way. And on October 1, 1553, the day of her coronation [t], he served the office of Lord Panterer of England, and on that account had, as his fee, a salt of gold and chrystal.

On Feb. 8, in the 3d and 4th of Philip and Mary, he was in commission with Edmund Bonner, Bishop of London, Thomas Thirlby, Bishop of Ely, Sir Edward Waldegrave, Knt. Master of the Queen's great wardrobe, and others [u], to enquire into all heresies and heretical opinions, heretical and seditious books, contempts, conspiracies, and of all false ru-

l Ibid. in famil. de Nevill. m Cole's Esc. lib. 3. n. 61. a. 14. in bibl. Harley. n Hall's chron. fol. 213. o Ibid. fol. 215. p Strype's memorials, vol. 2. p. 483. q Ibid. p. 431, 432. r Stow's annals, p. 611. and Hollinsh. p. 1086. s Speed's chron. p. 842. t Strype's memor. vol. 3. p. 37. and regist. Pykering. Qu. 28, in cur. prærog. Cant. u Burnet's hist. of the reformat. p. 283.

Windsor-Hickman, Earl of Plymouth.

mours, seditions, words, and sayings, raised or published against the King and Queen, or against the quiet government and rule of their people and subjects; and to take possession of all manner of such books, or writings, &c. and determine all matters relating thereto, as misbehaviours, misdemeanors, &c. committed in any church, chapel, or any other hallowed place within the realm. Or with-holding of any lands, tenements, goods, or ornaments, stocks of money, and other things, belonging to any of the said churches, &c. Also, to inquire out all such persons, as obstinately refuse to receive the sacrament, hear mass, &c.

On July 5, 1557, King Philip passing over to Calais, and from thence into Flanders, the Queen sending over forces under the Earl of Pembroke[w], this Lord Windsor was one of the commanders under him, and had with him Sir Edward Windsor, his son, who greatly signalized himself at the taking of St. Quintin's, and on Aug. 10, at the defeat given to the French who came to relieve it.

This Lord Windsor had a seat at Bradenham, in Buckinghamshire, where, for the most part of the summer, he resided, possessing it from his father, who became possessed of it the latter end of Henry VIIth's reign[x]. The family of Scot owned it in the reign of Edward IV. and continued lords thereof, till after 1496. But Andrews Windsor, Esq; was lord of the manor and patron of the church, in 1508, 24 Hen. VII.[y]

In 1521, 13 Hen. VIII. Sir Andrews Wyndsore presented the minister to the church of Bradenham, dedicated to St. Botolph; on the wall of which, over the burial-place of the lords of the manor, was painted the following inscription:

' Orate pro animâ Willhelmi Wyndefore Militis dom.
' Manerii de Bradenham, & Dominæ Margaretæ & Hæ-
' redis Walteri Blount Militis Dom. Mountjoye, & Paren-
' tum predicti Wilhelmi Wyndefore Domini Wyndefore qui
' Hanc capellam fieri fecit. A. D. 1542 An Regni Regis Hen-
' rici 34.'

Besides Margaret, mentioned in the above inscription, this William, Lord Windsor, had two other wives, viz. [z] Margaret, daughter and heir of William Sambourne, of Southcote, in Berkshire (whose ancestors were heirs of the families of Lushel and Drew) by whom he had seven sons and nine daughters: and [a] Elizabeth, second daughter and coheir of Peter

---

[w] Speed's chron. p. 855. and Stow, p. 631.   [x] Ex inform. B. Willis armig.   [y] Ibid.   [z] Ex stemmate, per Glover Somerf. and lib. geneal. in bibl. Lambeth.   [a] Ibid.

Coudray, of Harrierd, in com' Southamp. who bore to him a son Philip, and a daughter Elizabeth; who both survived him, and died without issue.

Thomas Windsor was his eldest son, who dying an infant, his second son was also named Thomas. Which Thomas Windsor was one of the persons of distinction created Knights of the Bath, at the coronation of Edw. VI. Feb. 20, 1547 [b]. On Feb. 4, 2 Edw. VI. he had a grant [c] of the office of bailiff and feodary of the liberties of the dutchy of Lancaster, in com' Buck. and Bedford, being in the patent wrote Sir Thomas Wyndsore, Knt. son and heir of William Lord Wyndsore. He was married, in 36 Hen. VIII. [d] to Dorothy, daughter of William Lord Dacre, of Greystock and Gillesland; and died in his father's life-time, without male issue by her.

By his last will and testament, bearing date November 8, 1552, 6 Edw. VI. [e] writing himself Sir Thomas Wyndsor, of Princes Risborough, in com' Buck. Knt. he bequeaths his manors of Princes Risborough and Darlington, after the decease of his wife, to Anne his daughter, and her heirs, and in default thereof, to his brother William Wyndsor; and that his uncle, Edmund Wyndsor, have the management, till he attains the age of twenty-one years. He bequeaths to the Lord, his father, his black horse; and constitutes his uncle, Edmund Wyndsor, and the Lady Dorothy, his wife, his executors. The probat bears date Jan. 16 following, and administration was granted to Dorothy, his widow, and Edmund Wyndsor.

Henry, third son of William Lord Wyndsor, died in his infancy, and was buried at Stanwell.

Andrews, fourth son, died in his father's life-time, and was buried at Bradenham.

Edward, fifth son, succeeded to the honour and estate, as I shall further shew.

Walter, sixth son, married Margaret, daughter of Sir Geffery Poole, Knt. and had issue, Edward Windsor, and William Windsor.

William, seventh son, was seated at Alberbourne, in Buckinghamshire, and by Elizabeth, his wife, daughter of William Somerset, Earl of Worcester, had issue, William, his son and heir.

[b] J. S. in offic. armor.   [c] Lib. pat. &c. 4 Edw. VI. ad 10 Eliz. in the duchy office in Lancashire, fol. 23.   [d] Cole's Esc. lib. 4. p. 135. in bibl. Harley.   [e] Ex regist. Tash. Qu. 1. in cur. prærog. Cant.

Windsor-Hickman, Earl of Plymouth.

His nine daughters were, 1. Elizabeth, married first to Henry, son and heir to Thomas Lord Sands; 2dly, to Sir George Pawlet, Knt. and 3dly, to Richard Scrope, of Hamilden, in com' Buckingh. Esq; 2. Eleanor, to Sir Christopher Brome, of Halton, in com' Oxon. Knt. 3. Bridget, to Edward Ferrers, of Badsley-Clinton, in com' Warw. Esq; who [f] died Aug. 11, 1564, leaving issue by her, Henry Ferrers, his heir, and lies buried in Tarbick church: 4. Mary, wife to William Scot, of the Mote, in com' Suff. Esq; 5. Dorothy, to Thomas Pauncefoote, of Haresfield, in com' Glouc. Esq; 6. Anne, 7. Ursula, and 8. Margaret, who died young, or unmarried: and 9. another Anne, wife of Sir Henry Grey, of Pergo, in com' Essex, who was lineal heir male of Henry, Duke of Suffolk, and created by James I. Baron Grey, of Groby, in com' Leicest. ancestor to the present Earl of Stamford.

The last will and testament of the said William, Lord Windsor, shews, that he had a sound judgment, with strict integrity and honour; also, that he improved his estate by divers purchases. Therefore I have taken an extract of what is most memorable therein, and of the manors and lands he died possessed of. It is dated [g] August 10, 1558, in the 5th and 6th of Philip and Mary; wherein he stiles himself, William Wyndesore, of Bradenham, in the county of Buckingham, Knt. Lord Wyndesore: and orders his body to be buried in the right-side of the quire, within the parish church of Bradenham, and the right-side of the same church, if he deceases within the county of Buckingham; but, if he dies elsewhere, within the realm, then his body to be buried in the conventual parish church of Friers, in Hounslowe, within the county of Middlesex, in such place as shall be thought most decent and convenient by his executors, if it shall so come to pass, that the church of Hounslowe, at the time of his decease, be a parish church. Also wills, that his burial entertainment, and anniversary, be conveniently kept in such church his body is buried in; according to his degree and estate, with such cloathing for the Lady his wife, their children, and menial and houshold servants, with such moneys as shall be appointed by his executors, at the several days of his burial and anniversary. And that vi l. xiii s. iiii d. be given among poor householders, the day of his interment; also, from and after his decease, there be yearly kept, the Monday next before the feast of St. Michael the Arch-angel, where his body shall be buried, one anniversary service, according to the godly order

[f] Dugdale's Warwicksh. p. 712.   [g] Ex regist. Wells, n. 41. Qu. 12.

Windsor-Hickman, Earl of Plymouth.

of the holy catholick church, with certain priests and clerks, to pray for the soules of him the said William Lord Wyndesore, Andrews Lord Wyndesore, his father, Thomas Wyndesore, Esq; his grandfather, and all their wives, ancestors, friends, and childrens souls, and all christian soules. And he wills that his son Philip, for ever yearly, the said Monday, or before, cause to be paid to the minister, or other governour or governers of the house of Hounslowe, for the time being, a yearly rent of xxxiii s. 4 d. out of his manor of Cranford le Mote, at Cranford St. John's, in the county of Middlesex, and, in default of payment thereof, the said minister or governour, &c. may destrain for it; and be divided among the priests and clerks, that shall sing and say mass or diridge, and amongst the poor householders of Hounslowe. He bequeaths to the vicar of Heriard, for his tythes forgotten, 13 s. 4 d.

He wills to Sir Edward Windsore, Knt. his eldest son and heir apparent, his arras, tapestry, beds and bedding, pillowes, sheets, blankets, &c. there and then being at Bradenham; also all his chapel stuff, apparell, and ornaments at Bradenham; and all the great kitchen stuff at Bradenham, as potts, pans, spittes, plates, dishes, &c. and all other necessaries. He bequeaths to Walter Windsor his son, and William Windsor his son, bedds, &c. also to Philip, his son, houshold stuff remaining at Heriard, in the county of Southampton. That his son William, when he is twenty-one years of age, have his indenture of the prebend and parsonage of Thame, towards his finding either at school, at Oxford, or in one of the inns of court, or of chancery; and further bequeaths, to him and his heirs, the manor of Monks-Risborough, with his copyhold lands in Ascote, in the county of Buckingham, and other lands called Lichingams, Brandes, and Champions.

He bequeaths to his son, Sir Edward Windsore, his lease of Towresay, and all the profits thereof, which he had of the late Edward Ferrers, of Badsley, his son-in-law; also all his estate, after the life of Lady Knightly, in the manors of Barleyham, Wilsham, Aldam, Taston, Darnesdon, and Barkings, in the county of Suffolk, and during all the term of the life of the said Lady Knightly, paying to her yearly two hundred marks, as by indenture appeareth. And for the disposition of his plate, he wills, that his said son Edward shall have that which was bequeathed to him, by the Lord Andrew Windsor, his late father; also much other plate, which he entails on him and his heirs male, and in default, according to the will of his father, Andrew Lord Windsor. He bequeaths several pieces of plate to his sons Walter, and William. And that his daughter Anne

Windsor-Hickman, Earl of Plymouth.

take to her husband John Danvers, if they be so contented. And, whereas there was owing to him, by the Earl of Oxford, a thousand marks, he wills his executors to get it into their hands at such times as it shall be due, and out of it pay his son, Walter Windsor, one hundred pounds, and the residue towards the performance of his will. He bequeaths to every gentleman, or gentlewoman, at the day of his death, xxvi s. 8 d. every yeoman xx s. and every other servant xxx s. iiii d.

He bequeathes to his son, Philip, his farm of Allesborne, in the county of Suffolk; and that all his stocks of cattle at Heriard, in the county of Southampton, remain to the Lady Elizabeth, now his wife, for her life, and after her decease, to Philip and Elizabeth, the children of the said Elizabeth, and him, the said Lord Windsor, and Mary Powlet, daughter to his said wife. Also, to his said son Philip, such plate as is severed and sorted at Bradenham, and a cup which King Philip gave him to his christning, and a standing cupp gilt and cover, given at his christning by the Bishop of Winchester, and a drinking cup of silver and cover, given him by the Lady Marquis of Winchester, his godmother. And his mind is, that the Lady Elizabeth, his wife, being his natural mother, shall have only the custody thereof during her life, putting in sufficient sureties to his executors, for the deliverance thereof to his son Philip, after her decease, and to his daughter Elizabeth, if the said Philip die before his said mother. He further wills, that his wife have, during her life, his house in Mogwell-street, in London, called Windsor-Place, with the garden, and all hangings of tapestery and arras during her life, and being unmarried; also his new lodging there, adjoining to London-wall, with the appurtenances in the ward of Cripplegate, London; and after her decease to his next heir male, to whom he gives the said new building and garden, and not to be severed from Windsor-Place; likewise the manor of Snaylesham, in Iklesham, and Gestling parishes, that she holds in jointure. He further wills, that all such debts as he owed, as also his father's that are unpaid, be well and truly contented by his executors with all convenient speed. That the Lady Elizabeth, his wife, Sir Thomas White, of Southwarnborow, and his executors, have the governance and finding of his said son Philip, and daughter Elizabeth, until his son comes to the age of twenty-one years, and his daughter to eighteen years.

He ordains executors of his will, Dr. White, Bishop of Winchester, with a legacy of x l. Lord Chidioke Poulet, 6 l. 13 s. 4 d. Sir John Baker, Knt. 13 l. 16 s. 8 d. Sir Thomas White,

White, of Southwarnborow, 10 l. and William Roper, Gent. and overſeers the Marquis of Wincheſter, Lord Treaſurer of England, to whom he bequeathes xx l. and Sir George Paulet, the other overſeer, 6 l. 13 s. 4 d. praying them to accept it in good part. The reſidue of his goods, chattels, &c. (except his harneſs, armory, weapons, gunns, ſhot and powder, and his tent, which he gives to his ſon, Sir Edward Windſor) he bequeaths to his ſon Philip, and Elizabeth his ſiſter; and, if they deceaſe before the age of twenty-one, then to remain to his ſon, Sir Edward Windſor, and his heirs male. He further bequeaths to his grandſons and grand-daughters ſeveral pieces of plate. And concludes, ‘ Provided always, and my full
‘ mind and will is, that if my ſaid executors, and every of
‘ them, do refuſe and deny to take on them the probation
‘ and execution of this my laſt will, contrary to ſuch truſt
‘ and confidence as I have in them put, as I do verily truſt
‘ they will not, then I will that my ſaid ſon, Sir Edward
‘ Windſore, ſhall in no wiſe attempt or make any enterprize in
‘ or concerning this my will, or the order or adminiſtration of
‘ any of my goods and chattells, debts or credits. But I will,
‘ that the ſaid Elizabeth, my wife, and Sir Thomas White,
‘ Knt. or the ſurvivor of them, ſhall, on ſuch refuſal, take
‘ on them the execution of my ſaid will, according to the
‘ purport and tenor of the ſame.’ He died poſſeſſed (as his will ſhews concerning the diſpoſitions of his manors, lands, &c.) of the manors of Bradenham and Penne, called Bealing's: alſo of lands, &c. in Cheping-Wycombe and Weſt-Wycombe, and Weſton-Turvile, called Molen's manor, and Butler's manor, in the towns of Weſton-Turvile and Puttenham, and Aſcot, in the counties of Bucks and Hertf. the manor of Millcourt, in the county of Southampton: the manors of Elmanſton, Amſtanton, Hatton, Bentley, Thurwaſton, Alkemanton and Alkemanton-Bentley, in the county of Derby: the manor of Maideley-Home, in the county of Stafford: alſo, the manors of Medeley, Houghton, and Belyngley, in the counties of York and Nottingham, immediately after the deceaſe of Dorothy, Lady Windſor, wife of Sir Thomas Windſor, Knt. and the manor of Mynchinhampton and Penberye, in the county of Glouceſter, together with the manors of Cranford St. John's, Cranford le Mote, with the appurtenances, in the county of Middleſex, which he wills to remain to his ſon Philip, and his heirs for ever, yielding and paying out of the premiſes, to the monaſtery of Hounſlow, forty pounds yearly, at the feaſts of our Lady and St. Michael; and, for lack of iſſue male of the ſaid Philip, to remain to William Windſor, and his heirs male; and, in default, to Sir Edward
Windſor,

Windsor-Hickman, Earl of Plymouth. 79

Windsor, and his heirs male. He also wills, that his executors pay for the making up of the friers house in Hounslow, and for the obtaining of the lease and reversion of the domains of the said house, which one Rone, the auditor, now hath.

He wills the manor of Southcote, with the lands in Birfield and Shinfield, in Berkshire, to the Lady Elizabeth, his wife, if she lives sole and unmarried, and to her heirs male, in default to Sir Edward Wyndsor, Knt. his eldest son, and his heirs male, with remainder to his sons Walter Windsor, and William Windsor, and their heirs male, in default to his own right heirs. He further bequeaths to Walter Windsor, his son, his manors of Lushill, the third part of Hendonweeke, and the manor of Sopworth, in Wiltshire, to him and his heirs male, in default to the right heirs of him, the said William Lord Windsor. And to his son, William Windsor, and the heirs male of his body (with like limitation) the third part of the manor of Langage, with the advowson, the manor of Chipenham, and all the lands purchased of Giles Wilson in Heydon-Wyke, Kerson, Mylford, Hepton, and Crowbridge, in Wiltshire and Somersetshire.

He bequeaths to Sir Edward Windsor, his son and heir, the advowson and parsonage of Monks-Risborough, with the glebe-land; and law-day, at Ascote, once in the year to be kept; and to him, or who shall be his next heir, his manor of Okebrook within Chadesden, in com' Derb. the manor of Tredberk, with Brodsley, in the counties of Worcester and Warwick: the manors of Hedeley and Hursmere, in Surry: the manor of Eton, near Windsor, in com' Buckingh. the manors of Bailham, Willesham, Goodeford, Rowes, Aldenham, Tafton-hall, and Brandeford, in the county of Suffolk: the manor of Farnham and White-Waltham, in Berkshire: the manor of Stoke-Doile, in com' Northamp. the manor of Bunkhurst, in Wiltshire: a tenement in Mogil-Street, and a tenement in Lothbury, called the Abby, and the house called Windsor-Place, sometime Westmoreland-Place, in Silver-Street, in London: the reversion of the manor of Boneforden, in Stoke-Pogey, &c. with lands in reversion in Stanwell, in Middlesex, sometime of the monastery of Ankerwike. All which he entails on his heirs males; and, in default, on the heirs males of his father, Andrews Lord Windsor.

The probat bears date December 10, 1558, and administration was granted to the Lady Elizabeth, his relict, Sir John Baker, Knt. the Lord John, Bishop of Winchester, Sir Chidioke Poulet, Knt. Sir Thomas White, Knt. and William Roper.

By

80 Windsor-Hickman, Earl of Plymouth.

By an inquisition taken at the castle of Gloucester, after his decease [h], it was found that he died on August 20, after the making of his will, and he [i] was buried at Bradenham on [k] the 29th following, very splendidly, according to his quality, says Strype.

His eldest son and heir, Sir Edward Windsor, succeeded to the honour, as 3d Lord Windsor, and the greatest part of his father's estate. He was made one of the Knights of the Carpet, October 2, 1553, the day after Queen Mary's coronation, when his uncle, Sir Edmund, beforementioned, [l] received the same honour.

In 1557, he embarked with King Philip, July 7 [m], and the town of St. Quintin, in Picardy, being besieged, and the French endeavouring to throw succours into the town, they were entirely routed, and two thousand slain, also many taken prisoners of great rank, on August 10. And on the 8th day after this victory, the town was taken by storm, and all therein put to the sword, or made prisoners, by the English, as Hollinshed [n] recites; this Sir Edward Windsor, with Henry Dudley, being the first that entered the town, and right valiantly behaved, and were the first that advanced the English banner on the wall, as Stow writes, and that Henry Dudley lost his life in the assault.

In 1566, 9 Eliz. the Queen visiting the university of Oxford [o], she, on her return, did this Lord Windsor the honour of a visit at his seat at Bradenham, where she was highly entertained. Miles Windsor, his kinsman, son of Thomas, son of Andrews Lord Windsor, was then, and as Wood relates [p], ' a tolerable Latin poet, but a better orator, as was
' sufficiently witnessed by his speech intended to have been
' spoken in C. C. C., when Queen Elizabeth was entertained
' by the Oxonian muses, 1566; and more especially by that
' which he most admirably well delivered before her at the Lord
' Windsor's house at Bradenham, a little after she left Oxon.
' Which giving the Queen great content, she, in a high man-
' ner, commended it before Dedicus Gosemanus de Sylva,
' the Spanish Ambassador, then present. And looking wist-
' fully on Windsor, said to Goseman, Is not this a pretty
' young man.' Wood further recites, ' That, at riper years,
' he applied himself to the study of history and antiquities:'
and gives him a fine character.

---

h Cole's Esc. lib. 4. p. 135. in bibl, Harley.   i Ex regist. Pykering, Qu. 28.
k Strype's memorials, vol. 3. p. 450.   l Ib. in appendix, p. 11.   m Stow's annals, p. 631.   n Chronicle, p. 1183.   o Wood's Athenæ Oxon. vol. 1. p. 416.   p Ibid.

Windsor-Hickman, Earl of Plymouth.

This Edward, third Lord Windsor, was likewise well read, and possessed of all moral virtues, as his last will and testament shews; which, containing many remarkable ꝗ particulars of his piety, charity, prudence, judgment, and strict honour, as well as the estate he died possessed of, and the care he took to preserve it in his family, has induced me to transcribe the greatest part thereof, as registered in the prerogative court of Canterbury. It bears date December 20, 1572; Whereby he orders his body, if he dyes in England, to be buried in the parish church of Bradenham, in com' Buck. with such order of funeral, as shall appertain to his degree and honour. He bequeaths to the poor of Bradenham, Great-Wycombe, and West-Wycombe, in com' Buck. five pounds, to be distributed the day of his burial; also, the like sume to the poor of Tardebrigge and Bordesly; and orders his executors, within one year after his decease, to pay all his debts and legacies, as also his father's and grandfather's debts and legacys, unpaid or unperformed. He bequeaths to his right entirely beloved Catharine, his wife, all her aparel and jewells particularly specified, with much houshold furniture, and much plate; and the use of all his houshold plate and jewells, furniture, stock, &c. at the time of his decease, during such time as she shall continue sole and unmarried; she providing two sufficient sureties with her, within three months next after his decease, to become bound with her to his executors, in the sume of two thousand marks, for the just answering thereof to his son Frederick, on the day of her marriage, or within one month next ensuing the time of her decease, which shall first happen: and his executors to deliver her a true inventory thereof; and his son Frederick to have them after her death or marriage.

He also bequeaths to his said son Frederick all the plate, furniture, &c. of his house at Bradenham, and all his armour whatsoever in England; likewise his chain of gold set with rubies, that he had of the gift of the late Queen Mary, when he came from St. Quintin's. Also a chain of gold wyre, with a clock hanging thereat, set with diamonds and emroddes; a salt of gold and chriftall, which the Lord, his father, by his office, as Lord Panterer of England, had at the coronation of Queen Mary. Likewise much other plate particularly specified, among which was a great and deep bason of silver of his grandfather's; a gilt cup, called the helmet; two standing pots, all gilt; ten standing cups, after the new making, of the Almain manner; four beer cups, all gilt, &c. And all to

---

ꝗ Ex regist. Pykering, Qu. 28. in cur. prærog. Cantuar.

be delivered to him when he shall accomplish the age of twenty-one years, and not before; and if he dyes before that age, then to be delivered to the next heir of his body, or of the Lord his father's body, to whom his barony and inheritance shall descend, when he shall come to the age of twenty-one years, and not before. And that his armour and plate shall go from heir male to heir male of his body, and of the Lord his father's body, one after another, for ever. To several of his chief servants he bequeaths annuities for life, to be paid out of his manors, lands, &c. in Sussex, on condition that they serve the Lady Catharine, his wife, or his son Frederick, being lawfully required; and, if they refuse, then to be frustrate, and of no effect. He also bequeathed to every gentleman, that should be his servants at the time of his decease, four marks each; and to every gentlewoman waiting on Lady Catharine, his wife, four marks; and to every man servant, not being a gentleman, and every woman servant, not a gentlewoman, forty shillings each; and that his houses and servants shall be kept by his executors, at his charge, in the same order that he shall leave them, two months after his decease. He bequeaths to Edward Windsor, his godson, eldest son of his brother, Walter Windsor, one hundred pounds, and to every of the rest of his children, fifty pounds each, to be delivered them at the age of sixteen years: and to the daughters of his sister Scot, fifty pounds each. He ordains executors, his son Frederick Windsor, Sir John Throckmorton, Knt. John Talbot, and Peter Vavasor, and bequeaths to Sir John, and the other two, fifty pounds each for their just and due execution of his will: And appoints overseers, Thomas, Earl of Sussex, Lord Chamberleyn of England, and the right honourable his very good Lord and Nephew, the Lord William Sandes, with Sir James Dyer, Knt. Lord Chief Justice of the Queen's court of Common Pleas. Beseeching them to extend their aid and furtherance towards the performance of this his last will and testament. And for a token of his good will boorn towards them, he bequeaths to the said Earl his best horse; and to the Lord, his Nephew, his second horse, with two field pieces of brass, and their carriages and furnitures. And to Sir James Dyer his best ambling gelding, or ten pounds, at his own election. He concludes,
' And thus I make an ende, touching my last will and testa-
' ment, of all my goods and chatels whatsoever. And as
' touching the order and disposition of all my manors,
' messages, lands, &c. First, my intent and meaning is,
' that all my manors of Southcote, and Pynsones, in Berk-
' shire; and all those my lands, &c. called Stokes, and
· Welmeres,

Windsor-Hickman, Earl of Plymouth.

' Welmeres, in Wiltshire; and all those my manors of Bent-
' worth-hall, Berkham, Asteley, Mulcourte, and Thraftons;
' and all my lands, &c. called Crowches, in the countie of
' Southampton, with all my other lands in the said countie.
' My manors of Crampford St. Johns, Crampeford le Mote,
' and Houndflow, in the countie of Middlesex, with all my
' lands, &c. in Crampford and Houndflow, and all my
' houses, lands, &c. within the citty of London. And my
' manor of Eaton, next Windsor, in Buchinghamshire, other-
' wise called the manor of Colle-Morton, in Eaton; and my
' manor of Wycombe in Great-Wycombe, in the said coun-
' tie of Buckingham, with the appurtenances. My manor of
' Bradenham, and Hitchenden, in the said countie. Also my
' manor of Hungrye-Bentley, in the countie of Derby. Which
' manors, lands, &c. here expressed, do in all amount to a
' full 3d part of all my manors, lands, &c. above all charges,
' and shall descend and come to my next heir; to the intent
' that the Queen's majestie may have the wardship, and livery
' thereof, according to the laws and statutes of this realm.
' And I will and bequeath the manor of Madeley-Holme, and
' all my lands, &c. in Madely-Holme, in the county of Staf-
' ford, unto my executioners beforenamed, untill my son
' Henry shall accomplish his full age of 21 years, to find him
' with meat and drink, cloathing and education;' and the
overplus to the discharge of his gifts and legacyes. And when
the said son Henry comes to his full age of twenty-one, to
enjoy the said manor, to him and his heirs for ever, in fee-
simple. In like manner he bequeaths to his son, Edward, his
manor of Gretworth, in the countye of Northampton.

He bequeaths to his executors, his manors, capital messuages, and farms of Bilinges in Penne, and Cooks in Ag-
mondesham, in the counties of Buckingham and Hertford,
untill his son Andrew shall accomplish his full age of twenty-
one years, to find him in education, &c. and if he lives to
that age, then to enjoy the said lands to him and his heirs for
ever, in fee-simple. And for the better performance of his
will, and payment of his legacies, he bequeaths to his executors, his manors of Michelhampton alias Michinhampton,
Avening, and Losmere, in the county of Gloucester; his
manors of Gate-Court, Gate-Glossams, Dixter, and Vdy-
mere, in the county of Sussex; and his lands, tenements,
&c. in the said countyes of Gloucester and Sussex, not therein
otherwise disposed of, for the term of xx years after his decease: and after the end thereof, to remain to his son Frederick, and the heirs males of his body lawfully begotten; in
default to the heirs males of the body of him the said Edward

Windsor-Hickman, Earl of Plymouth.

Lord Windsor; in default to the heirs males of the body of William, late Lord Windsor, his father; in default to the heirs males of his body of his grandfather, Andrews, late Lord Windsor; in default to the heirs males of the body of Thomas Windsor, Esq; deceased, father unto the said Andrews, late Lord Windsor; in default of such heirs, to the right heirs of his son, Henry, for ever. And for the further surety and sure payment of all his debts and legacies, he bequeaths to his said executors, his manors of Towresly, Weston-Molins, and Weston-Butlers, in the county of Buckingham. Also his manor of South-Mimms, in the county of Middlesex; his manors, lands, tenements, &c. in Weston-Turvil, in the county of Buckingham, untill one, that shall be heir male of his body, shall be of the age of twenty-one years: and entails the same on the heirs males, as before-mentioned, and in default to the right heirs of his son, Henry, for ever. And if any surplusage be, his said debts and legacys being paid, as he hopes, and is assured there will; then he bequeaths the same to such heir male of his body, that shall first accomplish the age of twenty-one years, towards the charge of his livery, or prymer seazone, and setting up of houshold. And where there must be 240 pounds by the year paid to the Lady, his mother-in-law, during her life, and xx pounds a year must be paid back again, during the time that his said mother-in-law, and Mr. Puttenham, her husband shall live together; His will is, that they be paid the said 240 pounds by his executors, on such days he ought to pay the same. And whereas he, the said Edward Lord Windsor, for the sum of five hundred pounds by him paid to William Lord Sands, had taken to farme of the said Lord Sands, the manors of Steane, and Hinton, in the county of Northampton, with their appurtenances, to hold the said manors, &c. immediately after the decease of Reynold Bray, Esq; and his wife, unto him the said Edward Lord Windsor, and to Edward, and Andrew Windsor, his sons, during the term of thirty-one years next following; his will is, that, immediately after his decease, the said Edward, and Andrew Windsor, his sons, shall occupye and enjoy the said manors, &c. And further his will is, that, after his decease, an almshouse be built at Bradenham, with rooms and chambers convenient for a master and six poor men; and that the parson of Bradenham, aforesaid, and his successors, shall be masters of the same almes house for ever: and that his executors, or the survivor of them, shall obtain and procure of the Queen, her heirs or successors (which he trusts it will please his Soverayn, the rather for charity sake, to grant) letters patents, whereby the parson of Braden-

Bradenham, and his succeffors, and six poor men, may be incorporated, by name of master and brethren of the hospital of Bradenham. And that there be good ordinances made and devised by his executors, for the better government, rule, and continuance of the same corporation. Also, that his executors, as soon as they can conveniently, build the said almes house, procure the said letters patent for corporation, and purchase lands and tenements, to the yearly value of forty pounds, to be assured to the said master and brethren, by licence by them in that behalf obteyned. And that of the said forty pounds a year, the parson of Bradenham, and his successors, masters of the said hospital for the time being, shall have, towards the augmentation of his living, twenty marks a year, and the forty marks remanent of the said forty pounds a year shall be to the six poor men, equally amongst them, towards their finding and living, to pray for him and his ancestors, and the prosperous estate of his posterity. Also, his will is, that if he calls to remembrance any thing to be added to this his last testament, that the same put in writing, &c. shall stand as parcel of this his last will and testament, as if herein expressed. In testimony thereof, he set his seal, &c.

And going the year after to the Spaw in Germany, for the recovery of his health, he there made a codicil, as follows:

' And whereas there is a clause in the latter end of my will,
' that if any thing be added thereunto, and subscribed with
' my hand and seal, that then, &c. Be it therefore known
' to all christan people, that this xviiith of June, being in
' perfect and good mind, I do add unto my said will these
' things following: First, I do bequeath my soule into the
' hands of Almighty God, my maker and saviour, hoping to
' be saved with the merits of his precious blood; and my body
' to be buried in the cathedral church of the noble city of
' Leage, and to have a convenient tombe to be made in to-
' ken of some remembrance of me. My heart to be inclosed
' in lead and sent into England, to be buried in the chapell
' of Bradenham, under the tombe of my lord and father, in
' token of a true Englishman. Item, I do bequeath unto my
' soveraign Lady and mistress, Queen Elizabeth, my cross of
' diamonds; in demonstration, that in my life-time I lived to
' dye, and to fight under the same banner. Next, to offer
' my body to be imployed in any her majestie's service, most
' humblie to desire her majestie, to be good to my poor wife
' and children. Item, I give unto my nephew, Thomas
' Sandes, my best gelding, with xx pounds in his purse, towards his journey into Italy. Item, I give unto my wife
' all my jewells in my jewell coffer, unbequeathed, with the
' cheyne

'cheyne of gold that I ufually wear. Item, I give to every man of mine, that attends on me at the Spawe, v pounds a peece. And this I make an end. Dated at the Spawe this xviiith of June, Anno D. 1573.'

By inquifition taken after his deceafe, at [r] Cirencefter, in Gloucefterfhire, September 19, 1576, 18 Eliz. it was found by the jury, that he died on January 24, 1574-5, 17 Eliz. feifed of the manors of Michinghampton alias Muchelhampton, Aveninge, Pynberie, and Lofemore, in the county of Gloucefter. Alfo, by inquifition taken at Weftminfter, November 29, 1577, 19 Eliz. he [s] was found to die on January 24, 17 Eliz. poffeffed of the manors of Cranford St. John's, and Cranford le Mote; the manor of Greneford alias Stickleton, in Greneford, held by patent, Auguft 4, 31 Hen. VIII. the manor of Hounflow, held of the King of his manor of Eaft-Greenwich, in free foccage; and the manor of South-Mymms, held of the King of his caftle of Hertford, in foccage, by fealty, and 3s. 4d. rent, all in the county of Middlefex. And by both inquifitions, Frederick, Lord Windfor, was found to be his fon and heir, and of the age of 16 years, February 2, after his father's deceafe.

The faid Edward Lord Windfor had to wife the Lady Catharine, daughter of John Earl of Oxford, and of Dorothy, his wife, daughter of Ralph Nevile, Earl of Weftmoreland, by whom he had three other fons, and four daughters, mentioned in the infcription on a noble monument erected to her memory, in the church of Tarbick, which is in Warwickfhire. Her effigies lies at length on a tomb, her head refting on a pillow, in a praying pofture, with a canopy fupported by pillars, with the figures of Humility, Zeal, and Fame, and the following infcription:

D. O. M. S.

Katherinæ, Vere, Oxoniæ filiæ, Weftmorelandiæ neptis, Staffordiæ Buckinghamiæ Abneptis, Windeforiæ conjugis, hic jacent cineres, Quæ ortu vero; partu clara, clarior virtute, Edvardo Charifs: Marito, Venetiis defuncto; ætate forma florens, xxxiii; vitæ anno; Viduam Caftitatem, more prifco incepit, ufq; ad fexagefimum Vitæ ultimum, fanctè tenuit: novo tunc flagrans amore novum quæfivit & Sponfom in cœlis; Chriftum. Terreftrem hæc terra tenet partem; Ætheream Æther. Obit. 17 Jan. 1599.

Sed ne Exemplar Caftitatis & Pudicitiæ, Honore merito, pofteri Exemplo hic carerent, Aviæ fuæ Digniffimæ, Thomas, ex Henrico filio nepos, hoc Monumentum poni curavit.

[f] Cole's Efc. lib. IV. p. 135.   [g] Ibid. p. 136.

Windsor-Hickman, Earl of Plymouth.

Ex Marito quatuor suscepit Filios, Fredericum dominum Windesore, qui coelebs obiit; Henricum dominum Windesore, è regione sepultum; Qui Annam cohæredem Thomæ Rivet Equitis Aurati uxorem duxit; Edwardum, qui Elizabetham Ardington; Andream, qui Annam Pecham. Quatuor item Filias; quarum Maria et Elizabetha infantili ætate obiere; Margareta eximio Johanni Talbot de Grafton in Comitatu Wigorniensi Armig: Catherina Roberto Audley de Berechurch Comitatu Effexensi Armig. nupsit.

Secundùm Misericordiam tuam memento mei, Tu propter bonitatem tuam Domine. Psal. 24. Vers. 8.

The said Lady Catharine was sole daughter and heir to the said John, Earl of Oxford, by his first wife; and indentures were signed between his Lordship and Edward Duke of Somerset, Protector of King Edward VI. and the realm, for her marriage to Henry the Duke's 2d son: But after the Duke's attainder and execution, a bill was brought into parliament, and enacted, in 6 Edw. VI. that two indentures [t], between the said late Duke of Somerset, and the said Earl of Oxford, should be void and of none effect, concerning the marriage between the said Henry and Catharine. And she was after married to the said Edward Lord Windsor.

Their eldest son Frederick, 4th Lord Windsor, shewed himself, from his youth, a Nobleman of spirit and honour; being in 23 Eliz. among the gallants of that age, expert in justings, barriers, and turney. The Earl of Arundel, in honour to the Queen, and for her Majesty's diversion, having challenged all comers to try their feats in arms in those exercises; among the defenders [u] were, first, the Earl of Oxford; second, this Lord Windsor; third, the famous Sir Philip Sidney, &c. Also, the year after, 24 Eliz. when the French commissioners came into England, to make overtures for a marriage between the Queen and the Duke of Alençon, the French King's brother, accompanied with a very great train of the Nobles of France, rich in apparel, chains and jewels, as Stow writes [w], sundry royal justs, &c.. were performed by the most noble gallants of that time, whereof he recites this Lord Windsor to be one of the number. And Seager in his discourse of honour, p. 196, gives an account of a royal combat fought on foot before her Majesty, January 1, 1581, when Monsieur, brother to the French King, the Earl of Sussex, the Earl of Leicester, the Count St. Aignon, Monf. Chamoullon, and Monf. Backqueville, were challengers; and the defenders were this Lord Windsor, with his brother, Henry

[t] Strype's memorials, vol. 2. p. 209.   [u] Seager, of honour military and civil, p. 295.   [w] Annals, p. 688, 689.

Windsor, the Lord Thomas Howard, the Lord Darcy, the Lord Sheffield, Sir Thomas Cecil, and others. This Lord was afterwards [x], with other noblemen, appointed, by the Queen, to attend the Duke of Alençon to Sandwich, in order to his embarkation, when for their own honour, and the honour of the nation, they had many followers in their trains And in 27 Eliz. this Lord Windsor, with his brother, Henry Windsor [y], accompanied Henry Earl of Derby, in his ambassy to Henry III. the French King, to invest him with the order of the Garter. The Earl took his leave of the Queen at Greenwich, Jan. 20, and with those who went with him, having been admitted to kiss her Majesty's hand, they landed at Calais on February 1, and from thence proceeded to Paris, were received by the King of France with great marks of honour [z], and, by the way of Boulogne, returned to Dover, March 12, and on the Tuesday following waiting on the Queen at Greenwich, had a gracious welcome home.

This Lord Windsor departed this life [a] on December 24 following, 1585, 28 Eliz. as by the inquisition appears, taken after his decease, at Finsbury, in com' Middlesex, May 7, 28 Eliz. when Henry, his brother, was found to be his heir. By his last will, dated December 2, 1585 [b], he orders his body to be interred with such decent and comely funeral, as appertaineth to his estate; and that the testament of his father, Sir Edward Windsor, Knt. Lord Windsor, whereof he, with John Talbot, Esq; were executors, be performed in every article. He bequeaths to his brother Harry, his heir apparent, all his plate, jewells, apparel, armor, chatels, leafes, utencills, and houshold stuff, whatsoever, within the realm of England. He also bequeaths, in acknowledgment of his bounden duty and thankfulness to the Queen's Majesty (Queen Elizabeth) for her most gracious favours, at sundry times bestowed upon him, the cross of diamonds, willed and bequeathed to her Majesty by his father; also one other jewell, full as good, or better, as a token of his loyalty and affection to her Majesty, with these words engraven in the same, " Dator, non Donum," wishing his ability could extend to a greater gift; but, notwithstanding, he humbly beseeches her Majesty to accept the same; and his very loving friend, Mr. William Cornwallis, to present it to her. He further wills, that his brother Harry make a sufficient grant, of a rent-charge of fifty pounds per

---

[x] Annals, p. 688, 689.   [y] Ashmole's order of the garter, p. 395, 406.
[z] Ibid. p. 411.   [a] Cole's Esc. lib. 4. p. 136.   [b] Ex regist. Windsor, N. 69.
Qu. 1, in cur, prærog. Cant.

ann. out of his manor of South-Mymmes, in com' Middlesex, to his brother, Edward Windsor, for term of his life: and a like grant to his brother Andrew Windsor.

He bequeaths to his sisters, Margaret, and Catharine, the summ of two hundred marks, to buy them jewells, at the time of their marriage; most heartily requesting his said brother, and heir, to have a brotherly care of them, and to augment the portions his father gave them, as far forth as conveniently he can, which he himself proposed, if God should lend him life. Also, that his said brother cause a bason and ewer of silver to be made, of the price of fifty pounds, to be delivered to his most loving and dear mother, as a token of his dutiful affection to her Ladyship.

He bequeaths to his very good Lord, the Lord Admiral of England (Earl of Nottingham) a nest of bowles of silver gilt, of the price of twenty pounds, or better, as a token of his thankfulness for all his friendships: also to the Lord Clifford, Earl of Cumberland, his best hawke, which he thinks to be the haggard: to George Farmour, Esq; his next best hawke: to the Lord Thomas Howard, his white jennet: to his good friend William Cornwallis, Esq; his grey courser: to his good friend John Packington, Esq; his best brown bay horse. He makes his brother Harry Windsor his executor, and bequeaths to him all his manors, lands, and tenements, whatsoever, lying in the counties of Middlesex and Southampton; and ordeynes the Lord Sandes, and William Cornwallis, Esq; overseers of his will.

The probat bears date December 22, 1585, which also shews he died in the same month and year, he made his will; and administration was granted to Henry, 5th Lord Windsor, his brother. Which Henry, 5th Lord Windsor, was aged 23 years, August 10, 1585, 27 Elizabeth [c], as found by inquisition, on succeeding to the estate of his brother. He was, as mentioned before, one of the defenders [d], in the royal combat fought before Queen Elizabeth, on January 1, 1581, when Monsieur, brother to the French King, &c. were challengers. He also went with his brother [e] in the ambassy of the Earl of Derby, with the habit and ensigns of the order of the Garter, to Henry III. King of France. Mr. Ashmole has given a relation [f] of the manner of investing the French King, and of their entertainments in their journey, and the honours paid to them. Whereof I shall now observe, that on Saturday, February 13, before their entry into Paris, they were met in the midway between that city and St. Dennis, by the Duke of Monpensier,

c Coles's Esc. lib. 4. p. 136.　　d Seager on honour, military and civ. p. 196.　　e Stow's annals, p. 700.　　f Hist of the garter, p. 406, & seq.

a Prince

a Prince of the blood, and other great Lords of France, to accompany the Earl of Derby, &c. to the hoftell of Anjou, where his Lordfhip, with the Lord Windfor, and his brother, were lodged; and three tables fumptuoufly furnifhed for them at the King's coft. The particular ceremonies at their audience of the King, and after, of the Queen-mother, I fhall omit, as too long; and only mention, that the King, on his inveftiture, ordered, for Queen Elizabeth's fpecial honour, that none fhould that day proceed before him but Englifh, and that fuch French as were appointed to go with them, and his own Nobility, fhould walk behind him. At night, at fupper, the Earl, with Sir Edward Stafford, the Queen's Ambaffador refident with the French King, fat at the end of the King's table, with the King, the two Queens (viz. Aloifia, the confort of Henry, and Elizabeth, dowager of the late King Charles IX.) and fix or feven great Ladies. At another table, right againft them, fat divers great Ladies, all on one fide; and the Lord Windfor, the Lord Sands, this Henry, his brother, with the Englifh gentlemen, on the other fide.

On Dec. 10, 1589 [g], the faid Henry Lord Windfor was one of the principal of the fix, that fupported the pall, at the funeral of Henry Lord Compton, at the church of Compton, in Warwickfhire. And by a letter from Rowland White, Efq; [h] to Sir Robert Sydney, at Flufhing, dated from court, June 2, 1597, he writes, that the Earl of Effex's patent is drawing for Lord Lieutenant of Ireland; and that the Earl of Southampton, and the Lord Windfor, the Lord Rich, &c. were to go with him into Ireland againft the rebels. On Feb. 19, 1601, the 43d of Elizabeth, he was [i] one of the Peers, on the trials of the Earls of Effex and Southampton; but I find no further mention of his Lordfhip till his deceafe, in the year 1605, when he was 43 years of age. The inquifition taken after his deceafe, at Bury St. Edmund in Suffolk, on Sept. 10, in 1605, 3 Jac. I. [k], fets forth, that he died on April 6, that year, and that Thomas Lord Windfor was his fon and heir, and born on Sept. 29, 1591. He was buried in the church of Tarbick, where a curious monument is erected to his memory, with his effigies lying at full length, under a canopy, fupported by pillars; on three of which are the figures of Charity, Wifdom, and Temperance. And his extraordinary and rare virtues, are defcribed in the infcription thereon, together with his marriage, and iffue, as follows:

[g] Funeral ceremonies, MS. Not. 31. in bibl. Joh. Anftis, armig. [h] Sydney's letters and memorials of ftate, vol. 2. p. 55. [i] Camden's Eliz. in hift. of Engl. vol. 2. p. 633. [k] Cole's Efc. lib. 4. p. 135.

Windsor-Hickman, Earl of Plymouth.

HIC IN SPE
RESURRECTIONIS
OBDORMIT

Prænobilis Henricus Baro Windsor de Bradenham, filius Edwardi dom. Windesor, & Catherinæ filiæ Johannis de Vere, Comitis Oxon. & Dorotheæ Radulphi Nevill com. Westmerlandiæ filiæ; Qui (Frederico fratre seniore moriente sine liberis) & paternam hæreditatem & honorem adiit: Titulis verò animi fortitudinem, in prosperis, in adversis patientiam adjunxit: Tàm acquisitione, quam procreatione verè nobilis. Duxit in uxorem Annam cohæredem Thomæ Rivet de Chipenham in com. Cantab. Militis filiam, ex Grisilda filia Domini Gulielmi Paget, Baronis de Beudesert, Custodis privati Sigilli Reg. regnatib. Mariâ, & Elizabethâ, ex qua & redditus satis amplos, & liberos (connubii benedictionem) suscepit bis binos maculos: cæteras quinque filias pars major eorum ante ipsos parentes, & in ipsorum cunabulis inter cœlestes cohortes ascripti sunt: Funebria parentum, & miseriam hujus mundi gustaturi, tres solummodo supervixere, Thomas, scilicet filius & hæres; Elizabetha senior nupta Dixeo Hickman de Kew in com. Surr. armigero; & Elizabetha junior consanguineo suo Andreæ Windesor armig. [1] Nobilitatem suam omnibus animi & corporis dotibus adornavit: Deo devotissimum, Principi obsequentissimum, uxori amantissimum, domesticis liberalissimum & suavissimum, omnibus charum semper se præbuit.

In hoc agro suo Tardebigiensi, & mansione de Hewell, in ipsa camera ubi primò spiravit expiravit, magna cum Christiana alacritate & fiduciâ Animam in manus Redemptoris placidè & quietè commendavit: Corpus in hac Ecclesiâ sepeliri curavit sexto die Aprilis inter Resurrectionis solemnia, post partum virginis M. D. C. V. Invictissimi nostri Britanniæ Monarchæ Jacobi, An. 3. Ætatis suæ circiter xliii.

Hoc qualecunque Monumentum, & Epitaphium, meritis suis non satis amplum, obsequii & amoris ergo, Patri verè Pio, verè Catholico, Thomas mœstissimus filius & hæres, multis cum lacrimis scripsit & posuit.

Beati qui in Domino moriuntur.

The said Thomas, sixth Lord Windsor, his only son and heir, was, in June, 1610, one of the young noblemen [m], chosen to be Knights of the order of the Bath, at the creation of Henry Prince of Wales.

---

1 He died without issue by her, and she was, 2dly, married to Sir James Ware, Auditor General of Ireland; and descendants from her, of the name of Ware, are yet existing in Ireland.   m Anstis's knighthood of the Bath, 4to, p. 61, & seq.

Windsor-Hickman, Earl of Plymouth.

In 1621, the Lords considering the numbers of Scotch Earls and Viscounts, King James had made, who assumed to take precedence of the English Barons, he was one [n] of the Peers that remonstrated to his Majesty, 'That whereas, at the im-
'portunity of some of his subjects of England, he had con-
'ferred on them honours, titles, and dignities, peculiar to
'other his Majesty's dominions; by which all the nobility
'in this realm, either in themselves, their children, or both,
'find they are prejudiced: They humbly desire they may pre-
'serve their birth rights, and take no more notice of those
'titles, than the law of the land doth; but may be excused,
'if in civil curtesey they give them not the respect or place as
'to noblemen strangers; they being born and inheritanced
'under our laws, yet procuring translation into foreign
'names, only to their prejudice, &c. therefore, in all hum-
'bleness, they present this to his gracious view, confident of
'his Majesty's equal favour.'

In 1623, he was [o] Rear Admiral in that fleet sent by King James, to bring Prince Charles out of Spain: at which time he nobly entertained, on ship-board, the Grandees of that court, to the great honour of the English nation: his equipage and expences in that employment (all at his own charge) standing him in no less than fifteen thousand pounds; which he chearfully underwent, being a person of a most free and generous spirit, much accomplished with learning, especially antiquities, and sundry useful observations, by his travels through France, Italy, and other foreign parts; and safely [p] landed his Highness at Portsmouth, on Oct. 5, 1623. At the funeral [q] of King James, on Saturday, June 18, 1625, he was one of the mourners then attending. Also was one of those loyal Peers, who, on a special summons from Charles I. attended his Majesty at York, in the year 1639; being called thither to advise what was best to be done with the Scots, who had then invaded the northern parts of this realm with a powerful army. And having married Catharine, daughter to Edward Earl of Worcester (Lord Privy Seal) died without issue, Dec. 6, 1642, and was buried with his ancestors in the church of Tarbick, in Warwickshire.

To him succeeded, in all his possessions, and at length to his peerage, as seventh Lord Windsor, Thomas-Windsor Hickman, Esq; the son of his eldest sister, before-mentioned; which Thomas-Windsor he had from his birth, in default of

---

[n] Wilson's life of King James, in hist. of Engl. vol. 2. p. 747. [o] Dugdale's additions to his Baronage of Engl. MS. penes meipf. [p] Rushworth's collect. vol. 1. p. 104. [q] Funeral ceremonies, Net, H. 10. p. 73. MS. in bibl. Joh, Anstis.

issue by himself, designed to be his heir [r], giving him, at his baptism, the christian name of Thomas-Windsor; and upon whom afterwards, by a special deed, dated in December, 1641, he settled his whole estate, on condition that he should assume the name and arms of the ancient and right noble family of Windsor.

Which Thomas-Windsor Hickman, being in minority at his said uncle's death [s], became ward to William, Viscount Say and Sele, then master of the court of wards and liveries. But upon that unparalleled defection of the English and Scotch, this Thomas (though then but 15 years of age) brought in to his Majesty a good troop of horse, which, at his own charge, he maintained, and from time to time recruited, during the long continuance of that rebellious war; and, behaving himself in several battles and sharp encounters, with great loyalty and valour; especially in that near Naseby, on June 14, 1645, where he stoutly charged, with the regiment of horse then under his command, through and through the enemy's army: and his Majesty, taking special notice thereof, commanded, that he, with the same regiment, should be his royal guard for that day.

But all being lost in the said fatal battle, and the King constrained to retreat to Ashby-de-la-Zouch, in Leicestershire, he there most graciously acknowledging the signal service of those horse in that unhappy fight (and, in particular, the merits of this Thomas-Windsor, for his dextrous conduct therein [t]) as a special testimony of his royal grace and favour to him, gave order to the Lord George Digby (then one of his principal Secretaries of State) to prepare a warrant for his royal signature, in order to a patent under the great seal, for reviving the title and dignity of Lord Windsor, to him the said Thomas-Windsor, and the descendants of his body lawfully begotten: but from that time forward, continual losses befalling the King, so that the rebels totally prevailed throughout all his Majesty's dominions, nothing was further done thereupon, until the happy restoration of Charles II. and then his Majesty (as expressed in his patent) taking into consideration the many good services performed by this Thomas-Windsor, throughout the whole course of that grand rebellion (among which, the raising the siege of his Majesty's garrison of High Ercall, in Shropshire, was not the least) as also his sufferings by imprisonment, plunder, and otherwise; did, by a declaratory patent under his great seal, bearing date,

r Dugdale, ut antea.   s Dugdale, præd.   t Ibid.

Windsor-Hickman, Earl of Plymouth.

June 16, 1660, the 12th year of his reign [u], restore unto him the said Thomas and his descendants, as aforesaid, the stile, title, and dignity, of Lord Windsor, with the like pre-eminence and precedence in all parliaments, and elsewhere, as the said Thomas, late Lord Windsor, or any of his ancestors, bearing that title, had heretofore of right used and enjoyed. And, on July 18 [w] following, constituted him Lord Lieutenant of Worcestershire.

Soon after which, being summoned, as Lord Windsor, to the ensuing parliament begun at Westminster, May 8, 16 Car. II. he sat there accordingly; and the next year following, was sent Governor to Jamaica, where having, with the forces under his command, beaten a body of 3000 Spaniards, and possessed himself of seven ships in the harbour of St. Jago de la Cuba, he at length took that strong town, as also the castle, with five hundred barrels of powder therein, and divers pieces of cannon: but not enjoying his health in that climate, by his Majesty's special leave, he returned home, bringing with him two of those guns to the Tower of London; and was shortly afterwards constituted one of his Majesty's Privy Council in Ireland: and the King taking into consideration his eminent services, he was, by letters patent [x] dated Dec. 6, 1682, advanced to the degree and dignity of Earl of Plymouth, with limitation to the heirs males of his body; at which time [y] he was Governor of the town and garrison of Kingston upon Hull. But after his creation [z], no parliament meeting till May 19, 1685, 1 Jac. II. he was then introduced into the house of Peers, as Earl of Plymouth. On the 26th of the same month [a], the Earl of Radnor reported from the Lords committee for privileges, ' That the Earl of
' Plymouth informed their Lordships, that his Lordship being
' to give an answer in Chancery, he offered it to Sir William
' Beversham, Master in Chancery, upon his honour; but he
' refused to take it, unless his man might hold a bible before
' his Lordship's face. But Sir Timothy Baldwin, another
' Master, immediately took the answer, without laying the
' book before him.

' That it is the opinion of the committee, that a Master in
' Chancery, refusing to take a Peer's answer in Chancery,
' upon his honour, without laying a bible before him, is a
' breach of the privileges of Peerage. And that your Lord-
' ships would be pleased to make an order to be recorded

[u] Pat. 12 Car. II. [w] Bill. Signat. 12 Car. II. [x] Pat. 34 Car. II.
[y] Bishop Kennet's life of Charles II. in hist. of Engl. vol. 3. p. 396. [z] Journal dom. procer. 1 Jac. II. [a] Ibid.

Windsor-Hickman, Earl of Plymouth.

'in Chancery, to prevent such inconveniencies for the future.' Whereupon the house agreed to the report, and made an order accordingly; and that Sir William Beversham attend the house to-morrow morning at ten of the clock in the forenoon, 'To receive the reprehension of the house, for his offence, in refusing to take the answer of the Earl of Plymouth, without laying a bible before him, and not upon his honour only. Accordingly, he kneeling at the bar, the Lord-Keeper, by command of the house, did reprehend him severely for breaking the privilege of Peerage, and of the house, in the case of the Earl of Plymouth. And promising never to commit the like again for the future, he was discharged.'

On July 15, 1685 [b], the King conferred on him the command of the fourth regiment of horse, then newly raised; and in October following, he [c] was sworn of the Privy Council, and took his place at the board accordingly. His Lordship departed this life on Nov. 3, 1687, and was buried in the church of Tarbick.

He first married Anne, daughter to Sir William Savile, of Thornhill, in com' Ebor. Bart. and sister to that learned Nobleman, George, Marquis of Hallifax, Lord Privy-Seal, and president of the council in the reign of Charles II. and by her had one son, Other, of whom hereafter, and two daughters; Lady Mary, married to Sir Thomas Cookes, of Bentley, in the county of Worcester, Bart. [d] who died in the 36th year of her age, and the 22d of her marriage, on Jan. 3, 1694, and was buried at Tarbick, under a very handsome monument: Anne, the second daughter, died an infant. His second Lady was Ursula, youngest daughter and coheir of Sir Thomas Widrington, of Sherburn Grange, in com' Northumb. Knt. She was born Novem. 11, 1647, and surviving the Earl, her husband, till April 22, 1717, was buried at Tarbick. They had issue 4 sons, and 5 daughters, of whom Thomas the eldest son, was created Lord Viscount Windsor in Ireland, June 19, 1699, 11 Will. III. and Baron Montjoy, in the Isle of Wight, Hants, Dec. 31, 1711, 10 Anne; but those titles are now extinct.

The honourable Dixey Windsor, 2d son by the Earl's 2d marriage, born in 1672, was one of the Fellows of Trinity College in Cambridge, and so well respected by the University,

---

[b] Millan's succession of Colonels. [c] Hist. of Engl. præd. p. 440. [d] Inscrip. tumuli, apud Tarbick.

96 Windsor-Hickman, Earl of Plymouth.

that they [e] chose him, in six succeeding parliaments, one of their representatives. In 1712, being constituted Store-keeper to the office of ordnance, a writ was ordered, July 8, that year, for a new election, and he was re-chose. On the accession of George I. he was [f], on Nov. 11, 1714, continued in his place of Store-keeper to the office of ordnance. And, being a leading member of the house of Commons, he was one of the committee, chosen by ballot [g], in January 1720-1, to enquire into all the proceedings relating to the execution of the South Sea act. He died at Broke-End, in the parish of Gamlingay, Cambridgeshire, on Octob. 20, 1743, and was buried in the church there; having acquired a general reputation for his integrity and honour. He married Dorothy, youngest daughter of Sir Richard Stote, of the county of Northumberland, Knt. and coheir to her brother, Bertram Stote, Esq; but left no issue by her.

The honourable Andrews Windsor, Esq; 3d son, born in 1678, [h] served in two parliaments for the borough of Bramber, in Sussex; and in that, summoned to meet on March 17, 1715, for the borough of Monmouth. Taking to a military life, he was constituted Colonel of the 28th regiment of foot, on Oct. 1, 1709 [i], and on Feb. 12, 1710, Brigadier General in the army; having served through the whole course of the war, in the reign of Queen Anne; but was removed from his military employments in 1715.

William, 4th son, died an infant.

Lady Ursula, eldest of the five daughters, born in 1673, was married, in Henry VIIth's chapel in Westminster-Abbey, March 28, 1703, to Thomas Johnson, Esq; and died, his widow, on Aug. 20, 1737. Lady Elizabeth, 2d daughter, was married, on July 21, 1720, to Sir Francis Dashwood, of West-Wycomb, in Buckinghamshire, Bart. Lady Mariana, 3d daughter, died on April 22, 1710, of the small-pox, and was buried at Ryegate, in Surry. Frances, and Catharine, also died unmarried.

Other, son and heir to the aforesaid Thomas, Earl of Plymouth, born A. D. 1660, died in the life-time of his father; and by Elizabeth, his wife, daughter, and at length sole heir, of Thomas Turvey, of Walcote, in Worcestershire, Esq; had issue two sons, Other, who succeeded his grandfather in his honours and estate; Henry, born May 31, 1681, who died

---

e Willis's not. parl. & parl. reg. n. 16.   f Pointer's chron. hist. p. 795.
g Tindal's continuat. of Rapin's hist. of Engl. vol. 4. p. 632.   h Parl. regist. n. 115, 193.   i Millan's succession of Colonels, &c.

Windsor-Hickman, Earl of Plymouth.

without issue; and a daughter Anne, who died unmarried, in 1701, aged 19, and lies buried at Tarbick.

Which Other, 2d Earl of Plymouth, born Aug. 27, 1679, was, on Nov. 21, 1710, constituted Custos Rotulorum of the county of Worcester, which he held till August, 1714, when John, Lord Somers, succeeded him. On June 23, 1713, he had his patent for Custos Rotulorum of Cheshire; and Septem. 4, 1713, his Lordship was made Lord Lieutenant of Cheshire, and of the counties of Denbigh, and Flint, held by him till Oct. 21, 1714, 1 Geo. I. when Hugh, Earl of Cholmondely, succeeded thereto. In 1720, his Lordship was chosen Recorder of Worcester; and having married Elizabeth, daughter and heir of Thomas Whitley, of Peel, in the county of Chester, Esq; had issue by her (who died June 11, 1711) Other, his successor, and Henry, who died without issue in 1741. His Lordship departed this life on Dec. 26, 1727, aged 47, and was buried in the vault in the chancel of Tarbick.

Other, his eldest son and heir, born on June 30, 1707, succeeded as Earl of Plymouth; and, on May 7, 1730, was married to Elizabeth, only daughter and heir of Thomas Lewis, of Soberton, in the county of Southampton, Esq; by whom he had issue Other-Lewis, his only son and heir, born on May 12, 1731. His Lordship deceased on Nov. 23, 1732, aged 25, and was buried at Tarbick; and his Lady died on Nov. 9, 1733. He was succeeded, in his honours and estate, by his only son, before-mentioned,

Other-Lewis Windsor, the present and 4th Earl of Plymouth, of his family, who had his first rudiments of learning at Eaton, near Windsor, from whence he removed, for his further education, to Queen's-College, in Oxford; and after his return from the University, his Majesty was pleased, March 30, 1750, to confer on his Lordship a grant of the several offices of constable of the castle of Flint, and comptroller of the records within the counties of Cheshire, and Flint; and of comptroller of the pleas, fines, and amerciaments, of the county of Carnarvon, in North-Wales.

His Lordship was married, at the royal chapel at St. James's, Saturday, August 11, 1750, to Catharine, eldest daughter of Thomas Lord Archer, by whom he had issue, 1st, Other Windsor, Lord Windsor, his son and heir, born at his Lordship's house in Hanover-square, on May 30, 1751; 2d, Thomas, born on May 19, 1752; 3d, Andrews, who was born at Hewel in Worcestershire, and died the same day; 4th, ———, born on Sept. 25, 1758; 5th, ———, born on Jan.

Windfor-Hickman, Earl of Plymouth.

Jan. 4, 1760; 6th, ———, born on May 12, 1764; 7th, Lady ———, born on Dec. 3, 1755; and, 8th, Lady ———, born on May 3, 1757.

His Lordſhip, when he came of age, was conſtituted Cuſtos Rotulorum of the county of Flint, and took the oaths, and his ſeat in the houſe of Peers, April 17, 1753; and on November 9, 1754, was conſtituted Lord Lieutenant, and Cuſtos Rotulorum, of the county of Glamorgan. After the acceſſion of his preſent Majeſty, he was, on June 23, 1761, continued Lord Lieutenant, and Cuſtos Rotulorum, of Glamorganſhire, and appointed Cuſtos Rotulorum of Flintſhire.

TITLES.] Other-Lewis Windſor-Hickman, Earl of Plymouth, and Baron Windſor, of Bradenham, in com' Buck.

CREATIONS.] Declared, and confirmed Baron, by letters patent June 16 (1660) 12 Car. II. and accordingly ſummoned to that parliament, May 8, (1661) 13 Car. II. Originally by deſcent and writ of ſummons to the parliament, Nov. 3 (1529) 21 Hen. VIII. and Earl of Plymouth, in com' Devon. Dec. 6 (1682) 34 Car. II.

ARMS.] Gules, a Saltire Argent, between twelve Croſs Croſslets, Or.

CREST.] On a Wreath, a Stag's Head guardant, Argent, eraced proper, attired, Or.

SUPPORTERS.] Two Unicorns, Argent, armed, creſted, tufted, and hoofed, Or.

MOTTO.] JE ME FIE EN DIEU.

CHIEF-SEATS.] At Hewel-Grange, in the counties of Worceſter and Warwick, 3 miles from Broomſgrove, and 80 from London; and at Peel-hall, in Cheſhire.

Windsor Earl of Plymouth

LUMLEY, Earl of Scarborough.

CAMBDEN, Sir William Dugdale, and other of our antiquaries, have obferved, that this family is denominated from Lumley-caftle, fituate on the bank of the river Weare (near Chefter on the Street) in the bifhoprick of Durham, and is defcended from Liulph (a nobleman of great figure in the time of King Edward the Confeffor) who married Algitha, daughter to Aldred, Earl of Northumberland.

This Liulph, being ftripped of his great poffeffions by the Normans, who ruled in all places with a fevere hand, quietly withdrew into the bifhoprick of Durham [a], where he was dearly beloved by the people, not only in refpect of his high parentage, but of his many eminent qualities; whereby he grew into fuch familiarity and credit with Walcher, Bifhop of Durham, and Earl of Northumberland, that he would do nothing in temporal affairs without his advice: but this credit that he had with the Bifhop was the caufe of his death; which is thus related in Anglia Sacra, and by another author, [b] from Simeon Dunelmenfis, who was a monk of Durham, and precentor of that church, A. D. 1164, 10 Hen. II.

Leofwin, the Bifhop's chaplain, and archdeacon, finding himfelf not fo often called to council as he was before his Lord's acquaintance with Liulph, conceived fuch envy, as that he procured one Gilbert (who had been made fheriff by his coufin the Bifhop) to murder the faid Liulph by night, in his manor-place, not far from Durham; which the Bifhop having notice of, and knowing it would be grievoufly taken of the people, he, as foon as he heard of the murder, fent letters and meffengers into the country, offering to purge himfelf of being concerned in it, according to the order of the canon laws; and gave out, that he had banifhed Gilbert, and others, out of Northumberland, who had committed the murder. But the people finding this to be a ftory, and that he had not banifhed the murderers, but received them into his houfe, and favoured them as before, they ftomached the matter highly; and a day being appointed, by the kindred of Liulph, for a conference with the Bifhop, at Gatefhead, concerning the murder, and the prelate, inftead of giving them fatisfaction, taking refuge in the church, they threatened to fet fire to the place, if the archdeacon and fheriff, who had

[a] Wharton's Anglia Sacra, vol. 1. p. 703. [b] Hollinfhed's chron. vol. 2. p. 12, 13.

alſo taken the ſame ſanctuary, were not delivered up. At length, by the perſuaſion of the Biſhop, Gilbert went out, and, with his aſſociates who ventured out with him, was inſtantly killed by the enraged multitude. The archdeacon refuſing to come out, Walcher himſelf ſtept forth, caſting the ſkirts of his gown over his face, and, whilſt he was addreſſing the populace in the mildeſt manner, was diſpatched with lances. Leofwin ſtill continued in the church, till it was in flames, and then coming out, almoſt ſcorched to death, was hacked in pieces. This happened on May 14, 1080, the 14th year of the reign of William the Conqueror.

The ſaid Liulph had iſſue four ſons, Ughtred, ꞌ Oſbert (whoſe daughter and heir Ormonda was married to Robert de Peſhale) Adam, who had, ᵈ by gift of William the Conqueror, Uldel and Gilcruce; and Odo, who being ſtiled ſon of Liulph, had ᵉ alſo, by gift of the ſaid King, Talentire and Caſtlerigge, with the foreſts between Galtre, and Græca. But from Ughtred is this family deſcended, he having iſſue Sir William de Lumley, and Matthew. Which Sir William, by Judith, his wife, daughter to Heſilden of Heſilden ᶠ, had iſſue another Sir William de Lumley, who had two ſons, William, ᵍ and Marmaduke, ʰ who was father of John Fitz-Marmaduke, Baron of Horden, in the biſhoprick of Durham, who, on Feb. 12, 1300-1, 29 Edw. I. ⁱ was among thoſe Barons that ſubſcribed a memorable letter to Pope Boniface VIII. (in anſwer to one he ſent to the King, 'commanding him to forbear fur-
' ther proceedings againſt the Scots, claiming withal the ſove-
' reign authority over them, as belonging to the church)' wherein they owned and claimed the dominion of Scotland, and peremptorily conclude, ' That the King, their Lord, ſhould in
' no wiſe undergo his holineſs's judgment therein, nor ſend
' his procurators (as was required) as though their King's title
' were dubious, to the prejudice of the crown, the royal dig-
' nity, liberties, cuſtoms, and laws of England, which by their
' oath and duty they were bound to obſerve, and would de-
' fend with their lives; nor could they permit, if the King
' would, any ſuch unlawful proceedings; and therefore be-
' ſought his holineſs not to concern himſelf farther in that mat-
' ter.' An exemplar of this memorable inſtrument, with their ſeveral ſeals, is preſerved in Corpus-Chriſti college library in Oxford; and the ſeal, of this John Fitz-Marmaduke, is a Feſs between three Parrots, circumſcribed, Johannes Filius Marmaduci; which arms the family ſtill retain.

c Ex ſtemmate.   d Dugd. Monaſt. vol. 1. p. 400.   e Ibid.   f Seager's Baron. MS.   g Ibid.   h Ibid.   i Hiſt. of Engl. vol. 1. p. 199.

I now

Lumley, Earl of Scarborough.   101

I now return to Sir William, eldeſt ſon of Sir William de Lumley, and Judith, his wife. Which Sir William [k] married the daughter and coheir of Walter de Audre, of Morton-Audre, in the biſhoprick of Durham, and by her was father of Sir Roger de Lumley, Knt.[l] who wedded Sibil, daughter and coheir of Hugh de Morewic, an ancient Baron in Northumberland, who, dying in 45 Hen. III. left the ſaid Sibil, Theophania, and Beatrix, his coheirs, and then in minority, [m] whoſe wardſhip and marriages, without diſparagement to them, were obtained of the King, by William de Latimer, for MCC marks.

The ſaid Roger de Lumley, with her the ſaid Sibil, in 4 Edw. I. made partition with the reſt of the coheirs, of thoſe Knights fees of her inheritance, [n] and left iſſue Sir Robert de Lumley, and Sir Roger de Lumley, ſecond ſon, anceſtor to the Lumleys of Harleſton and Clipſton, in com' Northampt.

Which Sir Robert de Lumley, in 26 Edw. I. on the death of his mother (then the [o] widow of Laurence de St. Maur) ſucceeded to the lands of her inheritance, viz. [p] the manors of Weſt-Chivington, Morewicke, and Bamburgh-caſtle, in the county of Northumberland; as alſo to divers lands, &c. within the liberty of Rediſdale, and in Hodiſpethe and Feling, in the ſame county; at which time it was certified, that he was her ſon and heir, and of the age of 26 years. In 27 Edw. I. he had [q] livery of the ſaid lands, on the payment of five marks for his relief. He married Lucia, eldeſt daughter [r] of Marmaduke de Thweng, a great Baron, lord of Kiltoncaſtle, and Thweng, with divers other manors in Yorkſhire, Lancaſhire, and Weſtmorland. Which Lucia was at length coheir to her brothers, William, Robert, and Thomas de Thweng, [s] who ſucceſſively ſucceeded to the barony of Kilton-caſtle, &c.

Their ſon and heir, Sir Marmaduke Lumley, took to wife [t] Margaret, daughter and heir of ——— Holland, by whom he had iſſue four ſons, Robert, Ralph, Thomas, and William; as alſo a daughter Iſabel, married to Sir William Fulthorp, Knt.

Which Robert, being under age at the death of his father, [u] was in ward to William Latimer, Lord Latimer, in 1374, 48 Edw. III. when (on the partition of the lands of Thomas de Thweng, Baron of Kilton-caſtle) being ſtiled ſon of Marmaduke de Lumley, ſon of Lucia, ſiſter to Thomas de Thweng, he had 8 l. 10 s. 6 d. yearly, out of thoſe lands that were aſ-

k Ex ſtemmate penes Præhon. Ric. nup. com' Scarborough.   l Ibid.   m Rot. pip. 45 Hen. III. Ebor.   n Ex ſtemmate.   o Rot. fin. 26 Edw. I. m. 2.   p Eſc. 26 Edw. I. n. 23.   q Rot. pip. 27 Edw. I. Northumb.   r Dugd. Baron. vol. 2. p. 58.   s Ibid.   t Rot. fin. 48 Edw. III. m. 9.   u Ibid.

signed to Catharine, youngeſt ſiſter of the ſaid Thomas de Thweng; as alſo the manors of Moreſſome Magna, Moreſſome Parva, Ocketon, Lythum, Merſke, Brotton, Hylderwell, Skynner-Green, Lyvertoun, North-Cave, Roteſe on the Wolds, Lound, Langtofe, Swaythorpe, Thorp juxta Kilton, Foxholes, Thweng, with the advowſon of the cnurch, Kilton Caſtle, Stotevil-Fee, and Bulme-Fee, all in com' Ebor. ʷ and died poſſeſſed of them on the Sunday before the Nativity of our Lord the ſame year, as is evident from the inquiſition taken after his death, at Giſburgh, in 49 Edw. III. before John Savile, the King's eſcheator for the ſaid county; when it was alſo proved, that Ralph de Lumley was his brother and heir, and of the age of 13 years. And by another inquiſition ˣ, taken in 7 Richard II. being wrote ſon and heir of Sir Marmaduke de Lumley, it appears, that he alſo died ſeized (beſides his lands in the biſhoprick of Durham) of the manors of Eaſt and Weſt Chivington, and Rovely, as alſo 40l. rent in Morewicke, with nineteen tenements and a water-mill in Huſband, in the county of Northumberland; and that Ralph de Lumley was his brother and heir, and at that time of the age of 21 years.

Which Ralph de Lumley was a Knight in 9 Richard II. ʸ and in the retinue of Henry de Percy, Earl of Northumberland, in that expedition then made into Scotland, wherein he ſo well behaved, that he ᶻ was made Governor of Berwick upon Tweed, in 10 Richard II. and ᵃ continued there in 11 Richard II. but in ᵇ 12 Richard II. was taken priſoner by the Scots. After which, ᶜ in 15 Richard II. he was Deputy-governor of Berwick, under Henry de Percy, Earl of Northumberland; and the year after, 16 Richard II. ᵈ obtained licence to make a caſtle of his manor-houſe at Lumley. He was ſummoned to parliament, ᵉ among the Barons of the realm, from the 8th year of Richard II. till 1 Henry IV. incluſive, when he was ᶠ attainted, and had his lands ſeized, for being concerned with Thomas de Holland, Earl of Kent, and other Lords, who not aſſenting to the depoſal of Richard II. joined in a confederacy againſt Henry IV. binding themſelves by indenture ſextipartite, ᵍ to be diligent and faithful to each other in their undertaking, and were ſworn to keep their deſign ſecret, and to attend carefully upon the execution of it ʰ. But

w Eſc. 49 Edw. III. p. 2. n. 5. x Eſc. 7 Rich. II. n. 51. y Rot. ſcoc. 9 Rich. II. m. 6. z Ibid. 10 Rich. II. m. 3. a Ibid. 11 Rich. II. m. 4. b Ibid. 12 Rich. II. m. 3. c Ibid. 15 Rich. II. m. 7. d Pat. 16 Rich. II. m. 22. e Clauſ. de iiſd. ann. f Rot. fin. 1 Hen. IV. m. 18. Eſc. 5 Hen. IV. n. 3. g Hiſt. of Engl. vol. 1. p. 277. h Ibid. p. 279. Hiſt. of Oxford, vol. 1. p. 201.

Lumley, Earl of Scarborough. 103

appearing in arms, [i] and the Lords taking their lodgings in the town of Cirencester, whilst their forces encamped without the town, were overpowered by the inhabitants, and carried prisoners to the Abbey, notwithstanding all means were used, by their servants and retainers, to further their escape. And our historians relate, that 28 Lords, Knights and Gentlemen, the chief leaders of the rebellion, were brought from thence to Oxford, to the King, who immediately caused them to be executed there. But this Lord Lumley, who was standard-bearer in this expedition, and stiled a Banneret, died in the field of battle; which is evident from the record, [k] whereby all his lands and tenements, which he held in fee-simple from Jan. 5, 1 Hen. IV. together with all his goods and chattels, were adjudged in parliament to be forfeited.

He married Eleanor, daughter of John Lord Nevil, of Raby, and sister of Ralph Earl of Westmorland. Which Lady, in her widowhood (2 Hen. IV.) had an assignment of 20l. per ann. during life, out of the customs at Hull, [l] which was confirmed by Hen. V. in 1413, the first year of his reign, with the further grant of the lands and tenements in Beautrone and Strauton in the bishoprick of Durham, and Holme in Holdernesse, with the appurtenances, in com' Ebor. Their [m] issue that survived, were four sons, Thomas, Sir John, William (stiled of Lumley, 15 Hen. VI.) and Marmaduke; as also three daughters, Elizabeth, wife of Adam Tirwhit, of Kittleby, in com' Linc. Esq; Margaret, wedded to Sir John Clervaux, of Croft, in Yorkshire; and Catharine, married to Sir John Chideock, of Chideock, in Dorsetshire.

Of the sons, I shall first take notice of Marmaduke, the youngest, who, having a learned education, was elected Master of Trinity-Hall, in Cambridge, [n] and Chancellor of that University, in 7 Hen. VI. also, on April 15, the year following (1430) had the temporalities of the Bishop of Carlisle delivered to him, and [o] was consecrated the next day Bishop of that see. In 11 Hen. VI. he was specially appointed to take care of the interests of the clergy of the King and kingdom, at the great council held at Basil; and in the King's letters of safe conduct, dated May 1, in the same year, he is stiled Marmaduke Lumley, Bishop of Carlisle, late rector of Stepney, in Middlesex, and executor of Sir John Lumley, Knt. On [p] December 18, in 25 Hen. VI. he was constituted Treasurer of England; and after having sat twenty years Bishop of Carlisle, was translated to the bishop-

[i] Rymer, vol. 8. p. 529.   [k] Pat. 1 Hen. IV. p. 3. m. 42.   1 MS. de famil. nob. not. L. 25. p. 378. in bibl. Joh. Anstis, arm.   [m] Le Neve's fasti. eccl. Ang. p. 390, 426.   [n] Ib. p. 334.   [o] Rymer's fœd. tom. 8. p. 590. [p] Pat. 25 Hen. VI. p. 2. m. 25.

rick of Lincoln, Feb. 5, 1450-1, 29 Hen. VI. which he enjoyed scarce a year, departing this life in his attendance on the King at London. He was a q great benefactor toward the building of Queen's-College in Cambridge, and bestowed 200 marks (a great sum in those days) on the library of that college, with a great many good books.

Thomas de Lumley, the elder brother of the Bishop, departed r this life on May 31, 1404. 5 Hen. IV. being then seized of the castle and manor of Kilton, with the manors of Lythum, Cotum, Thweng upon the Wolds, Oktone juxta Swathorpe, Okton-Holme in Holderneffe, in com' Ebor. and Haddefton, in com' Northumb. as alfo of the castle of Lumley parva, and manors of Stanley, Strauton, Riklefden, and Beautrone, in the bishoprick of Durham; leaving Sir John Lumley, Knt. his brother and heir, twenty years of age. But John Beaufort, Earl of Somerfet, s had a grant of several manors, lands and tenements, which his father was possessed of, to the value of 360 l. a great estate in that age.

The said Sir John Lumley, doing his homage in 6 Hen. IV. t had livery of all the castles, manors and lands, whereof Sir Ralph Lumley, his father, was seized at the time of his attainder; and the honour of Knighthood was conferred on him for his fervices in Scotland. He alfo served that monarch in his wars with the French, who, having experience of his fidelity, he u was fully restored in blood (tainted by the conviction of Ralph, his father) by act of parliament in the 13th year of Hen. IV. He alfo signalized himself with Hen. V. in his wars; and in the 10th year of the reign of that victorious monarch, loft his life in the field of battle, w with Thomas Duke of Clarence, the King's brother; who being betrayed by Andrew Forgufa, a Lombard, his fcout-master, that represented the numbers of the enemy to be inferior to what they were, precipitated himself into a battle at Baugy, in the province of Anjou, on Easter-Eve, April 13, 1421, and was there slain, together with this Sir John Lumley, Lord Lumley, the Earls of Tanquervile and Angus, and the Lord Rofs, who difapproved of this rash design; yet made proof of their duty and their valour, not only in obeying their General in his life time, but accompanying him in his death, no men ever behaving more courageously; but being four to one, were over-powered.

This Sir John Lumley, Lord Lumley, by Felicia, his wife, daughter of Sir Matthew Redman, x Governor of Berwick,

q Bp. Goodwin's account of English bishops, p. 247.   r Esc. 5 Hen. IV. n. 30.   s Rymer's fœd. tom. 8. p. 163.   t Clauf. 6 Hen. IV. m. 14. u Rot. parl. 13 Hen. IV.   w Hall's chron. p. 76. b.   x Froifart's chron. p. 265.

had

had issue a daughter Maud, married to Sir William Thirkeld, of Thirkeld, in Cumberland, Knt. and Thomas de Lumley, his son and heir.

Which Thomas, in 10 Hen. VI. on making proof of his ʸ age, had livery of his lands, when ᶻ John Swinburn, of the age of 60 years and more, deposed, that he was born at Morpeth, in Northumberland, on the feast of St. Michael the Arch-Angel, in 1408, and was of the age of 22 years and more, on ᵃ the feast of St. Michael last past. Also by inquisition in 10 Hen. VI. was found heir to his father Sir John Lumley, who died possessed of a messuage and lands, called Sulam, in the parish of Baryftany, in com' pal. Lanc. He was afterwards knighted for his services in the wars, and concerned in divers negociations. In 28 Hen. VI. he was ᵇ one of the guarantees for the King of England, on a treaty with the King of Scots; as also in 29 Hen. VI. and ᶜ again in another treaty between the said Princes, in 31 Hen. VI. And the King having experienced his fidelity, prudence, and conduct, ᵈ he was constituted Governor of Scarborough castle for life, in the 33d year of his reign. In 35 Hen. VI. he was again employed to treat with the Scots, on certain affairs then in agitation; ᵉ and was also a guarantee in another treaty in the 37th year of Hen. VI. 1459; but more of him I do not find in that reign. 'Tis likely, that the sufferings of his family, under the Lancastrians, induced him to take part with the house of York; for when Edw. IV. attained the crown, he petitioned the parliament for the reversion of the attainder of Ralph Lord Lumley, his grandfather; ᶠ which was accordingly repealed in the first year of the reign of that King, and he had summons to parliament among the Barons of the realm, till his death.

In the 5th year of Edw. IV. he was ᵍ constituted one of the commissioners to treat with James III. King of Scotland, about his marriage with some person of the King of England's allegiance, as also concerning certain wrongs, ʰ which had been done by the subjects of both nations to each other, contrary to the articles of truce. About that time also, he was at the siege of Bamburgh-castle, in the county of Northumberland, ⁱ then held out (with some other garrisons in the north) by the Lancastrians. And on Oct. 10, 1466, in 6 Edw. IV. the King, in regard of his fidelity, circumspection, and industry, ᵏ appointed him one of the commissioners to treat at Newcastle upon Tyne, with the deputies of the King of Scots, concerning certain grievances between the two

y Claus. 10 Hen. VI. n. 16.   z Esc. 10 Hen. VI. n. 56.   a Esc. 10 Hen VI. n. 42.   b Rymer, tom. 11. p. 253.   c Ibid. p. 300, 334.   d Pat. 33 Hen. VI. p. 2. m 12.   e Rymer's foed. vol. 2. p. 434.   f Rot. parl. 1 Edw. IV.   g Rot. scoc. 5 Edw. IV. m. o.   h Ibid. m. 4.   i Ex vet. rot. penes, W. Pienpoint, arm.   k Rymer's foed. vol. 2. p. 573.

nations,

106 *Lumley, Earl of Scarborough.*

nations. Having married Margaret, [1] daughter of Sir James Harrington (brother of Sir William Harrington Lord Harrington, [m] and Knight of the Garter in the reign of Hen. V.) he had iſſue by her, Sir George Lumley, his ſucceſſor; and three daughters, Joan, wife of Bertram Harbottle, of Harbottle in the county of Northumberland, Eſq; Margaret, married to Bertram Lumley of Ravenſholm, in the biſhoprick of Durham, and Elizabeth, wife of William Tylliot, Eſq;

Which George, Lord Lumley, was knighted before the 2d year of Edw. IV. [n] when he was ſheriff of the county of Northumberland, for that, and the ſucceeding year, 3 Edw. IV. An office in that age, of great power and truſt; for the ſheriffs of Northumberland never accounted to the King in his exchequer, till the 3d year of Edw. VI. but received the iſſues and profits of their bailiwick to their own uſe, with all other debts, fines, and amerciaments, within the ſaid county; and all emoluments accruing from alienations, intruſions, wards, marriages, reliefs, &c. which was chiefly to encourage them to be on their guard againſt the Scots. But that care being leſſened, by ſettling the Lords Wardens of the marches, [o] it was enacted in the 3d year of Edw. VI. that the ſheriffs of Northumberland ſhould be accountable for their office, as others, in the exchequer. In the 6th year of Edw. IV. this Sir George Lumley, and Sir Robert Folbery, [p] were elected Knights for the county of Northumberland, to the parliament ſummoned to meet at Weſtminſter; and in the return of the writ, are ſtiled Milites gladiis cincti. In the 8th year of Edw. IV. he was conſtituted ſheriff of Northumberland, and was [q] continued in that office four years ſucceſſively. In 20 Edw. IV. I find him bearing the title of Lord Lumley, being a principal commander of thoſe forces under the leading of Richard Duke of Gloucester the King's brother, which retook the town of Berwick (that had been ſurrendered to the Scots by Queen Margaret, to gain a ſanctuary for her huſband, Henry VI. when he was expelled England) and afterwards entering into Edinburgh, he was for his valour and conduct in that expedition, made [r] a Knight Banneret in Hooton-Field, on Auguſt 22, the ſame year, with the Lord Fitzhugh, the Lord Scroop of Maſham, and others. On the acceſſion of Hen. VII. he waited [s] on his majeſty in his progreſs,

---

[l] Ex ſtemmate. [m] Aſhmole's order of the garter, p. 610. [n] Fuller's worthies in Northumb. p. 312. [o] Rot. parl. 2 & 3 Ed. VI. cap. 34. [p] Pryn's brev. parl. p. 123. [q] Fuller's worthies, p. 313. [r] Nom. milit. MS. ſub manu Tho. Jekyl, armig. [s] MS. in bibl. Cotton. ſub effig. Julius, p. 12.

Lumley, Earl of Scarborough.

in the northern parts of the kingdom, in the first year of his reign. In the 13th year of Hen. VII. he was in that expedition with the Earl of Surrey, [t] against the Scots, who, with their King, were besieging Norham-castle, situated on the river Tweed, dividing England from Scotland; which siege they raised, and marching into Scotland, levelled several strong places, particularly Hayton-castle, one of the strongest fortresses between Berwick and Edinburgh, in sight of the Scots army. And on the espousals of the Princess Margaret, eldest daughter of Hen. VII. with James IV. King of Scotland, which was solemnized at Richmond by Earl Bothwell, on St. Paul's day, 1502-3, 18 Hen. VII. [u] his Lordship and his son met the Queen at Darneton [Darington] in Yorkshire, with several Gentleman in his retinue, and 80 Horsemen in his livery, and waited on her majesty as far as Berwick, where she was received by Sir Thomas Darcy the governor. After this, I find no further mention of him; but that he took to wife Elizabeth, [w] daughter and heir of Roger Thornton, Esq; a very wealthy merchant of Newcastle upon Tyne (who [x] founded the house of White-friars in Newcastle) by whom he had the lordships of Witton, in com' Northumb. Lulworth, and the Isle, in the bishoprick of Durham. But possessing those lands in right of his wife, there happened great suits and sharp contests, betwixt him and Giles Thornton, a bastard son to the said Roger, concerning the inheritance of them; in which quarrel the said Giles was killed by him at Windsor. He departed this life, in the [y] 23d year of Hen. VII. leaving issue three sons, Thomas, Roger, and Ralph (or John, according to some.)

His eldest son and heir, Thomas Lumley, appeared on the behalf of the clergy and commonalty of the [z] diocese of Durham, in 11 Hen. VII. when the three estates of the kingdom were summoned to meet at Westminster, Oct. 27 1495; and dying in the life-time of his father, left issue by Elizabeth Plantagenet his wife (natural daughter of Edward IV. by the Lady Elizabeth Lucy) [a] Richard his son and heir, John, [b] George, and Roger Lumley, of Ludworth in Durham, Esq; who left three daughters his coheirs, Agnes, married to John Lambton, of Lambton in Durham, Esq; Isabella. wife to Richard Conyers of Hordon, in Durham, Esq; and Margaret, wedded to Thomas Trollop of Thornly, Esq; The said Tho-

---

t Hall's chron. fol. 43, 44.   u MS. Not. G. 11. p. 48. in bibl. Joh. Anstis,
arm.   w Leland's Itin. vol. 5. fol. 89. & vol. 6. fol. 62.   x Ibid.   y Seager's baronagium geneal. MS.   z Rymer's fœd. tom. 12. p. 711.   a MS.
E. 6. f. 5. b. in offic. arm. -   b MS. Not. L. 25. in bibl. John Anstis.

mas

mas Lumley had also three daughters, ᶜ Anne, married to Ralph Lord Ogle of Bothal; Sibil, wife to William Baron Hilton, of Hilton, in the bishoprick of Durham, and Elizabeth espoused to Robert Creswell, of the county of Northumberland, Esq;

Richard Lumley, his eldest son and heir, succeeding his grandfather, had summons ᵈ to parliament among the Barons of the realm, in the first year of Hen. VIII. and married Anne, daughter of Sir John Conyers of Hornby-castle in com' Ebor. Knight of the Garter (sister to William Lord Conyers) by whom he left issue two sons, John Lord Lumley, and Anthony Lumley, of whom hereafter, as lineal ancestor to the present Earl of Scarborough.

This Richard, Lord Lumley, died ᵉ on Trinity Sunday (26 Maii) 1510, 2 Hen. VIII. seized of the manor and castle of Kilton, &c. in com' Ebor. and of the manors of Kirkeby in Kendale, Helsington, &c. leaving John his son and heir 18 years of age.

Which John Lord Lumley, in 1513, 5 Hen. VIII. on the invasion of this realm by James IV. King of Scotland, brought ᶠ a considerable strength to the Earl of Surrey, who came to York with 500 men only (his sovereign lying before Tournay, with most of his nobles) and was one of the principal commanders of the van-guard of the army, which on Sept. 9, engaged in the battle of Flodden, where the King of Scotland was slain. Our historians relate, that the van-guard wherein this Lord Lumley engaged, acquitted themselves with the greatest bravery; encountering with the Earls of Crawford, and Montrose, who had with them a great number of Lords, Knights and Gentlemen, and were both slain.

In the succeeding year (ᵍ 6 Hen. VIII.) he was summoned to parliament as Lord Lumley; and the year after ʰ had livery of all the lands of his inheritance. In the year 1520 (12 Hen. VIII.) he was ⁱ at the meeting between his sovereign, and the Emperor Charles V. at Canterbury; and crossing the seas, was, in June, the same year, at that great interview of the Kings of England and France, between Ardress and Guisnes. In the 14th year of Hen. VIII. he ᵏ was in that army under the leading of the Earl of Shrewsbury, intended to invade Scotland, had not a peace ensued; and the following year, ˡ was in that expedition under the Earl of Surrey, against the Scots, who with some French forces, having invaded the kingdom, were

c Ibid. d Clauf. de iisd. ann. in dorso. e Cole's Esc. vol. 1. p. 178. in bibl. Harley. f Hall's chron. fol. 38, 42. g Clauf. 6 Hen. VIII. in Dorf. h Pat. 7 Hen. VIII. p. 2. i MS. B. 5. p. 380. in bibl. Joh. Anstis, arm. k Hall's chron. fol. 103. b. l Ibid. fol. 115. b.

then

ther put to flight. In 21 Hen. VIII. he had summons to that parliament [m] which met at Westminster, November 3, the same year, and continuing by prorogation till the 27th of that King's reign, gave the first stroke to the dissolution of the monasteries in England. In 22 Hen. VIII. he [n] was among the Barons, who signed a memorable letter to Pope Clement VII. intimating, that unless he complied with the King in his divorce from Queen Catharine, the acknowledgment of his supremacy in England would be much endangered. But in 28 Hen. VIII. he was one of the chief of those Northern Lords, who appeared in the insurrection called, The pilgrimage of grace; and a pardon being offered by the Duke of Norfolk, at that time general of the King's forces sent to suppress them; he was [o] chosen to treat with the Duke, at Doncaster, and so well accommodated matters, that the leaders, and all who had been either authors or partakers in the tumult, [p] were permitted to repair each one to their own home, without being questioned for their offence; which the King confirmed. Yet soon after he had the mortification of losing his only son George Lumley, [q] who being concerned in another insurrection, with the Lord Darcy, Sir Thomas Percy (brother to the Earl of Northumberland) and others, was thereupon apprehended with them, committed to the Tower, and in June, 29 Hen. VIII. was arraigned at Westminster, before the Marquis of Exeter, High Steward of England, [r] and being found guilty of high treason, suffered death.

This John, Lord Lumley, [s] married Joan, daughter to Henry Lord Scroop of Bolton, and had issue George his only son before-mentioned, who took to wife Jane, second daughter and coheir of Sir Richard Knightly [t] of Upton in the county of Northampton, Knt. and by her (who afterwards wedded John Knottesford, of Malverne-Priory, in Worcestershire, Esq;) left issue John his son and heir, and two daughters, Jane wife of Geffery Markham, of Astwood, in com' Wigorn, Esq; who died without issue, and Barbara, who was twice married, 1st to Humphry Lloyd, of Denbigh, Esq; the ingenious Welsh antiquary, and father, by her, of Henry Lloyd, of Cheam in Surry, from whom the Rev. Dr. Robert Lumley Lloyd, of Cheam, who was also rector of St. Paul's Covent-garden, in Westminster, and died in Nov. 1730; and 2dly to William Williams, of ———— in Carnarvonshire Esq; by whom she also had issue.

[m] Rymer's foed. vol. 14. p 308.   [n] Ib. p. 406.   [o] Herbert's life of Hen. VIII. in hist. Eng. vol. 2. p. 207.   [p] Hall's, chron. fol. 231.   [q] Ib, fol. 231, 232.   [r] Godwin's annals of K. Hen. VIII. p. 155.   [s] Ex stemmate.   [t] Ibid.

The said John, son and heir of George Lumley, on the death of his grandfather, was then an infant: But on his petition in the first year of Edward VI. setting forth, 'That he 'was a person in lineage and blood corrupted, and deprived 'of all degree, estate, name, fame, &c. by reason of the 'attainder of George Lumley his father;' [u] it was enacted, 'That the said John Lumley, and the heirs male of his body, 'should have, hold, enjoy, and bear the name, dignity, state, 'and preheminence of a Baron of this realm, &c.' On Sept. 29, 1553, two days before the coronation of Queen Mary, he was made one of the Knights of the Bath, in company of the Earl of Devonshire, the Earl of Surry, the Lord Abergavenny, the Lord Berkley, and ten others, being first knighted by the Earl of Arundel (his father-in-law) Lord Steward of the houshold, who had commission from the Queen to confer that honour; and the oath administered to them [w] was, 'Right dere brother, gret worshyp be thys ordre unto you. 'Almyghty God geve you the presynge of al knyghthode. 'Thys is the ordre of Knyghthode: You shall honour God 'above al thyngs; yee shal be stedfast in the feith of holly 'church, and the same mayntain and defend to your power. 'You shall love your sovereygn above al earthly creatures: 'And for your sovereygn, and sovereygnes right and dygnitie, 'lyve and die. Yee shal defend wydows, maydens, and or- 'phelyns, in their ryght. Yee shal suffre no extortion as far 'furth as ye may; nor syt in place where any wrongful judge- 'ment shal be geven to your knowledge. And as grete ho- 'nour be this noble ordre unto you, as ever it was to any of 'your progenitours.' His Lordship and his Lady were at the coronation, he attending among the Barons, and she [x] being one of the six principals Ladies dressed in crimson velvet, that sat in the third chariot of state; next to whom rode ten Ladies in crimson velvet, their horses trapped with the same; coaches in that age being used by none of the nobility, and as Stow relates, [y] were not brought into England till the year 1564. On April 24, 1556. he, [z] and the Lord Talbot, introduced Osep Napea, ambassador from the Emperor of Russia, to his audience of leave of the Queen, who brought several rich presents from his master, and concluded a treaty of amity and commerce; being the first ambassador who came here from that court.

In the first year of Queen Elizabeth, he [a] was constituted one of the commissioners to receive the claims of all such, as

u Rot. parl. 1 Ed. VI. w Strype's hist. memorials, vol. 3. p. 35. x Ibid. p. 36. y Annals, p. 867. z Stow's annals, p 630. a Pat. 1 Eliz. p. 4. in Dorf.

held

Lumley, Earl of Scarborough.

held of the Queen in grand Serjeanty, and were required to perform their respective services. In 8 Eliz. [b] he was employed to treat with Cosmo Medicis, Duke of Florence, about 1125 *l*. owing to her father Henry VIII. and having received it with interest, the Queen gives the said Duke a discharge for it. After this I find no mention of him, till 12 Eliz. when, with his father-in-law, the Earl of Arundel, being privy to divers transactions, relating to the Queen of Scots; as also to her designed marriage with the Duke of Norfolk, [c] they were both taken into custody. 'Tis related by Camden [d], ' That a
' great many who observed the Queen's averseness to marriage,
' and that foreign Princes, who were enemies to England, con-
' sidered the Queen of Scots as the undoubted heir of the crown
' of England, believed it would tend more to the settlement
' of affairs, and the fixing the Queen of Scots to just measures
' of government, should she marry the Duke of Norfolk, the
' first Nobleman in England, a man of popular interest, and
' bred up in the protestant religion; than should she admit of a
' foreign Prince, who might, by her help, embroil both king-
' doms, and at last inherit them; whereas 'twas the general
' wish to have them united in a person of English blood, should
' the young King of Scots do otherwise than well.'

'Tis very likely, that his Lordship concurred in these affairs, out of the great regard he had for the Earl of Arundel, who, in his last will and testament (bearing date, December 30, 1579, the 22d year of Queen Elizabeth) recited, [e] ' That
' by deed dated the 14th of March, in 8 Eliz. he had freely
' gave to his son the Lord Lumley, all his goods, chattles,
' houshold-stuff and plate. And in consideration of the great
' love, care and affection, which he had always found his
' said son, the Lord Lumley, to bear to him; as also for and
' in consideration of his great travel and pains, taken for him
' about his business and affairs, during all the time sithence
' he was first known to him; and especially for that for him,
' and his causes, and for the discharge and payment of his
' debts, he had sold the most part of his own lands, tenements,
' and hereditaments, and patrimony, to him descended from
' his ancestors. And for that, and for the payment of the
' residue of his said debts, he hath charged, and bound him-
' self and his friends, in divers and sundry bonds, and great
' sums of money, which he knows cannot be paid and satis-
' fied, without his great charge. He therefore had convey-
' ed, given, aud assured to his said son Lumley, the inhe-

b Rymer's fœd. vol. 13. p. 655, 656.   c Cambden's Eliz. in hist. of England, vol. 2. p. 421, 436.   d Ibid. p. 419.   e Ex regist. vocat. Arundel, qu. 1. in cur. prærog. Cant.

' ritance

'ritance of the greater part of all his manors, lands, &c. as by the conveyance thereof, more at large appeareth. And finding the same love, care, and good disposition of his said son the Lord Lumley, still continuing towards him; he therefore not only ratifies and confirms, all and singular the conveyances made by him, to his said son Lumley, or to any other for his use; but also bequeaths to him, all and singular the manors, &c. conveyed to him, and the Lady Jane his wife, his daughter deceased, to have and to hold, to him and his assigns for ever. And he desires his very good friends, Sir Thomas Bromley, Knt. Lord Chancellor of England, and Sir Christopher Wray, Knt. Lord Chief Justice of England, that if any variance should happen between the Earl of Surry, and his said son the Lord Lumley, about any of the lands, &c. that they would do their best endeavours to continue good amity and friendship between them, and also order and divide between them, all and singular his lordships, manors, &c. to them or either of them, by him conveyed. He also constitutes his said son, the Lord Lumley, full and sole executor, and Sir Thomas Bromley, Lord Chancellor of England, overseer, desiring him to assist his executor with his best advice, and bequeaths to him plate to the value of 100 l and to Sir Christopher Wray, Lord Chief Justice, plate to the value of 40 l.'

The Lord Lumley erected a noble monument for the Earl, in the collegiate church of Arundel, with an inscription beautifully gilt, setting forth his honours and principal employments; and underneath is this memorial in capitals:

'Johannes Lumley, Baro de Lumley, Gener Pientissimus, Supremæ Voluntatis suæ Vindex, socero suavissimo, Et Patrono Optimo, Magnificentissime Funerato, non Memoriæ (Quam Immortalem Sibi Multifariis Virtutibus comparavit,) sed Corporis Mortalis Ergo, In Spem Felicis Resurrectionis Reconditi; Hanc illi propriis Armaturis Statuam Equestrem, Pro Munere Extremo, Uberibus cum Lachrymis Devotissime consecravit.'

In 29 Eliz. he was commissioned with other Lords, [f] for the trial of the Queen of Scots; and the next ensuing year was in commission [g] for the trial of secretary Davison, 'For contempt towards the Queen's majesty, breach of his allegiance, and neglect of his duty, in sending the warrant for putting the Queen of Scots to death, without her knowledge.' And the commissioners differing in their sentiments about the man, and his punishment, this Lord Lumley delivered his opinion, that the sentence was justy pronounced against the Queen of

[f] Cambden's Eliz. in hist. of Eng. vol. 2. p. 519.   [g] Ibid. p. 536.

Scots; but affirmed, 'That never in any age was there such a
contempt against a prince heard, or read of, that the Queen's
council, in the Queen's palace, in the council chamber near
the Queen, who was, as it were, president of the council,
should resolve upon a matter of such consequence, without
her advice or knowledge; when both they and Davison might
have had so easy access to her: Protesting, that if he had but
one only son, and he were in the same fault, he would cen-
sure him to be severely punished But being persuaded of
the man's ingenuous and honest intention, he would inflict
no heavier punishment upon him than the rest have done
before.' Which was, that he should be fined 10,000 l. and
imprisoned during the Queen's pleasure; whereunto the majo-
rity of the commissioners assented.

In 44 Eliz. [h] he was one of the Peers that sat on the trial
of Robert Devereux Earl of Essex. And on the accession of
James I. he was [i] constituted one of the commissioners for
settling the claims at his coronation; as also a commissioner,
[k] with other Lords, who were authorized to make Knights
of the Bath. Cambden [l] gives this character of him, 'That
he was a person of entire virtue, integrity and innocence;
and in his old age, a compleat pattern of true nobility.
Had so great a veneration for the memory of his ancestors,
that he caused monuments to be erected for them in the
collegiate church of Chester on the Street (opposite to
Lumley-castle) in order as they succeeded one another, from
Liulphus down to his own time; which he had either picked
out of the demolished monasteries, or made new.' He likewise took care, that his estate should descend to one of his
own name and blood, by his last will and testament, which
he made some time before his death (bearing date, January
28, 1605-6, the third year of James I.) as also by deeds of
settlement. 'By which testament, he [m] orders his body to
be buried in the church of Cheam, next unto Nonsuch,
in the county of Surry, whereof he was patron, [n] with as
little extraordinary charge, as conveniently might be; and
bequeaths to his kinsman and heir male, Richard Lumley,
eldest son and heir apparent of Roger Lumley, Esq; son
of Anthony Lumley, brother to John Lord Lumley his
grandfather, his castle of Lumley, and all such manors,
lands, and tenements in the county of York, which he had
made a lease of in trust to Sir Richard Lewknor, Knt. Ser-

h Ibid. p. 537.   i Ibid. p. 633.   k Rymer's foed. tom 16. p. 524.
l Cambden's Eliz. in hist of Eng. vol. 2. 533.   m Britannia enlarged by Bishop
Gibson, vol. 2. p. 950.   n Ex regist. vocat. Dorset, qu. 34. in cur. prærog. Cant.

'jeant at law, and Chief Justice of Chester, &c. and William
'Smith, Esq; his old and trusty servant, bearing date 20 Fe-
'bruary, in 37 Eliz. but that during his minority, the Lady
'Elizabeth his wife should have the profits, using her libe-
'rality towards the said Richard, his brethren and sisters.
'And if it should so happen, that she died during the minority
'of the said Richard Lumley, or any such heir male, to whom
'the said castle of Lumley should come to or remain; he then
'wills the custody of the said Richard Lumley, during his
'minority, to the before-named Sir Richard Lewknor, and
'William Smith, Esq; as also if the said Richard Lumley de-
'parted this life during his minority, that they should have
'the maintenance and education of such heir male, as had a
'right to the castle of Lumley, &c. He constitutes Elizabeth
'his wife sole executrix, and Sir Richard Lewknor, overseer,
'and orders them to distribute two hundred pounds, amongst
'poor people.'

His first wife was Jane, eldest of the two daughters and co-heirs of Henry Fitz-Allan Earl of Arundel, by whom [o] he had issue Charles, Thomas and Mary, who died infants, and lie buried with their mother in the chancel of the church of Cheam. His last Lady was Elizabeth, daughter of John Lord Darcy of Chich, who survived him without having issue. He departed this life on April 11, 1609, and according to his desire, was buried in the vault, under the chancel of the church of Cheam, [p] having a noble monument of white mar-ble erected to his memory, against the north-east side thereof, adorned with the arms of the several families his ancestors had married into.

Thus the ancient Barony of Lumley, for want of issue male of his Lordship, expired with him, the attainder of his father George Lumley, Esq; not being repealed, by that act of the first year of Edw. VI. which restored him to the title of Lord Lumley. But the reverend Dr. Robert Lumley Lloyd, of Cheam in Surrey, lineally descended from Barbara, sister to the said John Lord Lumley, petitioning his late Majesty to be called to the upper house of parliament, in right of his descent from Ralph Lord Lumley, summoned to parliament in the 8th year of Richard II. which petition being referred by his Majesty to the house of Peers, and the said Dr. Lloyd heard by his council [q] thereupon, it was reported as follows; The Lord Delawar (Die Lunæ 23 Martii 1723) reporting from the Lords committee for privileges, the claim of the said Dr. Lloyd; as also the evidence of Richard Earl of Scarborough,

---

o Sandford's geneal. hist. p. 421. p Ib. p. 424, 425. q Journal dom. procer.

who was heard by his council againſt it, and inſiſted that the Earl is well intitled to the ſaid Barony of Lumley; the houſe of Peers came to this reſolution, ' That the petitioner (Dr. Lloyd) ' hath not any right to a writ of ſummons to parliament, as ' prayed by his petition.'

The honour of Baron Lumley, being therefore again revived in the perſon of Richard Lumley, Lord Viſcount Lumley, father of Richard Earl of Scarborough: I ſhall firſt deduce his deſcent, before I proceed to treat of his advancement to that dignity. That Anthony Lumley, Eſq; was ſecond ſon of Richard Lord Lumley, is evident from [r] the inquiſition of the court of wards, in 7 Jac. I. as alſo the will of the laſt Lord Lumley, [s] and other authorities; and that he left iſſue (by his wife, a daughter of Richard Gray, of the county of Northumb. Eſq;) Roger Lumley, Eſq; his ſon and heir.

Which Roger Lumley, Eſq; [t] married Anne, daughter of —— Kurtwich, Eſq; and left iſſue three ſons, Richard, George, and John, recited in the ſettlement of John Lord Lumley, in 6 Jac. I. Alſo a daughter Elizabeth, married to Sir William Langley, of Higham Gobions, in com' Bedford, Bart. [u] and by her was father of Sir Roger Langley, of Sheriff Hutton, in Yorkſhire, Bart.

Richard Lumley, eldeſt ſon and heir of the ſaid Roger Lumley, was the chief heir male of the family, after the deceaſe of John Lord Lumley, in the year 1609, and inherited the greateſt part of the eſtate of his anceſtors, by deed of ſettlement, and the laſt will and teſtament of the ſaid Lord Lumley. He was firſt knighted by King James at Theobalds, July 19, 1616, and was created Lord Viſcount Lumley of Waterford, in Ireland, [w] by letters patent bearing date, July 12 (1623) 4 Car. I. In the time of the rebellion, adhering to the King, he made his houſe of Lumley-caſtle a garriſon, and being a principal commander of the forces under Prince Rupert, marched with him into the Weſt of England; was at the ſiege of Briſtol, and remained there [x] at the time it was ſurrendered to the parliament's forces, Sept. 10, 1645. He [y] afterwards compounded for his eſtate for 1955 l. 10 s. He was alſo among thoſe loyal Peers, who [z] ſubſcribed a memorable declaration, juſt before the meeting of the parliament, that reſtored Charles II. which (as Lord Clarendon obſerves) very much contributed to it, by appeaſing the minds of many peo-

r Inq. 30 Maii, 7 Jac. I.   s Sandford's geneal. p. 421.   t Ex ſtemmate.   u Sir William Dugdale's viſ. de com' Ebor. 1665.   w Pat. 4 Car. I.   x Ruſhworth's collect. vol. 6. p. 75.   y Liſt of compounders, Ed. 1655, in letter L.   z Baker's chron. 7th edit. p. 700, 701.

Lumley, Earl of Scarborough.

ple who had incurred guilt. His Lordship married Frances, daughter of Henry Shelley, of Warminghurft-Park in Suffex, Efq; (a younger branch of the family, feated at Michaelgrove, the feat of the prefent Sir John Shelley, Bart.) by whom he had iffue a fon John, and a daughter Julia, married firft to Alex. Jermyn, of Lordington in Suffex, Efq; by whom he had a daughter and heir Frances (married firft to Francis More, Efq; fon and heir of Sir Henry More, of Fawley in Berks, Bart. and 2dly, to John Shuckburgh of Barton in com' Warw. Efq;) and by her fecond hufband Sir Chriftopher Conyers, of Hordon, in the palatinate of Durham, Bart. had alfo an only daughter named Julia, married to Sir William Blacket, of Newcaftle upon Tyne, Bart. and afterwards to Sir William Thompfon, Knt. Recorder of London, and one of the Barons of the Exchequer. This Richard, Lord Vifcount Lumley, was buried in the vault at Cheam, with his kinfman, John Lord Lumley, leaving Richard, his grandfon, heir to his honour and eftate, John his only fon and heir dying in his life-time. Which John Lumley, Efq; married Mary, daughter, and at length one of the heirs, of Sir Henry Compton of Bramble Teigh in Suffex, Knt. of the Bath (youngeft fon of Henry Lord Compton, anceftor to the Earl of Northampton) and of Cecily his wife, daughter of Robert Sackvile, Earl of Dorfet. They both lie buried in the church of St. Martin's, Weftminfter; and had iffue two fons, Richard, and Henry Lumley; as alfo three daughters, Elizabeth, married to Richard Cotton, of Water Gate in the county of Suffex, Efq; Frances and Anne, who died unmarried.

Henry Lumley, youngeft fon, married firft Elizabeth, daughter of .... Thimelby, of the county of Lincoln, Efq; and 2dly, Anne, daughter of Sir William Wifeman, of great Canfield hall in Effex, Bart. and of Arabella his wife (daughter of Sir Thomas Hewit, of Pifhiobury in com' Hertf. Knt. and Bart.) fifter and co heir to George Hewit, Lord Vifcount Hewit of Gowran, in the province of Leinfter in Ireland. He diftinguifhed himfelf in feveral campaigns in the reign of King William, [a] particularly at the battle of Landen, July 29, 1603, where his regiment of horfe, by the noble ftand they made, faved his Majefty from being taken prifoner. He ferved likewife all the war, under the late Duke of Marlborough, and was promoted to the rank of Lieut. Gen. Feb. 24, 1702-3; and at length his great merit raifed him to be General of of the horfe; and he was likewife Colonel of the King's regiment of horfe, and governor of Jerfey; to which he was

---

[a] Hift. of Eng. vol. 3. p. 514.

appointed

appointed April 13, 1703. In the battle of Audenard, July 11, 1708, he very much diſtinguiſhed himſelf, being then Lieut. General; and with Lieut. Gen. Bulau, were ordered by the Duke of Marlborough the next morning, with 40 ſquadrons of horſe, and a conſiderable body of foot, to purſue their rearguard; but the French flinging themſelves in the highway towards Ghent, they were followed only by 4 battalions and the 40 ſquadrons, and encountering them, a great number of the enemy were killed and taken, the regiment of Riſbourgh entirely ruined, and two entire companies taken. Alſo Brigadier Pourriene, who commanded the laſt brigade, was taken priſoner, with many officers. He departed this life on October 18, 1722, and was buried in the vault of the family of Hewit, in the church of Sabridgworth in Hertfordſhire. And his Lady continued a widow till her death, March 4, 1736-7.

Richard Lord Viſcount Lumley (eldeſt ſon of John Lumley, and grandſon and heir of Richard Lord Viſcount Lumley) having all the advantages of education, both at home and abroad, rendered himſelf ſo acceptable from his firſt ſetting out in the world, that he was particularly taken notice of by Charles II. and diſtinguiſhed among the moſt polite men of the age. The firſt opportunity which offered of ſerving his country, was in the year 1680, when an expedition was intended againſt the Moors, and to raiſe the ſiege of Tangier; which long voyage, and dangerous enterprize, his Lordſhip readily engaged in; ᵉ and on June 12, the ſame year, was actually embarked at Portſmouth to go on that ſervice, under the Earl of Mulgrave (after Duke of Buckinghamſhire) who was appointed commander in chief. But other meaſures being concerted, and the expedition laid aſide, his Lordſhip returned to court, and ſoon after (on September 11, 1680) was ᶠ conſtituted Maſter of the horſe to Queen Catharine, conſort to Charles II. In that ſtation he ſo far recommended himſelf, that his Majeſty, in conſideration of his great merit, and approved fidelity, and his deſcent from noble anceſtors, antient Barons of this kingdom, advanced him ᵍ to the ſtate and degree of Baron of Lumley-Caſtle, in the county palatine of Durham, and to the heirs male of his body, and for lack of ſuch iſſue, to Henry Lumley his brother, and the heirs male of his body, by letters patent, bearing date May 31, 1681, 33 Car. II. But no parliament ſitting during the remainder of that reign, his Lordſhip was not introduced till May 19, 1685, in the firſt year of James II. ʰ when he was brought into the houſe of

ᵉ Pointer's chronol. hiſt. of Eng. p. 278.   ᶠ Hiſt. of Eng. vol. 3. p. 380.
ᵍ Bill ſign. 33 Car. II.   ʰ Journ. dom. procer. 1 Jac. II.

118 *Lumley, Earl of Scarborough.*

Peers, between the Lord Colpeper, and the Lord Baron of Wefton, having received his writ of fummons, on Feb. 14 preceding.

On the infurrection raifed by the Duke of Monmouth in the weft, he had the command of a regiment of horfe, and being fent into thofe parts, had a principal fhare in gaining the victory at Sedgemore, July 6, 1685; and the Duke of Monmouth, with the German Count who accompanied him, and the Lord Grey, were [i] by his vigilancy difcovered, and furrendered themfelves prifoners to his Lordfhip. Neverthelefs, when he obferved King James's defign was to introduce popery, and that our religion and laws were in danger of being fubverted, by the arbitrary meafures then taken, he forfook the court, [k] appeared on the behalf of the feven Bifhops at their trial, June 29, 1688, and was among thofe of the chief nobility, who had the courage to confult with Monf. Dykvelt (whom the Prince of Orange intrufted to manage his affairs in England) and to concert with him fuch advices and advertifements, as might be fit for the Prince to know, whereby he might govern himfelf by them; [l] and often met at the Earl of Shrewfbury's, where they confulted how to proceed, and drew the declaration, on which they advifed his Highnefs to engage. It alfo [m] appears, that he was principally intrufted by Admiral Ruffell, afterwards Earl of Orford, who went over to Holland, and had the Prince's direction for the management of the grand affair of the revolution.

When matters were concluded on, [n] his Lordfhip, with the Duke of Devonfhire, and the Earl of Danby, undertook for the North; and retiring into their feveral counties, the Lord Lumley, by his intereft and friends, [o] fecured the important town of Newcaftle, which declared for the Prince foon after his landing. He was afterwards no lefs inftrumental, by his intereft and arguments in the houfe of Peers, in gaining the vote, that the throne was vacant, as alfo, that the Prince and Princefs of Orange fhould be declared King and Queen of England. For which fervices, on Feb. 14, 1688-9, the day after their Majefties were proclaimed, he was fworn of the Privy-council, [p] and declared one of the Gentlemen of the King's bed-chamber. Alfo, on April 10, 1689, before their coronation, was advanced to the dignity of Vifcount Lumley, of Lumley-caftle; and finally, on April 15, 1690, to the title of

[i] Bp. Burnet's hift. of his own time, p. 644. [k] Hift. of Eng. vol. 3. p. 514. [l] Bp. Burnet's hift. p. 712. [m] Ibid p. 763. [n] Ibid. p. 766. [o] Ibid. p 791. [p] Hift. of Eng. vol. 3. p. 550.

Lumley, Earl of Scarborough. 119

Earl of Scarborough ; and was likewise constituted Captain and Colonel of the first troop of horse-guards. In the year 1690, [r] he attended King William into Ireland, was at the battle of the Boyne, July 1 ; and afterwards [s] waited on his Majesty at the great congress of Princes at the Hague, and came back with him to England.

In the year 1691, he returned again to Holland, and waited on the King in his several campaigns in Flanders, till the conclusion of the peace of Ryswick, Sept. 11, 1697, and was declared Lieutenant-General of his forces. Being in waiting on the King at his decease, he, [t] and the Lord Lexington, had the care of his body. His Lordship, in that reign, [u] was likewise Lord-lieutenant of the county palatine of Durham, county of Northumberland, and Custos Rotulorum of the same, as also Lord-lieutenant and Custos Rotulorum of the town and county of Newcastle upon Tyne, and Vice-admiral of the sea coasts of Durham and Northumberland : in which posts he was continued by Queen Anne, who, on June 24, 1702, appointed him Lord-lieutenant of the counties of Durham and Northumberland. He was also sworn of her Privy-council, and constituted one of the commissioners to treat of a union between the two kingdoms of England and Scotland ; and, pursuant to that act, was sworn of the Privy-council at Kensington, Aug. 18, 1708.

On the accession of King George I. his Lordship was found to be among those Peers, intrusted by his Majesty with the government of these kingdoms, till his arrival. On [x] March 9, 1715-16, he was appointed Chancellor of the dutchy and county palatine of Lancaster, which he resigned in May, 1717 ; and thereupon had the office of Vice-treasurer, Receiver-general, and Paymaster-general of all his Majesty's revenues in the kingdom of Ireland, with the power to act by sufficient deputies. And his Lordship, having no intention to go over, procured an act of parliament, which passed the royal assent, July 6, 1717, to enable him to take in Great-Britain the usual oath to qualify himself for the said office. He departed this life on Dec. 17, 1721, and was buried with his ancestors in the church of Chester-in-the-Street, in the bishoprick of Durham ; and having married Frances (only daughter and heir of Sir Henry Jones, of Aston, in com' Oxon. Knt. and of his wife Frances, daughter of Henry Bellasis, Esq; eldest son of Thomas Lord Viscount Fauconberg) had issue seven sons and four daughters :

r Hist. of Engl. vol. 3. p. 598. s Ibid. p. 612. t Ibid. p. 837.
u Dale's cat. of the nobility, p. 84. x Bill sign. 1 Geo. I.

1. Henry

Lumley, Earl of Scarborough.

1. Henry Lord Vifcount Lumley, who was elected to parliament for the borough of Arundel, in 7 Q. Anne, and dying of the fmall pox on July 24, 1710, was buried near his grandfather, in the church of St. Martin's in the Fields.
2. Richard, 2d Earl of Scarborough.
3. William, who was brought up in the fea-fervice, and killed in an engagement in the Mediterranean, April 9, 1709.
4. Thomas, 3d Earl of Scarborough.
5. Charles Lumley, Efq; who was made Groom of the bedchamber to his late Majefty Dec. 22, 1727, and died on Aug. 11, 1728, being then member for Chichefter.
6. John, who was one of the Grooms of the bedchamber to Frederick Prince of Wales, and member of parliament for Arundel in Suffex; alfo appointed, on Feb. 1, 1731-2, Colonel of a company of grenadiers in the Coldftream regiment of foot-guards. He departed this life in Octob. 1739, and was interred in the burial vault of St. Martin's church in the Fields, London.
7. James, member in two parliaments for the city of Chichefter, and Arundel; who, in May, 1734, was conftituted Avener and Clerk-marfhal of his Majefty's horfe; and was appointed, with Colonel Henry Berkeley, Commiffioners for executing the office of Mafter of the horfe; alfo one of the Grooms of the bedchamber to Frederick Prince of Wales.

Lady Mary, married to George Montagu, Earl of Hallifax.

Lady Barbara, married to the honourable Charles Leigh, of Leighton-Beaudefert, in com' Bedford, Efq; brother to Thomas, late Lord Leigh, of Stonely, in com' Warw. and Knight of the fhire in parliament for the county of Bedford, who had no iffue by her Ladyfhip, who died January 4, 1755.

Lady Anne, married to Frederick Frankland, Efq; member of parliament for the borough of Thirfk, in Yorkfhire, and died without iffue, in Feb. 1739-40.

And Lady Henrietta, who died unmarried in 1757.

The Lady Frances, their mother, was one of the Ladies of the bedchamber to Queen Mary, and Queen Anne; and died on Nov. 26, 1737.

Richard, late Earl of Scarborough, was elected one of the members for Eaft-Grinfted, to the parliament called in the feventh year of Queen Anne; and for the borough of Arundel, in two other parliaments, whereof the laft was fitting on the demife of the Queen. On the acceffion of her fucceffor to

the

Lumley, Earl of Scarborough. 121

the throne, he was appointed (Sept. 21, 1714) one of the Gentlemen of the bedchamber to his Royal Highnefs the Prince of Wales, and prefently after was conftituted Mafter of the horfe; and was alfo Captain and Colonel of the firft troop of grenadier guards. On March 10, 1714-15, he was called by writ to the houfe of Peers, and took his place according to his father's patent of creation, whom he fucceeded in the year 1721, as well in his honours, as Lord-lieutenant and Cuftos Rotulorum of the county of Northumberland, and Lord-lieutenant and Cuftos Rotulorum of the town and county of Newcaftle upon Tyne. On May 2, 1721, he ftood proxy for Erneft Auguftus, Duke of York, at the baptifm of the Duke of Cumberland; and, on the Earl of Cadogan's fucceeding the Duke of Marlborough as Colonel of the firft regiment of foot-guards, his Lordfhip was conftituted Colonel of the fecond regiment of foot-guards, June 22, 1722. On June 9, 1724, his Lordfhip was elected one of the Knights-companions of the moft noble order of the Garter, and inftalled at Windfor, on July 28 following.

On our late Sovereign's acceffion to the throne, he was, on June 15, 1727, conftituted Mafter of the horfe to his Majefty, and fworn one of the Privy-council; alfo Lord lieutenant and Cuftos Rotulorum for the county of Northumberland, and Vice-admiral of the county of Durham. In 1733-4, he refigned his poft of Mafter of the horfe; and departing this life, at his houfe in Grofvenor-fquare, was interred in St. George's chapel, in Audley-ftreet, Feb. 4, 1739 40. Dying unmarried, his titles and eftate defcended to Sir Thomas Lumley Saunderfon, Knight of the Bath, his next brother and heir.

Which Thomas, Earl of Scarborough, was appointed, Nov. 28, 1721, his Majefty's Envoy extraordinary and Plenipotentiary to the King of Portugal; where he demeaned himfelf with that honour and integrity, as won him the regard of that Monarch, and the love and efteem of all his Majefty's fubjects there. On June 8, 1723, obferved as the birth-day of his then Majefty, he gave a magnificent entertainment to the Nobility and foreign Minifters: on July 6 following, he had audience of leave of their Portuguefe Majefties, having obtained permiffion to pafs into England, for the fummer, on his private affairs. In the year 1724, being again in his embaffy in Portugal, on the birth-day of his Royal Highnefs the Prince of Wales, our late moft gracious Sovereign, he diftinguifhed himfelf on that occafion; of which the following account is given in our Gazette, N° 6324; ' That

' he

' he entertained the foreign Ministers, Nobility of Portu-
' gal, and other persons of distinction, at dinner. In the
' evening there was a concert of vocal and instrumental
' musick, at which were a great appearance of Ladies, who
' were afterwards conducted to a fine collation, followed
' with a ball, that held till morning. The whole enter-
' tainment passed with a magnificence suitable to the oc-
' casion.'

On June 17, 1725, he was installed a Knight-companion of the most honourable order of the Bath. He was also appointed, in May, 1738, Treasurer of the houshold to Frederick, Prince of Wales, and as such walked at his funeral procession, April 13, 1751. He was elected to parliament for the borough of Arundel, in Sussex, in 1722, and returned one of the Knights for Lincolnshire, in the parliament summoned to meet at Westminster, Novemb. 28, 1728, [i] also for the said county in the next parliament, summoned to meet, June 13 [k], 1734. Enjoying the estate of James Saunderson, Earl of Castleton (who died without issue, May 24, 1723) he, by act of parliament, took the surname of Saunderson, in pursuance of the will of the said Earl. His Lordship married the Lady Frances, daughter of George Hamilton, Earl of Orkney (one of the Ladies of the bedchamber to her Royal Highness the Princess of Wales) by whom he had issue two sons, Richard, now Earl of Scarborough, and the honourable George Lumley, who died Dec. 11, 1739; also three daughters, Lady Anne; Lady Frances, married, in June, 1753, to Peter, Earl of Ludlow, in Ireland; and Lady Harriot, who died Nov. 6, 1747. And his Lordship deceasing, March 15, 1752, was succeeded by his only son Richard, the present Earl of Scarborough.

Which Richard, now Earl of Scarborough, and Colonel of the northern battalion of the Lincolnshire militia, married, Dec. 12, 1752, Barbara, sister to Sir George Saville, of Rufford, in Nottinghamshire, Bart. and by her has issue three sons, 1st, George-Augustus, Viscount Lumley, baptized Oct. 24, 1753, at his Lordship's house in Grosvenor-square; the sponsors being their Royal Highnesses the Prince of Wales (the present King) Princess Augusta, and the Marquis of Hartington, late Duke of Devonshire: 2d, ———, born on April 3, 1757: 3d, ———, born on June 22, 1760. His Lordship has also two daughters, viz. Lady

[i] British parl. reg. No. 103.   [k] Ibid.

Frances-

Lumley Earl of Scarborough 59

Lumley, Earl of Scarborough.

Frances-Barbara-Ludlow, born on Feb. 25, 1756; and Lady ———, born on June 1, 1758.

TITLES.] Richard Lumley-Saunderson, Earl of Scarborough, Viscount and Baron Lumley, of Lumley-castle.

CREATIONS.] Baron Lumley, of Lumley-castle (in the bishoprick of Durham) May 31 (1681) 33 Car. II. Viscount Lumley, of Lumley-castle, April 10 (1689) 1 Will. & Mar. and Earl of Scarborough, April 15 (1690) 3 Will. & Mar.

ARMS.] Argent, a Fess Gules, between three Parrots, or Popinjays, proper, collar'd of the 2d; being the arms of the ancient Barons Thweng, from one of the heirs whereof his Lordship is lineally descended. But the ancient arms of Lumley are, Gules, six Martlets, Argent.

CREST.] On a wreath, in her Nest proper, a Pelican feeding her Young, Argent, vulned proper.

SUPPORTERS.] Two Parrots, with Wings expanded, proper (i. e. Vert) beaked and membred, Gules.

MOTTO.] MURUS ÆNEUS CONSCIENTIA SANA.

CHIEF-SEATS.] Sandbeck, near Tickhill, in the West-Riding of Yorkshire, 150 miles from London; and Glentworth, in Lincolnshire, 8 miles from Lincoln, and 134 from London.

ZULEISTEIN, Earl of Rochford.

THE houſe of Naſſaw has produced heroes, allied to the greateſt Princes of Europe, and renowned both in the cabinet, and the field: but the brevity needful for the work I am engaged in, not permitting me to treat farther than what immediately relates to the deſcent of this noble family, I ſhall only obſerve, that Henry-Frederick de Naſſaw, Prince of Orange, and grandfather to William III. Prince of Orange, Stadtholder of the United Provinces, King of England, &c. had a natural ſon, Frederick de Naſſaw, whom he endowed with the Lordſhip of Zuleiſtein, and who thereupon took that ſurname. In 1669, the aforeſaid William, Prince of Orange, coming in the winter to the court of England, was accompanied by the ſaid Monſ. Zuleiſtein: on which Biſhop Burnet [a] obſerves, ' That King Charles the ſecond tried the Prince in point
' of religion (as the Prince told him) and ſpoke of all the pro-
' teſtants as a factious body broken among themſelves, ever
' ſince they had broken off from the main body; and wiſhed he
' would take more pains and look into things better, and not be
' led by his Dutch blockheads. The Prince told all this to
' Zuleiſtein his natural uncle. They were both amazed at it,
' and wondered how the King could truſt ſo great a ſecret, as
' his being a papiſt. The Prince told me, he never ſpoke of
' this to any other perſon, till after his death,'

Monſ. Zuleiſtein was General of the foot, in the ſervice of the States-General, when his country was invaded by the French, in 1672. In that diſmal conjuncture, when the Prince of Orange was made Stadtholder, his firſt action was an attack on Naerden [b], and, in order thereto, he detached General Zuleiſtein, to take quarters between Utrecht and Naerden. Whereupon the Duke of Luxemburgh marched the next day to relieve the beſieged, and with between eight and nine thouſand men, fell on the quarter of General Zuleiſtein, but was repulſed with loſs, and forced to retire. The town was after battered, and reduced to ſuch extremities, that they ſent to capitulate. In which interval, the Duke of Luxemburgh, having been reinforced, marched through waters, by the guide of ſome peaſants, and again attacked the quarters of General Zuleiſtein, and after a bloody and reſolute diſpute,

[a] Hiſt. of his own times, 8vo, vol. 1. p. 383. [b] Lives of the Princes of Orange, p. 135.

the General was slain, Octob. 12, 1672, dying valiantly fighting [c], and refusing quarter from the enemy.

He took to wife Mary (daughter of Sir William Killigrew, of the county of Cornwall, Bart. and Chamberlain to Queen Catharine, consort of Charles II.) who came over with the Princess Mary, mother of King William. He had issue by her William-Henry, his son and heir.

Which William-Henry de Zuleistein was greatly confided in by the Prince of Orange, who sent him to King James II. on the birth of the Prince of Wales, to congratulate him thereon, and to inform himself of the state of the nation [d]. 'Whereupon he brought him such positive advices, and such an assurance of the invitation he had desired, that he was fully fixed in his purpose to prepare for his intended expedition into England.' And when the Prince embarked, he come over [e] in the same ship with him. And on his landing, marching with him to Windsor, he was sent by him to King James at Feversham [f], to desire him to continue there or at Rochester, or set him at full liberty to go whithersoever he pleased; but King James setting out before his arrival there, he missed him on the way. However, on the King's return to Whitehall, three Lords being sent by the Prince, with a message to the King, for his remove from thence, he readily agreed thereto; and when they were gone from him as far as the Privy-chamber, he sent for them back again [g], and told them, 'He had forgot to acquaint them with his resolutions before the message came, to send my Lord Godolphin next morning to the Prince, to propose his going back to Rochester; finding by the message Monf. Zuleistein was charged with, that the Prince had no mind he should be at London; therefore desired he might rather return to Rochester, than go to any other place.' Which being made known to the Prince, he consented to it.

On Feb. 14, 1688-9, the day after King William and Queen Mary had been proclaimed, their Majesties named their Privy-council, and at the same time filling up some of the chief officers of their court, Monf. Zuleistein [h] was appointed Master of the robes to his Majesty. On Sept. 12, 1690, he was constituted [i] Lieutenant-general of horse and foot, and served both in Ireland and Flanders. At the battle of Landen, July 29, 1693, where his [k] Majesty was in the utmost danger, his enemies surrounding him on all sides, he distinguished himself by his gallant behaviour, and was wounded and taken prisoner.

c Hist. of Engl. vol. 3. p. 319.   d Ibid. vol. 2. p. 481.   e Ibid. vol. 3. p. 526.   f Ib. p. 536. and Burnet's hist. p. 544.   g Hist. of Engl. ut antea, p. 537.   h Ib. p. 550.   i Ex collect. Greg. King Lanc. fecial.
k Hist. of Eng. p. 655.

Whereupon his Majesty, taking into consideration his faithful services and eminent abilities, as also his near alliance in blood to him, was pleased to create him Baron of Enfield, in the county of Middlesex, Viscount Tunbridge, in Kent, and Earl of Rochford, in the county of Essex, by letters patent, dated May 10, 1695, in the 7th year of his reign.

His Lordship constantly attended his royal master, on his going over to Holland: and on that Prince's death, March 8, 1701-2, he retired to his seat at Easton, in Suffolk (which, with the estate he had purchased of Sir William Wingfield) and staid in England to settle his affairs, till the latter end of the summer, before he embarked for Holland, arriving at the Hague from England, August 23, 1702. Afterwards, for the most part of his life, he lived retired at Zuleistein; except in 1705, when his Lordship, with the Duke of Shrewsbury, and the Earl of Sunderland, took the advantage of a convoy, attending the Duke of Marlborough's passage to England, and embarking on board the yacht, sailed on Dec. 27 from Brill, and arrived at St. James's the 30th following. After which, I find no further mention of his Lordship, till his decease, which was at Zuleistein, in [1] 1708.

He married Jane, daughter and heir of Sir Henry Wroth, of Durans, in Enfield, in the county of Middlesex, and of Loughton-hall, in Essex, great-grandson of Sir Robert Wroth, Knt. by the Lady Mary Sidney, his wife, eldest daughter of Robert, Earl of Leicester. And the said Sir Robert was son and heir of Sir Robert Wroth, and Susan his wife, daughter and sole heir of John Stonard, of Loughton, in the county of Essex, Esq; and of Sir Thomas Wroth, [m] by Mary his wife, daughter to Richard Lord Rich, ancestor to the late Earls of Warwick and Holland: by which Lady his Lordship had issue 4 sons, and 4 daughters;

1. William-Henry, Earl of Rochford.
2. Frederick, Earl of Rochford.
3. Maurice, a Colonel of foot, in the service of George I. and died in 1722.
4. Henry, who died unmarried ... April, 1741, and was buried at Easton, in Suffolk, leaving his estate to his nephew, William-Henry, Earl of Rochford.

Of the daughters; 1. Lady Anne died unmarried, and was buried in St. Michael's chapel, in Westminster-Abbey, Feb. 15, 1700.

[1] Annals of Queen Anne, ann. 1704, p. 352, tificates, I 16. p. 222, in offic. armor.   [m] Cambden's funeral certificates

2. Lady Mary, married to the Heer Harvelt, one of the chief Nobles of the Province of Gelderland, second son to the famous General, Godart de Ginkell, Earl of Athlone.
3. Lady Elizabeth, who died unmarried, 1722.
4. Lady Henrietta, wedded to Godart, second Earl of Athlone, and elder brother of the Heer Harvelt, before-mentioned.

The eldest son, William Henry, Earl of Rochford, took early to arms, being in 1702, a volunteer in the expedition under the Duke of Ormond to Cadiz, and behaved with great gallantry, on the attack of the fort of Rodendallo; the taking whereof greatly contributed to the destroying the galleons at Vigo. He[n] distinguished himself by many brave actions, under the Duke of Marlborough, when Lord Viscount Tunbridge; particularly at the battle of Hochstet, or Blenheim, Aug. 2, 1704; and was sent by his Grace, to England, with the particulars of that glorious victory.

In 1708, succeeding his father in his honours and estate, he came into England, and was constituted, May 10, 1710, Brigadier-general of her majesty's forces; and being Colonel of a regiment of dragoons, he went over to Spain soon after, where he served that campaign, and was unfortunately killed at the battle of Almenara, July 27, 1710; having behaved with great gallantry. His Lordship, dying unmarried, was succeeded in his honours and estate, by Frederick, his next brother and heir, then one of the nobles of the province of Utrecht.

Which Frederick, Earl of Rochford, came into England the same year; where for the most part he resided, to the time of his decease, leading a retired life, honoured and esteemed among the Peers, and by all who knew him, for his affable deportment, and friendly character. His Lordship departing this life, at his house in Great Queen-street, Lincoln's-inn-fields, June 14, 1738, in the 56th year of his age, was buried at Easton in Suffolk; and having married Bessey, daughter of Richard Savage, Earl Rivers (who died on August 18, 1712, and by his will left her his estate) had issue by her Ladyship (who 2dly wedded the Rev. Mr. Carter) two sons

1. William-Henry, now Earl of Rochford, born Sept. $\frac{15}{27}$ 1717.
2. The honourable Richard Savage de Nassaw, born June 1, 1723, and in December, 1751, taking to wife Elizabeth, daughter and heir of Edward Spencer, of Rendlesham, in com' Suffolk, Esq; the widow and relict of James Duke of Hamil-

[n] Annals of Q. Anne, 1708, p. 352.

128   Zuleiſtein, Earl of Rochford.

ton and Brandon, to whom ſhe was 3d wife; and hath iſſue by her Grace; 1. a daughter Lucy, born on November 3, 1752; 2. a ſon born July 28, 1754, named William-Henry, and a 2d ſon, —— born on Sept. 5. 1756.

William-Henry, the preſent and 4th Earl of Rochford, in 1738, was by his Majeſty appointed one of the Lords of his bed-chamber; and was conſtituted Vice-admiral of the coaſts of Eſſex. In 1749, he was ſent Envoy-extraordinary and Plenipotentiary to the King of Sardinia, where he reſided with great reputation. His Lordſhip took an opportunity, during his reſidence at Turin, to make a tour with his Lady, through the principal cities of Italy, in order to diſcover the diſpoſition of the ſeveral Italian courts, and arrived at Rome, April 5, 1753. The year after, his Lordſhip having obtained a permiſſion to return to England, for a few months, on his private affairs, had his audience of leave of his Sardinian majeſty, and all his royal family; and with his Lady leaving Turin, March 26, 1754, came by the way of Paris to England, landing at Dover, April 26 following: and on Sept. 5 enſuing, his Lordſhip embarked at Harwich for Holland, in his return to Turin, where it was intended his Lordſhip ſhould reſide ſometime longer; but on the Earl of Albemarle's dying ſuddenly at Paris, an expreſs was ſent for him to return to England; which he obeyed with great expedition; for notwithſtanding the inclemency of the ſeaſon, his Lordſhip leaving Turin, Feb. 12, 1755, arrived at his houſe in Berkeley-ſquare, on the 28th of the ſame month. The next day his Lordſhip waited on his majeſty at St. James's, and was moſt graciouſly received: and the day after, March 2, the King, as a reward for his ſervices he had rendered during his miniſtry at Turin, was graciouſly pleaſed to appoint his Lordſhip Groom of the Stole, and firſt Lord of his Bedchamber. Alſo, on the 11th of the ſame month, he was by his Majeſty's command, ſworn of his moſt honourable Privy Council, and took his place at the board accordingly: and on April 26 following was appointed one of the Lords Juſtices for the adminiſtration of the government, during his Majeſty's ſtay beyond the ſeas. On April 6, 1756, his Lordſhip was conſtituted Lord Lieutenant and Cuſtos Rotulorum of the county of Eſſex, and Vice-Admiral of the coaſts of the ſame county. In theſe three laſt offices he was continued by his preſent Majeſty, as well as in the liſt of Privy Counſellors: and on June 8, 1763, his Lordſhip was declared Ambaſſador extraordinary to the court of Spain; where he now reſides in that quality, with an equal attention to the intereſt of his country and the dignity of his Sovereign.

Zulestein Earl of Rochford

Zuleiftein, Earl of Rochford.

His Lordfhip married the honourable Lucy Young, one of the maids of honour to her Royal Highnefs the Princefs of Wales, and daughter of Edward Young, of Durnford in Wiltfhire, by his wife Lucy, fifter to John, Lord Vifcount Chetwynde. Her Ladyfhip is of a very antient family; her anceftors, as is evident from records, having been poffefled of Durnford, without any intermiffion, from the reign of King Henry II.

TITLES.] William-Henry Zuleiftein, de Naffaw, Earl of Rochford, Vifcount Tunbridge, and Baron of Enfield.

CREATIONS.] Baron of Enfield in com' Middlefex, Vifcount Tunbridge, in Kent, and Earl of Rochford, in com' Effex, May 10 (1695) 7 Will. III.

ARMS.] Quarterly, 1. Azure, Semée of Billets, and a Lion Rampant, Or, for Naffaw; 2. Or, a Lion rampant, Gules, crowned with a ducal Coronet, Azure, for Deitz; 3. Argent, a Fefs, Gules, for Vianden; 4. Gules, two Lions paffant guardant in pale, Or, for Catznelboge; over all, in an Efcutcheon, Gules, three Zules, Argent, and fometimes a Lion Rampant, Sable.

CREST.] In a ducal Coronet, Or, a pair of Buck's-horns, Gules.

SUPPORTERS.] Two Lions, Erminois, ducally crowned, Azure.

MOTTO.] SPES DURAT AVORUM.

CHIEF-SEATS.] At Eafton, in the county of Suffolk, 6 miles from Woodbridge; at St. Ofyth, in the county of Effex, 12 miles from Colchefter; and at Zuleiftein, in Holland, 15 miles from Utrecht.

KEPPEL, Earl of Albemarle.

Arnold-Jooft van Keppel, created Earl of Albemarle, was descended of an ancient family in Guelderland, one of the United Provinces, being a younger son of Bernard van Pallant, Lord of Keppel, by Agnes-Charlotte-Elizabetha his wife, daughter to Jacob van Waffenar, Lord of Opdam. His elder brother the Baron Pallant, and Lord of Keppel, was killed at the battle of Eckeren, June 30, N. S. 1703, unmarried: and his younger brother Rabo, who was Lieutenant-General in the service of the States-general, Colonel of a regiment of foot, Postmaster-general of the province of Guelderland, Bailiff of Boisleduc, and one of the Nobles of the province of Over-Iffel, died in 1733, leaving issue one son, Arnold-Jooft.

The said Arnold-Jooft, who was created Earl of Albemarle, attended King William into England, in the year 1688 (being then page of honour to his Highness) and was afterwards made one of the Grooms of his bed-chamber, and Master of the robes. On March 25 (N. S.) 1691, being one of the Grooms of the King's bed-chamber, he was sent from the Hague to compliment the Elector of Bavaria, on his arrival in Flanders: and attending on his Majesty in several campaigns, wherein he distinguished himself by his courage and fidelity, he was by letters-patent, bearing date Feb. 10, 1695-6, 8 William III. created Baron Ashford, of Ashford in Kent, Viscount Bury, in com' pal. Lanc. and Earl of Albemarle, a town and territory in the dukedom of Normandy, heretofore belonging to Stephen the son of Odo, descended from the Earls of Champagne, whom William the Conqueror made Earl of Albemarle, as being the son of his half-sister by the mother's side, and gave to him, for the further maintenance of his estate, the territory of Holderneffe in Yorkshire. And when his issue failed, the Kings of England honoured others, who had greatly deserved of them, with the same title, tho' they had long since lost their estate in Normandy. He was a Major-general, before the year 1697; when his Majesty, in his camp at Promelles, June 17, ordered the Earl of Albemarle, with a considerable detachment, to cover the left wing of the army, which foraged towards Lovain.

In the year 1699, on the resignation of the Earl of Scarborough, he was constituted Colonel of the first troop of horse-guards. On July 14, 1699, he introduced the Sieur Galefky, Envoy from the King of Poland, to a private audience of his

his Majesty, in his bed-chamber at Loo, in Holland; which fine seat that King afterwards made him a present of. On May 14, 1700, he was elected one of the Knights companions of the most noble order of the Garter, being then one of the Lords of the bed-chamber to his Majesty; and was installed at Windsor on June 5 following.

King William held his Lordship in the highest esteem, and bequeathed to him, in a codicil annexed to his last will and testament, the lordship of Breevost, and 200,000 guilders, the only legacy he gave from the Prince of Nassaw Friezland, whom his Majesty made his heir. In Sept. 1701, his Lordship, with the Earl of Galway, reviewed the forces encamped on the Moerdike, near Nimeguen, and continuing there and at the Hague, set out from thence, in March 1701-2, to view the frontier places against the French. And receiving there the melancholy news of the King's decease, he arrived in England, June 26, 1702.

His Lordship having waited on the Queen, and being deeply affected with the death of his royal master, retired to his native country, and on his arrival in Holland, took his place, as a member of the Nobles, in the assembly of the States-general.

In 1702, he was declared General of the Dutch forces; and taking his leave of the States-general at the Hauge, August 3, joined the army on the 7th.

In 1705, he came into England, and attending on the Queen, when she visited the university of Cambridge, he was, on April 16, created Doctor of Laws there. He returned to Holland soon after; and on June 11, left the Hague to join the army under Monsieur Auberquerque; being also that year at the forcing of the French lines near Tirlemont, July 18, N. S. He was at the battle of Ramellies, May 23, N. S. next year, and took up his winter quarters at Brussels. On April 20, 1708, the States-general declared his Lordship General of horse; and on July 11, that year, he was in the memorable battle of Oudenard; and soon after, Augustus King of Poland, and the Landgrave of Hesse-Cassel, arriving in the camp at Helchin, the Duke of Marlborough entertained them, August 19, with the review of the first line of his army; after which they dined with the Earl of Albemarle. At the siege of Lisle, the Duke of Marlborough having advice that thirty of the enemies squadrons were marched, through Tournay, to intercept a convoy of ammunition, sent out from Brussels for the siege, the Earl of Albemarle was immediately ordered to march with the like number of squadrons towards Gramont, for security of that convoy, and to take a 1000 horse more from Oudenard, if necessary. And accordingly his Lordship brought the convoy safe to Menin, and joined the army Sept. 12. After which, the French investing Brussels, during the siege of Lisle, the Duke of Marlborough, having passed the Scheld to its relief, raised the siege: but encountering with a party of the enemy, under M. de Hautefort, Nov. 28, 1708, his Lordship's horse was shot under him. In 1710, he had her Majesty's leave to dispose of his troop of horse-guards, which, by her favour, he had hitherto kept; and accordingly (for a valuable consideration) by agreement between him and the Earl of Portland, the Queen conferred it on that Earl, who was afterwards created Duke of Portland. On Aug. 27, 1711, the Earl of Albemarle, with nine battalions and 1100 horse, conducted the second convoy of ammunition and artillery to the siege of Bouchain: and commanding at the battle of Denain, July 24, 1712, N. S. was made prisoner, but soon released. Prince Eugene, arriving at the Hague, on Nov. 2 following, took up his abode in his Lordship's house, till one he had taken was fitted up, for the winter season. On the demise of Queen Anne, Aug. 1, 1714, his Lordship was sent by the States-general to Hanover, to congratulate her successor on his happy accession to the crown of these realms: and, after his return, was one of those Noblemen deputed by their High Mightinesses, to receive the King, and his Royal Highness the Prince, in September, on the frontiers of the United Provinces. His Lordship had also the honour to entertain them at his fine seat at Voorst; and in October, that year, when the Princess of Wales (the late Queen Caroline) came from Hanover, she was received and attended by his Lordship to Rotterdam, where she embarked for England. In 1716, his Lordship continuing his instances in favour of such of the Swifs, in the Dutch service, who were not on the foot of stipulation, with any of the Cantons, they were, by his endeavours, kept in their service, the battalion, of which he was Colonel, being of that number. In 1717, he was nominated by the Nobles of Holland, to compliment the Czar Peter on his arrival; and he was received and complimented by his Lordship, at Amsterdam [a], August 2, 1717.

His Lordship was a member of the Nobles of Holland, as also Deputy-Forester of that province, General of the horse, and of Swissers, in the service of the States-general, Governor of Boisleduc, Colonel of a regiment of carabiniers, and of a regiment of Swissers; and departed this life, very much regretted, in the 48th year of his age, at the Hague, on May 30, N. S.

[a] Help to history.

Keppel, Earl of Albemarle. 133

30. N. S. 1718. He married, in Holland, in the year 1701, Ifabella, fecond daughter of S. Gravemoor, General of the forces of the States-general; who, furviving his Lordfhip. died at the Hague, Dec. 2, 1741; and by whom he had an only fon, born at Whitehall, June 5, 1702, who had the names of William-Anne, from her Majefty Queen Anne, who honoured him with ftanding godmother in perfon; alfo a daughter named Sophia, born at Tournay, on July 2, 1711, married to John Thomas, Efq; brother to Sir Edmund Thomas. of Wenvoe-caftle, in Glamorganfhire, Bart.

Which William-Anne, fecond Earl of Albemarle, having been educated in Holland, returned into England in the 16th year of his age; and was, by George I. on Aug. 25, 1717, conftituted Captain of a company, with the rank of Lieutenant-colonel, in the firft regiment of foot-guards. In Jan. 1722, he went back to his patrimony in Holland; and on June 13, that year, was vifited at his fine feat at Voorft, in Guelderland, by the Bifhop of Munfter. In October, 1722, his Lordfhip was declared one of the Lords of the bedchamber to the Prince of Wales. In 1725, he was made one of the Knights-companions of the moft honourable order of the Bath. And on March 31, 1727, was appointed Aid de Camp to the King. On his late Majefty's acceffion to the throne, June 11, 1727, he was continued in his place of Lord of the bedchamber; and on Nov. 22, 1731, the command of the 29th regiment of foot, then at Gibraltar, was conferred on him. On Dec. 8, the fame year, his Lordfhip (with other Peers) attended Francis-Stephen, Duke of Lorrain (the prefent Emperor of Germany) to Greenwich, where he embarked, in the Fubbs yacht, for Holland, after refiding fome time at our court. On June 4, 1733, he was conftituted Captain and Colonel of the third troop of horfe-guards; and Governor of Virginia, on Sept. 26, 1737. On July 2, 1739, he was made a Brigadier-general; and on Feb. 20, 1741, he was conftituted Major-general of his Majefty's forces. On April 14, 1742, his Lordfhip was appointed commander of thofe forces then ordered to the Netherlands, whereof John Earl of Stair, Field-marfhal, was to take the command; and they arrived fafely at Oftend on May 21 following. On Aug. 29, the fame year, his Lordfhip again commanding the troops fent to the Netherlands, got into Oftend, with moft of the fhips, though with great difficulty, being in a violent gale of wind. On Feb. 26, 1742-3, he was promoted to the rank of Lieutenant-general, and in that command, behaved with great gallantry at the battle of Dettingen, June 27, N. S. 1743.

Keppel, Earl of Albemarle.

His Lordship made the campaign in 1744, with Marshal Wade: and in 1745, when his Royal Highness, the Duke commanded, was in the battle of Fontenoy, where he was wounded. On April 16, 1746, he had the command of the right wing at the battle of Culloden; and on his Royal Highness's leaving Scotland, he was constituted General and Commander in chief of all his Majesty's forces there, August 23, 1746; on which day his Lordship arrived at Edinburgh, having marched with the troops under his command, from Fort Augustus, on the 13th before, and settled them in their quarters at Perth and Stirling. On July 2, N. S. 1747, he was with his Royal Highness in the battle of Vall; in the account whereof, published in our Gazettes, it is recited, that the Earl of Albemarle did all that could be expected from an officer, as the behaviour of the British infantry (then under his command) shewed. In 1748, he again went over with his Royal Highness; and soon after the conclusion of the peace, his Lordship was appointed Ambassador and Plenipotentiary to the French court; being then General in chief of the forces in Scotland. On July 12, 1750, he was installed, at Windsor, a Knight of the most noble order of the Garter, by his proxy, Sir Charles Eggleton, Knt. and afterwards coming into England, was, July 12, 1751, sworn of his Majesty's most honourable Privy-council, and took his place at the board accordingly, being then Groom of the Stole to his Majesty. On March 30, 1752, he was appointed one of the Lords Justices, during his Majesty's abode in his German dominions.

His Lordship, whilst Ambassador at the French court, lived very magnificently; but being suddenly taken ill, departed this life at Paris, Dec. 22, 1754, and his body being landed at the Tower, on Monday, Feb. 19, 1755, was on Wednesday following privately buried in South-Audley-street chapel, near Grosvenor-square.

The French King shewed his esteem for his Lordship, by sending to Monf. Ruvigni de Cosne, Secretary of the ambassy from England, at Paris, his picture set with diamonds, to be presented to the present Earl of Albemarle, which he intended for the late Earl, had not death carried him off before he had finished his ambassy.

His Lordship, on Feb. 21, 1722-3, was married at Caversham (a seat of the Earl of Cadogan) near Reading, to the Lady Anne, daughter of Charles Lennox, first Duke of Richmond, Lennox, and Aubigny; and by her Ladyship (who was one of the Ladies of the bedchamber to her late Majesty) had issue 8 sons, and 7 daughters.

1. George,

1. George, Lord Viscount Bury, now Earl of Albemarle.
2. Augustus, brought up in the sea-service, who was with Commodore Anson [b] in the South-seas; and at the taking the town of Paita, where he was in great danger; having on a jockey cap, one side of the peak was shaved off close to his temple by a cannon ball, which however did him no other injury. On Dec. 11, 1744, he was made Captain of one of his Majesty's ships, and during the remainder of the war, took several of the enemy's privateers. In 1751, he was Commodore of a squadron in the Mediterranean; and on May 1, that year, sailed from fort St. Philip's, in the island of Minorca, to settle the differences between the English merchants and the Dey of Algiers. On his arrival, the Dey acknowledged to him, ' That one of his officers had been guilty of ' a very great fault, which tended to embroil him with his ' chiefest and best friends; wherefore he should never more ' serve him by sea or land, and hoped the King, his master, ' would look on it as the action of a fool or madman, and ' he would take care nothing should happen again in the like ' nature, that they may be better friends than ever.' Which declaration was sent to England, and published by order of the Lords of the Admiralty, May 22, 1751. He also concluded treaties with the states of Tripoly, and Tunis; and before the end of the year 1752, he arrived at Portsmouth, from the Mediterranean, with all the ships under his command, having been upwards of three years on that station.

This gallant seaman, having further signalized himself by his courage and conduct upon every occasion, after the rupture with France in 1755, was pitched upon to conduct the second expedition against the island of Gorée, on the western coast of Africa, being at the same time invested with the command of the land-forces destined for that enterprize, consisting of the second battalion of George Lord Forbes's regiment (76th) of foot, on the Irish establishment: and, after several delays and misfortunes, arriving off the said island on Dec. 28, 1758, employed his time so well, that Mr. St. Jean, the French Governor, with the garrison, surrendered at discretion the next day. Commodore Keppel, having sent off the French captives, and placed a sufficient number of British troops for the defence of the island, under Major Newton, departed, on Jan. 12, 1759, for Senegal (which had been reduced by Commodore Marsh, and Major Mason, in May preceding, before their unsuccessful attempt upon Gorée) and there reinforced the garrison, leaving Lieutenant-colonel Richard

[b] Anson's voyage, p. 270.

Worge (who had come out with him) Governor, in the place of Major Mason. When Mr. Keppel had sufficiently provided for the security of these African conquests, he set sail for England, on January 23, and arriving at Spithead on March 3, proceeded to London, where he was most graciously received by his Majesty. After that, he was employed in the bay of Biscay, under Sir Edward Hawke, and was with that brave officer, when he defeated the French fleet, commanded by M. Conflans, on Nov. 20, 1759, off Belleisle; on which occasion Mr. Keppel, in the Torbay of 74 guns, engaged and sunk the Theseus, carrying the same number of guns, but of a greater caliber. In Feb. 1760, he was nominated Colonel of the Plymouth division of marines. The conquest of Belleisle being concerted, Commodore Keppel got the command of the squadron appointed for the cover of the siege; and sailing from Spithead on March 29, 1761, contributed, by his prudence and bravery, not only to making good the landing of the troops in that month, but also to the reduction of the citadel of Palais, the capital of that island, on June 7 following; the military operations at which did infinite honour to the besiegers and besieged. When the British ministry, after the declaration of war against Spain, on Jan. 4, 1762, resolved on the conquest of the city of Havannah, in the island of Cuba, Mr. Keppel was nominated to act as Commodore, in that important service, under that experienced and gallant officer Sir George Pococke, Knight of the Bath; who sailed from St. Helen's on March 5, 1762. When the British fleet arrived off that island, on June 6, Sir George appointed Mr. Keppel to remain, eastward of the Havannah, with seven sail of the line, and some small frigates, to protect and conduct the debarkation of the forces: and in his letters to the Lords of the Admiralty, dated July 14, and Aug. 19, acquainted their Lordships, that Commodore Keppel executed the duty entrusted to him, with an activity, judgment, and diligence, no one man could surpass. After that place surrendered to the British arms, on August 13, Mr. Keppel, who was promoted to the rank of Rear Admiral of the Blue, in Novem. that year, was very successful in taking many valuable prizes, both French and Spanish. At the general election, in 1761, he was returned one of the members for Windsor, having served in the former parliament for Chichester, in the room of his brother, when he succeeded to the Peerage: and is one of the Grooms of his Majesty's bedchamber.

3. James, who died young.

4. William,

4. William, Gentleman of the horse to his late Majesty; and, Dec. 21, 1752, was made a Captain in the first regiment of foot-guards, with the rank of Lieutenant-colonel. On July 21, 1760, he was nominated 2d Major of that regiment, with the rank of Colonel of foot; and in Jan. 1762, got the command of the 56th regiment of infantry, with which he embarked in March following in the fleet fitted out against the Havannah, having the rank of Major-general in that expedition. On Aug. 14, the day after the capitulation for the surrendering of the Havannah, he took possession of the fort La Punta; and being left commander, after his eldest brother sailed for Europe, re-delivered the possession of the city of Havannah to the Spanish troops, on July 7, 1763, according to the articles of peace, concluded at Paris, Feb. 10 preceding; soon after which, he embarked for England, and, after a short voyage landed at Portsmouth.

5. Frederick, who was appointed Canon of Windsor, on April 23, 1754; officiated as one of the Chaplains in ordinary to their late and present Majesties; and in Octob. 1762, was promoted to the bishoprick of Exeter. His Lordship, in Sept. 1758, married ———, one of the natural daughters of Sir Edward Walpole, Knight of the Bath, 2d son of Robert, Earl of Orford; and by her has ———, a daughter, born on June 18, 1759, and ———, a son, born on Nov. 14, 1762.

6. Thomas; and, 7. Edward, both deceased; the latter in Jan. 1745, aged 9 years.

8. Henry, youngest son, an officer in the army.

His Lordship's daughters were, 1. Lady Sophia; 2. Lady Mary; 3. Lady Anne; 4. Lady Naffaw (who all four died unmarried) 5 Lady Caroline, married to Mr. Adair, on Feb. 22, 1759; 6. Lady Elizabeth, wedded, on June 7, 1764, to Francis, Marquis of Tavistock, son and heir apparent of John Ruffel, Duke of Bedford; and, 7. Lady Amelia, who died young.

George, the eldest son, 3d Earl of Albemarle, was born on April 8, 1724; and, betaking himself to a military life, was, after he had been some time in the army, appointed Captain-lieutenant in the 3d or royal regiment of dragoons. On April 7, 1743, his Lordship was promoted to the same office in the 2d regiment of foot-guards, with the rank of Lieutenant-colonel of infantry; and on June 4, 1745, was advanced to the command of a company in the same regiment, with the rank of Colonel. He served as Aid-de Camp to the Duke of Cumberland, at the battle of Fontenoy, May 11, N. S. that year; and being with his Highness at the battle of Culloden,

on

Keppel, Earl of Albemarle.

on April $\frac{16}{27}$, 1746, was sent express with the news of that affair to the King, who, on that occasion, made him an handsome present, and afterwards constituted him one of his Aid-de-Camps. His Lordship was, at that time, and has continued ever since, one of the Lords of the bedchamber to the Duke of Cumberland; and on Nov. 1, 1749, got the command of the 20th regiment of foot, which he kept till he got that of the 3d regiment of dragoons, soon after his succession to the Peerage. Being appointed a member of the Privy-council, and Governor of the island of Jersey, by the present King, he took the usual oath, and his seat at the Council-board, on Jan. 28, 1761; and at the same time had the oaths administered to him as Governor of the said island. On Feb. 1, 1756, his Lordship was advanced to the rank of Major-general, and to that of Lieutenant-general, on April 1, 1759. His Lordship, in 1762, was Commander in chief of the land-forces, at the reduction of the Havannah, where he acquired laurels and an increase of fortune. Having settled every thing to his mind at that conquest, he embarked for England on board the Rippon man of war, and arriving at Portsmouth on Feb. 20, 1763, took post to Windsor, where he visited his Royal Highness the Duke of Cumberland; and proceeding thence to London, waited on their Majesties on the 23d at St. James's, and was graciously received.

His Lordship, on the death of the honourable James Brudenell, 1746, was elected, in his room, member for Chichester to the last session of the 9th parliament of Great-Britain; and sat for the same city in the two succeeding parliaments, until he succeeded his father, as Earl of Albemarle, &c. on Dec. 22, 1754.

TITLES.] George Keppel, Earl of Albemarle, Viscount Bury, and Baron Ashford, of Ashford.

CREATIONS.] Baron Ashford, of Ashford, in Kent, Viscount Bury, in Lancashire, and Earl of Albemarle, in Normandy, Feb. 10 (1696) 8 Will. III.

ARMS.] Gules, three Escallop-Shells, Argent.

CREST.] In a ducal Coronet, Or, a Demi-Swan close, proper.

SUPPORTERS.] Two Lions, ducally crowned, Or.

MOTTO.] NE CEDE MALIS.

CHIEF-SEATS.] At Durhams, near Barnet, in the county of Middlesex; and at Voorst, and Loo, in Holland.

Keppel Earl of Albemarle

COVENTRY, Earl of Coventry.

THE first of the name of Coventry, that I meet with, was Henry Coventry, [a] Sheriff of London, in 1260, 45 Hen. III. But as Sir William Dugdale, and other of our antiquaries, agree, the present Earl of Coventry is descended from William Coventry, of the city of Coventry, whose son John Coventry, being a mercer of London, and of an opulent fortune, was Sheriff thereof, [b] with Robert Whittingham, in 1416, 4 Hen. V. and Lord Mayor of London in 1425, 4 Hen. VI. He was [c] one of the executors of Richard Whittingham, who was four times Mayor of London; and who having begun to build Newgate, and the Library of the Grey-Friars at Christ church, London, with that at Guildhall, they were all finished by his three executors.

This John Coventry is much [d] commended, in our chronicles, for his discreet carriage in the debate betwixt Humphry, Duke of Gloucester, and Henry Beaufort, Bishop of Winchester; and lies buried in the church of St. Mary-le-Bow in Cheapside, London, [e] where a monument was erected to his memory, with this inscription, much to his commendation.

> Magnificus, sed justificus,
>   miseris & amicus,
> Vir speciosus, Vir
>   generosus, virque prudicus,
> Et peramabilis, et
>   venerabilis, atque piarum
> Vis, dux, lex, lampas,
>   flos Major Londoniarum;
> In terræ ventre jacet
>   hic John rite Coventre
> Dictus, quem necuit
>   veluti decuit lue plenus
> Bis Septingenus
>   tricenus, si trahis unum,
> Martius in sole
>   triceno, si trahis unum,
> Virginis a partu, carnis
>   modo mortuus artu;
> Vivis erit Cœlis tuba
>   clanxerit ut Gabrielis, Amen.

[a] Stow's Survey of London, p. 543. [b] Ibid. p. 561, 563. [c] Ibid p. 256.
[d] Weaver's Funeral monum. p. 402. [e] Stow ut antea, p. 270.

From him in lineal descent, [f] was Vincent Coventry, of Caffington, near Yarnton, in Oxfordshire, whose son and heir Richard Coventry, Esq; married a daughter of ―――― Turner, and had issue two sons, John, who had the estate at Caffington, and left a family; and Thomas.

Which Thomas, born anno 1547, had his education in Baliol-College in Oxford; and on June 2, 1565, was [g] created Batchelor of Arts. He afterwards became a member of the Inner-Temple, London; and in 38 Eliz. was [h] chosen Autumn-reader of that house: but a great plague then raging in London, he read not till the Lent following. On May 17, 1603, 1 Jac. I. he was sworn [i] Serjeant at Law, having been elected to that degree in the reign of Queen Eliz. and in 3 Jac. I. was [k] constituted King's Serjeant; also the same year one of the [l] Justices of the court of Common-pleas, in which post he continued till his death, which was on December 12, 1606, and was buried at Croome d'Abitot, in Worcestershire, where a monument is erected to his memory.

He had issue by [m] Margaret his wife, daughter and heir to ―――― Jeffreys, of Earles Croome, alias Croome d'Abitot, in Worcestershire, three sons; Thomas his son and heir; William, who left a family, seated at Ridmarley in Worcestershire; and Walter, ancestor to the present Earl of Coventry: as also four daughters; Margaret; Joan, married to ―――― Rogers, of the county of Surry, Esq; Catharine, espoused to William Child, Esq; and Anne, wedded to George Frampton, Esq;

Thomas, son and heir of the last mentioned Thomas, born at Croome-d'Abitot in Worcestershire, in 1578, became, at the age of fourteen, a [n] Gentleman-commoner of Baliol-college in Oxford, where he continued three years, and then was entered a member of the Inner-Temple; where, pursuing his father's steps in the laudable studies of the municipal laws, he was chosen Autumn-reader of that society, 14 Jac. I. and the same year, on November 17, was [o] elected Recorder of the city of London: also on March 14 following, [p] constituted Sollicitor-general; and received [q] the honour of knighthood two days after at Theobalds.

In 18 Jac. I. he was made [r] Attorney-general; and from thence [s] advanced to that eminent office of Lord-keeper of the great Seal of England, by Charles I. on November 1, 1625.

[f] Ex stemmate. [g] Wood's Fast. Oxon. vol. 1. p. 723. [h] Dugd. orig. Jurd. p. 166. [i] Stow's Annals, p. 824 [k] Pat. 3 Jac. I. p. 2. [l] Dugd. orig. Jurid. p. 102. [m] Ex stemmate. [n] Wood's Athenæ Oxon, p. 534. [o] Ibid. [p] Pat. 14 Jac. I. p. 3. [q] Philpot's Cat. of Knights, p. 62. [r] Pat. 18 Jac. I. p. 16. [s] Dugd. chron. Ser. p. 104.

On April 10, 1628, he was dignified with the ^{ت} degree of a Baron of this realm, by the title of Lord Coventry of Aylesborough in com' Wigorn.

He died at Durham-house in the Strand, in London, on January 14, 1639-40, and Feb. 17, ^{u} was conveyed from thence, with great funeral solemnity, to his interment at Croome d'Abitot, near his father, on March 1 following. The Earl of Clarendon, in his history of the Rebellion, says of him, ^{w} ' That he discharged all the offices he went through,
' with great abilities, and singular reputation of integrity;
' that he enjoyed his place of Lord Keeper with an universal
' reputation (and sure justice was never better administred) for
' the space of about sixteen years, even to his death, some
' months before he was sixty years of age:' ' Which was
' another important circumstance of his felicity; that great
' office being so slippery, that no man had died in it before for
' near the space of forty years: nor had his successors for some
' time after him much better fortune. And he himself had use
' of all his strength and skill (as he was an excellent wrestler
' in this kind) to preserve himself from falling in two shocks:
' the one given him by the Earl of Portland, Lord High-trea-
' surer of England; the other by the Marquis of Hamilton,
' who had the greatest power over the affections of the King,
' of any man of that time.

' He was a man of wonderful gravity and wisdom; and
' understood not only the whole science and mystery of the
' law, at least equally with any man who had ever sat in that
' place; but had a clear conception of the whole policy of the
' government both of church and state; which, by the unskil-
' fulness of some well meaning men, justled each the other
' too much.

' He knew the temper, disposition, and genius of the king-
' dom most exactly; saw their spirits grow every day more
' sturdy, inquisitive and impatient: and therefore naturally
' abhorred all innovations; which, he foresaw, would produce
' ruinous effects. Yet many, who stood at a distance, thought
' he was not active and stout enough in opposing those inno-
' vations: For though by his place he presided in all public
' councils, and was most sharp sighted in the consequence of
' things; yet he was seldom known to speak in matters of
' state, which, he well knew, were, for the most part, con-
' cluded before they were brought to that public agitation:
' never in foreign affairs; which the vigour of his judgment
' could well have comprehended: nor indeed freely in any

t Pat. 4 Car. I. p. 39. u Hist. Eng. vol. 3. p. 97. w Vol. 1. p. 45.

' thing,

'thing, but what immediately and plainly concerned the juf-
' tice of the kingdom ; and in that, as much as he could, he
' procured references to the Judges. Though in his nature he
' had not only a firm gravity, but a feverity and even fome
' morofity; yet it was fo happily tempered, and his courtefy
' and affability towards all men fo tranfcendent, and fo much
' without affectation, that it marvelloufly recommended him
' to men of all degrees ; and he was looked upon as an ex-
' cellent courtier, without receding from the native fimplicity
' of his own manners.

' He had in the plain way of fpeaking and delivery, without
' much ornament of elocution, a ftrange power of making
' himfelf believed (the only juftifiable defign of eloquence) fo
' that though he ufed very frankly to deny, and would never
' fuffer any man to depart from him with an opinion that he
' was inclined to gratify, when in truth he was not; holding
' that diffimulation to be the worft of lying : yet the manner
' of it was fo gentle and obliging, and his condefcenfion fuch,
' to inform the perfons whom he could not fatisfy, that few
' departed from him with ill-will and ill-wifhes.

' But then this happy temper, and thofe good faculties, ra-
' ther preferved him from having many enemies, and fupplied
' him with fome well-wifhers, than furnifh him with any
' faft and unfhaken friends, who are always procured in courts
' by more ardour and more vehement profeffions and applica-
' tions than he would fuffer himfelf to be entangled with : fo
' that he was a man rather exceedingly liked, than paffionately
' loved; infomuch that it never appeared that he had any one
' friend in the court, of quality enough to prevent' or divert
' any difadvantage he might be expofed to. And therefore it
' is no wonder, nor to be imputed to him, that he retired
' within himfelf as much as he could ; and ftood upon his de-
' fence, without making defperate fallies againft growing mif-
' chiefs; which, he knew well, he had no power to hinder,
' and which might probably begin in his own ruin. To con-
' clude; his fecurity confifted very much in his having but lit-
' tle credit with the King; and he died in a feafon the moft
' opportune, in which a wife man would have prayed to have
' finifhed his courfe, and which in truth crowned his other
' fignal profperity in the world.'

This noble Lord married two wives. By his firft, Sarah, daughter to Edward Sebright of Besford, in com' Wigorn, and fifter to Sir Edward Sebright, of the fame place, Bart. he had iffue, Thomas his fucceffor ; and Elizabeth, married to Sir John Hare, of Stow-Bardolph in Norfolk. By Elizabeth,

his

his second wife, daughter to John Aldersey, of Spurstow in com' Cestr. and Widow of William Pitchford, Esqrs; he had four sons; John, Francis, Henry, and William: also four daughters; Anne, married to Sir William Savile, of Thornhill, in Yorkshire, Bart. father, by her, to George, created Marquis of Halifax; Mary, to Henry-Frederick Thynne, of Longlete it Wiltshire, Esq; ancestor to the present Lord Viscount Weymouth; Margaret, to Anthony Earl of Shaftsbury, being his first wife, but had no issue by him; and Dorothy, to Sir John Packington, of Westwood in the county of Worcester, Bart. These Ladies were all very eminent for their piety, virtue, and great capacities; the youngest of them being a Lady of that incomparable understanding, as well as piety, that she is said to be the author of The Whole Duty of Man: and their brothers were as conspicuous for their talents and abilities in parliament, and at the cabinet.

Therefore, before I proceed to treat of Thomas Lord Coventry, his successor, I shall give what I find remarkable of his sons by the second marriage; 1. John, the eldest son got, from his father, the manors of Clifton-Camvyle and Hampton, in Staffordshire, purchased from Sir Walter Heveningham of Aston, in the same county. He had [x] to wife Elizabeth, daughter and co-heir of John Colles of Barton in the county of Somerset, Esq; widow of Herbert Doddington, second son, and after heir, to Sir William Doddington of Bremer, in com' Southampt. Knt. This Lady was 19 years of age [y], at the decease of her father, Sept. 5, 1627, 3 Car. I. and by her second husband had issue Sir John Coventry of Pitminster in the county of Somerset, and of Mere in the county of Wilts, made Knight of the Bath at the coronation of Charles II. and was a member in that parliament, called the long-parliament, for the borough of Weymouth in Dorsetshire, and in all other parliaments of Charles II. On December 21, 1670, a violent and inhuman attempt was made on his person, as the preamble to the act sets forth, for ' Preventing malicious maiming and ' wounding,' which has been since called the Coventry-act; and by which the persons so offending are to suffer death. Bishop Burnet, in the history of his own time, [z] and other relations, give us this account of it. Sir John Coventry was one of those members of the house of Commons, who struggled much against the giving money; and it being then usual, after such bills had failed in the main vote, for those, who opposed, to endeavour to lay the money on funds unacceptable and deficient; it was proposed to lay a tax on the Play-houses, which

---

[x] Coles Esc. lib. 1. p. 316. in bibl. Harley.   [y] Coles Esc. ibid.   [z] P. 269, 270.

were

were then deemed nefts of proftitution. This was oppofed by the court: It was faid, 'The players were the King's fer-
'vants, and a part of his pleafure.' Whereupon Sir John Coventry afked, 'Whether did the King's pleafure lie among
'the men, or the women that acted?' This was carried with great indignation to the court. It was faid, 'This was the
'firft time that the King was perfonally reflected on: If it
'was paffed over, more of the fame kind would follow; and
'it would grow a fafhion to talk fo. It was therefore fit to
'take fuch fevere notice of this, that no body fhould dare to
'talk at that rate for the future.' The Duke of York told Bifhop Burnet, 'He faid all he could to the King to divert
'him from the refolution he took; which was to fend fome of
'the guards, and watch in the ftreets where Sir John lodged,
'and leave a mark upon him.' The fact, by bills of indict-ment, was found to be commited by Sir Thomas Sandys, Knt. Charles Obryan, Efq; Simon Parry and Miles Reeves, who were fled from juftice, not daring to abide a legal trial. 'As
'Coventry was going home, they drew about him; he ftood
'up to the wall, and fnatched the flambeau out of his fer-
'vant's hands; and with that in one hand, and his fword in
'the other, he defended himfelf fo well, that he got credit by
'it. He wounded fome of them; but was foon difarmed,
'and then they cut his nofe to the bone, to teach him (as they
'faid) to remember what refpect he owed to the King; and
'fo they left him, and went back to the Duke of Monmouth's,
'where Obryan's arm was dreffed: That matter was executed
'by orders from the Duke of Monmouth; for which he was
'feverely cenfured, becaufe he lived then in profeffions of
'friendfhip with Coventry; fo that his fubjection to the King
'was not thought an excufe for directing fo vile an attempt
'on his friend, without fending him fecret notice of what
'was defigned. Coventry had his nofe fo well needled up,
'that the fcar was fcarce to be difcerned. This put the houfe
'of Commons into a furious uproar: They paffed a bill of
'banifhment againft the actors of it; and put a claufe in it,
'that it fhould not be in the King's power to pardon them;
'and that it fhould be death to maim any perfon. This gave
'great advantages to all thofe that oppofed the court; and
'was often remembered, and much improved by all the angry
'men of thofe times.' He died unmarried, and endowed an hofpital at Wivelifcomb in com' Somerfet, for twelve poor people.

Francis, fecond fon of the fecond venter, married 3 wives; by the two laft he had no iffue: but by his firft, Elizabeth, daughter and coheir to John Manning of Warbleton. in

Suffex, Efq; and widow of Robert Cæfar, Efq; one of the Six-clerks in Chancery, he had iffue, befides two fons that died young, Francis, who died unmarried in 1686; and two daughters, Elizabeth, married to Sir William Keyt of Ebrington in com' Glouc. Bart. and Ultra-Trajectina, to Sir Lacon-William Child, of Weft-Coppice in Shropfhire, Knt.

Henry Coventry, third fon, of the fecond marriage, [a] had his education in All-fouls college in Oxford, where he was created both [b] Mafter of Arts, and Batchelor of Law. He afterwards [c] fuffered greatly for his loyalty during the rebellion; fo that foon after the reftoration of Charles II. he was made one of the Grooms of his bed-chamber, and on September 4, 1664, fent Envoy Extraordinary to Sweden, where he continued near two years, arriving at Whitehall on June 21, 1666. The year following, he and Denzil Lord Hollis were fent Ambaffadors Extraordinary to Breda, where they concluded a peace with France, Denmark, and the States-General. In the year 1671, he went again Ambaffador to Sweden; and on his return from thence, was on July 3, the year following, conftituted one of his Majefty's principal Secretaries of State, and fworn of the Privy-council; in which eminent office he behaved himfelf with much honour and integrity; but declining in his health thro' the neceffary fatigue of that employment, of which this public notice was given in the Gazette, N. 4185; Whitehall, Feb. 11, 1679, His Majefty was, this afternoon, pleafed to declare in council, that Mr. Secretary Coventry has long folicited him, on account of his infirmity of body, for his leave to refign his place of one of his principal Secretaries of State; that his Majefty had at laft been prevailed upon to grant it, though with fome unwillingnefs, becaufe of the great fatisfaction his Majefty had always had in his fervices; and that his intention was he fhould ever continue in his Privy-council. After this, he never accepted of any public employment, but lived retired to his death, which was at his houfe in the Hay-Market, near Charing-Crofs, in Weftminfter, on December 7, 1686, in the 68th year of his age, and unmarried; leaving his eftate to Henry Coventry, Efq; brother to William Earl of Coventry, and to his nephew Mr. James Thynne: Alfo by his will (which bears date, September 16, 1686) bequeaths his lands in Hampton-Lovet, in com' Wigorn; to the burgeffes of Droitwich, for the erecting and maintaining an hofpital for twenty-four poor people.

[a] Wood's fafti chron. vol. 1. p. 892.   [b] Ibid. 887.   [c] Ibid. p. 892.

Coventry, Earl of Coventry.

William, the youngest son, in 1642, at 16 years of age [d], became a Gentleman-commoner of Queen's-college in Oxford; and after he had continued there some time, he travelled beyond the seas, and at his return, adhering to Charles II. was made secretary to the Duke of York, also secretary to the Admiralty; and elected a burgess for the town of Great Yarmouth in Norfolk, to the parliament which met at Westminster, May 8, 1661; and also to that parliament which was summoned in 1678. In 1663, he was created Doctor of the civil-law at the university of Oxford. He was sworn of the Privy-council, and received the honour of Knighthood on June 26, 1665, and made one of the Commissioners of the Treasury on May 24, 1667; being, as Bishop Burnet relates, [e] 'A man of great notions and eminent virtues; the best speaker in the house of Commons, and capable of bearing the chief ministry, as it was once thought he was very near it, and deserved it more than all the rest did.' However, as he was too honest to engage in the designs of that reign, and quarrelling with the Duke of Buckingham, a challenge passed between them; upon which he was forbid the court, and retired to Minster-Lovel, near Whitney, in Oxfordshire, where he gave himself up to a religious and private course of life, without accepting of any employment, tho' he was afterwards offered more than once the best posts in the court. He died unmarried at Somerhill, near Tunbridge-wells, in Kent (where he had went for the benefit of the waters, being afflicted with the gout in the stomach) and was buried at Penshurst, in the same county, under a monument erected to his memory; and the inscription recites, that he died the 9th calends of July 1686 (June 23) aged 60. By his last will he gave 2000 l. for the relief of the French protestants then lately come into England, and banished their country for the sake of their religion; also 3000 l. for the redemption of captives from Algiers.

I now return to Thomas, 2d Lord Coventry, only son and heir of Thomas Lord Coventry, Lord-keeper of the Great-seal of England, by his first wife. He married Mary, daughter to Sir William Craven, Knt. and sister to William Earl of Craven, by whom he had issue two sons; George his succeslor, and Thomas the first Earl of Coventry. She died in childbed, in the 29th year of her age, on October 18, 1634: and his Lordship continued a widower to his death, which hap-

---

[d] Wood's Athenæ Oxon. vol. 2. pag. 601, 170, 265.   [e] In Hist. of his own times, p.

pened in the 55th year of his age, at his houſe in Lincoln's-Inn-Fields, London, on October 27, 1661, and was buried at Croome-d'Abitot by his Lady, where a monument is erected to their memory, with theſe inſcriptions.

Candide & Conſtanter.
D. O. M.
S.
Thomas Dominus Coventrye, Baro Coventrye de Alleſborough, Paterni nominis, honoris, opum, & virtutum, Hæres & promotor;
Inconcuſſæ erga Deum, Principem et Patriam fidei,
Æquiſſimæ in arduis, et bonis rebus mentis,
Magnificus elegantiarum cultor.
Erga ſuos Pater-familias vigilantiſſimus,
Erga Clientelas Dominus æquus, et bonus,
Erga pauperes benignus,
Erga omnes juſtus,
Ubique inculpatus.
Hic
Juxta Clariſſimam Conjugem
Gulielmi Domini Craven
Illius Herois ſororem,
Sepulturæ Majorum ſuorum additus
Ætatis Lv.
Anno Chriſti 1661
In obitum

Clariſſimæ mulieris Mariæ, Thomas Coventrye filii natu maximi Thomæ Baronis Coventrye de Alleſborough, Domini Cuſtodis magni ſigilli Angliæ, piæ Uxoris; Fæmina equidem admodum admiranda, Cui forma, (et quæ ſexui rarior) Virtutis prodigus Deus. Vultus ultra fœmineum, venuſti animi ultra maſculum Generoſi, famæ illibatæ, vitæ integerrimæ, fælicis acuminis, judicii nervoſi, eloquii facilis, linguæ bene moderatæ, paſſionum tranquilla victrix. Dotum denique omnium non tantum prudens, ſed et tranquilla moderatrix, quatuor liberorum fœcunda Mater. Ad ultimum fatale invenit puerperium, filium, invitâ Lucinâ, potius ad funus quam vitam enixa, quocum dum dividere tentat vitam perdit, ipſaque brevi poſt Infantem intervallo, communi comitata uctu fato ceſſit.

Obiit 18° Octobris 1634, Ætatis ſuæ 29.

His eldeſt ſon, George, 3d Lord Coventry, on June 3, 1660, was conſtituted Cuſtos Rotulorum of the county of Worceſter. By Margaret, daughter of John Earl of Thanet (whom

Coventry, Earl of Coventry.

(whom he wedded on July 18, 1653) he had issue three sons; John, who succeeded him; Thomas, born August 27, 1659, and died January 17, 1660; and William, born July 6, 1661, who died July 14, 1664: also two daughters, Anne, born July 28, 1656, who died young; and Margaret, born at Hothfield-House in Kent, September 14, 1657, married to Charles Earl of Wiltshire (then son and heir to Charles Marquis of Winchester) after Duke of Bolton, and died without children, in the fourth year of her marriage, and in the 24th year of her age, anno 1683.

This George Lord Coventry, died at his house in Lincoln's-Inn-fields, on December 15, 1680, being then 52 years of age, and was buried in the South-isle of the parish-church of Croome-d'Abitot. To him succeeded John, 4th Lord Coventry, his only surviving son, who was born at Croome-d'Abitot, on September 2, 1654; and dying unmarried in the 33d year of his age, July 25, 1687, was buried in the church of Croome-d'Abitot, where a monument is erected to his memory, with the following inscription, which shews his excellent virtues and great worth.

Sacrum est hoc Marmor
Johanni Domino Coventrye
Nil opus est sculpsisse Baronem Coventrye de Allesborough:
Custodem Rotulorum, Regnantibus Carolo et Jacobo secundis;
Et vanam multorum honorum pompam.
Non eget titulis, aut epitaphio,
Ad famam, aut luctum faciendum.
Dicto tam charo nomine,
Fluent lacrymæ, nascetur veneratio:
Et qui norunt vivum, è vivis præreptum lugebunt.
Desideratum Cromæ numen adorabunt,
Nam supra artem, et omni Nobilitate efficacius,
Defuncti immortalitati consecrabunt,
Viventis notissimæ virtutes.
In Deum, Ecclesiam, parentes non ficta, sed vera pietas,
Inexpugnabilis erga Regem, nullis illecebris tentanda, nullis artificiis vincenda fidelitas.
Castitas (heu) nimiùm severa,
In sui, amicorum, familiæ, et seculi detrimentum.
Temperantia ità quotidianis periculis exercitata, et probata,
Ut nullo modo solicitanda videretur; nec unitis epularum, vini, aut ingenuis viribus superanda.
Venusti corporis amplitudinem mirum in modum illustrabat.
Animi magnitudo non Vulgaris,
Incomparabili morum suavitate, et candore perfusa.

Unde

Coventry, Earl of Coventry.

Unde familiarium suffragio, facilè pronunciabatur, ficut revera
fuit,
Mortalium Optimus, et Maximus.
Datam hominibus fidem fanctiffimè colebat.
Singularem exhibuit facerdotibus honorem;
Et rebus facris juftiffimam reverentiam.
Sanabat ille fpoliatæ gementifque Matris Ecclefiæ Anglicanæ
vulnera;
Quacùnque enim per terras ipfius ingruebat facrilegium,
(Authoribus ipfis, aut authorum nepotibus femper lethale:)
Ut primum innotuit fagaci patrono, virus expulit, hæreditatem
luftravit;
Et lætus, lubenfque reftituit infame lucrum, et fatale.
Regendis affectibus tam egregius Artifex fuit, et Magifter,
Ut non magis famulorum dominus æftimaretur, quam fui.
Juramento, vel imprecatione nè femel unquàm vitiavit labra.
Nullis ille fimultatibus vexatus,
Nifi quas juftiffimus arbiter cognovit aliorum gratiâ;
Et fælicitur compofuit litigantium beneficio.
Illum unum ornare confpirabat fimul omne gentilitium decus;
Judicis integritas,
Cuftodis fapientia.
Hofpitalitas Avi,
Charitas Patris.
Sic immortalium Gloriæ maturus, in cœlum evectus eft;
Ob has Clariffimas virtutes,
Diademate puriffimi luminis, Æternum Coronandus,
Anno ætatis 33° Julii 25 1687.
Suis fumptibus erexit optima Mater ornatiffima Margareta,
DominaCoventryeDotaria, Marito cunctifque liberis Mœftiffima
fuperftes :
Johannis Tufton Comitis de Thanet filia Natu Maxima :
Georgii Coventrye Baronis Coventrye de Allefborough Uxor.
Pietate verò Nobilior quam genere,
Et bonis operibus illuftrior quam fortunâ.

The title and eftate defcended to Thomas Coventry, Efq;
uncle to John, and only brother to the faid George Lord
Coventry.

Which Thomas, feated at Snitfield, in Warwickfhire, was
elected to parliament for the borough of Warwick, in the
reign of James II. and by the fpecial grace and favour of
King William, was advanced, on April 26, 1697, to the title
and dignity of Earl of Coventry, and Vifcount Deerhurft,
with limitation of thofe titles to William, after Earl of Co-

ventry, Thomas and Henry his brothers, and their issue-male, grandsons of Walter Coventry before-mentioned. He was Lord-lieutenant of the county of Worcester, and dying on July 15, 1699, in the 70th year of his age, was buried at Croome-d'Abitot, having had issue by Winifride his first wife, daughter of Pierce Edgcumbe, of Mount-Edgcumbe, in com' Devon, Esq; several children; whereof two sons, Thomas, and Gilbert, survived him. This Lady dying on June 11, 1694, he married secondly, in July, 1695, Elizabeth, daughter of Richard Graham, Esq; who survived him without issue; and in May, 1700, was re-married to Thomas Savage, of Elmley-castle, in com' Wigorn. Esq; The said Elizabeth erected a noble monument at Elmley, to his memory, with the following inscription:

Candide et Constanter.
M. S.

Prænobilis Domini Thomæ
Comitis Coventriæ, Vicecomitis Deerhurst,
Baronis Coventrye de Allesborough,
Hujus Comitatus Custodis Rotulorum,
Necnon Decani et Capitalis Ecclesiæ Vigornien.
Et Burgi de Evesham Primarii senascalli.
Tho. Baronis Coventry filius fuit natu secund.
Georgii Baronis Frater, Johannis Patruus,
Et ejusdem, sine prole decedentis,
In avita dignitate, successor.
Varia Reipublicæ munia
Tum Militaria tum Civilia præstitit.
Familiam Censu jam Celebrem, pluribus fundis
Et Comitis et Vicecomitis Titulis,
Regnante Gulielmo III. ornavit et auxit.
E priori Conjuge, Winifreda Piercei Edgecombe
De Mount-Edgecombe in Com. Devon. Arm. Filia
Liberos superstites reliquit Thomam
Honorum hæredem Dignissimum et Gilbertum.
Pietatem, Justitiam, Liberalitatem,
Animique Constantiam semper et enixe coluit.
Dierum tandem et Gloriæ satur,
Sese à seculo quasi subduxit,
Ut solutus cæteris curis Deo ac sibi vacaret.
Sic Cœlos anhelans,
Immortalitati maturam
Efflavit animam,

xv Julii

Coventry, Earl of Coventry.

xv Julii An°
MDCXCIX.
Æt. LXX.

Elizabetha Comitiſſa ejus Dotaria,
E Nobili Grahamorum Familia prognata,
Ricardi, filii Ricardi Graham de Com. Norf.
Armi' pro Rege Carolo Primo
Strenue Dimicantis Capitanei, Filia;
Hcc amoris finceri, fummæ Obſervantiæ,
Gratique demum animi Pignus,
Pro tenerrimo Domini et Mariti erga ſe affectu,
Nulla licet beata prole, Mœſtiſſima poſuit;
Et poſt obitum Corpus ſuum
Cum Dilectiſſimo Marito hic recondi voluit.

Obiit   Die   Ann. Dom. MDCC.

    Thomas, 2d Earl of Coventry, his eldeſt ſon, was married, on May 4, 1691, to Anne, daughter of Henry Duke' of Beaufort, and by her (who died at Snitfield, Feb. 17, 1763, aged 90) had two ſons; Thomas, his ſucceſſor, and John, born Aug. 23, 1705, who died the next year. This Lord died in Auguſt, 1710, and was ſucceeded by Thomas, his only ſurviving ſon, born April 7, 1702, who dying at Eaton-college, Jan. 28, 1711-12, his titles and eſtate devolved on Gilbert, his uncle.

    Which Gilbert, 4th Earl of Coventry, married, to his firſt wife, Dorothy, daughter to Sir William Keyt, of Ebrington, in com' Glouc. Bart. by whom he had an only daughter, Anne, married to Sir William Carew, of Anthony, in Cornwall, Bart. and died in January, 1733-4. He married, ſecondly, Anne, daughter to Sir Strenſham Maſter, of Codnorcaſtle, in Derbyſhire, Knt. but dying without iſſue-male, on Octob. 27, 1719, he was ſucceeded in the honours of Viſcount Deerhurſt and Earl of Coventry, and the greateſt part of his eſtate, by William Coventry, of the city of London, Eſq; then one of the Clerks of the Green-cloth, and a member for the borough of Bridport, lineally deſcended from Walter Coventry, youngeſt brother to Thomas, firſt Lord Coventry; the iſſue-male of William Coventry, of Ridmarley, in Worceſterſhire (the ſecond brother of the ſaid Lord) failing.

    Which Walter had iſſue a ſon of his own name, Walter Coventry, Eſq; who, by Anne his wife, daughter of Simon Holcombe, of the county of Devon, Eſq; had iſſue four ſons; Walter, who died on April 5, 1677: William, late Earl

Coventry, Earl of Coventry.

of Coventry: Thomas, who first married Mary, daughter and heir of John Green, of Millen, in the parish of Hambleton, in com' Bucks, Esq; by whom he had issue one son, Thomas, Counsellor at law, and a Director of the South-sea company, who was returned to the last and present parliaments for Bridport, in Dorsetshire, and married Margaret, daughter to Thomas Savage, of Elmley-castle, in Worcestershire, Esq; The said Thomas had also, by his wife Mary, a daughter, called after her mother, successively wedded to Henry Barker, of Chiswick, in Middlesex, Esq; and to Philip Bearcroft, D. D. and Master of the Charter-house: and took to his second wife Anne-Maria, daughter of the reverend Thomas Brown, of Polston, in com' Wilts, and by her (who died Decem. 17, 1726, aged 32, and was buried at Hambleton) had issue two sons; the reverend Francis Coventry, who died unmarried; George, an officer in the first regiment of foot-guards, and four daughters. Henry, youngest son of Walter Coventry and Anne Holcombe, married Anne, daughter of Mr. Coles, of the city of Oxford, and had issue one son, Henry Coventry, Esq; who died December 29, 1753.

Which William, 5th Earl of Coventry, was elected a member for the borough of Bridport, in Dorsetshire, in the three last parliaments of Q. Anne, as also to the first parliament of Geo. I. On April 15, 1717, he was constituted one of the Clerks-comptroller of the Green-cloth; in which post, 1719, he attended his Majesty to Hanover; and the same year succeeded to the title of Earl of Coventry. On March 22, 1719-20, he was sworn of the Privy-council, and took his place at the board. He was at the same time sworn Lord-lieutenant of the county of Worcester, and Custos Rotulorum of the same; and likewise, on ª March 2, 1727-8, upon his late Majesty's accession. His Lordship married Elizabeth, daughter to Mr. John Allen, of the city of Westminster, by whom he had issue three sons, Thomas-Henry, Viscount Deerhurst, deceased; George-William, now Earl of Coventry; and John-Bulkeley Coventry, late member for Worcestershire. Her Ladyship died Nov. 23, 1738. And his Lordship, departing this life March 18, 1750-1, was succeeded by his eldest surviving son,

George-William, 6th Earl of Coventry, who, on June 17, 1751, was appointed Lord-lieutenant of the county and city of Worcester, and Custos Rotulorum of the same: and took the oaths and his seat in the house of Peers, Jan. 19, 1753. He was Lord of the bedchamber to his late Majesty;

ª Bill signet. Geo. II.

Coventry Earl of Coventry

Coventry, Earl of Coventry.

and was continued in that office by the prefent King; as alfo in thofe of Lord-lieutenant and Cuftos Rotulorum of the county and city of Worcefter.

His Lordfhip, on March 5, 1752, married Maria, eldeft daughter of John Gunning, Efq; by his wife Bridget, daughter of John Bourk, Lord Vifcount Mayo, in Ireland, and fifter to Elizabeth, Dutchefs of Hamilton. By her Ladyfhip (who died on October 1, 1760) his Lordfhip had iffue one fon, ———, Lord Vifcount Deerhurft, born on April 28, 1758; alfo four daughters, viz. Lady Anne-Elizabeth, who died on Auguft 22, 1756, aged about three years; Lady Maria-Alicia, born in December, 1754; Lady Anne-Margaret; and Lady ———, born on March 18, 1757.

His Lordfhip remained a widower till Septem. 26, 1764, when he took to his fecond wife, Barbara, fifter to John Lord St. John, of Bletfoe, and daughter to John Lord St. John, of Bletfoe, by his Lady Elizabeth, daughter of Sir Ambrofe Crawley, Knt. Alderman of London.

TITLES.] George-William Earl of Coventry, and Vifcount Deerhurft.

CREATIONS.] Vifcount Deerhurft, and Earl of Coventry, April 26, 1697, 9 William III.

ARMS.] Sable, a Fefs Ermine, between three Crefcents, Or.

CREST.] On a Wreath, a Garb, Or, and thereon a Dunghill-Cock perched, Gules, Comb, Wattles and Legs, Or.

SUPPORTERS.] Two Eagles, Wings expanded, Argent, membered and beaked, Or.

MOTTO,] CANDIDE ET CONSTANTER.

CHIEF-SEAT.] At Croome-d'Abitot, 6 miles from Worcefter, and 110 from London.

VILLIERS,

VILLIERS, Earl of Jersey.

THE name of this family, variously written Villers, Villiers, Vileres, Vylers, &c. is doubtless descended of the ancient noble house of Villers*, Seigniours of Lile-Adam, in Normandy, and came into England at the time of the conquest, in 1066; for soon after, Pagan de Villers was Lord of Crosby, in com' Lanc. and was also possessed of Newbold, in com' Nottingh. which his posterity held till the reign of Edw. III. But Crosby went ª away to the Molineuxes, by Beatrix, a daughter and heir of the elder line, married, about the time of King John, to ᵇ Robert Molineux, of Sefton, in Lancashire, from whom descended the Lord Viscount Molineux, of Ireland, and Sir Charles Molineux, of Teversall, in Nottinghamshire, Bart. This Pagan was a witness to the foundation-charter of Roger of Poictou to the monastery of Lancaster, and flourished in the reign of William II. and Hen. I. Gilbert de Villers, probably son of Pagan, ᶜ and William Villers, were witnesses, with Roger, Bishop of Chester, to a charter of Robert, son of Nicholas de Stafford ᵈ. After him, 1 meet with another Gilbert Villers, to whom King John, in the 2d year of his reign, granted, for homage and service, all the mediety which he possessed in the vicarage and mill of Mesnacel.

Cotemporary with him was Roger, or rather Robert, living in 9 John, who had issue Robert, father of William, who in 7 Edw. I. together with Robert Pierpont, Roger de Lewknor, Roger de Covert, and many more, were, by a Quo warranto, to ᵉ deliver, to the Abbey of Bec Herlowin, the manour of Preston; and soon after, in 13 Edw. I. William de Villers was witness to a deed without date, whereby Master William de Montfort grants to John de Montfort, the manours of Preston and Uppingham in com' Rutland.

* Of that house were the renowned Pierre de Villiers, and Jaques de Villiers; the first Grand Master of France, in 1390, under Charles VI. and the latter Provost of Paris, in the same reign; besides divers other eminent persons. ª Thoroton's antiq. of Nott.   ᵇ Ex stem. famil. Molineux.   ᶜ Dugd. Baron. vol. 1. p. 731.   ᵈ Ex lib. prior. de Kenilworth.   ᵉ Quo warr. com' Suff. 7 Edw. I.

Villiers, Earl of Jersey.

This William was son of Alexander; for in 14 Edw. I. he impleaded Andrew de Nevil for the manour of Riggesby, &c. whereof his father Alexander died seized; whereunto answer was made, that the said Alexander had an elder son named Richard [f].

Of this family also was Benedict le Vilar, who died seized of the manours of Borshal and Brehall, of the honour of Wallingford, leaving John his son and heir, then three years old, as [g] appears by inquisition in com' Bucks, taken in 20 and 21 Edw. I.

But the first that was written of Brokesby, in Leicestershire, was another Alexander de Vylers, who by his attorney appeared against Gilbert de Glen, chaplain, in a plea against him, that he should [h] pay eight marks, the arrears of an annual rent of four marks then owing. This Alexander was father to Sir Nicholas de Villers, a renowned warrior, who, in 1268, following Edw. I. into the Holy Land, relinquished his paternal coat of arms, viz. Sable, three Cinquefoils, Argent, and instead thereof assumed the Cross of St. George, the patron of his country, and five Escallop-shells on it, to shew the cause of his expedition, being ancient badges of those Crossades. By his wife Maud, daughter and coheir to Sir John Hyde, of Hyde-hall, in Sabridgeworth, Hertfordshire, Knt. (by his wife Elizabeth, daughter of John Sudley, Lord Sudley) and widow of Thomay Jocelyn, Esq; ancestor to the present Viscount Jocelyn, in Ireland, he had two sons, Sir Francis, and Geoffery, hereafter mentioned.

Sir Francis de Villers served Edw. II. and Edw. III. in their wars, and died without issue, leaving Agnes his wife surviving, whom Edw. III. in consideration of the services of her husband (stiling him Franciscus charæ memoriæ) recommended to the Abbess [i] of Barking to provide for.

Geoffery succeeded his brother in the estate of Brokesby, in 20 Edw. III. and in the 26th year of that King's reign, was one of the Knights for the county [k] of Leicester, in the parliament held at Westminster.

His son Sir John de Villers had two wives; 1. Joan, one of the three sisters and coheirs to Simon Pakeman, of Pakeman's-Place in Kirby, in com' Leicest. Esq; by whom he had issue a daughter, Beatrix, married to Sir John Bagot, of Blithfield, in Staffordshire, Knt. (and by her, ancestor to Sir Walter Wagstaffe Bagot, Bart.) and three sons, Richard, John, and Alex-

---

f De Banco. trin. 14 Edw. I. Rot. 57. de com' Linc.   g Esc. de iisd. ann. n. 14 & 20.   h De Banco. Hill. 25 Edw. I. Rot. 96.   i Claus 5 Edw. III. p. 2.   k Pryn's brief regist. p. 218.

ander;

ander; 2dly, Margaret, living in 1392, 15 Rich. II. at which time Richard, eldeſt ſon of the ſaid John, died, viz. on the Sunday next before the feaſt of the Nativity of St. John Baptiſt, then ſeized of the manour of Brokeſby, with the appurtenances, alſo of the advowſon of the church held of the King, as of the honour of Cheſter, by the ſervice of half a Knight's fee, leaving iſſue John, his ſon and heir,[1] aged eleven years and a half.

The ſaid John married Joan, daughter to William Mering, of Mering, in Nottinghamſhire, and died on the feaſt of St. Catharine, Nov. 25, 1416, 4 Hen. V. ſeized of a meſſuage called Pakeman's-Place, ſeven cottages, four virgates and an half of land in Kirby, held of the King in capite; a meſſuage and two virgates in Barton, of Reginald Lord Grey, of Ruthyn; alſo of a moiety of a meſſuage, &c. in Ravinſton, with one cottage in Wiggeſton, and the manour of Brokeſby, with the advowſon, the manours of Athen, and Howby, by Knights ſervice, and a pair of gilt ſpurs; [m] leaving John his ſon and heir, twelve years old and above, at the time of the inquiſition. This John died in ward to the King, and William his brother and heir ſucceeded.

Which William married Joan, ſiſter and coheir to John Bellers, Eſq; of Kirkby-Bellers, in the county of Leiceſter, and died in 20 Hen. VI. having iſſue by her, among others, John, and Bartholomew Villiers, who married Margaret, daughter and coheir of John Clarke, of Whiſſendine, in com' Rutland, where he was buried.

John, the eldeſt ſon, died in his father's life-time, having married Elizabeth, daughter to John Sothill, of Everingham, in com' Ebor. by whom he had iſſue a daughter Elizabeth, and four ſons, 1. John; 2. Thomas, who made his will 6 Hen. VII. and died without iſſue; 3. Chriſtopher, who was ſeated at Burſtal, and died without iſſue, Aug. 5, 1508, the 23d year of that King, ſeized of the manours of Kilby, and Cowdon-Magna, and lands in Harborough, in Leiceſterſhire, having ſettled in truſtees the ſaid manours after his own life on his younger nephews, George and Thomas, and their heirs male, for ever; as [n] alſo the manour of Howby, on them and their brother William, by a like entail. William Villers, clerk, was the fourth ſon of the ſaid John.

John Villers, Eſq; (ſon and heir of the aforeſaid John) ſucceeded his grandfather in the lordſhip of Brokeſby, in 20 Hen. VI. In 1487, 2 Hen. VII. he brought [o] forces to the aid of

---

[1] Eſc. 15 Rich. II. n. 64. [m] Eſc. 4 Hen. V. n. 22, [n] Eſc. 30 Hen. VIII. [o] Polyd. Virg. p. 573. n. 40.

the King, againſt the Earl of Lincoln, Lambert Simnel, and other adherents, and behaved with great valour in the battle of Stoke, near Newark-upon-Trent, June 16, when they were defeated, and the Earl of Lincoln ſlain. In 6, 10, and 15 of Hen. VII. he was Sheriff of Lincolnſhire and Warwickſhire; and was afterwards [p] made Knight of the Bath at the marriage of Prince Arthur the King's ſon, Nov. 14, 1501. He died on December 2, 1506, 22 Hen. VII. leaving iſſue, by Agnes his wife, daughter to John Digby of Colſhil, in com' Warw. Eſq; a daughter Winifrid, to whom her father gave lands for life, in 36 Hen. VIII. and ſeven ſons; 1 Sir John, 2. George, 3. Thomas, 4. William, of whom hereafter; 5. Edward, who died poſſeſſed of lands at Flower and Howthorp, in com' Northamp. June 26, 1513, 5 Hen. VIII. and is the progenitor to the Villers of Howthorp, and to thoſe of Dowſby and Groby; Leonard and Bartholomew, 5th and 6th ſons, died without iſſue; and Anthony Villers, 7th ſon, was of Cotneſs in com' Ebor. and died [q] poſſeſſed of that manour in 1547, 1 Edw. VI.

Sir John, the eldeſt ſon and heir of Sir John, enjoyed the inheritance of Brokeſby, and having been knighted, was Sheriff of Leiceſterſhire and Warwickſhire, in 23 and 29 Hen. VIII. and the next year was found couſin and next heir to his uncle Chriſtopher aforeſaid, in the manour of Bourſtal, [r] aged then 50 years and above. This Sir John died on December 8, 1544, 36 Hen VIII. ſeized of the manours of Brokeſby, and Howby, and the advowſons of thoſe churches: having, by a fine levied in 32 Hen. VIII. between Alexander Villers, and Richard Holme, querents, he and Dorothy his daughter and heir apparent (by Elizabeth his wife, daughter to John Wingat) deforcients, ſettled the ſaid manours and rent in [s] Brokeſby, Howby, and Sevelby, on himſelf in tail male; and in default, to his brothers George, Thomas, William, and Leonard. He died ſeized alſo of lands and tenements in Rotherby, Turſington, Dalby, Wiggeſton, Staunton, and Swannington; Dorothy, his ſaid daughter, the wife of Francis Brown, Gent. being found heir to them, and aged 28 years old and upwards.

His laſt will bears date May 24, 1544, reciting, that he intended, by the grace of God, ſhortly to paſs the ſeas unto the realm of France, to ſerve the King's Majeſty in his wars againſt the French King. He orders his body to be buried in the chancel of the pariſh church of St. Michael of Brokeſby, if

p Nom. equit. in bibl. Cotton. Claudius. c, 3. Ebor. r Ibid. præd. 30 Hen. VIII. q Eſc. 2 Edw. VI. com. s Eſc. 36 Hen. VIII. Leiceſt.

it should fortune him to die in Leicestershire, or else to be buried where it shall please God. And that his executors cause a great stone, then lying in the chancel of Brokesby church, to be laid on his father and mother, and cause two images of latin, with their arms, to be set on the same stone with scripture round about it; as also another stone of the like value to be laid over him, if he should die in England. He divided his estate between his brothers, Edward, Thomas, William, and George Villers, and his daughter Dorothy, to whom he left his lands at Fulnethy, Lessington, Newbell, and Swinthorpe, in the county of Lincoln, as also his manour of Covenham in the same county: and bequeaths to his good Lord Sir Edward Montague, Knt. Lord Chief Justice (with whom he leaves his will) his bason and ewer of silver, and his best ambling gelding, desiring him to be a good Lord to all his friends; and constitutes his brother, George Villers, sole executor, leaving him the residue of his goods not bequeathed. Which will was proved the last of January 1544.

George his brother, by virtue of the fine, as next heir male, succeeded to the manours of Brokesby, and Howby, and the advowsons (as also of the manour of Siwolby in fee-tail, and of the manour of Burstal, upon the death of John Villers, alias Twyford) of all which he died possessed, Aug. 29, 1546, 38 Hen. VIII. He left issue by Joan his wife, daughter to John Harrington, of Bagworth, in com' Leicest. Richard his son and heir, aged 3 years, t who died without issue, and a daughter Elizabeth, heir to her brother, wife to Sir Edward Waterhouse, who also died without issue; so that Thomas, 3d son of Sir John Villers, Knight of the Bath, and brother to the said George, mentioned in the entail, became possessed of Brokesby; but leaving only one daughter, Dorothy, married to William Smith, in com' Leicest. Esq; the entailed estate devolved on

William Villers, Esq; his brother, who likewise became possessed of Brokesby, as the next heir male; and having married Coletta, daughter and heir to Richard Clarke, of the county of Bucking. Esq; Widow to Richard Beaumont of Cole-Orton, in com' Leicest. Esq; died on Nov. 1, 1558, 5 and 6 Phil. and Mary; and the inquisition taken 1 Eliz. at Leicester, mentions, that Sir John Villers, long before his death, was seized of Brokesby and Howby, and of 40 messuages, 20 cottages, 20 tofts, 2 water-mills, 1000 acres of land, 500 of meadow, 2000 of pasture, and other lands and possessions in Brokesby, Howby, and Siwolby in that county, and in the

t Esc. 38 Hen. VIII.

advowsons of the churches of Brokesby and Howby; reciting the said entail made in 32 Hen. VIII. as also a settlement made by Christopher Villers, Esq; on himself for life; remainder to his nephews, George, Thomas, and this William, of the manours of Kelby and Great Bowden, and of lands in Harborough; all which descended to the said William, who was likewise possessed of the manour of Howby in com' Leicest. with other lands there; and left issue

George Villers, his son and heir (aged 14 years at his father's death) who was Sheriff of Leicestershire in 1591, 33 Eliz. and having received the honour of Knighthood, departed this life Jan. 4, 1605-6, 3 Jac. I. He was seized of the manours of Brokesby, Howby, Godby-Marward, and the grange of Godby, which he settled, with the capital messuage called the farm of Howby, on his first wife and her issue male by him, &c. And being likewise seized in all the tythes of herbage, grain and hay, and all other tythes arising in Cadewell, and Wikeham in com' Leicest. he settled the same on himself for life; remainder to John, George, and Christopher (sons by his 2d wife) and their heirs male; remainder to his own right heirs.

His first wife was Audrey, daughter and heir to William Sanders, of Harrington in com' Northamp. Esq; which Lady died May 1, 1587, 29 Eliz. and had by him three daughters; Elizabeth, married to John Lord Butler of Bramfield; Anne, to Sir William Washington of Pakington in com' Leic. and Frances, who died unmarried: also two sons, Sir William, hereafter mentioned, and Sir Edward Villers, Knt. who was president of Munster in Ireland; and from him are descended the Viscounts and Earls of Grandison, of the surname of Villiers; as also the present Earl of Jersey. The second wife to Sir George Villers was Mary, daughter to Anthony Beaumont, of Glenfield in com' Leicest. Esq; a younger son of William Beaumont of Cole-Orton, in the same county: and the said Elizabeth, surviving him, was created Countess of Buckingham, in 16 Jac. I. and became, secondly, wife to Sir William Rayner; and lastly to Sir Thomas Compton, Knight of the Bath, and brother to William 1st Earl of Northampton. Sir George had issue by her a daughter Susan, married to William Fielding, Earl of Denbigh, and ancestor to the present Earl; and three sons, 1. John, created Baron Villers of Stoke, and Viscount Purbeck, and by Frances his wife, daughter to Sir Edward Coke, Lord Chief Justice, had a son Robert, at whose death, those titles became extinct, for want of issue: 2. George, who was at length, Duke and Marquis of Buckingham, Earl of Coventry, Viscount Villers, &c. Knight of the Garter, and a favourite of two succeffive Kings, viz. James I. and Charles I. and was the greateft ornament and glory of his family: 3. Chriftopher, youngeft fon, who was, on Sept. 24, 1623, 21 Jac. I. created Earl of Anglefey and Baron of Daventry, whofe fon Charles Earl of Anglefey died without iffue, anno 1659, leaving Sufan his fifter and heir, who was married to Thomas Savile Earl of Suffex.

Sir William Villiers of Brookefby, Bart. (the eldeft fon of Sir George, by his firft wife) was Sheriff of Leicefter, in 6 Jac. I. and created a Baronet on July 19, 1619, 17 Jac. I. which became extinct in his grandfon Sir William Villiers, Bart. who died without iffue on February 27, 1711, aged 67 years; having fold the manour of Brookefby to Sir Nathan Wright.

But forafmuch as George Duke of Buckingham, beforementioned, was the principal advancer of his family to the honours before recited; I fhall, from proper vouchers, give an account of his rife, and of the principal actions of his life [x]. He was born at his father's feat of Brookefby on Auguft 28, 1592, and having at home been educated according to his genius, in the courtly accomplifhments of fencing, dancing, and the like ornaments of youth, he at the age of 18 years, for his further improvement, travelled into France, from whence, after three years abode, he returned into England. It was about this time that Robert Ker, Earl of Somerfet, began to decline in the favour of James I. a Prince of more learning and knowledge than any other of that age, and who really delighted in books, and in converfation of learned men; yet it was obferved, of all wife men living, he was the moft delighted and taken with handfome perfons and fine clothes; fo that Mr. Villers no fooner appeared at court, than the gracefulnefs of his perfon recommended him to the King's efteem. He firft entertained him (ann. 1613) as his Cup-bearer at large, and the following fummer admitted him in ordinary; which place adminiftred frequent occafions of his being in the King's prefence; and thereby he became a partaker in that converfation and difcourfe, with which King James always abounded at his meals.

He acted very few weeks in that ftation before he was mounted higher, and in one day (viz. on April 23, 1615) both knighted and made one of the Gentlemen of the bedchamber. Soon after this, it luckily, for his advancement, fell out, that the Earl of Somerfet had been concerned, or at leaft privy to a horrible murther (the poifoning of Sir Thomas Overbury) on which both he and his wife, after a trial by

[x] Reliquæ Wottonianæ, p. 74. & Clarend. hift. of the rebellion.

their Peers, were condemned to die. Whereby, being without a rival in the King's affections, he was presently advanced to new honours, and became the most absolute favourite to two Kings that ever this nation beheld. In the year 1616, he was made Master of the horse, Knight of the Garter, and created Baron of Whaddon, and Viscount Villiers, on August 27, that year: also on January 5, 1616-17, he was made Earl of Buckingham, and on the succeeding New-Year's Day was advanced to the title of Marquis of Buckingham. On Jan. 30, 1617-18, he was made Lord High Admiral, and shortly after Chief Justice in Eyre of all the parks and forests south of Trent, Master of the King's-Bench office, High-Steward of Westminster, and Constable of Windsor-Castle.

With these great honours and as great employments, he was likewise the sole dispenser of the King's favours, so that he exalted all his own numerous family and dependants. And tho' he was a person of a most flowing courtesy, and of great affability to all men, yet at first he so failed in duty to Charles, Prince of Wales, that his Highness conceived great indignation against him, which he had the art thoroughly to remove; and entirely fixed himself in favour, by being the sole contriver of that extraordinary journey into Spain, in 1623, by Prince Charles and himself. The Spaniards disrelished him for the great familiarity he used towards the Prince; which, together with his personal animosity against the Duke of Olivares, the sole favourite at the Spanish court, was one reason that this journey entirely dissolved the Spanish match so many years in agitation. During his abode in Spain, he added to his other titles those of Earl of Coventry, and Duke of Buckingham, by patent dated May 18, 1623, 21 Jac. I. and on his return from thence, he was made Lord Warden of the Cinque-Ports, and Steward of the manor of Hampton-Court.

The Prince's arrival in England brought not only infinite delight to the King, but was accompanied with the most universal rejoicing over the whole kingdom, that the nation had ever been acquainted with; in which the Duke had so full a harvest, that the imprudence and presumption of carrying the Prince into Spain was totally forgotten, or not remembered with any reference to him; and the high merit, and inestimable obligation, in bringing him home, was magnified and celebrated by all men in all places: Yet our historians observe, the conclusion of this journey was so contrary to the King's inclinations, that he never after really affected the Duke, but retained as sharp a memory of it, as his nature was capable of. This indisposition of the King towards him was exceedingly increased during the sitting of the parliament, after the Prince's return out of Spain, in which the Duke endeavoured to appear very popular; and having gained the leading men of both houses to espouse his interests, he engaged the King in a war with Spain, and totally ruined the Earl of Middlesex, Lord High Treasurer of England, who presuming on the King's displeasure against him, had dared to dispute his commands.

At these things, though the King inwardly repined, yet he was so far from thinking fit to manifest it (except in whispers to very few men) that the Duke executed afterwards the same authority in conferring all favours and graces, and in revenging himself on those who had manifested any unkindness towards him; insomuch as he prevailed with the King to restrain the Earl of Bristol (against whom he had a particular dislike on account of the match with Spain) on his first arrival, without permitting him to come into his presence, which he had positively promised and resolved to do; and in the end suffered his Attorney-general to exhibit a charge of high-treason, in his Majesty's name, against the said Earl, who was thereupon committed to the Tower.

Shortly after this, viz. on March 27, 1625, died King James at Theobalds, of an ague; ' Which meeting (as my
' Lord Clarendon says) many humours in a fat unwieldy body,
' of 58 years old, in four or five fits carried him out of the
' world. After whose death many scandalous and libellous
' discourses were raised against the Duke, without the least
' colour or ground; as appeared upon the strictest and most
' malicious examination that could be made, long after in a
' time of licence, when no body was afraid of offending
' Majesty, and when prosecuting the highest reproaches and
' contumelies against the royal family was held very meri-
' torious.'

This change brought no diminution to the power of the Duke, for he continued in the same degree of favour with the son, which he enjoyed for many years under the father. ' A
' rare felicity; seldom known, and in which the expectation
' of very many (as my Lord Clarendon observes) was exceed-
' ingly disappointed; who knowing the great jealousy and in-
' dignation that the Prince had heretofore conceived against
' the Duke, for having been once very near striking him, ex-
' pected that he would now remember that insolence, of which
' he then so often complained: without considering the oppor-
' tunity the Duke had, by the conversation with the Prince,
' during his journey into Spain (which was so grateful to him)
' and whilst he was there, to wipe out the memory of all for-
' mer oversights, by making them appear to be of less magni-
' tude

' tude than they had been underſtood before, and to be ex-
' cuſable from other cauſes ; ſtill being ſevere enough to him-
' ſelf for his unwary part, whatſoever excuſes he might make
' for the exceſs ; and by this means to make new vows for
' himſelf, and to tie new knots to reſtrain the Prince from fu-
' ture jealouſies. And it is very true, his hopes in this kind
' never failed him : the new King from the death of the old,
' even to the death of the Duke himſelf, diſcovering the moſt
' entire confidence in, and even friendſhip to him, that ever
' King had ſhewed to any ſubject ; all preferments in church
' and ſtate given by him ; all his kindred and friends pro-
' moted to the degree in honour, or riches, or offices, that he
' thought fit, and all his enemies and enviers diſcountenanced,
' as he appointed.'

 The new King ſent him over to France, to conduct into England the Princeſs Henrietta Maria, whom he had married by
his proxy; and accordingly the Duke came to Paris on May
24, 1625. ' In this embaſſy his perſon and prudence were
' wonderfully admired (as the Earl of Clarendon writes) and
' eſteemed, and in which he appeared with all the luſtre the
' wealth of England could adorn him with, and outſhined all
' the bravery that court could dreſs itſelf in, and over-acted
' the whole nation in their own moſt peculiar vanities ; he
' had the ambition to fix his eyes upon, and to dedicate his
' moſt violent affection to, a Lady of a very ſublime quality,
' and to purſue it with moſt importunate addreſſes: inſomuch,
' as when the King had brought the Queen his ſiſter as far as
' he meant to do, and delivered her into the hands of the
' Duke to be by him conducted into England ; the Duke, in
' his journey, after the departure of that court, took a reſo-
' lution once more to make a viſit to that great Lady, which
' he believed he might do with much privacy. But it was ſo
' eaſily diſcovered, that proviſion was made for his reception ;
' and, if he had purſued his attempt, he had been without
' doubt aſſaſſinated ; of which he had only ſo much notice, as
' ſerved him to decline the danger. But he ſwore in the in-
' ſtant, That he would ſee and ſpeak with that Lady, in
' ſpight of the ſtrength and power of France.'

 And from the time that the Queen arrived in England, June
13, he took all the ways he could to undervalue and exaſperate
that court and nation, by cauſing all thoſe, that fled into England
from the juſtice and diſpleaſure of that King, to be received and
entertained here, not only with ceremony and ſecurity, but
with bounty and magnificence ; and the more extraordinary
the perſons were, and the more notorious their King's diſplea-

sure was towards them (as in that time there were many Lords and Ladies in those circumstances) the more respectfully they were received and esteemed. He omitted no opportunity to incense the King against France, and to dispose him to assist the Hugonots, whom he likewise encouraged to give their King some trouble.

'He also (as observed by Lord Clarendon) took great pains
' to lessen the King's affection towards his young Queen, be-
' ing exceeding jealous left her interest might be of force
' enough to cross his other designs. And in this stratagem he
' so far swerved from the instinct of his nature, and his pro-
' per inclinations, that he, who was compounded of all the
' elements of affability and courtesy towards all kind of peo-
' ple, had brought himself to a habit of neglect, and even of
' rudeness towards the Queen.

'One day, when he unjustly apprehended that she had
' shewed some disrespect to his mother, in not going to her
' lodging at an hour she had intended to go, and was hindered
' by meer accident; he came into her chamber in much paf-
' sion, and after some expostulations rude enough, he told
' her, She should repent it. Her Majesty answering with some
' quickness; he thereupon replied insolently to her, That there
' had been Queens in England, who had lost their heads:
' and it was universally known, that during his life the Queen
' never had any credit with the King, in reference to any pub-
' lic affairs.'

Soon after his return from France, a parliament was called, in which he had the unhappiness to see himself represented as the public grievance of the nation; and though he in a well-composed speech made answer to whatever objections might be laid to his charge, yet finding the house of Commons resolute in maintaining their proceedings, it so transported him, that he prevailed with his Majesty to put an end to their sitting, by an abrupt dissolution on August 12, 1625. However, it being resolved to carry on the war with Spain, he and the Earl of Holland were sent to the Hague, to negociate a league, with the United Provinces, against the Emperor and King of Spain; where after a month's stay, they returned into England. But whilst he was abroad, he purchased a choice collection of Arabian manuscrips, gained in remote parts, through the industry of Erpinius, a most excellent linguist; after whose death, they being in the disposal of his widow, she had sold them to the Jesuits at Antwerp, had not the Duke interverted the bargain, by giving for them 500l. to the poor widow; 'A mixed act
' (saith Sir Henry Wotton, in his account of the Duke) both
' of

'of bounty and charity; and the more laudable, being much out of his natural element.' These, with other benefactions, he intended to have bestowed on the University of Cambridge, whereof he was Chancellor; but being prevented by an untimely death, were nevertheless presented thereto by his Dutchess.'

At the coronation of Charles I. Feb. 2, 1625-6, he was Lord High-constable for that day; and a parliament meeting four days after, he was impeached of high crimes and misdemeanours in thirteen articles, all which he immediately answered, civilly couched, and though his heart was big, favoured of an humble spirit; but the King, being impatient of all proceedings against him, chose rather to dissolve the parliament, than to part with the Duke, though it was at a time when he was actually engaged in a war with Spain. 'For they (as the Lord Clarendon writes) who flattered him most before, mentioned him now with the greatest bitterness and acrimony; and the same men who had called him our Saviour, for bringing the Prince safe out of Spain, called him now the corruptor of the King, and betrayer of the liberties of the people, without the least crime imputed to him, to have been committed since the time of that exalted adulation, or that was not then as much known to them, as it could be now: so fluctuating and unsteady a testimony is the applause of popular councils!'

This transported him with indignation, and created in him a greater contempt of parliaments, than he had before shewn, and which he did not forbear to publish in the most open manner. Such as had given any offence, were imprisoned or disgraced, and new projects were set on foot for money, which served only to offend and incense the people, and brought little supplies, yet raised a great stock for expostulation, murmur, and complaint; many persons of the best quality (excepting Peers) being committed to several prisons, with unheard-of circumstances, only for refusing to pay money required of them by those extraordinary ways. And the Duke himself would passionately say, and frequently do many things, which only grieved his friends, and incensed his enemies, and gave them ability to do him harm.

And notwithstanding the King engaged in a war with Spain, yet in a month after the dissolution of the parliament, a new war was precipitately entered into with France; and the fleet, which had been sent to surprise Cadiz, was no sooner returned without success, and with much damage, than it was repaired, and the army reinforced to invade France. The Duke was personally employed both as Admiral and General, and made a descent

descent on the isle of Rhée, hoping in that service to recover the good will of the public, which by his own example he saw might quickly be won or lost. It is observed by Sir Henry Wotton, that his deportment, in this expedition, 'was noble 'throughout, to the gentlemen a fair respect, bountiful to 'the soldier, according to any special value which he spied in 'any, tender and careful of those that were hurt, of unques- 'tionable courage in himself, and rather fearful of fame than 'danger. In his countenance, which is the part that all eyes 'interpret, no open alteration, even after the succours he ex- 'pected did fail him; but the less he shewed without, the more 'it wrought intrinsically, according to the nature of suppressed 'passions: for certain it is, that to his secretary Dr. Mason, 'whom he layed in a pallet near him, for natural ventilation 'of his thoughts, he would, in the absence of all other ears 'and eyes, break out into bitter and passionate eruptions, pro- 'testing, that neither his dispatches to divers Princes, nor the 'great business of a fleet, of an army, of a siege, of a treaty, 'of war, of peace, both on foot together, and all of them 'in his head at a time, did not so much break his repose, as 'a conceit, that some at home under his Majesty, of whom 'he had well deserved, were now content to forget him. 'Of their two forts, he could not take the one, nor would 'he take the other; but in the general town he maintained 'a seizure and possession of the whole, three months and 'eighteen days; and at the first descent on shore, he was not 'immured within a wooden vessel, but countenanced the 'landing in his long-boat, defeating near 200 horse, gen- 'tlemen of family and great resolution, and 2000 foot; as, 'all circumstances well balanced on either side, may surely 'endure a comparison with any of the bravest impressions in 'antient time.'

Rushworth, in his Collections, relates, that he first blocked up the citadel, in hopes of starving the garrison, which was in want of provisions; but the French finding means to throw in supplies, he after besieged it in form. And refreshments of men, &c. being still poured in, about the middle of October, the Duke called a council to consult of a retreat, when it was judged proper to embark: however, on the instance of Sou- bize, and the French protestants, he continued the siege; and on Novem. 6, made a general storm of the citadel and works, wherein many men were lost, and the rest forced to retire. This ill success, with advice, that, notwithstanding our ship- ping, the French were come with a great body into the island, caused the Duke to hasten his retreat.

On Nov. 8, 1627, the army marched, but the troops of the enemy appeared equal in number for foot, and far stronger in horse. Yet, notwithstanding their strength, and the advantage of falling on an army on a retreat, which had endured much hardship and received many discouragements, the enemy dared not to engage in a plain field, when the Duke several times drew up the troops in their march, and made a stand in hopes of a battle. But the wary French commander shunned the hazard of a fight on equal terms, foreseeing a greater advantage with less hazard: for no sooner were the English entered into a narrow causey and lane, having on each hand deep ditches and salt-pits, but the enemy observed the advantage, and advanced with great fury on a weak rear-guard of horse, and quickly put them to a retreat; who in that narrow causey disordered the foot, and the enemy thereupon followed close, and did much execution on the English. Those, who escaped the sword, were drowned in the salt-pits and ditches; and the croud was so great on the bridge (the enemy pursuing them over) that many English were drowned in the river. Yet in this discomfited condition, the Duke, by an extraordinary courage and conduct, rallied his forces, and drew up a smart body, that faced about to fight the enemy; and the French (not daring to engage, but on great advantage) were obliged to retreat over the bridge. The next day the army was shipped, and the Duke, having promised the Rochellers to come again to their relief, set sail for England, and met with the Earl of Holland, as he was setting out of Plymouth, coming with a supply. When this unfortunate action was known and published throughout the nation, the cry of the people was so great, and the King's necessity so pressing (the mariners coming in multitudes to the court at Whitehall, in great disorder and confusion, crying out for pay, and hardly to be appeased) that a parliament was necessitated to be called. They were no sooner met, March 17, 1627-8, than the Duke's excessive power was voted to be the cause of all the evils and dangers to the King and kingdom; and a remonstrance of grievances drawn up, wherein he was charged as the principal occasion of them; but the parliament adjourning till Oct. 20, 1628, he in the interval not only endeavoured to allay the prejudice raised against him in the house of Commons, but also to regain the good-will of the public, and repair his lost honour by a second expedition against the French. Accordingly, in August he came to Portsmouth, intending, as soon as all things were ready, to embark for the relief of Rochelle, then straitly besieged by the French King.

Villiers, Earl of Jersey.

Whilst he was preparing to embark, he was assassinated at the age of 36 years and 3 days, when he was in the highest favour with his Sovereign, the house and town full of his servants and dependants, and the King and court but about six miles from him. John Felton committed the fact, without any other inducement or encouragement than what the melancholy of his nature, and the belief that he should do God and his country good service, by destroying an enemy to both, might suggest to him. He had been Lieutenant of a foot company, whose Captain was killed at the isle of Rhée, on which he conceived that it ought to have been conferred on him; and on refusal by the Duke of Buckingham, gave up his commission, withdrawing from the army; and resided at London, when the Duke was voted by the Commons an enemy to the public; which, together with a certain book then published by one Egglestone, a Scottish physician, representing the Duke unworthy to live in a Christian court, was the reason (as he alledged at his examination) that he first resolved to kill the Duke; for which purpose he bought an ordinary knife of no greater price than ten-pence, and sewed the sheath to the lining of his pocket, that he might in an instant draw forth the blade with one hand, for the other was maimed. Thus prepared, partly on horseback, and partly on foot, for he was indigent of money, he came to Portsmouth, where attending as a suitor, and watching his opportunity, as the Duke after breakfast came from an inner chamber, discoursing with Sir Thomas Fryar, a Colonel in the army; in the very moment as Sir Thomas withdrew from the Duke, this assassin gave him, with a back blow, a deep wound into his left side, leaving the knife in his body; which the Duke pulled out, and without using any other words, but ' The villain hath killed ' me,' instantly fell down dead, the knife having pierced his heart.

Being thus barbarously murdered on Saturday, Aug. 23, 1628, his bowels were interred at Portsmouth, and a handsome memorial of him erected there, by his sister, the Countess of Denbigh. His body was brought to York-house, where he lay some time in an illustrious manner, on a hearse; and after was sumptuously entombed on the north side of Henry VII's chapel in Westminster-Abbey, where a most noble monument is erected to his memory.

The Earl of Clarendon, in the first volume of his history of the rebellion, writes, ' That he was of a noble nature, and ' generous disposition, and of such other endowments, as made ' him very capable of being a great favourite to a great King,
' and

' and underſtood the arts of a court, and all the learning that
' is profeſſed there exactly well. That he was of a moſt flow-
' ing courteſy and affability to all men who made any addreſs
' to him; and ſo deſirous to oblige them, that he did not
' enough conſider the value of the obligation, or the merit of
' the perſon he choſe to oblige; from which much of his miſ-
' fortune reſulted. He was of a courage not to be daunted,
' which was manifeſted in all his actions, and in his conteſts
' with particular perſons of the greateſt reputation; and eſpe-
' cially in his whole demeanor at the iſle of Rhée, both at the
' landing, and on the retreat: in both which, no man was
' more fearleſs, or more ready to expoſe himſelf to the higheſt
' dangers.'

This great Duke took to wife, eight years and two months before his death, the Lady Catharine Manners, daughter and ſole heir to Francis Earl of Rutland, and by her (who afterwards married Randal Macdonald, Marquis of Antrim) had iſſue three ſons, and a daughter Mary, who by patent, bearing date Aug. 31, 1627, 3 Car. I. had the title of Dutcheſs of Buckingham limited to her, in default of iſſue male of her father. She was firſt married to Charles Lord Herbert, ſon and heir to Philip Earl of Montgomery; ſecondly, to James Stuart, Duke of Richmond and Lenox, in Auguſt, 1637; and thirdly, to Thomas Howard, brother to Charles Earl of Carliſle; but by neither of them left iſſue.

The ſons were Charles, who died an infant, and was buried in Weſtminſter-Abbey, on March 17, 1626; George Duke of Buckingham; and the Lord Francis Villiers, born after his father's deceaſe, on April 2, 1629, who, on his return from his travels in the year 1648, engaging with the Earl of Holland, to riſe on the behalf of Charles I. was unfortunately ſlain on July 7, the ſame year, in a ſkirmiſh with the rebels at Kingſton upon Thames, and was buried three days after in his father's vault in Weſtminſter-Abbey; being, as the Earl of Clarendon writes, a youth of rare beauty, and comelineſs of perſon.

The eldeſt, George Duke of Buckingham, being very young on his father's murder, was ſent to travel, during the time of the civil wars; and returning to England whilſt Charles I. was under reſtraint, he and his brother, the Lord Francis Villiers, before-mentioned, thought themſelves obliged to venture their lives and fortunes for the King the firſt opportunity, and thereupon engaged with the Earl of Holland. The Duke had a commiſſion under him of General of the horſe, and behaved with great gallantry: and on their defeat at Kingſton upon Thames, happily found a way into London, where he lay concealed till

he

he had an opportunity to secure himself, by being transported into Holland, where the Prince of Wales at that time was, who (as the Earl of Clarendon writes) received him with great grace and kindness.

The parliament at Westminster voted, that for his levying war, he should be proceeded against as a traitor, and that his estate should be sequestered; and it was accordingly assigned for the payment of the forces under General Lambert. The house of Lords shewed that favour to him, as to send a message to the Commons, to desire their concurrence with them, that he might be indemnified from his late engagement, if he returned within fourteen days; which was rejected.

After the murder of the King, when the Scottish commissioners waited on Charles II. at Breda, to invite him into their kingdom, the Duke of Buckingham, who had waited on him from his arrival in Holland, was permitted to go over with him to Scotland; and on their arrival there, in June, 1760, when all his Majesty's English servants were removed from his person, the Duke was only excepted.

When the King was preparing to march into England, he granted a commission to the Duke to raise a regiment of horse, and one of foot, out of the English that should repair to him. And after their march to Worcester, perceiving that very few of quality or distinction repaired to his Majesty, he remonstrated to the King, that it would be more to his interest to remove the Scottish General; alledging it would not consist with the honour of any Peer of England to receive his orders: and thereupon asked his Majesty, to confer that command on himself. Which the King refusing to do, the Duke was so discontented (as Lord Clarendon writes) that he came no more to the council, scarce spoke to the King, neglected every body else, and himself: insomuch as for many days he scarce put on clean linen, nor conversed with any body; nor did he recover this ill humour whilst the army stayed at Worcester.

On Septem. 3, 1651, there was a general engagement with Cromwell's forces near that city, when the Duke was on the King's right-hand, and behaved with exemplary valour. And on the loss of the day, retired with his Majesty northward, who had then an intent of going into Scotland; but on consultation with the Duke, the Earl of Derby, the Lord Wilmot, &c. it was thought more convenient to conceal himself in Boscobel-house: whereupon his Majesty, with the Duke, the Earl of Derby, and others, in all about sixty horse, marched thither; and having left the King, as they hoped,

hoped, in fecurity, the Duke with the Earl of Derby, &c. went forward, to overtake General Lefley, with the main body of Scotch horfe. But being met by the rebels, he, with the Earl of Derby, the Earl of Lauderdale, and moft of them, were taken prifoners.

The Duke (whilft the rebels were plundering thofe noble perfons) with the Lord Livingfton, Colonel Blague, Mr. Marmaduke Darcy, and Mr. Hugh May, forfook the road firft, and foon after their horfes, and betook themfelves to a by-way, and got into Bloore-Park, near Chefwardine, about five miles from Newport, where they received fome refrefhment at a little obfcure houfe of Mr. George Barlow; and afterwards met with two honeft labourers in an adjoining wood, to whom they communicated the diftrefs which the fortune of war had reduced them to; and finding them like to prove faithful, the Duke thought fit to imitate his royal mafter, delivered his George, which was given him by the Queen of England, to Mr. May (who preferved it through all difficulties, and after reftored it to his Grace in Holland) and changed habit with one of the workmen; and in this difguife, by the affiftance of Mr. Barlow and his wife, was after fome days conveyed by one Nicholas Matthews, a carpenter, to the houfe of Mr. Hawley, an hearty cavalier, at Bilftrop, in Nottinghamfhire, from thence to the Lady Villiers's houfe at Brokefby, in Leicefterfhire; and after many hardfhips and encounters, his Grace got fecure to London, and from thence had the good fortune to efcape a fecond time into Holland, where on his arrival he was taken for the King; and it was thought good policy to publifh that his Majefty was arrived.

On the King's arrival in France, the Duke of Buckingham went to him there, but afterwards coming into England, was apprehended and committed to the Tower, on Aug. 24, 1658. He continued confined till July 29, 1659, when he was difcharged, on his giving fecurity to be faithful to the government. Neverthelefs, on Auguft 13 following, he was again taken up (on Sir George Booth's rifing) with the Earl of Oxford, the Lords Delawar, and Falkland, who were all fent to the Tower, except the Duke of Buckingham. And on May 4, 1660, the Commons agreed to an order of the Lords, to reftore him to his eftate.

On May 29, the day of the King's triumphant entry into London, the Duke of Buckingham and General Monk rode together, bare-headed, before his Majefty. And whilft he was in Holland, having been elected a Knight-companion of the moft noble order of the Garter, he was inftalled at

Windfor,

Windsor, on April 15, 1661. He was afterwards Master of the horse to the King; and in 1667, on the Earl of Clarendon's withdrawing himself, was reputed his Majesty's Prime Minister. He had, as he was often admitted to familiarities with the King, endeavoured, with all his wit and humour, to make Lord Clarendon, and all his counsels, appear ridiculous.

In 1670, the Marshal Bellefond being sent from the court of France, to condole the death of the Dutchess of Orleans, the Duke of Buckingham was sent to return the compliment; but really to conclude a treaty with the French, to declare war against the Dutch. The King of France treated him in so particular a manner, knowing his vanity, that he went in, without reserve, to what he proposed, and consented to the French fleet's coming into our seas and harbours; which afterwards improved the mariners of that nation, and learnt them the way of fighting at sea.

On declaring of war against Holland, March 17, 1671-2, Clifford, Ashley, Buckingham, Arlington, and Lauderdale, had the chief management of affairs, and from the initial letters of their names, were called the Cabal. When the French had almost reduced the States, the Duke of Buckingham and the Earl of Arlington were sent to Utrecht, in July, 1672, to bring the King of France to better terms than he had offered; but in vain. The next year, the nation being in a ferment about the war, and money being wanted, those who had the chief concern in the ministry, were for saving themselves (a parliament being called that year) so that the Duke was the only person his Majesty confided in; but by bringing in Sir Thomas Osborne (afterwards Earl of Danby) he found himself neglected, in proportion as that Nobleman rose in credit with the King.

In Feb. 1676-7, he was committed to the Tower, by order of the house of Lords, for questioning the legality of the parliament, after their long prorogation. Being afterwards, on his submission, discharged, he, with Shaftsbury, Essex, and Hallifax, were, as Bishop Burnet writes, the governing men among the Lords.

By a strange conduct, and an unsteady temper, he could not long fix in any friendship, or to any design, which gave his enemies great advantages; so that towards the latter end of the reign of Charles II. he was sunk very low in the opinions of most people, as well as in his estate, which he wasted by all manner of ways, and died in a poor cottage in Yorkshire, without issue, April 16, 1687. His wife was Mary, daughter and

heir

heir of Thomas Lord Fairfax, of Cameron, the famous parliament General, by his wife, daughter and coheir to Horatio Lord Vere, of Tilbury. He wrote the Rehearsal, a celebrated comedy, and several poems, which shew his wit and gallantry; but he gave himself up to a monstrous course of studied immoralities, as Bishop Burnet writes in the history of his own times; and that he was for subjects submitting in all things to the King's motion, and thought all that opposed him, or his ministry in parliament, were rebels in their hearts; and he hated all popular things, as below the dignity of a King. He says further of him, that in the Dutch wars the King having discovered to the Duke the Earl of Ossory's design on Helvoetsluys, his Grace employed all his wit to make it appear ridiculous, as hating both the Duke of Ormond and Lord Ossory, and would have seen the King and all his affairs perish, rather than the person he hated should have the honour of such merit: and thereupon the King ordered the design to be laid aside; so easy was he to the man of wit and humour.

I now return to Sir Edward, second son of Sir George Villiers, by his first wife, Audrey, daughter to William Sanders. This Edward received the honour of Knighthood [a] at Windsor, on Sept. 7, 1616, and in 1620, was sent Ambassador to Bohemia; also on March 10, 1622, [b] was, by the interest of his brother the Duke of Buckingham, advanced to the Presidentship of Munster, in Ireland, in the room of the Earl of Thomond, deceased. He lived there (saith Sir Henry Wotton) in singular estimation for his justice and hospitality; and died (Sept. 7, 1626) with as much grief of the whole province, as ever any Governor did, before his religious Lady, who was of a sweet and noble disposition, adding much to his honour. He was buried in the Earl of Cork's chapel at Youghall, where these lines were put up to his memory:

> Munster may curse the time that Villiers came,
> To make us worse, by leaving such a name;
> Of noble parts, as none can imitate,
> But those whose hearts are married to the state:
> But if they press to imitate his fame,
> Munster may bless the time that Villiers came.

The said Sir Edward's Lady was Barbara, eldest daughter of Sir John St. John, of Lidiard Tregose, in com' Wilts, and niece to Sir Oliver St. John, created Viscount Grandison,

[a] Philpot's cat. of Knights. [b] Cox's hist. of Ireland, part. 2. p. 39.

in Ireland, Jan. 3, 1620, with limitation of that honour to her pofterity; and by her had iffue Sir Edward Villiers, and three daughters; 1ft, Barbara, married to Thomas Wenman, fon and heir of Philip Lord Vifcount Wenman, and after his deceafe, to James Howard, Earl of Suffolk; 2. Anne; and, 3. Ellen. Sir Edward had alfo four fons,

1. William, who fucceeded his father in eftate, and in 1630, his uncle in the title of Vifcount Grandifon. On the breaking out of the rebellion, he adhered to Charles I. and fignalized himfelf on feveral occafions; but being wounded at the fiege of Briftol, July 26, 1643, he was carried to Oxford, where he died in Auguft following, in the 30th year of his age; and has a noble monument erected to his memory in the cathedral of Chrift-church (where he was buried) by Barbara, Dutchefs of Cleveland, his only daughter and heir, who was married to Roger Palmer, Earl of Caftlemain, in Ireland, by whom fhe had no iffue; but to Charles II. who, on Aug. 3, 1670, created her Dutchefs of Cleveland, &c. fhe bore Charles Duke of Cleveland and Southampton, Henry Duke of Grafton, and George Duke of Northumberland; Anne Palmer Fitzroy, 3d wife of Thomas Lennard, Earl of Suffex; Charlotta Fitzroy, married to Henry Lee, Earl of Litchfield; and Barbara, a nun. The Earl of Clarendon, in his hiftory of the rebellion, mentioning this William Lord Vifcount Grandifon, fays, ' He was a young man of fo virtuous a habit of
' mind, that no temptation or provocation could corrupt him;
' fo great a lover of juftice and integrity, that no example,
' neceffity, or even the barbarities of this war, could make
' him fwerve from the moft precife rules of it; and of that
' rare piety and devotion, that the court, or camp, could
' not fhew a more faultlefs perfon, or to whofe example
' young men might more reafonably conform themfelves.
' His perfonal valour and courage of all kinds (for he had
' fometimes indulged fo much to the corrupt opinion of ho-
' nour, as to venture himfelf in duels) was very eminent,
' infomuch as he was accufed of being too prodigal of his
' perfon; his affection, zeal, and obedience to the King,
' was fuch as became a branch of that family.' And he was wont to fay, ' That if he had not underftanding enough to
' know the uprightnefs of the caufe, nor loyalty enough to
' inform him of the duty of a fubject, yet the very obli-
' gations of gratitude to the King, on the behalf of his houfe,
' were fuch, as his life was but a due facrifice. And there-
' fore, he no fooner faw the war unavoidable, than he en-
' gaged all his brethren, as well as himfelf, in the fervice;
' and

Villiers, Earl of Jersey.

' and there were then three more of them in command in
' the army, where he was so unfortunately cut off.'

2. John, who succeeded his brother William in the honour, but died without issue male.

3. George, who, on the death of his brother John, was Lord Viscount Grandison, and deceased in December, 1699, aged about 40 years; and was succeeded by John, his grandson and heir, who was created Earl Grandison, of Limerick, Sept. 11, 1721, 7 Geo. I.

4. Edward, of whom I am principally to treat, being ancestor to the present Earl of Jersey. This Gentleman, on the breaking out of the civil wars, engaged himself in the royal cause [c]; and when it was resolved to take the command of the fleet from the Earl of Northumberland, and to send letters to all the captains, with orders to observe the commands of Sir John Pennington, the whole dispatch to the fleet was committed to the care of Mr. Edward Villiers, whose diligence and dexterity (as Lord Clarendon says) his Majesty found fit for any trust; but though he delivered his letters to the several captains, and punctually executed his orders, this design, through the ill management of superior officers, put the whole command of the fleet into the parliament's hands. He was afterwards a Lieutenant-colonel in his Majesty's army, in divers engagements, more particularly in the battle of Newbury, Sept. 20, 1643, where he was wounded: and having by these and other services recommended himself to Charles II. he was honoured with knighthood at Whitehall, April 7, 1680, and made Knight-marshal of his houshold, on the death of Sir Edmund Wyndham; also Colonel of the Dutchess of York's regiment, and Governor of Tinmouth-castle. He had likewise a grant, from Charles II. of the royal house and manour of Richmond; and his Lady was governess of the Princesses Mary, and Anne, after Queens of Great-Britain. King James continued him in his post of Knight-marshal, and having a mind to nurse the Pretender in the old palace of Richmond, he, on a valuable consideration, resigned it to him. He lived to see his eldest son advanced to the post of Master of the horse to Queen Mary, on the revolution brought about by King William; and was buried in Westminster-Abbey, on July 2, 1689. He married the Lady Frances, daughter to Theophilus Howard, Earl of Suffolk, by whom he had two sons, and six daughters.

Edward, his eldest son, was created Earl of Jersey.

[c] Clarend. hist. of the rebellion.

Henry, youngeft fon, firft a captain under his father in the Dutchefs of York's regiment, afterwards Colonel of a regiment of foot, and conftituted Governor of Tinmouth-caftle, July 8, 1702, was father of Henry Villiers, Efq; his only furviving fon, who was alfo Lieutenant Governor of that caftle, and died on May 29, 1753, having wedded, 1ft Arabella, daughter and heir of John Roffiter, of Somerby in Lincolnfhire, Efq; and 2dly, Mary, daughter to —— Fowke, Efq; and fifter to Lieut. General Thomas Fowke.

Elizabeth, eldeft daughter, was Maid of Honour to Mary Princefs of Orange, and married, in 1695, to the Lord George Hamilton, third fon to William Duke of Hamilton, after created Earl of Orkney; and died at his houfe in Albemarle-ftreet, April 19, 1733.

Catharine, fecond daughter, was married in King Henry VII's chapel in Weftminfter-Abbey, on July 20, 1685, to James Lewis de Puiffar, Marquis of Puiffar in the kingdom of France: and after his death to William Villiers, a younger fon to George Vifcount Grandifon.

Barbara, third daughter, wedded to John Berkeley, Vifcount Fitzharding.

Anne, fourth daughter, to William Bentinck Earl of Portland.

Henrietta, fifth daughter, on May 23, 1695, to John Earl of Breadalbane in Scotland, and died on Feb. 1, 1719-20.

Mary, fixth daughter, was wedded to William Earl of Inchiquin, in Ireland.

Edward, eldeft fon and heir of the laft Sir Edward, waited on the Princefs Mary into Holland, after her marriage with the Prince of Orange, with whom he came into England, in 1688; and on their being proclaimed King and Queen of England, was on the firft fettlement of their houfhold, in Feb. 1688-9, made Mafter of the horfe to the Queen. On May 27 following, being then a Knight, he was chofen by her Majefty to compliment the Dutch Ambaffadors on their arrival, who were fent by the States-General to congratulate their Majefties on their acceffion to the throne. And the death of his father happening foon after, he fucceeded him in his place of Knight-Marfhal; alfo advancing farther in their Majefty's favour, he was on March 20, in the 3d year of their reign, created Vifcount Villiers of Dartford, and Baron of Hoo, both in the county of Kent. At the funeral of Queen Mary, March 5, 1694-5, he led a mourning horfe, attended by two Equerries; but his place of Mafter of the Horfe determining by her death, he was fent Envoy-Extraordinary and Plenipotentiary to the
congrefs

congress at the Hague, where on September 9, 1695, he had his public audience of the States-General; and in April, 1697, he was constituted one of the Lords Justices of Ireland, being also about the same time appointed one of the Plenipotentiaries for the treaty of Ryswick; and soon after, Oct. 29, 1697, he received the character of his Majesty's Ambassador extraordinary to the States-General; and to create the greater lustre to his employments, was created Earl of Jersey, on October 13 following. He had, shortly after, his audience of leave of the States-General; and returning into England, was sworn of the Privy-council, Nov. 25, 1697. The year following he succeeded the Earl of Portland, as Ambassador extraordinary to the Court of France; and making his public entry into Paris on January 4, N. S. 1698-9, with great magnificence, had two days after his public audience. He continued at that court till the beginning of May 1699, about which time he embarked for England; and after his arrival, on May 14, was constituted one of his Majesty's principal Secretaries of State. And his Majesty declaring in council his intention of going over to Holland the 31st of the same month [b], he was declared one of the Lords Justices for the administration of the government. And before the end of the year, being sent for by his Majesty to attend him at Loo, he arrived there from England, Oct. 4, 1699. That year he was appointed one of the Plenipotentiaries for the second treaty of partition; and on June 24, made Lord-chamberlain of his Majesty's houshold.

On the accession of Queen Anne, he was sworn of her Privy-council, and on April 14, 1702, constituted Lord-chamberlain of her houshold, and created Doctor of the civil laws in August, that year, when the Queen was at Oxford. His Lordship continued in his post of Lord-chamberlain till April, 1704; and after had no public employment, dying in the 56th year of his age, on August 26, 1711, the day he was to have been named Lord Privy-seal, being likewise designed one of the Plenipotentiaries to the congress at Utrecht.

His Lordship married Barbara, daughter to William Chiffinch, Esq; Closet-keeper to Charles II. by whom he left issue two sons, William his successor, and Henry; also a daughter Mary, married to Thomas Thynne of Old Windsor, in Berks, Esq; by whom she was mother of Thomas, 2d Lord Viscount Weymouth, and was secondly the wife of George Granville, Lord Lansdown, and died on Jan. 17, 1734-5.

William, second Earl of Jersey, was elected one of the Knights for Kent to the parliament in 1705, his father being

[b] Hist. of Engl. vol. 3. p. 769.

Villiers, Earl of Jersey.

then alive: and married Judith, only daughter to Frederick Hern of the city of London, Esq; by whom he had two sons, William now Earl of Jersey, and Thomas Lord Hyde of Hindon; also an only daughter, Lady Barbara, married, in 1725, to Sir William Blacket, of Newcastle on Tyne in com' Northumb. Bart. but he dying on August 27, 1728, she was married on March 13, 1728-9, to Bussy Mansel, Esq; uncle to Thomas last Lord Mansel, and on July 16, 1757, to George Venables Vernon, Esq; The Countess their mother survived her Lord several years; and departing this life, was buried in St. Bridget's church, London, on July 31, 1735.

William, now Earl of Jersey, succeeded his father on July 13, 1721. His Lordship was one of the Gentlemen of the bedchamber to Frederick, Prince of Wales (at whose funeral, April 13, 1751, he was one of the six supporters of the pall) and on May 12, 1740, was appointed Lord Chief Justice in Eyre of all his Majesty's forests, chases, parks, &c. on this side Trent. His Lordship married, on June 23, 1733, the Lady Anne Egerton, daughter to Scroop Duke of Bridgwater, and relict of Wriothesley Duke of Bedford; and by her, who died on June 16, 1762, had issue Frederick-William, Lord Viscount Villiers, who was born on March 25, 1734, and died in October 1742, and George Bussy, now Lord Viscount Villiers, born on June 9, 1735.

The said George Bussy, Viscount Villiers, was, on his uncle's being created Lord Hyde, in 1756, elected member for Tamworth in Staffordshire in his room; and was again chosen for the same place at the general election in 1761. His Lordship, on March 21, 1761, was declared one of the Lords of the Admiralty; but resigned in April, 1763.

TITLES.] William Villiers Earl of Jersey, Viscount Villiers of Dartford, and Baron of Hoo.

CREATIONS.] Baron of Hoo in Kent, and Viscount Villiers of Dartford, in the said County, March 20 (1690-1) 3 Will. and Mary, and Earl of the Island of Jersey, Octob. 13 (1697) 9 Will. III.

ARMS.] Argent, on a Cross of St. George, Gules, 5 Escallop Shells, Or.

CREST.] On a Wreath, a Lion rampant, Argent, and ducally crown'd, Or.

SUPPORTERS.] Two Lions, Argent, crown'd with ducal Coronets, Or, each having a plain Collar, Gules, charged with three Escallop Shells, of the second.

MOTTO.] FIDEI COTICULA CRUX.

CHIEF-SEAT.] At Middleton Stony, Oxfordshire.

POULETT,

Villiers Earl of Jersey

POULETT, Earl Poulett.

HAVING treated of the original of this family in that of the Duke of Bolton's, I shall begin with Sir Thomas Paulett, or Poulett ª, eldest son of Sir John Paulett, by Elizabeth his wife, daughter and co-heir of William Creedy of Creedy, in com' Devon, Esq;

Which Sir Thomas Poulett, married Alice, daughter and heir of William Paulett of Beer-Paulett (descended from the second son of William Paulett, by the heir of Beere) and in her right had the manor of Beere-Paulett, and left issue John her son and heir, who by his wife Adonia Cale of Somersetshire, was the father of Sir Thomas Paulett or Poulett (for the name has been wrote differently) ᵇ who married Margaret, daughter and heir of Henry Burton, Esq; by Alice his wife, daughter and heir of John de Boys, and had issue two sons, Sir William Paulett, and John Paulett of Gothurst in com' Somers. also a daughter Elizabeth, married to Robert Burton, and secondly to William Bigberye, Esquires.

His eldest son Sir William Paulett (knighted by Henry VI. for his valiant behaviour in the wars of France) married Elizabeth daughter and heir of John Deniband (or Dewriband according to some) of Henton (commonly Hinton) St. George, in the county of Somerset, Esq; by whom he became possessed of that lordship, which came by the Giffards, who had it by the heir of Poutrals; and the Denibands were of Pescayth in Monmouthshire. He had issue four daughters, and one son Sir Amias Paulett. Of the daughters, Elizabeth married Sir John Paulett, the Duke of Bolton's ancestor; and Anne was the wife of Sir William Carey of Cockington, predecessor to Lord Hunsdon, &c.

Which Sir Amias was knighted for his gallant behaviour at the battle of Newark on Trent, June 16, 1587, 2 Hen. VII. when the Earl of Lincoln and Lambart Simnell were defeated. He was likewise one of the ᶜ commanders of those forces against Perkin Warbeck: and in 15 Hen. VII. bearing the title of one of the Knights of the King's body, was ᵈ commissioned with Robert Shirburn, Dean of St. Paul's, in consideration of their loyalty, industry, foresight, and care, to receive all such persons into favour, as were adherents to Perkin Warbeck, by fine or otherwise, as to them shall seem most proper. 'This commission they managed so discreetly, that (as Hollinshed observes ᵉ) 'Equity therein was very well, and justly executed.'

---
a MS. in bibl. Lambeth, entit. desc. of Nobility.   b Ibid.   c Hollinshed's chron. p. 784.   d Rymer's fœd. tom. 12. p. 766.   e Chron. p. 785.

It is further memorable of him, that in the reign of Henry VII. when Cardinal Wolfey was only a fchool-mafter at Limington in Somerfetfhire, Sir Amias Paulett, for fome mifdemenour committed by him, clapped him in the ftocks: which the Cardinal, when he grew into favour with Henry VIII. fo far refented, that he fought all manner of ways to give him trouble, and obliged him (as Godwin in his annals obferves [f]) to dance attendance at London for fome years, and by all manner of obfequioufnefs to curry favour with him. During the time of his attendance, being commanded by the Cardinal not to depart London without licence, he took up his lodging in the great gate of the Temple towards Fleet-ftreet. And in 7 Henry VIII. when the Cardinal was made [g] Lord-Chancellor, he re-edified the faid gate (now called the Middle-Temple gate) and fumptuoufly beautified it on the outfide with the Cardinal's arms, cognizance, badges, and other devices, in a glorious manner, thereby hoping to appeafe his difpleafure. Having been fo great a benefactor to the fociety of the Middle-Temple, he [h] was chofen Treafurer thereof in 12 Hen. VIII. and departed this life in 1538, 30 Hen. VIII. having about feven years before fold the manour of Paulett, the ancient inheritance of his family, to the Earl of Shaftefbury's anceftor. His laft will bears date, April 1, 1538, and the probate thereof June 25 following [i]. He orders his body to be buried in the church of Cherfcomb, in com' Somerf. and was a benefactor to the cathedral church of Wells, and to the churches of Henton, Cherfcomb, Chard, Crookhorne, Ylminfter, South-Peterton, Dynington, and the abbey and convent of Ford. He bequeaths all his lands, goods, &c. to his fon and heir Sir Hugh Paulett, Knt. whom he made fole executor, charging him to be loving to his fons John and Henry, and to help them to preferment.

He married two wives, firft, Margaret, daughter of John Paulett, Efq; grandfather of William Marquis of Winchefter; and fecondly, Lora, daughter of William Kellaway of Rockborn in com' Southamp. Efq; but had iffue only by the laft, viz. the three fons mentioned in his will; and one daughter Elizabeth, married firft to John Sidenham, Efq; fecondly to William Carfwell, of Carfwell, in Devonfhire, Efq; and thirdly to Henry Copplefton, Efq;

Sir Hugh Paulett, his eldeft fon, was knighted for his fervices in the French wars, at taking the Brey at the fiege of Boulogne, 1544, in the prefence of Hen. VIII. In 30 Hen. VIII. in

---

[f] P. 28. [g] Dugd. orig. jurid. p. 188. [h] Ibid. p. 221. [i] Ex regift. Dingley in cur prærog. Cant.

consideration of his services [k], he had a grant from the King, to him and his heirs, of the manour and borough of Samford-Peverell in Devonshire; and on February 24, 31 Hen. VIII. was [l] made supervisor of all the manours, messuages, lands, &c. belonging to Richard Whiting, late Abbot of Glastonbury, attainted. On May 11, 33 Hen. VIII. he had [m] a grant to him and his heirs of all the King's lands, tenements, woods, &c. called Upcrofte, and Combe, in Crukerne in the county of Somerset. He was Sheriff of Dorset and Somersetshire, in 29 and 34 Henry VIII. and 1st of Edward VI.

In 3 Edward VI. he was [n] Knight-Marshal of that army commanded by the Lord Russel (Lord Privy-Seal) sent against the rebels of Devonshire and Cornwall, who had besieged the city of Exeter; and being defeated by the King's forces, fled into Somersetshire, where this Sir Hugh followed them, and at King's-Weston again vanquished them, and took their leader prisoner. For these services he was, the year following, [o] made Governor of the isle of Jersey, and of Mount-Orguil castle.

In the 6th year of Q. Elizabeth, he was one of the principal commanders, who so valiantly defended Newhaven against the French [p], and when Montmorency, Constable of France, by a trumpet to the Earl of Warwick, summoned him to surrender; this Sir Hugh Paulett was sent by the Earl to assure the Constable, that the English were prepared to suffer the last extremity, before they would yield up the town without the Queen's orders. And when the forces were greatly reduced by the plague and pestilence, so that the Queen, in compassion to those brave soldiers that were living, gave directions to the Earl of Warwick to surrender the town [q], Sir Hugh Paulett was the principal of the commissioners that managed the conferences with the Constable of France, for the capitulation.

Dr. Fall, in his account of the island of Jersey, writes, That this Sir Hugh Paulett was Treasurer to Henry VIII's army at the siege of Boulogne; Governor of Havre de Grace, when the town was in the hands of the English; reputed one of the best and most experienced Captains of his time, and a zealous promoter of the reformation in the island of Jersey, of which he was Governor 24 years, and was succeeded by his son Sir Amias Paulett, in 13 Eliz.

He married Philippa, daughter and heir of Sir Lewis Pollard of King's Nympton in Devonshire, Knt. by whom he had issue

[k] Priv. Sigill. 30 H. VIII. [l] Bill. Signat. 31 H. VIII. [m] Priv. Sigill. 33 H. VIII. [n] Hollinshed, p. 1026. [o] Rymer, tom. 15. p. 261. [p] Cambden's hist. of Q. Eliz. in hist. of Engl. v. 2. p. 292. [q] Stow's Annals, p. 655.

three sons, Sir Amias Paulett, Nicholas, and George, father of Richard, wedded to Philip Carteret, Earl Granville's anceftor; as alfo a daughter Jane, wife of Chriftopher Copplefton, of Copplefton in Devonfhire, Efq;

His eldeft fon, Sir Amias Paulett, fucceeded him in the government of the ifle of Jerfey, as was faid before; and was knighted in 18 Eliz. In the year 1576, 19 Eliz. he was [r] Ambaffador to the French King; and in 27 Eliz. the keeping of Mary Queen of Scots [s] was chiefly committed to his fidelity, who fo honourably difcharged his truft therein, that when Secretary Walfingham moved him to fuffer one of his fervants to be bribed by the agents of the Queen of Scots, the better to gain intelligence, he would on no terms confent to it. In 29 Eliz. being one of the Privy-council, and Governor of the ifle of Jerfey, he was in [t] commiffion for the trial of the Queen of Scots. And in the year after, on the Eve of the feaft of St. George, was [u] fworn. at Greenwich, Chancellor of the moft noble order of the Garter: And was alfo Cuftos Rotulorum of the county of Somerfet.

He died in 1588, and was buried on the north fide of the chancel in the church of St. Martin in the Fields, London, where a noble monument was erected to his memory, of the Ionick order, with his effigies carved at full length, lying in armour, fenced with iron rails, and this infcription:

Honoratiffimo Patri Amitio Pouleto, Equiti aurato, Infulæ Jerfiæ præfecto, apud Chriftianiffimum Regem quondam legato, Nobiliffimi Ordinis Garterii Cancellario, & fereniffimæ Principis Elizabethæ Confiliario, Antonius Pouletus filius hoc Pietatis Monumentum mœrens pofuit.

Gardez la Foy.

Quod verbo fervare fidem, Poulette, folebas,
   Quam bene conveniunt hæc tria verba tibi?
Quod gladio fervare fidem, Poulette, folebas,
   Quam bene conveniunt hæc tria figna tibi?
Patria te fenfit, fenfit Regina fidelem,
   Sic fidus civis, ficque Senator eras.
Te fidum Chriftus, te fidum Ecclefia fenfit,
   Sic fervas inter multa pericla fidem.
Ergo quod fervo Princeps, Ecclefia nato,
   Patria quod fido cive fit orba dolet.
Interea Chriftus defuncti facta coronat,
   A quo fervatum viderat effe fidem, &c.

The reft is not legible.

---

[r] Fall's account of Jerfey, p. 91.   [s] Cambden's hift. præd. p. 501.   [t] Ibid. p. 501.   [u] Afhmole's ord. of the garter, p. 521.

*By the inquisition taken on Jan. 15, 1588-9, 31 Eliz. at the city of Wells, in the county of Somerset, it appears that Sir Amias Poulett, Knt. died on September 26, 1588, 30 Eliz. and was at the time of his decease, seized of the manour of George-Hinton, with appurtenances in Henton; the manours of Bymyngton, Henton-park, and farm of Combe; the manours of Chafcomb, Knolle, Illeigh, Stocklinch, Shepton, Roade, Sherfton, and Stalleigh, with the advowson of the church; the manour of Curry-Mallet, and Ruton, and advowson of the church and park of Curry-Mallet, by patent of July 5, in 8 Eliz. all in the county of Somerset; and the rectory with advowson of the church and park of Curry-Mallet, by patent July 6 in 8 Eliz. also one fourth of the manour of Crewkherne, and one fourth of the hundred of Crewkherne, all in the county of Somerset; one third of the manour of Marftland-Vale, in the county of Dorset; the manours of Stamford-Peverell, Uplomyn, with the advowson of the church, Halberton, and Boyes, in the county of Devon; and a granary, with garden-land to the fame belonging, containing one acre, in Clerkenwell in the county of Middlesex. And that Anthony Poulett was his son and heir, and then of the age of 25 years, by his wife Margaret, daughter and heir of Anthony Hervey, of Columb-John in com' Devon. Esq; and the said Anthony Hervey died on ˣ May 23, 1564, 6 Eliz. possessed of the manour of Wyndford-Ryvers in com' Somerf. which he had of the gift of Gertrude Courtney, Marchioness of Exeter, in 5 Phil. & Mar. and that his daughter and heir, Margaret, was of the age of 28 years, and married to Amias Paulett, Esq; all which is evident from the inquisition taken after his decease, July 22. He had issue by her three sons, Hugh, who died in his infancy, Sir Anthony Paulett, and George Paulett of Gothurst in com' Somerf. in right of his wife Elizabeth, daughter and heir of Edward Paulett, of the same place, Esq; lineally descended from John Paulett of Gothurst, brother to Sir William Paulett before mentioned, who first resided at Henton St. George. Also three daughters, Joan, married to Robert Heydon, of Bowood in com' Devon. Esq; Sarah, first wife of Sir Francis Vincent, of Stoke-Dabernon in Surry, Knt. and Bart. and Elizabeth, who died unmarried.

His eldest surviving son and heir, Sir Anthony Poulett, was also ʸ constituted Governor of the isle of Jersey, on the death of his father; was likewise Captain of the guard to Queen Eliz. who conferred the honour of knighthood on him; and in 1600, the 42d year of that reign, he departed this life; Sir Walter

w Coles Efc. Lib. 5. N. 61. A. 16. p. 328. in bibl. Harley.   x Ibid. Lib. 1. n. 61. a. 12. p. 31. in bibl. Harley.   y Fall's account of Jersey, p. 94.

Raleigh being on his deceafe [z] appointed Governor of Jerfey, on Auguft 26, the fame year. He [a] married, in 1583, Catharine, fole daughter to Henry Lord Norreys, Baron of Rycot, by whom he had iffue John his fon and heir, and Henry fecond fon, from whom the family at Prefton, and thofe that were of Taunton in Somerfetfhire, defcended; and two daughters, Margery, married to John Sidenham, of Combe in the county of Somerfet, Efq; and Sufan, the wife of Sir Peter Prideaux, of Netherton in Devonfhire, Bart.

Which John Poulett, Efq; being a very accomplifhed gentleman, of quick and clear parts, and a bountiful houfe-keeper (as Fuller in his Worthies of England relates [b]) K. Charles I. configned Monf. Soubize unto him, who gave him and his retinue many months liberal entertainment. After which he was by letters-patent, bearing date June 23, 1627, 3 Car. I. advanced [c] to the dignity of a Baron of this realm, by the title of Lord Poulett, of Henton St. George. He was [d] knighted with his eldeft fon, Sir John Poulett, by the Earl of Lindfey, on board his Majefty's fhip the Mary-honour, on September 27, 1635, with four other perfons of quality; being in that fleet then fent out to fecure our commerce, the Spanifh bullion, &c. in Englifh bottoms, which was expected home, and thought to be in danger from the Hollanders, who had lately made a league with France againft Spain. Which fervice our fleet performed.

In the year 1640, he was fummoned to that council appointed to meet at York, to advife his Majefty what method fhould be taken with the Scots, who had then invaded the northern parts of the kingdom. And this meeting producing a treaty at Rippon, he was appointed by the King, with feventeen other Peers, commiffioners for that purpofe, being (as Lord Clarendon writes [e]) all popular men, and not one of them of much intereft in the court, except the Earl of Holland. But when the parliament, that met foon after, engaged in defigns (as he thought) prejudicial to his Majefty's intereft, he manifefted the greateft diflike thereof, and immediately repaired to his Majefty at York; where he, with many other Lords and Counfellors, on June 15, 1642 [f], fubfcribed a declaration, difavowing any intention, either in the King, or themfelves, of raifing war againft the parliament. And an unnatural rebellion openly breaking out foon after, he moft loyally engaged both himfelf and his eldeft fon in the royal

[z] Rymer, tom. 16. p. 398. [a] Hollinfhed, p. 1355. [b] In com' Somerfet. p. 32. [c] Pat. 3 Car. I. p. 36. [d] Cat. of Knights, p. 152. [e] Hift. of the Rebell. 8vo. v. 1. p. 155. [f] Ibid. p. 655, 656.

cause; and having accepted of a commission to raise a regiment of 1,500 foot, he [g] accompanied the Marquis of Hertford into the west of England, by whose great reputation, and the interest of this Lord Poulett, with some other gentlemen of prime quality there, his Majesty hoped to form an army in those parts able to relieve Portsmouth, then besieged by the parliament's forces; ' they being (as Lord Clarendon writes) [h] like to give 'as good examples in their persons, and to be followed by as 'many men, as any such number of gentlemen in England 'could be.' However, after having, with less than 1000 men, withstood an army of 7000, commanded by the Earl of Bedford, and finding themselves unable, by reason of his coming, to draw more forces together, the Marquis and the Lord Poulett [i] transported themselves into Wales, where they [k] raised 21000 foot, and one regiment of horse.

In the year 1644, he was one of the principal commanders that besieged Lyme in Dorsetshire [l], which, after many gallant attacks, being almost reduced, was supplied with provisions by the Earl of Warwick, and the siege raised soon after by the Earl of Essex. Thereupon the parliament voted, that 1000 l. per annum, out of the Lord Poulett's estate, should be given to the inhabitants, in recompence for their service. The same year [m] he met his Majesty a mile from Exeter, in order to conduct him to that city; and on September 30, following, had the honour to [n] entertain him at his seat at Henton St. George. The year following the King was unsuccessful in all his undertakings, and the kingdom being reduced to the obedience of the parliament, he endeavoured to compound for his estate. But the houses of Peers and Commons differing in their opinions, the Lords [o] thinking fit to pardon him, and the Commons dissenting, he on April 20, 1646 [p], obtained leave to stay at Exeter, until he should compound with the parliament, or get a pass to transport himself out of England. However, on May 2 following, after a sharp debate, he, at the request of the General, was [q] permitted to compound; and the same day, on a petition from the town of Lyme, it was ordered they should have reparation out of his estate for the losses they had suffered by him. How far this was complied with, appears not; but his composition was not settled till three years after, when on March 6, 1648-9 [r], it was voted to be 4,200 l. and at the same time Sir John Paulett his son was likewise allowed to compound for 3,760 l.

[g] Ibid. p. 681. [h] Hist. præd. p. 715. [i] Ibid. v. 2. p. 20. [k] Hist. præd. p. 127. [l] Whitlock's memorials, p. 86. [m] Walker's historical disc. p. 47. [n] Ibid. p. 98. [o] Whitlock præd. p. 202. [p] Ibid. p. 207. [q] Ibid. p. 208. [r] Ibid. p. 278.

Poulett, Earl Poulett.

This noble Peer departed this life on March 20, 1649, having taken to wife Elizabeth, daughter and coheir to Christopher Ken, of Ken-court, in com' Somerf. Efq; who survived him, and was married secondly to John Afhburnham, of Afhburnham in com' Suff. Efq; (anceftor to the prefent Earl of Afhburnham) by whom fhe had no iffue: but by the Lord Paulett fhe had three fons and five daughters, viz. John his fucceffor; Francis, who married Catharine, daughter to Robert Creighton Bifhop of Bath; and Amias: Florence, married to Thomas Smith, of Long-Afhton in Somerfet, Efq; fecondly to Colonel Thomas Pigot of the kingdom of Ireland; Margaret, firft to Dennis Rolle, of Stephenfon in com' Devon. Efq; fecondly to Sir Richard Cholmley of Grofmont in com' Ebor. Knt. Banneret, Governor of Axminfter for Char. I. and laftly to Colonel Edward Cook of Highnam in com' Glouceft. Sufan, to Michael Warton of Beverley in com' Ebor. Efq; Helen, to William Wilmot, fon and heir to Sir George Wilmot of Charleton in Berkfhire, Knt. and dying May 12, 1651, was buried in Wantage church in the fame county, where a monument is erected to her memory; Elizabeth, youngeft daughter, was married firft to William Afhburnham of Afhburnham in com' Suff. Efq; anceftor by her to the prefent Earl; and afterwards to Sir William Hartop, of Rotherby in com' Leiceft. Knt.

John, fecond Lord Poulett, his eldeft fon and heir, received the honour of knighthood in his father's life-time, as before obferved; and being elected Knight of the fhire for the county of Somerfet to that parliament, which met on Nov. 3, 1640, he eminently manifefted his loyalty to his fovereign during the civil wars. He had the command of a regiment of foot, after the rebellion broke out in Ireland, and ferved fome time in that kingdom. But in the year 1643, it was [s] tranfported out of Munfter for the fervice of the weft, where he ferved. In 1645, he was befieged in the caftle of Winchefter (where the Lord Ogle commanded in chief) by Cromwell, who firft fummoned them to furrender, but being refufed, he battered it fo long with his guns, that he made a breach in the walls fit to enter, on which the caftle was delivered up, Oct. 14, and the officers and foldiers conveyed to Woodftock. He afterwards compounded for his eftate; and having lived to fee the reftoration of Charles II. departed this life at his manour-houfe of Court de Weeke, in Somerfetfhire, on September 15, 1665, in the 50th year of his age, and was buried at Hinton St. George.

[s] Clarendon præd. vol. 4. p. 468.

He married two wives; firſt, Catharine, daughter and co-heir to that famous General Sir Horatio Vere, Knt. Lord Vere, of Tilbury in Eſſex, widow of Oliver St. John, Eſq; by whom he had iſſue two ſons, John and Horatio; and three daughters, Elizabeth, married to Sir John Sydenham, of Brimpton, in com' Somerſ. Bart. who, dying anno 1669, was buried at Brimpton; Vere died unmarried; and Catharine, wedded to Mr. Secretary Johnſton. His Lordſhip married ſecondly Anne, ſecond daughter and coheir to Sir Thomas Brown, of Walcote, in com' Northamp. Bart. by whom he had iſſue two ſons, Amias, and Charles; alſo four daughters, Anne, Florence, and Mary, who all died young, and Margaret, married to Francis Fulford, of Fulford, in Devonſhire, Eſq;

John, his eldeſt ſon and heir, ſucceeded him in honour and eſtate. On July 6, 1674, he was appointed Lord-lieutenant of the county of Dorſet, and dying about the year 1680, left iſſue by his firſt wife Eſſex, eldeſt daughter to Alexander Popham, of Littlecote in com' Wilts, Eſq; two daughters, Catharine, ſecond wife to William Lord Lempſter, and Letitia, to Sir William Monſon, of Broxburn, in Hertfordſhire, Bart. by whom ſhe had no iſſue. By his ſecond Lady, Suſan, daughter of Philip Earl of Pembroke, he had iſſue John, his only ſon and heir.

Which John, 4th Lord Poulett, ſoon after the acceſſion of Queen Anne to the throne, was ſworn of her Privy-council; and having been one of the commiſſioners for the treaty of union, anno 1706, was the ſame year, on Dec. 29, created Viſcount of Hinton St. George, and Earl Poulett. For ſome years his Lordſhip declined accepting of ſeveral places of great diſtinction; and at length Queen Anne deſired to have him appointed firſt Lord-commiſſioner of the Treaſury, which his Lordſhip accepted of on Aug. 8, 1710; in which high ſtation he continued till the year 1711, when, on June 13, he was declared Lord-ſteward of her Majeſty's houſhold. He was alſo appointed, June 10, 1702, Lord-lieutenant of the county of Devon, and Cuſtos Rotulorum of Somerſetſhire, March 2, 1712-13. On Oct. 26, 1712, at a chapter then held, he was elected a Knight-companion of the moſt noble order of the Garter, but was not inſtalled till Auguſt 4 following; when his Lordſhip was Lord-ſteward of the houſhold, Lord-lieutenant and Cuſtos Rotulorum of Devonſhire, and Cuſtos Rotulorum of Somerſetſhire. He lived in the latter part of his life at his country ſeats, and died on May 28, 1743, in the 81ſt year of his age.

His Lordship married Bridget, daughter and coheir to Peregrine Bertie, of Waldershare, in Kent, Esq; brother to Robert Earl of Lindsey, and uncle to Robert Duke of Ancaster, and by her had four sons, and four daughters; 1. John Lord Viscount Hinton, late Earl Poulett; 2. Peregrine, who on a vacancy was chose member for Bossiney, in May, 1737, and died member for Bridgwater, Aug. 26, 1752; 3. Vere, now Earl Poulett; 4. Lady-Anne, so named by her Majesty Queen Anne, his godmother; 5. Lady Bridget, married, on May 21, 1724, to Polexfen Bastard, of Catley, in Devonshire, Esq; 6. Lady Catharine, who was wedded, on June 26, 1725, to John Parker, Esq; son and heir of George Parker, of Burrington, in the county of Devon, Esq; and died on Aug. 12, 1758; 7. Lady Susanna; and, 8. Lady Rebecca.

Which John, Lord Viscount Hinton, succeeded his father in his honours and estate, as second Earl Poulett. He was called up by writ to the house of Peers, Jan. 17, 1733-4, by the title of Lord Poulett, Baron of Hinton St. George, with precedence according to the creation of John Lord Poulett, June 23, 3 Car. I. and was appointed one of the Lords of his Majesty's bedchamber. On March 21, 1743, he was constituted Lord-lieutenant and Custos Rotulorum of the county of Somerset; but in March, 1755, resigned his place of Lord of the bedchamber. On the accession of the present King, his Lordship was continued in his offices of Lord-lieutenant and Custos Rotulorum of Somersetshire, and enjoyed them at his death, which happened on Novem. 3, 1764, when he was also Colonel of the first battalion of the militia of that county, and Recorder of Bridgwater.

His Lordship dying a bachelor, his estate and titles devolved on his brother Vere, before-mentioned, now third Earl Poulett, who was elected, in 1741, one of the members for the borough of Bridgwater, to the ninth parliament of Great-Britain, and on Novem. 16, 1764, was chosen Recorder of Bridgwater.

His Lordship, in 1754, married Mary, daughter of Richard Butt, of Arlingham, in Gloucestershire, Esq; and by her has ———, Lord Viscount Hinton, born on April 7, 1756; and another son, born in May, 1761.

TITLES.] Vere Poulett, Earl Poulett, Viscount and Baron Poulett, of Hinton St. George.

CREATIONS.] Baron Poulett, of Hinton St. George, in the county of Somerset, June 23, 1627, 3 Car. I. Viscount of the same place, and Earl Poulett, Dec. 24, 1706, 5th of Q. Anne.

ARMS.]

Poulet Earl Poulet.

Poulett, Earl Poulett.

ARMS.] Sable, three Swords in Pile, their Points in base, Argent, Pomels and Hilts, Or.

CREST.] On a Wreath, an Arm embowed, and brandishing a broad Sword, all proper.

SUPPORTERS.] On the dexter Side a Savage Man; on the sinister a Woman, both proper, wreathed about their Temples and Loins with Ivy, Vert.

MOTTO.] GARDEZ LA FOY.

CHIEF-SEATS.] At Hinton St. George, in the county of Somerset, 2 miles from Crokehorn, and 133 from London. And at Buckland, in the county of Dorset, 6 miles from Dorchester, and 96 from London.

GODOLPHIN, Earl of Godolphin.

THIS family is denominated from Godolphin (anciently written Godolghan) in the county of Cornwall, as is evident, [a] as well from ancient records, as from the white eagle, which the name in Cornish imports, and has been constantly borne in their coat of arms.

John de Godolphin, who was living about the time of the Norman conquest, being, among other his possessions, lord of the manour of Godolphin, and residing there, was from thence denominated. And [b] by his wife Margaret, daughter of Roger Treworgan, of Treworgan, in Cornwall, had issue Richard his son and heir, father of James de Godolphin, whose son, John de Godolphin, left issue Thomas de Godolphin, whose successor Edward de Godolphin, [c] marrying Maud, daughter of William Boteler, of Carnanton, Esq; had issue William de Godolphin, from whom proceeded Thomas de Godolphin, his son and heir, father of Edward de Godolphin, of Godolphin, Esq;

Which Edward [d], by his wife Christian, daughter of Thomas Prideaux, Esq; had issue Alexander Godolphin, Esq; who married Mary, daughter of Sir John de Tregour, and had William his son and heir, father of David Godolphin, of Godolphin, Esq;

Which David Godolphin, Esq; taking to wife Meliora, daughter of John Cowling, of Trewerveneth, Esq; left issue only Eleanor, his daughter and heir [e], married to John Rinsey, Esq; [f] of an ancient family in the same county, but being a great heiress, it was covenanted, that his descendants should bear the name of Godolphin. They had issue Thomas Godolphin, of Godolphin, Esq; who took to wife Isabel, daughter of ——— Benne, of Boskenna, in com' Cornub. Esq; and was succeeded by John, his son and heir.

Which John Godolphin, Esq; married Elizabeth, daughter of John Beauchamp, of Bennerton, in com' Cornub. Esq; and by her was father of a son of his own name, John Godolphin, Esq; who wedded Elizabeth, daughter of John Killigrew, Esq; and was succeeded by his son and heir, another John Godolphin, Esq; [g] who was Sheriff of Cornwall in 19 Henry VII.

a Carew's survey of Cornwall, p. 253.   b Seager's Baronagium genealog. in stemmate hujus fam. MS. in bibl. Cotton.   c Ibid.   d Ex stemmate.
e Seager ut antea.   f Ibid.   g Fuller's worthies, p. 100.

and in 23 Hen. VII. he and Sir Robert Willoughby, Lord Brook, Steward of the mines in Cornwall and Devonshire [h], had a pardon for all forfeitures, penalties, &c. relating to the tin-works and courts. He married Margaret, daughter of John Trenouth, Esq; and had issue a daughter Elizabeth, wedded to William Canell, Esq; as also two sons, William and John Godolphin, whose descendants were seated at Morewale and Treweryeneth, in the county of Cornwall.

The eldest son, William Godolphin, Esq; [i] married Margaret, daughter and one of the three coheirs of John Glinne, of Moreval, and Lowewater, by whom he had issue two sons, Sir William Godolphin, and Thomas Godolphin, Esq; from whom the present Earl of Godolphin is lineally descended.

Sir William Godolphin was a person of great note in the reign of Hen. VIII. who, for his services, conferred on him the honour of knighthood, and [k] constituted him Warden and chief Steward of the Stannaries. He lived to a great age; was several times chosen one of the Knights of the shire [l] for Cornwall, in the parliaments of Hen. VIII. and Edw. VI. He was also Sheriff of the said county [m] in 21, 25, 30 Hen. VIII. 3 Edw. VI. and 10th year of Queen Elizabeth. He likewise acquired much fame, by his conduct and intrepidity, in several military commands [n], particularly at the siege of Boulogne. Mr. Carew, in his Survey of Cornwall, ranks this Sir William Godolphin among the principal worthies of that county, giving this account of him [o]: ' He demeaned himself ' very valiantly beyond the seas, as appeared by the scars he ' brought home, no less to the beautifying of his fame, than ' the disfiguring of his face.' He took to wife Blanch, daughter of Robert Langden, Esq; by whom he had three daughters, Margaret, married to Sir Robert Verney; Grace, married to Sir John Sydenham, of Brimpton, in com' Somers. and Anne, wedded to Sir John Arundel, of Talvern, in com' Cornub. but leaving no issue male, the estate devolved on his nephew Francis Godolphin, Esq; son and heir of his brother Thomas Godolphin, Esq;

Which Thomas Godolphin was at the siege of Boulogne, with his brother Sir William Godolphin; and on Thursday, Aug. 14, 1544, he [p], Mr. Harper, and Mr. Culpepper, were hurt with one shot from the town. He married ——, daughter of Edmund Bonithon, Esq; and left issue two sons, Francis, and

h MS. de com. Cornub. p. 240. not. p. 33. in bibl. J. Anstis, arm. gart. reg. arm.   i Leland, p. 498.   k MS. de com. Cornub. ut antea, p. 286. l Willis's Not. parl. v. 2. p. 12.   m Fuller's worthies, p. 208, 209.   n Carew's survey of Cornw. p. 153.   o Ibid. p. 61, 62.   p Rymer's fœd. tom. 15. p. 45.

Godolphin, Earl of Godolphin.

William Godolphin, Esq; one of the members for Helston, in the parliament of the 28th of Queen Elizabeth, and had to [q] wife one of the two coheirs of Gaurigan. Francis Godolphin, eldest son, succeeded his uncle Sir William Godolphin, in the ancient inheritance of the family, and was knighted by [r] Queen Elizabeth, at Richmond, on Sunday, Nov. 20, 1580. His knowledge in the laws, his love for justice and equity, and his affection to her Majesty's government, raised him to all the posts of honour, consistent with a country life, which he rather chose, than an attendance on the court, where his great abilities might have further advanced him. He was returned one of the Knights for the county of Cornwall [s], to the parliament held in 31 Eliz. and served for the [t] borough of Lestwithiel in the next parliament, which met at Westminster in 35 Eliz. In that reign he was the first in the commission of the peace [u], and of the quorum; as also the first [w] in the lieutenantcy of the county of Cornwall, and Colonel of a regiment of 12 companies, armed with 470 pikes, 490 muskets, and 240 calivers. He was also Governor of Scilly, which (as Mr. Carew, my [x] author, saith) by her Majesty's order, ' was reduced to a more defensible
' plight by him, who with his invention and purse, bettered
' his plot and allowance, and therein so tempered strength with
' delight, and both with use, as it serveth for a sure hold, and
' a commodious dwelling.' This most ingenious Knight, having always the good of his country in his thoughts, entertained a Dutch mineral man [y], and taking light from his experience, built thereon far more profitable conclusions, practising a more saving way to make tin of what was, before, rejected for refuse. He likewise undertook the coinage of silver out of mines in Wales, and Cornwall; and Charles I. (for he was living on his accession to the throne) for his encouragement, and saving of expence, granted [z] him the power of coinage, at Aberrusky, in Cornwall; and the pence, groats, shillings, half-crowns, &c. of this silver, had the ostrich feathers (the cognizance of the Prince of Wales) for distinction, stamped on them. He likewise distinguished himself in the defence of his country, in July, 1595, shewing the greatest courage, and most approved conduct, in resisting the Spaniards, who landed near Pensance in Cornwall, of which Mr. Carew gives a very particular account [a]; and acknowledged, in his survey of Cornwall [b], ' That from him he gathered sticks to

q Carew, p. 150.　　r MS. in bibl. Cotton. Claudius, c. 3. p. 247.　　s Willis ut antea, p. 12.　　t Ibid. p. 42.　　u Carew, p. 88.　　w Ibid. p. 83.
x Ibid. p. 55.　　y Fuller's worthies, p. 211.　　z Ibid. in Wales, p. 20.
a Carew, p. 157.　　b Ibid. p. 13.

build

'build that nest, and was assistant unto him in that playing
'labour ᶜ,' as he termeth it; and gives this memorable character of him about the latter end of the reign of Queen Elizabeth:
 'Sir Francis Godolphin, Knt. whose zeal in religion, up-
'rightness in justice, providence in government, and plentiful
'house-keeping, have won him a very great and reverent re-
'putation in his country; and these virtues, together with his
'services to her Majesty, are so sufficiently known to those
'of highest place, as my testimony can add but little light
'thereunto. But by his labours and inventions in tin mat-
'ters, not only the whole country hath felt a general benefit,
'so as the several owners have thereby gotten very great profit
'out of such refuse works, as they before had given over for
'unprofitable; but her Majesty hath also received increase
'of her customs by the same, at least to the value of 10,000 l.
'Moreover, in those works, which are of his own particular
'inheritance, he continually keepeth at work 300 persons, or
'thereabouts; and the yearly benefit, that out of those his
'works accrueth to her Majesty, amounteth, communibus
'annis, to 1000 l. at the least, and sometimes to much more.
'A matter very remarkable, and perchance not to be matched
'again, by any of his sort and condition in the whole
'realm.'

He married Margaret, daughter of John Killigrew, of Arn-
wick, in com' Cornub. Esq; by whom he had three sons, William, his heir; John, of whom afterwards; and Francis, who
died without issue; as also six daughters, Blanch, married to
ᵈ George Keckwith, of Catch-French, Esq; (a seat so named
from a memorable accident) a gentleman of continual large
and inquisite liberation to the poor, beyond the imitation of
any other in the shire, faith Mr. Carew; Ursula, second daughter, wedded to John Credye, Esq; Thomasin, third daughter, the first wife of Sir George Carew, afterwards, on Feb.
5, 1625-6, created Earl of Totnefs; Jane, Elizabeth, and
Margaret. He married, to his second wife, Alice, relict of
Sir John Gianville, a Justice of the King's-bench, and mother
to Sir Francis Glanville, of Kilworthy, in com' Devon. Knt.
She was also relict of this Sir Francis, in 1625.

John, second son of Sir Francis Godolphin, and Margaret
Killigrew, before-mentioned, wedded Judith, daughter of
Thomas Meredith, of Ashley-castle in Cheshire, Esq; and by
her was father of two sons, Sir William Godolphin, his heir,
of whom afterwards; and John Godolphin, LL.D.

ᶜ Carew, p. 153.   ᵈ Ibid. p. 109.

Godolphin, Earl of Godolphin.

The said John Godolphin, LL.D. married four wives, but had only issue by the first, Mary Tregoss, and the fourth, Rebecca Wallis, by whom he was father of a daughter, named Rebecca, after her mother, and wedded to Samuel Edwards, of Frodesley, in Shropshire, Esq; By his first wife, he had a son, Colonel Sidney Godolphin, Governor of Scilly, and Auditor of Wales; who, by his wife Susannah Tannat, of Aber-Tannat, in Shropshire, was father of one son, Tannat Godolphin, who died in the army in Flanders, aged 21. This Sidney had also, by his said wife, five daughters, 1. Margaret; 2. Mary, wedded to Henry Godolphin, D.D. Provost of Eaton-college, and Dean of St. Paul's cathedral, hereafter-mentioned; 3. Penelope, first married to Francis Hoblyn, of Wanswhyden, in Cornwall, Esq; (by whom she was mother of Thomas Hoblyn, Esq; member for Bristol, in 1747) and, 2dly, to Sir William Pendaws; 4. Elizabeth, who died unmaried; and, 5. Frances, who died young in 1754.

Sir William Godolphin, eldest son and heir of John Godolphin, Esq; and Judith Meridith, before-mentioned, by ———, his wife, daughter of ———, had, 1. Francis Godolphin, of Coulston, in Wiltshire, Esq; 2. Sir William Godolphin, who died Ambassador in Spain; and, 3. Sir John Godolphin, who, by ———, his wife, daughter of ——— ———, was father of Elizabeth Godolphin, who died Maid of Honour to Queen Catharine, the consort of King Charles II.

Francis Godolphin, of Coulston, Esq; eldest son of Sir William Godolphin, wedded Elizabeth, daughter and coheir of Nicholas Johnson, Esq; and by her had two sons, and one daughter, viz. William, who was Governor of Scilly, and died without issue; Francis, 2d son, continuator of the line; and Elizabeth, married to Charles Godolphin, Esq; Commissioner of the Customs, and Regifter-general of all the trading-ships belonging to Great-Britain, of whom more fully afterwards.

Francis, 2d son, was Governor of Scilly: and by ———, his wife, daughter of ——— ———, had two sons, and three daughters, viz. Major William Godolphin, of Coulston aforesaid; Francis Godolphin, Esq; who was Deputy-governor of Scilly, and died a batchelor; Elizabeth, married to ——— Burston, Esq; Barbara, married to the Rev. Mr. Mappletoft; and Mary, to Capt. Cobb.

William Godolphin, eldest son and heir of Sir Francis Godolphin, and his wife, Margaret Killigrew, mentioned before, was one of those gentlemen of quality, who accompanied Robert Earl of Essex, in his expedition to Ireland against the rebels,

Godolphin, Earl of Godolphin.

rebels, A. D. 1599; and for his valour at Arclo [e], was, with William Courtney, Esq; knighted by the said Earl, on his return to Dublin. He set out with great reputation, having, besides a very liberal education, travelled into most parts of Europe, and attained several languages. Mr. Carew [f] makes this honourable mention of him; 'That he had so enriched 'himself with sufficiency for matters of policy, by his long 'travels; and for martial affairs, by his present carriage in 'Ireland, that it is better known how far he outgoeth most 'others in both, than easily to be discerned; for which he de-'serveth principal commendation.' He had so far signalized himself by his valour and conduct, that on the Spanish invasion, in the latter end of the year 1600, he was in such esteem with the Lord Montjoy, Lord deputy of Ireland, that he entrusted him with the command of his own brigade of horse, in the decisive battle between the Queen's forces, and the Spaniards and rebels [g], fought on Dec. 24, within a mile of Kinsale; which victory was principally owing to his gallant service, having broke through the whole body of Spaniards [h], entirely routed them, taking their chief commander prisoner, whereupon the Irish immediately threw away their arms, and fled. In this action he was [i] slightly wounded in the thigh with a halbert; but in six days after was so well recovered of it, that when Don John d'Aquila, commander of the Spaniards in the town of Kinsale, offered a parley, desiring the Lord-deputy, [k] that some gentlemen of special trust and sufficiency might be sent into the town to confer with him, and to receive his proposals, he was [l] employed in the negociation (related verbatim by Stow, in his [m] annals) which was brought to a conclusion on Jan. 2, 1601, the Spaniards agreeing to quit all places in that kingdom.

Sir William Godolphin afterwards performed divers services against the rebels; and on March 20, 1601-2, for the great trust reposed in him [n], and the good opinion had of his discreet judgment, he was specially appointed to confer with the Earl of Tyrone, and receive (according to his request) his humble submission to her Majesty. In the year 1603, he [o] commanded in the province of Leinster; and the rebels being subdued, he returned into England, soon after the death of Queen Elizabeth.

In the first parliament called by King James, he was unanimously elected one [p] of the Knights for the county of Corn-

e Jekyl's cat. of Knights, MS.   f Survey, p. 62.   g Cox's hist. Irel. p. 445.
h Stow's annals, p. 799.   i Ibid. p. 800.   k Stow præd.   l Speed's chron. p. 902.   m Ibid. p. 801, & seq.   n Morison's itinerary, part 2. p. 248.   o Ibid. p. 297.   p Willis, p. 13.

wall, on the deceafe of Sir Jonathan Trelawney, Knt. and departing this life, A. D. 1613, left iffue, by Thomafin his wife, daughter and heir of Thomas Sidney, of Wrighton, in com' Norf. Efq; one daughter, Penelope, baptized in the parifh of St. Margaret's, Weftminfter, July 13, 1607, married to Sir Charles Berkeley, Lord Vifcount Fitzharding; and three fons, Francis, Sidney, and William Godolphin, all eminent for their valour, conduct, and fobriety.

William q, the youngeft, had the command of a regiment, and performed many fignal fervices for Charles I. in feveral remarkable actions in the Weft. And Sidney, the fecond fon, loft his life in the royal caufe at Chagford in Devonfhire: ' A young gentleman of incomparable parts (as the Earl of ' Clarendon relates r) who being of a conftitution and educa- ' tion more delicate and unacquainted with contentions, upon ' his obfervation of the wickednefs of thofe men in the houfe ' of Commons, of which he was a member, out of the pure ' indignation of his foul againft them, and confcience to his ' country, had, with the firft, engaged himfelf with that party ' in the weft: and though he thought not fit to take command ' in a profeffion he had not willingly chofen, yet as his advice ' was of great authority with all the commanders, being al- ' ways one in the council of war, and whofe notable abilities ' they had ftill ufe of in their civil tranfactions, fo he expofed ' his perfon to all action, travel and hazard; and by too for- ' ward engaging himfelf (in this action at Chagford) received ' a mortal fhot by a mufket, a little above the knee, of which ' he died in the inftant, leaving the misfortune of his death ' on a place, which could never otherwife have had a men- ' tion in the world.' He was buried s in the chancel of the church of Okehampton, in Devonfhire, on Feb. 10, 1642-3. In the year 1624, he became a ftudent in Exeter college, Oxford, and by his incomparable wit, and exact judgment, gained the love and efteem of all the learned in the Univerfity. The famous Mr. Hobbes t gives this fhining character of him: ' There is not any virtue that difpofeth a man either to the ' fervice of God, or to the fervice of his country, to civil fo- ' ciety, or to private friendfhip, that did not manifeftly ap- ' pear in his converfation; not as acquired by neceffity, or ' affected upon occafion, but inherent and fhining in a gene- ' rous conftitution of his nature.' And the fame author, in another place, writes thus of him: ' I have known clearnefs ' of judgment, and largenefs of fancy, ftrength of reafon, and

q Clarendon's hift. of the rebellion, 8vo, vol. 3. p. 134, 269.   r Ibid. p. 135.
s Wood's Athenæ Oxon. p. 24.   t In his preface to the Leviathan.

graceful

Godolphin, Earl of Godolphin.

'graceful elocution, a courage for the war, and fear for the
' laws, and all eminently in one man, and that was my moſt
' noble and honoured friend Mr. Sidney Godolphin, who
' hated no man, nor hated of any, was unfortunately ſlain in
' the beginning of the late civil war, in a public quarrel, by
' an undiſcerned and undiſcerning hand.' Yet Lord Clarendon obſerves [u], ' That of all men living, there were no
' two more unlike than Mr. Godolphin and Mr. Hobbes, in
' the modeſty of nature, or integrity of manners; but Mr.
' Godolphin deſerved all the elogy he gives of him.' He was
one of the moſt eminent poets of his time, and among other
his compoſitions, he tranſlated, into Engliſh verſe, The Paſſion
of Dido for Æneas, as it is incomparably expreſſed in the
fourth book of Virgil, printed at London, 1658, and publiſhed
by the celebrated Edmund Waller, Eſq;

Francis Godolphin, Eſq; the eldeſt ſon, ſucceeded to a great
eſtate on the death of his grandfather Sir Francis; he was baptized in the pariſh of St. Margaret's Weſtminſter, Dec. 27, 1605,
and returned to parliament for the county of Cornwall in the firſt
of Charles I. and for the borough of St. Ives, in the third year
of that King; [w] as alſo to that parliament, which met at
Weſtminſter, Nov. 3, 1640; when diſcerning the artifices of
ſome of the leading members of that houſe, tending to the
ruin of the eſtabliſhed government, both in church and ſtate,
he retired to his ſeat in Cornwall, ſecured the iſland of Scilly
for the King, and raiſed a regiment of foot, the command
whereof was given to his brother Colonel William Godolphin,
before-mentioned. He afterwards waited on his Majeſty at
Oxford, and was among thoſe members [x], who met there by
his royal appointment in Jan. 1643-4.

He was one of [y] the 43 Noblemen and Gentlemen, who
ſigned a declaration, Jan. 27, 1643-4, of ſuch means as might
moſt probably ſettle the peace of the kingdom, at Oxford.

The iſland of Scilly was under his command, till after the
King was a priſoner to his rebellious ſubjects; and then, finding all places given up to the predominant party, and that it
was impoſſible to maintain himſelf againſt their power, he ſurrendered on honourable conditions, Sept. 16, 1646. The
Commons voted, on Jan. 4, 1646-7, ' That Mr. Godol-
' phin, Governor of Scilly [z], upon his ſurrender of that iſland,
' with all forts, &c. ſhould enjoy his eſtate, and be free from
' arreſts for any acts of war.' His ſequeſtration was taken
off from the preceding Michaelmas; but was to ſue out his

---

[u] In his brief view and ſurvey of Mr. Hobbs's Leviathan.   [w] Willis, p. 130.   [x] Annals of K. Charles, p. 878.   [y] Ruſhworth's hiſt. collections, p. 3, & 566.   [z] Whitlock's memorials, p. 237.

pardon

pardon under the Great Seal, and take the negative oath and covenant [a].

For his known loyalty, he was created one of the Knights of the Bath, at the coronation of Charles II. and having married Dorothy, second daughter of Sir Henry Berkeley, of Yarlington, in com' Somerf. Knt. had issue by her sixteen children, whereof William, his eldest son and heir, succeeded him in his estate.

Which William Godolphin, of Godolphin, Esq; was created a Baronet, on April 29, 1661, and enjoying a great fortune, chose retirement from all public business, and celibacy, to the time of his death, which happened at his house in Suffolk-street, on Aug. 17, 1710; and was buried on Sept. 3 following, in the south isle of Westminster-abbey, leaving his estate to his nephew, Francis Earl of Godolphin.

Francis, second son, also died unmarried in the reign of Charles II.

Of Sidney, third son, I am principally to treat.

Henry Godolphin, fourth son of Sir Francis, had his education in All-Souls college, in Oxford, and took his degree of Doctor of Divinity, on July 11, 1685. On Oct. 30, 1695, he was instituted Provost of Eaton college; and on July 18, 1707, was installed Dean of the cathedral church of St. Paul. He died at Eaton, near Windsor, Jan. 29, 1732-3, in the 84th year of his age, and enjoyed the use of his faculties to the last. He was very exemplary for his piety and charity; a great encourager of learning and virtue, without distinction of party; and so careful in the choice of the persons he preferred, that he was hardly ever deceived in any instance. He has left many marks of his munificence at Eaton college, of which he was Provost 37 years; and was a great benefactor to the bounty of Queen Anne, for the augmentations of small livings, to which he gave at one time 4000 l. The corporation of the sons of the clergy likewise partook largely of his bounty, having given twice, within a very few years, 500 l. and to their collection, on Thursday before he died, 100 l. besides great sums given in private charity, for the relief of poor families, and single persons in distress. As he was Dean of St. Paul's, in 1726, being desirous to retire, he resigned that dignity, in favour of Dr. Hare, afterwards Bishop of St. Asaph, and Chichester; so uncommon an instance of generosity and friendship, that nothing more need be added to compleat his character. He married Mary, daughter of Col. Sidney Godolphin, Governor of Scilly, and Auditor of Wales, before-men-

[a] Journ. of parl. vol. 5. p. 42.

tioned:

tioned: and left issue, Henry, who died on June 3, 1722; and William Godolphin, Esq; who, in February, 1733-4, married the Lady Barbara, youngest daughter of William Bentinck, Earl of Portland, by his second Lady; and she dying without issue, on April 15, 1736, he married, on May 28, 1748, Lady Anne, second daughter of John Earl Fitz-William. He also left one daughter Mary, married, in 1730, to William Owen, of Porkington, a gentleman of very considerable estate near Oswestry, in Shropshire; and Francis Godolphin, of Baylis, in com' Buckingh. heir apparent to the Barony of Helston.

Charles Godolphin, fifth son, was chosen one of the members for Helston, in that parliament which assembled at Oxford on March 21, 1680-1, and served in every parliament after, both in the reigns of King James and King William. He was one of the Commissioners of the Customs for several years, in the reigns of K. William and Q. Anne, appointed thereto by that Queen, Jan. 23, 1711-12; and was also Register-general of all trading-ships belonging to Great-Britain. He married Elizabeth, daughter of Francis Godolphin, of Coulston, in Wilts, Esq; before-mentioned; and died in the year 1720. Against the wall, on the west side of the cloisters, in Westminster-abbey, is a large neat marble monument erected to his memory, and, within the pediment, the arms of Godolphin, impaling Godolphin, below which is the following inscription:

Here rest in hope of a blessed Resurrection, CHARLES GODOLPHIN, Esq; Brother to the Right Honourable SIDNEY Earl of GODOLPHIN,
Lord High-Treasurer of Great Britain, who died July 10, 1720, aged 69.
And Mrs. GODOLPHIN his Wife, who died July 29, 1726, aged 63.
Whose excellent Qualities and Endowments can never be forgotten.
Particularly the publick-spirited Zeal with which he served his Country in parliament, and the indefatigable Application,
Great Skill and nice Integrity, with which he discharg'd the Trust of a Commissioner of the Customs for many years.
Nor was she less eminent for her Ingenuity, Wit, sincere Love of her Friends, and Constancy in Religious Worship.
But as Charity and Benevolence were the distinguishing Parts of their Characters,
So were they most conspicuously display'd by the last Act of their Lives.

Godolphin, Earl of Godolphin.

A pious and charitable Inftitution by him defign'd and ordered,
And by her compleated to the Glory of God, and for a bright Example to Mankind.

The endowment whereof is a rent-charge of one hundred and eighty pounds a year, iffuing out of lands in Somerfetfhire ; and of which one hundred and fixty pounds a year are to be for ever applied, from the 24th of June, 1726, to the educating eight young gentlewomen, who are fo born, and whofe parents are of the church of England ; whofe fortunes do not exceed three hundred pounds, and whofe parents, or friends, will undertake to provide them with decent apparel; and after the death of the faid Mrs. GODOLPHIN, and WILLIAM GODOLPHIN, Efq; her nephew, fuch as have neither father or mother; which fame young gentlewomen are not to be admitted before they are eight years old, nor to be continued after the age of nineteen ; and are to be brought up in the city of New Sarum, or fome other town in the county of Wilts, under the care of fome prudent governefs, or fchoolmiftrefs, a communicant of the church of England ; and the overplus, after an allowance of five pounds a year, for collecting the faid rent-charge, is to be applied to the binding out one or more poor children apprentices, whofe parents are of the church of England.

In perpetual memory whereof, Mrs. FRANCES HALL, Executrix to her Aunt Mrs. GODOLPHIN, has, according to her Will, and by her Order, caus'd this Infcription to be engraven on their Monument, 1727.

I now return to Sidney Godolphin, third fon of Sir Francis, who by his wifdom, unblemifhed integrity, and many rare accomplifhments, rofe to high honours, and left a fhining example to pofterity. He was from his youth in the fervice of Charles II. who, when Prince of Wales, coming into Cornwall, there took particular notice of him ; and after his reftoration, made him one of the Grooms of his bedchamber [b]. In the year 1663, being in waiting on the King at Oxford, he had the degree of Mafter of Arts conferred on him. He was returned for Helfton, in Cornwall, in that called the long parliament, which began at Weftminfter, May 8, 1661, and ferved for that borough, and St. Maws, in all parliaments whilft he continued a Commoner. In February, 1678, the

[b] Wood's Fafti Oxon. p. 830.

French

Godolphin, Earl of Godolphin.

French King having taken Ghent and Ypres, it gave such an alarm to Holland, as disposed them to a peace on any terms, whereof Charles II. having notice by his ministers, he [c] dispatched Mr. Godolphin immediately into Holland, to bring the last and surest account he could get of the States resolution on that grand affair, and to return with the greatest speed he could. He performed this commission so much to the satisfaction of his Majesty, and his ministry, that the King seeming resolved to go into a war against France, he [d] was again posted into Holland about the middle of April, to know the final resolutions of the States-general. He had been there but a very short time, before he wrote to court, that the Dutch absolutely desired the peace, even upon the terms proposed by France; and had resolved to send Monsieur Van Lewen to England, to dispose the King to be contented with them.

Soon after Mr. Godolphin's return, Sir William Temple was appointed to go into Holland, on the resolution of the King and council, to enter into a war against France, in case the French persisted in their refusal to evacuate the towns they were to deliver to the Spaniards by a time prefixed. And upon this dispatch, Sir William Temple remarks [e], ' That Mr. Godolphin, ' who had been so lately in Holland, told him, that if he ' brought the States to the treaty his Majesty proposed on this ' occasion, he would move the parliament to have his statue ' set up.' Thus heartily did Mr. Godolphin engage, to stop the growth of the power of France, which he then thought was dangerous to Europe. And Sir William Temple, in a letter to him from the Hague (July 29, N. S. 1678) after giving an account of his negociation, makes this conclusion: ' In short, the King is once more at the head of all the affairs ' in Christendom: what use he will make of it, is in his own ' hands, and those of his ministers and servants that are about ' him. Among whom, as I know no man that wishes better ' at heart to his Majesty and his kingdoms than you do, so I ' am sure no man can wish better to you in all points than I do, ' nor more desire the occasions of expressing the sincere truth ' and passion, as well as esteem, wherewith I am, and shall ' be always, &c.' On the dismission of the Earl of Danby, from being Lord High-treasurer of England, he was constituted (March 26, 1679) one of the Commissioners of the Treasury; and by his notable dexterity in business, and assiduity, was soon after, [f] considered as one of the ablest men belonging to

[c] Temple's memoirs, part 2. p. 213.   [d] Ibid. p. 315.   [e] Memoirs, p. 330.   [f] Bp. Burnet's hist. of his own times, p. 487.

the court, and sworn, Feb. 4, 1679-80, one of his Majesty's Privy-council.

When the house of Commons grew warm in the prosecution of the popish plot, and were often addressing the King, to bestow pensions on one or other of the evidences, without raising the necessary supplies for his Majesty's service, he thought it became him to take notice of it, and among other particulars said, 'That since they were so forward in their ad-
'dresses to his Majesty, to give such pensions, he thought it
'would be necessary for them to consider of the means to en-
'able him to do it.' By his prudent management, he gained a great ascendant in the council, and Sir William Temple informs us [g], 'That the Earl of Sunderland, Mr. Hyde, and Mr. Go-
'dolphin, were esteemed to be alone in the secret management
'of the King's affairs, and looked upon as the ministry.'

In the year 1680, finding the parliament insisting on the exclusion of the Duke of York, he declared [h] openly for it; as at that time the interest of England, and affairs of Europe, made a league against France indispensibly necessary, which could not be done, without a good understanding at home. And on the debate in council, concerning the Duke's stay, or going back into Scotland before the parliament met [i], he joined absolutely in the reasons and advices of his going away; and tho' the rest of the council were of the contrary opinion, yet the King fell in with his and Lord Sunderland's reasons. He [k] excused himself from carrying his Majesty's message to the house (Jan. 4, 1680-1) 'That he could never consent to the
'exclusion of the Duke,' and thereupon Sir William Temple delivered it. But so far was it from giving satisfaction, that the house resolved and declared, 'That until a bill be passed,
'for the exclusion of the Duke of York, they cannot give
'any supply to his Majesty, without danger to his Majesty's
'person, extreme hazard of the protestant religion, and un-
'faithfulness to those by whom they were entrusted.'

On the resignation of Sir Leoline Jenkins, one of his Majesty's principal Secretaries of State, April 14, 1684, he was sworn into that office on the 17th of that month, in the council held at Hampton-court. But not liking his place of Secretary of State, and desiring to be again in the Treasury, where his management had given great satisfaction both to the King and people, he was, by his Majesty, declared first Commissioner of the Treasury, on August 24 following. And in consideration of his great merit and services, was, on Sept. 8, 1684, advanced to the dignity and title of a Baron of this king-

[g] Memoirs, part 3. p. 87. [h] Burnet, p. 481. [i] Temple, part 3. p. 115. [k] Ibid. p. 130.

dom, by the name and ſtyle of Baron Godolphin, of Rialton in the county of Cornwall.

On the acceſſion of James II. to the throne, when the Earl of Rocheſter was conſtituted Lord High-treaſurer of England, he was declared Lord-chamberlain to the Queen. But on the removal of the Earl of Rocheſter, his Lordſhip was again appointed one of the Commiſſioners of the Treaſury, Jan. 5, 1686-7.

On the landing of the Prince of Orange, and King James being reſolved to go in perſon to the Weſt, his Lordſhip was in the number of thoſe, to whom he committed the adminiſtration of affairs in his abſence. And on the King's return from Saliſbury to London, the Marquis of Hallifax, the Earl of Nottingham, and the Lord Godolphin, were ſpecially deputed by King James, to go to the Prince, and to aſk him what it was that he demanded ; whereupon waiting [1] on his Highneſs at Hungerford, after conferring with the Earls of Oxford, Shrewſbury, and Clarendon, they received the Prince's anſwer, on Sunday, December 8, 1688. On their coming to London, they were much ſurpriſed to hear of the ſudden departure of his Majeſty, who after, his return from Feverſham to Whitehall, and miſſing of Monſ. de Zuleſtein (who was ſent to deſire his ſtay at Rocheſter) he made choice of the Lord Godolphin to wait on his Highneſs, to propoſe his going back to Rocheſter.

In the debate on the vacancy of the throne, his Lordſhip, and many other noble Peers, out of their tender regard to the ſucceſſion, voted for a Regency : Nevertheleſs, when their Majeſties King William and Queen Mary were on, Aſh-Wedneſday, Feb. 13, 1688-9, proclaimed King and Queen of England, knowing his great abilities and integrity, they conſtituted him one of the Lords-commiſſioners of the treaſury; and the management thereof ſeemed wholly to depend on his Lordſhip, none of the other Commiſſioners (who where Charles Lord Mordaunt, afterwards Earl of Peterborough, Henry Lord Delamere, afterwards Earl of Warrington, Richard Hambden, Eſq; and Sir Henry Capel) having ever been employed in that intricate office before. He was alſo ſworn of their Majeſty's Privy-council, Feb. 16, 1688-9 ; and in November, 1690, on an alteration in the commiſſion of the treaſury, his Lordſhip was conſtituted firſt Lord-commiſſionnr of it, the other four being Sir John Lowther, Vice-chamberlain of the Houſhold, Richard Hambden, Eſq; Chancellor of the Exchequer, Sir Stephen Fox, and Thomas Pelham, Eſq; after Lord Pelham.

[1] Burnet's hiſt. p. 794, 795.

In the year 1695, his Lordship was declared one of the seven Lords Justices, for the administration of the government, during the King's absence beyond the seas; as he was the year following, as also in the year 1701, when he was again made first Lord Commissioner of the Treasury, having been removed from that board in the year 1697.

On the accession of Queen Anne to the throne of these realms, he was constituted, on May 6, 1702, Lord High-Treasurer of England; and on the 12th went to Westminster-Hall, where the usual oaths were administered to him, as well in the court of Chancery, as the Exchequer. Under his Lordship's administration in this high office, public credit revived, which before was in a sinking condition, and the war was carried on with success, and the nation entirely satisfied with his prudent management. He omitted nothing that could engage the subject to bear the burthen of the war with chearfulness. He was also one of those faithful and able counsellors, who advised her Majesty to declare in council, ' That she judged the selling
' of offices and places in her houshold, and family, to be high-
' ly dishonourable to her, prejudicial to her service, and a dis-
' couragement to virtue and true merit, which could and
' should recommend persons to her royal approbation; and
' that her Majesty was resolved to prevent such selling of the
' same, &c.' And so true a friend was his Lordship to the established church, that considering how contemptible some of its clergy were, by the poor allowance for their support, he likewise advised her Majesty to settle her revenue of the first-fruits and tenths of the clergy to augment small vicarages.

His Lordship was much concerned at the heats and animosities about the bill to prevent occasional conformity, thinking it an ill time for such disputes, when all parties ought to unite against the common enemy. At that time it was, that there rose to a great height the distinction of High and Low Church; and tho' his Lordship voted for that bill, yet the party, that espoused it, gave out that he made interest against it. But the esteem, he had gained by his wisdom and counsels, was apparent in the addresses of congratulation to her Majesty on the glorious victory obtained at Hockstet, August 13, 1704. In that from Fowey in Cornwall, presented by the honourable George Granvile, Esq; after Lord Lansdown, complimenting his Grace the Duke of Marlborough, ' That he had not only
' retrieved the reputation of the English arms, but raised it to
' a degree of glory greater than ever, and has his veins full of
' the blood of their countrymen;' It is further added, ' Nor
' do we esteem it a less happiness, that the same Providence
' furnished your Majesty with a person from among us, to be
' entrusted

'entrusted with the management of the revenues, whose fru-
'gal and faithful administration has appeared to be such, both
'in that high station, and in your councils, that your people
'might almost believe themselves in full peace at home, were
'it not for the fame of the victories abroad.'

The Queen had so great a sense of his services, that at a chapter held on July 6, the same year, at St. James's, her Majesty and twelve Knights companions being present, his Lordship was elected a Knight of the most noble order of the Garter, and on December 30 was installed at Windsor, in the chapel-royal of St. George, at Windsor, by George Duke of Northumberland, Constable of Windsor castle, and the Earl of Pembroke, Lord President of the council, commissioned by the Sovereign; and a grand entertainment was made for the company in the guard chamber of the castle. On April 16, 1705, he was constituted Lord-lieutenant, and Custos Rotulorum of the county of Cornwall. And his Lordship so managed affairs before the end of the same year, that her Majesty was impowered by the parliaments both of England and Scotland, to appoint commissioners to treat about a Union. The commission for England bore date April 10, 1706, and his Lordship was the fourth nominated.

This grand affair was set on foot by James I. but no Prince before her Majesty, nor any councils but hers, could effect it: for by the assiduity and dexterity of the Lord Godolphin, all obstacles were removed, and the long desired union of the two kingdoms happily brought to bear. It is to his Lordship's honour, that tho' he had a great share in the favours of four succeeding Princes, he never sought new titles: But having done great services, her Majesty now thought it highly necessary to advance such a faithful servant to the dignity of an Earl, by the style and title of Earl of Godolphin, and Viscount Rialton, by letters patent bearing date December 29, 1706.

On the incorporating of the two kingdoms, the treasury of Scotland being entirely determined, her Majesty was pleased to constitute the Earl of Godolphin, Lord High-treasurer of Great-Britain. Yet soon after, some persons having endeavoured to lessen his Lordship in her Majesty's esteem, the house of Commons in their address, of March 13, 1708, expressed themselves to this effect: ' That there could be nothing so dan-
' gerous and fatal to the safety of her Majesty's person and the
' security of the present happy establishment, as those persons
' who endeavored to create divisions and animosities among her
' faithful subjects; or by any artful methods lessen her just
' esteem for those who, so eminently, and in so distinguishing
' a manner, commanded her armies, and managed her treasure,
' to

'to the honour and glory of her Majesty abroad, and entire
'satisfaction of her people at home; and therefore they begged
'leave to beseech her Majesty to discountenance all such per-
'sons and designs, in the most remarkable manner.' To which
address her Majesty made answer, 'That she thought all those,
'who endeavoured to make divisions among her faithful sub-
'jects, must be her's and the kingdom's enemies; and that
'she should never countenance any persons who should go
'about to lessen the just esteem which she had for those,
'who had done, and continued to do her the most eminent
'services.' And further to satisfy the nation, the Queen
removed, from their offices, several persons, who at that time
were thought to be forming a party in opposition to the Lord
High-treasurer.

But such was the inveteracy of many of the clergy, on their
mistaken notions of the church being in danger (by his Lordship's bringing some, into offices, who were known friends to
the protestant religion and succession) that they continually
maligned him; and Dr. Sacheverel's sermon and trial having
spirited up the change among the people, her Majesty on Aug. 8,
1710, was persuaded to remove his Lordship from the office of
Lord High treasurer of Great-Britain; to the great regret of
all her Majesty's allies.

His Lordship laboured under an indisposition of the stone
and gravel for some years, the pains whereof growing more
violent upon him, he departed this life, aged 67, at his Grace
the Duke of Marlborough's house at St. Alban's, Sept. 15,
1712; and on the 8th of the next month, was buried in Westminster-Abbey, where his daughter-in-law, the late Dutchess
of Marlborough, erected a monument to his memory, against
the south wall of the south isle, on which is his busto.

The character of this great man has been so fully described
by several hands, that words can't be more properly adapted,
to leave a greater reverence to his memory. He was a great
encourager of literature, and a good judge of poetry. He promoted Dr. Davenant for his ingenious Essays on peace at home
and war abroad: And having a sight of Mr. Addison's poem
on the glorious campaign of the Duke of Marlborough, when,
it was carried on as far as the applauded simile of the angel,
he so far approved of it, that he bestowed on the author,
in a few days after, the place of Commissioner of the appeals,
vacant by the removal of the famous Mr. Locke to the
council of trade, which was also done by his Lordship's
interest.

He married Margaret, at that time maid of honour to
Catharine Queen of England, fourth daughter and one of
the

the co-heirs of Thomas Blague, Esq; (Groom of the bed-chamber to Charles I. and Charles II. Colonel of a regiment of foot, and Governor of Wallingford during the civil war; Colonel of a regiment, and Governor of Yarmouth and Landguard fort, after the restoration) and by her had issue Francis, 2d Earl of Godolphin, of whom she died in child-bed, and was buried at Breage in com' Cornub. September 16, 1678. And his Lordship was so much affected with her death, that he ever after continued a widower.

Which Francis Earl of Godolphin was born on September 3, 1678, and in his younger years was bred at Eaton school, and afterwards at King's-college in Cambridge. As soon as his Lordship came of age, he was returned to parliament for the borough of Helston, and was chose one of the Knights of the shire for the county of Oxford, in the parliament of the 7th year of Queen Anne. In the year 1702, he was made one of the Tellers of the Exchequer. On January 6, 1704-5, at the splendid entertainment made by the Lord Mayor and court of Aldermen, for the entertainment of John Duke of Marlborough, after his glorious success against the enemy at the battle of Hockstet (on August 13, N. S. preceding) his Grace was accompanied in one of her Majesty's coaches by his Lordship, the Duke of Somerset, and the Prince of Hesse, followed by a great train of other coaches; and in 1705, was made Lord-warden of the Stannaries in Cornwall. On his Lordship's resignation of his place of one of the Tellers of the Exchequer, he was constituted Cofferer to Queen Anne, as he was like-wise (on October 3, 1714) to King George I. who on October 14, 1715, appointed him Lord-lieutenant and Custos Rotulorum of Oxfordshire. On May 25, 1723, his Lordship was declared Groom of the Stole, and first Gentleman of the bed-chamber to his Majesty; who the next day making known his intentions to his Privy council, that some affairs called him abroad for the summer, his Lordship was appointed one of the Lords-justices, and of the privy-council, during his Majesty's absence: And was also one of the Lords-justices, when the King went abroad in the years 1725, and 1727. On the accession of our late Sovereign, he was again, July 24, 1727, appointed Groom of the Stole, and first gentleman of his Majesty's bed-chamber, and Lord-lieutenant of Oxfordshire; which honour he resigned in January, 1734-5. On July 7, 1733, his Lordship was appointed Governor of the islands of Scilly; and on January 23, 1734-5, (8 George II.) was created Baron of Helston in the county of Cornwall, and to his heirs male, with remainder to the heirs male of Henry Godolphin, Doctor

208 Godolphin, Earl of Godolphin.

Doctor in Divinity, late Dean of St. Paul's, and Provost of Eaton college, beforementioned. Likewise on May 16, 1735, his Lordship was sworn Lord Privy-seal, which he afterwards resigned: However he was again admitted a member by his late Majesty; and at the accession of the present King, was continued at that board, and in the government of Scilly.

His Lordship married the Lady Henrietta, eldest daughter and coheir of his Grace, John, Duke of Marlborough, who for his unparelleled services to the nation, and the confederated powers of Europe, had his honours entailed by act of parliament on his daughters, and their heirs male, by virtue whereof she was Dutchess of Marlborough, on her father's decease; and was one of the Ladies of the bedchamber to her Majesty Queen Anne. Her Grace departed this life on October 24, 1733. His Lordship had issue by her,

1. William Marquis of Blandford, who had all the advantage of education at home, and travelled thro' most parts of Europe for his greater accomplishment. In April 1720, his Lordship accompanied by the Lord Spencer, were at Geneva, and from thence passed into Italy. He was one of the representatives for the borough of Woodstock in the parliament summoned to meet on November 18, 1727; and in the year 1730, was complimented by both the universities of this kingdom, with the degree of Doctor of laws; that of Cambridge was conferred on him at their public commencement. His Lordship on April 25, 1729, married Maria Catharina daughter of Peter D'Jong, of the province of Utrecht, and sister to the Countess of Denbigh, by whom he had no issue; and departed this life at Oxford, of an apoplectic fit, on August 24, 1731. And his Lady on June 1, 1734, was married to the late Sir William Wyndham, Bart.

Henry, second son, died young; as did a daughter, the Lady Margaret.

The Lady Henrietta, married to Thomas Pelham Holles, Duke of Newcastle: And

The Lady Mary, married to Thomas Duke of Leeds.

TITLES.] Francis Godolphin, Baron Godolphin, Baron of Helston, Viscount Rialton, and Earl of Godolphin.

CREATIONS.] Baron Godolphin of Rialton in Cornwall, by Letters Patent, September 8 (1684) 36 Car. II. Baron of Helston in the county of Cornwall, January 23 (1734-5) 8 George II. Viscount of the same place, and Earl of Godolphin in the aforesaid County, December 29, 1706, 5 Anne.

ARMS.]

Godolphin Earl of Godolphin.

Godolphin, Earl of Godolphin.

ARMS.] Gules, an Eagle with two Heads difplayed, between three Fleurs-de-lis, Argent.
CREST.] On a Wreath, a Dolphin naiant, embowed, proper.
SUPPORTERS.] Two Eagles, reguardant, with their Wings difplayed, Argent.
MOTTO.] FRANCHA LEALE TOGE.
CHIEF-SEATS.] At Godolphin in the county of Cornwall, 4 miles from Market-Jew, and 276 from London; at Tilfheade in the county of Wilts, 4 miles from Eaft-Lavington, and 86 from London; at Gogmagog, 10 miles from New-market, 4 from Cambridge, and 52 miles from London.

CHOLMONDELEY, Earl of Cholmondeley.

THAT names of men and places have been variously written, is well known to all who have looked into our records, whereof there is an instance in this family of Cholmondeley, denominated from the lordship of Cholmondeley, in the hundred of Broxton, in Cheshire, the name having been written twenty-five several ways; viz. Chelmundele, Chelmundelly, Chelmonsleigh, Chelmundelegh, Cholmoneleigh, &c. as is evident from divers old deeds in the custody of the present Earl of Cholmondeley. In Domesday-Book (which contains an account of the lands, lordships, &c. in the several counties in England, except Westmoreland, Cumberland, Northumberland, and Durham, and was begun [a] in the 14th of William the Conqueror, as the Red-book in the Exchequer manifests, but not finished till the 20th, as the book itself declares) it was wrote Calmundelei, and at that time was part of the possessions of Robert, son of Hugh, Baron of Malpas. Which Hugh also held in Cestrescire, as the same book testifies (besides the lordship of Calmundelei) the manours of Bedesfeld, Burwardestone, Hurdingebery, Depenbeche (now called Malpas) Tillestone, Christestone, Eghe, Hantone, Lawechedone, Dochintone, Cetelea, Brosse, Overtone, Cuntitone, Socheliche, Tusigeham, Bicheley, Bieretone, Burwardesley, Creuhalle, Tidnistane, Bristone, Bolebery, Tivertone, Spurrestowe, Fentone, Sudctone, Butelege, and Coeneche. But the said Robert dying without issue male, the Barony of Malpas, with the lordship of Calmundelei, &c. devolved on his only daughter and heir Lettice, married to Richard de Belward [b], whose son (or grandson) William de Belward, was married to Beatrix, daughter of Hugh Kiviliock, the fifth Earl of Chester, and coheir to her brother Randal, Earl of Chester. He was, in right of his mother, Baron of Malpas, though it is said by some, that he had only half of the barony; but it is agreed by Sir William Dugdale, [c] and other of our antiquaries, that he left issue three sons, David, Robert, hereafter mentioned, and Richard.

David, who from being clerk (or secretary) to the Earl of Chester, was sometimes wrote le Clerk, as also de Malpas, succeeded his father at Malpas; and after the Earldom of Chester

[a] Spelman's glossary, p. 176. [b] Records, &c. hujus fam. MS. p. 103, 104. penes Fraehon. Geo. com' Cholmondeley. Egerton de Oulton, arm. [c] Ex stemmate penes Joh.

Cholmondeley, Earl of Cholmondeley.

was annexed to the crown, d was Sheriff of the county of Chester, in 36 Hen. III. bearing the name of David de Malpas. He left issue Sir William de Malpas, who died without lawful issue; e Philip, second son, who seating himself at Egerton, left that surname to his posterity, from whom the family of Egerton is descended, whereof the present Duke of Bridgwater is derived.

Peter, another of the sons of the said David, took the name of Clerk; and his posterity, seated at Thornton, bore that surname, as was customary in those times. f Which line terminated in the reign of Edw. III. in six daughters and coheirs of Sir Peter le Clerk; Ellen, the wife of Sir Thomas Dutton, of Dutton (who had issue by her, amongst others, Lawrence, who continued the line at Dutton, which ended in 1614, in a daughter Eleanor, wife to Gilbert Lord Gerard, of Gerards-Bromley, and secondly, to Robert Lord Viscount Kilmurry, of the kingdom of Ireland;) Elizabeth, of Hammon-Fitton, of Bollyn-Murick; Maud, of Henry de Beeston, of Beeston; Margaret, of Sir William de Goulbourne (descended from David de Golbourne, g another of the sons of the before-mentioned David de Malpas) Beatrix, of Thomas de Sansbury, who died without issue, 20 Rich. II. and Emme, of Hugh de Weverham.

I now return to Robert, second son of William, Baron of Malpas, of whom I am principally to treat, being the direct ancestor to this family of Cholmondeley, as all antiquaries agree. Which Robert, having, by the gift of his father, the lordship of Cholmondeley, and fixing his residence there h, assumed that surname (as was most usual in those times) which his posterity have ever since retained. He married Mabel, daughter of Robert Fitz-Nigel, Baron of Halton, with whom he had the Lordship of Christleton, and a release of the hospital of Cholmondeley. i Their son and heir was Sir Hugh de Chelmundeleigh, as the name was then wrote in a charter k, without date, of Robert, son of Liulph, and Mabilla his wife, whereunto the said Sir Hugh de Chelmundeleigh, and Robert his son, were witnesses. He had a release l from Ranulph, Earl of Chester, for himself and his heirs, of all right of suits of court, and justice, owing to the hundred of Broxstone, for his lands in Cholmundeley. Which release is without date (as in old times was usual) but is witnessed by Philip de Orebie, Justice of Chester, in the m beginning of the reign of Hen. III.

d Leicester's antiquities of Cheshire, p. 178.   e Ex stemmate de famil. de Egerton, penes Joh. Egerton, præd.   f MS. de famil. de Cholmondeley, præd. p. 104.   g Ex stemmate de Egerton.   h Dugdale's Baronage, vol. 2. p. 474.   i Ibid.   k Cart. penes Hen. Manwaring de Croxton, arm. l Ex script. Tho. Aston de Aston, Bar.   m Leicester's antiquities of the shire, p. 178.

Cholmondeley, Earl of Cholmondeley.

and many others. The said Sir Hugh is also mentioned in a fine, in 14 Hen. III. ⁿ between Sibil, daughter of William de Goldburne, and William Clerk, of Handley, levied before William de Vernon, then Justice of Chester. He married Felice, natural daughter of Ranulph de Blundeville, Earl of Chester and Lincoln, ᵒ by whom he had the before-mentioned Robert, his son and heir; Richard, second son; and a daughter, Felice.

Which Robert, in several old deeds, is written lord of Cholmondeley; and Simon de Cristelton, styling him nepoti suo, ᵖ releases to him his claim of two bovates of land, with the appurtenances in Christelton, which Sir Hugh de Chelmundeley, brother to him the said Simon de Christelton, gave to him. Which land this Robert de Chelmundeley gave by charter to the abbey of Chester, with his body to be buried in the church-yard of St. Werburgh; Richard de Chelmundeley, his brother, releasing his claim thereto, as is evident from charters entered in the ledger book of the abbey of Chester. He married Beatrix, daughter to Urian St. Peire, ᑫ or (as others) daughter of David le Clerk, baron of half the barony of Malpas, and sister to Idonea, the wife of Urian de St. Peire, by whom he had issue Richard, his son and heir.

Which Richard is wrote lord of Cholmondeley, in a deed without date, ʳ wherein he grants to Hugh, his son and heir, all his lands in Cholmondeley, Wythall, &c. He married Margery, sister and coheir of Richard de Kingsley, ˢ and daughter of Sir Richard de Kingsley (lord of Kingsley, Norley, Newton, Codington, and of the bailwick of Delamereforest) who was great-grandson of Randle de Kingsley, who had the foresterfhip of Delamere, of the grant of Randle, the first Earl of Chester of that name. The said Margery is mentioned in 29 Hen. III. as one of the coheirs of Richard de Kingsley, her brother, and surviving her husband, grants, by deed without date, ᵗ to Hugh de Camera, her kinsman, and his heirs, one plow-land in Aston, paying one pair of white gloves yearly, at the feast of the Nativity of St. John Baptist, and one lance every second year; whereunto are witnesses, Robert de Celmundele, and others; and her seal, appendant, is a branch of a tree, circumscribed, in old characters, S. Margaria Celmundele. She had issue three sons (of whom Richard, the eldest, died without issue) and several daughters.

n Fines 14 Hen. III. in offic. prothon. Cestr.   o Ex stemmate.   p MS. ut antea, p. 6.   q MS. p. 86.   r Ex collect. Will. Vernon de Shakerley.   s Ex stemmate de Kingsley.   t Cart. penes Tho. Aston de Aston, Bar.

The

Cholmondeley, Earl of Cholmondeley. 213

The eldest surviving son was Hugh de Cholmondeley, mentioned in several deeds, in the reign of Edw. I. and in the 6th year of Edw. II. being in the commission of the peace, was present at the castle of Chester, [u] when David le Cooper was executed for burglary, committed at Cholmondeley and Burwardesley. In 8 Edw. II. he was the first witness [w] with Richard de Fulhurst, Sheriff of Cheshire, and other persons of note, to a deed of Wintiliana le Constantin, dated at Tushingham; as also to another deed in 9 Edw. II. dated at Malpas. He married Catharine, daughter of William de Spurstow, and left issue Richard, his son and heir; William, hereafter-mentioned; Robert, and Thomas, who writes himself son of Hugh de Cholmondelegh, in a charter, [x] granting to John de Burton, chaplain, all his lands and tenements, with the appurtenances in Burton, near Tervyn, which he had of the gift of Hugh, son of Richard, son of Simon de Burton; dated at Burton, the Friday after the feast of St. Hilary, MCCCXXV.

Robert is also wrote son of Hugh de Cholmundelegh, in a writ of error, 23 Edw. III. [y] concerning lands in Wyncham, near Picmer, wherein he and Alice his wife (daughter and coheir to John de Wasteneys, of Wyncham, in Cheshire) were, with others, plaintiffs. Also in 35 Edw. III. he [z] gave in trust to Hugh del Halgh, chaplain, his property in all his lands in Chorley, Werlefton, Berkesford, and Wich-Malbank, to which charter, John de Delves, then Lieutenant and Justice of Chester, was a witness. He left issue two sons, William, and John, [a] wrote son of Robert de Cholmundeley, of Chorley, in 13 Hen. IV. at which time he had the guardianship of John, son and heir of William Crew de Sond. He succeeded his brother William, at Chorley, in the 4th year of Hen. IV. [b] as appears by inquisition taken after his death; and in the 9th year of Hen. V. is wrote John de Cholmondeley de Chorley, and, [c] with Robert his son, grants to Margaret, wife of Edmund de Munsale, a moiety of the village of Wyncham. From the said Robert, who married a daughter of Sir Robert Needham, of Shenton, descended John Cholmondeley, of Chorley, who, by Joan his wife, daughter and coheir of Thomas Heyton, [d] was father to Sir Richard Cholmondeley, and Roger Cholmondeley, lineal ancestor to the Cholmondeleys, of Whitby, in Yorkshire.

u Placita com' Cestr. 6 Edw. II.   w Ex collect. Will. Vernon de Shakerley, gen.   x Cart. penes Jonath. Bruyn de Stapleford, armig.   y Ex origin in Castro Cestr.   z Ex collect. W. Vernon de Shakerley, a record in Castro Cestr.   a Ibid. in 13 Hen. IV.   b Esc. 4 Hen. IV. in Castro Cestr.   c Ex collect. W. Vernon de Shakerley, præd.   d Ex stemmate.

Cholmondeley, Earl of Cholmondeley.

Which Sir Richard Cholmondeley was famous for his valour and conduct, shewed on several occasions, in the reigns of Hen. VII. and Hen. VIII. He was knighted by the Earl of Surrey, in 12 Hen. VII. [e] for his services against the Scots, who had received and assisted Perkin Warbeck; and for his great merit was, by Hen. VII. constituted Lieutenant of the castle of Berwick, and afterwards Governor of the town of Kingston upon Hull; and on Sept. 9, 1513, 5 Hen. VIII. [f] commanded the forces of that garrison, at the battle of Brampston, or Flodden-field, wherein James IV. King of Scotland, was slain, with most of his Nobles, and the flower of his country. And so serviceable was his conduct that day, that he received a letter from the King, dated Nov. 27, at Windsor: also for his services in this battle, he was made Lieutenant of the Tower of London; and in an act (6 Hen. VIII.) [g] concerning the King's General-receivers of his revenues, is this memorable clause: ' Provided, That this act extend not to
' hurt and prejudice the grant made by our dear father King
' Henry the seventh, by his letters patent the 16th year of his
' reign, unto Sir Richard Cholmley, Knt. now being Lieute-
' nant of our Tower of London, and late Lieutenant of our
' castle of Berwick upon Tweed, by whatsoever name or names,
' or surnames, addition or additions, the said Sir Richard is
' named, called or known, to be Supervisor-general of all and
' singular our castles, lordships, manours, lands, called Rich-
' mond, Sheriffe-Hooton, Midlam, Barney-castle, Wakefield,
' Sandall, Connesborow, Hatfield, Thorne, Cottingham, Rose,
' and Rascall, with all and singular the members and appurte-
' nances, and members in the shire of York, according to the
' tenor and effect of the said grants; and with the fees and re-
' wards in the said letters patent, contained and specified; this
' present act, or any other act, made, or to be made in this pre-
' sent parliament, to the contrary notwithstanding.'

By his last will and testament, [h] bearing date Dec. 26, 1521, in 13 Hen. VIII. (the probate whereof is on March 24 following) he orders his body to be buried in the same chapel where Sir John Risley, Knt. lieth buried, within the chapel of our Blessed Lady of Barking, besides the Tower of London, if the master and wardens will thereunto agree with his executors. But if they do not agree thereto, that then his body be buried in the church of the Crossed Friars, besides the Tower of London, before the image of our Lady, in the same church, if the

e Nom. Equit, MS. in bibl. Cotton. sub effig. Claudius C. 3. f Hall's chron. fol. 38. b. g Rot. parl. 6 Hen. VIII. h Ex regiftr. vocat. Manwaring, qu. 22. in cur. prærog. Cantuar.

Cholmondeley, Earl of Cholmondeley.

Prior will confent; or elfe in fome other convenient place within the faid church. He bequeaths his manours of Thornton upon the Hill, Wykton, and Hefell, in the county of York, Blincolgoe, in the county of Cumberland, and Forfett, in the county of York, to Elizabeth his wife, for term of her life, and after her deceafe, to Roger Cholmley his brother, and his heirs male, and in default thereof, to Richard Cholmley, of Cholmley, in the county of Chefter. And all the reft of his manours, lands and tenements, in England, Calais, or Berwick, to his faid brother Roger, and to the heirs male of his body; and for default of fuch iffue, to remain to his right heirs for ever, except lands and tenements of the yearly value of 20 l. which he wills to his natural fon, Roger Cholmley, of Lincoln's-Inn, and the heirs males of his body lawfully begotten; and for default of fuch iffue, to remain to Roger his brother as aforefaid; and in default, to his right heirs for ever. And except lands and tenements in the city of London, of 12 l. yearly value, which he bequeaths to the mafter and wardens of the chapel of our Lady of Barking, or fuch place where he fhall be buried, for a prieft to fing and fay Mafs, and pray for his foul, his wife's foul, his friends fouls, and all Chriftian fouls, with a yearly obiit and anniverfary. And except all his lands and tenements within the county of Effex, and in the city of London, which he wills to his fon Roger Cholmley, of Lincoln's-Inn, and to the heirs male of his body lawfully begotten; and in default of fuch iffue, to remain to his faid brother Roger, and his heirs male; and in default, to Richard Cholmley, of Cholmley, and to the heirs males of his body; and in default, to his right heirs. He leaves fmall legacies to his coufins Richard Cholmley, and William Cholmley; and to his faid brother Roger Cholmley, one hundred pounds of his beft plate, and his beft china: and all other plate, &c. not mentioned in his will, he bequeaths to Elizabeth his wife, whom he conftitutes his fole executrix, and appoints Sir Henry Wyat, Sir John Dauntefey, and Sir Richard Brooks, Knts, and his brother Roger Cholmley, overfeers.

Which Roger Cholmley (brother to Sir Richard) was Knt. for the body of Hen. VIII. and died April 28, 1538; and by his wife Catharine, daughter of Sir Robert Conftable, of Flamborough, in Yorkfhire, Knt. father to Sir Richard Cholmley, of Thornton, who was conftituted [1] Conftable of Scarborough-caftle, in 2 Edw. VI. and by his firft wife Margaret, daughter of William Lord Conyers, had iffue Roger Cholmley, anceftor to the Cholmleys, of Brandefby, and

[1] Privat. figill. 2 Edw. VI.

Thornton; and by his second wife Catharine, [k] daughter to Henry Clifford, Earl of Cumberland, relict of John Lord Scroope of Bolton, had issue Sir Henry Cholmley, ancestor to the Cholmleys, of Whitby, in Yorkshire.

Roger Cholmley, natural son of Sir Richard, being bred to the study of the laws, in Lincoln's-Inn, was so famed for his knowledge and abilities, that after a gradual rise, he became Lord Chief Justice of England. In 15 Hen. VIII. he was chosen Lent-reader of the society of Lincoln's-Inn, [l] and in 20 Hen. VIII. Double reader thereof; also in 23 Hen. VIII. [m] constituted a Serjeant at Law. In 36 Hen. VIII. [n] King's Serjeant; and the year following was promoted to the office of Lord Chief Baron [o] of the Exchequer; and finally on March 21, 6 Edw. VI. Lord Chief Justice of the King's Bench. An inscription over the door of the chapel at Highgate, in the county of Middlesex, informs us, ' That he instituted and ' erected, at his own charges, a public and free grammar ' school in that town, and procured the same to be established ' and confirmed, by the letters patent of Queen Elizabeth, ' endowing the same with a yearly maintenance.' He left issue two daughters, his coheirs, Elizabeth, married to Sir Leonard Beckwith, of Selbie-abbey, in Yorkshire; secondly, to Christopher Kenn, Esq; and Frances, wife to Sir Thomas Russel, of Strensham-court, in Worcestershire.

I now return to Richard, eldest son of Hugh de Cholmundeley, by Catharine, his wife, daughter of William de Spurstow. Which Richard, by his charter [p] without date, releases to Richard, son of Pagan, and his heirs (in consideration of five marks) a quit-rent of 10 s. per ann. for land held of him in Christleton-Parva, but reserves for homage and service a pair of white gloves yearly, on the feast of St. John Baptist, according to the charter of Robert de Cholmundeley, granted to the said Richard, son of Pagan. And being also wrote Richard, son of Hugh de Cholmundeley, [q] was summoned in 13 Edw. II. to the court of pleas at Chester, to answer Thomas, Abbot of St. Werburgh, why he destrained the chattles of the said Abbot, in Wardhull demesnes, in Halghton. To which he pleaded, that the seizure was just, it being not in the town of Halghton, but in Rowe-Chiistleton, the lordship of which town belonged to him the said Richard de Cholmundeley. On what account he had this controversy with the Abbot, does not appear; but the same year he summoned the said Abbot,

[k] Seager's Baronagium geneal. MS. [l] Dugdale's origin. juridiciales, p. 251. [m] Cronica series, p. 83. [n] Pat. 36 Hen. VIII. p. 18. [o] Pat. 37 Hen. VIII. p. 17. [p] Ex collect. Ra. Holme de Cestr. gen. [q] Placita com' Cestr. 13 Edw. II.

Cholmondeley, Earl of Cholmondeley. 217

and William de Bebynton, to anſwer why they ſeized and detained his chattles at Hull, near Wadeſdale, in Row-Chriſtleton: whereunto the Abbot pleaded, that he took them not in Chriſtleton, but in Halghton demeſnes, belonging to the manours of Huntington, and Halghton. He was living in 9 Edw. III. being then wrote Richard de Cholmundeley, ſenior, and with Mabilla his wife, were [r] deforciants, in a fine levied before William de Clinton, Juſtice of Cheſter. Alſo in 31 Edw. III. Richard, ſon of Hugh de Cholmundley, [s] claimed view of frank-pledge, waifs, ſtrays, &c. in Cholmundeley; and the ſame year being ſtyled Richard lord of Cholmondley, [t] claimed the privilege of holding courts for trial of all manner of pleas within his demeſnes of Cholmondley and Chriſtleton. He left iſſue, Richard, his ſon and heir, who departed this life without iſſue, in 35 Edw. III. and by inquiſition [u] taken after his death, William, ſon of Hugh de Cholmondley, was found to be his next heir; and that Maud, wife of Richard de Cholmondley, father of the ſaid Richard, held in dower four meſſuages, and 60 acres of land in Cholmondley.

Which William married Elizabeth, daughter to Sir William de Brereton, of Brereton, Knt. and was dead in 49 Edw. III. when the ſaid Sir William de Brereton, Knt. had, in conſideration of the ſum.[w] of 166 l. 13 s. and 4 d. payable to the King within the term of ſeven years, the guardianſhip of Richard, ſon and heir of William de Cholmondeley, and his marriage, without diſparagement; as alſo the reverſion of the dowry (when it ſhall happen) of Maud, wife of the late Richard de Cholmondley. And if the ſaid Richard, ſon and heir of William de Cholmondley, ſhould die before he attained his full age, that he the ſaid Sir William de Brereton ſhould have the guardianſhip and marriage of Catharine and Margery, ſiſters of the aforeſaid Richard de Cholmondley.

Which Richard de Cholmondley married two wives, Anne, daughter of John Bromley, of Badington, and Alice, daughter of Richard de Henhull, of Henhull. Which Richard de Henhull dying in 11 Rich. II. the ſaid Alice was found (by the inquiſition taken after his death) to be his daughter and coheir, [x] and then the wife of Richard de Cholmondelegh, as the name at that time was wrote. His ſon and heir was William de Cholmondley, [y] who died before him in 10 Hen. IV. having iſſue by his wife Maud, daughter of Sir John Cheyney, of Willaſton in Wirral, in com' Ceſtr. Knt. (and coheir to her mother Maud, daughter and co-

---

[r] Fines in Prothon. offic. Ccſtr. 9 Edw. III.   [s] Placita com' Ceſtr. 31 Edw. III.   [t] Ibid.   [u] Eſc. 35 Edw. III. in caſt. Ceſtr.   [w] Cart. penes Will. Domini Brereton de Brereton.   [x] Eſc. 11 Rich. II. in caſt. Ceſtr. [y] Ex ſtemmate in MS. præd.

218 *Cholmondeley, Earl of Cholmondeley.*

heir to Thomas de Capenhurft) [z] Richard his fon and heir, and John Cholmondley, fecond fon, of Copenhall in Staffordfhire, anceftor to the Cholmondleys of Copenhall, and others. Richard de Cholmondeley, eldeft fon, is mentioned [a] in the fine rolls in 4 Ed. IV. as one of the Juftices in the county of Chefter, before whom fines were levied, as alfo in 22 Ed. IV. [b] when he was wrote Richard de Cholmondelegh, fenior; and likewife in 2 Hen. VII. He departed this life in 4 Hen. VII. [c] as the inquifition taken after his death fhews; and having married Ellen, daughter of John Davenport, of Davenport, Efq; had iffue Richard, his fon and heir.

Which Richard de Cholmondley, married Eleanor, fifth daughter of Sir Thomas Dutton, of Dutton, and fifter and coheir to John her brother, who died before he was of full age. [d] Which family of Dutton, defcended from Huddard Lord of Dutton, brother to Nigel, Baron of Halton, and were inriched by the marriages of the heirs of Minfhul, of Minfhul, and of Sir Piers Thornton, of Thornton in Chefhire. A Quo Warranto was brought in 15 Hen. VII. [e] againft William de Wilbraham, Thomas Booth, and Richard Belputon, feoffees of and in the lands and tenements of Richard de Cholmondelcy, of Cholmondeley, Efq; to anfwer to the Prince and Earl of Chefter, by what authority they claimed view of frank-pledge in the manour of Cholmondley, and waifs and ftrays there, and to be difcharged from fuit or fervice to the Earl's court, and of the hundred of Dunfton, & de uno Judice, &c. Whereunto they produced an exemption as to the fuit of court, & de uno Judice, by the charter of Ranulph Earl of Chefter and Lincoln, granted to Hugh de Cholmondley, wherein he was difcharged of thofe fervices; and as to view of frank-pledge, waifs and ftrays, they pleaded prefcription. This Richard de Cholmondley was a benefactor to the church of Badeley; upon which account, his figure, according to the cuftom of thofe times, was painted in glafs, in the higheft window on the fouth fide next the chancel. He is pourtrayed kneeling before a defk, and a book before him, with the arms of his family, viz. ' Gules, ' two Helmets in chief, Argent, garnifh'd, Or ; and in bafe a ' Garb of the third,' and underneath was this infcription in the year 1670. ' Orate pro bono ftatu ..... et .... Richardi ' Cholmondley ....'
He left iffue a fon of his own name,

[z] Ibid.   [a] Fines 4 Ed. IV. in caftro Ceftr.   [b] Ibid. 22 Ed. IV. and 2 Hen VII.   [c] Efc. 4 Hen VII.   [d] Ex ftem. de Dutton in MS. præd. p. 100.
[e] Quo warranto 15 H. VII. in offic. prothon. Ceftr.

Richard

Cholmondeley, Earl of Cholmondeley.

Richard Cholmondley, Efq; one of the Juftices before f whom fines were levied, from 17 Hen. VII. to 24 Hen. VIII. and who, in 30 Hen. VIII. departed this life, g feized (as the inquifition fhews, taken March 20, the fame year) of the manours of Cholmondley, Church-Minfule, and Afton; and of divers other manours and lands in Gildon, Sutton, Broughton, Pulton-Lancelyn, Whitley, Hawarden, Copenhurft, Laerton, Chorley, Badeley, Bikerton, Malpas, Hampton, Ebnall, Tufhingham, Bradeley, and Kinderton. He repaired the chancel of Cholmondley in the beginning of the reign of Hen. VIII. and on the fcreen of it his arms are cut, and this infcription; 'Orate pro bono ftatu Richardi Cholmundley et ' Elizabeth Uxoris ejus, facelli factoris, Anno Domini Mille- ' fimo quingentefimo quarto decimo.' He married, firft, Elizabeth daughter to Sir Roger Corbet, of Morton Corbet, in com' Salop, Knt. by whom he had iffue an only daughter Maud, wedded to Sir Peter Newton, Knt. But by his fecond wife Elizabeth, daughter to Sir Randle Brereton of Malpas, chamberlain of Chefter (who furvived him, and was afterwards married to Sir Randle Mainwaring, of Over-Pever, Knt.) he had feveral children, whereof thefe daughters were married, viz. Catharine, to Richard Preftland, of Preftland and Wardhill, in Chefhire, Efq; Agnes, to Randle Mainwairing of Carington, Efq; and Urfula, to Thomas Stanley of Wever, Efq; Hugh Cholmondley was his eldeft fon and heir; and Randle Cholmondley, a younger fon, being educated in the ftudy of the laws at Lincoln's-Inn, was elected Autumn reader of that fociety, in 5 Edw. VI. but did not read, becaufe of the peftilence. h In 6 Edw. VI. he was Lent-reader of the faid fociety; and in 4 and 5 Philip and Mary, Double reader thereof; i at which time he was Recorder of the city of London. In the laft year of King Philip and Queen Mary, k he was elected Serjeant at law: Alfo in the firft year of Queen Elizabeth, was Treble reader of the fociety, whereof he was a member, l and was then called by that Queen's writ to be Serjeant at law. His learning and knowledge in the laws appear from his being fo often Reader of this fociety; but he died without iffue on April 25, 1563.

Hugh Cholmondley, his elder brother, m was 25 years of age at his father's death, in 30 Hen. VIII. He was in that expedition made into n Scotland under the Duke of Norfolk, 36 Hen. VIII. and for his valiant behaviour there, received the

---

f Fines in offic. prothon. Ceftr. de iifd. ann.   g Efc. 30 Hen. VIII.   h Dugdale's orig. jurid. p. 252.   i Ibid.   k Dugdale's chron. feries, p. 91.
l Pat. 1 Eliz. p. 4.   m Efc. 30 Hen. VIII.   n Dugdale's Baronage, vol. 2. p. 474.

Cholmondeley, Earl of Cholmondeley.

honour of knighthood at Leith. In the reign of King Philip and Queen Mary, [o] he raised, at his own expence, 100 men, to march against the Scots, under the Earl of Derby, who in Sept. 1557, was sent to oppose them, on their invading England, and threatening to besiege Berwick. He was a person of great honour, [p] and for his admirable gifts of wisdom, temperance, continency, liberality, hospitality, and godly departure at his end, left few who were his equals; and his death was lamented by all sorts of people, having for fifty years together [q] been esteemed the father of his country, by the good offices he did to all who applied themselves to him, which appears from many arbitrations on record, that were left to his determination. He was five times Sheriff of Cheshire, [r] as also Sheriff of Flintshire, for some years, and a long time one of the two only Deputy-lieutenants of Cheshire; and for a good space Vice-president of the marches of Wales, in the absence of the famous Sir Henry Sidney, Knt. Lord-deputy of Ireland. He departed this life in the 83d year of his age, on January 6, 1596-7, the 39th year of Queen Elizabeth, seized (as the inquisition taken after his death [s] shews) of the manour of Cholmondley, and of 22 messuages, four cottages, two water-mills, and one wind-mill, &c. in Cholmondley; as also of the manour or barony of Wich-Malbank, with all the rents, reversions, services, &c. the manour of Barkesford, alias Basford, with the appurtenances, and the several manours of Moldsworth, Bickley, Norbury, with Alhurst, Aston juxta Mondrem, Church-Minsule, two parts of the manour of Copenhurst, the manours of Newbald and Edleston juxta Wich Malbank, and the fourth part of the vill of Burwardsley; with divers lands and tenements in Henhull, alias Hendle, Barton, Haughton, Horton, Tilston, Rowton, alias Row-Christleton, Wirswall, Bradley Boughton, Haslington, Badington, Chowley, Plumley, two messuages and two salt-works in North-Wich, and lands in Worleston, Wrenbury, Frith, Egerton, Church-Shocklack, and Shocklach-Oyat, Audlim, Swanbach, Golbourne, Bellow juxta Tattenhall, Church-Copenhall, Monks-Copenhall, Woodbanke, alias Rough-shot-wicke infra Great Saughall, Bebyngton. St. Ann's Heys, in the Parish of Plumstall, &c. Backford, Newhall; and of one capital messuage called Cholmondley-house, in the parish of St. John Baptist in the suburbs of the city of Chester: also of the manours of Hinton and Madford in Somersetshire, and lands in Shropshire and Flintshire. He lies buried in the chancel of the family in the church

---

[o] Strype's historical memorials, p. 433, 435.   [p] King's description of Cheshire, p. 54.   [q] Fuller's Worthies in Cheshire, p. 187.   [r] King, ut antea.   [s] Esc. 39 Eliz. in the Exchequer of Chester.

Cholmondeley, Earl of Cholmondeley.

of Malpas, and a noble monument is erected there, his effigies, with his Lady by him, lying thereon.

He married two wives, but by Mary his laſt Lady, daughter to Sir William Griffith of Pentrin, relict of Sir Randle Brereton of Malpas, he had no iſſue. His firſt Lady was Anne, daughter and coheir to George Dorman of Malpas, [t] by Agnes his wife, daughter and heir of Thomas Hill of Malpas, ſon of Humphry Hill, and of Anne his wife, daughter and coheir of John Bird of Chorlton, by Catharine his wife, aunt and heir of David de Malpas of Hampton and Bickerton, in com' Ceſtr. and the ſaid Humphry Hill was lineally deſcended from Hugh Hill, who in the reign of King Edward III. married Eleanor, daughter and coheir of Hugh de Wloukeſlow, lord of Wloukeſlow, in com' Salop; and the coats of arms, of theſe heireſſes, the preſent Earl of Cholmondeley has a right to quarter. Sir Hugh had iſſue (by the aforeſaid Anne) three ſons, and one daughter; Frances, married to Thomas Wilbraham of Woodhey in com' Ceſtr. Eſq; father (by her) of Sir Richard Wilbraham, Knt. and Bart. whoſe male iſſue terminated in Sir Thomas Wilbraham, who had two daughters his coheirs, viz. Grace married to Lionel Talmaſh, firſt Earl of Dyſart, and Mary, to Richard Newport, ſecond Earl of Bradford, and father by her of the two laſt Earls. Of Sir Hugh's three ſons, only the eldeſt left iſſue, who was named after his father, Hugh.

Which Hugh Cholmondley, of Cholmondley [u], was knighted in the life-time of his father, in 1588, the memorable year of the Spaniſh invaſion, and at his father's deceaſe in 39 Eliz. was [w] forty-ſix years of age and more. He [x] was heir to his virtues, as well as to his eſtate, and gave many proofs of an honourable benevolence, and a ſteady adherence to the proteſtant religion, and the intereſts of his country. Before he was 21 years of age, he headed [y] 130 men, raiſed by his father's intereſt and expence, and marched with them for the ſuppreſſion of that rebellion in the North, begun [z] in the 12th year of Queen Elizabeth, under the leading of the Earls of Weſtmorland and Northumberland, for reſtoring the Romiſh religion: And the Queen's forces having put them to flight, thoſe Earls, with other of the conſpirators, were attainted in parliament. He was twice the Queen's Eſcheator of the county of Cheſter, [a] viz. in 33 Eliz. and [b] 41 Eliz. as alſo Sheriff of

---

[t] Ex ſtem. de famil. Hill. in MS. præd. p. 105. [u] MS. de Equit penes meip. [w] Eſc. 39 Eliz. [x] Fuller's Worthies, p. 187. [y] MS. hujus famil præd. p. 88. [z] Cambden's hiſt. of Q. Eliz. in hiſt. of Eng. vol. 1. p. 422. [a] Leiceſter's antiq. of Cheſh. p. 187. [b] Bundle of inquiſitions in the Exchequer at Cheſter.

the

the same county; and in 42 Eliz. was in a special commission, with c the Lord Chancellor Egerton, Thomas Lord Buckhurst, Lord Treasurer of England, and others, for the suppression of schism. He increased his estate by his marriage, and by divers purchases, as appears by the inquisition after his death, in 43 Eliz. d which shews that he departed this life on the 23d of July the same year, and that Robert Cholmondley, Esq; was his eldest son and heir, and of the age of seventeen years, on the 16th of June last past. He lies buried with his ancestors in the chancel of the family, in the church of Malpas, where his Lady had also sepulture, who lived many years after him, deceasing on the 15th of August, in the first year of King Charles the first. Her name was Mary, and she was sole daughter and heir of Christopher Holford, of Holford, Esq; by Elizabeth his wife, daughter and coheir of Sir Randle Manwaring, of Pever and Badeley in Cheshire, elder brother to Philip Manwaring, Esq; of whom descended Sir Thomas Manwaring, Knt. and Bart. The said Christopher Holford was grandson e and heir to Sir John Holford, and of Margery his wife, sole daughter and heir of Ralph Brereton of Escoyd, second son of Randle Brereton, grandson and heir of Sir Randle Brereton of Malpas Knt. f and of Alice his wife, daughter and coheir to William de Ipston, by Maud, heir to Sir Robert Swynerton, Knt. by Elizabeth his wife, daughter and coheir to Sir Nicholas Beake, and of Jane his wife, only daughter of Ralph Earl of Stafford, by his second wife Catharine, daughter and coheir of Sir John de Hastang of Chebsey, in com' Staff. And this family of Cholmondley, by the marriage of the Holfords with the daughter and heir of Brereton, is also maternally descended from Alice, fourth daughter of David Earl of Huntingdon, third son of Henry Earl of Huntingdon, son of David, King of Scotland; the Earldom of Huntingdon g being for some time in the royal line of Scotland. And the said Alice was also by her mother h descended from the Earls of Chester, she being eldest daughter of Hugh Kiveilock Earl of Chester, and sister and heir of Randle Earl of Chester.

The said Mary, Lady Cholmondley, had a great contest with George Holford of Newborough, about the lands that descended to her by the death of her father Christopher Holford, Esq; which, i after it had continued for above forty years, was at length, by the mediation of friends, composed; and on the partition, she had the manours and lordships of Holford, Bulk-

c Rymer's fœdera, vol. 16. p. 386.   d Esc. 43 Eliz. in scac. Cestr.   e Ex stem. de famil. de Holford.   f Ex stem. de fam. Brereton & Ipston.   g Dugdale's Baronage, vol. 1. p. 608, 609.   h Ibid. p. 33, & 45.   i Leicester's antiq. of Cneth. p. 344.

ley, and other large poffeffions. This Lady in her widowhood refided at Holford, which fhe rebuilt and enlarged; and by conducting,' with fpirit, the great fuit before mentioned, was ftiled by James I. ' The bold Lady of Chefhire.' She had iffue, by Sir Hugh Cholmondeley, fix fons and three daughters; Mary, married to Sir George Calveley of Ley in com' Ceftr. Knt. Lettice, wife to Sir Richard Grofvenor of Eaton, Knt. and Bart. and Frances, wedded to Peter Venables, Baron of Kinderton. Of the fons, three died unmarried. The others were Robert: Hugh, anceftor to the prefent Earl of Cholmondeley: and Thomas, feated at Vale-Royal, who married Elizabeth daughter and heir of John Minfhull of Minfhull, Efq; and departing this life on January 3, 1652, was buried at Minfhull, having had iffue Thomas Cholmondeley of Vale-Royal; Robert, fecond fon, who died on September 4, 1658; Francis third fon; Mary, married to Thomas Middleton, Efq; eldeft fon of Sir Thomas Middleton of Chirk-caftle; Catharine, wife to Charles Mainwaring of Ightfield, in com' Salop, Efq; and Elizabeth, who died unmarried. The faid Thomas, eldeft fon, was one of the Knights of the fhire for the county of Chefter in the reign of Charles II. and by his firft wife Jane, daughter of Sir Lionel Talmafh, Knt. and Bart. (grandfather of Lionel firft Earl of Dyfart of his name) had iffue one fon Robert, and three daughters; Elizabeth, married to Sir Thomas Vernon, of Hodnet in com' Salop. Bart. Jane, who died unmarried; and Mary wedded to John Egerton of Oulton in com' Ceftr. Efq; His fecond wife was Anne, daughter of Sir Walter St. John (and fifter to Henry, late Lord Vifcount St. John) and by her (who died in Dec. 1742, aged 92) had iffue two fons and a daughter; Charles who fucceeded to the eftate, and Seymour, who married Elizabeth, eldeft daughter of John Lord Afhburnham, widow of Robert Cholmondeley, of Holford, Efq; and dying on July 26, 1739, at Arden in Chefhire, left no iffue by her. His daughter was Johanna, married to Amos Meredith, Efq; fon and heir to Sir William Meredith, of Henbury in Chefhire, Bart. Robert, eldeft fon of the faid Thomas Cholmondeley, married Elizabeth, fifter to Sir Thomas Vernon, Bart. and deceafing, leaving one daughter Elizabeth, married to John Atherton of the county palatine of Lancafter, Efq; the eftate devolved on his brother Charles Cholmondeley, of Vale-Royal, Efq; one of the Knights for Chefhire in eight feveral parliaments, who married Effex, eldeft daughter of Thomas Pitt, Efq; (and fifter to the late Countefs Stanhope) by whom he had iffue (who lived to maturity) four daughters; Effex, Jane, Mary, and Elizabeth; of whom Jane was married in Auguft, 1732, to the 3d fon of Owen Merrick, Efq; of Bodorgan

gan in Anglesey, for which he was member 1 Geo. I. and one son Thomas, his heir, one of the Knights for the county of Chester, in this and the former parliament.

I now return to Robert, eldest son of Sir Hugh Cholmondeley: which Robert being a well-deserving person, and enjoying an ample estate, was, upon June 29 (1611) 9 Jac. I. advanced to the dignity of a Baronet, being the 36th in order of creation; also by Charles I. was advanced to the degree of a Viscount of the kingdom of Ireland, by the title of Viscount Cholmondeley of Kellis in the province of Leinster in that realm, A. D. 1628. 'And afterwards, [k] in consideration of his special
'service, in raising several companies of foot in Cheshire, in or-
'der to the quenching those rebellious flames which began to
'appear anno 1642, and sending many other to the King, then
'at Shrewsbury (which stood him in high stead in that memora-
'ble battle of Kineton, happening soon after) as also raising other
'forces for defending the city of Chester, at the first siege thereof
'by his Majesty's adversaries in that county, and courageous ad-
'venture in the fight at Tilston-Heath; together with his great
'sufferings, by the plunder of his goods, and firing his houses;'
was by letters patent bearing date at Oxford, September 1, 21 Car. 1. created a Baron of the kingdom of England, by the title of Lord Cholmondeley of Wiche-Malbank (commonly called Nantwiche) in com'Cestr. And by other letters-patent, bearing date on March 5 next ensuing, was created Earl of the province of Leinster, in Ireland. When the royal power was at an end, and the whole kingdom was under the obedience of the parliament, he was suffered to compound for his estate, [l] but paid no less a fine for the enjoyment of it, than 7,742 l. He was revered for his liberal hospitality, his conduct in the government of his country, and other virtues. He married Catharine, daughter of John Lord Stanhope of Harrington, but died without lawful issue, on Oct. 2, 1659, and was buried by his Lady (who deceased on June 15, 1657) on the 8th of the same month, in the chancel of the family at Malpas. Whereupon Robert his nephew, son of Hugh his brother, became heir to his estate.

Which Hugh Cholmondeley, Esq; married Mary, daughter of Sir John Bodville, of Bodville-castle in Carnavonshire, and aunt to the Lady Viscountess Bodmin, mother to Russel Robarts, Earl of Radnor. He departed this life at Bodville on Sept. 11, 1655, and was buried with his ancestors at Malpas, having had issue, two sons, and three daughters; but none left progeny, except Robert his eldest son.

k Bill. Sign. 21 Car. I.   l Lloyd's memoirs of loyalists, p. 681.

Cholmondeley, Earl of Cholmondeley.

Which Robert Cholmondeley, Efq; fucceeding his uncle the Lord Cholmondeley and Earl of Leinfter, was, for his own great merits, and the fervices of his anceftors, dignified with the title of Vifcount Cholmondeley, of Kellis, formerly enjoyed by his faid uncle, by letters patent bearing date [c] March 29, 1661, in the 13th year of Charles II. His Lordfhip married Elizabeth, daughter and coheir of George Cradock, of Caverfwell-caftle, in Staffordfhire, Efq; and departing this life in May, 1681, had iffue by her, Hugh, late Earl of Cholmondeley, Robert, fecond fon, who died at Weftminfter-fchool, and was buried in the Abbey church of Weftminfter, Feb. 14, 1678. George, third fon, fucceeded his brother as Earl of Cholmondeley; and Richard, fourth fon, buried in Weftminfter-abbey, A. D. 1680; alfo one daughter, Elizabeth, married to John Egerton, of Egerton, and Oulton, in com' Ceftr. Efq; eldeft fon and heir of Sir Philip Egerton, fecond furviving fon of Sir Rowland Egerton, of Egerton, Knt. and Bart. and of his Lady Bridget, daughter of Arthur Lord Grey, of Wilton.

Hugh, the eldeft fon, fucceeded his father as Vifcount Cholmondeley, of Kellis in Ireland, and joining with thofe perfons, who oppofed the arbitrary meafures of James II. he was, on the acceffion of King William and Queen Mary to the throne of thefe realms, created Lord Cholmondeley, of Namptwich, by letters patent dated April 10, 1689, with limitation of the honour, for want of iffue male, on the honourable George Cholmondeley, his brother. On March 29, 1705, he was fworn of the Privy-council to Queen Anne, and on Dec. 27, 1706, advanced to the dignity of Vifcount Malpas, and Earl of Cholmondeley, with the like entail on his faid brother George, late Earl of Cholmondeley. On April 22, 1708, his Lordfhip was conftituted Comptroller of her Majefty's houfhold: and on May 10 following, when a new Privycouncil was fettled, according to an act of parliament, on the union of the two kingdoms, he was again fworn thereof; alfo on Oct. 6, the fame year, appointed Treafurer of her Majefty's houfhold. He was alfo conftituted, by her Majefty, Lord-lieutenant and Cuftos Rotulorum of the county of Chefter, and city and county of Chefter, and Lord-lieutenant of North-Wales; but was removed from his employments in the year 1713.

On the acceffion of George I. his Lordfhip was conftituted Treafurer of his houfhold, and fucceeded to the feveral ho-

[c] Dale's cat. of the nobility, p 160.

nours and trusts, from which he was removed in 1713; but dying unmarried, on Jan. 18, 1724-5, was succeeded in his estate and honours by his only brother George, as 2d Earl of Cholmondeley.

Which George, 2d Earl of Cholmondeley, after being well grounded in learning at Westminster-school, and at Christ church in Oxford, betook himself to a military life; being, in 1685, made Cornet of horse; and on King William's accession to the crown, was made one of the Grooms of his bedchamber. His Lordship served in all the wars of that reign; and in Ireland, at the battle of the Boyne, July 1, 1690, commanded the horse-grenadier guards; likewise, at the battle of Steenkirk, on Aug. 3, 1692, when his Majesty attacked the French army in their camp, his Lordship particularly distinguished himself, and was wounded. And his Majesty, in his camp at Promelles, on June 17, 1697, declaring three Colonels Brigadiers-general of horse, Colonel Cholmondeley was the first of them. In the first year of Queen Anne, on July 1, 1702, he was constituted Major-general of her Majesty's forces, and Governor of the forts of Tilbury and Gravesend. Also, on Jan. 1, 1703-4, was declared Lieutenant-general of her Majesty's horse forces.

On George I's accession to the throne, his Lordship was continued in his government of Gravesend and Tilbury forts, as also Colonel of the horse-grenadier guards. On Feb. 11, 1714-15, he was constituted Captain and Colonel of the third troop of horse-guards; and on March 15 following, created Baron of Newborough, in the county of Wexford, in Ireland, being the first Peer of that kingdom created by his then Majesty, who taking further into consideration his great merits and services, was pleased to advance his Lordship to the Peerage of this kingdom, by the title of Baron of Newburgh, in the isle of Anglesey, by letters patent bearing date July 2, 1716. On succeeding his brother in his estate and titles, his Majesty, on March 20, 1724-5, was pleased to appoint his Lordship Lord-lieutenant of the county of Chester, and of the city of Chester, and also Custos Rotulorum of the said county of Chester; and likewise Lord-lieutenant of the counties of Denbigh, Montgomery, Flint, Merioneth, Carnarvon, and Anglesey. His Lordship was also constituted, on March 25, 1725, Governor of the town and fort of Kingston upon Hull; and on April 15, 1727, made General of the horse; likewise, in October, 1732, appointed Governor of the island of Guernsey. He departed this life, at his house, at Whitehall, on May 7, 1733, and was succeeded

by

by George, his eldest son and heir, by Elizabeth his wife, daughter to the Heer Van Baron Ruytenburgh, by Anne-Elizabeth his wife, daughter of Lewis de Naſſaw, Lord of Beverwort, and niece to Henry de Naſſaw, Seignior de Auverquerk, Velt-marſhal of the forces of the States-general, and father of Henry, late Earl of Grantham. The ſaid Elizabeth was naturalized by act of parliament, which had the royal aſſent, Jan. 21, 1703-4. And by her (who died on Jan. 16, 1721-2) his Lordſhip had iſſue another ſon, James, who wedded the Lady Penelope Barry, daughter and heir of James, 4th Earl of Barrimore, of the kingdom of Ireland, and of Elizabeth, his 2d wife, daughter and heir of Richard Savage, late Earl Rivers.

Of this James Cholmondeley, who is now General of foot in his Majeſty's forces; I ſhall obſerve, that he bore the rank of Major on his firſt entrance into the army, his commiſſion bearing date May 12, 1725: and on April 6, 1731, he was conſtituted ſecond Lieutenant-colonel in the 3d troop of horſe-guards, in which poſt he continued till Jan. 17, 1740-1, when he was appointed Colonel of the 48th regiment of foot, then ordered to be raiſed. And on Dec. 18, 1742, was promoted to be Colonel of the 34th regiment of foot. In June, 1744, the regiment being ordered into Flanders, he made the campaign that year. In 1745, he was at the battle of Fontenoy, May 11, N. S. and in July after, was made Brigadier-general of his Majeſty's forces, in which ſtation he ſerved the remainder of the campaign. On the apprehenſion of the progreſs of the rebellion in Scotland, his Majeſty thinking it proper to recall part of his forces from abroad, he was one of the General-officers, who came over with ten battalions of foot, which arrived at Graveſend, about the time that the news came of Sir John Cope's forces being defeated at Preſton-Pans, on Sept. 21, that year. Soon after, he was ſent to Cheſter, to take upon him the command of two battalions of foot, newly arrived from Ireland, who marched under his conduct, till they joined the army of Marſhal Wade, then in Yorkſhire, under whom he ſerved as a Brigadier-general. And when Lieutenant-general Henry Hawley was ſent to take upon him the command of Marſhal Wade's army, the major part of which was immediately ordered for Scotland, to form, with ſome other forces, an army to ſubdue the rebels, there likewiſe he was one of the four Generals, who were entruſted with the command of this army, Lieutenant-general Hawley, Major-general Huſke, and Brigadier-general Mordaunt, being the other three; and greatly ſignalized himſelf

self at the battle of Falkirk, on Jan. 17, 1745-6: but the great fatigue he underwent in this action, joined with the extreme feverity of the weather, unfortunately deprived him of the ufe of his limbs for fome time. He was conftituted Major-general of his Majefty's forces, on Sept. 23, 1747, and promoted to the rank of Lieutenant-general, on May 2, 1754; and thence to that of General of foot in March, 1765. In 1747, he was made Colonel of a regiment of dragoons in Ireland, and from thence was conftituted Colonel of the regiment of horfe-carabineers in Ireland; and on Jan. 16, 1750-1, was appointed Colonel of the Inniſkilling regiment of dragoons, fo denominated, from their fignal behaviour at that place, when raifed there 1689.

The faid George, 2d Earl of Cholmondeley, had alfo, by the fame Lady, three daughters, the Lady Henrietta, unmarried; Lady Elizabeth, married, on Jan. 23, 1730-1, to Edward Warren, of Poynton, in Chefhire, Efq; (and had iffue by him, who died in September, 1737, one fon, Sir George Warren, Knight of the Bath, and a daughter) and Lady Mary, unmarried.

His eldeft fon, George, the prefent Earl of Cholmondeley, was a member of the houfe of Commons, in two parliaments, before he fucceeded his father; firft, on the deceafe of John Smith, Efq; in 1724, [d] for the borough of Eaftlow, in Cornwall; and was chofe for Windfor, in the fucceeding parliament fummoned to meet on Nov. 28e, 1727. On the revival of the moft honourable order of the Bath, he was, on June 17, 1725, inftalled one of the Knights-companions; and on May 13, 1727, appointed Mafter of the Robes to his Majefty. On the acceffion of the late King, he was conftituted one of the Commiffioners of the Admiralty, and Governor of Chefter. And on the eftablifhment of the houfhold of Frederick, late Prince of Wales, was appointed Mafter of his horfe. His Lordfhip, fucceeding his father, was alfo conftituted, on Nov. 2, 1727, Lord-lieutenant of North-Wales, and Lord-lieutenant and Cuftos Rotulorum of the county of Chefter, alfo Chamberlain of Chefter. In May, 1735 (having refigned his poft of Mafter of the horfe to the Prince) he was conftituted one of the Commiffioners of the Treafury; and in May, 1736, was appointed Chancellor of the dutchy of Lancafter, and fworn of the Privy-council. On Dec. 10, 1743, his Majefty having been pleafed to grant to his Lordfhip the office of Keeper of his Majefty's Privy-feal (in the room of John Lord Gower) he was, three days after, fworn

[d] Britifh parl. reg. No 31. [e] Ibid. No. 4.

into

sworn into the said office at St. James's, his Majesty being present in council, and took his place at the board accordingly. And on resigning it, his Lordship was, on Dec. 27, 1744, appointed joint Vice-treasurer, Receiver-general, and Paymaster-general of Ireland, and Treasurer of war in the same kingdom, having resigned the Privy-seal to the said Lord Gower. In 1745, at the breaking out of the rebellion in Scotland, his Lordship raised a regiment of foot for his Majesty's service. His Lordship married, on Sept. 14, 1723, Mary, only lawful daughter of Sir Robert Walpole, first Earl of Orford; and by her Ladyship, who died in 1732, had issue three sons, viz. 1. George, late Lord Viscount Malpas; 2. Robert; and, 3. Frederick, who died in his infancy, April 29, 1731.

Robert Cholmondeley, the second son, born on Nov. 2, 1727, was some time an officer in the army: but preferring an ecclesiastical to a military life, he entered into holy orders; and beside the church-livings of St. Andrew's in Hertford, and Hertingfordbury, near that town, enjoys the office of Auditor-general of his Majesty's revenues in America. He married ———, and has issue.

His Lordship's eldest son and heir, George Lord Viscount Malpas, born on Oct. 17, 1724, served as a volunteer at the battle of Fontenoy, on May 11, 1745, N. S. and immediately after was appointed Aid-de-camp to Sir John Ligonier, and after had a company of foot conferred on him, in Lieutenant-general Howard's regiment of foot. On the rebellion that happened at that time, he was appointed Lieutenant colonel of the regiment of foot raised by his father, the Earl of Cholmondeley, for the suppression of the rebels. He served in the present parliament for Corffe-castle, in Dorsetshire, and for Bramber, in Sussex, in the former; and was Colonel of the Cheshire militia, and of the 65th regiment of foot. His Lordship married, on Jan. 19, 1746-7, Hester, daughter and heir of Sir Francis Edwards, of Grete, and of the College in Shrewsbury, both in the county of Salop, Bart. whose descent (as asserted by the heralds of Wales) is from one of the Barons of the Prince of Powis, descended from the King of Powis, who derived his pedigree from Gurthiern (named by the English, Vertigern) Earl of Euryain and Ewyas, in Herefordshire, and after King of the Britains, about the year 450. His Lordship died on March 15, 1764, leaving, by his said Lady, one son, George-James, now Lord Viscount Malpas, born in 1749; and a daughter, ———, born in 1755.

Cholmondeley, Earl of Cholmondeley.

TITLES.] George Cholmondeley, Earl of Cholmondeley, Viscount Malpas, and Viscount Cholmondeley, of Kellis, Baron Cholmondeley, of Wich-Malbank, alias Namptwich, and Baron of Newburgh.

CREATIONS.] Baron Cholmondeley, of Wich-Malbank, alias Namptwich, April 10 (1689) 1 Will. and Mar. Viscount Malpas, and Earl of Cholmondeley, all in the county of Chester, Dec. 27 (1706) 5 Q. Anne, and Baron of Newburgh, in the isle of Anglesey, in North-Wales, July 2 (1716) 3 Geo. I. Also Baron of Newburgh, in com' Wexford, March 15 (1714) 1 Geo. I. and Viscount Cholmondeley, of Kellis, in the county of East-Meath, March 29 (1661) 13 Car. II. Irish honours.

ARMS.] Gules, two Helmets in chief, proper, garnished, Or; in Base, a Garb of the third.

CREST.] On a Wreath, a Demi-Griphon, rampant, Sable, beaked, winged, and membered, Or, holding an Helmet, proper.

SUPPORTERS.] On the dexter Side, a Griphon, Sable, its Beak, Wings, and Fore-Legs, Or; on the sinister, a Wolf of the second, gorged, with a Collar perflew, Vaire.

MOTTO.] CASSIS TUTISSIMA VIRTUS.

CHIEF-SEAT.] At Cholmondeley, in the county of Chester, 3 miles from Malpas, and 160 from London.

HARLEY,

Cholmondeley Earl of Cholmondeley. 66

HARLEY, *Earl of Oxford, and Earl Mortimer.*

SOME have deduced the house of Harlai, in France (one of the most eminent in that kingdom) from a branch of this ancient and noble family in England: and according to Moreri, there are French authors of this opinion; for he acknowledges,[a] 'It has been reported, they are derived from our 'country: though others maintain, that they are denominated 'from the town of Arlai, in the Franche Compte of Burgundy, 'and pretend to have proof thereof.'

The family of Harley, in England, is undoubtedly more ancient than the Norman conquest; and has been so illustrious, that those in France may be descended from it; though the name may neither be of Saxon, or British, much less of French extraction: for from Hursla, a barbarous Latin word, signifying a wood, comes Hurley, and so it changed into Harley,[b] a town in Shropshire (the ancient seat of this family) according to the learned Sir Henry Spelman. Though others have affirmed Harley to be a Saxon name, and of the same signification with Locus Exercitus.

In an ancient obiit, or ledger book of the abbey of Pershore, in Worcestershire, is a commemoration of a noble warrior of this name,[c] who, commanding an army under Ethelred, King of England, in his wars against Swane, King of Denmark, gave the Danes a great defeat near that town, about the year 1013, and thereby preserved it from spoil and destruction.

We find also, that before[d] the Norman conquest, Sir John de Harley was possessed of Harley-castle and lordship, and having married Alice, daughter of Sir Titus de Leighton,[e] by Letitia his wife, daughter of Hugh le Brune, left issue,

Sir William de Harley, Knt. who is the first mentioned in the visitation of Shropshire, in the college of arms, as lord of Harley in that county. He was one [f] of those eminent persons who attended Godfrey de Bulloigne, Robert Curthoese, Duke of Normandy, Alan, Lord High-steward of Scotland, and others of note, in the first memorable expedition to the Holy-Land, anno 1098, where they obtained many victories against the Saracens, and conquered Jerusalem. In honour of which, this Sir William was with them made Knights of the Sepulchre,

---

a Grand Dict. tom. 3.   b Ed. Llwyd's antiq. of Shrop. MS. p. 226.   c Ex collect. Hug. Thomas, MS.   d Ibid.   e Vincent's visitat. de Salop. ann. 1623. MS. p. 246.   f Ibid. p. 198.

an order of Knighthood inftituted upon that occafion. He died in England, and was buried in the abbey of Perfhore, where his tomb is ftill remaining, and the only ancient monument there, which was not demolifhed at the diffolution of abbeys in the reign of Hen. VIII. and it is obfervable, that the fhield on his effigies is plain, without any arms, according to the cuftom of the moft ancient times. He married Catharine, daughter of Sir Jafper Croft, who was alfo a Knight of the Sepulchre, [g] and by her left iffue,

Nicholas de Harley, who had to wife Margaret, daughter of Sir Warren de Boftock, of Boftock, in com' Ceft. by whom he had iffue William de Harley, who married Joan, daughter of Sir John de la Bere, Knt. of Kinnerfley and Clonger, in com' Salop, and by her was father of Nicholas de Harley, who wedded Alice, daughter of Ralph Preftrop, of Preftrop, in Shropfhire, and from them proceeded Robert de Harley; their fon and heir.

Which Robert married Alice, daughter and heir of Sir Roger Pulifdon, of Pulifdon, in com' Salop, by whom he had iffue Sir Richard de Harley, continuator of the line, and Malcolm de Harley : all which defcents are in the vifitation of Shropfhire, before-mentioned ; but our public records have not been generally preferved till the reign of Hen. III. [*]

The youngeft fon Malcolm de Harley, or Harleigh, as it was fometimes wrote, was chaplain to Edw. I. and much in his favour, being employed in the management of the revenues of that glorious monarch, and was his Efcheator on this fide Trent, an office of great honour and truft in thofe days. In 11 Edw. I. he, and Sir Guifchard de Charne, or Charran, had the cuftody of the bifhopric of Durham, and accounted for the iffues thereof to the King during the vacancy[h], viz. from June 13 to Sept. 4, the fame year, and paid into the Exchequer 1319 l. for rents of affize of the manours in the ferm of the city of Durham, and in certainties for guard of burgs and ovens, or bake-houfes ; alfo 1193 l. 19 s. 1 d. for tallage

---

[g] Vincent ut fupra. [*] Henry, lord of Harley, died in 1281, 9 Edw. I. and by Joan, his wife, had fix fons, all monks : John, the eldeft, became profeffed in the monaftery at Worcefter, October 21, 1279, Annal. Wigorn. in Anglia Sacra, vol. 1. p. 502. This John, on his father's death, obtained an indulgence of 1185 days, in his convent, for the fouls of his parents. The other five brothers were, Richard, a monk, at Beaulieu, in Hampfhire; William, at Hales-abbey, in Gloucefterfhire; Walter, at Bordefley, in Worcefterfhire; Nicholas, at Rufford, in Nottinghamfhire; and Roger, in a convent beyond fea, Ibid. p. 505. Sir Richard, mentioned above as continuator of the line, was, perhaps, brother and heir to this Henry, father of the fix monks, though he is ftyled lord of Harley before the 9th of Edw. I, but, that might be by the refignation of Henry. [h] Madox's hift. of the Excheq. p. 496, 497.

affeffed

Harley, Earl of Oxford, and Earl Mortimer. 233

affeffed upon the manours of the bifhopric, and other fums for divers other parts of the revenue thereof; in all, 2620 l. 7 s. 9½ d. In 1296, 24 Edw. I. the King grants to this Malcolm de Harleigh. (as it was then wrote) ftyling him his beloved Clerk [i], the marriage of Margaret, eldeft daughter, and one of the heirs, of Brian de Brampton, deceafed, for his nephew Robert de Harleigh, fon of Richard, dated at Vghtragharder (Auchterarder) June 21. On Aug. 22, 1297, 25 Edw. I. [k] he was with the King at fea, in the fhip called Cog. Edward, near Winchelfea, and was one of the witneffes to the King's delivery of the Great-feal to John de Benefteed, in the faid fhip. And attending that monarch abroad, who did not return to England till March 14, 1298, died foon after: for the King, by writ of Privy-feal, 26 Edw. I. [1] reciting that he was his Efcheator on this fide Trent, and that Philip de Willoughby, the Treafurer's Lieutenant, and the Barons of the Exchequer, would probably feize his goods and chattels, he commands them to leave enough in the hands of his kindred for the honourable interment of his body; and that they fhould fend fome fit perfon to all places where he had any goods, to take a true and exact inventory of them, that the King, when he fhould be certified thereof, might give fuch orders therein as he thought proper. Accordingly [m] Thomas de Boyvil was affigned, by letters patent, to take an inquifition concerning the goods of the faid Malcolm, and the Treafurer's Lieutenant was ordered to deliver to Richard de Harley, his executor, 48 l. 14 s. 11 d. for the exequies and burial of the deceafed. He built [n] that houfe now called Clifford's-Inn, behind St. Dunftan's church, in Fleet-ftreet; which being feized by the King, for certain debts due from the faid Malcolm, it was granted, in 3 Edw. II. to Robert de Clifford, Lord Clifford, who made it his habitation, and had thence the name of Clifford's-Inn; Ifabel, the widow of the faid Robert, having demifed it to the ftudents of the law. But though that houfe was feized by the King, yet his poffeffions were more than fufficient to difcharge all his debts; for it is evident, fome of his lands devolved on his brother and his defcendants.

I now return to Richard de Harley, elder brother to the faid Malcolm, and his executor, as before related. The firft mention I find of him is in 40 Hen. III. when he was attached to anfwer to a plea [o] of Richard, fon of Robert de Clifton, that he, with others, came into the wood of the faid Richard, fon of

i Pat. 24 Edw. I. m. 14. k Rymer's fœd. vol. 2. p. 791, 813. l Hift. of the Excheq. p. 665, 666. m Ibid. n Dugdale's orig. jurid. p. 187.
o Placita jur, & affif. in com' Salop, anno 40 Hen. III, rot. 7.

Robert,

Robert, in Beldefworth, and that his men, in the said wood, beat and abufed the faid Richard and his men, contrary to the peace, &c. And thereupon Richard de Harleigh pleaded, that the wood was his wood, and, finding fome trees felled, he carried them away, as he lawfully might. However, by confent, a perambulation was made between the wood of the faid Richard, fon of Robert de Clifton, and the wood of the faid Richard de Harleigh, in Harleigh. And that Odo de Hodenet, Stephen de Buterlegh, Peter de Muneton, and William de Leighton, four Knights, reviewed the fame perambulation, begun on the fouth of the land of the priory of Wenlock, between the wood and the plain, by an old hedge, to a great elm; and awarded, that the faid Richard de Harleigh may make a hedge from the elm through part of that wood to the green oak, and from thence to the withered oak, and fo to another withered oak in the plain.

In the fame year, he [p] was among thofe of the county of Salop, who, holding lands in capite by Knight's fervice, to the value of 15 l. per ann. and not being Knights, were fummoned to take that degree, or fine for the fame.

In 1264, 48 Hen. III. the Barons, with Simon Montfort, Earl of Leicefter, having taken Prince Edward prifoner, at the battle of Lewes, May 14, his Highnefs was held in cuftody in Hereford-caftle, when Roger Mortimer, Lord of Wigmore, contrived his efcape; and, being affifted by this Sir Richard Harley [q], they iffued out from Wigmore-caftle, and delivered him. It appears from our hiftorians [r], and other authorities, that Mortimer fent the Prince a fwift horfe, with intimation, that he fhould obtain leave to ride out for his recreation into a place called Widmerfh, and upon fight of a perfon mounted on a white horfe, at the foot of Tillington-hill, and waving his bonnet, he fhould hafte towards him with all fpeed. Accordingly the Prince, on the fignal, fetting fpurs to that horfe, overwent thofe about him; and Mortimer meeting him with five hundred armed men, chaced them back to the gates of Hereford, and brought him in fafety to his caftle of Wigmore. Afterwards they were in that great battle of Evefham, fought on Aug. 6, 1265, 49 Hen. III. where the Barons were vanquifhed, and Simon Montfort, their leader, flain. Which victory was a principal means of putting an end to that bloody war, and of advancing this family, when the faid gallant Prince afcended the throne.

[p] MS. Not. b. 5. p. 68. in bibl. Joh. Anftis, arm. [q] Hift. de la Maifon de Harley, par M. Moret, MS. fol. 4. [r] Mon. Ang. vol. 2. p. 223. & MS. in bibl. Bodl. med. 10. 120. b.

Harley, Earl of Oxford, and Earl Mortimer. 235

In 56 Hen. III. he was ˢ Coroner of Shropshire, an officer, in those days, of great trust. In 3 Edw. I. it was found, by verdict of the hundred of Condover, that Richard de Harley ᵗ held the manour of Harley for three hides of land. He was married before 20 Edw. I. for ᵘ in that year he is mentioned with Burga his wife, in a plea concerning a free tenement and lands in Great-Wenlock. In 21 Edw. I. he was summoned to attend the King at Bristol, on the marriage of his daughter to the Earl of Barr ʷ; as appears by a writ in the White Tower.

In 1297, 25 Edw. I. he was ˣ summoned to be ready with horse and arms, to attend the King at London, on Tuesday after the Octaves of St. John Baptist, to go with him beyond the seas. In the same year, ʸ a fine was levied by him and Burga his wife, and Adam la Bolde, of the manour of La Bolde, granted to them by the said Adam, which they convey to him again for life, paying a rose annually, remainder to the said Richard de Harleye, and Burga, and their heirs. She was the sole daughter and heir ᶻ of Sir Andrew de Willey, son and heir of Warrin de Willegh, or Willey, by Petronella his wife, daughter and heir of Robert, son of Odo, Lord of Kinlegh, in com' Salop. And by this ᵃ match, divers fair lordships accrued to this family, as Willey, Gretenton, Walderhope, Walle under Eywood, and Rushbury; beside what came by the heir of Kenlegh.

In 27 Edw. I. the King sent him ᵇ a letter, styling him his beloved and faithful Richard de Harlegh, commanding him to be at Berwick upon Tweed, with such foot-soldiers as he had raised, to march against the Scots.

In 28 Edw. I. this ᶜ Sir Richard Harley, Robert Corbet, and Robert de Roscale, were the three Knights chosen for Shropshire, whom the ᵈ King (to satisfy his Earls and Nobles) impowered, as Justices in the said county, to punish all offences against the articles of Magna Charta, the Charter of the Forest, and the Statute of Winton, not punishable by the common laws of the realm. And the same year being chosen ᵉ one of the representatives of the county of Salop, in the parliament held at Westminster, he had a writ directed to the sheriff, for his expences.

s Plac. jur. & assisæ, & plac. coron. apud Salop. 56 Hen. III. rot. 13.
t Inter inqui pro hundred, in cur. recept. scac.   u Plac. jur. & assis. apud Salop. 20 Edw. I, rot. 15.   w Ex collect. Hug. Thomas.   x MS. in bibl. Cotton. sub. effig. Claudius, c. 2.   y Int. pedes fin. com' Salop. 25 Edw. I. in cur. recept. scac.   z Vincent's visit. ut supra.   a Ex collect. W. Holman de com' Essex.   b Madox's Baronia Angl. p. 257. c. 2. & claus. 27 Edw. I. m. 6. dorso.   c Pat. 28 Edw. I. m. 14.   d Pryn's hist. of K. John, Hen. III. & Edw. I. p. 830.   e Pryn's 4th part of a brief regist. p. 10.

In

In 29 Edw. I. he [f] was Sheriff of Shropſhire, and had a ſpecial letter [g] from the King, to attend him with horſe and arms at Berwick. And it is probable he was then made a Knight Banneret; for, among the collections of the late Sir Henry St. George, Garter King at Arms, are the names of the Knights, who ſerved Edw. I. in his wars in Scotland, with their arms curiouſly painted, taken from an old roll, wherein this [h] Sir Richard Harley is mentioned, with his arms,. Or, a Bend, cotiſed Sable.

In 30 Edw. I. he [i] obtained a grant of free warren within his lordſhips of Harleigh, Kenleigh, Willeigh, Gretenton, Hatton, Wilderdehope, Ruſhbury, and La Bould. He was [k] alſo in that year Sheriff of Shropſhire, which was then an office of great truſt and power.

In 33 and 34 Edw. I. [l] attending again in parliament, as repreſentative of the county of Salop, he had his expences allowed: and, in 35 Edw. I. was elected, with John de Dene, Knights for Shropſhire, being the longeſt parliament in that King's reign: yet, as Pryn obſerves (in his fourth part of A Brief Regiſter, &c. p. 28.) it laſted not full two months; but in that ſpace made ſome good laws, and tranſacted ſeveral grand affairs, occaſioned by the Scots rebellion, and crowning Robert Bruce their King; the marriage of Prince Edward, and divers weighty public affairs.

In the reign of Edw. II. he was elected in four ſeveral parliaments, one of the Knights for the county of Salop [m], viz. in the fourth, fifth, eighth, and ninth, of that Monarch. In 3 Edw. II. he [n] was one of the three, with the Sheriff of Shropſhire, to whom the King directed his letters, to put in execution the articles for obſerving the ſtatute made in the parliament held at Winchester. In 1311, 5 Edw. II. having the cuſtody of the lands of the Knights-Templars, and of the Biſhop of Litchfield and Coventry, he had [o] command from the King, to pay the iſſues thereof into the Treaſury, on the morrow of St. Hilary. In 7 Edw. II. he [p] and William de Mortimer, were aſſigned Juſtices of aſſize for the county of Salop, and cauſes were tried before them, on the Wedneſday before the feaſt of St. Ethelbert, the King and Martyr.

---

f Fuller's worthies in eod. Com.　g Ryley's plac. parl. p. 482. & clauſ. 29 Edw. I.　h MS. n. 20. p. 34. in bibl. Joh. Vicecom. Percival.　i Ed. Lwyd's ant. of Shrop. MS.　k Fuller, ut antea.　l Pryn's 4th part; ut ſupra.　m Pryn, p. 74.　n Clauſ. 3 Edw. II. m. 7. & Ryley's plac. parl. in append. p 523.　o Rymer's fœd. tom. 5. 297.　p Aſſiſa cap. apud Salop. 7 Edw. II. in cur. recept. ſcac.

This

Harley, Earl of Oxford, and Earl Mortimer.

This Sir Richard Harley died q about 13 Edw. II. and Burga, his widow, was ftyled Lady of Willegh, and Kinlet, in Shropſhire, in an acquittance dated 14 Edw. II. whereby fhe releafed to the monks of Wenlock, certain rents due to her. They had iffue, Robert; Malcolm; and Henry, who was a prieſt; and probably r John Harley, Sheriff of Worcefterfhire in 40 Edw. III.

Of Henry it is related s, that in 2 Edw. III. he had a great conteft concerning the deanery of Bridgenorth, occafioned by having obtained a grant of the fame, upon fuggeftion, that Thomas de Eyton, the Dean, was dead. But he appearing before the King, the grant was revoked, with a fpecial mandate for reftoring of the rightful Dean. Whereupon the Sheriff certified, that both Thomas de Eyton, and Henry de Harley, had raifed great numbers of men in arms, in order to difpute the right by force; on which the King commanded the Sheriff to charge both parties to defift, fuperfeding the mandate for reftoring Thomas de Eyton, till both appeared in the court of Chancery. The parties accordingly appeared, and Thomas de Eyton was reftored.

Of Malcolm de Harley, the fecond fon, I find a fine t was levied in 5 Edw. III. between him and Burga his mother, of the manour of Gretynton, and fixteen acres of land, and 40 s. rent, in Rufhebury, the right of the faid Malcolm, which he conveys to the faid Burga, to hold for life, and after her deceafe, to remain to Philip de Harley and his heirs. Alfo, in the fame year, a fine u was levied between the faid Burga, who was the wife of Richard de Harleye, and Philip de Harleye, of two mills, and 23 acres of land, with the appurtenances, in Borewardefleye, and a third part of the manour of Borewardefleye, and the advowfon of the church, the right of the faid Philip, which he conveys to the faid Burga for life, and after her deceafe, to Malcolm de Harleye, and his heirs.

It is probable this Philip was another fon of Sir Richard Harley; and w in 10 Edw. III. I find Philip de Harley parfon of the church of Stircheley, and in 42 Edw. III. parfon of the church of Rufhbury.

I now return to Robert de Harley, eldeft fon of Sir Richard. In 24 Edw. I. his uncle, Malcolm de Harley, obtained for him the marriage of Margaret, eldeft daughter and coheir of Brian de Brampton, as before-mentioned; and in 1309, 2 Edw. II. on proof that his wife x Margaret was then of full age, the

---

q Ex collect. Hug. Thomas.   r Fuller in cod. com.   s Llwyd's antiq. of Shropfhire, MS.   t Penes fin. com' Salop. 5 Edw. III.   u Pedes fin. ejuſd. comit. & ann.   w Fin. Salop, 10 Edw. III. & 42 Edw. III.   x Clauf. 2 Edw. II. m. 19.

King commanded Walter de Gloucester, his Escheator beyond Trent, to deliver them full seisin of those lands that were in his province, viz. the manour of Brampton, and the hamlet of Weston, with their appurtenances, in the marches of Wales; the manour of Buxton, with the appurtenances; 33 s. rent, with the appurtenances in Stowe, in the same marches; lands in the park of Kinlet, in com' Salop, and the manour of Ashton, with the appurtenances, in com' Hereford.

Brian de Brampton, father of the said Margaret, died y on 14 kalends of June (May 19) 1293, 21 Edw. I. and her only sister Elizabeth was married to Sir Edmund de Cornwal, grandson of Richard Earl of Cornwal, King of the Romans, brother to Hen. III.

As from this match he acquired a great estate, and their seat of Brampton-castle having since been the chief seat of the descendants of the said Sir Robert Harley, I hope it won't be thought a digression, if I give some account of the ancient and noble family of Brampton, or Bramton, as it is now wrote.

The before-mentioned Brian de Brampton z was the only son and heir of Sir Walter de Brampton, eldest son and heir of Sir Brian de Brampton, lord of Brampton, Drayton, Bucton, Pedwardyn, Wiston, Hermeston, Ayston, Kynlet, Foxcot, Walton, and Adrington, by hereditary succession; and in right of Alice his mother, was lord of Botteley and Condover. He was usually called the noble Brian, in respect of his noble descent, and qualities. He married Emma, daughter, and at last one of the heirs of Thomas, Lord Corbet, Baron of Caus. And he was the son of Brian de Bramton, styled Senior, by Alice his wife, daughter and one of the coheirs of Walter de Remenyle, Lord of Botteley and Condover, in com' Salop. This Brian de Bramton, senior, was of such eminence, that in 17 Hen. III. the King a requiring hostages of the Barons Marchers for their fidelity, Ralph de Mortimer delivered him Henry, son and heir of this Sir Brian, for his faithful demeanor, and he was thereupon committed to the custody of William de Stutevil; and it may be, he died under confinement; for Walter was at length the heir of the said Sir Brian, who, in 39 Hen. III. had a b grant of free warren in his manours and lands of Brampton, Bucton, Stanage, Weston, Pictes, and Ashton, in com' Hereford and Salop; also at Wauton in Somersetshire. He made his will on the vigil of the apostles Simon and Jude, in 46 Hen. III. and is therein

---

y Ex stem. sub manu Joh. Anstis, arm. gart. reg. arm. and Rad. Brook.
z Ibid. & ex collect. Nich. Jekyl de Cast. Hedingham in com' Essex, arm. & Rad. Brooke secial. Ebor.   a Clauf. 17 Hen. III. m. 8. in dorso.   b Cart. 36 Hen. III. & transcrip. ejusd. in cur. recept. scac. in baga Peramb. Forest.

Harley, Earl of Oxford, and Earl Mortimer.

styled Senior. He was the son of Brian de Bramton, by Alice his wife, daughter of Walter de Nova Meinil, who gave with her, in free marriage, four virgates of land in Foxcott, in the territory of Idelburi; to which were witnesses, E. Bishop of Hereford, Hugh de Mortimer, William de Mortimer, Philip de Mortimer, William de Burley, and others. John de Brampton was his father, and, by Maud his wife, was related to most of the great men of that age; she c being the widow of Roger Mortimer, Lord of Wigmore, and the daughter of William de Breos, Lord of Brecon (now wrote Brecknock) by Eva his wife, daughter and coheir of William Marshal, Earl of Pembroke, by Isabel his wife, daughter and heir to Richard Strongbow, Earl of Pembroke, who married Eva, daughter and sole heir of Dormack Mac-Morough, King of Leinster, in Ireland. And the said Richard Strongbow was the son of Gilbert de Clare, grandson of Richard Fitz-Gilbert, Earl of Brion in Normandy, and of Rose his wife, sister and heir to Walter Gifford, Earl of Buckingham. And the before-mentioned William de Breos was the son of Reginald de Breos, by Grisold, daughter and coheir to William Brewer, Lord of Torbay; and he, of William de Breos, son of Philip de Breos, by Berta, second daughter, and at length coheir to Walter Earl of Hereford, son of Walter, Earl of Hereford, and of Sibil his wife, daughter and sole heir of Bernard Newmarch, Lord of Brecon (by conquest, and by gift of William Rufus) and of Neast, daughter to Traham ap Cradock, King of North-Wales. And the last-mentioned Philip de Breos, was grandson and heir of William de Breos, Lord of Breos in Normandy, and of Bramber, in com' Sussex, who married Agnes, daughter to Waldron, Earl of St. Clare.

By the foregoing account it appears, how nobly Sir John de Brampton was related by Maud, his wife; and Sir Brian de Brampton, his father, had to wife, Maud, daughter and heir of Sir John de St. Vallerie, lineally descended from Reginald de St. Vallerie, at the time of the conquest. And the said Sir Brian was [d] son of Brian, son of Barnard de Brampton, surnamed Vnspec, Lord of Kinlet, in com' Salop, in the reign of Hen. I.

I now return to Sir Robert Harley, who, by his Lady aforesaid, was not only allied to the before-mentioned noble families, but she was also near in blood to the great family of Mortimer; being lineal heir (as I have already shewed) to Sir John de Brampton, and Maud his wife, one of the heirs of William de Braeose, or Brewes, Lord of Brecknock; who had

[c] Ex collect. Hug. Thomas & visitat. de com' Salop.   [d] Vincent's visitat. de com' Salop.

240 *Harley, Earl of Oxford, and Earl Mortimer.*

for her ᵈ firſt huſband Roger Mortimer, Lord of Wigmore, by whom ſhe had iſſue Edward Mortimer, Lord of Wigmore, father of Roger, Earl of March, the great favourite of Queen Iſabel, mother of Edw. III.

In 11 Edw. II. this Sir Robert Harley had the following remarkable grant: ' Sachez nous ᵉ Roger de Mortimer Seigneur
' de Wygemore avoir donne & grante a noſtre chier Bachiler,
' Monſieur Robert de Harley, pour ſon bon ſervice & pour
' cent livres de argent, la gard du corps Gilbert filz & heir
' Sir Johan de Lacy, enſemblent ove le marriage meſmes celuy
' Gilbert deyns age eſteant en noſtre garde, &c. Donne à
' Penebrugge l'an du regne la Roye Edward filz le Roy Edward
' unzyme.' Cambden, in his Britannia, fol. 176, makes a queſtion, whether theſe Bachelors were not of a middle degree, between Knights and Eſquires. In pat. 8 Rich. II. p. 1. m. 4. Jonn de Clanvou is ſtyled Bacalarius Regis. And the word is uſed, 13 Rich. II. ſtat. 2. cap. 1. where it ſignifieth the ſame with Knight-bachelor.

In 14 Edw. II. ᶠ he had livery of the lands of which his father died poſſeſſed; and in 17 Edw. II. he is ſtyled Chevalier in two fines; the one ᵍ between Hugh de Bramton, of Ludlowe, Quer. and the ſaid Robert and Margaret his wife, Deforc. concerning a meſſuage in Ludlowe, the right of the ſaid Hugh, and the heirs of Margaret. The other was ʰ between Robert de Harley, Chevalier, and Margaret his wife, Quer. and Joan, who was the wife of Gilbert de Lacy, Deforc. who grants to the ſaid Sir Robert and Margaret, for life, the manours of Bramton and Bukton, and after their deceaſe, to remain to Brian, ſon of the ſaid Sir Robert and Margaret, and the heirs of his body; and if the ſaid Brian dies without heir male, to remain to the heirs of the bodies of the ſaid Robert and Margaret, remainder to the right heirs of the ſaid Margaret.

In the ſame year all Knights, and others, who bore ancient arms from their anceſtors, were returned into Chancery; and, in the liſt of thoſe for Shropſhire, ⁱ are Sir Robert Harley, and Malcolm Harley, his brother; from which it may be inferred, that his chief reſidence was then at the caſtle of Harley, no mention being made of him in Herefordſhire.

In 18 Edw. II. ᵏ he was appointed to array thoſe forces raiſed in Shropſhire, for the ſervice of the King, againſt the French in Gaſcony: and was ˡ one which that King chiefly confided in, for ſuppreſſing the Knights-Templars.

d Vincent's viſitat. de com' Salop. & Dugd. Baron. vol. 1. in famil. de Mortimer. e Cowel's law interpreter, ſub tit. Bachelor. f Clauſ. 14 Edw. II. g Pedes fin. com' Salop. 17 Edw. II. h Ibid. i MS. in bibl. Cotton. Claud. c. 2. k Rymer's fœd. tom. 4. p. 78. l Ex collect. Hug. Thomas.

Soon

Harley, Earl of Oxford, and Earl Mortimer.

Soon after the accession of Edw. III. Roger Mortimer, Earl of March (to whom he was of kin) coming to a violent death, I presume it might some way affect him; for I find no mention of him [m] till 12 Edw. III. when he was elected one of the Knights for Shropshire, in the parliament then held: in the same year, the King commissioned him [n] to march 50 archers, and 50 pikemen to Ipswich, being the quota that John de Warren, Earl of Surry, as Lord of Bromfield and Yale, was to furnish for the King's service. And, by another commission of the same date, he [o] was appointed by the King to muster those forces, and to see that they were well cloathed all in a livery, and well armed.

He was again elected one of the [p] Knights for Shropshire, to the parliaments held in 13 and 15 Edw. III. In 16 Edw. III. by a fine levied between him and Margaret his wife, and Philip de Harley [q], he settled the manours of Bramton, and Buckton, with the appurtenances, after the decease of himself and Margaret his wife, on his son Brian and his heirs, with remainder to the right heirs of the said Robert and Margaret. In 18 Edw. III. Joan, who was the wife of Gilbert de Lacy [r], by a fine then levied, settled messuages, lands, and rents, in Ashton, in com' Hereford, on this Sir Robert Harley and Margaret his wife, for their lives, remainder to Walter, son of the said Robert and Margaret, and the heirs of his body, remainder to the heirs of the said Robert and Margaret, remainder to the right heirs of the said Margaret.

In 21 Edw. III. on the death of Beatrix, wife of Peter, Lord Corbet, of Caus, who died seized [s] of the barony of Caus, the manours of Munsterley, Yokethul, Wentenouse, Shelve, Bynnewesson, Foxton, Chelme, Over-Gother, Nether-Gother, and Baghetrese, in com' Salop, it was found, that Thomas Corbet, ancestor to the said Peter, died seized of the said manours, and left a son Peter, and three daughters, Alice, Venice, and Emme; likewise, that the said Peter had issue Peter, his son and heir, who married her the said Beatrix: And that the beforementioned Alice became the wife of Robert de Stafford, who had issue by her Nicholas, his son and heir, and he Edmund, and he Ralph, then Lord Stafford (viz. at the time when the inquisition was taken) and that Emme, the other sister, had issue Walter de Bramton, her son and heir, and he Brian, who left two daughters his coheirs, Margaret, the wife of Sir Robert de Harley, and Elizabeth, wife of Edmund de Cornwal; and were next heirs to the before-specified Peter Lord Corbet,

---

m Pryn's brev. parl. p. 75.　n Rymer, tom. 5. p. 7.　o Ibid. p. 8.
p Pryn ut supra.　q Pedes fin. com' Salop. 16 Edw. III.　r Fin. com'
Heref. 18 Edw. III.　s Esc. 21 Edw. III. n. 55.

Ralph Lord Stafford being then 32 years of age, Margaret 46, and Elizabeth 42. The said Peter Lord Corbet, in 27 Edw. I.[t] was found, by inquisition, to be one of the next heirs of Roger de Valletort, a great Baron in the west; and [u] died, the year following, seized of the barony of Caus, with its members; which barony, by the death of Peter, son of the said Peter, as before-mentioned, has been ever since in abeyance between the families of the Lord Stafford (whence branched the Dukes of Buckingham) this family of Harley, and that of Cornwal. And in 21 Edw. III. the coheirs [w] came to an agreement; Ralph, Lord Stafford, had, for his purparty, the castle of Caus entirely, with the appurtenances; the Knights fees being likewise parted amongst them. Sir Robert Harley had for his share, the manours of Yokethul, also Yokelton, Wentnore, Stretton, Chelme, with a moiety of two water-mills, and one fulling-mill, and of the fourth part of the manour of Byn-Weston. He died in 23 Edw. III. 1349, possessed of the manours of Harley, Willegh, and divers other manours, leaving Robert his son and heir; and had also two other sons, Brian and Walter, as the authorities before-mentioned make appear; and one daughter Joan, married to Gilbert de Lacy, Lord of Frome-castle, in Herefordshire, who was in wardship to him, and was son and heir of Sir John de Lacy, and Joan his wife.

It is also probable, that Andrew Harley was one of his sons, and had that name from his mother's father. It is certain [x], that Andrew Harley was one of the Knights of the shire for the county of Hereford, in 7 Rich. II. as also in 9 Rich. II. when he is styled Chevalier.

Robert de Harley, his eldest son, is styled Fatuus (or the Simple) in the genealogy and records. In 23 Edw. III. Hugh de Parrok and Richard More, by deed, dated at Harley, [y] grant to Robert Harley and Joan his wife, the manours of Harley, Gretingdon, Kenle, Cherlecote, Bolde, Yokelton, Stretton, Shelve, Wentenere, and the 4th part of the forest of Caus, which they had by the feoffment of the said Robert. In 35 Edw. III. by the name of Robert, son and heir of Margaret, wife of Robert de Harley, he [z] gave 25 marks to the King for his relief for the fourth part of the [a] barony of Caus. In 37 Edw. III. by a final agreement between Hugh Parok, plaintiff, and Robert de Harley and Joan his wife, deforcients, a settlement was made of the manours of Harley, Gretington, and Wyleleye (as then wrote) on him and the said Joan his wife, and the heirs of their bo-

[t] Esc. 27 Edw. I. n. 32. [u] Esc. 28 Edw. I. n. 40. [w] Clauf. 21 Edw. III. m. 19. [x] Pryn ut supra in com' Heref. [y] Ex collect. R. Glover, Somers. [ ] Fin. 35 Edw. III. Ex collect. W. Holman. [a] Inter ped. fin. com' Salop. 37 Edw. III.

dies,

dies, with remainder to the right heirs of the said Joan. Also the same year by [b] another final agreement, wherein Hugh le Yonge, clerk, and Hugh Parrock, vicar of the church of Shawebury, being plaintiffs, they settled the manours of Yokelton, Shelve, and Wentenere, and the 4th part of the forest of Caus, on the said Robert and Joan, for their lives, with remainder to Fulk, son of Robert Corbet, of Morton, and his heirs, remainder to the right heirs of the said Joan: but, by another final agreement the next ensuing year, they [c] granted the premises to the said Fulk Corbet, to hold for their lives, in consideration of an annual allowance of 60 l. during both their lives. In 39 Edw. III. [d] he granted to John Delves, Chevalier, a Knight's fee, and seven shillings rent, with the appurtenances, in Deryngton, together with the homage and service of Richard de Deryngton, and his heirs, in the said town. And in 41 Edw. III. [e] reciting, that Fulk, son of Robert Corbet, of Morton, Knt. holds the manours of Yokelton, Shelve, Wentenore, and the 4th part of the forest of Caus, for life, by demise of the said Robert and Joan his wife, and that the premises, after the decease of the said Fulk, ought to revert to the said Robert and Joan, and the heirs of Joan; they granted the reversion thereof to Roger, son of Robert Corbet, of Morton, Knt. and to the heirs male of his body, remainder to the said Robert and Joan, and the heirs of Joan. In 48 Edw. III. [f] it is set forth, that Robert de Harley, cousin and heir of Malcolm de Harley, held the moiety of the manour of Ashdon, with the appurtenances, of the heir of Robert de Mortimer, late Earl of March, the King's ward, by the service of a moiety of one Knight's fee. But not long after he departed this life, as is evident from a final agreement in 50 Edw. III. [g] between Joan, widow of the said Robert de Harley, plaintiff, and Peter de Cornewall, deforcient, whereby the said Peter grants the reversion of the manour of Cherlecote (then held by Brian de Cornewall, Chevalier, and others, for the life of the said Brian) together with the manours of Yokelton, Shelve, and Wentenore, and the 4th part of the forest of Caus (then also held by Fulk Corbet, for life, with remainder to Roger his brother, if he survives him) to the said Joan, and her heirs. She [h] was daughter of Sir Robert Corbet, of Morton Corbet, Knt. and survived her husband many years. In 4 Rich. II. being styled Joan, [i] widow of Robert de Harley, she claimed the 3d part of the manours of Bueld, and Cherlecote, as her dower, against Hamond de Peshall, and Alice his wife; and her claim was

b Inter ped. fin. com' Salop. 37 Edw. III.   c Ibid. 38 Edw. III.   d Ibid. 39 Edw. III.   e Ibid. 41 Edw. III.   f Ibid. 48 Edw. III.   g Ibid. 50 Edw. III.   h Vincent's visitat. de com' Salop,   i Ex collect. R. Glover, Somers. fecial.

allowed.

allowed. She was alfo living [k] in 13 Hen. IV. They had iffue an only daughter and heir [l] Alice, married to Sir Hamond de Pefhall, of the county of Stafford, Knt. and carried the caftle and lordfhip of Harley, and a great eftate, out of the family; and the faid Alice likewife left iffue Elizabeth, her fole heir [m], married 1ft to Henry Grendon [n], who died poffeffed of the manour of Harley, &c. In 24 Hen. VI. fhe fecondly was married to Sir Richard Lacon, Knt. who had iffue by her William Lacon, of Willey [o], from whom defcended thofe of the name at Willey, and Kinlet, Thongland, Holloway, and Mounflow, in Shropfhire.

Having brought the iffue of Robert de Harley to a period, I now return to Brian Harley, his brother. Which Brian Harley being in the wars with France, he there received the honour of Knighthood; and was a perfon of fuch eminence, that [p] Edward the Black Prince recommended him to his father Edw. III. to be chofen a Knight of the Garter; but he died before his election. He [q] married Eleanor, daughter to Sir Roger Corbet, of Morton, fifter to his eldeft brother's wife; and, by agreement with his brother, [r] divided the inheritance of the family. I have before mentioned, that the paternal eftate in Shropfhire went away with his brother's daughter and heir. And by the faid agreement, this Sir Brian was heir to his mother's eftate, viz. Brampton, Bucton, Byton, and other lands in Wiggefmoreland. He left iffue one fon, [s] Bryan de Harley, and a daughter, [t] Eleanor, married to Sir John Bromwick, of Bromwick-caftle, in Herefordfhire, Knt. Eleanor his wife was fecondly [u] married to Thomas Cotes, as appears by an award made in 7 Rich. II. by Sir John Burley, Knt. and others, betwixt her faid hufband Thomas Cotes, and her fon Bryan Harley. She was alfo living in 16 Rich. II. [w] when, ftyling herfelf Eleanor, relict of Sir Brian de Harley, Knt. fhe gave to Roger Swinnerton, Lord of Chebbefey, all her right in the manour of Haymes, in the county of Stafford.

Bryan de Harley, Efq; fucceeding his father, was denominated of Brampton-caftle, in Herefordfhire; he was Governor [x] of Montgomery and Dolverin caftles, in the reign of Hen. IV. which he bravely defended againft the famous Owen Glendourdwy, who was forced, by his valour, to return from them; in memory whereof he changed his creft, which was ' a Buck's ' Head proper, to a Lion rampant, Gules, iffuing out of a

k Vincent's vifitat. de com' Salop. l Ibid. m Ibid. n Ibid. o Efc. 24 Hen. VI. n. 35. p Ex collect. Hug. Thomas. q Vifitat. &c. com' Salop. præd. r Ex ftemmate fub manu Joh. Anftis, arm. s Ibid. t Vifit. de com' Salop. præd. u Ex collect. Hug. Thomas. w Ex collect. R. Glover, Somerf. x Ex collect. Hug. Thomas.

Harley, Earl of Oxford, and Earl Mortimer.

'Tower, triple towered, proper.' He married Isolda, second daughter of Sir Ralph Lyngen, of Stoke, Knt. by whom he had issue two sons, Richard and Jeffery. In 23 Rich. II. having made a feoffment of his manour of Byton, to Sir Henry Mortimer, Sir Hugh Burnel, Knts. and others, in trust for his said wife and his heirs by her, those feoffees, in 3 Hen. IV. confirm the said manour to her for life, with remainder to Richard Harley, her son. But the said Richard, dying unmarried, [y] was succeeded by Jeffery, his brother and heir.

Which Jeffery de Harley, of Brampton-castle, Esq; married [z] 1st, Joan, daughter of Johan ap Harry, of Poston, Esq; by whom he had issue Margaret, wife of Hugh Wolley: and 2dly married [a] Julian, daughter of Sir John Burley, of Burley, Knt. nephew and heir to Sir Simon Burley, Warden of the cinqueports, Constable of Dover, Lord-chamberlain, and of the Privycouncil to Rich. II. and Knight of the most noble order of the Garter; whose brother, Sir Richard Burley, was also Knight of the Garter, as was also Sir John Burley, their father; and it is remarkable, that the father and sons were Knights of the Garter at the same time. From this marriage proceeded two sons, John; and Brian, killed at Brampton, on Palm-Sunday, by certain felons of Radnorshire. The said Jeffery Harley, by his last will [b], bearing date Jan. 10, 1448-9, 26 Hen. VI. bequeathed, to his eldest son John, his manours of Brampton, and Buxton; and to his younger son Brian, his manour of Byton; and to his daughter Joan, several legacies.

John Harley, his eldest son, engaging on the part of the house of York against that of Lancaster, in those bloody contests which then happened [c], was knighted in the field of battle, at Gaston, near Tewksbury, by Edw. IV. on May 9, 1471, the 11th year of his reign. He [d] was Sheriff of Shropshire, in 21 Edw. IV. and was buried in Brampton church, where a monument was erected to his memory, and that of his son Richard, with their statues of alabaster, but defaced in the civil wars, in the reign of Charles I.

Cotemporary with this Sir John Harley, was [e] Sir Walter Harley, slain anno 1461, in a battle between the houses of York and Lancaster; and Robert Harley [f] was also a commander in the battle of Mortimer's-cross, near Wigmore, in Herefordshire, Feb. 2, 1460-1, in which Owen Tudor was taken prisoner.

[y] Ex stemmate ut supra. [z] Ibid. [a] Ex collect. H. Wanley. [b] Ex stemmate per Anstis & Holmand. [c] Ex collect. Hug. Thomas. [d] Jekyl's cat. of Knights, MS. [e] Fuller's worthies. [f] Ex collect. Hug. Thomas.

246 *Harley, Earl of Oxford, and Earl Mortimer.*

The said Sir John Harley was living in 10 Hen. VII. as appears by a deed [g], wherein William Hoskins conveys lands, in Byton, to him and Joan his wife. She was the daughter of Sir John Hackluit, of Eyton, Knt. by whom he left issue Richard, his son and heir; and had also a daughter Alice, wife of Richard Monington, Esq; and 2dly, to William Tomkins, of Monington.

His only son Richard Harley, Esq; in the 14th year of Hen. VII. [i] was Sheriff of the county of Salop. He married Catharine, sister of Elizabeth, Lady Monteagle, and daughter of Sir Thomas Vaughan, of Tretower-castle, in Brecknockshire, who, by order of the Duke of Gloucester, afterwards Rich. III. was beheaded at Pomfret, with the Earl Rivers, and others, anno 1483, for their fidelity to the young King Edw. V. This Richard Harley, Esq; by his marriage aforesaid, was related to most of the best families in Wales; [k] the Welch genealogists deriving the said Sir Thomas Vaughan from the ancient British Princes of Hereford, Brecknock, and Radnor, before the Norman or Saxon conquests; and from the noble families of the Clares and Mortimers, as also from all the Princes of Wales.

By the inquisition taken at Wigmore, [l] June 27, 1529, 21 Hen. VIII. after the death of the said Richard, it appears, that Sir John Harley, Knt. in consideration of a marriage between the said Richard, his son and heir apparent, and Catharine, daughter of Sir Thomas Vaughan, Knt. made a settlement of the manour of Brampton, the town of Bucton, parcel of the said manour, the manour of Over-Pedwardyne, and divers messuages, &c. in Over-Pedwardyne, Nether-Pedwardyne, Walforde, and Borysforde, six burgages, and certain lands and tenements thereto belonging, in the town or borough of Wigmore, together with divers other messuages, lands, and tenements, in Lengthalle-Erlys, Alfortune, Kyntone, and Leyntwardin, in the lordship of Wigmore, in trust for the use of him the said John Harley, Knt. and Joan his wife, for their lives, remainder to the use of Richard Harley, his son and heir, and the heirs of his body, remainder to the right heirs of the said Sir John [m]; and that the said Richard died on March 11, before the taking of the inquisition, leaving John Harley, his son and heir, 38 years old and upwards: and had also two other sons, William, and Thomas; and a daughter Catharine, married to Roger Hopwood, Esq;

g Ex collect. Hug. Thomas.   h Ibid. & visitat. de com' Salop.   i Ibid. Fuller's worthies in eod. com.   k Ex stemmate sub manu Hug. Thomas. l Esc. 21 Hen. VIII.   m Esc. ut supra.

The

Harley, Earl of Oxford, and Earl Mortimer. 247

The said John Harley, Esq; born in 1491, 7 Hen. VII. was, in his father's life-time, [n] a commander in the wars against the Scots, and signalized himself in the battle, when James IV. King of Scotland, was killed at Flodden-field, Sept. 9, 1513. He married, in the 11th of Hen. VIII. Anne, daughter of Sir Edward Crofts, Knt. by whom he had issue John Harley; Thomas, Rector of Brampton; William; Edward; Margaret, wife of Thomas Adams, of Electon, in Shropshire; Joyce, and Elizabeth. After her decease, he wedded Anne, daughter of Sir Edward Rouse, of Worcestershire, Knt. by whom he had issue Alice, wife of Simon Macklew. In 1541, he covenanted for his son's marriage, as hereafter particularised: and died on August 6, 1542, leaving John his son and heir, who was 21 years of age, on Oct. 29 following, as is evident from the inquisition.

But, before I proceed to treat of him, it will be here proper to give some account of John Harley, Bishop of Hereford. He was of a younger branch of this family, born towards the beginning of Hen. VIII's reign, and admitted Fellow of Magdalen's college, about 1537 [o], being then B. A. and master of the free-school joining to that college. Afterwards, proceeding in the faculty of divinity, he took holy orders, became preacher to the Earl of Warwick (afterwards Duke of Northumberland) and tutor to his children. He was a zealous preacher, in Oxford, against the Roman catholicks, upon the entrance of Edw. VI. [p] and at length chaplain to that Prince; who, for his effectual promotion of the reformed religion, gave him a prebendship of Worcester, anno 1551: after which, he was Rector of Upton upon Severn, and Vicar of Kederminster, in Worcestershire; lastly elected Bishop of Hereford, and consecrated on May 26, 1553; but was deprived by Queen Mary [q] a few months after, for refusing to hear Mass, and being married. As to his merits and abilities, we have incontestible evidences of them, given by the famous John Leland [r], who knew him personally, and has highly extolled him in a Latin poem, for his great virtue and learning, especially in the classical authors and poets, and for the delicacy of his own poetical compositions; but what he has particularly published, neither this author, Bayle, nor Pits, relate. He removed from place to place, to avoid persecution, and comfort the distressed remnant of protestants; but died in one of these journies about England, 1554, in the reign of Q. Mary.

n Ex collect. Hug. Thomas.   o Athen. Oxon. vol. 1. fol. 681.   p Idem & hist. & antiq. univ. Oxon. lib. 1. p. 265.   q Godwin, de præsul. Angl. r In encomiis, trophæis, &c. eruditor. in Anglia virorum, &c. p. 107.

I now return to John, eldest son and heir of John Harley, Esq; who died on August 6, 1542. Which John Harley, Esq; on his father's decease, was in ward to the King ten weeks, and being at full age on Oct. 29, 1542, 34 Hen. VIII. thereupon sued * out a special livery of all the manours and lands his father died possessed of, viz. the manour of Bucton, with the appurtenances in Bucton; the manours of Pedwarden, and Borisforde, held of the King as of the honour of Wigmore, by the service of one Knight's fee; the manour of Byton, with the appurtenances, and other lands and tenements in Byton, held of Richard Cornwall, Esq; as of his manour of Stepleton, in scoccage by the rent of 6 d. Also lands and tenements, and a mill, with the appurtenances, in Walford, Lentwarden, Atfortone, Wigmore, Bucktone, and Yetone, held of the King in scoccage: also lands and tenements in Kingtone: the manour of Bramton-Brian, with its appurtenances, held of the King as of the honour of Wigmore, by the service of one Knight's fee; and Bucton-park, with its appurtenances, all in Herefordshire: the manour of Lysse, and its appurtenances, in the county of Southampton; tenements in Bukenhille, half the manour of Dowr, tenements in Nether-downe, in Brome, and in Wynds, in com' Salop; tenements in the Reves, and in Blackbich, in Radnorshire.

His father, on March 30, 1541, 32 Hen. VIII. covenanted with Richard Warncomb, of Hereford, Esq; for a marriage to be solemnized between his said son John, and Maud Warncomb, before the feast of Pentecost then next ensuing, and settles upon them in present, the manours of Byton, in com' Hereford, and Lysse Stormy, alias Lysse Harley, in com' Southampton, with the reversion of Bramton-Brian, Pedwardin, Boresford, Bucton, Walford; and the lordship of Nether-down, in com' Montgomery, after the expiration of thirty years; during which time the profits thereof was to provide portions for younger brothers and sisters. This Maud Warncomb was at length coheir to her brother † James Warncomb, Esq; who died possessed of the manour of Lugwardin, in com' Heref. (purchased by his father, Richard Warncomb, Esq; of Sir John Bridges, in 31 Hen. VIII.) and divers other manours and lands. And, on the division of the estate, she had, for her share, the manours of Aylton and Pickfley, with lands in Bodenham, Webton, Gothermet, Leyntall, Starks, and Elton; and several houses in Hereford, and Leominster.

* Pat. 34 Hen. VIII. ex collect. Humph. Wanley, to Lugwarden, &c. MS. † Warncomb's title

Harley, Earl of Oxford, and Earl Mortimer. 249

By the said Maud, he had issue John Harley, Esq; slain in the French wars; Thomas, William, and Richard: also three daughters; 1 Catharine, first married to John Cresset, of Upton-Cresset, and afterwards to John Cornwall, Baron of Burford in Shropshire; 2dly, Elizabeth, wife of Giles Nanfan, of Birch-Morton, in Worcestershire; and 3 Jane, married to Roger Minors, of Triago, in com' Heref. Esqrs. The said John Harley, Esq; was sheriff of Herefordshire, in 3 Edw. VI. and again in 3 Eliz. He was [u] a zealous Romanist, and is said to have given some protection, at Brampton Castle, to Parsons and Campian the Jesuits. Yet it appears that he was Constable of Conway-Castle, in the reign of Queen Elizabeth [w]. Sir Henry Sidney, Lord-deputy of Ireland, and president of Wales, in a letter to Secretary Cecil (dated August 8, 1568) desired he might have Queen Elizabeth's letter to Harley, Constable of Conway-Castle, to receive such Irish prisoners, or pledges, as he should send him, to be confined in the said castle.

His will bears date in December, 1580, and Maud, his wife's, anno 1589; but if he lived to be 85 years of age, as is asserted [x], he did not die till the year 1606, as may be computed from his age before-mentioned on his father's decease. When his body was opened to be embalmed, a stone was taken out of it, that weighed above 16 ounces, and was long kept in the family.

His eldest surviving son Thomas Harley, Esq; of Brampton, born about the year 1548, lived, during his father's life, at Wigmore-Castle; was in [y] the commission of peace, A. D. 1585, [z] high Sheriff of Herefordshire, in the 36th of Elizabeth, as also in the last year of that Queen, and in the first of James I. in which year he had [a] a grant, from his Majesty, of the honour and Castle of Wigmore. He was likewise, [b] in that reign, of the council to William Lord Compton, President of Wales; and very considerable in his time for his affluence of fortune, and great abilities; but chiefly distinguished himself by the sagacity of his councils to King James I. against the measures then in pursuit [c], as tending to involve his Majesty, or his son, in a war with his people; which accordingly came to pass, though above 20 years after, and he lived not himself to see his predictions verified. After this sincere delivery of his sentiments, he retired from the court, and service of the state, though not without marks of honour and favour from

---

u Introduction to the life of Sir Robert Harley, Knight of the Bath, MS. w Sidney's state letters, &c. vol. 1. p. 36.   x Ex collect. Hug. Thomas.   y Abstract of Humph. Wanley's extracts of the Harleian family.   z Fuller's worthies in Heref.   a Pat. 1 Jac. I. p. 9. m. 18.   b Rymer's fœd. vol. 17. p. 30.   c Vide Plato Redivivus.

Charles

Charles I. and employed his plentiful fortune in acts of hospitality.

He lived to a great age, dying in March, 1631, and was buried on the 19th of the same month, at Bramton. He married Margaret, daughter of Sir Andrew Corbet, of Morton-Corbet, Knt. by whom he had issue Sir Robert Harley, Knight of the Bath. And, surviving her, he married, secondly, Anne, daughter to Walter Griffith, of Burton-Agnes, in Yorkshire, Esq; sister to Sir Henry Griffith, Knt. by whom he had issue James Harley; and Thomas, who was baptized at Brampton, Sept. 6, 1601, and was buried at Leintwarden the same year. The said James Harley married, on Oct. 10, 1610, Anne, daughter and coheir to John Gardiner, Esq; of Brampton [d], by whom he had issue Anne, baptized at Bramton, on July 16, 1615. He buried his wife there, on June 18, 1618, and dying himself at Berrington, soon after, was buried near her, on July 14 following; and their daughter aforesaid, on March 27, 1619 [e].

Sir Robert Harley, only surviving son of Thomas, was born at Wigmore-castle, [f] and baptized on March 1, 1579. His mother died when he was very young, and he received his first instructions in literature from his uncle Richard Harley, a man of noted wit and learning, by whom being accomplished for the University, his father sent him to Oriel-college, in Oxford, where he studied under the care of an able tutor, Mr. Cadwallader Owen. He continued there four years, and took his degree of Bachelor of Arts [g] : and thence removed to the Middle-Temple, in London, where he associated with men of the first rank in that society, and resided there till the coronation of James I. at which he was made one of the [h] Knights of the Bath, on July 15, 1603. He was in the next year, on July 16, made Forester of Boringwood, alias Bringwoodforest, in com' Hereford [i], with the office of the Pokership, and custody of the forest or chase of Prestwood, for life. In an abstract of the King's revenues [k], are these entries relating thereto :—To Sir Robert Harley, for keeping Boringwood, alias Bringwood-forest, in com' Hereford, 6 l. 2 s. 8 d. per ann. for the Pokership 30 s. 5 d. by the year; and for keeping the forest of Prestwood, 18 s. by the year. In the 7th of Jac. I. he obtained a grant to himself, his heirs, and assigns, for ever, for a weekly market [l], and a fair annually, at Wigmore, in Herefordshire. He was elected Knight for the said county,

---

d Regist. de Bramton Brian. e Ibidem. f Ibid. g Introduction to the life of Sir Robert Harley, Knight of the Bath, MS. h Philpot's catal. of Knights. i Pat. 2 Jac. I. p. 21. k Printed 4to, 1651. l Pat. 7 Jac. I. p. 27.

Harley, Earl of Oxford, and Earl Mortimer. 251

ᵐ in the 21ft year of James I's reign, and was put into the commiffion of the peace, as his father ⁿ had been in the 1ft of Charles I. On Sept. 12, 1626, the 2d year of that King's reign, he ᵒ had a grant of the office, and offices, of mafter, and worker of monies, to be be coined in the Tower of London, during life; and on Nov. 8 following, an ᵖ indenture was made, between the faid King Charles I. and Sir Robert Harley, Knight of the Bath, for coining the monies of filver and gold, ᑫ according to his letters patent. To this office was annexed a falary of four thoufand pounds per ann. as Whitlock obferves; ʳ and that after the King's murder, the parliament having ordered a new coin to be ftamped, Sir Robert Harley refufed to coin with any other ftamp than that of the King: whereupon the parliament ordered a trial of the Pixe to be made at Sir Robert Harley's expence; and removed him from his place. While he enjoyed it, to the great improvement of our coin, he introduced that famous artift, Thomas Symonds, to be engraver of the dies for the mint.

Being, by his Lady, related to that famous General, Horace Lord Vere, of Tilbury (one of the grandfons of John, the 15th Earl of Oxford) there was fuch an intimacy between them, ˢ that the faid Lord, in his will, dated Nov. 10, 1634, ftyling him his much refpected friend, makes him the firft of his truftees, by indenture, Oct. 20, 1634, which he alfo confirmed by his will. He was one of the leading members, as reprefentative for the county aforefaid ᵗ, in the parliaments of Charles I. alfo Captain of a troop of horfe in the parliament's fervice, and had confiderable influence in the public affairs, as may further appear in the printed hiftories of thofe times. ᵘ In April, 1642, he was chofen, by the King, one of the Commiffioners and Council for the advifing, ordering, and difpofing all things concerning the government and defence of the kingdom of Ireland. It appears, by books dedicated to him, that he was a great patron of religion and learning; an enemy to oppreffion, bigotry, and hypocrify; and protected the puritan minifters againft the violence of the courts of high commiffion, and ftar-chamber.

He was thrice married; firft, to Anne, daughter of Charles Barret, of Belhoufe, in Aveley, in Effex, Efq; by whom he had a fon named Thomas, who died young; and fhe was buried at Cuxton, near Rochefter in Kent, where there is a handfome monument erected for her. Secondly, he married Mary,

m Ex collect. Br. Willis, arm.   n Ex collect. H. Wanley.   o Pat. 2 Car. I. p. 21. n. 17.   p Ibid. p. 24. n. 5.   q Ex collect. Nich. Jekyl, de Caft. Henningh. in com' Effex, arm.   r Memorials of K. Charles, fol. 388. s Ex regift vocat. Sadler quire 45, in cur. prærog. Cantuar.   t Ex collect. B. Willis, arm.   u Pat. 4 April, 18 Car. I.

daughter

Harley, Earl of Oxford, and Earl Mortimer.

daughter to Sir Francis Newport, of High Ercal, in com' Salop, afterwards Lord Newport, by whom he had issue John, born at Bramton-castle, on Oct. 18, 1607, and afterwards buried at Bucknel; also eight children more, who all died young [w]. This Lady Mary, their mother, was buried at Brampton-Brian, on Aug. 5, 1622. He took to his third wife Brilliana, second daughter of Edward Viscount Conway (one of the greatest men of that age, both in camp and state) by Dorothy his wife, daughter to Sir John Tracy, of Todington, in com' Gloucester, Knt. sister to Mary, wife of that renowned General, Sir Horace Vere, Lord Vere, of Tilbury; by which his family became related to the Veres, Earls of Oxford, Holleses, Earls of Clare, and several other noble families. This marriage was solemnized on July 22, 1623: and, by the said Lady Brilliana, he had issue, 1. Sir Edward Harley, hereafter mentioned; 2. Sir Robert Harley, Knt. [x] who married, on Feb. 6, 1670, Edith, daughter of ———— Pembrugge, Esq; and widow of Major Hinton, but died issueless, and was also buried at Bramton, on Nov. 18, 1673; 3. Thomas Harley, of Kinsham-court, in com' Hereford, Esq; who, by Abigail his wife, daughter of Sir Richard Saltinstall, Knt. had four sons, who died issueless. Sir Robert had also four daughters; Brilliana, wife of James Stanley, second son of Sir Robert Stanley, Knt. who was second son to William Earl of Derby; Dorothy, wife of William Mitchell, in the county of Norfolk, Esq; Margaret and Elizabeth, who died unmarried.

His Lady Brilliana, so christened, because born while her father was Governor of the Brill, was highly celebrated for her prudence and valour in the late civil wars; having [y] so heroically defended her husband's castle of Bramton, against the powerful army which invaded it; that they were, after many attacks, obliged to raise the siege, merely through her skilful management of treaties with the adversaries, and exemplary courage, which animated the defendants; well becoming a descendant from her warlike ancestors. This siege of Bramton was begun on July 26, 1643, [z] and lasted seven weeks, in which time most of the town was burnt; and this gallant Lady dying in October following, the castle was a second time besieged. And then, after a long and brave defence, though made by Sir Robert Harley's servants only, and the besiegers cannon having laid all the walls and outworks in ruin, it was surrendered and burnt; as was also his castle of Wigmore (the ancient seat of the Mortimers) together with the church

---

[w] Regist. de Brampton-Brian. [x] Ibid. [y] Ex collect. H. Thomas.
[z] The old register of Bramton, at the end.

of Brampton; alfo his two parks and warren laid wafte; befides above 40 dwelling-houfes deftroyed. And as the family has been ever addicted to the love of literature, as well as the exercife of arms, an extraordinary library of manufcript and printed books, which had been collected from one defcent to another, alfo perifhed in Brampton-caftle, and the faid demolition and fack thereof; the whole lofs amounting, as it has been computed, to above 50,000 l. Sir Henry Lingen's eftate (who had befieged the caftle, and burnt the town of Bramton, &c.) was afterwards laid under fequeftration, and the profits thereof ordered to make fatisfaction for thofe great damages. Yet fo honourable, fo compaffionate was Colonel Harley, that, after an inventory had been taken of all the perfonal eftate and goods, he waited on the Lady Lingen (Sir Henry being dead) and having afked, ' whether that was a perfect ' inventory, and fhe had figned the fame,' he prefented it to her, with all his right thereto. Sir Robert Harley wanted not fortitude, hereditary and acquired, to fuftain thefe difafters; living feveral years after them, and at laft died of thofe infirmities, the ftone and gout, to which the old age he arrived at is moft commonly incident, on Nov. 6, and was interred with his anceftors at Bramton-Brian, [a] on Dec. 10 following, anno 1656. His funeral fermon was preached the day of his interment, by the Rev. Mr. James Froyfeld, who, foon after publifhing the fame, dedicated it to his fon, Colonel Edward Harley, we refer thereto for his further deferved praife. Among other hardfhips in his old age, he was imprifoned by the army, on the following occafion : ' On Dec. 6, 1648, he and his fon Colonel Edward Harley having voted, ' That the ' King's anfwer to the propofitions from both houfes, was a ' ground for them to proceed upon, to the fettlement of the ' kingdom's peace,' the army the next morning feized on one and forty of the principal members then fitting; and Sir Robert, with his fon Colonel Harley, being two of them, were conveyed into their great victualling-houfe, near Weftminfterhall, called Hell, where they kept them all night, without any beds, and were after driven as prifoners (through fnow and rain) to feveral inns in the Strand, and there confined under guards of the foldiers. See Dugdale's view of the troubles, p. 362.

Colonel Edward Harley fucceeded his father, as his eldeft fon and heir, in his eftate and virtues: and, being a man of great integrity, was defervedly advanced to great honour. He was baptized at Wigmore, on Oct. 21, 1624, and was edu-

[a] Regift. de Bramton.

cated

cated at Magdalen-hall, in Oxford, tho' he did not abide long there. [b] He was one of the Knights of the shire for Hereford, with his father, in the last parliament called by Charles I. and, upon the eruption of the civil war, he was Colonel of a regiment, which he raised himself. In one of his first engagements, in the year 1642, he was shot with a musket-ball, which he bore in his body 58 years, even to his grave. He distinguished his valour and expertness in arms, in several battles; and, in the year 1644, [c] was made Governor of Monmouth; also, the year after, of Cannon-Frome, a garrison between Worcester and Hereford. In 1647, [d] he was one of the eleven members in the house of Commons, who, by reason of their firmness in promoting a peace with the King, were impeached by the army of high treason: ' For that, by their power in the house, the ordinance for disbanding the army did pass;' and threatened, if they were not expelled, they would march up to Westminster: whereby the rest of the members were so intimidated, as to exclude them the house. But, being some time after again admitted, he, with his father, Sir Robert Harley, were, by the army, made prisoners, on Dec. 7, 1648, as already mentioned in the account of Sir Robert. In 1656, being chosen by the county of Hereford one of their representatives in parliament; and Oliver Cromwell having secluded him, with several other members who would not be subservient to him; he was one of those who signed and published a remonstrance, ' [e] That they would not be frighted or flattered to betray their ' country, and give up their religion, lives, and estates, to be ' at his will, to serve his lawless ambition.' And, in very pathetic terms, set forth the depredations of Cromwell, and the power he had assumed; protesting, that the assembly at Westminster was not the representative body of England; and ' That all such members as shall take on them to approve the ' forcible exclusion of other chosen members, or shall sit, vote, ' or act, by name of the parliament of England, while, to their ' knowledge, many of the chosen members are so by force ' shut out, ought to be reputed betrayers of the liberties of ' England, and adherents to the capital enemy of the com- ' monwealth.'

In the parliament, which restored Charles II. he was one of the members for the county of Hereford. He approved himself such a faithful assertor of the royal cause, and was so instrumental to the restoration, that meeting the King at Dover, upon his first return to his dominions, his Majesty made

---

[b] Ex collect. B. Willis, arm.   [c] Whitlock's memor. p. 102.   [d] Ibid. p. 256. and Kennet's hist. of Engl, vol. 3. fol. 168.   [e] Whitlock, p. 643.

him Governor of Dunkirk; and he went directly to take possession of it, that the town might not fall into the hands of the French, as General Monk told him otherwise it would. He also preferred a petition to the council, which Mr. Annesley reported to the house of Commons, on June 29, 1660, [f] and was referred to a committee, to take into consideration the establishment of a government at Dunkirk, what number of men would be necessary to be continued, and upon what pay; and thereupon to prepare an establishment, and report it to the house, with their opinion, how provision may, with most conveniency, be made for the settled payment thereof.

His said government of Dunkirk was soon after confirmed by the King; the warrant was made to him for life, which he chose to have altered to during pleasure, telling the then Sollicitor-general, that he would never serve any Prince longer than he desired. The commission was therefore drawn up in these words (of which there are copies in the offices of records:)

'CHARLES the second, by the grace of God, King of
' England, Scotland, and Ireland, defender of the faith,
' &c. To all to whom these presents shall or may come, greet-
' ing. Know ye, that we, reposing especial trust and confi-
' dence in the great industry, judgment, approved abilities,
' and good affections, of our trustie and welbeloved Colonell
' Edward Harley, have constituted, ordained, and appointed,
' and by these presents, of our especiell grace, certain know-
' ledge, and meere motion, doe constitute, ordeyne, and ap-
' point the said Colonell Edward Harley, Governour of our
' town, port, and guarison of Dunkirke, and Mardyke, in
' West Flaunders, and of all the forts, fortifications, and our
' other strong holds and havens thereunto belonging: to have
' and to hold the said office or place of Governour of our said
' towne, porte, and guarison of Dunkirke, and Mardyke, and
' of all the forts, fortifications, and other strong holds there-
' unto belonging, unto the said Colonell Edward Harley, du-
' ring our pleasure; with all privileges, profits, allowances,
' duties, fees, emoluments, perquisites, commodities, thereunto
' incident and belonging, in as large and ample manner, and
' forme, as any person or persons heretofore exerciseing and ex-
' ecuting the said office of Governour of our said towne, porte,
' and guarison of Dunkirke, and Mardyke, formerly enjoyed and
' received, for the exercise and execution thereof. And for

[f] Journ. dom. com.

'the

'the better ordering and governing of all and every of our offi-
'cers and fouldiers already placed, or hereafter to be placed
'within our faid towne, porte, and guarifon of Dunkirke,
'and Mardyke, and the forts thereunto belonging, wee do by
'thefe prefents give full power and authoritie to the faid Colo-
'nell Edward Harley, from time to time, upon any juft occa-
'fion, to remove, difplace, and cafhiere all and everie officers
'and fouldiers, officer and fouldier nowe placed, or hereafter
'to be placed in our faid towne and guarifon of Dunkirke,
'and Mardyke, for the defence and fafeguard thereof, who,
'for contempt and difobedience, or any reafonable caufe, fhall
'deferve the fame; and, in his and their places fo removed,
'to admit and place others as often as occafion fhall require,
'and to put in execution the law martiall againft notorious
'offenders, for the prevention of all mutinies, rebellions, and
'infurrections, within our faid towne and guarifon of Dun-
'kirke and Mardyke, and other the places aforefaid : and from
'time to time to doe and execute all and every fuch lawful act
'and acts, thinge and thinges whatfoever, as may tend to the
'fafetie and well governing of our faid towne guarifon of Dun-
'kirke, and Mardyke, and other the places aforefaid, in as
'ample manner and forme, as any perfon or perfons formerly
'Governour or Governours of the faid towne and guarifon
'have lawfully executed and performed. And further, for
'that the faid Colonell Edward Harley may have urgent oc-
'cafions fometimes to abfent himfelf from his faid charge and
'command, we have given and graunted, and by thefe pre-
'fents doe give and graunt unto the faid Colonell Edward
'Harley, in cafe of fuch his abfence, full power and authoritie
'to nominate, fubftitute, and appoint, one or more deputie
'or deputies, for whom hee the faid Colonell Edward Harley
'will be anfwerable: to which deputie or deputies, we do
'hereby give full power and authoritie, in the abfence of the
'faid Colonell Edward Harley, to doe and execute all the
'powers and authorities hereby given to the faid Colonell Har-
'ley, in as large and ample manner as the faid Colonell Harley
'might or ought lawfully doe and execute, if hee were
'prefent. Willinge and hereby ftreightly chargeinge and
'commanding all our officers, as well civill as martiall, and
'all, and all manner our loveinge fubjects within our faid
'towne, porte, and guarifon of Dunkirke and Mardyke, and
'places aforefaid, to be aydeing, affiftant, and obedient unto
'the faid Colonell Edward Harley, or any other authorifed, by,
'or under him as aforefaid, in the due execution of his faid
'office and place, as they and everie of them will anfweare
'the contrary att their perills. In witnefs whereof, wee have
'caufed

'caufed thefe our letters to be made patents. Witnefs our
'felfe at Weftminfter, the fourteenth day of Julie, in the
'twelfth yeare of our reign.'

By the Kinge,

HOWARD.

During the fhort fpace of time he held this government of Dunkirk, he [g] recruited the garrifon to above nine thoufand men, and began many fortifications, which were afterwards perfected by the French. And, as a fingular pattern of incorruptible fidelity, be it remembered, to his lafting glory, that no honours, no rewards, could make him act contrary to the intereft of his country. He was fo far from uniting with thofe who confented to the fale of Dunkirk to the French, that he ftrenuoufly oppofed it; and, by his intereft, got the [h] houfe of Commons to pafs a refolution to prepare an act that it fhould never be alienated, but be made a part of the King's hereditary dominions. Nor could he be prevailed on by threats, or promifes, or even by great bribes, to relinquifh that refolution. And it muft be more particularly remembered, [i] that he refufed the dignity of Peerage; alfo an offer made him, by a certain great man, of ten thoufand pounds, to be paffive in the furrendery of that place, and forbear his profecution of a law, to annex Dunkirk to the crown of England. However, the court being determined to fell the town, he received the following order at Dunkirk, on May 25, by the hands of Major Floyd:

Charles R.

WHEREAS, we have given commiffion to our right trufty and well-beloved Andrew, Lord Retorfort, to bee Governour of the faid garrifon, and to take charge of the faid garrifon, with all the forts and ftrengths thereof, and of the ordnance, amunition, and other furniture of war, in or belonging to the faid garrifon : thefe are to require you, Sir Edward Harley, Governor of the faid garrifon of Dunkirke, upon fight hereof, to furrender and deliver up the faid garrifon of Dunkirke, with all the forts and ftrengthes therein, or therewith under your command; and all the ordnance, arms, amunition, ftoares, and other furniture and utenfils of war, with all provifions, cloathes and neceffaries belonging to the faid garrifon, or now therein for publique ufe, or in any of the forts and ftrengths, that are under your command, unto Andrew

---

g Hift. de la Maifon de Harley, par Monf. Moret, MS. h Kennet's hift.
of Engl. vol. 3. p. 259.   i Moret ut fupra.

Lord Retorfort aforesaid, for our service; taking the said Lord Retorfort's receipt for all the particulars you shall so deliver up unto him, which shall be your discharge for the same. Given at our court at Whitehall, this 22d day of May, in the 13th year of our reign.

To our trusty and well-beloved Sir Edward Harley, Knight of the Bath.

By his Majesties command,

WILL. MORICE.

Having seen the Lord Retorfort's discharge, here follows an exact copy of it.

I Doe heirby certify, that in obedience to his Majesties ordres of the tuentie tuo of May, 1661, to the richt honorable Sir Edward Harley, he hath surrendred and delyvered up to me his Maiesties garrison of Dunkerk, with all the forts and strengths thereunto belonging, and all the ordonnances, armes, ammunition, stores and other furniture and ustencelles of warr, with all provisions or other necessaries belonging to the sayd garrison. For the which I have given, to the said richt honorable Sir Edward Harley, this my recept to serve for his discharge. At Dunkerk, this tuenty eicht May, 1661.

RETORFORT.

It appears that the King allowed 1200 l. weekly, for maintaining the garrison of Dunkirk, and Mardyke, [k] and that Sir Edward Harley left in the hands of Thomas de la Vall, Deputy-treasurer of Dunkirk, 127,752 l. 15 s. for which the Lord Retorfort, his successor, afterwards Earl of Tiviot, gave his receipt, bearing date May 29, 1661.

Upon the expence of the King's marriage, and that of settling the Queen-mother in a splendid court at Somerset-house, France took the opportunity to compleat their bargain for Dunkirk. 'The first motion to the King for complying there-
'with, as my author says, [l] he was assured by a knowing man,
'was the great expence in keeping it; which Rutherfort the
'Governor had increased to an exorbitant degree, since the
'dismission of Sir Edward Harley.' It was sold for 500,000 l. and ingloriously put into the possession of the French, under the government of the Count D'Estrades, [m] the English Governor (Rutherfort) with two companies guarding the gates, at their entrance, and delivering the keys.

[k] Sir Edward Harley's account of the expences and treasure at Dunkirk, MS. [l] Echard's hist. of England, vol. 3. p. 84. [m] Kennet's hist. of England, vol. 3. p. 259.

Lord Lansdown, in his vindication of General Monk, gives this account of Sir Edward Harley: 'General Monk foresaw 'early what might happen to be the fate of Dunkirk, and 'took his precautions in the very beginning to preserve it, by 'placing Sir Edward Harley in the command, a man of pub- 'lic spirit, firm to the interest of his country, and not to be 'biassed, tempted, or deluded to be assistant in any thing 'contrary to it. This appeared plainly afterwards; for the 'first step taken, as soon as the treaty was projected, was to 'remove that gallant man, and place another Governor in 'his stead.'

When Sir Edward Harley returned into England, and had delivered up his accounts, which appeared unexceptionable to the council, he took his leave of the King on that occasion, and told him before the Duke of Albemarle, that the guns, stores, arms, and ammunition he left at Dunkirk, were worth more money than the French were to give for the place. He also told the King, he should leave him one thing more, which his Majesty might not think of, [n] and that was 10,000 l. he had saved in an iron chest against a siege, or any other exigence which might happen. Upon the whole, he acquitted himself so honourably, that the King was pleased to give him the following gracious release:

CHARLES the second, by the grace of God, King of England, Scotland, France, and Ireland, defender of the faith, &c. To all to whome theise presents shall come greeting. Whereas our trusty and well-beloved Sir Edward Harley, Knight of the Bath, hath performed and done unto us many eminent and acceptable services, which wee do hereby, and shall allways acknowledge, particularly in his singular care, and conduct, and vigilance, while hee was Governour for us of the towne, port, and garrison of Dunkirk, and Mardike, in West Flanders, and of all forts, fortifications, and other strong holds and havens thereunto belonging. And whereas the said Sir Edward Harley having, in obedience to our comand, delivered up the said garrison of the said towne of Dunkirk, and Mardike, into the charge of our right trusty and right wellbeloved cousin, Andrew Earl of Tiveot (then Lord Rutherford) did present to the Lords of our Privy-council, an accompt of the disbursements of money, during his the said Sir Edward Harley's service there, with a true state of the ragiments, money, victualls, artillery, amunition, and all other provisions belonging to the said garrison, and received from him by the

[n] Ex collect. Joh. Freind, M. D. MS.

said Earl of Tiveot. Which accompt the said Lords of our councell did approve and cause to be entered into the councell book. Know yee therefore, that wee of our especiall grace, certain knowledge, and meere motion, have remised, released, pardoned, and quit-claimed: and by theise our letters patents for us, our heirs and successors, doe remit, release, pardon, and for ever quit-clayme, unto the said Sir Edward Harley, his heirs, executors, and administrators, all and all manner of actions, suites, complaints, impeachments, accompts, debts, prosecutions or demands whatsoever, or causes of actions, suites, complaintes, impeachments, accompts, debts, prosecutions, or demands whatsoever, either in law or equity, to us, our heirs and successors, belonging, or in any wise aperteyning, for, touching, or concerning any cause, matter, or things whatsoever, acted or done, or suffred to be acted or done, or omitted or neglected to bee done by him, the said Sir Edward Harley, during his government aforesaid; or for, touching, or concerning any matter, cause, or thing whatsoever, belonging or relating to his said government of the said town, port, and garrison of Dunkirk, and Mardike, in West Flanders aforesaid. And of the forts, fortifications, and other strong holds and havens thereunto belonging. And our further will and pleasure is, and by these presents for us, our heires and successors, Wee doe give and graunte to the said Sir Edward Harley, his heirs, executors, and administrators, that he, they, and all and every of them, his, theire, and all and every of theire mannors, lands, tenements, and hereditaments; and his, theire, and all and everie of theire goods, chattells, rights, and credits, shall be and are by theise presents, and from henceforth for ever freed and discharged, of and from all, and all manner of actions, suit, quarrells, impeachments, accompts, debts, prosecutions, and demands whatsoever, allready comenced, or levyed, or hereafter to be comenced, prosecuted, or levyed on the behalf of us, our heires and successors, for any cause, matter, or thing whatsoever, touching, belonging, or relating to his the said Sir Edward Harley's said government of the said towne, port, and garrison of Dunkirk, and Mardike, and the forts, fortifications, and other the strong holds and havens thereunto belonging: any statute, provision, lawe, grant, commission, constitution, decree, or whatsoever to the contrary thereof, in any wise notwithstanding; although expresse mention of the true yearly value or certeinty of the premisees, or any of them, or of any other guifts, or grants by us, or by any of our progenitors or predecessors heretofore made, to the said Sir Edward Harley, in theise presents, is not made, or any other statute, act, ordinance, provision, proclamation,

mation, or restriction heretofore had, made, enacted, ordeyned or provided, or any other matter, cause, or thing whatsoever to the contrary thereof in any wise notwithstanding. In witness whereof, wee have caused theise our letters to be made patents. Witnes our selfe at Westminster, the third day of December, in the fifteenth year of our reigne.

By writt of Privy Seale,
HOWARD.

When Charles II. made a creation of Peers upon his restoration, Sir Edward Harley had the offer of a warrant for a Viscount, which he, with great modesty and duty to the King, declined accepting of, and gave this reason for it, 'left 'his zeal and his services, for the restoration of the ancient 'government, should be reproached, as proceeding from am- 'bition, and not conscience:' and so nice was he in this point, that his being made Knight of the Bath was done without his knowledge; he being then at Dunkirk, and the King inserted his name in the list with his own hand.

He was one [o] of the members for the town of Radnor, and for the county of Hereford, in all the parliaments of Charles II. was much regarded in the house of Commons for his sound reasoning, and generally closed the debate; as may be found [p] in the printed books, which record the transactions of parliament in those times.

He was also elected for the county aforesaid, in several parliaments called by King William, to the time of his death, which happened at Bramton-Brian, on Dec. 8, 1700, [q] and was buried in that church in the family vault.

He was twice married: first, on June 26, 1654, to Mary, daughter of Sir William Button, of Parkgate, in Devonshire (by his second wife, the daughter of Arthur Ascot, of Tetcote, in com' Devon, Esq;) by whom he had issue four daughters, viz. Brilliana, wife to Alexander Popham, of Tewkesbury, in com' Gloucester, Esq; Martha, wife to Samuel Hutchins, of London, Merchant; and two Maries, who both died young. His second wife was Abigail, daughter of Nathanael Stephens, of Essington, in Gloucestershire, Esq; by whom his children were [r] allied to Sir Francis Walsingham, the famous Sir Philip Sidney, and the great Earl of Essex. By this wife he had four sons, and one daughter.

o Ex collect. B. Willis, arm. 1680.   q Regist. de Brampton, par M. Moret.

p Debates of the house of Commons, 8vo,   r Histoire de la Maison de Harley,

1. Robert, Earl of Oxford, &c.
2. Edward Harley, of Eywood, in com' Hereford, Esq; whose character and eminent virtues, in public and private life, cannot be more justly set forth, than by inserting the inscription placed on his monument in the church-yard of Titley, in which parish his seat of Eywood is situated.

Under this STONE,

By his own Appointment, Lye humbly interr'd
The Reliques of the honourable Edward Harley, Esq;
Of Eywood, in the County of Hereford, second son of
Sir Edward Harley, Knight of the Bath, of Bramton
Brian, in the same County, and Brother to the Right
Honourable Robert, Earl of Oxford: He married
Sarah, third Daughter of Thomas Foley, of Witley,
in the County of Worcester, Esq. by whom he had
three Sons and one Daughter.

He was Recorder of Leominster, above forty years,
And Represented that Borough near 30 Years in Parliament,
In which his Skill in the Law,
And unwearied Application to Business,
And extensive Knowledge of public Affairs,
Join'd with a calm and unprejudic'd Judgment,
A steady and unbiafs'd Adherence to the Constitution,
And a disinterested Zeal for the Good of his Country,
Made him justly Esteemed,
One of the great Supports and Ornaments of it.

In 1702, He was advanced by Queen Anne,
To be one of the Auditors of the Imprest.
Which important Place he executed to his Death,
With great Care, Integrity, and Ability;
And, by his Regulation of the National Accounts,
His Service to the Public remains after his Death.
Yet his Affiduity in Civil Imployments,
Neither lessen'd his Attention to Religion,
Nor interrupted his daily Course of Devotion;
The Discharge of his Duty, as a Christian,
Was the Source and Center of all his Desires.

His Hospitality was Great,
His Liberality Greater,
His Charity private and without Ostentation,
Nor ever made known but where it cou'd not be conceal'd.

He augmented several small Livings
In this County, and in Monmouthshire;
He maintain'd several Charity Schools in Both;
And endowed one for Ever at Bramton Brian,
The Place of his Birth.

From his known Zeal to promote Christian Knowledge,
And particularly the Instruction of Youth,
In the Year 1725
He was chose Chairman of the Trustees
For the Charity Schools in London.

The whole Tenour of his Life was strictly Moral,
Without Dissimulation, Pride, or Envy;
His Deportment Affable and Humble,
His Conversation Chearful and Instructive.
He was faithful and constant to his Friends,
Charitable and Forgiving to his Enemies,
Just and Beneficent to all.
And the great Example of Piety and Religion,
(Which shone thro' his Life, and was most conspicuous on his deathBed)
Is the great Consolation and Blessing,
He has transmitted to his Posterity.

He was born the 7th of June, 1664.
And died on the 30th of August, 1735.

The issue, mentioned in the above inscription, were, Edward, 3d Earl of Oxford: Robert, who died an infant: Robert, who was chosen member for Leominster, in the two parliaments called in 1710, and 1713; is Recorder of the said borough; and has served in the last and present parliaments for Droitwich: and Abigail, married to the Hon. John Verney, late Master of the Rolls.

3. Nathanael, the youngest surviving son of Sir Edward Harley, was baptized on March 6, 1665, and bred a merchant. He died at Aleppo, in January, 1719-20. Sir Edward had also a son named Brian, who died young; and a daughter named Abigail, born in 1664, who died unmarried, on Oct. 4, 1726.

His eldest son, Robert Harley, Esq; was born in Bowstreet, in the parish of St. Paul, Covent-Garden, on Dec. 5, 1661.

He was educated under the Reverend Mr. Birch, at Shilton, near Burford, Oxfordshire, which, tho' a private school, was remarkable for producing, at the same time, [s] a Lord High Treasurer, [t] a Lord High Chancellor, [u] a Lord Chief Justice of the Common Pleas; and ten members of the house of Commons, who were all cotemporaries, as well at school, as in parliament. Here he laid that foundation of extensive knowledge, in human and divine learning, in which he afterwards became so eminent.

At the revolution, Sir Edward Harley, and this his eldest son, raised a troop of horse at their own expence, and marched to Worcester, of which place Sir Edward was made Governor, by the gentlemen of the county; and his two sons were sent, by him, to tender his and their services to the Prince of Orange, and to give his Highness an account of the posture of affairs in those parts.

After the accession of William and Mary, the said Robert Harley, Esq; was first [w] chosen, on a vacancy, member of parliament for Tregony, in Cornwall, and afterwards served for the town of Radnor, from 1690, till he was called up to the house of Lords. On Nov. 13, 1690, [x] he was ordered to bring in a bill, for the better ease of Sheriffs in passing their accounts, and in the execution of their office; and on Dec. 26 following, was chosen, [y] by ballot, one of the nine members of the house of Commons, commissioners for stating the public accounts. On Nov. 3, 1691, on his motion, the Commons resolved, [z] ' That the paying the army any otherwise than by the musters of effective men, is a great wasting of their Majesty's treasure, and ordered a bill for paying the army according to the musters of effective men; and for better payment of quarters, and preventing false musters, and punishing mutiny and desertion.' And Mr. Harley [a] presented the bill to the house, on Nov. 10 following. He was also chosen one of the arbitrators for uniting the two India companies.

In 1694, the house of Commons made it their first business to order Mr. Harley, Novem. 19, to prepare and bring in a bill, ' For the frequent meeting and calling of parliaments;' which they had been so earnest for in former sessions [b]. And he drew up and presented the bill, Nov. 22, which met with so ready a concurrence in the house, that it was sent up to the Lords, Dec. 13, who, on the 18th of the same month, agreed to it without any amendments. On Feb. 11, 1700-1,

[s] Earl of Oxford. [t] Lord Harcourt. [u] Lord Trevor. [w] Willis's notit. parliament, vol. 2. p. 116. [x] Vote of the house of Commons, No. 37. [y] Bp. Kennet's hist. of Engl. vol. 3. p. 609. [z] Vote, No. 8. [a] Ibid. [b] Kennet's hist. of Engl. vol. 3. p. 666.

he was chosen Speaker of the house of Commons. That parliament being diffolved the fame year by King William, and a new one called, he was again chosen Speaker on Dec. 31 following. Also, in the firft parliament called by Queen Anne, he was elected Speaker, whereby he had that dignity in three fucceffive parliaments.

On April 17, 1704, he was fworn of her Majefty's Privy-council; and, on May 18 following, fworn in council one of the principal Secretaries of State, being also Speaker of the house of Commons at the fame time. In 1706, he was appointed one of the Commiffioners for the treaty of union with Scotland, which took effect; and refigned his place of principal Secretary of State, in February, 1707-8. On Auguft 10, 1710, he was conftituted one of the Commiffioners of the Treafury, also Chancellor and Under-Treafurer of the Exchequer. And, having three days after been again fworn in the Privy-council, he was, on March 8 following, in great danger of his life; the Marquis of Guifcard, a French papift (then under examination of a committee of the Privy-council at Whitehall) ftabbing him with a penknife which he took up in the clerk's room, where he waited before he was examined; Guifcard was thereupon imprifoned, and died in Newgate on the 17th of the fame month. Whereupon an act of parliament paffed, making it felony, without benefit of clergy, to make an attempt on the life of a Privy-counfellor, in the execution of his office; and a claufe was inferted, ' to juftify and indemnify all perfons, who in affifting
' in defence of Mr. Harley, Chancellor of the Exchequer,
' when he was ftabbed by the Sieur de Guifcard, and in fecur-
' ing him, did give any wound or bruife to the faid Sieur de
' Guifcard, whereby he received his death.' And, both houfes of parliament having addreffed her Majefty on the occafion, they expreffed their great concern ' at the moft barbarous and
' villainous attempt made upon the perfon of Robert Har-
' ley, Efq; Chancellor of your Majefty's Exchequer, by the
' Marquis of Guifcard, a French papift, at the time when he
' was under examination for treafonable practices, before a
' committee of your Majefty's council. We cannot but be
' moft deeply affected, to find fuch an inftance of inveterate
' malice againft one employed in your Majefty's council, and
' fo near your royal perfon. And we have reafon to be-
' lieve, that his fidelity to your Majefty, and zeal for your
' fervice, have drawn on him the hatred of all the abettors of
' popery and faction. We think it our duty on this occafion,
' to affure your Majefty, that we will effectually ftand by and
' defend your Majefty, and thofe who have the honour to be
' employed

'employed in your service, against all public and secret attempts of your enemies, &c.'

Whereunto her Majesty returned this answer:

My Lords and Gentlemen,

'I take this address very kindly from you, on the occasion of that barbarous attempt on Mr. Harley, whose zeal and fidelity in my service must appear yet more eminently, by that horrid endeavour to take away his life, for no other reason, that appears, but his known opposition to popery and faction. Your warm concern for the safety of my person, and the defence of those employed in my service, is very grateful to me, &c.'

The wound he had received, confined him for some weeks; and the house of Commons being informed, that it was almost healed, and that he would in a few days come abroad, they came, on April 11, to this unanimous resolution, 'That, when the right honourable Robert Harley, Esq; Chancellor of her Majesty's Exchequer, attends the service of the house, the Speaker do, in the name of this house, congratulate the said Mr. Harley's escape and recovery from the barbarous and villainous attempt made upon him by the Sieur de Guiscard.'

And, attending the service of the house on April 26, the Speaker (William Bromley, Esq;) addressed himself to him in the following speech:

Mr. Chancellor of the Exchequer,

'When the barbarous and villainous attempt made upon you by the Sieur de Guiscard, a French papist, was communicated to this house, they immediately declared, They were most deeply affected to find such an instance of inveterate malice against you. And observing, how you have been treated by some persons, they concluded, they had reason to believe, that your fidelity to her Majesty, and zeal for her service, had drawn upon you the hatred of all the abettors of popery and faction.

'In this opinion they must be abundantly confirmed, since the Lords, and the Queen, have concurred with them.

'Sir, if your fidelity to her Majesty, and zeal for her service, could ever be doubted, and wanted any testimonials to prove them, you have now the most ample, and the most undeniable, that can be given; and, after these, it would be an unpardonable presumption in me, to imagine I could add

'to

'to them, by saying any thing of your faithful discharge of those great trusts you have been honoured with; to which your eminent abilities at first recommended you, and your distinguishing merits have since justified her Majesty's wife choice.

'Your very enemies, Sir, acknowledge this, by their unwearied and restless endeavours against your person and reputation.

'God be thanked, they have been hitherto disappointed, and have not been able to accomplish what their inveterate, but impotent, malice had designed against both.

'And, may the same providence, that has wonderfully preserved you from some unparalleled attempts; and that has raised you up to be an instrument of great good in a very critical juncture, when it was much wanted; continue still to preserve so invaluable a life, for the perfecting of what is so happily begun; that we may owe to your counsels, and to your conduct (under her Majesty) the maintenance and firm establishment of our constitution in church and state.

'These expectations, Sir, have filled this house with an inexpressible satisfaction for your escape and recovery, which they have unanimously commanded me to congratulate. I do therefore, in the name of this house, congratulate your escape and recovery from the barbarous and villainous attempt made upon you by the Sieur de Guiscard.'

To which Mr. Harley returned the following answer:

Mr. Speaker,

'The honour this house has done me, which you have expressed in so obliging a manner, is a sufficient reward for the greatest merit. I am sure it so far exceeds my deserts, that all I can do or suffer for the public, during the whole course of my life, will still leave me in debt to your goodness. By the acceptance you have vouchsafed my poor service, how noble an encouragement, worthy of you, has this house given all our fellow-subjects, to exert themselves in the glorious cause of preserving the constitution in church and state, and in loyalty to the best of sovereigns? This, without doubt was your view; and this may convince all, who are designedly obstinate, how dear the true interest of the nation is to this honourable assembly. Sir, the undeserved favour I have received this day, is deeply imprinted in my heart; and, whenever I look upon my breast, it will put me in mind of the thanks due to God, my duty to the Queen, and that debt of gratitude and service I must always owe to this ho-

' nourable houfe, to you, Mr. Speaker, and to every particu-
' lar member.'

The next day the Commons ordered their Speaker's fpeech to Mr. Harley, and his anfwer, to be printed. And having formed a fcheme to fatisfy all public and national debts and deficiencies, by eftablifhing the company, now called the South Sea company, her Majefty Queen Anne, refolving to reward his many eminent fervices, was pleafed to advance him to the Peerage of Great-Britain, by the ftyle and titles of Baron Harley, of Wigmore, in com' Hereford, Earl of Oxford, and Earl Mortimer, with remainder, for want of iffue male of his own body, to the heirs male of Sir Robert Harley, Knight of the Bath, his grandfather, by letters patent, bearing date May 24, 1711, in the 10th year of her reign. The preamble of the faid patent is as follows:

' Whatever favour the equity of a Prince can beftow on a
' Gentleman, defcended from an illuftrious and very ancient
' family, framed by nature for great things, improved by edu-
' cation in all manner of learning for greater, exercifed by long
' experience in bufinefs, verfed in very different employments
' of the commonwealth, with extraordinary reputation, and
' not without danger: fuch has our trufty and well-beloved
' Counfellor, Robert Harley, juftly deferved of us: he being
' the only man, who, by a full houfe of Commons, was chofen
' Speaker for three fucceffive parliaments; and, at the fame
' time that he held the chair, was one of our principal Secre-
' taries of State: his capacity fitting him for the management
' of thofe two important offices, which, though they feemed
' to difagree in themfelves, were eafily reconciled by one who
' knew how, with equal weight and addrefs, to temper and
' turn the minds of men; fo wifely to defend the rights of the
' people, without derogating from the prerogative of the crown;
' and who was thoroughly acquainted how well monarchy could
' confift with liberty. Having run through thefe two employ-
' ments at the fame time, after fome breathing-while, he took
' care of our Treafury, as Chancellor of our Exchequer; put
' a ftop to the growing embezzlement of the public money,
' which was fpreading far and wide, like a contagion; pro-
' vided for the fettling a new trade to the South Seas; and hav-
' ing, with wonderful fagacity, very lately, and in a very good
' time, retrieved the languifhing condition of our Exchequer;
' and thus reftored the public credit, merited the applaufe of
' the parliament, filled our citizens with joy, and us (for our
' intereft is ever the fame with that of our people) with no
' fmall fatisfaction: for thefe reafons, we determine to con-
' fer

'fer on a Gentleman, who has deserved so well of us, and all
'our good subjects, those honours which were long since due
'to him and his family; being induced thereto by our own in-
'clination, and the general voice of all Great-Britain. Since
'therefore the two houses of parliament have declared, that
'the fidelity and affection he has expressed in our service, have
'exposed him to the hatred of wicked men, and the desperate
'rage of a villainous parricide; since they have congratulated
'his escape from such imminent dangers, and put us in mind,
'that he might not be preserved in vain, we willingly comply
'with their desires, and grant him, who comes so honourably
'recommended by the hearty votes of our parliament, a place
'among the Peers; to whom, by the noble blood, and long
'train of his ancestors, he is so nearly allied; and that, with
'all felicity, he take his title from the city, where learning
'flourishes in so high a degree; himself the ornament of learn-
'ing, and patron of learned men. Know, &c.'

In regard to the latter part of his Lordship's character, it may justly be observed, that he was not only an encourager of literature, but the greatest collector, in his time, of all curious books in print and manuscript, especially those concerning the history of his own country; which were preserved, and much augmented, by the late Earl his son. But, the Harleyan library being so much celebrated for its usefulness, by other authors, I need only refer my reader to the description of it, in the preface to Bishop Nicholson's English Historical Library, folio; and to what I have cited in my several accounts relating to the noble families, whereof I have treated.

On Tuesday, May 29, 1711, being the anniversary of the nativity and restoration of Charles II. the Queen appointed the Earl of Oxford, &c. Lord High Treasurer of Great-Britain; her Majesty having thought fit to pitch on that auspicious day, for the inauguration of a Prime Minister, to whose wisdom, vigilance, and integrity, the restoration of public credit was principally owing. On June 1, his Lordship, attended by the Dukes of Newcastle, Buckingham, Shrewsberry, Somerset, Ormond, Beaufort, Schomberg, Queensbury, and Hamilton; the Earls of Northampton, Rivers, Winchelsea, Scarsdale, Clarendon, Cardigan, Rochester, Anglesey, Yarmouth, Jersey, Poulett, Cholmondeley, Marr, and Loudon; the Lords Dartmouth, De la Warr, Guilford, Butler of Weston, Hallifax, and Guernsey; with the officers of the Exchequer, took the oath in the court of Chancery; after which, his Lordship went to the court of Exchequer, and took also the usual oath as Lord High Treasurer; on which occasion

Sir Simon Harcourt, the Lord-keeper, addressed himself to his Lordship in the following speech:

'My Lord Oxford;

'The Queen, who does every thing with the greatest wisdom, has given a proof of it in the honours she has lately conferred on you, which are exactly suited to your deserts, and qualifications.'

'My Lord,

'The title, which you now bear, could not have been so justly placed on any other of her Majesty's subjects. Some of that ancient blood, which fills your veins, is derived from the Veres: and you have shewed yourself as ready to sacrifice it, for the safety of your Prince, and the good of your country, and as fearless of danger, on the most trying occasions, as ever any of that brave and loyal house were. Nor is that title less suited to you, as it carries in it a relation to one of the chief seats of learning: for when your enemies, my Lord (if any such there still are) must own, that the love of letters, and the encouragement of those who excel in them, is one distinguishing part of your character.'

'My Lord,

'The high station of Lord-Treasurer of Great-Britain, to which her Majesty has called you, is the just reward of your eminent services. You have been the great instrument of restoring public credit, and relieving this nation from the heavy pressure and ignominy of an immense debt, under which it languished; and you are now entrusted with the power of securing us from a relapse into the same ill state, out of which you have rescued us. This great office, my Lord, is every way worthy of you; particularly on the account of those many difficulties, with which the faithful discharge of it must be unavoidably attended, and which require a genius like yours to master them. The only difficulty which even you, my Lord, may find insuperable, is how to deserve better of the crown and kingdom, after this advancement, than you did before it.'

On August 15, 1711, at a general court of the South Sea company, he was chosen their Governor, of which he had been the chief founder or regulator. On October 26, 1712, he was elected a Knight-companion of the most noble order of the Garter, and installed at Windsor, on August 4 following. He was also one of the Governors of the Charterhouse, and Custos Rotulorum of the county of Radnor. On July 27, 1714, he resigned his staff of Lord High Treasurer of Great-Britain, at Kensington, into the Queen's hands, who died on August 1, that year.

On June 10, 1715, his Lordship was impeached, by the house of Commons, of high treason, and high crimes and misdemeanors; and was committed to the Tower by the house of Lords, on July 16, the same year: where he suffered a severe and long confinement, till July 1, 1717, when, after a public trial, he was unanimously acquitted by his Peers.

Mr. Pope hath celebrated his memory, in the following lines:

> A soul supreme, in each hard instance try'd,
> Above all pain, all anger, and all pride;
> The rage of power, the blast of public breath,
> The lust of lucre, and the dread of death.

After his Lordship's decease, the following character was also justly given of him.

'During the time he was Prime Minister, notwithstanding such a weight of affairs rested on him, he was easy and disengaged in private conversation. He was endowed with great learning, and was a great favourer and protector of it. Intrepid by nature, as well as by the consciousness of his own integrity; he would have chosen rather to fall by an impeachment, than to have been saved by an act of grace; sagacious to view into the remotest consequence of things, by which all difficulties fled before him. He was a courteous neighbour, a firm and affectionate friend, and a kind, generous, and placable enemy, sacrificing his just resentments, not only to public good, but to common intercession and acknowledgment. He was a despiser of money, and, what is yet more rare, an uncorrupted Minister of state, which appeared, by not having made the least accession to his fortune.'

His Lordship married, first, Elizabeth, daughter of Thomas Foley, of Witley court, in the county of Worcester, Esq; and sister to Thomas, the first Lord Foley, by whom he had issue, Edward, his son and heir, 2d Earl of Oxford, &c. and two daughters: Lady Elizabeth, married, on Dec. 15, 1712, to Peregrine Hyde Osborne, Marquis of Carmarthen, afterwards Duke of Leeds, by whom she died in childbed of the present Duke

Duke of Leeds; and Lady Abigail, youngeſt daughter, married to George, Earl of Kinnoul, in Scotland, and Baron Hay, of Pedwarden, in England. His Lordſhip took to his ſecond wife Sarah, daughter to Thomas Middleton, Eſq; a ſon of Sir Hugh Middleton, Bart. but by her had no iſſue: and departing this life in the 64th year of his age, on May 21, 1724, was ſucceeded in honour and eſtate by Edward, his only ſon, before-mentioned; and his ſecond Lady ſurviving him, died in June, 1737.

Which Edward, ſecond Earl of Oxford, &c. married, on October 31, 1713, the Lady Henrietta Cavendiſh Holles, only daughter and heir of his Grace John Holles, Duke of Newcaſtle.

His Lordſhip was eminently diſtinguiſhed for his diſintereſtedneſs, both in public and private life; and was reſpected as one of the principal patrons of the age, for his encouragement of literature, and learned men. He made a moſt valuable addition to the rich magazine of manuſcripts, collected by the Lord Treaſurer, his father, eſpecially in the hiſtory and antiquities of England, both eccleſiaſtical and civil. He collected, beſides, an invaluable treaſure of original letters and papers of ſtate, written by the greateſt Princes, Stateſmen, and Scholars, as well of foreign nations, as of Great-Britain. But I ſhall be the leſs particular on this head, becauſe Mr. Humphry Wanley, ſometime his Lordſhip's librarian, has given a ſhort view of his manuſcript collections, in the preface of Biſhop Nicholſon's Engliſh Hiſtorical Library. His printed books were the moſt choice and magnificent that were ever collected in this kingdom. There were in his library the firſt printed books of all countries, and eſpecially of our own. Many printed upon vellum, and otherwiſe, in the grandeſt manner, and enriched with the moſt coſtly ſculptures. The printed books alone have been reckoned above forty thouſand volumes. As none were ever more zealous to collect whatever rarities in literature would be moſt ſerviceable to the learned, ingenious, and knowing part of mankind; ſo none was more communicative thereof, as may ſufficiently appear, in the numbers of authors who have made ſuch reſpectful references to the volumes in the Harleyan library. The valuable collection of manuſcripts was preſerved by his Lady, the right honourable Henrietta-Cavendiſh Holles, Counteſs of Oxford, at her houſe in Dover-ſtreet; till her Ladyſhip, for the ſervice of the public, conſented to the parliament's making a purchaſe thereof in 1754. His Lordſhip was a true lover of his country, as his conduct in the ſenate manifeſted: and departing this life, aged 42, at his houſe in Dover-ſtreet, on Tueſday, June 16, 1741, was buried in

Weſt-

Harley, Earl of Oxford, and Earl Mortimer. 273

Weftminfter-abbey. He left iffue, an only daughter and heir, Lady Margaret-Cavendifh Harley, married, in 1734, to his Grace William Duke of Portland. Leaving no male iffue by his Lady (who furvived him till Dec. 8, 1755, and lies buried with him) his honours devolved on Edward Harley, Efq; then Knight of the fhire for the county of Hereford, fon and heir of Edward Harley, of Eywood, in com'. Hereford, Efq; before-mentioned, one of the Auditors of the Impreft, who was next brother to Robert, firft Earl of Oxford and Earl Mortimer, Lord High Treafurer of England, according to the limitation of the patent.

The faid Edward Harley, who thus fucceeded as 3d Earl of Oxford and Earl Mortimer, &c. ferved as one of the Knights in parliament for the county of Hereford, from the firft parliament, called in 1727, by the late King, inclufive, until he became intitled to a feat in the houfe of Peers. In 1746, his Lordfhip was elected High-fteward of the city of Hereford, in the room of Henry Duke of Beaufort, deceafed: and on April 12, 1748, was, in convocation, prefented, by the Univerfity of Oxford, with the degree of Doctor of the Civil Law. His Lordfhip, in March, 1725, wedded Martha, eldeft daughter of John Morgan, of Tredegar in Monmouthfhire, Efq; and fifter to the late Sir William Morgan, Knight of the Bath: and by her Ladyfhip had iffue five fons, 1. Edward Lord Harley, the prefent and 4th Earl of Oxford, &c. 2. The honourable Robert Harley, who was born on Sept. 10, 1727, and died a batchelor, at Bath, on Jan. 12, 1760: 3. The hon. and rev. John Harley, who was born on Sept. 29, 1728, and conftituted Archdeacon of Salop, in February, 1760: 4. The hon. Thomas Harley, Efq; of whom afterwards: and, 5. The hon. and rev. William Harley, who was born on May 30, 1733, and is Vicar of Uffington in Berkfhire, and Rector of Everley in Wiltfhire. This Earl of Oxford had alfo, by the fame Lady, two daughters, viz. Lady Sarah, who died unmarried, on April 28, 1737, in the 7th year of her age; and Lady Martha, who was born on Nov. 23, 1736, and married, on April 20, 1764, to Charles Millborne, of the Priory, near Abergavenny, in the county of Monmouth, Efq;

The hon. Thomas Harley, Efq; the 4th fon, before-mentioned, of Edward, 3d Earl of Oxford, was born on Auguft 24, 1730; and on March 15, 1752, married Anne, daughter of Edward Bangham, Efq; Deputy-auditor of the Imprefts, and member for Leominfter, in 1710. By this Lady he had two fons, and five daughters, viz. Thomas, who died on Jan. 17, 1763; Edward; Henrietta, who died on July 4, 1759; Martha; Anne; Sarah; and Elizabeth.—At the general election,

tion, in April, 1761, being an eminent merchant, he was chosen one of the four citizens of London to the 12th parliament of Great-Britain: and on May 5, that year, was elected Alderman of Portsoken-ward, in the city of London, in the room of Sir William Calvert, Knt. deceased. On June 23, he was chosen one of the Sheriffs of London and Middlesex; and having been sworn in at Guildhall, on Sept. 26 following, was sworn at the Exchequer on the 29th, when he entered into his office, which he discharged with spirit and integrity. He is also one of the Governors of the London Lying-in Hospital, in Aldersgate-street, of which he was elected Treasurer in 1762, and President in 1764.

The Earl of Oxford died at Bath, on April 11, 1755, having, through the whole course of his years, behaved with great honour, and integrity, in public as well as private life. He was succeeded by his eldest son,

Edward, Lord Harley, the present and 4th Earl of Oxford, &c. who was born on Sept. 2, 1726; and on July 15, 1747, was elected, to the 10th parliament of Great-Britain, one of the Knights for the county of Hereford, for which he was also returned to the next parliament, which first met on business, May 31, 1754, and sat till his father's death. On April 12, 1748, he had the degree of Doctor of the Civil Law conferred on him, in convocation of the University of Oxford. Soon after the accession of the present King, he was made one of the Lords of the bedchamber: and is also a Fellow of the Royal Society, and one of the Trustees of the British Museum.

His Lordship married, on July 11, Susannah, eldest daughter of William Archer, of Welford in Berkshire, Esq; (who represented that county in the 8th parliament of Great-Britain, with great honour and fidelity, until he died, on June 30, 1739, aged 59) but as yet hath no issue by her Ladyship.

TITLES.] Edward Harley, Earl of Oxford, and Earl Mortimer, and Baron Harley, of Wigmore.

CREATIONS.] Baron Harley, of Wigmore, in com' Hereford, Earl Mortimer (the name of a family) and Earl of the city of Oxford, May 24 (1711) 10 Queen Anne.

ARMS.] Or, a Bend cottised, Sable.

CREST.] On a Wreath, a Castle, Argent, triple-towered, with a Demi-Lion, rampant, Gules, issuing out of the Battlements of the middle Tower.

SUPPORTERS.] Two Angels, proper, habited in long Robes, their Hair and Wings, Or.

MOTTO.] VIRTUTE ET FIDE.

CHIEF-SEATS.] Eywood, and Brampton-Brian, both in the county of Hereford.

SHIRLEY,

Harley E. of Oxford & Mortimer.

SHIRLEY, Earl Ferrers.

THIS family is descended from Sasuvalo (whose name shews him to have been of an old English stock) [a] the founder and endower of Nether-Eatendon church, in com' Warw. That he was an eminent man, is obvious, from his possessions in Warwickshire, Lincolnshire, Northamptonshire, and Derbyshire, in the time of the Conqueror; few being allowed to enjoy more at that change than a part of their estate, and even obliged to hold that, by military and other services, from their new Lords. Therefore, if we may guess at his authority, by the extent of his estate, he must have been no less than a Thane, in the time of the Saxons, when not little more than five hides of land, as Selden observes, was an estate for some who were so dignified. He had issue two sons, Henry, who was a benefactor to the canons of Kenilworth, in com' Warw. and died without issue; and Fulcher, who had issue Henry.

Which Henry succeeded in the inheritance, and [b] gave Idenbrock to the Monks of Bildwas, in com' Salop; and though he had issue Fulcher, yet he [c] appointed his younger brother Sewall his heir to the lands of his father and uncle, by fine levied in 4 Rich. I. de Baroniis Fulcheri & Henrici, as the record testifies.

The said Sewall was a Knight, and took the surname of Etendon, or Eatendon, from the place of his abode. He married Maud, daughter of ———— Ridel, of Haloughton, in com' Leicest. and had issue Henry, who attended William, 3d Earl Ferrers, and of Derby, anno 1202, 4 Joh. in that King's service, into Poictiers; and in 7 Joh. was restored to the manour of Edensoure, in com' Derb. of which he had been deprived when he was on that voyage. He founded a chantry in the church of Etendon, and was succeeded by Sewall, his son and heir, who was a Knight, and had issue James, his son and heir, who first assumed, in the reign of Hen. III. the surname of Shirley, and by that name had free warren granted to him in all his demesnes at Shirley in Derbyshire, and Etendon. He was afterwards knighted; and having married Agnes de Wauton, had issue, [d] by her, Sir Ralph.

[a] Dugdale's antiq. of Warwicksh. p. 475. [b] Cart. antiq. R. n. 20.
[c] Dugdale ut antea.   [d] Ibid.

Shirley, Earl Ferrers.

Which Sir Ralph, his fon and heir, in 7 Edw. I. held the manour of Eatendon aforefaid, in com' Warw. of Edmund Earl of Lancafter, the King's brother, by the fervice of two Knights fees. In 9 Edw. I. he was of full age. In 28 Edw. I. he had the cuftody of the counties of Salop and Stafford, with the caftle of Shrewfbury, committed to his charge; and was Sheriff of the counties of Derby and Nottingham, in the 27th, 28th, and 30th of Edw. I. In 1301, 29 Edw. I. he was fummoned to attend the King at Berwick upon Tweed, on Midfummer-day, well-appointed with horfe and arms, to march againft the Scots. In 3 Edw. II. he was conftituted one of the Juftices in the county of Warwick for the gaol-delivery; and in 5 Edw. II. ferved in two parliaments, held that year, as a reprefentative for that county. In 6 Edw. II. he was difcharged from the office of Coroner, on account of his ill ftate of health; but in 8 Edw. II. he was Governor of Horfton-caftle, in com' Derb. and in 16 Edw. II. a Commiffioner for levying a fifteenth in com' Warw. The next year he was in the lift of thofe Knights and men at arms, whofe names were then certified in the Chancery.

He married [e] Margaret, daughter and one of the coheirs of Walter de Waldefhof, Butler to Edw. II. and dying in 20 Edw. II. left iffue Ralph, his fon and heir, a Commiffioner for affeffing and collecting a fifteenth and tenth, granted in 11 Edw. III. and in the 12th, was appointed to collect the fcutage due to the King for the Scotch expedition. In 14 Edw. III. he ferved as one of the Knights in parliament for the county of Warwick; and to him fucceeded his fon and heir Sir Thomas Shirley.

Which Sir Thomas Shirley, Knt. dying in 1362, 36 Edw. III. left iffue, by Ifabella, daughter of Ralph Lord Baffet, of Drayton, Hugh Shirley, who was a Knight in 1 Hen. IV. and Mafter of the King's hawks. He was made Chief-warden of Higham-Ferrers park, in com' Northamp. by John (of Gaunt) Duke of Lancafter; and in 22 Rich. II. Conftable of Donnington-caftle, by Henry Duke of Lancafter (afterwards Hen. IV.) He married Beatrix, fifter and heir to John de Brews, of Weft-Nefton, in com' Suffex, and was killed on July 21, the eve of St. Mary Magdalen, in 1403, 4 Hen. IV. in the battle of Shrewfbury, fighting on the King's part againft the gallant Henry Lord Percy, furnamed Hotfpur, who fell alfo in the fame engagement.

He left iffue Ralph, his fon and heir, then 12 years old, who in 3 Hen. V. was retained to ferve the King in perfon in his

---

[e] Dugdale's antiq. of Warwickfh. p. 466.

army in Guyen, with 6 men at arms and 18 archers; and the next year with 8 men at arms and 16 archers, and was about that time knighted; for in 8 Hen. V. being then Sheriff of the counties of Nottingham and Derby, he was then styled a Knight. He married Joyce, daughter and sole heir to Thomas Basset, of Brailsford, Esq; by whom he had issue Ralph, his son and heir, who died on St. Stephen's day, 1466, 6 Edw. IV. having had issue by his second wife Elizabeth (sister to the Lord Montjoy) Ralph, from whom descended those of the name in Sussex; and by his first wife Margaret, daughter and coheir of John de Staunton, of Staunton-Harold, in com' Leic. had John, his son and heir, who married Eleanor, daughter of Sir Hugh Willoughby, of Middleton, in com' Warw. and Wollaton, in com' Nott. and died on May 18, 1485, 2 Rich. III. leaving Ralph his son and heir, 26 years old, who, for his valour in the battle of Stoke, in com' Nott. June 16, 1487, 2 Hen. VII. was made a Banneret; to which battle [f] he brought forces to the King's aid, when the Earl of Lincoln was slain. In 7 Hen. VII. he was retained to serve the King in his wars beyond sea for one year; and died on Jan. 6, 1516-7, 8 Hen. VIII. By his last will and testament [g], which bears date four days before his death, writing himself Sir Rauf Shirley, of Staunton-Harold, in com' Leic. Knt. he orders his body to be buried at the discretion of his executors, and that 1000 Masses be said the day of his burial, or shortly after, for the health of his soul, and all Christian souls; also, that alms be distributed among 3000 poor people. He bequeaths to Jane, his wife, his manours of Shirley and Brailesford, with the lands, rents, and services; as also other lands, in full of her jointure and dower, for term of her life: and his manour of Barnham to the monastery of Gerondens, for the term of 50 years.

It also appears by his will, that he had five brothers, and that he was possessed of the manours of Staunton-Harold, Rakedale, and Willowes, Burton, Long-Whatton, Ratelyff, Dunton, Esterleyke, Sutton-Bonyngton, and Newton-Regis; and bequeathed lands in Melbourne and Worthington, to the chantry of St. Catharine in St. Michael's church in Melbourne for ever, to pray for his soul; also to Lincoln church, 10 shillings, and to every house of friars in Leicester, 10 shillings. He bequeaths all his household furniture, plate, &c. to his wife, and his son Francis, to be divided equally between them; and ordains executors, his cousin Sir Richard Sackvil (to whom he bequeaths a cross of gold, hanging at his chain) his brother Robert Ha-

[f] Polyd. Virg. p. 573. No. 20.   [g] Ex regist. Ayloff. qu. 1.

fylryg

fylryg (hufband to Elizabeth, his fifter) Sir James Smith, his prieft, and Thomas Herbert.

He married four wives, but had no iffue by his firft and third ; and by his fecond wife Elizabeth, daughter and coheir to Thomas Walfh, of Wanlip in Leicefterfhire, had only a daughter, Anne, married to Sir Thomas Poultney, of Mifterton, in com' Leiceft. Knt. By his laft wife Jane, daughter to Sir Robert Sheffield, Knt. anceftor to the late Duke of Buckinghamfhire, he had Francis, his fon and heir, beforementioned.

Which Francis was [h] Sheriff of the counties of Warwick and Leicefter, in 4 Phil. and Mary; and having lived [i] to an advanced age, famous for his charity and hofpitality, died on July 27, 1571, 13 Eliz. and was buried in the church of Breedon on the Hill, in Leicefterfhire, where a monument was erected to the memory of him, and Dorothy his wife, who furvived him but a fhort time, as appears by her laft will and teftament [k], bearing date Auguft 9, 1571, and the probate thereof, May 16 following. She was daughter of Sir John Gifford, of Chillington in Staffordfhire, Knt. and married to her firft hufband John Congreve, Efq; but had iffue by the faid Francis Shirley, three fons, John Shirley, Efq; hereafter mentioned, Edward, who died young, and Ralph: alfo three daughters, Caffandra, married to Walter Powtrell, of Weft-Hallum in com' Derb. Efq; Elizabeth, to Thomas Cotton, of Conington in Huntingdonfhire, Efq; father, by her, to the famous Sir Robert Cotton, Knt. and Bart. the great Collector of the records, now repofited in the Britifh Mufeum, formerly called Montagu-houfe; and Anne, to John Brook, of Madely in Shropfhire, Efq;

John Shirley, eldeft fon and heir, died, A. D. 1570, in the life-time of his father, aged 35 years, and was buried in the church of Breedon, before-mentioned, where a monument is erected to his memory, reciting, that he married ———, fole daughter and heir of Thomas Lovett, Efq; and that by her he had five fons, and three daughters.

George Shirley, Efq; (eldeft fon and heir of the faid John) fucceeded his grandfather in his eftate, and was created a Baronet [l] on May 22, 1611, 9 Jac. I. on the firft erection of that dignity, being the 4th in order of precedency. He married Frances, daughter to Henry Lord Berkeley, anceftor to the prefent Earl of Berkeley, a Lady [m], who to her noble defcent

---

h· Fuller's worthies. i Ex infcript. tumul. k Ex regift. Daper.
qu. 16. collect. T. Meller, Gent. l Pat, 9 Jac. I. m Ex infcript.
tumul.

added

added many extraordinary virtues; and dying in the 31ſt year of her age, on Dec. 29, 1595, was buried in the church of Breedon, where a monument is erected by her affectionate huſband; who married, 2dly, Dorothy, daughter of Thomas Wroughton, of Wilcot in com' Wilts, Eſq; and relict of Sir Henry Upton, of Farringdon in com' Berks, Knt. but by her had no iſſue. He had, by his firſt wife, four ſons, and one daughter, Mary, who died unmarried. The two eldeſt ſons, John and George, died young: Henry ſucceeded his father, and Thomas, the youngeſt ſon [n], received the honour of Knighthood at Whitehall, on May 22, 1622, and is characteriſed by Sir William Dugdale [o], to have been ' a great lover ' of learning, and eſpecially affected to antiquities, in the ' ſtudy whereof he attained to much knowledge, and thereby ' gave no ſmall luſtre to his ancient and worthy family.' He married [p] Mary, daughter to Thomas Harpur, of Chepnor in Oxfordſhire, Eſq;

Sir George Shirley, Bart. departed this life at [q] Stanton-Harold, on April 27, 1622, 20 Jac. I. and was buried at Breedon. To him ſucceeded Henry, his eldeſt ſurviving ſon and heir.

This Sir Henry Shirley, Bart. (who was Sheriff of Leiceſter, the laſt year of James I.) married, in 1615, Dorothy, youngeſt of the two daughters of that great but unfortunate favourite to Queen Elizabeth, Robert Earl of Eſſex, and ſiſter and coheir to her brother, Robert Earl of Eſſex, the famous General to the parliament. It is by this alliance, that the Earls Ferrers quarter the arms of France and England with their own; the Earls of Eſſex being maternally deſcended from Richard Plantagenet, Earl of Cambridge, grandſon to King Edw. III. and grandfather to King Edw. IV. and alſo from Thomas Plantagenet, Duke of Glouceſter, youngeſt ſon of Edw. III. Sir Henry Shirley, by the ſaid Dorothy (who, in 1634, took for a ſecond huſband, ——— Stafford, Eſq;) had two ſons, Charles, and Robert; alſo one daughter, Lettice, married to William Bourke, Earl of Clanrickard, in Ireland. By the inquiſition, taken at Leiceſter, April 18, 1633 [r], it appears, that he died on Feb. 8, 1632, ſeized of the manours of Aſtwell, Falcot, Billing-manour, alias Gifford's-manour, Brookes-manour, alias Mamſey-manour; alſo of the manours of Stanton-Harold, Syleby, and Ragdale, with the impropriation, the manour of Willows and rectory, all in Leiceſter-

---

n Philpot's cat. of Knights. collect. T. Meller. q Ibid. in bibl. Harley.

o In antiq. of Warw. p. 477.   p Ex r Cole's Eſc. lib. 3. n. 61. a, 14. p. 153.

shire; the manours of Etenton, Oxhill, Fulridie, and Whatcoate, in Warwickshire; the manours of Sutton-Boneryton, in Nottinghamshire; and the manours of Shirley, and Bray-Jefford, in Derbyshire: all which devolved on his son and heir, Sir Charles Shirley, Bart. aged nine years, on Sept. 9, 1632.

Which Sir Charles dying unmarried, about the year 1646, was succeeded in title and estate by Sir Robert Shirley, Bart. his brother and heir. Which Sir Robert, for his loyalty to Charles I. was imprisoned in the Tower of London by Oliver Cromwell, where he died during his confinement, not without suspicion of poison, leaving issue, by Catharine his wife, daughter to Humphrey Okeover, of Okeover, in the county of Stafford, Esq; two sons, Seymour his successor, and Robert, afterwards Earl Ferrers: also two daughters, Catharine, married to Peter Venables, of the county of Chester, Esq; commonly called Baron of Kinderton; and Dorothy, to George Vernon, of Sudbury in Derbyshire, Esq;

Sir Seymour Shirley, Bart. marrying Diana, daughter of Robert Bruce, Earl of Aylesbury, left issue an only son, who surviving his father but a short time, the title of Baronet devolved on Robert, his uncle (youngest son to Sir Robert Shirley, before-mentioned) afterwards created Earl Ferrers.

Which Sir Robert Shirley, Knt. was born at East-Sheen, in Surry, during his father's aforesaid confinement in the Tower; and on Dec. 14, 1677, 29 Car. II. was summoned to parliament by the title of Lord Ferrers of Chartley, which honour, by the death of Robert Devereux, the 3d and last Earl of Essex of that family, Sept. 13, 1646, was immerged in the issue of his two sisters and coheirs, and so continued till Cha. II. was pleased to restore that title, with the precedency thereto belonging (from 27 Edw. I.) to this Sir Robert Shirley, grandson and heir of Dorothy, the youngest of those two sisters. He was introduced into the house of Peers on Jan. 28, 1677-8 [s], and took his place according to the ancient writ of summons, Feb. 6 (1298) 27 Edw. I. He was Master of the horse, and Steward of the houshold to Queen Catharine, consort of King Charles II. and was sworn of the Privy-council to King William, on May 25, 1699. In the reign of Queen Anne, he was again sworn of the Privy-council, on Nov. 25, 1708, according to the act for the union of the two kingdoms; and on Sept. 3, 1711, was advanced to the titles of Viscount Tamworth, and Earl Ferrers, by reason of his descent from the ancient and noble family of Ferrers.

[s] Journal Dom. Procer.

His Lordship departed this life on Dec. 25, 1717, having had issue, by his first wife Elizabeth, daughter and heir to Laurence Washington, of Carefden in Wiltshire, Esq; ten sons, and seven daughters; and this Lady dying on Oct. 2, 1693, was buried at Stanton-Harold; whereupon he married to his 2d wife, in August, 1699, Selina, daughter of George Finch, of the city of London, Esq; and by her (who died on March 20, 1762) had five sons, and as many daughters, viz. the hon. Robert Shirley, Esq; born May 27, 1700, who was elected, on the accession of our late Sovereign, a member of parliament for the borough of Stamford in Lincolnshire, and died unmarried in July, 1738; George, who died an infant; another George, born in 1705, of Lower-Eatington in Warwickshire, who married ———— ————, and had a son born at Lower-Eatington, and baptized Nov. 29, 1750, by the name of George; Sewallis, born in 1709, Comptroller of the houshold to Queen Charlotte; and John, born in 1712. The five daughters were, the Lady Selina, married to Peter Bathurst, of Clarendon-park in Wiltshire, Esq; brother to Allen, 1st Lord Bathurst; the Lady Mary, to Charles Tryon, of Bullwick in Northamptonshire, Esq; the Lady Anne, on May 17, 1729, to Sir Robert Furnefs, of Walderfhare in Kent, Bart. the Lady Frances, and the Lady Steuarta.

The seven daughters by the first marriage were, the Ladies Elizabeth and Catharine, who died in their infancies; the Ladies, Elizabeth, married to Walter Clarges, Esq; brother of Sir Thomas Clarges, of Afton in Hertfordshire, Bart. Anne-Eleanora, and Catharine, who died unmarried in October, 1736; and Dorothy, married to John Cotes, son and heir of Charles Cotes, of Woodcot in Shropshire, Esq; Likewise of the ten sons by the first marriage, only three survived their father, Washington, the second son, late Earl Ferrers; Henry, ninth son, late Earl Ferrers; and Laurence, tenth son, born on Sept. 26, 1693; the rest all dying in their infancies, except Robert, the eldest son, born on Sept. 4, 1673.

Which Robert married, 1st, Catharine, daughter of Peter Venables, Baron of Kinderton; and she deceasing in her nonage, he married, 2dly, in September, 1688, Anne, daughter of Sir Humphry Ferrers, of Tamworth-castle in Warwickshire, Knt. by whom he had issue three sons, Robert, Ferrers, and Thomas, and a daughter Elizabeth, Countess of Northampton, and Baroness Ferrers of Chartley, as heir to her father: and the said Robert dying of the small-pox, on Feb. 25, 1698-9, Robert, his son and heir, born on Dec. 28, 1692, became heir apparent to his grandfather, and was elected Knight of the shire for the county of Leicester in the last parliament

liament called by Queen Anne; and furviving both his brothers, died of the fmall-pox, on July 5, 1714, unmarried, leaving his fifter, the Countefs of Northampton, his heir.

Whereupon the hon. Wafhington Shirley, fecond fon of Robert Earl Ferrers, fucceeded his father in the Earldom of Ferrers. His Lordfhip was born on June 22, 1677, and on April 12, 1725, was conftituted Lord-lieutenant of Staffordfhire, alfo Cuftos Rotulorum of the faid county, on April 27 following; and again, on Nov. 17, 1727. He married Mary, daughter of Sir Richard Levings, Bart. one of the Judges of the Kings-Bench in Ireland, and by her, who died in France in January, 1739-40, left iffue three daughters, his coheirs; Lady Elizabeth, who was married, on June 24, 1725, to Jofeph Gafcoigne-Nightingale, of Enfield, in the county of Middlefex, Efq; and by him had a fon, and a daughter, of whom fhe died in childbed, and was interred in Weftminfter-abbey, on Aug. 26, 1731. Her hufband furviving her, deceafed on July 15, 1752, at Enfield. Lady Selina, 2d daughter, was wedded, on June 3, 1728, to Theophilus Earl of Huntingdon; and Lady Mary, youngeft daughter, on June 29, 1730, was married to Thomas Needham, Lord Vifcount Kilmurry, of the kingdom of Ireland. This Wafhington Earl Ferrers, departed this life on April 14, 1729, and leaving no heir male, the title devolved on Henry, his next brother and heir, who was born on April 14, 1691, and in May, 1731, was appointed Lord-lieutenant and Cuftos Rotulorum of Staffordfhire: but the faid Henry, 3d Earl Ferrers, dying, in Auguft, 1745, unmarried, the title devolved on his nephew Laurence, fon and heir of Laurence Shirley, tenth fon of Robert Earl Ferrers.

Which Laurence married Anne, 4th daughter to Sir Walter Clarges, of Afton in Hertfordfhire, Bart. by whom he left iffue, Laurence, late Earl Ferrers; Wafhington Shirley, now Earl Ferrers; Robert, Walter, and Thomas; and two daughters, Elizabeth, and Anne.

Which Laurence, Earl Ferrers, on Septtember 16, 1752, married Mary, youngeft daughter of Amos Meredith, Efq; fon and heir of Sir William Meredith, of Henbury in Chefhire, Baronet of Nova-Scotia, and fifter to Sir William Meredith, the prefent Baronet, member for Wigan in the parliament fummoned in 1754, and for Liverpool, in that which convened in 1761: but there being a domeftic uneafinefs between his Lordfhip and his Lady, her Ladyfhip was allowed a feparate maintenance by act of parliament. His Lordfhip, though he was at times a very intelligent perfon, and a Nobleman converfant in the conftitution of his country,

Shirley, Earl Ferrers.

try, yet, as was endeavoured to be proved on his trial, on divers occasions, exhibited suspicious symptoms of a constitutional insanity of mind. He shot Mr. Johnson, his land-steward, with a pistol, at his seat at Stanton-Harold, in Leicestershire, in January 1760; for which, being tried in Westminster-hall, by his Peers, on April 16 and 17, following, he received sentence, on Friday the 18th, to be executed the next Monday, and to have his body dissected and anatomized, the evidence of his insanity not being satisfactory to their Lordships: but the right hon. the Lord Henley, now Earl of Northington, who acted as High-steward at that awful solemnity, with consent of the Peers, respited his Lordship's execution till Monday, May 5. At receiving sentence, this unfortunate Nobleman begged his Peers to recommend him to mercy: and after he was carried back to the Tower, he applied, by letter, to the King, that he might suffer there, where the Earl of Essex, Queen Elizabeth's favourite, and one of his ancestors, had been beheaded. This application, he said, he made with the greater confidence, as he had the honour to be related to his Majesty, and to quarter part of his arms: but all application from himself and friends proving ineffectual, his Lordship was, on May 5, conveyed from the Tower, in his wedding-suit, to a scaffold erected for that purpose, at the usual place of execution, which was covered with black baize, and suffered with great firmness and composure.

His Lordship dying without issue, the estate and titles devolved on his brother, Washington, who took his seat in the house of Peers, on May 19, 1760. This Washington, 5th Earl Ferrers, betaking himself to a maritime life, was, on April 19, 1746, appointed a Captain in his Majesty's navy, in which station he gave eminent proofs of courage and conduct: and the Royal Society, on Dec. 14, 1761, enrolled him among their number, on account of the accurate observations he had made on the transit of Venus over the Sun, on June 6 preceding, and had communicated to that learned body, with other useful discoveries, tending to the improvement of mathematical knowledge.

TITLES.] Washington Shirley, Earl Ferrers, Viscount Tamworth, and Baronet.

CREATIONS.] Baronet, May 22 (1611) 9 Jac. I. Viscount Tamworth, in com. Staff. and Earl Ferrers, Sept. 3 (1711) 10 Queen Anne.

ARMS.] Quarterly, 1st and 4th, Paly of six, Or, and Azure, a Canton Ermine: 2d and 3d, France and England, quarterly, within a Border, or.

CREST.]

Shirley, Earl Ferrers.

CREST.] On a Wreath, the Buſt of a Saracen, ſide-faced, and couped, proper, wreathed about the Temples, Or, and Azure.

SUPPORTERS.] On the dexter ſide, a Talbot Ermine, his Ear, Or, and his ducal Collar, Gules. On the ſiniſter, a Rein-deer, of the laſt, attired, Argent, gorged with a ducal Coronet, and billeted, Or.

MOTTO.] HONOR VIRTUTIS PRÆMIUM; and MALGRE L'ENVIE.

CHIEF-SEATS.] At Stanton-Harold, in Leiceſterſhire, 2 miles from Aſhby de la Zouch, and 100 from London; at Aſhwell, in the county of Northampton, 2 miles from Brackley, and 58 from London; at Chartley-caſtle, in Staffordſhire, 3 miles from Stafford, and 135 from London.

Shirley Earl Ferrers

Wentworth, Earl of Strafford.

ALL genealogists agree, that the surname of this noble family is of Saxon original, and that it was taken from the lordship of Wentworth, in the wapentake of Strafford, in the county of York, where, at the time of the conquest, A. D. 1066, lived Reginald (or Rynold) de Winterwade (as wrote in Domesday-book). He had a son named Henry, whose son Richard had Michael, whose son Henry had a son named Hugh, who, dying in the year 1200, 2 Joh. left a son William Wyntword, of Wyntword, who married Emma, the daughter and heir of William Wodehous de Wodehous; and from that time, they were called Wentworth, of Wentworth-Woodhouse. William Wentworth, of Wentworth-Woodhouse, son to William, married Beatrix, daughter of Gilbert Thakel, and by her had two sons, William, his heir, and Richard de Wentworth, who was Bishop of London, and Chancellor of England, A. D. 1338. William, the eldest son, who, in 1288, married Dyonisia, daughter of Peter de Rotherfield; and after her decease, wedded Lucy, daughter of Sir Adam de Newmarch, by whom he had no issue: but by his first Lady he was father of two sons, William, his successor; and John, who had Elmsall with his wife ——, daughter and heir to ——— Elmsall, of Elmsall, in Yorkshire; and dying without issue, left that estate to his nephew, John. William de Wentworth succeeded his father, William, in 1295, and in 1303, obtained a writ, from Edw. I. for turning a high road near his house. He married Isabel, daughter and coheir of William Pollington, of Pollington in Yorkshire; and by her (whose estate was partitioned in 1307) he had two sons, Sir William, his heir; and John, who, by the gift of his uncle John, aforesaid, inherited Elmsall, and by Joan, his wife, daughter of Richard de Teys, of Burgh-Walleys in Yorkshire, was patriarch of the Wentworths of Elmsall, Kirby, Barons and Viscount Wentworth, and the knightly family seated at Bretton, with their several branches.

Sir William Wentworth, the eldest son and heir, married Isabel (by some called Lucy) daughter and heir of Robert Hooton (or Hutton) of Hooten-Roberts in Yorkshire, by his wife Lucy, daughter and coheir to Sir Edward Skelton; and by the said Isabel, was father of another Sir William, who wedded Lucy, daughter and coheir of Walter, son and heir of Henry de Tynneslow (alias Tinsley) of Tynneslow in Yorkshire, by Lucy his wife, daughter and heir of Walter le Brett. Thomas Wentworth, fon and heir of the faid Sir William and Lucy, married Ifabel, daughter of Sir William Fleming, of Waith, Knt. which barony is in the Marquis of Rockingham's titles. His fon William married Ifabella, daughter of Sir Thomas Rerefby, of Thriberg, in com' Ebor. Knt. whofe fon Sir Thomas taking part with King Hen. VI.ᵃ when he came out of Scotland (whither he was forced to fly by Edw. IV.) brought forces to his affiftance; and valiantly behaving, at the battle near Hexham, April 3, 1463, was taken prifoner, with the Duke of Somerfet and others, the King himfelf narrowly efcaping, but foon after taken in difguife. This Sir Thomas married Joan, daughter of Sir Richard Redman, of Harwoodtower, Knt. in the 8th of Hen. VI. and left iffue two fons, William and John. William Wentworth, Efq; in 39 Hen. VI. wedded Ifabella, daughter of Sir Richard Fitz-Williams, of Aldwark in Yorkfhire, and by her had four fons, Sir Thomas, his fucceffor; Ralph, George, and William; befides a daughter Elizabeth, fucceffively the wife of Thomas Lea, of Middleton, Efq; and Henry Arthington, Efq; He died A. D. 1477, 17 Edw. IV. and was fucceeded by his eldeft fon,

Thomas, who received the honour of Knighthood, for his bravery at the action near Guinegafte, commonly called The Battle of Spurs, becaufe the French made more ufe of them, than their fwords, at that encounter, on Aug. 16, 1513, 5 Hen. VIII.

Being very rich, he was ufually called Golden Thomas, and paid a fine to be excufed from being created a Knight of the Bath. In 1528, he obtained an uncommon licence from Hen. VIII. to wear his bonnet, and be covered in his prefence, becaufe he was infirm. He died on Dec. 5, 1548, 2 Edw. VI. aged 70: and having, in 5 Hen. VIII. wedded Beatrix, daughter of Sir Richard Woodrove, of Wolley, Knt. and widow of John Drax, of Woodhall, Efq; had by her five fons, 1. William, his heir; 2. Gervafe; 3. Michael Wentworth, Efq; who was of Mendham in Suffolk, Comptroller to the Queen; and by Ifabel, his wife, daughter and heir of Percival Whitley, of Whitley in com' Ebor. Efq; was progenitor of the Wentworths, of Wooley in Yorkfhire: 4. Thomas Wentworth, of Scorby, Efq; who married Grace, daughter of John Gafcoigne, of Lafingcroft, Efq; and by her had a fon of his own name; and, 5. Bryan Wentworth,

ᵃ Hollinfhed's chron. p. 666.

Efq;

Efq; Sir Thomas had alſo three daughters, viz. Elizabeth, wedded to Ralph Durham, Efq; Iſabel, to Nicholas (or, according to others, Richard) Wombwell, of Thunnercliffe, Efq; and Beatrice, to James Wyrrall (or Worrall) of Lowerſtall, Efq; both in the county of York.

William Wentworth, Efq; the eldeſt ſon of Sir Thomas, of Wentworth-Woodhouſe, married Catharine, daughter of Ralph Beeſton, of Beeſton in Yorkſhire, Efq; in 1546, and by her was father of four ſons, 1. Thomas, his ſucceſſor; 2. Michael; 3. William; and, 4. Gervaſe: and alſo of four daughters, 1. Margaret, eſpouſed to Lancelot Montfort, of Kilnhurſt, Efq; ſon and heir to Chriſtopher Montfort, Efq; by his firſt wife, and by him mother of an only child, Beatrice Montfort; 2. Muriel, the ſecond wife of the ſaid Chriſtopher Montfort, to whom ſhe bore a ſon Thomas; 3. Elizabeth, who died unmarried; and, 4. Beatrice, wedded to John Savile, of Wathe, Efq; This William died on Dec. 4, 1549, 3 Edw. VI. as found by inquiſition taken [b] after his deceaſe, at Wakefield, in com' Ebor. on June 21 following; and that he died, ſeized of the manour of Wentworth, Woodhouſe-hall, in Wentworth; the manour of Frezehouſe in Wentworth, parcel of the monaſtery of Bolton in Craven; the manours of Pollington, Hooton, Berbrythall in Grayſebroke; half the manours of Tynneflowe, and Waithe; and divers other lands and tenements in Yorkſhire.

Thomas Wentworth, Efq; the eldeſt ſon and heir of the ſaid William, was then about two years of age. This Thomas was High-ſheriff of the county of York, in 25 Eliz. and died on Feb. 14, 1586-7, the 29th of her reign, poſſeſſed of lands to the then value of ſix thouſand pounds a year, in the ſaid county. He married Margaret, daughter and heir of Sir William Gaſcoigne, of Gawthorpe, Knt. (grandſon of Sir William Gaſcoigne, Knight of the Bath) by his wife Joan, daughter and heir of John Nevil, Lord Ferrers, of Overſley. By this match came the manour and ſeat of Gawthorpe, Cuſworth, &c. and alſo the claim to the baronies of Newmarch, and Overſley, his Lady being deſcended from the noble families of Nevil, Ferrers, and Newmarch, who inherited thoſe titles. He left iſſue, Sir William Wentworth, his heir, and four daughters, 1. Elizabeth, the wife of Thomas Danby, of Farnley, Efq; 2. Barbara, who died unmarried; 3. Margaret, firſt wedded to Michael, ſon and heir of John Lord Darcy (of whoſe deſcendants, under the title of Holderneſſe) and, 2dly, to Jaſper Blythman, of New-Lathes, Efq; by whom

[b] Cole's Eſc. lib. 5. n. 16. a. 16. p. 379. in bibl. Harl.

she had no issue; and, 4. Catharine, espoused to Thomas Gargrave, of Nostel-Priory in Yorkshire, Esq;

Sir William Wentworth, the son and successor of the aforesaid Thomas, of Wentworth-Woodhouse, Gawthorpe, &c. and the 19th in paternal descent from Reginald de Wintewade, served the office of High-sheriff for the county of York, in the last year of Queen Elizabeth; and on June 29, 1611, 9 Jac. I. was created a Baronet, being the 22d in precedence. By Anne, his wife, daughter and heir of Sir Robert Atkins, of Stowell in Gloucestershire, Knt. he had eight sons, five of whom died unmarried. Sir George Wentworth, the 8th and youngest son, was, with Sir George Wentworth, of Wooley, Knt. returned for Pontefract, to the parliament in 1640; but, together with him, disabled from sitting, on account of their loyalty to Charles I. by whom he was knighted, made General of the forces in Ireland, and a Privy-counsellor in that kingdom. He married ——, daughter of Sir Francis Ruishe, of Sarre in the isle of Thanet, in Kent, Knt. and by her had Ruishe-Wentworth, of Sarre, Esq; (living in 1681) who, by Susan, his wife, daughter to ——— Adye, of Dodington in Kent, Esq; was father of Mary, his only child and heir, the first connubial consort of Thomas Lord Howard, of Effingham. The two eldest surviving sons were, Sir Thomas Wentworth, the renowned Earl of Strafford; and Sir William Wentworth, Knt. ancestor to the present Earl of Strafford, of both whom more at large, after giving an account of their three sisters. Mary (or, according to others, Margaret) was wedded to Sir Richard Hooton, of Goldesburgh in Yorkshire, Knt. Anne, to Sir Gervase Savile, of Thornhill in Yorkshire, Knt. and Bart. and Elizabeth, to James Dillon, Earl of Roscommon in Ireland, the celebrated Poet, who died sine prole. Sir William Wentworth, their father, departed this life in 1614 (his Lady having died in July, 1611) and was succeeded by his eldest son,

Sir Thomas Wentworth, Bart. who makes such a conspicuous figure in the English annals, both as Commoner and Peer, and in the cabinet as well as the field. He was returned one of the Knights for the county of York, to the parliaments summoned in 12 and 18 Jac. I. and 1 and 3 Car. I. having immediately served the office of Sheriff for that county before his last election. He appeared among the anti-courtiers, till he saw their aim was to overturn the constitution in church and state: and then heartily concurred with the King's Ministers; which so exasperated the popular demagogues, that they never left pursuit of him, till they brought him to the block. On July 22, 1628, he was created Baron Wentworth, of Wentworth-Woodhoufe; and on Dec. 10 following, promoted to the degree of Vifcount Wentworth. He was, in 1629, made a Privy-counfellor, Lord-lieutenant of the county of York, and Prefident of the North. In Feb. 1632-3, his Lordfhip was nominated Lord-deputy of Ireland, where he reftored the ftate of the country, and effected a conformity between the churches of England and Ireland; the convocation there having paffed a canon for receiving the articles of religion eftablifhed in the Englifh convocation, in the time of Queen Elizabeth. He alfo raifed eight regiments in that kingdom, for the fervice of his Sovereign; but before he could difpofe them into neceffary quarters, he was recalled, to command as Lieutenant-general in the army raifed againft the Scots; who, at the folicitation of the Englifh puritans, threatened England with an invafion. On Jan. 12, 1639 40, 15 Car. I. he was further dignified with the titles of Baron Raby, of Rabycaftle, and Earl of Strafford; foon after appointed Lord-lieutenant of Ireland, and elected Knight of the Garter, on Sept. 12, 1640. The puritan intereft prevailing in the Englifh parliament, which met on Nov. 3, 1640, and the chiefs of that party being confcious, that his Lordfhip would be a great, if not an infurmountable, obftacle to their views againft monarchy and epifcopacy, it was refolved to get rid of him, before they avowed their defigns. Soon after the meeting of the parliament, they impeached his Lordfhip of high treafon; and in the mean time, they practifed every method, to deprive him of the evidence of thofe who could have exculpated him. However, when he was brought to trial before his Peers, on March 22, 1640 1, his profecutors were not able to make good their charge againft him, according to the common laws of the land, notwithftanding the many artifices and endeavours they had ufed, to fift out evidence againft him; and therefore they proceeded againft him by attainder, which paffed through both houfes, but not without difficulty, and with an exprefs declaration, that it fhould not ferve for a precedent in time coming. The tumultuous means made ufe of to force the bill through the two houfes, and the methods practifed to extort his Majefty's affent, are fo amply narrated in hiftory, that it may be fufficient to fay, that, the royal fanction being given by commiffion, on May 10, 1641, his Lordfhip was, on the 12th, conducted to the fcaffold on Tower-hill, where he fuffered decapitation with fuch refolution, magnanimity, and compofure, as became the great and good man.

The preamble to his patent fets forth, that he was lineally defcended from John of Gaunt, and from the ancient Barons of Newmarch and Overfley, &c. His anceftors, either by father or mother, had matched with divers houses of honour; as with Maud, Countess of Cambridge, daughter to the Lord Clifford of Westmorland, Margaret, daughter and heir to the Lord Philip de Spencer, the Lords D'arcy of the North; Latimer, Talboys, Ogle, Ferrers Earl of Derby, Quincy Earl of Winchester, Beaumont Earl of Leicester, Grantmesnil Baron of Hincley, and Lord High Steward of England, Peverel Earl of Nottingham, Leofrick Earl of Mercia, and from Margaret, Dutchess of Somerset, grandmother to Hen. VII.

He married, 1st, the Lady Margaret Clifford, daughter to Francis Earl of Cumberland, by whom he had no issue; but by his 2d wife, the Lady Arabella, daughter to John Holles, Earl of Clare, he had one son, William, and two daughters, viz. the Lady Anne, married to Edward Watson, Lord Rockingham, from whom the late Earls of Rockingham, and the present Marquis of Rockingham, are descended; and also Arabella, married to John Maccarty, Viscount Mount-cassel, in Ireland (a younger son of Donald, Earl of Clancarty) to whom she had no issue. He had, by his 3d wife, Elizabeth, daughter of Sir Godfrey Rhodes, of Great Houghton in Yorkshire, a daughter named Margaret, who died unmarried. His son William was restored to his father's honours, &c. by patent, on Dec. 1, 1641, the 17th of Charles I. and soon after the restoration, an act passed, reversing his father's attainder; in the preamble whereof, the injustice done to that Earl and his family is set forth. He was also made Knight of the Garter.

This William Earl of Strafford married, 1st, the Lady Henrietta-Maria Stanley, daughter of James Earl of Derby, who was beheaded by the rebels; and 2dly, the Lady Henrietta, daughter to Frederick-Charles du Roy, Knight of the Elephant, and Generalissimo of the forces of the King of Denmark; but dying in October, 1695, without issue by either, he left his estate to Thomas Watson, Esq; 2d son of Edward Lord Rockingham, and the Lady Anne, above-mentioned, ordering him to use and bear the name and arms of Wentworth.

The principal male branch of this illustrious family thus expiring, all the titles of Peerage became extinct, except the dignity of Baron of Raby, which (having been taken out by Thomas, Earl of Strafford, with remainder to his brothers, in failure of his own issue-male) devolved, together with the baronetage, on Thomas Wentworth, Esq; grandson of Sir William Wentworth, Knt. 2d surviving son of Sir William Wentworth, of Wentworth-Woodhouse, &c. Bart. who married

ried Anne, daughter and heir of Sir Robert Atkins, of Stowell in Gloucefterſhire, Knt.

The ſaid Sir William Wentworth, Knt. was feated at Aſhby-Puerorum, in Lincolnſhire; and having been knighted, took arms for Charles I. was a commander of thoſe forces under William Cavendiſh, Marquis of Newcaſtle, who were befieged in York for three months; and at the breaking up of the fiege, this Sir William Wentworth was killed at the battle of Marſton-moor.

He married Elizabeth, daughter and coheir of Thomas Saville, of Northgate-Head in Wakefield, Eſq; (founder of the ſchool there) in com' Ebor. and by her had iſſue Sir William Wentworth, of Northgate-Head in Wakefield, High Sheriff of Yorkſhire, 24 Car. II. and father of the late Earl of Strafford; and Thomas, who died young; alſo one daughter, Anne, married to Edward Skinner, of Thornton-college in Lincolnſhire, Eſq;

Sir William, laſt named, married Iſabella, daughter of Sir Allan Appſley, Knt. Treaſurer of the houſhold to the Duke of York (afterwards King James II.) by whom he had iſſue five ſons, and ſix daughters; and departed this life in July, 1693, leaving his Lady ſurviving, who having lived to be 80 years of age, died, after a ſhort indiſpoſition, at her houſe in Twickenham, on July 31, 1733.

William, his eldeſt ſon, taking early to arms, was a Cornet in James II's army; and going over to the Prince of Orange, at the revolution, was made Captain of a troop of horſe, and ſerved in Flanders to the time of his death, dying unmarried, anno 1693, and was buried at Bruſſels.

Thomas, his 2d ſon, was created Earl of Strafford.

Peter Wentworth, Eſq; 3d ſon, feated at Henbury in Gloucefterſhire, was Equerry, firſt to the Duke of Gloucefter, after to Prince George of Denmark, Queen Anne, King George I. and Queen Caroline. He married Juliana, only daughter of Thomas Horde, of Cote, in the county of Oxford, Eſq; by his 2d wife, daughter of Sir Eraſmus de la Fountain, of Kirby-Bellers, in com' Leiceſt. Knt. and granddaughter to Baptiſt Viſcount Campden, and at length one of the coheirs to her uncle John de la Fountain, who died on Jan. 10, 1738-9, and had iſſue by her ſons and daughters, to the number of eleven, who all deceaſed unmarried, except his daughter Henrietta, married to Thomas Arundel, ſon and heir of Francis Arundel, of Stoke-Bruers-park, in com' Northamp. Eſq; whom ſhe ſurvived, he dying without iſſue on Septem. 27, 1733; and his ſon and heir, William

Wentworth, of Henbury in Dorsetshire, born in March, 1700. Which William had a Cornet's commission in the Royal regiment of dragoons, when he was but two years old, and remained in the regiment 43 years; being at length Captain of a troop in it, at the battles of Dettingen, and Fontenoy. He was Gentleman Usher, and Daily Waiter to Frederick Prince of Wales; and is Gentleman Usher of the Privy-chamber to the Princess Dowager of Wales. He was married, on Oct. 23, 1731, to Susannah, daughter of John Slaughter, of Upper-Slaughter-hall, in com' Glouc. Esq; by whom he has issue a son Frederick-Thomas, and two daughters, Caroline, and Augusta.

Paul, 4th son to Sir William Wentworth, was killed at the siege of Namur, in 1695, unmarried.

Allan, 5th son, was Page of honour to King William, and a Cornet in his brother's, the then Lord Raby's regiment of dragoons, at 17 years of age; and was killed, mounting the breach in the attack on the citadel at Liege, Oct. 23, 1702, acting then as volunteer.

Elizabeth, eldest daughter, died young. Frances-Arabella, 2d daughter, Maid of honour to Queen Mary (wife of James II.) was married to Walter Lord Bellew, of the kingdom of Ireland. Anne, 3d daughter, Maid of honour to Queen Anne, when Princess of Denmark, was wedded to James Donolan, of the kingdom of Ireland, Esq; Isabella, Maid of honour to Queen Anne, and after one of the bedchamber-women, was espoused to Francis Arundel, of Stoke-Bruers-park, in com' Northamp. Esq; Mary died young; and Elizabeth, 6th daughter, was married to John Lord Arundel, of Trerife.

Thomas, the eldest surviving son of Sir William Wentworth, and 22d in paternal descent from Reginald de Wintewade, on the death of his cousin, William Earl of Strafford, in 1695, inherited the dignity of Baronet by descent, and the Barony of Raby, which (as said before) was limited to the brothers of Thomas Earl of Strafford.

At the time of the revolution, * being then a younger brother, he was made Cornet in the Lord Colchester's (afterwards Earl Rivers) regiment of horse, and his commission was signed by the Prince of Orange, on Dec. 31, 1688, before he was declared King: and was (though then very young) commanded into Scotland, where he made his first campaign in the Highlands, against the Lord Dundee, who routed King William's troops at Killycrankie, on July 16, 1689, but lost

* Ex script. Tho. nuper com' de Strafford.

his own life. He afterwards served in every campaign with King William im Flanders, where his elder brother, who was his Captain, died of a fever at Brussels, contracted in the field; and his two younger brothers, Paul and Allan, were killed in his presence, one at the siege of Namur, and the other at Liege, as before mentioned.

His Lordship was commanded on the detachment that made the van-guard at the battle of Steinkirk, which appeared before the French by break of day, on Aug. 3, 1692, and rested in their fight till after sun-set, and then made the rear-guard of the army: and of the squadron of which he was, there came not 50 off alive, out of 250. Whereupon, on the report of his behaviour in that action, by Major-general Dumprie, in the Dutch service, who commanded that van-guard, King William desired the Lieutenant-colonel of that regiment, who was then a Groom of his bedchamber, to bring him into his presence; and then promised him, in person, to advance him in the army, and made him his Aid-de-camp.

At the battle of Landen, on July 29, 1693, he was one of the four or five, who, standing by King William to the last, accompanied him over the river Manhain, after the defeat of his army. And at the end of that campaign, on Oct. 4, his Majesty gave him a commission of Guidon and Major in the first troop of horse-guards. Also soon after, on Jan. 20, 1693-4, made him Cornet and first Major in the said troop of guards, and Groom of his bedchamber.

On the decease of William Earl of Strafford, he succeeded to the title of Lord Raby, and was [d] introduced into the house of Peers, on Nov. 25, 1695. On June 13, 1697, his Majesty gave him the royal regiment of dragoons. And in 1698, when King William went to meet the Duke of Zell at the Goor, his Lordship was chosen to be one of the few of his court to attend him thither, where he was in great danger of his life; for at a hunting of wild beasts, he (like a young man of spirit) went alone to attack a wild boar, who at his second thrust threw him down, ripped up his breeches from the knee to the binding, cut his shirt, and some part of his flesh, and would have torn him to pieces, had not King William sent the two huntsmen, that were his only seconds, to his relief, who with their spears killed the wild boar upon him. It was then at Zell, his Lordship first saw and became acquainted with the Princess Sophia, her son, the Elector of Hanover, and her grandson, afterwards George II. then a youth.

[d] Journ. Dom. Procer.

In 1701, he was sent by King William to congratulate Frederick I. King of Prussia, when, by the Emperor's consent, he assumed that title; and when King William, on Feb. 26, 1701-2, had the fall from his horse (of which he died) his Lordship was then seeing his regiment at Greenwich embark for Flanders; but on his return, was every day with his Majesty till he expired, on March 8 following.

In 1702, the first year of Queen Anne, he served with his regiment in Flanders, and was then made Brigadier-general of her forces. But the year after, at the earnest request of the King of Prussia, he was sent (though against his inclination, it being in time of war) Envoy-extraordinary to that King. His Lordship arrived in the Maes, on April 21, N. S. 1703, and after went to Arnheim, to review his regiment quartered there, and from thence waited on the Duke of Marlborough. Returning from the army to the Hague, in the beginning of May, he set out on his journey two days after; and on Jan. 1, 1703-4, was made Major-general. The Duke of Marlborough, after the battle of Hockstet, on August 13, N. S. 1704, arriving at Berlin, on Nov. 22, was met without the town by his Lordship, who, on the 25th, gave his Grace an entertainment, at which the King, with the Margrave his brother, were present.

In 1705, he had the character of Ambassador-extraordinary to the King of Prussia, and made his public entry into Berlin, on April 7, 1706: and the same year (though in that post) he served the campaign under the Duke of Marlborough, when he forced the French lines, and took Menin, Ostend, &c. In his return from the army, he waited on the Elector of Hanover, arriving there on Oct. 3, and after a week's stay, proceeded on his embassy to Berlin: and whilst there, he was, on Jan. 1 (1706-7) constituted Lieutenant-general of her Majesty's forces. Also, on Jan. 14, N. S. following, the King of Prussia, with the Prince and Princess Royal (daughter of the Elector of Hanover) dined with his Lordship at Berlin; which was the first time of their Royal Highnesses dining abroad after they were married. And on June 9, 1707, the King and the Prince Royal did his Lordship the honour to sup with him, at his house of retirement near Berlin. He had, the same year, credential letters to the Imperial court, to which the Queen had a mind to remove him, to have his service there; but at the pressing desire of the King of Prussia, he was continued Ambassador-extraordinary at his court, till he succeeded the Lord Viscount Townshend as Ambassador-extraordinary to the States-general, viz. in March, 1710-11.

And

And a treaty of peace being then in agitation, his Lordship was sent for to England, to concert measures relating thereto; and on his arrival, was sworn of the Privy-council, on June 14, 1711.

And her Majesty, taking into consideration his great merits and services, was pleased to advance him to the dignities of Earl and Viscount, by the style and title of Earl of Strafford, Viscount Wentworth, of Wentworth-Woodhouse, and of Stainborough, in com' Ebor. with remainder to his brother, Peter Wentworth, Esq; and his issue male, by letters patent bearing date Sept. 4, 1711, 10 Queen Anne; the preamble to the patent, reciting his services, as follows:

'When we consider what a great incitement it is to men, 'truly noble, to pursue virtue, that the memory of their good 'actions should be honoured with the splendor of titles, we 'could not but give those testimonies of our approbation to 'the merits of our very faithful and beloved Counsellor Tho- 'mas Lord Raby, which, from the equity of a Prince, who is 'the favourer of good men, might seem agreeable to the bright- 'ness of the approved loyalty of his ancestors, and his own 'peculiar glory, which he hath acquired both at home and 'abroad; we gratefully call to mind his renowned great uncle 'the noble Earl of Strafford, who being of a lively genius in 'council, and courageous in arms, and as it were the strongest 'support to the royal dignity of our grandfather, of most glo- 'rious memory, was taken off by the false and unjust accu- 'sations of wicked men, but afterwards restored to the glory 'and immortal nobleness of his name, by a very honourable 'vote of the English parliament; when by a solemn order they 'acquitted that very deserving Gentleman of the crimes ob- 'jected against him, without precedent, in a manner never 'heard of before; and justly thought, that whatever was so in- 'juriously proceeded against him ought to be erased and obli- 'terated out of the public records. Since the male issue of that 'excellent man has been extinguished, it was pleasing to us, 'notwithstanding, to see his virtue revive in one of the same 'blood. And therefore we have thought fit to advance the 'Lord Raby, who is not more allied in blood than in like me- 'rit, to the same dignity of titles; for if we consider him as 'one experienced in the arts of peace and war, he will not be 'thought, by no means, undeserving of so great an honour; 'bred up a soldier almost from his very childhood, he has 'gained the reputation of an extraordinary courage, thro' all 'the scenes of the fatigues and dangers in the camp; and be- 'ing now placed in the high station of Lieutenant-general of 'our forces, seems to have made an easy step to the height of 'military

'military preferment; but since we have called him thence to
'the management of affairs of state, we have found him, by
'experience, no less ready for his high ability in civil employ-
'ment, than for his valour in arms. First, at the desire of
'the King of Prussia, we sent him to the court of Berlin with
'the character of our Envoy extraordinary; in which station
'he behaved himself for several years with such signal applause,
'that we thought fit to honour him with the title of our Am-
'bassador-extraordinary to the same King. We had also deter-
'mined him to take care of our affairs in the august court of the
'King of the Romans; but the King of Prussia a second time
'requesting his presence, we were unwilling to call him from
'thence, where he was so very useful to us, and peculiarly ac-
'ceptable to the said Prince: but since, for eight years past, he
'has happily devoted himself to the common interest of us, and
'all the confederates, with the utmost fidelity and dexterity;
'the most important concerns of the armies, and difficult af-
'fairs of the Christian world, required us to send to the Hague
'a Gentleman so well qualified for so great a province: where-
'fore we ordered him to go to the High and Mighty Lords
'the States-general of the United Provinces, in the quality of
'our Ambassador-extraordinary and Plenipotentiary, which
'post he has begun to manage with double penetration and
'prudence; and especially after the death of Joseph, at that
'time Emperor, he entered upon such measures, according
'to his usual sagacity, with the said States-general, as were
'very suitable to the present posture of affairs, and agreeable
'to our mind. Therefore, that he may enjoy some mo-
'numents of our royal favour, as the reward of a life
'employed for the good of his country, and all Europe, and
'which may be an incentive to his future race of glory:
'Know ye, &c.'

His Lordship soon after returned to the Hague, and being again sent for by her Majesty, arrived at London on May 15, 1712; after which, having received instructions to go to the army (tho' Ambassador-extraordinary and Plenipotentiary for the treaty of Utrecht) he accordingly left London on June 23 following, being ordered by the Queen first to the Hague, to invite the States-general to join with her Majesty in a cessation of arms, on the French giving up Dunkirk to the English. On their refusing to comply with the Queen's measures, he went, pursuant to his instructions, with a very few domestics (not staying for an escort) up to the late Duke of Ormond, then encamped at Chateau Cambresis, and in his way thither was in some danger, being stopped and examined by several parties, as well French and Spaniards, as Dutch, Imperi-
alists,

alifts, &c. Having executed his commiffion, by feeing the ceffation of arms declared between the French and Englih on Dunkirk's being put into the Queen's hands, he returned to Utrecht, through Lifle, Tournay, Oftend, Bruges, Ghent, and Bruffels, and had all the honours paid him as to a crowned head, as well by the Dutch as the others, being faluted by a treble difcharge of the cannon round the towns as he paffed, and by part of the feveral garrifons under arms to receive him. After having ftaid two days at Bruffels, to give the neceffary orders (the Catholic Netherlands being then equally under the adminiftration of the Queen and States-general) he paffed thro' Antwerp, where, on his arrival, he was faluted by the cannon round the town and works, was met by the Governor of the town, and carried to his palace, where he lay, and was moft magnificently treated. The Magiftrates waited on him in their formalities, made him a handfome fpeech, and prefented him with feveral large flagons of wine, and other things, brought in by the feveral burghers of the town, and their under officers, in great numbers; and the next morning, on his departure, he was again faluted with a treble difcharge of cannon round the town and ramparts, as at his entrance.

On his arrival at Utrecht, the negociation for the treaty of peace was continued by his Lordfhip, and the Lord Privy-feal (Dr. John Robinfon, then Bifhop of Briftol, and afterwards of London) with the feveral minifters of all the foreign powers of Europe. And being again fent for to England, he was, at a chapter held at Windfor, on Oct. 26, 1712, elected a Knight-companion of the moft noble order of the Garter; but being again fent in her Majefty's fervice beyond the feas, was inftalled by proxy at Windfor, on Aug. 4 following. Whilft he was abroad[e], he was highly efteemed by feveral foreign Princes, efpecially by the Princefs Sophia, who often, with the Queen of Pruffia, dined with him at Berlin: and, when abfent, kept almoft a continual correfpondence by letters. And the Kings of Denmark, and Poland, having an interview with the King of Pruffia, thofe three Kings, with the Queen of Pruffia, dined together at his Lordfhip's, and made him a prefent of their pictures at full length in one piece, in memory of his having treated three Kings and a Queen at the fame time.

He was, at the demife of Queen Anne, on Aug. 1, 1714, Plenipotentiary for the treaty of Utrecht; and by a diftinct appointment, Ambaffador-extraordinary and Plenipotentiary to the States-general, Lieutenant-general of her Majefty's forces,

[e] Ex inform; Tho, nuper com' de Strafford.

Wentworth, Earl of Strafford.

Colonel of the 1st regiment of foot-guards, first Lord of the Admiralty, appointed Aug. 29, 1712, and of her Cabinet and Privy-council. The treaties of Utrecht were signed at his Lordship's house at Utrecht (though in the Annals of Queen Anne, by mistake, it is printed as signed at the Lord Privy-seal's house) between Great-Britain, France, Spain, Portugal, Prussia, the States-general, Duke of Savoy, and all the allies, except the Emperor, on April 11, 1713.

As first Lord of the Admiralty, he was, by act of parliament, one of the Lords Justices for the administration of the kingdom, till the arrival of the King from Hanover, who, on his coming to the Hague, to embark for England, shewed him particular marks of his esteem, even so far as to come publicly with the Prince of Wales, to the Earl's house, where he played at ombre with his Lady, amongst a great many foreign Ministers, and many other persons of distinction. And when the King was stepping into the boat, to embark for England, it was observed, he took leave of the Earl in a most kind and distinguished manner. [a] But after his Majesty's arrival in England, on Sept. 18, 1714, things took another turn, &c. and on Oct. 11, his Lordship was superseded at the Admiralty-board by the Earl of Orford. However, he continued at the Hague in his public character, till Dec. 20 ensuing; when, in a public audience, taking leave of the States-general, he was, before his departure, presented with a gold medal and chain, valued at 6000 guilders, and landed in England on Jan. 1 following.

His Lordship married [b], on Sept. 6, 1711, at Bradenham, Anne, sole daughter and heir of Sir Henry Johnson, of Bradenham, in the county of Bucks, Knt. also of Tudington in Bedfordshire, and of Freeston-hall in Suffolk (who died on Sept. 29, 1719) by his first wife Anne, daughter to Hugh Smithson, Esq; son of Sir Hugh Smithson, of Stanwick, in the county of York, Bart. by whom he had issue one son, William, his successor, and three daughters; Lady Anne, who had Queen Anne for her godmother, and in April 1733, was married to the right hon. William Conolly, Esq; one of his Majesty's Privy-council of the kingdom of Ireland, and a member of parliament as well in England as Ireland: Lady Lucy, married, in 1747, to George Howard, Esq; cousin to Francis, 5th Lord Howard of Effingham; and Lady Henrietta, married, in December, 1743, to James Vernon, Esq; son of James Vernon, Esq; Clerk of the Council, and nephew to Admiral Vernon.

[a] Ex scrip. Tho. super com' de Straff.   [b] Ex regist. ecclef. de Bradenham.

Wentworth, Earl of Strafford.

His Lordship departed this life at his seat in Yorkshire, in Nov. 1739, and was succeeded by William, his only son and heir. Their mother, the Countess of Strafford, died on Sept. 19, 1754, in her house at Twickenham, in Middlesex.

Which William, now Earl of Strafford, married, on April 28, 1741, the Lady Anne, 2d daughter and coheir of John Campbell, Duke of Argyle; but as yet hath no issue.

TITLES.] William Wentworth, Earl of Strafford, Lord Viscount Wentworth, of Wentworth-Woodhouse, and of Stainborough, Baron of Raby, Newmarch, and Overlsey, and Baronet.

CREATIONS.] Baronet, June 29 (1611) 9 Jac. I. Baron Raby, of Raby-castle, in the bishopric of Durham, Jan. 12 (1639-40) 15 Car. I. Viscount of Stainborough, in com' Ebor. and Viscount Wentworth, of Wentworth-Woodhouse, and Earl of Strafford, in the said county, Sept. 4 (1711) 10 Queen Anne.

ARMS.] Sable, a Cheveron between three Leopards Heads, Or.

CREST.] On a Wreath, a Griphon passant, Argent.

SUPPORTERS.] On the dexter side, a Griphon, Argent; on the sinister, a Lion, Or.

MOTTO.] EN DIEU EST TOUT.

CHIEF-SEATS.] At Wentworth-castle, in the county of York, 9 miles from Wakefield, and 124 from London; at Boughton, in the county of Northampton, 2 miles from Northampton, and 56 from London; and at Twickenham, in the county of Middlesex, 2 miles from Brentford, and 10 from London.

LEGGE,

LEGGE, Earl of Dartmouth.

THIS family is said to come out of Italy into England, where there remain several of that name, as also in Naples, and other parts [a]. Those of Venice removed from Ravenna, about the end of the tenth century; and such was their noble descent, and so great their wealth, that they were thought worthy of a place among the patricians in the year 1297, and have a magnificent palace near the church of the Misericordia, in that city; a further proof of their eminency, and the several great offices they have borne in the Empire, confirm it.

When they came to England, is not ascertained. Hugh de la Lega, and Richard, son of Osbert, were [b] Sheriffs of Bedfordshire and Buckinghamshire, from the 10th to the 16th of Hen. II. and William de la Lega (as the name is wrote in our ancient records) was Sheriff of Herefordshire, in 17 Hen. II. Those of Herefordshire have always been esteemed the elder branch; but those of Legg's-Place, near Tunbridge in Kent [c], were resident there for many generations before Thomas Legge, who lived in the reign of Edw. III. and is the direct ancestor to the present Earl of Dartmouth. Which Thomas was of the company of Skinners of London, and Sheriff of that city, anno 1343 [d], and twice Lord-Mayor, viz. anno 1346, and 1353. He was returned [e] one of the burgesses in parliament for that city, in 1349, and 1352. In 1338, he lent Edw. III. 300 l. [f] towards carrying on the war with France, which was a considerable sum in those days, and more than any citizen advanced, except the Lord-Mayor, and Simon de Frauncis, who lent each 800 l. the next year.

He married Elizabeth [g], one of the daughters of Thomas Beauchamp, Earl of Warwick, and had issue by her, two sons, Simon, and John, who was a Serjeant at arms in 1373, 17 Edw. III. [h] and had then the King's præcipe directed to William de Weston and himself, to receive from Roger de Beauchamp, Constable of the castle of the Devizes, the two sons of Charles de Bloys, and to deliver them to Robert de Morton, Lieutenant of Collard de Aubrichecourt, Constable of Nottingham-castle, there to remain as hostages, till the pretensions to the duchy

a Hist. de Venise, par le Sieure Amelet de la Houssaie, t. 2.   b Fuller's Worthies.   c Speed's map of Kent.   d Stow's survey of London.   e Ex coll. B. Willis, arm.   f Stow's survey.   g Ex stemmate in fam. Beauchamp, MS.   h Rymer, tom. 7. p. 26.

Legge, Earl of Dartmouth. 301

of Britany should be cleared. In 1381, being then in the Tower, with Simon Sudbury, Archbishop of Canterbury, and others, he [i] was there surprized by Wat Tyler and his rebels, taken from that place, and beheaded on Tower-hill. He was [k] Knight of the shire for the county of Surry, in 2 Rich. II. and had issue [l], from whom those of the name in Norfolk descended, of which family was Dr. Thomas Legge, Master of Caius and Gonville college in Cambridge.

SimonLegge, the eldest son, married Joan, daughter of John Clavering, son of Roger Clavering, of the city of London [m]; and in Cobham church, in Kent, is an exhortation to pray for the souls of Thomas Legge, and this Simon Legge, whose son Thomas married [n] Margaret, daughter of Sir John Blount, Knt. Governor of a garrison in Aquitaine [o], who, being besieged, in 14 Hen. IV. by the Mareschal of France, with 300 men, overthrew the Mareschal's army, consisting of 4000 fighting men, and took prisoners 12 persons of note, and others to the number of 120. The said Thomas had issue, by his wife aforesaid [p], Richard, William, and John. The first died a bachelor, and was buried in Cobham church, after having spent the greatest part of his estate in the wars between Hen. VI. and Edw. IV.

John, the 3d son, [q] took advantage of his brother William's absence in Ireland, and got possession of his brother Richard's estate after his death, which occasioned a long suit. But neither William, nor his heirs, ever recovered it. He married Eleanor, a daughter of ———— Talboys, of Kyme, in com' Linc. of which family was the Lord Talboys in the reign of Hen. VIII. In that reign was Robert Legge, who [r] married Edith, daughter of John Boys, of Godneston in Kent, who was, 2dly, the wife of Robert Colwell, and 3dly, of Sir Christopher Barker, Knt. Garter King of Arms. She died in Sept. 1550, 4 Edw. VI. surviving her husband, Sir Christopher; and, as appears by his will, had issue only by her husband Colwell, viz. three sons.

William Legge, the 2d son of Thomas, went into Ireland [s], where he married Anne, only daughter of John, son of Miles Lord Birmingham, of Athenree, and had issue by her, Edward, his son and heir; and dying, aged 92, was buried at Caffils in Ireland.

i Stow's annals. k Pryn's brev. parl. p. 88. l Ex script. Will. com' Dartmouth. m Weaver's fun. mon. n Ex script. ut antea. o Hollinshed's and Speed's chron. p Ex script. præd. q Ibid. r Anstis's regist. Gar. vol. 2. p. 378, 379. s Ex script. præd.

Which

Which Edward was [t] sent by his father into England on the law-suit with his uncle John; but being unsuccesful, he made a voyage, in 1584, with Sir Walter Raleigh, to the Indies; and on his return into Ireland, had a company given him in Sir Henry Danvers's regiment. He was afterwards made Vice-president of Munster, when Sir Charles Blount, Lord Montjoy, Knight of the Garter (afterwards Earl of Devon) was Lord-lieutenant, to whom he was related; and often transacted affairs with the Earl of Tir-Oen, being in favour with both parties. He had issue by Mary his wife, daughter of Percy Walsh, of Moyvallie, six sons, and seven daughters, and died in the 74th year of his age, anno 1616. He was the first Protestant of his family; but most of his children were brought up Roman Catholics by his wife, who outlived him several years.

1. Elizabeth, his eldest daughter, never married, but lived to 105 years. She was well versed in the Latin, English, French, Spanish, and Irish tongues.

2. Mary, married to —— Spragge, was mother of Sir Edward Spragge, Admiral of the Blue, who commanded the rear under Prince Rupert, and lost his life in the 3d and last engagement with the Dutch, on Aug. 11, 1673.

3. Margaret, wife of —— Fitz-Gerald, Esq; lived above 100 years, and was buried in Ireland.

4. Eleanor, married to —— Davys, Esq; son of Sir John Davys, Attorney-general, in Ireland, to James I.

5. Susannah, wife of —— Nugent, Esq; by whom she had issue, and was interred in Ireland.

6. Anne, espoused to —— Anthony, Esq; and died in the 112th year of her age, in 1702.

7. Jane, married to —— Usher, Esq; and had issue.

Thomas Legge, 2d son of the aforesaid Edward and Mary, died young, and was buried in Ireland.

Richard Legge, 3d son [u], was Ensign in the regiment of Montjoy Blount, Earl of Newport, in the first expedition against the Scots, in 1639, and afterwards Lieutenant-colonel of that regiment [w], and taken prisoner when the Earl of Derby was defeated by Lilburn, at Wigan, in com' Lanc. on Aug. 25, 1651. After the restoration, he [x] was sent with forces under the Earl of Peterborough, to take possession of Tangier: and was Ranger of Whichwood-forest, in Oxfordshire, and died unmarried.

---

[t] Account of this family, by Col. John Legge, MS.   [u] Rushworth's collect.   [w] Baker's chron. continued by E. P.   [x] Ex script. Will. com' Dartm.

Legge, Earl of Dartmouth.

John Legge, 4th son [y], was a Lieutenant-colonel in the Marquis of Antrim's regiment in Ireland, temp. Car. I. And on the accession of Charles II. by the cruel murder of his royal father, on Jan. 30, 1648, being then in Ireland, he was sent by Prince Rupert, Prince Maurice, and the Marquis of Ormond, then Lord-lieutenant, from Kinsale, to hasten his Majesty's coming into Ireland; but the ship he was in being taken [z], he was for a long time imprisoned at Plymouth, and by a court-martial condemned to die. Whitlock [a] gives the following account, on July 16, 1649, ' that ' the fleet, before Kingsale, took a vessel of Prince Rupert's, ' of 11 guns, and in her, Legg, Sir Hugh Windham, Capt. ' Darcy, and 60 men, and ammunition. On 21 July, letters ' from Plymouth, of Col. Legg, Sir Hugh Windham, and ' others, being brought thither prisoners, to know the plea- ' sure of the house concerning them. Ordered, that Col. ' Legg be committed in Bristol, and Sir Hugh Windham to ' the Mount, for high-treason.' However, he was afterwards released; and was Deputy-governor of Jersey, in the reign of James II. and Ranger of Whichwood forest aforesaid, where he died in 1702, aged 109 years. He married Anne Allot, and had issue two sons, and four daughters.

Edward, 5th son, died in his infancy.

Robert, 6th son, was [b] sent by Charles I. into Holland with the Queen, to provide arms and ammunition; and on her return, she gave this account of her army, from Newark, June 27, 1644. ' I carry with me 3000 foot, 30 companies of ' horse and dragoons, 6 pieces of cannon, and 2 mortars. ' Harry Jermyn commands the forces which go with me, as ' Colonel of my guards, Sir Alexander Lesley the foot under ' him, Gerard the horse, and Robin Legge the artillery.' He was in most of the battles during the civil war, and received several wounds. In 1645, he [c] was Colonel of foot, and taken prisoner by Colonel Massey, at the storming of Evesham. He was much trusted by the King and Queen, on all hazardous occasions, both their Majesties having a good opinion of his courage and fidelity, which he never forfeited. He [d] married a daughter of Sir Daniel Norton, of Southwick in Hampshire, by whom he had no issue. In order to the restoration of Charles II. he had Portsmouth delivered to him by Colonel Norton, his wife's brother, the government of which he

---

y Ex script. Will. com' Dartmouth. z Cox's hist. of Ireland, vol. 2. p. 2.   a Memorials, p. 399.   b Rushworth's collections, vol. 2. and Ludlow's memoirs, part 3.   c Whitlock's memorials, p. 142.   d Ex script. W. com' Dartmouth.

possessed to his death, which happened soon after, and was buried there.

I now return to William Legge, eldest son to Edward Legge and Mary Walsh. He was [e] brought out of Ireland by Henry Danvers, Earl of Danby, President of Munster, his godfather, who had promised (his father being infirm) to take care of his education, and was sent by him, to serve as a volunteer under Gustavus Adolphus, King of Sweden; and after, served under Prince Maurice, of Orange, in the Low-Countries. On his return to England, he was first [f] constituted, on Nov. 30, 2 Car. I. Keeper of the King's Wardrobe during life; and soon after made Groom of the bedchamber. And when Danvers, Earl of Danby, was fined 5000 l. in the court of Star-chamber (for having felled timber in Whichwood-forest, without licence) he desired, as a favour to him, that 2000 l. thereof might be given to Colonel William Legge, saying, it was what he designed to leave him as a legacy, and which he should not be able to perform when he had paid his fine; and thereupon the King granted it. In 1639, he had a commission to be Lieutenant-general of the Ordnance, in the first expedition against the Scots; and in 1640 [g], brought up that petition from the army, to which his Majesty subscribed C. R. whereupon he was examined by the house of Commons, and ordered into custody as a delinquent; but was allowed his liberty [h], giving 10,000 l. bail for himself, with the Earls of Cumberland, and Newport, 5000 l. each, for his appearance. The parliament soon after publishing a declaration, mentioning the King's attempting to incense the northern army against them, &c. his Majesty, in answer thereto, said, ' He signed Capt. Legge's petition to satisfy the army [i].' And immediately after, removing northward, the Earls of Pembroke and Holland having waited on him at Royston, from the parliament, March 9, 1642, they reported, on their return, that the King, on reading that part of their message concerning Capt. Legge, said, ' That's a lie.' And on going with the King to York, and being with him, when his Majesty demanded entrance into Hull, on April 23, the parliament thereupon remanded him. However, in that year, he [k] was constituted Serjeant-major and Captain of a troop of cuirassiers in Prince Rupert's regiment, and was taken prisoner at Dunsmore-heath, by Major Ballard. However, he was soon at li-

[e] Ex script. W. com' Dartm.   [f] Pat. 2 Car. I. p. 21. n. 27.   [g] Husband's collect. and Whitlock's mem. p. 44.   [h] Nalson and Rushworth's collect.   [i] Whitlock, p. 54, 55.   [k] Ex script. W. com' Dartm.

Legge, Earl of Dartmouth.

berty; for, as Rushworth writes, he joined Prince Rupert at Bridgnorth, with 1120 musketteers, before the fight between the Prince and Sir John Meldrum, at Newark, on March 21, 1643. And in April following, was wounded and taken prisoner at Litchfield (as Echard writes) and soon after again released. For, in the first battle at Newbury, on Sept. 20, 1643, having valiantly behaved, and the night after attending his Majesty in his bedchamber, the King presented him with a hanger he had that day worn, which was in an agate handle set in gold, and would have knighted him with it, had he consented [l]; but the hanger was kept in his family, till the house at Blackheath was robbed, in 1693.

In 1644 [m], he was Governor of Chester; and Dec. 25, that year, was made [n] Governor of Oxford, in the room of Sir Arthur Afton. He [o] had a regiment of foot, and another of cuirassiers; also a commission to be Governor in chief of the city and county of Oxford, with power for impressing what soldiers he pleased in the counties of Bucks and Berks. On April 16, 1645, [p] being then one of the Grooms of the King's bedchamber, and Governor of Oxford, he was admitted Doctor of Laws of that University; and on Oct. 8 following, surrendered it to Sir Thomas Glenham, his Majesty taking him with him when he left Oxford. When King Charles made his escape from Hampton-court, he, with Sir John Berkeley, and Mr. Ashburnham, were the only persons to whose fidelity the King committed himself. The Earl of Clarendon relates, that Ashburnham alone seemed to know what they were to do, the other two having received only orders to attend. Whereupon he had no hand in that unfortunate step, of carrying the King over to the isle of Wight, in which the other two were involved; for [q] he staid with the King at Titchfield-house, while Ashburnham and Sir John Berkeley went to Col. Hammond. And on that, the Earl of Clarendon gives him the following character: ' Legge had so general a
' reputation of integrity and fidelity to his master, that he never
' fell under the least imputation or reproach with any man:
' he was a very punctual and steady observer of the orders he
' received, but no contriver of them; and tho' he had in truth
' a better judgment and understanding than either of the other
' two, his modesty, and diffidence of himself, never suffered
' him to contrive bold counsels.'

l Ex script. præd. m Ibid. n Wood's Athenæ Oxon. vol. 1. p. 728.
o Ex script. præd. p Wood's Fasti Oxon. vol. 2. p. 728, 733. q Hist.
of Eng. vol. 3. p. 170.

Cromwell sent a warrant to Col. Hammond for securing Mr. Legge, Mr. Ashburnham, and Sir John Berkeley, [r] but the Colonel desired to forbear the execution thereof, till he might know the pleasure of the houses; ' In regard (as he said) if ' those Gentlemen should be apprehended, it would be very ' difficult for him to secure the person of his Majesty.' And that the King said, ' If these Gentlemen should be taken from ' him, and punished as evil doers, for counseling him not to ' go out of the kingdom, but rather to come to this place, ' for the more conveniency as to settlement of peace, and for ' endeavouring it accordingly, in attending him hither, he ' cannot but himself expect to be dealt with accordingly, his ' case being the same:
' That these Gentlemen have engaged their honours not to ' depart from him: and having cast themselves upon him, in ' case they should be removed from thence, it would much re-' flect upon him.'

On May 19, 1648, he [s] was committed prisoner to Windsor-castle, but was soon after released; and during the treaty of the isle of Wight, he was nominated, among others, to attend his Majesty; but on Aug. 31 following, he was with Mr. Doucet, the only two disapproved of by the parliament. And engaging in that design of the Earl of Holland's, to restore the King, he was wounded, and taken prisoner with the Earl, at St. Neots in Huntingdonshire. King Charles was so sensible of his sufferings, and had so great an esteem of his fidelity, that a little before his death, he charged the Duke of Richmond to tell the Prince of Wales from him, that whenever he was restored to his right, he should be sure to take care of honest Will. Legge; for he was the faithfullest servant that ever any Prince had.

After the unfortunate death of that King, he and his family suffered great hardships, and being imprisoned in Plymouth, he was, by order of parliament, in 1649 [t], removed to Bristol, with a charge of high-treason, and from thence was sent to Arundel-castle, in Sussex; from whence he applied to the Speaker, Lenthall, for leave to go abroad; who obtained it for him; and in return, Colonel Legge, on the restoration, was very instrumental in procuring Lenthall's pardon, who, when he died, left him, by his will, 200 l. as a legacy.

As he had eminently distinguished his loyalty to Charles I. so was he not backward in espousing the interests of his son and successor, Charles II. accompanying him, in 1650, into Scotland, where he was committed prisoner to Edinburgh-

r Whitlock's memorials, p. 282.   s Ibid. p. 305.   t Ibid. p. 399.

castle,

castle, and so continued, till the King made his escape from St. Johnstown, when, to gratify his Majesty, he was released. At the battle of Worcester, on Sept. 3, 1651, he was wounded and taken prisoner [u], and had been certainly executed, if his wife had not contrived his escape out of Coventry-gaol, by hiring an old woman to carry him her cloaths, which he put on, and brought a close-stool pan, well filled, under his arm, the stench of which occasioned the guards to stand clear, and let him pass unregarded.

In the protectorship of Oliver Cromwell, he, with the Earl of Oxford, and others, were committed to prison, being betrayed by Manning, who corresponded with Thurloe, Cromwell's secretary, with a design to get money from them, and thereupon informed against such, whose fidelity to the King was most notorious. In 1659, when risings were designed throughout the kingdom, he had a commission to raise a regiment of foot, with several blank commissions, to dispose of as he thought fit. He was also commissioned, with Arthur Annesley, after Earl of Anglesey, John Mordaunt, soon after created Viscount Mordaunt, Sir John Greenvile, afterwards Earl of Bath, and Sir Thomas Peyton, to promise pardon to all those who shall endeavour his Majesty's restoration, except those who sat as Judges on his father. The said commission was dated at Bruxels, March 11, 1659 [w], wherein they were also empowered, by writing under their hands, &c. to promise, in his Majesty's name, such rewards as they thought proper, which he would ratify, confirm, and perform. They were so active in this commission, that most of the nobility and gentry of England and Wales were engaged by them in the King's service, and a day in July [x] fixed for their rising; but that being deferred to August 1, the design took air; and only Sir George Booth, with his friends, appeared in Cheshire, and the Earl of Litchfield, with some others, in Surry. The King was in such expectation of the success, that he went from Bruxels to Calais, and had a shalop ready for his transportation, on hearing any considerable body of men were in arms for him. In 1660, just before the meeting of the parliament, he subscribed that declaration of the nobility and gentry, whereby they promised not to retain any resentments for former ill treatment.

After the restoration, the King told him the message he had received from his royal father, by the Duke of Richmond, which, he said, must always intitle him to any marks of favour he

[u] Ex script. præf. p. 649, 650.   [w] Baker's chronicle, edit. 1. 84. p. 64.   [x] Ibid.

could give him, and offered to create him an Earl before his coronation; which he modeftly declined, having a numerous family, with a fmall fortune: but told the King, he hoped his fons might live to deferve his Majefty's favour. On which he was reftored to his place in the Bedchamber, and Lieutenancy of the Ordnance, with a commiffion to be Superintendant, with General's pay. Alfo was conftituted Treafurer of the Ordnance, and Colonel of an independent company of foot in the Tower of London. All thefe were granted in 1660 to him, during his life.

The next year he was [y] chofen member of parliament for Southampton: and obtained a grant of the King's houfe in the Minories (formerly an abbey) London, the lieutenancy of Alice Holt, and Woolmer-forefts in Hampfhire, for forty-five years; alfo, of lands in com' Lowth, in Ireland, to a confiderable value, with a penfion of 500 l. per ann. for his own and his wife's life. And when Prince Rupert went to Vienna, he conftituted him his fufficient and lawful Attorney and Commiffioner for him and in his name, and to his ufe, to act, manage, perform, and do all and all manner of matters and things whatfoever, which doth or may any way concern him, either with his Majefty, the parliament, or any other perfon or perfons whatfoever. In 1663, he was made Woodward of Chute-foreft, in com' Wilts. He died of a fever, at the faid houfe in the Minories, near the Tower, on Oct. 13, 1670, in the 63d year of his age, and was buried in the vault in the Trinity-chapel in the Minories, with great folemnity; Prince Rupert, the Dukes of Buckingham, Richmond, Monmouth, Newcaftle, and Ormond, with moft of the court, being prefent at his funeral: and a monument of white marble is erected there to his memory.

He married Elizabeth, eldeft daughter of Sir William Wafhington, of Packington in Leicefterfhire, by Anne, daughter of Sir George Villiers, of Brookfby in the faid county, and fifter to the firft Duke of Buckingham of that family. She died in 1688, in the 76th year of her age, and was buried in the vault in the Trinity-chapel in the Minories, by her hufband. They had iffue three fons, George, William, and Edward, and two daughters, whereof Mary, the eldeft, was married to Sir Henry Gooderick, of Ribfton, in the county of York, Knt. and Bart. who was Envoy-extraordinary to Spain, in the reign of Charles II. and Lieutenant-general of the Ordnance, and Privy-counfellor to William III. by whom fhe had no iffue. She died aged 70 years, and was buried in the vault with

[y] Ex fcrip. præf.

her father, though it is mentioned (by miftake) on Sir Henry Gooderick's monument, in Ribfton chapel, that fhe was buried there. Sufannah, 2d daughter, was married, on April 25, 1678, in Hen. VII's chapel in Weftminfter-abbey, to Thomas Bilfon, of Mapledurham, in the county of Southampton, Efq; by whom fhe had iffue one daughter, that died in her infancy, and two fons, Leonard Bilfon, and Thomas Bilfon, both which died in her life time, without iffue; Thomas, by a fall from his horfe; and Leonard, in 1715, who left the remainder of his whole eftate, after Thomas Bettefworth, and the heirs male of his body lawfully begotten, to Henry Legge, 4th fon to William Earl of Dartmouth, provided he take the name of Bilfon.

William, 2d fon to the faid William Legge, was [y] page of honour to Charles II. Groom of his bedchamber, Captain of a troop of horfe, in the regiment of horfe-guards commanded by Aubrey de Vere, Earl of Oxford. And in 1680, was fent by the King to Heffe-Caffel, to ftand godfather, as his proxy, to Prince Charles, the Landgrave's fon. In the reign of James II. he was Lieutenant-colonel in the Queen's regiment of horfe, Governor of Kinfale in Ireland, and member of parliament for Portfmouth. He married Mary Pool, widow of ——— Townfhend, Efq; but had no iffue by her; and dying in Dublin, in the 48th year of his age, was buried there.

Edward Legge, 3d fon, died in his infancy, and was buried at Stoke, in com' Middlefex, where his mother refided during the abfence of his father beyond the feas.

George Legge, eldeft fon and heir, was fent to fea [z] at the age of feventeen, under the care of Sir Edward Spragge. He commanded the Pembroke in 1667, the Fairfax in 1671, and the Royal Catharine in 1672. In the Dutch wars he was wounded, taking and deftroying feveral of their fhips. In 1669, he had the command of his father's independent company of foot; and in 1672, was made Lieutenant-governor of Portfmouth, under his Royal Highnefs James Duke of York. In 1673, Governor of Portfmouth, Mafter of the horfe, and Gentleman of the bedchamber to the Duke of York. In 1677, he had a grant of 300l. per ann. as Affiftant to the office of Ordnance. And before the end of that year, was conftituted Colonel of a regiment of foot, and Lieutenant-general of the Ordnance. Soon after, he was made Mafter of the Ordnance; and on March 3, 1680-1, was fworn of the Privy-council to Charles II. In 1682, he had a commiffion for viewing all the

[y] Ex fcript. præf.   [z] Ibid.

forts and garrisons in England, and for commanding in chief. And before the end of the same year, was, by letters patent dated Dec. 2, in the 34th year of his reign, advanced to the degree of a Baron of this realm, by the title of Baron of Dartmouth, in the county of Devon, to hold and enjoy to himself and the heirs male of his body; and for default of such issue, to William Legge, Esq; one of the Grooms of the royal bedchamber (brother to him the said George) and to the heirs male of his body: which remainder the King particularly ordered himself, in justice (as he was pleased to say) to the memory of old Colonel Legge, whose modesty ought not to prejudice his children. The preamble to the patent imports: [a] 'That his Majesty remembering the great merits of William Legge, one of the Grooms of the royal bedchamber to his late father King Charles the first, especially in that unparalleled rebellion raised against him; in which, being a person of singular skill and experience in military affairs, as also a valiant and expert commander, he faithfully served him in most of the battles and sieges of those unhappy times. Also performed several eminent services to the said King, since his most happy restoration. And further considering, that George Legge, eldest son of the said William, following his father's steps in divers military employments, especially in sundry sharp and dangerous naval fights, wherein he did freely hazard his life; for which respect, being made General of the Ordnance and Artillery, and one of his most honourable Privy-council, his Majesty thought fit to dignify him with some farther honour.'

The following year he was [b] sent Admiral of the whole English fleet, to demolish Tangier, having a commission to be Captain-general of all his Majesty's forces in Africa, and Governor of that city. Bishop Burnet recites [c], ' After the King had kept Tangier about 20 years, and had been at a vast charge in making a mole before it, in which several undertakers had failed, but the work was now brought near perfection, which seemed to give us the key of the Mediterranean; he, to deliver himself from the charge, sent Lord Dartmouth with a fleet to destroy all the works, and bring home all our men.' On his return, he had, as a reward of his many faithful services, a grant from his Majesty, of 10,000 l. He also obtained, from Charles II. a grant to hold a fair twice a year, and a market twice a week, upon Black-heath, in the parish of Lewisham in Kent.

[a] Dugdale's additions to his Baronage, MS. penes meipf. ipsi.   [c] Hist. of his own times, vol. 2. p. 264, 265.   [b] Ex script.

During

Legge, Earl of Dartmouth.

During the reign of James II. he was Mafter of the Horfe, General of the Ordnance, Conftable of the Tower of London, one of the Lords of the Privy-council, Colonel of the royal regiment of Fufiliers, and Captain of an independent company of foot. He was alfo High-fteward of Dartmouth, and Kingfton upon Thames, and Recorder of Litchfield. In the year 1687, attending the King in his progrefs, and the city of Coventry prefenting his Majefty with a large gold cup and cover, he immediately delivered it to the Lord Dartmouth, telling him, 'there was an acknowledgment from the city of Coventry, for his father's fufferings in their town;' where, during the civil wars, he had endured a long imprifonment. He [d] refigned his poft of Mafter of the Horfe on Dec. 16, 1687. And in the fucceeding year, he was made Admiral of the fleet of England, then fet out to intercept the Dutch fleet bringing over the Prince of Orange: which employment he accepted out of gratitude to the King, who, as Bifhop Burnet writes (in his hiftory of his own times) loved him, and in whofe fervice and confidence he had long been. The Bifhop alfo fays, ' [e] that he was indeed one of the worthieft men of his court, but he was much againft the conduct of his affairs; yet he was refolved to ftick to him at all hazards.'

After the Prince had landed, it is recited in our Gazettes, that he paffed by Portfmouth, on Nov. 18, 1688, and after bad weather, returned to Spithead on Nov. 23 following, with 43 fhips of war; the reft of the fleet being put into other ports. Afterwards he failed from thence for the Downs, on Dec. 29, and leaving there feveral men of war, under the command of the Lord Berkeley, his Lordfhip, with the reft of the fleet, failed for the Buoy of the Nore.

Yet, notwithftanding he brought the fleet fafe home, and had acted by order of King James when he was in power, he was deprived of all his employments at the revolution; and in 1691, committed prifoner to the Tower of London, where, after three months imprifonment, he departed this life fuddenly of an apoplexy, on Oct. 25, that year, in the 44th year of his age. When he was dead, Lord Lucas, who was Conftable of the Tower, made fome difficulty of permitting his body to be removed, without order; on which, application being made to King William, he was pleafed to direct, that the fame refpect fhould be paid at his funeral, that would have been due to him, if he had died poffeffed of all his employments in that place. And accordingly the Tower guns were

[d] Journal per Greg. King, Lanc. fecial, MS. penes meip. p. 498. [e] Hift. præd.

Legge, Earl of Dartmouth.

fired when he was carried out, to be interred near his father in the vault in the Minories, where a monument of white marble is erected to his memory, by Barbara, his Lady, who died on Jan. 28, 1717-18, in the 68th year of her age, and was buried in the same vault with him. She was daughter and coheir of Sir Henry Archbold, of Abbots-Bromley in Staffordshire, and by her Lord had issue one son, William, Earl of Dartmouth, and seven daughters.

Mary, the eldest, was maried, on Nov. 12, 1685, in Hen. VII's chapel, in Westminster-abbey, to Philip Musgrave, Esq; eldest son of Sir Christopher Musgrave of Edenhall, in Westmorland, Bart. and after his decease, to John Crawford, Esq; son to Commissary-general Crawford; and died on Feb. 25, 1753. The other daughters were, Elizabeth, Barbara, Susannah, and Anne, the youngest; besides the 5th and 6th, who died in their infancies.

William, late Earl of Dartmouth, only son to George Lord Dartmouth, was born on Oct. 14, 1672. He was Lieutenant of Alice-Holt, and Woolmer-forests, till King William granted the reversion, after the term of Colonel William Legge's grant for 45 years, to Emanuel How, Esq; Groom of his bedchamber; on which he surrendered the remainder of his term for a valuable consideration. He [f] took his place in the house of Peers, on Nov. 22, 1695. On the accession of Queen Anne, he was constituted one of the Lords Commissioners for Trade and Plantation, on June 14, 1702; and on the 18th following, was sworn of her Privy-council, at St. James's. In 1710, he was sworn one of her Majesty's Principal Secretaries of State, and constituted Keeper of the Signet of Scotland, in commission with James Duke of Queensberry. Also the following year, on Sept. 5, was advanced to the dignities of Viscount Lewisham, in Kent, and Earl of Dartmouth. In 1713, he was appointed Lord Keeper of the Privy-seal; and on the demise of Queen Anne, as such, was one of the Lords Justices of Great-Britain, being at the same time High-steward of Dartmouth, and one of the Governors of the Charter-house.

His Lordship married, in July, 1700, the Lady Anne Finch, 3d daughter to Heneage, Earl of Aylesford, and by her Ladyship, who died on Nov. 30, 1751, had issue six sons, and two daughters; the Lady Barbara, married, on July 27, 1724, to Sir Walter Baggot, of Blithfield in Staffordshire, Bart. and the Lady Anne, married, in Oct. 1739, to Sir Lister Holt, of Aston in Warwickshire, Bart.

[f] Journ. dom. procer.

His Lordship's eldest son, George Lord Viscount Lewisham, married Elizabeth, sole daughter and heir of Sir Arthur Kaye, of Woodsome in Yorkshire, Bart. by his wife Anne, eldest daughter and coheir of Sir Samuel Marrow, of Berkeswell in Warwickshire, Bart. And having been elected a member in the parliament that sat first on business on Nov. 28, 1727, for Great-Bedwin in Wiltshire, died of the small-pox at his house in Holles-street, Cavendish-square, London, on August 29, 1732. By his said Lady (who wedded Francis, now Earl of Guilford) he had issue a daughter that was still-born; secondly, a son, Arthur Legge, who died on Oct. 6, 1729, aged two years and ten weeks; also a son, William, Lord Viscount Lewisham, now Earl of Dartmouth; and two daughters, Anne, and Elizabeth; whereof Anne was, on Nov. 23, 1760, married to James Brudenel, brother to George Montagu, Earl of Cardigan.

Heneage Legge, 2d son, born in 1703-4, was admitted a Student in the Inner-Temple, at the age of 19; and on Dec. 12, 1734, chosen High-steward of the city of Litchfield. In Feb. 1739, he was sworn one of the King's Council; and in 1749, constituted one of the Barons of the Exchequer. In June, 1740, he was married to Catharine, daughter and one of the coheirs of Mr. Jonathan Fogg, Merchant of London, and niece to Sir John Barnard, Knt. Alderman of London, by whom he had issue, whereof a daughter, Anne, died on July 30, 1752.: the said Heneage departed this life on Aug. 29, 1759, and his Lady on Nov. 12 following.

William Legge, 3d son, died in his infancy.

The right hon. Henry Bilson Legge, 4th son, was born in March, 1708: but of him afterwards, under the title of Stawell.

Edward Legge, 5th son, was entered a volunteer on board the Royal Oak, on May 31, 1726, in the 16th year of his age; and constituted Lieutenant of the Deptford man of war, on March 5, 1733-4. After a gradual rise, he was Commodore of a squadron in the West-Indies, and died there in 1747 [g], when he was elected member of parliament for Portsmouth.

Robert, 6th son, died in his infancy.

Their noble father, William Earl of Dartmouth, who had behaved with the strictest honour and integrity, throughout the whole course of his life, deceased at his house on Blackheath in Kent, on Dec. 15, 1750, in the 79th year of his age,

[g] Brit. parl. reg. n. 157.

Legge, Earl of Dartmouth.

and was succeeded in his honours and estate by William, his grandson and heir, now Earl of Dartmouth.

The said William, the present and 2d Earl of Dartmouth, for his more polite education, travelled through France, Italy, and Germany; and, on his return to England, took the oaths and his seat in the house of Peers, on May 31, 1754. His Lordship, who is Doctor of the Civil Law, Fellow of the Royal Society, and Recorder of Litchfield, married, on Jan. 11, 1755, Frances-Catharine, only daughter and heir of Sir Charles Gunter-Nicholl, Knight of the Bath: and by her has four sons, and a daughter, viz. George Viscount Lewisham, born on Oct. 4, 1755; ———, born on Feb. 4, 1757; ———, born on May 7, 1761; ———, born on Jan. 24, 1765; and Lady ———, born on May 18, 1759.

TITLES.] William Legge, Earl of Dartmouth, Viscount Lewisham, and Baron of Dartmouth.

CREATIONS.] Baron of Dartmouth in Devonshire, by letters patent, Dec. 2 (1682) 34 Car. II. Viscount Lewisham in Kent, and Earl of Dartmouth aforesaid, Sept. 5 (1711) 10 Queen Anne.

ARMS.] Azure, a Buck's Head, caboched, Argent.

CREST.] In a ducal Coronet, Or, a Plume of five Ostrich Feathers, party per pale, Argent and Azure.

SUPPORTERS.] On the dexter side, a Lion Argent, semee of Fleurs de Lis, Sable, and crowned, as the Crest. On the sinister, A Buck Argent, semee of Mullets, Gules.

MOTTO.] GAUDET TENTAMINE VIRTUS.

CHIEF-SEATS.] At Sandwell-hall in Staffordshire, 5 miles from Wolverhampton, and 117 from London; and at Blackheath in Kent, 1 mile from Greenwich, and 5 from London.

Legge Earl of Dartmouth.

Paget, Earl of Uxbridge.

THIS family was anciently feated in Staffordshire, whereof Lewis Paget, Esq; was [a] one of the Gentlemen of that county, who, in 11 Hen. VII. signed a certificate relating to the office of Master of the Game of Caukewood: but the first who attained to the dignity of Peerage, was William Paget, a person of very great and eminent abilities, whose father, Mr. Paget, one of the Serjeants at Mace of the city of London, born near Wednesbury in Staffordshire, had issue two other sons, John, and Robert; also one daughter, Anne, married to —— Smith, Esq;

The said William, who was created Lord Paget, was [b] born at London; and having been [c] educated under the famous Lilly, in St. Paul's school, was sent to the University of Cambridge [d], where, in Trinity-hall, he had his academical education: from whence he went into the family of the noted Stephen Gardiner, Bishop of Winchester, as appears from these lines Leland writ to him:

Tu Gardineri petiisti tecta diserti,
Eloquii sedem, Pieriique chori.

Which is, that being young, 'he went into the learned Gar-
'diner's family, which was the very seat of eloquence, and of
'the muses.' From his family he went to study in the University of Paris, and after some stay, returned again into the Bishop's house. Soon after, in respect of his learning and merits, he was employed by Hen. VIII. in several important affairs; for in 21 Hen. VIII. he was [e] sent into France, to obtain the opinions of the learned in that kingdom, concerning the King his master's divorce from Queen Catharine; and in 23 Hen. VIII. on [f] Nov. 8, he obtained a grant of the office of Warden and Constable of the castle, Keeper of the park, and Bailiff of the manour of Maxstok, in Warwickshire, during the minority of Peter Compton, Esq; Also the same year was made [g] one of the Clerks of the Signet; which title he bore in 26 Hen. VIII. when he had licence [h] from the King to import 400 casks of wine from Gascony. In the year 1537, 29 Hen.

---

[a] Ex origin. penes Tho. dom. Aston. p. 210. [b] Fuller's worthies in London. [c] Strype's memorials, vol. 2. p. 379. [d] Ibid. vol. 3. p. 282. [e] Herbert's life of Hen. VIII. in hist. of Eng. vol. 2. p. 140. [f] Priv. Sig. 23 Hen. VIII. [g] Pat. 23 Hen. VIII. p. 1. [h] Bill sig. 26 Hen. VIII.

VIII. the King [i] sent him privately (with instructions to take France in his way) into Germany, with Christopher Mount, to prevail on the protestant German Princes from agreeing with the Emperor, but rather, to refer all their differences to him and the French King. This employment required an extraordinary prudence, the voyage being to be performed in a disguised habit, and the King's Ambassador in France, and the French King (Francis I.) were first to be acquainted of it, with whose directions they had orders to comply. In this arduous negociation, he behaved himself so much to the King's satisfaction, that in 32 Hen. VIII. he was [k] made Clerk of the Privy-council. Also the same year was [l] constituted one of the Clerks of the Signet for life, and [m] Clerk of the Privy-seal, with the fee of 30 l. per ann. likewise soon after, [n] Clerk of the parliament for life.

The year following, he was [o] constituted Clerk of the Privy-council for life, and [p] sent Ambassador into France. In 1543, 35 Hen. VIII. on May 19, he and one Thomas Knight, Esq; were [q] constituted Clerks of the parliament for life, with the salary of 40 l. per ann. and soon after, he received the honour of Knighthood; for he bears that title on Jan. 19 following, when the King granted [r] to him, and his heirs, the lordships of Bromley, and Hurst, in the county of Stafford. Also in the same year he was [s] made one of the Principal Secretaries of State. In 36 Hen. VIII. on June 26, he was [t] commissioned, with the Lord Chancellor Wriothesley, and the Duke of Suffolk, to treat with Matthew Earl of Lenox, about certain affairs relating to the government of Scotland, and to treat of a marriage between that Earl and the Lady Margaret, the King's niece. The same year he [u] attended King Henry at the siege of Bulloign; and on his return into England, after the surrender of that town, he had a [w] grant (with John Mason, Esq;) of the office of Master of the Posts, within and without the realm, to occupy by themselves or deputies; and was [x] joined in commission with the Earl of Hertford, to conclude a general peace with the French King, who demanding restitution of Bulloign, the treaty was immediately broke off. But being again set on foot the following year, he was then sent Ambassador into France; and while it was in agitation, received the following letter from the King, which forasmuch as it shews

i Herbert, p. 210.   k Pat. 32 Hen. VIII. p. 2.   l Priv. sig. 32 Hen. VIII.   m Ibid. p. 6.   n Priv. sig. 32 Hen. VIII.   o Bill fig. 33 Hen. VIII.   p Herbert, p. 228.   q Priv. sig. 35 Hen. VIII. r Bill fig. 35 Hen. VIII.   s Pat. 35 Hen. VIII. p. 5.   t Rymer's foed. tom. 15. p. 28.   u Ibid. p. 55.   w Pat. 36 Hen. VIII. p. 16.   x Herbert, p. 249.

how greatly he was esteemed, and that it gives an infight into the politics of those times, I shall here [y] insert it verbatim.

'Trustie and right wel-beloved, we greet you well:

'And having receyved your letters of the 22 of this instant, by the which we do at good length understand the'ole discourse and conference which passed the day before betweene yow and Brewno, with th' ordre which yow intende to observe in propo.inge th' overture for the Treux; we have thought good, as wel to signifie unto yow that we take your proceedings in very thankfull parte, and lyke your devyse for proponinge the overture of the treux very well, as also t'advertife you for answer of such things, as ye desired to know our further pleasure in this sorte, ensueing.

'First, you shall understand that having perus'd th' articles or capitulations, which you sent unto us, and having altered and added certain points of importance therein, we do remit the same unto you to be concluded upon in such forme, as they be now conceyved, yf you may induce the French Ambassadors thereunto, or otherwise to be altered and qualified by your common agreement in some words and terms, so as the substaunce of the matters do remayn.

'And touching the comprehension of the Scots, our pleasure is that you shall travell as earnestly as ye may, to have this treux concluded without any comprehension of them, whom we wold most gladely, and think it necessary to be left out, for without that this treux, serving the French King to many purposes, should be to us every way over much prejudicial; and therefor lyke as we for our part can be pleased to conclude this treux generally with them, without comprehension of any States or Princes, so we think it reason that they shall conclude with us after the lyke sorte; for it hath not been seen in any treatie of treux that we have made with any Prince in all our time, that any other Prince hath byn comprehended.

'And further you may also declare to th' Ambassadors, aswel French as of the Protestants, how that by such treaties of amitie as be between us and our good brother th' Emperor, we may not in any wise comprehende the Scots in this or any other treatie of treux, or peace.

'As for the time of commencement of the said treux, although we see not how we may give assured notice thereof to all our subjects, being, as we have heretofore signified un-

[y] Rymer, tom. 15. p. 82.

'to

'to you, difperfed in fundry places and companies, before the
'firft day of Marche, and therefore think the day appointed
'in youre former inftruction, to be a very mete tyme for the
'begynning of the fame; yet if they fhall fhew themfelves
'much defirous to have the treux begyn, rather we be pleafed
'to affent thereunto. Mary you muft tell them withal, that
'we cannot affure them to give perfect nottice to our men
'before the faid day, and therefore yf for want of knowledge
'of the treux (which neverthelefs fhall be publifhed with as
'much fpeed as may be) any prejudice fhall enfue to any of
'the French King's fubjects, we doubt not they will of their
'wifdoms impute the fame to their own hafty abridging of the
'tyme, and not to thofe which fhall then be found ignorant
'of the fame; and therefore for the avoiding of all fuch oc-
'cafions of ane quarrels, and to th' intent all things might
'be fully obferved according to the agreements, we thought
'the firft day of Marche to be a mete day for begynnyng of
'the faid treux, th' ende whereof you may always forefee to be
'agreed upon the laft of October, according to your former
'inftructions, notwithftanding you fhall perchance, at their
'inftaunce, fomewhat prevent the commencement of the
'fame.

'Thyrdly, Touching a further meeting of the Proteftants,
'and other commiffioners for Us and the French King, primo
'Maii, or fuche other tyme as fhall be agreed upon, except
'we faw a gretter appearaunce of fome conformite in the French
'King than hath yet been fhewed hitherto, we neither thinke
'it mete to trouble the Proteftaunts with any other reforte to a
'nue affemblie, nor mynde to make now any appointment for
'the tyme of any fuch nue convention, whereof (the French
'King being foe much wedded to his oun will as he is) there
'is no lykelihood of any fructe to enfue : And yet, yf in the
'mean time we may by any means perceive that the French
'King will relent his obftinacye, and come on more roundly
'to fome reafonable and honorable conditions for a peax, we
'would not only be very glade to ufe the mediation of the
'Proteftaunts in the mayntainyng of the fame, but alfo give them
'well to underftond, that we do both repofe a more ample
'and fuller confidence in them, then the Frenche Kinge either
'doeth or will do, whatfoever he pretendeth and woold make
'them believe; and woold alfo in the concluding thereof ufe
'their advife before any others, not doubting but we fhall find
'them as much addicted to th'advancement of our affayres, as
'the French King's.

'Fourthly, As touching Brewno, we will you fhall allure and
'procure him to ferve us earneftly as moche as fhall be poffible

'for

' for you to do; and as for his penfion for this begynnyng, we
' be pleafed to graunt unto him five or fix hundred crownes
' by the yere, the leffe or the more to be at your difcretion;
' and as his fervice fhall appere hereafter acceptable unto us,
' fo peradventure to encreafe it. And for the firft payment
' thereof, we will you take ane years penfion of fuch our trea-
' fure, as remayneth in our treafourer of Calacy's hands, or is,
' or fhall be brought from our fervaunt Thomas Chamberlayn,
' unto our faid Treafourer, withe taking his othe yf yt may be,
' otherwyfe his promyfe in writing, to do us fervice. You may
' (yf he condefceend thereunto) fecretely delyver nnto him
' with a ciphre, to advertyfe us of the ftate of things in Al-
' mayne, from time to time as occafion fhall ferve; giving him
' fuch goode woordes withall on our behalfe, as may bothe
' encourage him to ferve us truelye, and diligently, and minif-
' ter hope unto him of more ample benefite at oure hands, if
' he fhall fhew himfelfe no lefs willinge to the advauncement
' of our affayres, and diligenfe in our fervice, then we have
' conceived good trufte of him.

' Finallye, yf in the end of this your long conference, the
' French Commiffioners will neither come on more roundly
' in the conditions of peax, nor affent to any treux in fuche
' forte as we have prefcribed unto you, but will break off; our
' pleafure is, that you fhall both give immediate nottice thereof
' to our Ambaffadors with the Emperor, and alfo give know-
' ledge of the fame to our officers at Bulloyn, Guyfnes, and
' Callys, to the intent every of them may fee the better to the
' garde of their peeces, and alfo by what meanes, and confider
' with what nombers the ennemy may be moft troubled; ad-
' vertyfing us of their opinions therein, to the intent we may
' further difpofe as to us fhall be thought convenient.

' Yeven undre our fignet, at our honour of Hampton-
' Courte, the twenty-fixth daye of Decembre, the thirty-fe-
' venth yere of our reigne.'

   Dorf.————To our truftye and right wel-beloved Coun-
    faillour, Sir William Paget, Knight, oon of our two
    principal Secretaryes.

At length, on June 7 following, this Sir William Paget, the Lord Lifle, High Admiral of England, and Doctor Wotton, Dean of Canterbury [a], concluded a peace with the French; by which the King gained the advantage of keeping Bulloign for eight years, without moleftation. Shortly after which,

a. Rymer, tom. 15. p. 93.

the King, lying on his death-bed, bequeathed to him a legacy of 300l. [b] conſtituted him one of his executors, and appointed him one of the Council to his ſucceſſor Edw. VI.

Being now of great authority, and in high repute for his wiſdom and learning, the Earl of Hertford (after Duke of Somerſet) protector of the King's perſon and dominions, contracted [c] with him an intire friendſhip, whereby he had a greater opportunity of exerciſing his extraordinary abilities to the public advantage. On Feb. 17[d], 1546-7, 1 Edw. VI. he was elected a Knight-companion of the moſt noble order of the Garter, at a chapter held in the Tower of London, and was inſtalled at Windſor on May 22 following. On March 4, 1546-7, being ſtyled Knight of the Garter, and Principal Secretary, he was [e] commiſſioned to fix the boundaries in the marches of Bulloign; and ſoon after exchanged his place of Secretary, for the Comptrollerſhip of the Houſhold. In 2 Edw. VI. he [f] obtained a grant of Exeter place, without Temple-bar (formerly belonging to the Biſhops of that ſee) as alſo a certain parcel of ground lying within the garden of the Middle-Temple, adjoining thereto. Which houſe he transformed into a new fabric for his own habitation, calling it Paget-houſe; but it retained the name no longer than it continued in the poſſeſſion of his family, being by after owners called Leiceſter-houſe, and Eſſex-houſe. The next year, with the Biſhops of London, Rocheſter, and others, he was [g] delegated to viſit St. George's chapel in Windſor, Wincheſter college, the dioceſe of Oxon, and that univerſity; and to order matters for the improving of good literature, and honour of thoſe places. Alſo in that year he was [h] ſent Ambaſſador to the Emperor Charles V. to prevail on him to enter into a confederacy againſt the French. And arriving at Bruſſels on June 19, 1549, 3 Edw. VI. [i] he was received by his Imperial Majeſty with extraordinary reſpect, but did not ſucceed in his negociations, the Emperor being unwilling to contribute any aſſiſtance. On his return into England, though he ſucceeded not in his embaſſy, yet he greatly raiſed his reputation in the Emperor's court, as appears by Sir Philip Hoby's letters to the Protector, when reſident Ambaſſador there: in which are [k] theſe expreſſions concerning him; 'That he was generally grateful to all the Emperor's court, a few of England's back friends only excepted, who miſtruſted much, leſt he had compaſſed ſomewhat to their diſadvantage. And the ra-

b Rymer, tom. 15. p. 104. c Strype, vol. 2. p. 10. d Anſtis's regiſt. of the Garter, vol. 1. p. 441. e Rymer, tom. 15. p. 138. f Pat. 2 Edw. VI. p. 2. g Rymer ut antea, p. 183. h Strype's memor. vol. 2. p. 155. i Ibid. k Ibid. p. 162.

'ther they were driven to conceive this opinion, becaufe his
'entertainment had been fuch, and fo refpectful, as well with
'the Emperor as his council. And he was fo generally com-
'mended, and well reported of by all, and the fame of his
'prudent handling himfelf, fo fpread abroad every where, as
'they could not think, but that of fuch toward likelihood,
'fome great effect muft needs follow.' He alfo added, 'That
'fhould he not perhaps be fufpected of adulation, he might
'find fufficient matter to confume a long time in difcourfing
'of his gravity and prudence, ufed as well in fetting forth,
'and well-handling his charge towards the Emperor, and
'his Counfellors, as in his behaviour generally towards all
'others. Whereby he had purchafed to himfelf love and cre-
'dit with all men, and not a little for the King's Majefty's
'honour and eftimation, in thofe parts.'

The fame year having been called by writ to the houfe of
Peers, by the title of Lord Paget, of Beaudefert, in com' Staff.
[l] he took his place in parliament on Dec. 3; being then
Comptroller of the Houfhold, and Chancellor of the duchy
of Lancafter. And on Jan. 19 following, was folemnly [m] created
to that honour; alfo immediately after, appointed one of the
Commiffioners to conclude a peace with the French King,
Henry II.

But notwithftanding thefe his extraordinary fervices, he was
[n] committed to the Fleet, on Oct. 21, 1551, 5 Edw. VI. and
on Nov. 8 following, fent to the Tower, by the procurement
of the ambitious Duke of Northumberland, who at that time
afpired to an abfolute command; and having refolved to remove thofe out of his way, whofe credit or intereft might be
any impediment to his evil purpofes, he firft committed the
Duke of Somerfet, and foon after this Lord Paget, between
whom an inviolable friendfhip had been maintained for feveral years. The unfortunate Duke foon after loft his head,
being [o] principally charged with defigning to murder the Duke
of Northumberland, and fome other Lords, at Paget-houfe.
And it was generally expected, that the Lord Paget would be
called in queftion for the fame; but whether Northumberland
was fufficiently fatisfied with the facrifices already made, or
that the Lord Paget's innocency would bear the teft, he contented himfelf with only difgracing this able Minifter of State.
Whereupon, on April 22 following, being the eve of St.
George's feaft, he was [p] divefted of the enfigns of the Garter,

l Journal of parl. m Hollinfhed, p. 1061. n Strype, vol. 2. p. 281.
o Heyward's life of Edw. VI. in hift. of Eng. vol. 2. p. 315. p Afhmole's
order of the Garter, p. 285.

on pretence of defect in blood, and arms, for three defcents: but the Liber Cæruleus, in the regiftry of the Knights kept at Windfor, obferves, it was not fo much thofe caufes, as the prevalence and practice of the Duke of Northumberland, by which he had been unjuftly and undefervedly put out of the order.

Neither was this difgrace thought fufficient: for money being extremely wanting at that time, he foon after was charged with felling the King's lands and timber-wood without commiffion; and that he had taken great fines for lands belonging to the crown, and applied them to his own ufe; with other things accumulated againft him. Whereupon he furrendered his office, and [p] fubmitted himfelf in the Star-chamber, on June 16, to be fined at the King's pleafure: and his mulct was fet at 6000 l. This he endured (faith Sir John Hayward [q]) with a manly patience, as knowing right well, that he held all the refidue of his eftate on courtefy of thofe who hated him at the heart. But in December following he [r] obtained a general pardon of all offences and tranfgreffions, and other negligences, except debts due to his Majefty in the court of Exchequer, the Augmentation, the Wards, and the Firft-fruits and Tenths. At which time an [s] indenture was made between the King and him, whereby he was to pay to his Majefty 100 l. per annum, and 1000 l. at Chriftmas next, and the fame fum the Chriftmas following. Yet in February enfuing he [t] had a difcharge for the payment of 2000 l. and the next month obtained a grant from the King to him, and his pofterity for ever, of the coat of arms now borne by the family, which had been taken from him, on pretence that it was given him by a King of Arms, who had not fufficient power to grant the fame.

On King Edward's death, July 6, 1553, he [u] joined with the Earl of Arundel, the chiefeft champion of Queen Mary; and after fhe had been proclaimed Queen in the city of London, accompanied with 30 horfe, rode poft with him that night, to certify her of the gladfome tidings of her fubjects loyal intentions. Whereupon he was [w] fworn of the Privy-council (with the faid Earl) on her coming to the Tower; and had a [x] fpecial pardon; and was, with others, commiffioned to [y] hear and determine all fuch claims as fhould be made on the day of her coronation. She alfo reftored him to the noble order of the Garter, the enfigns whereof having not with more difgrace been taken from him, than with honour

[p] Strype, p. 381.   [q] Life of Edw. VI. p. 311.   [r] Strype, vol. 2. p. 382.   [s] Ibid.   [t] Ibid.   [u] Godwin's annals, p. 272.   [w] Strype, vol. 3. p. 16.   [x] Bill. fign. 1 Mar.   [y] Rymer, tom. 15. p. 383.

restored to him, and that by as great and absolute authority as did deprive him of them; namely, by decree in a chapter holden at St. James's, on Sept. 27, anno 1 Mariæ, so that, as Ashmole [z] observes, the honour might be said to have been rather wrongfully suspended, than justly lost: for in confirmation of his restoration, he had the garter buckled on his leg again by two of the Knights companions present, and the collar of the order put about his shoulders, with the George depending thereat; and a command then also given Garter, to take care that his atchievements should be again publicly set up over his stall at Windsor; being the same he before possessed, viz. the ninth on the Sovereign's side. Mr. Ashmole further observes, ' That the records of the order brand this de-
' gradation of injustice; it being inferable, that when honour
' is conferred on the score of virtue and great endowments,
' the consideration of these supplies the defect and obscurity or
' extraction. Whence it came, that the then Sovereign (whose
' prerogative it was to declare and interpret the statutes) being
' at that time present in chapter, thought fit to qualify the
' law, and gave him this honourable commendation, " That
" he had highly deserved of the nation by his prudence and
" counsel."

The Queen also the same year bestowed on him divers grants [a], as the rectory and advowson of Alcestre in com' Leic. the marriage of Thomas Willoughby, and the reversion of the manour of Great Marlow in Buckinghamshire. In March, 1553-4, 1 Mariæ, he was [b] commissioned, with others, to treat with the Ambassadors of Charles V. Emperor of the Romans, about a treaty of marriage between the Queen and Philip Duke of Austria, son of the said Emperor. In the 2d year of Queen Mary, soon after her marriage with King Philip, he was sent Ambassador (with Sir Edward Hastings) to the Emperor, then at Brussels, to signify [c] from their Majesties of England, their joint longing to see Cardinal Pole, ' That by his authority he
' might rectify the church of England, wonderfully out of
' tune, by reason of the schism wherewith it had been afflicted.'
They came to Brussels on Nov. 11 [d], and returned with the Cardinal to Westminster on the 24th.

On Jan. 29, 2 and 3 Phil. and Mar. he was [e] constituted Lord Privy-seal. And in 1555, on May 18, he went over to Calais with Cardinal Pole, the Earl of Arundel, and others, to [f] treat with the commissioners of the said Emperor, and

z Order of the Garter, p. 285.   a Bill. sign. & privat. sigill. cod. an.
b Rymer, tom. 15. p. 370.   c Godwin, p. 307.   d Strype, vol. 3. p. 156.   e Pat. 2 & 3 Phil. & Mar. p. 8.   f Strype, vol. 3, p. 217, 218.

Henry II. King of France, and to mediate a peace between them. On May 23 they met at Mark, lying between Calais, Ardes, and Gravelin; but all the pains they took to reconcile their differences had but little effect.

On Queen Elizabeth's accession to the throne, Nov. 17, 1558, at his own request (as Cambden [g] writes in his life of Queen Elizabeth) he quitted the public service, though in her favour, 'she retaining an affection and value for him, though he was 'a strict zealot of the Romish church.' By his [h] last will and testament, bearing date Nov. 4, 1560, wherein he styles himself William Lord Paget, Knight of the Garter, Lord Paget of Beaudessert, he orders his body to be buried at Drayton, in com' Middlesex, if he deceased within 40 miles; or at Burton in Staffordshire, if he died within 40 miles of that place, with such funeral solemnities as his executors think convenient. He bequeathed to the Lady Anne, his wife, the use of the furniture of his houses in London, and West Drayton in Middlesex, as long as she lived unmarried, and after her decease, to his son and heir, Sir Henry Paget, Knt. to whom he bequeathed the use of his great standing cup, with the cover, double gilt, weighing 100 ounces and a half, and to remain from heir to heir, as an heir-loom. And to his sons Thomas, and Charles Paget, and to every one of his children living at his decease, a pair of gilt pots of the value of 20 l. He leaves, besides other legacies, annuities to his sons Charles, and Thomas, and his daughter Eleanor Palmer. The residue of his estate he bequeaths to his son and heir Sir Henry Paget, with his mansion-house without Temple-bar, called Pagetplace, and lately Exeter-place; and appoints him his sole executor. Which will was proved on July 1, 1563.

He departed this life, aged 57, on June 9, 1563, and was buried at Drayton; but his Lady, and his son Thomas, erected a very stately monument to his memory, above the choir in the cathedral of Litchfield, which, together with that beautiful church, was destroyed in the time of the rebellion against Charles I. but by the care, and at the cost of the Lord Hatton, a draught of it was taken, whereon the following inscription was engraven:

Illustri Heroi piæ memoriæ, Domino Gulielmo Paget, Equiti maxime honorati ordinis Garterii, Regulo seu Baroni de Beaudesert; potentissimi Principis Henrici Octavi ad Carolum Quintum Imperatorem, semper augustum, & Franciscum, Gal-

[g] Hist. of Eng. vol. 2. p. 394. præerog. Cant. [h] Ex regist. Chayre qu. 27. in cur.

Paget, Earl of Uxbridge.

lorum Regem Chriſtianiſſimum, Legato ſapientiſſimo, ejuſdem Principis principi Secretario, & Conſiliario fideliſſimo; inter alios hujus potentiſſimi Regni Adminiſtratori, in Teſtamento Regio nominato: Ducatus Lancaſtriæ (regnante Edvardo) Cancellario digniſſimo: Hoſpitii Regii Cenſori, ſeu Contrarotulatori prudentiſſimo: Privati Sigilli ſereniſſimæ Reginæ Mariæ Cuſtodi ſanctiſſimo: Illuſtriſſimæ Reginæ Elizabethæ Seni chariſſimo, Senatori graviſſimo; & optime de Patria ſua, & bonis omnibus merito. Necnon Dominæ Annæ fideliſſimæ Conjugi ſuæ, & Domino Henrico utriuſque chariſſimo Filio, & Katharinæ, Henrici uxori dulciſſimæ; prædicta Anna clariſſima Fœmina & Domina Catherina, uxor dicti Henrici ſuaviſſima; & prænobilis Vir Dominus Thomas Paget in præſentia Regulus de Beaudeſert, de ſententia & ultima voluntate dictorum Gulielmi & Henrici, animis libentiſſimis, & ſummo ſtudio officii memores poſuere. Vixit Annis 57, ob. 9 Junii, 1563.

This great man, William, Lord Paget, married Anne [i], daughter and ſole heir of Henry Preſton, Eſq; ſon and heir of Laurence Preſton, 2d ſon to Thomas Preſton, of Preſton, in com' Ebor. She ſurvived many years [k], and was buried by him at Weſt-Drayton, with great funeral ſolemnity, on Feb. 15, 1586. Their iſſue were four ſons, Henry, Thomas, Charles, Edward, which laſt died young; alſo ſix daughters, Etheldred, married to Sir Chriſtopher Allen, Knt. Joan, to Sir Thomas Kitſon, of Hengrave in Suffolk, Knt. Anne, to Sir Henry Lee, Knt. Eleanor, to Jerome Palmer, Eſq; and ſecondly to Sir Rouland Clerk, Knt. Dorothy, to Thomas Willoughby, of Wollaton in com' Nottingh. Knt. and Griſild, to Sir Thomas Rivet, of Chippenham in Camb. Knt. and ſecondly to Sir William Waldgrave, of Smallbridge in com' Suffolk, Knt.

His eldeſt ſon, Henry, 2d Lord Paget, was [l] made one of the Knights of the Bath, at the coronation of Queen Mary; and being ſummoned to parliament in 8 Eliz. [m] took his place there on Sept. 30. By his laſt teſtament [n], dated on Nov. 27, 1568, 11 Eliz. he orders his body to be buried in the pariſh church of Weſt-Drayton, in com' Middleſex, near to the place where the body of his father lay interred; appointing that a convenient tomb ſhould be erected over the graves of his father, and mother, and his own grave. He bequeaths to the Lady, his mother, the ring with a diamond, which he had

i Ex ſtemmate.   k MS. collect. Guil. Dethick, Gart. not. A. 31. in bibl. Joh. Anſtis, arm.   l Strype, vol. 2. p. 35.   m Journ. of parl.   n Ex regiſt. Sheffield, qu. 11.

of the gift of his very good Lord the Earl of Leicester. And if he happens to decease without issue male, he bequeaths to Elizabeth, his daughter, 500l. and if the Lady Catharine his wife be with child, and it be a daughter, 500l. but if no issue male, then 500l. more. He ordains all his furniture within his mansion-houses of Paget-place, and Drayton, in Middlesex, Beudesert, and Burton, in the county of Stafford, shall continue to such as shall be owners thereof. He bequeaths to his brothers, Thomas and Charles Paget, all his books, if he deceases without issue male; constitutes the Lady Catharine, his wife, sole executrix, and overseers, his brother Thomas Paget, Henry Knevet, John Vaughan, and Richard Cooper, Esqrs. And by a codicil, dated Nov. 13, 1568, he bequeathed all his right and term of years, he had to come in all those woods called great Great-hedge, situate in the parish of Icknam, in the county of Middlesex, and in the parsonage of Harmondsworth, in the said county, after the decease of the Lady his mother, to such as at the time of her decease shall inherit the manour of West-Drayton, for the better maintenance of hospitality in the mansion house there. He died on Dec. 28, ensuing; and the probate of his will bears date on May 4, 1569. He had issue, by Catharine his wife, daughter of Sir Henry Knevet, of Buckenham, in com' Norf. Knt. one daughter, Elizabeth, who was four months old at the death of her father, and died on June 29, 1571, 13 Eliz. His relict was, 2dly, married to Sir Edward Cary, of Aldenham in Hertfordshire, Knt. who was, by her, father to Henry, the first Lord Viscount Falkland.

Whereupon Thomas, his brother, succeeding him in this honour, had summons ᵒ to parliament in 13 Eliz. and took his place there on April 4. But in 27 Eliz. being zealously affected to the Romish religion, and letters having been intercepted, which betrayed his being a well-wisher to the Queen of Scots ᵖ, he, on the apprehension of Francis Throgmorton, privately (with Charles Arundel, a courtier) withdrew into France, where, as Cambden writes, ‘ They heavily bewailed
‘ and complained amongst themselves, that the Queen was,
‘ without any fault or desert of theirs, alienated from them,
‘ by the subtil artifices of Leicester and Walsingham : that
‘ they were unworthily disgraced, and ignominiously used :
‘ that strange kinds of tricks and cheats were invented, and
‘ secret snares so closely laid, that they must, whether they
‘ would or no, and before they were aware, be involved in
‘ the guilt of high treason: and that there was at home no

ᵒ Journ. of parl.   ᵖ Cambden, p. 497.

‘ hope

'hope at all of any safety.' And Cambden acknowledges, that at that time some subtil ways were taken, to try how men stood affected.

Hollinshed [q] relates, that Charles Paget, this Lord's brother, was a principal agent for the Roman catholics, as it was proved on examination of the Earl of Northumberland's case, viz. that in September, 1583, he came privately from beyond the sea, to the Earl of Northumberland at Petworth, where the Lord Paget met him; and that on Throgmorton's being committed to the Tower, the Earl of Northumberland prevailed on the Lord Paget to quit the realm, and provided him a ship on the coast of Sussex, wherein he embarked.

Thereupon, in the parliament holden at Westminster in 29 Eliz. he was [r] attainted, with his brother Charles, and their lands and possessions confiscated, whereby the Earl of Leicester got a grant of Paget-house. He died at Brussels in 1589, 32 Eliz. his death, as Cambden [s] observes, 'proving a sad and 'universal loss to the commonwealth of learning.' He married Nazaret, daughter of Sir John Newton, of Barr's-court, in the county of Somerset, Knt. ancestor to the late Sir Michael Newton, Knight of the Bath, husband to Margaret, late Countess Coningsby, who died on June 11, 1761: and by the said Nazaret, his wife, had issue William, his son and heir. She was the relict of Sir Thomas Southwell, of Norfolk, Knt. and died at London, on April 16, 1583.

Which William was knighted before the 39th of Eliz. when he accompanied [t] the Earl of Essex in that signal expedition of taking the town and island of Cales. And in the parliament held in the 1st of James I. was restored to his lands and honours. He married Lettice, daughter and coheir to Henry Knollys, of Kingsbury in Warwickshire, Esq; by Margaret, his wife, daughter and coheir of Sir Ambrose Cave, Knt. of the Privy-council to Queen Eliz. and Chancellor of the duchy of Lancaster, 4th son of Richard Cave, of Stanford in Northamptonshire, Esq; ancestor to Sir Thomas Cave, Bart. And the said Henry Knollys was a younger son to Sir Francis Knollys, Knight of the Garter, and Treasurer of the houshold to Queen Elizabeth. By this Lady, the Lord Paget had issue three sons, William, his successor; Henry, and Thomas, who both died unmarried; also four daughters, whereof Margaret was married to Sir William Hicks, of Ruckholt, in com' Essex, Bart. Dorothy died unmarried; Catharine, wife to Sir Anthony Irby, of Boston, in com' Linc. Knt. and Anne, first wedded to Sir Simon Har-

---

[q] Chron. p. 1406, 1407.   [r] Cambden, p. 526.   [s] Ibid. p. 558.
[t] Ibid. p. 593.

court, of Stanton-Harcourt in com' Oxon, Knt. anceftor, by her, to the prefent Earl Harcourt; and afterwards to Sir William Waller, of Ofterley-park, in com' Middlefex, Knt. who was the famous General of the parliament's forces, and of the family of the Wallers of Buckinghamfhire. The faid William Lord Paget departing this [u] life on Aug. 29, 1629, was buried with his anceftors at Drayton, and was fucceeded by William, his fon and heir, as the inquifition fhews, taken after his deceafe, at Burton upon Trent, in com' Staff. on Aug. 13, in 5 Car. I. and that he died poffeffed of the manour of Berbfwick, Beaudefert, Longdon, Whittington, Burton upon Trent, Branfon, Hermylow, Wightmere, Stretton, and Boudend, in Staffordfhire; alfo of the manours of Weft-Drayton, and Harmondfworth, in Middlefex; Ever, alias Iver, Leving, and Great-Marlow, in Bucks; and the manours of Nynfell, and Stapnell, in the county of Derby.

Which William was [w] 19 years of age on Sept. 13 preceding the death of his father, and was made Knight of the Bath at the coronation of Charles I. He was one of the Lords, who, after the expedition againft the Scots [x], figned a petition to the King (dated Aug. 18, 1640, and delivered at York) wherein they fet forth their zeal to the King and kingdom, and offered to his Majefty's wifdom, feveral grievances of the fubject, the dangers thereby to the church and ftate, and to his own perfon, and the means to prevent them. ' For remedy, they
' humbly befeech his Majefty to fummon a parliament, whereby
' the caufes of thefe grievances may be taken away, and the
' authors and counfellors of them punifhed. That the prefent
' war may be compofed without blood, to the honour and fafety
' of the King, the comfort of his people, and the uniting of
' both realms.'

In 1642, he was [y] appointed, by the parliament, Lord-lieutenant of the county of Buckingham. But foon after, as the Earl of Clarendon writes [z], ' being convinced in his confcience,
' fled from them, and befought the King's pardon. And for
' the better manifefting the tendernefs of his compunction, and
' the horror he had of his former guilt, he frankly difcovered
' whatfoever he had known of their counfels; and aggravated
' all the ill they had done, with declaring it to be done to worfe
' and more horrid ends, than many good men believed to be
' poffible for them to propofe to themfelves.' And at the battle of Edgehill, on Oct. 23, 1642, the [a] regiment raifed by

[u] MS. Cole's etc. lib. 1. p. 329. in bibl. Harl. [w] Ibid. [x] Whitlock's mem. p. 35. [y] Ibid. p. 56. [z] In hift. of the rebell. 8vo. vol. 1. part 2. p. 652. [a] Saunderfon's life of King Charles, p. 584.

Paget, Earl of Uxbridge. 329

him, for the King, did great service. He was [b] one of the Lords, who, at Oxford, on Jan. 27, 1643-4, signed a declaration, by the King's command, of the most probable means to settle the peace of the kingdom. He lived some years after the restoration of the royal family, departing this life on Oct. 19, 1678, at his house in the Old Palace-yard, Westminster, and was buried with his ancestors at Drayton.

He married the Lady Frances Rich, eldest daughter to Henry Earl of Holland, who was beheaded by the rebels, on March 9, 1648-9, and by her had three sons, and seven daughters, William, 6th Lord Paget, Henry, and Thomas, whereof the 2d married a daughter of ——— Sandford, of Sandford, in com' Salop, Esq; and settling in Ireland, had issue Thomas Paget, Esq; (one of the Grooms of the bedchamber to his late Majesty, so appointed on Dec. 22, 1727, and Brigadier-general of his Majesty's forces, and Colonel of a regiment of foot, whose Lady died on Feb. 15, 1740-1, whose only daughter was married in April, 1737, to Sir Nicholas Bayley, of Placenywyd, Bart. member for Anglesey, in the parliaments summoned in 1747, and 1754) and a daughter, Dorothy, married to Sir Edward Irby, of Boston, in the county of Lincoln, Bart. father, by her, to Sir William Irby, Bart. of whom in his place as Lord Boston. The seven daughters were, Isabella, who died unmarried; Lettice, wedded to Richard Hampden, of Great-Hampden, in com' Bucks, Esq; Elizabeth, who died unmarried; Frances, espoused to Rowland Hunt, of Boreatton, in com' Salop, Esq; Penelope, married to Philip Foley, of Prestwood, in com' Stafford, Esq; Diana, married to Sir Henry Ashhurst, of Waterstock, in com' Oxon, Bart. and Anne, youngest daughter, who died unmarried.

William, 6th Lord Paget, his eldest son and heir, so succeeding his father, took [c] his seat in the house of Peers, on Nov. 25, 1678. He was one of the Lords, who, in 1681, [d] signed that petition to the King, wherein they represented, ' That his ' Majesty, on the 21st of April, 1679, having called to his ' council many honourable persons, and declared his being ' sensible of the evil effects of a single ministry, &c. he would ' for the future, refer all things to his council, and the parliament, whereby they hoped to see an end of their miseries; but to their unspeakable grief, found their expectations frustrated, the parliament then subsisting being dissolved, before it could perfect what was intended for their relief and secu-

[b] Rushworth's hist. collect. p, 3. vol, 2, p. 566.   [c] Journ. dom. procer,
Hist. of Eng. vol, 3, p. 384.

' rity.

'rity. And that hearing his Majesty, by the private fugges-
' tions of some wicked persons, &c. (without the advice of
' the Privy-council) had been prevailed on to call a parlia-
' ment to meet at Oxford, where neither Lords nor Commons
' can be in safety, &c. they, out of a just abhorrence of such
' dangerous and pernicious counsel (which the authors have
' not dared to avow) and the apprehension of the calamities
' that may ensue, make it their most humble prayer and ad-
' vice, that the parliament may not sit at Oxford, where it
' cannot be able to act with that freedom which is necessary,
' &c.' The King frowned on the deliverers of this petition,
and persisted in his resolution of holding the parliament at Oxford.

In the reign of James II. he was one of the Peers, who
e appeared in Westminster-hall, at the trial of the seven Bishops, on June 29, 1688; which had an effect in their favour,
both on the Judges and the Jury. On the landing of the
Prince of Orange, he was one of the Peers who f petitioned
the King, ' That in the deep sense of the miseries of a war
' in the bowels of the kingdom, they thought themselves
' bound in conscience, humbly to offer to his Majesty, that,
' in their opinions, the only visible way to preserve his Majesty
' and the kingdom, would be the calling of a free parliament,
' wherein they should be most ready to promote such counsels
' and resolutions of peace and settlement in church and state,
' as might conduce to his Majesty's honour and safety, and to
' the quieting the minds of his people.' He was afterwards
one of the Lords, who voted for the vacancy of the throne,
and settling the crown on the Prince and Princess of Orange.
Whereupon, on their accession, he was, in March, 1688-9,
constituted Lord-lieutenant and Custos Rotulorum of the
county of Stafford, and appointed Envoy-extraordinary to the
Emperor. He arrived in that character at the Hague, on Oct.
3, 1689, and remained at the court of Vienna till February,
1692-3; when, being appointed Ambassador-extraordinary to
the Grand Signior, he travelled through Hungary and the
Turkish territories to Constantinople.

On Feb. 28, O. S. he had audience of the Grand Vizier;
and of the Grand Signior, on March 8 following, 1692-3,
who honourably received him. And the Vizier being deposed,
he had audience of the new Vizier, on March 25, 1693,
when the proposition he made relating to peace was well received, and a speedy answer promised. His Lordship was held
in great esteem during his residence at the court of Constanti-

e Hist. of Eng. vol. 3. p. 513.   f Ibid. p. 529.

nople, and by his prudent negociations, at length concluded a peace between the Emperor and the Grand Signior. About the middle of August, 1698, he arrived in the Turkish camp near Belgrade, and having prevailed for a neutrality to be obferved about the place for treating of peace, he left the Turkish camp on Oct. 19, for Carlowitz, which was appointed for the treaty. On Jan. 26, 1698-9, the peace between the Imperialists, the Poles, and the Turks, was signed; and soon after, the peace between Muscovy, the state of Venice, and the Turks; whereby all Europe was in tranquillity. His Lordship's great abilities shined through the whole negociation; and he spared no cost in the entertainment of the several mediators, or omitted any thing that might tend to the honour of his King or country. The Grand Signior expressed a great veneration and esteem for his Majesty of Great-Britain, and assured his Lordship, he should ever retain a grateful memory of the good offices of his mediation, presenting him with a very rich vest, and a fine Turkish horse, with costly furniture.

His Lordship left the Grand Signior's court, at Adrianople, in May, 1702; and reaching Vienna in July, staid there till towards the end of November, to adjust matters relating to a dispute between the Emperor and the Grand Signior, about the limits of their respective territories in the province of Bosnia. Having now fully settled that affair, his Excellency had audience of leave of the Emperor and Empress; and setting out for England, arrived at London in April, 1703. Before his return from his embassy, he was, on June 24, 1702, appointed Lord-lieutenant of the county of Stafford; and dying in an advanced age, at his house in Bloomsbury-square, on Feb. 26, 1712-13, was buried in the church of St. Giles in the Fields, Middlesex. He married, in the life-time of his father, Frances, daughter of the honourable Francis Pierpoint, Esq; a younger son of Robert Earl of Kingston, by whom he had issue, William, who died vita patris, unmarried; and Henry, Earl of Uxbridge. Her Ladyship died on Sept. 2, 1749, aged near 100.

Which Henry, Earl of Uxbridge, was elected (in his father's life-time) one of the Knights of the shire for the county of Stafford, in the 7th year of King William, as also in the 10th, 12th, and 13th of that King; likewise in the several parliaments in the reign of Queen Anne, whilst a commoner. In 1702, when George Prince of Denmark was constituted Lord High-Admiral of England, he was appointed one of his Council in the affairs of the Admiralty; and on June 13, 1711,

was

was declared Captain of the Yeomen of the Guard; and the next day, sworn of her Majesty's Privy-council. In the same year, on Dec. 31 (his father then living) he was created a Peer of Great-Britain, by the style and title of Lord Burton, Baron of Burton, in the county of Stafford. And on Feb. 26, 1712-13, succeeding his father in honour and estate, was constituted Lord-lieutenant and Custos Rotulorum of the county of Stafford. On April 17, 1714, her Majesty appointed his Lordship to be her Envoy-extraordinary to the Elector of Hanover (afterwards King George I.) and to the Princess Sophia, Electress and Dutchess dowager of Hanover. And the same year, on the accession of that Prince to the British throne, he was continued Captain of the Yeomen of the Guard, and Lord-lieutenant of the county of Stafford. Also, on Oct. 19, the same year, he was created Earl of Uxbridge, in the county of Middlesex. And in September, 1715, resigned his employments. His Lordship married Mary, daughter and coheir to Thomas Catesby, of Whiston, in the county of Northampton, Esq; by whom he had issue Thomas-Catesby, his only son and heir. But his Lady dying suddenly at Isleworth, in February, 1735-6, he married, 2dly, anno 1739, Elizabeth, daughter to Sir Walter Bagot, of Blithfield, Bart. but had no issue by her; his Lordship deceasing in August, 1743.

Which Thomas-Catesby, Lord Paget, was one of the Gentlemen of the Bedchamber to his late Majesty, when Prince of Wales; and on his accession to the throne, was, on July 4, 1727, continued in the same post. He was elected to parliament for the county of Stafford, in the two parliaments called by George I. His Lordship married, on May 3, 1718, the Lady Elizabeth, sister to Scroop, Duke of Bridgwater, by whom he had issue two sons, Henry, successor to his grandfather, and present Earl of Uxbridge; and George, who died at Colchester, in the 17th year of his age, in April, 1737, and was buried at Drayton. And his Lordship died at Drayton, near Uxbridge, in January, 1741-2.

The said Henry, the present and 2d Earl of Uxbridge, was born in 1719, and succeeded his grandfather in his titles and estate, in August, 1743. His Lordship is unmarried.

TITLES.] Henry Paget, Earl of Uxbridge, Baron Paget, of Beaudesert, and Baron of Burton.

CREATIONS.] Baron Paget, of Beaudesert in com' Stafford, Jan. 19 (1550) 4 Edw. VI. Baron of Burton in the same county,

Paget Earl of Uxbridge

Paget, Earl of Uxbridge.

county, Dec. 31 (1711) 10 Queen Anne; and Earl of Uxbridge in com' Middlesex, Oct. 19 (1714) 1 Geo. I.

ARMS.] Sable, on a Cross ingrailed, between four Eagles, displayed, Argent, five Lions passant of the first.

CREST.] On a Wreath, a Demi-Tyger rampant, Sable, gorged with a ducal Coronet, and tufted and maned, Argent.

SUPPORTERS.] Two Tygers, as in the Crest.

MOTTO.] PER IL SUO CONTRARIO.

CHIEF-SEATS.] At Dawley, in the county of Middlesex, 3 miles from Uxbridge, and 14 from London; and at Beaudesert, in the county of Stafford, 3 miles from Litchfield, and 97 from London.

BENNET, Earl of Tankerville.

IN 9 Edw. III. [a] William Bennet, going beyond the seas in his Majesty's service, in the retinue of William de Montacute, had the King's protection to hold from Sept. 12, till Christmas following. And of this family, anciently seated in Berkshire, was John Bennet, who, in 12 Hen. VI. 1433 [b], was returned among the Gentlemen of that county, who made oath for the observance of the laws then made for themselves and retainers.

In [c] All-hallows church, in Wallingford, Berkshire, now entirely pulled down, was a monument with this inscription:

' This is the monument of Thomas Bennet, of Clapcot,
' Esq; who had issue Thomas Bennet, Knight, Citizen and
' Alderman of London, his third sonne, who gave twenty
' pounds yearly for ever to fifteen poor people of the town of
' Wallingford.'

This Thomas Bennet, of Clapcot, near Wallingford, in com' Berks, Esq; had issue, by Anne his wife, daughter of ———— Molines, of Mackney, in com' Oxon, Richard Bennet, his son and heir, and Thomas Bennet, his 3d son, Sheriff of London, anno 1594, 36 Eliz. and Lord Mayor of that city in 1603, 1 Jac. I. [d] in which year, on July 26, he received the honour of Knighthood at Whitehall. He left issue, by Mary his wife, daughter of Robert Taylor, Sheriff of London, in 34 Eliz. three sons, Simon, Richard, and John; and two daughters; Anne, married to William Duncomb, of Brickhill in Buckinghamshire, Esq; and Margaret, to Sir George Crooke, Knt. Justice of the Common Pleas. Simon, the eldest son, seated at Beechampton in Buckinghamshire, married Elizabeth, daughter of Sir Arthur Ingram, Knt. and was created a Baronet, on July 17, 1627. Richard, the 2d son, was an eminent merchant of London, and had issue, by Elizabeth his wife, daughter of William Cradock, of Staffordshire, Esq; (after his decease, remarried to Sir Heneage Finch, Knt. Recorder of London) Simon Bennet, of Beechampton, in the county of Bucks, Esq; his son and heir, who marrying Gratiosa, daughter of Gilbert Morewood, of London, merchant, had issue three daughters his coheirs, viz. Elizabeth,

[a] Rymer's fœd. vol. 4. Greg. King. Lanc. Fecial.
[b] Fuller's worthies in Berksh.
[c] Ex collect.
[d] Philpot's cat. of Knights, p. 25.

Bennet, Earl of Tankerville.

married to Edward Osborn, Lord Latimer, eldest son of Thomas Earl of Danby, but died without issue; Grace, wedded to John Bennet, of Abington in Cambridgeshire, Esq; and Frances, espoused to James Cecill, Earl of Salisbury.

I now return to Richard Bennet, eldest son and heir of Thomas Bennet, of Clapcot before-mentioned. Which Richard married Elizabeth, daughter of Thomas Tisdale, of Deanly, in the county of Berks, Esq; and had issue Ralph Bennet, his son and heir, from whom those of Moreden, in Surry, derive their descent Sir John Bennet, Knt. 2d son, ancestor to the present Earl of Tankerville. Thomas, 3d son, Alderman of London, who, dying in 1622, left issue two sons, whereof Richard, the eldest, by his first wife, left an only daughter, Jane, married to James Scudamore, eldest son and heir of John Lord Scudamore; likewise, by his 2d wife, had an only daughter, Dorothy, married to Sir Henry Capel, Knight of the Bath, created Lord Capel, of Tewksbury; but died without issue. Thomas, the 2d son of the said Thomas, was seated at Baberham, in Cambridgeshire, and was created a Baronet, on Novem. 22, 1662; but this title is now extinct.

Sir John Bennet, Knt. 2d son of Richard Bennet, was seated at Dawley, in the county of Middlesex, and was ᵉ created on July 6, 1589, 31 Eliz. Doctor of Laws, by the University of Oxford, having been one of the Proctors there. He was afterwards Vicar-general in spirituals to the Archbishop of York, and Prebendary of Langtoft, in the church of York. In 42 Eliz. bearing the title of Doctor of Laws, he was ᶠ in commission, with the Lord Keeper Egerton, the Lord Treasurer Buckhurst, and several other Noblemen, for the suppression of heresy. He was also, in the 43d of that reign, returned to parliament for the city of York, and was a leading member of the house of Commons, as appears from several of his speeches (as also conferences with the Lords) in Townshend's collections. He was also one of the learned Council in the Northern Court ᵍ at York, in 15 and 41 Eliz. and 1 Jac. I. from whom he received ʰ the honour of Knighthood, before his coronation, on July 23, 1603, at Whitehall: and in that reign was ⁱ made Chancellor to Queen Anne (consort of King James) Judge of the prerogative court of Canterbury, and Chancellor to the Archbishop of York. In the beginning of the year 1617, he was sent Ambassador to Brussels,

e Wood's fast. Oxon, vol. 1. p. 763. f Rymer's fœd. tom. 17. p. 386.
g Drake's Eboracum, p. 369. h Philpot's cat. p. 13. i Wood's fast. præd.

to question the Archduke, in behalf of his master the King of Great-Britain, concerning a libel wrote and published, as it was supposed, by Erycius Puteanus, who neither apprehended the author, nor suppressed the book, until he was solicited by the King's Agent there; only interdicted it, and suffered the author to fly his dominions. In 1620, being intitled Judge of the prerogative court of Canterbury, he was in a special commission with the Archbishop of Canterbury, and other Noblemen, to put in execution the laws against all heresies, great errors in matters of faith and religion, &c. And the same year, bearing the title of Chancellor to the Archbishop of York, he was commissioned with the Archbishop of York, and others, to execute all manner of ecclesiastical jurisdiction within the province of York. This Sir John Bennet, who died, A. D. 1627, in the parish of Christ-church, London, married Anne, daughter of Christopher Weeks, of Salisbury, in Wilts, Esq; and by her [k] (who departed this life on Feb. 9, 1601, and was buried in the cathedral of York, where a monument is erected to her memory) had four sons, and two daughters. His eldest son and successor was Sir John Bennet, of Dawley. Sir Thomas Bennet, Knt. 2d son, Doctor of the Civil Law, and Master in Chancery, married, [l] first, Charlotte, daughter of William Harrison, of London, by whom he had two daughters, who died unmarried; but by his 2d wife, Thomasine, daughter and coheir of George Dethick, Esq; Counsellor at Law, son of Sir William Dethick, Garter King of Arms, son and heir of Sir Gilbert Dethick; he had issue Thomas Bennet, of Salthorp, in com' Wilts, Esq; who married Martha, daughter of John Smith, of Tidworth, in com' Southamp. Esq; Matthew, 3d son of Sir John Bennet, died unmarried.

The eldest son, Sir John Bennet, of Dawley, [m] received the honour of Knighthood in the life-time of his father, at Theobalds, on June 15, 1616. He married Dorothy, daughter of Sir John Crofts, of Saxham, in the county of Suffolk, Knt. by whom he had issue six sons; John, his son and heir; Henry, 2d son, created Earl of Arlington by Charles II. on April 22, 1672; who left issue an only daughter and heir, the Lady Isabella, Countess of Arlington, by descent, and the mother of Charles, 2d Duke of Grafton: Robert, 3d son, who died without issue: Charles, 4th son, who, marrying Anne, daughter of Richard Wigmore, of Upton-court, in Herefordshire, Esq; had issue one son, and two daughters.

[k] Drake's Eboracum, p. 511.
[m] Philpot's cat. of Knights, p. 52.
[l] Ex collect. Greg. King, Lanc. Focial.

Bennet, Earl of Tankerville.

Thomas, the 5th, and Edward the 6th sons, both died issueless. He had also two daughters, Dorothy, married to Benjamin Bacon, of London, Merchant; and Elizabeth, wedded to Sir Robert Carr, of Sleeford, in Lincolnshire, Bart.

Which John, the eldest son of Sir John, was made Knight of the Bath, at the coronation of Charles II. and was Lieutenant, and afterwards Captain, of the Band of Pensioners, in that reign. And his Majesty taking into consideration [n] the constant and faithful services performed to Charles I. his royal father, of blessed memory, in the rebellious times; as also to himself, by John Bennet, of Harlington, in the county of Middlesex, whom, at his coronation, he created Knight of the honourable order of the Bath, in further augmentation of his honour, did, by letters patent, bearing date on Nov. 24, in the 34th year of his reign, advance him to the degree and dignity of a Baron of this realm, by the title of Lord Ossulston, Baron of Ossulston, the name of one of the hundreds in the county of Middlesex. He died on July 28, 1685, in the 70th year of his age, leaving one son, and two daughters; and was buried in Harlington church, in com' Middlesex, whereof he was patron, and where a monument is erected to his memory. He married two wives, 1. Elizabeth, Countess of Mulgrave, daughter of Lionel Cranfield, Earl of Middlesex; and, 2. Bridget, daughter of John Howe, of Langor, in the county of Nottingham, Esq; and sister to Scroop, Lord Viscount Howe, in Ireland: and by the last had issue only, as above.

The son was Charles, who succeeded him in honour and estate; and the daughters were, Dorothy, who died unmarried; and Annabell, wedded to John Cecil, Earl of Exeter.

Which Charles, Lord Ossulston, took his place in the [o] house of Peers, on Dec. 12, 1695; and was created Earl of Tankerville, by Geo. I. by letters patent dated Oct. 19, 1714, the first year of his reign. On Dec. 9, 1715, he was constituted, by his Majesty, Chief Justice and Justice in Eyre of all the forests, chases, parks, and warrens, South of Trent: and on Feb. 27, 1720-21, was made a Knight of the most ancient and noble order of St. Andrew, or the Thistle. In July, 1695, he married the Lady Mary, only daughter of Ford, Lord Grey of Wark, Earl of Tankerville, by his wife, the Lady Mary, 4th daughter of George Earl of Berkeley: by which Lady, who died on May 31, 1710, he had issue four sons, and three daughters, viz.

n 11 Bill sign. 34 Car. II.   o Journ. Dom. Procer.

Charles Earl of Tankerville; John, who died an infant; Henry, and Grey, who died unmarried.

Lady Bridget, married to John Wallop, Lord Vifcount Lymington, firſt Earl of Portſmouth, and died on Oct. 12, 1738, leaving iſſue: Lady Annabella, wedded to William Paulet, Eſq; eldeſt ſon of the Lord William Paulet; and Lady Mary, married, on Aug. 6, 1720, to William Wilmer, of Sywell, in com' Northamp. and died on May 24, 1729, leaving three ſons, Charles, George, and Bennet.

The ſaid Charles, Earl of Tankerville, departed this life in the 48th year of his age, on May 21, 1722, and was ſucceeded by Charles, his eldeſt ſon and heir.

Which Charles, Earl of Tankerville, on Feb. 28, 1728-9, was appointed one of the Gentlemen of the Bedchamber to his Royal Highneſs Frederick Prince of Wales; and on May 16, 1730, was inveſted with the enſigns of the moſt ancient and noble order of St. Andrew, or the Thiſtle. In September, 1731, he was appointed Captain of the Yeomen of the Guard; and reſigning his poſt, in 1733, was made Maſter of the Buck-Hounds. After which he was appointed, in June, 1737, one of the Lords of the Bedchamber to the King, which he ſoon after reſigned. On May 1, 1740, he was ſworn Lord-lieutenant of the county of Northumberland, and of the town and county of Newcaſtle upon Tyne. His Lordſhip married Camilla, daughter to Edward Colvile, of Whitehouſe, in the biſhopric of Durham, Eſq; after one of the Ladies of the Bedchamber to her late Majeſty Queen Caroline; and lately to the Princeſs Auguſta, now Princeſs of Brunſwick: and by her he had iſſue two ſons, and one daughter; Charles, Lord Oſſulſton; George, born in 1727, to whom his late Majeſty was godfather; and the Lady Camilla, married, on Jan. 11, 1754, to Gilbert-Fane Fleming, Eſq; ſon of Gilbert Fleming, Eſq; His Lordſhip was taken ſuddenly ill, on the road from Alborough-hatch in Eſſex, to London, on March 14, 1753; and, notwithſtanding all poſſible aſſiſtance, died the ſame night. To him ſucceeded Charles Lord Oſſulſton, his eldeſt ſon, now 3d Earl of Tankerville.

Which Charles, 3d Earl of Tankerville, had all advantages of education, and ſet out on his travels in May, 1734; and whilſt abroad, was made an Enſign in the third regiment of foot-guards, in October, the ſame year. In 1736, he returned to England, and on Sept. 1, 1739, a company in General Wentworth's regiment of foot was conferred on him. In 1740, his Lordſhip embarked in the expedition to the Weſt-Indies, under the command of John Lord Cathcart; and being

Bennet Earl of Tankerville.

Bennet, Earl of Tankerville.

ing with his Majesty's forces before Carthagena, was at the attack of Fort St. Lazarre, on April 2, 1741; and behaving with great intrepidity, he was, on the 30th of the same month, constituted Major of the regiment commanded by Colonel Cotterell. On April 11, 1743, his Majesty was pleased to appoint him Lieutenant-colonel, with the command of a company in the first regiment of foot-guards: and on succeeding his father, he took his place in the house of Peers, on March 28, 1753.

His Lordship married, on Sept. 23, 1742, Alicia, 3d daughter of Sir John Astley, of Pateshull in Staffordshire, Bart. by whom he had issue three sons, 1. Charles Bennet, Lord Ossulston, who was born on Nov. 15, 1743, and returned from his travels in October, 1764: 2. John Grey Bennet; who died an infant: and, 3. ———, born on April 15, 1757. His Lordship has also two daughters, viz. Lady Camilla-Elizabeth, and Lady Frances-Alicia. The said Lady Camilla-Elizabeth was married to ——— Count Donkoff, a Polish Nobleman, Captain of Horse in the Dutch service, and nearly related to the Princes Czartorinski, and to Stanislaus, Count Poniatowski, the present King of Poland: but was left a widow, on Sept. 4, 1764, about a month after her nuptials.

TITLES.] Charles Bennet, Earl of Tankerville, and Baron of Ossulston.

CREATIONS.] Baron Ossulston, of Ossulston, in com' Middlesex, Nov. 24 (1682) 34 Car. II. Earl of Tankerville (a castle in the duchy of Normandy) Oct. 19 (1714) 1 Geo. I.

ARMS.] Gules, a Bezant between three Demi-Lions, rampant, Argent.

CREST.] On a Wreath, a Scaling-Ladder, Or; which is an ancient Crest of the family: but sometimes they used the following—On a Wreath, a Demi-Lion, rampant, Argent, the Head, Gules, holding in his Paws a Bezant; and sometimes, out of a mural Coronet, Or, a Lion's Head, Gules, charged with a Bezant on his Neck.

SUPPORTERS.] Two Lions, Argent, each charged on its Shoulder with a Bezant, and crowned ducally, Or.

MOTTO.] HAUD FACILE EMERGUNT.

But his Lordship now chuses the Motto of his grandfather, Ford Lord Grey, Earl of Tankerville, viz.

DE BON VOULOIR SERVIR LE ROY.

CHIEF-SEAT.] At Chillingham-castle, in Northumberland.

FINCH, Earl of Ailesford.

I AM now to treat of Heneage Finch, Lord Guernsey, and Earl of Ailesford, 2d son of Heneage, Earl of Nottingham: which Heneage, Earl of Ailesford [a], after his education in Christ-church, in Oxford, was entered in the Inner-Temple, for the study of the laws, wherein he was such a proficient, that, on Jan 13, 1678, he [b] was constituted his Majesty's Solicitor-general; from which office he was removed by James II. on April 21, 1686.

He was afterwards the principal of those eminent Council, who pleaded in behalf of the seven Bishops, who were tried on June 29, in Trinity-term, 1688, for refusing to authorise the reading King James's declaration for abrogating test and penal laws, and on that account were committed to the Tower. On which occasion [c] Mr. Finch argued strenuously against their commitment, and the power of the King in dispensing with the laws mentioned in that declaration: and that the Lords the Bishops could not in prudence, honour, or conscience, so far make themselves parties to it, as the solemn publication thereof in the time of divine service (as they were commanded) must amount to.

He was elected, for the University of Oxford, to that parliament which met at Westminster, on March 6, 1678-9; and returned a member for the borough of Guilford, in Surry, to that which met on May 19, 1685, 1 James II. [d] Also chosen for the University of Oxford, in the convention parliament, and in all the subsequent parliaments whilst he continued a Commoner, except in the 10th of Will. III. when by reason of his ill state of health, he declined being elected.

In August, 1702, the 1st of Queen Anne [e], he was chosen to compliment her Majesty on the part of the University, on her coming to the city of Oxford; and in consideration of his great merits and abilities [f], was created Baron of Guernsey (an island on the French coast belonging to the county of Southampton) by letters patent dated on March 15, 1702-3, and was sworn of the Privy-council [g], on the 20th.

On the accession of George I. he was created Earl of Ailesford, by letters patent, dated Oct. 19, 1714; being the same year constituted Chancellor of the duchy of Lancaster, and

---

a Wood's Athenæ Oxon, vol 2. p. 540.   b Dugdale's chron. series.
c Trial of the seven Bishops.   d Willes's notitia parl. MS.   e Annals of Queen Anne.   f Pat. 2 Queen Anne.   g Pointer's chron. p. 485.

sworn

Finch, Earl of Ailesford. 341

sworn of the Privy-council. Which office his Lordship resigned on Feb. 29, 1715-16. And departing this life on July 22, 1719, was buried at Ailesford in Kent.

His Lordship married Elizabeth, daughter and one of the coheirs of Sir John Banks, of Ailesford in the county of Kent, Bart. by whom he had issue nine children.

1. Lady Elizabeth, who was married to Robert Benson, late Lord Bingley, and died on Feb. 26, 1757, aged 80.
2. Lady Mary, who died unmarried.
3. Lady Anne, married to William Earl of Dartmouth.
4. Heneage, 2d Earl of Ailesford.
5. The hon. John Finch, who was returned member for the borough of Maidstone, to the parliament summoned to meet on May 10, 1722; also chosen in the succeeding parliaments to the time of his decease. On April 30, 1726, he married Elizabeth, daughter and heir of John Savile, of Methley-hall in Yorkshire, Esq; and deceasing on Jan. 1, 1739-40, left issue one son, John Savile Finch, Esq; and a daughter, Mary.
6. Lady Martha.
7. Lady Frances, married, on Oct. 16, 1716, to Sir John Bland, of Kippax-park in com' Ebor. Bart. by whom she had issue the present Sir John Bland, Bart.
8. The hon. Henry Finch, who died on July 15, 1757, unmarried.
9. Lady Essex, deceased unmarried.

Which Heneage, 2d Earl of Ailesford, was constituted Master of the Jewel-office, on June 11, 1711, and continued in the same place under George I. till he voluntarily resigned it, when his father quitted his place of Chancellor of the duchy of Lancaster. His Lordship, whilst a Commoner, was elected one of the Knights for the county of Surry, in the 9th and 12th years of Queen Anne; also in the first year of her successor, till he succeeded his father in 1719. And having married Mary, daughter and heir of Sir Clement Fisher, of Packington, in com' Warw. Bart. had issue one son, and four daughters; Heneage, Lord Guernsey; Lady Anne; Lady Mary, married to William, Lord Viscount Andover, son and heir of Henry Bowes, Earl of Suffolk and of Berkshire; Lady Elizabeth; and Lady Frances, married, on April 2, 1741, to Sir William Courtenay, of Powderham-castle in Devonshire, afterwards created Viscount Courtenay. His Lady, the Countess of Ailesford, died at Bath, in May, 1740; and he himself, on June 29, 1757.

His Lordship's son and successor, Heneage Lord Guernsey, now 3d Earl of Ailesford, was, on a vacancy, elected, in 1739, one of the Knights for the county of Leicester; and in the succeed-

succeeding parliament, summoned to meet on June 25, 1741, was chose for Maidstone in Kent; also in that which first met on May 31, 1754. He married, on Oct. 6, 1750, Lady Charlotte Seymour, youngest daughter of Charles Duke of Somerset, by his 2d wife, the Lady Charlotte Finch, daughter of Daniel Earl of Winchelsea and Nottingham; and by her was father of six sons; 1. Heneage Lord Guernsey, born on July 15, 1751, N. S. 2. Charles, born on June 4, 1752; 3. William, born on May 27, 1753; 4. John, born on May 22, 1755; 5. ———, born on April 26, 1756; 6. ———, born on March 11, 1760; and one daughter, Lady Charlotte, born on May 28, 1754.

TITLES.] Heneage Finch, Earl of Ailesford, and Baron of Guernsey.

CREATIONS.] Baron of Guernsey, in com' Southamp. by letters patent bearing date on March 15, 1702-3, and Earl of Ailesford in Kent, Oct. 19, 1714, 1 Geo. I.

ARMS.] Argent, a Chevron between three Griphons, passant, Sable.

CREST.] On a Wreath, a Griphon passant, Sable.

SUPPORTERS.] On the dexter side, a Griphon, Sable, gorged with a ducal Collar, Or: and on the sinister, a Lion of the second, ducally gorged, Azure.

MOTTO.] APERTO VIVERE VOTO.

CHIEF-SEATS.] At Ailesford, in the county of Kent, 4 miles from Rochester, and 28 from London; at Albury, in the county of Surry, 4 miles from Guilford, and 24 from London; and at Packington, in the county of Warwick.

HERVEY,

Finch Earl of Aylesford

HERVEY, Earl of Bristol.

THE surname of Hervey, or Harvey, written anciently with Fitz (i. e. son of Harvey) is derived from Robert Fitz-Harvey, a younger son of Harvey, Duke of Orleans, who is recorded among those valiant commanders [a], who accompanied William the Conqueror in his expedition into this kingdom, in 1066, and were rewarded by him with lands, &c.

This Robert Fitz-Harvey had several sons; one of them [b], Robert, writing himself son of Hervey, gave lands to the Abbot of Abington, which Hen. I. confirmed. Likewise, in the same reign lived Hervey [c], who, being Bishop of Bangor, was translated to the bishopric of Ely, and made the first Bishop of that see, in 1109, 10 Hen. I. wherein he sat 22 years, departing this life on Aug. 30, 1131.

Of the same lineage was Count Hervey, a Briton, a famous [d] soldier, and Governor of the castle of the Devizes, in the reign of King Stephen, which he held out against the Earl of Gloucester, and powerfully assisted that King in his wars with Maud, the Empress; but was at length forced to retire beyond the seas with a few attendants.

After him was Hervey de Yuon, who married a daughter of William Goieth, that died in his journey to the Holy Land [e]. Which Hervey delivered certain castles in France unto Hen. II. despairing to keep them against Theobald, Earl of Chartres, who, by aid of the French King, sought to dispossess him in 1169. He afterwards accompanied King Henry in his conquest of Ireland, as appears by the roll collected by William Cambden, in his observations of Ireland.

Our genealogists agree, that Henry was son of the said Harvey de Yuon; and I find his name among other persons of note, who were witnesses to Roger de Clare's grant to Rievaulx-abbey [f], in com' Ebor. in 1190, being styled Hen. fil. Harvei. This Henry [g] embarked for the Holy Land with Rich. I. who, in that expedition, subdued the isle of Cyprus, restored to the Christians the city of Joppa [h], and in many battles put the Turks to flight. He was held in much esteem by King John, as [i] appears by his grant to him of the forester-

---

a Stow's annals, edit. 1614. p. 104, 107.   b Mon. Ang. vol. 2. p. 106.
c Godwin's cat. of Bishops, p. 201.   d Tyrrel's hist. of Eng. vol. 2. p. 69.
e Hollinshed's chron. vol 3. p. 75.   f Mon. Ang. vol. 2. p. 731.   g Seager's Baronagium, MS. in stem. hujus fam.   h Stow's annals, p. 159.   i Ex evid. fam. penes Joh. com' Bristol.

ship of New-forest, Achilles Garth, and other lands. By his wife Alice, daughter to Henry, son of Ivo, he had issue Osbert de Hervey [k], who held lands in Helnfestune, as is evident by the register of the monastery of St. Edmundsbury, fol. 174. b. and being styled son of Hervey [l], is mentioned as one of the King's Justices at Norwich, with Roger le Bigot, in the 3d year of the reign of Rich. I. as also [m] one of the Justices itinerant at Huntingdon, on the octaves of the Assumption of the Virgin Mary, the same year; and fines were levied before him [n] to the octaves of St. Martin, in the 7th of King John, when he departed this life, leaving Adam, his son and heir, under age.

Which Adam de Hervey was in ward to Hen. III. and by his appointment (as was usual in those times) was married to [o] Juliana, daughter of John de Fitzhugh, by whom he had issue John de Hervey, his son and heir, who, by marrying Joan, [p] daughter and heir of John Harman, or (as others) Hammon, of Thurley, in Bedfordshire, became possessed of that lordship, and is the direct ancestor to those of the name now existing.

But there was another branch of this family seated at Boxted, in Suffolk [q], whereof William de Hervey was Sheriff of the counties of Norfolk and Suffolk, in the 32d of Hen. II. Also for the two first years of the reign of Rich. II. an office in that age of great power and trust; insomuch that Prince Edward, eldest son of Hen. III. in the 52d year of his father's reign, [r] was Sheriff of Bedfordshire, and continued so for five years. The said William Hervey left issue a son, who [s], in a charter without date, styling himself William Hervey of Boxted, son of William, grants to Peter, son of Geoffrey, divers lands in Boxted, whereto is appendant an oval seal of six bars, circumscribed, 'Sigillum Willielmi Hervii;' and to another charter without date, is an oval seal appendant, with this inscription, S. WILLI HERVY DE BOXTEDE. He [t] married Beatrice, daughter of Thomas de Weyland, about 8 Edw. I. by whom he had a daughter Amy, married to Robert Leyes, whose daughter and heir, Beatrix, was married to Thomas Badwelle, who thereby attained the manour of Boxtede.

I now return to John Hervey, who, by his marriage aforesaid, with Joan, becoming possessed of Thirley, or Thurley, in the hundred of Willy, in Bedfordshire, made it his principal residence; and departing this life in 21 Edw. I. [u] was succeeded by John, his son and heir.

k Apparatus geneal. MS. in bibl. Harley, p. 636. l Ib. p. 746. m Mon. Ang. vol. 2. p. 854. n Dugdale's origin. jurid. p. 41. o Seager præd. p Ibid. q Fuller's worthies. p. 267. r Ibid. p. 122. s Apparatus geneal. præd. p. 152, a. t Ibid. u Ex stemmate præd.

Hervey, Earl of Bristol. 345

Which John Hervey, of Thurley, Esq; taking to wife Margaret, daughter and heir of Sir John de Nernuytt, of Burnham, in com' Bucks (son of Thomas de Nernuytt [w], by Alice his wife, daughter and heir of Thomas Buckland, of Buckland, in com' Devon) did thereby greatly increase his inheritance, which descended to John Hervey, his son and heir.

The said John Hervey married Margery, daughter of Sir William Colthorpe, Knt. And in 1386, the 10th of Rich. II. was, with Ralph Fitz-Ralph [x], elected Knight of the shire for the county of Bedford, in the parliament then held, and attending sixty-three days, had 25 l. 4 s. allowed for their expences. In 4 Hen. IV. he was authorised [y], with Sir William de Roos, Sir Richard de Grey, and others of great note, to treat with Owen Glendowr, and his council, and to conclude with him, what they should conceive most expedient to be done, for the redemption of Reginald Lord Grey, of Ruthyn (ancestor to the late Duke of Kent) then prisoner with the said Owen. And the King, on Dec. 8, 1404, 6 Hen. IV. [z] grants licence to Gerard Braybroke, Knt. John Hervey, and others, to found a collegiate-church at Northill, in Bedfordshire (in the room of the parish-church there) to celebrate divine service for the souls of Sir John Traylly, Knt. and Reginald his son, deceased. The Lady of this John Hervey survived him, and being after wife to Sir John Argentine, died in the 5th year of Hen. VI. She had, by [a] her first husband, Sir Nicholas Hervey, slain at the battle of Tewksbury, on May 4, 1471, fighting on the part of Prince Edward, son of Hen. VI. as also Thomas Hervey, who inherited the estate. Cotemporary [b] with whom was William Hervey, who served under Hen. V. in France, and was in the famous battle of Agincourt, on Oct. 24, 1415.

Thomas Hervey, of Thurley, Esq; married Joan, daughter to William Paston, one of the Justices of the King's Bench (ancestor to the late Earl of Yarmouth) by whom he had issue [c] John Hervey, of Thurley, Esq; who in 1461, 1 Edw. IV. had a grant [d] from the King, of the office of Master of his Ordnance, with the wages of two shillings a day for himself, and six-pence a day for his clerk; and six-pence a day for his other servants in the said office. He took to wife Christian, daughter of John Chichley, Chamberlain of London, nephew and heir of Henry Chichley, Archbishop of Canterbury, founder of All-Souls-

w Jekyll's lib. Baron. MS. p. 225. x Pryn's 4th part of a brief reg. p. 392.
y Pat. 4 Hen. IV. p. 1. m. 28. & Rot. parl. 4 Hen. IV. n. 13. z Mon. Ang. vol. 3. p. 141. a Stow's annals, p. 424. b MS. Not. B. 5. p. 263. in bibl. Joh. Anstis, arm. c Visit. de com' Suff. in bibl. Harley, Not. 5. B. 11.
d Clauf. 1 Edw. IV. m. 1.

college

college in Oxford, and Cardinal of St. Eufebius [e], who died on April 12, 1443. From that marriage proceeded several sons and daughters, viz. John Hervey, of Thurley, Efq; John Hervey junior, Efq; who married Margaret, daughter and heir of William Wickham, relict of William Fines, Lord Say; Edward Hervey, Richard Hervey; Ifabella, a nun at Elftoe, in Bedfordfhire; Anne, Chriftian, Alice, Margery, and Florence

John Hervey, of Thurley, Efq; (fon and heir of John) was [f] wedded to Alice, daughter of Nicholas Morley, of Glind, in Suffex, and left iffue two fons, George, and Thomas Hervey, anceftor to the prefent Earl of Briftol.

George Hervey, the eldeft fon, fucceeding at Thurley, was [g] twice Sheriff of the counties of Bedford and Buckingham, viz. in 24 Hen. VII. and 8th of Hen. VIII. He had a brave fpirit, and fignalized himfelf in feveral martial exploits, particularly at the fieges of Teroven and Tournay, and in that battle, which our hiftorians call the Battle of Spurs, from the fwiftnefs of the French in running away [h], on Aug. 16, 1513. For his valiant behaviour in thefe actions, he was knighted by Hen. VIII. on Oct. 13, after his entrance into Tournay. In 1520, the 12th of the fame King, he was retained to attend his Sovereign [i] into France, with one chaplain, eleven fervants, and eight horfes, in his retinue; in which year there was a meeting [k], firft of the Emperor Charles V. who came over into England and was received by the King at Dover; and afterwards of the Kings and Queens of England and France, at a camp between Guifnes and Ardès; and likewife with the fame Emperor, and his aunt the Duchefs of Savoy, at Graveline and Calais.

This Sir George Hervey's laft will and teftament bears date on April 7, 1520, which was juft before his intended voyage; but he did not depart this life till fix years after, as fhould feem [l] by the probate thereof, dated on May 8, 1526. ' He orders his
' body to be buried in the parifh church of Thurley, or in the
' monaftery of Elmftow, if he fhould deceafe there; and that
' a marble ftone of the price of four marks fhould be laid over
' the bodies of John Hervey and his wife, one of the daugh-
' ters and heirs of Sir John Nernuytt, Knight, who lie there
' buried. Alfo, that his executors caufe the image of our Lady,
' that ftandeth within the chancel of Thurley, to be painted,

---

[e] Godwyn's cat. of Bifhops, p. 110.   [f] Vifit. de com' Suff. præd.   [g] Fuller's worthies in com' Bedford, p. 124.   [h] Nom. equit. in bibl. Cott. Claudius, c. 3. p. 91. and Jekyll's cat. of Knights, p. 24.   [i] MS. not. b. 5. in bibl. Joh. Anftis.   [k] Stow's annals, p. 510.   [l] Ex regift. vocat. Ayloofe, qu. 3. in cur. prærog Cant.

' and

' and provide a new tabernacle to set her in, and that they find
' an honest priest for the space of twenty years in the said
' church, to pray for the souls of his father and mother, and
' others his friends.

' He further directs his executors, to uphold his manour-
' place of Thurley, and bequeaths to them for the performance
' of his will, all his manours, lands, and advowsons, in the coun-
' ties of Huntingdon, Bedford, Bucks, Oxon, and Hertford-
' shire. He wills his lands in Fleetmarston, to Margaret Smart,
' for the term of her life, remainder to Gerard her son, and
' the heirs males of his body; and in default thereof, to his
' nephew John Hervey, of Highworth, Esq; He also bequeaths
' his manour of Thurley to the said Gerard, when he arrives at
' the age of twenty-five years, provided he marries by the ad-
' vice of his executors, Sir William Parr, Knight, John Hervey,
' and John Lee, Esquires; and appoints supervisors of his will,
' Sir Henry Gray, Knight, Sir Edmund Bray, and Sir William
' Paston, Knights.'

From the said Gerard, who took the name of Harvey, and was elected for the town of Bedford, to the parliaments in the [m] first of Edw. VI. as also in the reign of Philip and Mary, and was knighted [n], descended the Harveys of Thurley, in the county of Bedford.

But the chief heirs male of the family are the Herveys of Highworth, or Ickworth (as it is now written) descended from Thomas Hervey, only brother of Sir George Hervey, before mentioned. Which Thomas Hervey, Esq; served Hen. VIII. in his wars, and was [o] one of the Council of the city of Tournay, under Sir John Russel (after Earl of Bedford) the Governor, at the time of the delivery of it to the French King, Francis I. in 1519. He acquired the manour of Ickworth, and other possessions, by marriage with Jane, daughter and heir of Henry Drury, of Hawsted and Ickworth, &c. Esq; Which manour of Ickworth anciently belonged to a family of the same name, whereof Thomas Ickworth made his will the Thursday after St. John Baptist, in 1373, and was a bene-factor to the repair of the church of Ickworth, to the monks of Thetford, the brethren of Thetford, and the brethren of Bakewell; and left issue Agnes de Ickworth, his daughter and heir, who was married to ———— Drury, of Hawsted. The said Jane, surviving him, was secondly married to Sir William Carew; but by her first husband had issue John Hervey, Esq; [p]

[m] Willis's not. parl. in eod com. [n] Visit. de com' Essex in bibl. Harley, not. 90. a. 13. [o] Strype's memorials of Hen. VIII. vol. I. p. 7. [p] Ex-regist. Ayloof, præd.

executor and adminiftrator to the laft teftament of his uncle Sir George Hervey, in 18 Hen. VIII. who, dying without iffue, was fucceeded by William, his brother.

Which William Hervey, of Ickworth, Efq; took to wife Joan, daughter of John Cocket, of Ampton, in the county of Suffolk, and departing this life in 1538, in the 30th of Hen. VIII. was buried in the middle ifle of St. Mary's church in St. Edmundfbury, as appears by this infcription:

> Pray for the Soule of William
> Harvye, Efq; Obiit 1 Aug. 1538.

He had iffue feveral fons and daughters, viz. Elizabeth, Joan, and Margaret; John Hervey, of Ickworth, Efq; eldeft fon; and Sir Nicholas Hervey, 2d fon, who was of the Privy-chamber to Hen. VIII. and fo much in his favour, that in 1520, the 12th of his reign, he was one of thofe Gentlemen [q] who were appointed to furnifh the days of jufts, when the King, and feven he had appointed, challenged the French King, and as many on the part of France; on which occafion feats of arms were performed for thirty days, at a camp between Guifnes and Ardes. Likewife, in 18 Hen. VIII. when the King, for the entertainment of the French Ambaffadors, had appointed a folemn juft, he [r] named Sir Nicholas for one of the challengers; and he is ftyled the Valiant Efquire; for he received the honour of Knighthood after this, and was Hen. VIII's [s] Ambaffador in the Emperor's court at Gaunt, in the 23d of his reign. Having married Elizabeth, daughter of Sir Thomas Fitz-Williams, Knt. and widow of Sir Thomas Maleverer, he had iffue Sir Thomas Hervey, who was Knight-marfhal to Queen Mary, and left only two daughters. But Sir Nicholas, by his 2d Lady [t], Bridget, daughter and heir of Sir John Wiltfhire, of Stone-caftle in Kent, Knt. relict of Sir Richard Wingfield, of Kimbolton-caftle in Huntingdonfhire, Knight of the Garter, had iffue Sir George Hervey, of Markfhall in Effex, Lieutenant of the Tower, from whom the Harveys now of Markfhall defcend. But Henry Hervey, Efq; was eldeft fon of Sir Nicholas by his laft Lady, and taking to wife Jane, daughter of James Thomas, of the county of Glamorgan, Efq; had iffue William, his fon and heir, who diftinguifhed himfelf on feveral occafions, and for his eminent fervices, was at length advanced to the dignity

[q] Stow's annals, p. 509.   [r] Hall's chron. fol. 155. b.   [s] Ibid. fol. 200.
[t] Vifit. de com' Effex, præd.

Hervey, Earl of Bristol. 349

of a Peer of this Kingdom, by the title of Lord Hervey, of Kidbrook.

He first signalized himself in 1588 [u], in the memorable engagement of the Spanish armada, wherein he was principally concerned in boarding one of the Spanish galleons, killing the captain, Hugh Moncada, with his own hands. He was [w] afterwards knighted, on June 27, 1596, with many other persons of note, who had valiantly behaved in taking the town and island of Cales (or Cadiz); and the year following, embarking [x] again with the Earl of Essex, and Sir Walter Raleigh, was present at the taking the town of Fyal. In 1600 [y], he commanded one of the Queen's ships, and brought succours to the Lord-president of Munster, then reducing the rebels in Ireland, who were in expectation of assistance from the Spaniards. He staid some time in that kingdom, and behaved himself in several actions with great bravery and conduct [z]: particularly with 70 foot and 24 horse, he defeated 160 foot and 18 horse of the rebels, killing and taking 60 of them, without the loss of one man. He was also very serviceable at the siege of Kinsale (possessed by the Spaniards in 1601) and on the surrender thereof, on Jan. 9, 1601-2, he was sent to take possession of the castles of Dunboy, Castlehaven, and Flower, pursuant to the capitulation. Being afterwards made Governor of Carbry, from Ross to Bantry, he took in Capeclear-castle, and performed many successful acts, till the rebels were entirely reduced.

For which services, King James advanced him [a] to the dignity of a Baronet, on May 31, 1619, the 17th of his reign, and [b] the year following created him a Peer of the kingdom of Ireland, viz. Baron of Ross, in com' Wexford, by letters patent dated Aug. 5, 1620. Lastly, ' By reason of his eminent services at home and abroad, both in the times of King ' James and King Charles I. as well in council as in the wars, ' and other foreign expeditions' (as the patent [c] expresses) was created a Baron of this realm, by the title of Lord Hervey, of Kidbrook, in the county of Kent, on Feb. 7, 1627-8, 3 Car. I. He first took to wife Mary, relict of Henry Wriothesley, Earl of Southampton, and daughter of Anthony Brown, Viscount Montacute, by whom he had no issue: they were married in 1597, as appears [d] from a letter to Sir Robert Sidney, dated from court, on Friday, May 20, that year. He 2dly

---

u Baker's chron. 2d edit. p. 544. b.   w Stow's ann. p. 775.   x Brown's hist. of Q. Eliz. p. 181.   y Cox's hist. of Ireland, p. 426.   z Ibid p. 431, 443, 446, 451.   a Pat. 17 Jac. I.   b Pat. 18 Jac. I.   c Pat. 3 Car. I. p. 6.   d Sidney's state papers, vol. 2. p. 53.

married,

married [e], on Feb. 5, 1607, at Cripplegate church, London, Cordelia, daughter and coheir of Brian Annefley, of Lee in Kent, Efq; by whom he had three fons, William, flain in the German wars; John, who died in Ireland; and Henry, who died young: alfo three daughters, Dorothy and Helen, who died unmarried; and Elizabeth, who became his fole daughter and heir, and was wedded to John Hervey, of Ickworth, Efq; hereafter mentioned. This Lord Hervey, departing this life in June, 1642 [f], was buried with great folemnity on July 8 following, in St. Edward's chapel in Weftminfter-abbey, and his titles became extinct.

I now return to John Hervey, of Ickworth, Efq; eldeft fon of William, father of Sir Nicholas, grandfather to the faid Lord Hervey. Which John took to wife, Elizabeth, daughter of Henry Pope, of Milden-hall, in com' Suff. Efq; and [g] departing this life on July 11, 1556, 3 and 4 Phil. and Mar. was fucceeded at Ickworth, by William his eldeft fon: but he had, befides the faid William, a numerous iffue, viz. [h] John Hervey, 2d fon; Nicholas, 3d fon; Clement and Thomas, 4th and 5th fons; Robert, 6th fon; Francis, 7th fon; Chriftopher, 8th fon; and John, 9th fon: alfo fix daughters, Jane; Elizabeth; Mary; Anne; Urfula, married [i] to Henry Vefey, of Ifelham, in Cambridgefhire, Efq; from whom, by intermarriages, the prefent Sir Thomas Wilfon, of Eaftbourne, in Suffex, defcended; and Bridget.

The faid William Hervey, Efq; eldeft fon, was born in [k] 1509, 1 Hen. VIII. and having taken to wife Elizabeth, daughter to John Poley, of Boxted, in com' Suffolk, Efq; departed [l] this life on Nov. 2, 1592, and was buried at Ickworth. He had three daughters; Urfula, who died young; Elizabeth, married to William Haward, of St. Edmundfbury, Efq; and Bridget, married to —— Collins, of the fame town; as alfo five fons, John Hervey, his fucceffor at Ickworth; Francis Hervey, who married Mary, daughter of Sir Thomas Nevil, of Holt, in Leicefterfhire; William, Ambrofe, and Thomas.

Which John Hervey, Efq; was born in the year 1555, and by his wife Frances, daughter and coheir of Edmund Bocking, of Bocking, in Effex, Efq; who died before him, on Feb. 22, 1620, had iffue two fons, William, and Robert; as alfo three daughters, Frances, who deceafed in 1619; Elizabeth, who alfo died unmarried on April 22, 1623; and Mary, efpoufed to Giles Allington, of Horfeheath, in Cambridgefhire,

[e] Ex regift. eccl. paroc. de Cripplegate.   [f] Ex regift. de coll. eccl. Weftminfter.   [g] Cole's efc. lib. 2. p. 118. MS. in bibl. Harley.   [h] Vifit. de com' Staff. præd.   [i] MS. g. 18. p. 5. in coll. arm.   [k] Ex fcript. penes Joh. com' Briftol.   [l] Ibid.

Hervey, Earl of Bristol. 351

Efq; and departed this life on Sept. 4, 1626. This John Hervey lived to the 75th year of his ᵐ age, deceasing in 1630, and was succeeded by William, his son and heir.

Which William Hervey, knighted at Whitehall, on April 30, 1608, married Susan, daughter of Sir Robert Jermyn, of Rushbrook, in com' Suff. Knt. (grandfather to Sir Henry Jermyn, Earl of St. Albans) on ⁿ Sunday, March 21,'1613-14, in St. Mary's church, St. Edmundsbury, on which day of the month and week he was born in the same town, in 1585. In 1618, the 16th of James I. he was in commission with the ᵒ Lord Chancellor, Edward Earl of Worcester, Lord-keeper of the Privy-seal, with other Lords and persons of note, to survey Lincoln's-inn-fields, and to cause such uniform and comely buildings to be erected, and such walks, partitions, and plots to be made, both for health and pleasure, as they should approve of. In the 3d ᵖ of Car. I. he was elected to parliament for St. Edmundsbury; but being in years, lived afterwards retired from public business, without concerning himself in the civil wars, and departed this life on Sept. 30, 1660. His first Lady dying ᑫ on Feb. 6, 1637, he married, secondly, Penelope, daughter of Thomas Darcy, Earl Rivers, relict first of Sir George Trenchard, of Wolverton, in Dorsetshire, and secondly, of Sir George Gage, of Firle, in Sussex, Bart. but had issue only by his first wife, viz.

His first child still-born at St. Edmundsbury, on April 17, 1644, and buried in the chancel of St. Mary's church in the same town.

2. Judith Hervey was born at his house in Southgate-street, in St. Edmundsbury, on April 20, 1615, married to James Reynolds, of Bumpsted, in Essex, Esq; and died on July 12, 1679.

3. John Hervey, who succeeded his father, of whom I shall further treat.

4. Anne Hervey was born at St. Edmundsbury, on April 9, 1618, and died on Dec. 12, 1619.

5. William Hervey was born at St. Edmundsbury, on Whitsunday, May 15, 1619, and died at Cambridge, on Sept. 23, 1642. He was fellow-collegian with Mr. Cowley, in that University, who bemoans his death in an excellent copy of verses ʳ, the most celebrated in all his works.

6. Mary Hervey was born at Ickworth, on May 22, 1620, married to Sir Edward Gage, of Hengrave, in com' Suff. Bart. and died on July 13, 1654.

m Ex script. penes Joh. com' Bristol.   n Ex autog. penes Joh. com' Bristol.
o Rymer's fœd. tom. 17. p. 119, 120.   p MS. de parl. penes, B. Willis, arm.
q Ex autog. præd.   r Bp. Spratt's life of Cowley.

I   7. Susan

7. Sufan Hervey was born at Ickworth, on July 14, 1621, and was fecond wife to Sir Thomas Hanmer, of Hanmer, in Flint, Knt. and Bart.

8. Kezia Hervey was born at St. Edmundſbury, on Nov. 11, 1621, married to Thomas Tyrrel, of Gipping, in com' Suff. Efq; and died on Nov. 22, 1659.

9. Catharine Hervey was born at St. Edmundſbury, on Jan. 24, 1623, and died on Jan. 16, 1625.

10. Thomas Hervey was born in Northgate-ſtreet, St. Edmundſbury, on May 25, 1625, and will be mentioned hereafter, being anceſtor to the preſent Earl of Briſtol.

11. Nicholas Hervey was born at St. Edmundſbury, on July 12, 1627, and died on March 22, 1629. And,

12. Henry Hervey was born at St. Edmundſbury, on June 18, 1631, and died on Sept. 8 following.

I now return to John Hervey, the eldeſt ſon of Sir William. He was born at Ickworth, his father's ſeat in Suffolk, on Sunday, Auguſt 18, 1616, and had all the advantages of education, which he improved by travelling, and polite converſation. Robert Sidney, ſecond Earl of Leiceſter, who was Ambaſſador in Denmark, and France, and Lord-lieutenant of Ireland, and one of the moſt learned Noblemen of the age, formed ſuch a judgment of Mr. Hervey's accompliſhments, that while he was Ambaſſador in France, he entertained him in his houſe as a companion, as appears from a letter of his Lordſhip's dated at Paris, on Dec. 22, 1636, to Sir John Coke, Secretary of State, of what had paſſed at his audience, telling him [s], ' he will receive it by Mr. Hervey, a Gentleman who
' hath beſtowed his company upon me, ever ſince I came out
' of England.' The friendſhip between him and the Earl of Leiceſter, was very remarkable, as the letters paſt between them ſhew. Mr. Hervey from London, on Jan. 12, 1652 [t], tells his Lordſhip, ' It was more than ſixteen years, that he
' had the honour to be his Lordſhip's, by all the beſt titles
' that any thing is poſſeſt, you having for every day in that
' time, given more than a valuable conſideration for me;
' and I having in every minute of thoſe days voluntarily re-
' ſigned myſelf to you, ſo that the whole power in me, and
' over me, has for thus long abſolutely remained in your
' Lordſhip, &c.'

The Earl of Leiceſter, from Penſhurſt, on Jan. 20, ſent the following complimental anſwer; which ſhewing how much he was eſteemed by him, as alſo his great worth and excellencies, in juſtice to his memory I inſert it.

s Sidney's ſtate papers, vol. 2, p. 680.   t Ibid.

SIR,

Hervey, Earl of Bristol.

SIR[t],

'Take heed what you give or acknowledge to have given me, for though I confefs it is juft to reftore, and that you are worthy of any thing that can be given you, yet if the gift be of yourfelf, I fhall never confent to the revocation of it, nor be perfuaded to reftore yourfelf to you again; for I fhall efteem my propriety in you more than the brevets or letters patents of Kings, or the donation of Conftantine; and you fhall be but a Vfu fructuary of yourfelf. Or if in the time of my poffeffing you, I imploy not my intereft fo far as your favour would admit me, it is for fear of increafing that debt, which already is grown too great for me to pay, or recompenfe in all my life, and can never be difcharged by heirs, executors, or affigns. You have no way to refcue or help yourfelf but by my incapacity; for how liberal foever the donator be, it is but an offer, and not a gift, unlefs the donatary be capable of receiving it, which I acknowledge I am not; and therefore againft my will you muft in a manner be free ftill. But though I feem to let you loofe becaufe I have not roome fit to receive you in, nor bands worthy to hold you with; for all my merit is not better than the line of a cobweb, yet I will do my beft to detain you; that is by an exchange of myfelf, for yourfelf, which is unequal I confefs, but I have no more, if I had I wou'd make the bargain better for you. And howfoever I may feem to gain another advantage by this exchange, becaufe I have told you I will not part with you on any terms; and you have fo little reafon to value me, that it is likely enough you would give me myfelf again for afking, and fo might remain mine, and I not yours: Yet I affure you that I mean no fuch matter; but I like my condition fo well, that I am refolved to be ever:

Yours, &c.

LEYCESTER.'

Having heartily concurred in the reftoration of Charles II. he was conftituted Treafurer of the Houfhold to Queen Catharine, his confort; and was in the peculiar efteem of his Majefty, and in the greateft intimacy with the moft ingenious, as well as greateft men in the kingdom. In parliament, he was

[t] State papers, ut antea, p. 681.

one of the leading members; and Bishop Burnet relates of him, 'That he was ᵘ one whom the King (Charles II.) loved 'personally, and yet, upon a great occasion, he voted against 'that which the King desired. So the King chid him severely 'for it. Next day another important question falling in, he 'voted as the King would have him. So the King took no-'tice of it at night, and said, you were not against me to-day. 'He answered, No, Sir, I was against my conscience to-day,' Which was so gravely delivered, it was much talked of, being about the time of the Popish plot. He was a particular favourer of men of letters; and the famous Mr. Cowley ʷ, by his recommendation, was taken into the service of his kinsman, Henry Earl of St. Albans, Lord Chamberlain of the Household to Charles II. and was his great patron. This Mr. Hervey married Elizabeth, daughter and sole heir of William Lord Hervey, of Kidbrook, before-mentioned, but dying without issue, on Jan. 18, 1679, his estate devolved on his only surviving brother,

Sir Thomas Hervey, who was knighted by Charles II. and elected for St. Edmundsbury to the three last parliaments called ˣ by that Prince, as also to that called by James II. and to all others, to the time of his death. He shewed himself, in all parts of life, one of the best of men, and was particularly remarkable for his piety, chastity, charity, and other Christian and moral virtues, whereby he was in the esteem of all that knew him; and having lived to the 70th year of his age, died on May 27, 1694, and was buried with his ancestors at Ickworth.

He married, in 1658, Isabella, daughter of Sir Humphry May, Vice-chamberlain of the Houshold to Charles I. which Lady died on June 5, 1686; and they had issue, William Hervey, eldest son, who was born on Oct. 31, 1661, and died on June 14, 1663; John Hervey, who was created Earl of Bristol; Thomas, who was born on Jan. 13, 1668, betaking himself to a military employment, served in Ireland under King William; and dying at St. Edmundsbury, on Dec. 29, 1695, was buried at Ickworth: Isabella Hervey, eldest daughter, born Aug. 23, 1659, was married to Gervase Elwes, son and heir of Sir Gervase Elwes, of Stoke, in com' Suff. Bart. 2. Elizabeth, born on Sept. 16, 1660, and died on Feb. 18, 1673: 3. Kezia, born on April 24, 1664, married to Aubrie Porter, of St. Edmundsbury, Esq;

ᵘ Hist. of his own times, p. 385.   ʷ Bp. Sprat's life of Cowley.   ˣ MS. de parl. præd.

Hervey, Earl of Bristol.

John Hervey, eldest surviving son, created Earl of Bristol, was born on Aug. 27, 1665, and married, in the life-time of his father, on Nov. 1, 1686, Isabella, daughter and sole heir of Sir Robert Carr, of Sleeford, in com' Linc. Bart. Chancellor of the duchy of Lancaster, and of the Privy-council to Charles II. On the death of Henry Goldwell, Esq; he was elected in his place for St. Edmundsbury, in that parliament which first met in the 2d of William and Mary, and was chosen for the same place in a new parliament, which met at Westminster on Nov. 22, 1695, and in all other parliaments called by King William; as also in that of the first year of Queen Anne. Having distinguished himself in the house of Commons, he was, for the nobleness of his extraction, the antiquity of his family, and his many eminent virtues, advanced to the dignity of a Baron of this realm, by the style and title of Lord Hervey, of Ickworth, in the county of Suffolk, by letters patent bearing date March 23, in the 2d year of the reign of Queen Anne. And having strenuously asserted the succession of King George I. to the crown of these realms, was, in consideration thereof, and his many eminent qualities, created Earl of Bristol, on Oct. 19, 1714, the first year of his reign.

His Lordship had two wives, Isabella, before-mentioned, by whom he had issue two daughters, and one son, Carr Lord Hervey, born on Sept. 17, 1691, who was educated at Clarehall, in Cambridge; and as soon as he came of age, he was elected to parliament for the borough of St. Edmundsbury, as also in the first parliament called by George I. and was of the Bedchamber to his late Majesty, when Prince of Wales. He died unmarried at the Bath, where he went for the recovery of his health, on Thursday, Nov. 14, 1723.

Isabella, eldest daughter, died unmarried in Nov. 1711; and Elizabeth, 2d daughter, of whom her mother deceased in childbed, on March 7, 1692-3, died an infant.

In 1695, his Lordship married Elizabeth, sole daughter and heir to Sir Thomas Felton, of Playford, in the county of Suffolk, Bart. Comptroller of the Houshold to her Majesty Queen Anne; and by her (who died on May 2, 1741, having been one of the Ladies of the Bedchamber to her late Majesty Queen Caroline, and had served her in the same station, when Princess of Wales) had issue eleven sons, and six daughters, viz.

1. John, Lord Hervey, of whom I shall hereafter treat.
2. Thomas, born on Jan. 20, 1698, who was a member in two parliaments for the borough of St. Edmundsbury, and

was one of the Equerries to her late Majesty. Also on May 23, 1738, constituted Superintendant of all his Majesty's gardens of every his royal palaces, &c. He married, in 1744, Anne, daughter and heir of Francis Coghlene, Esq; Counsellor of law, of the kingdom of Ireland, and hath issue by her one son, William-Thomas Hervey.

3. William, born on Dec. 25, 1699, Captain in his Majesty's navy; and on Nov. 27, 1729, married to Elizabeth, daughter of Thomas Ridge, of Portsmouth, in com' Southamp. Esq; which Lady died in child-bed, on July 13, 1730, of a daughter, named Elizabeth.

4. Henry, born on Jan. 5, 1700, who was a Cornet in the Lord Mark Ker's regiment of dragoons; and on March 2, 1730, was married to Catharine, sister and heir to Sir Thomas Aston, of Aston, in com' Cest. Bart. Whereupon, soon after he went into holy orders, was Doctor of Divinity, and took the name of Aston; as does his son, Henry Hervey-Aston, who is seated at Aston, and married.

5. Charles, born on April 5, 1703 (twin with a daughter, Henrietta, who died young) is D. D. and Prebendary of Ely. He married, on Dec. 31, 1743, Martha-Maria Howard, daughter of ——— Howard, of St. Edmundsbury, in Suffolk, Esq;

6. A son, still-born on July 6, 1704.

7. James-Porter, who was born on June 24, 1706, and died unmarried.

8. Humphrey, who was born on June 3, 1708, and died soon after.

9. Felton, who was born on July 3, 1710, and died on the 16th following.

10. Felton, born on Feb. 12, 1711-12, member in two parliaments for St. Edmundsbury, who was one of the Equerries to her late Majesty, and in December, 1737, was appointed Groom of the Bedchamber to his Royal Highness the Duke of Cumberland. He married Dorothy, daughter of Solomon Ashley, Esq; and relict of Charles Pitfield, Esq; and by her, who died on Nov. 8, 1761, had issue a son, Felton-Lionel Hervey (constituted, with him, Joint-Remembrancers of the court of Exchequer in England, on Feb. 17, 1759) and a daughter, ———, born on Aug. 23, 1756.

11. James, born on March 5, 1712-13, who died unmarried.

His first daughter, Lady Elizabeth, was married to the hon. Bussy Mansel, Esq; son and successor of Thomas Lord Mansel, fel, and died in the 29th year of her age, on Dec. 3, 1727, without issue.

2. Lady Anne: 3. Lady Barbara, died unmarried, on July 24, 1727: 4. Lady Louisa-Carolina-Isabella, who was married, on Sept. 23, 1731, to Sir Robert Smith, of Smith-street, in the city of Westminster, Bart. and, 5. Lady Henrietta, died in August, 1732.

His Lordship departed this life on Jan. 20, 1750-1, and was succeeded in his honours and estate, by his grandson and heir, George-William, now Earl of Bristol, son and heir of John Lord Hervey, his eldest son.

Which John Lord Hervey, born on Oct. 15, 1696, was, in consideration of his great merits, called up by writ to the house of Peers, as Lord Hervey, of Ickworth, and took his place on June 12, 1733, according to his father's creation. His Lordship was chosen one of the members for St. Edmundsbury, in the first parliament called by our late Sovereign; and on May 6, 1730, was appointed Vice-chamberlain of his Majesty's Houshold, and two days after, sworn of his most honourable Privy-council. On May 1, 1740, his Majesty having been pleased to deliver the custody of the Privy-seal to his Lordship, the oath of Keeper of the Privy-seal was administered to him at St. James's, and his Lordship took his place at the Council-board accordingly. On May 12 following, he was nominated one of the Lords Justices for the administration of the government, during his Majesty's absence.

His Lordship married, on Oct. 25, 1720, Mary, daughter of Brigadier-general Nicholas Le Pell, then one of the Maids of honour to Caroline, then Princess of Wales. He had issue by her four sons,

1. George-William, born on Aug. 31, 1721, now Earl of Bristol.

2. Augustus-John Hervey, born on May 19, 1724, chusing a maritime life, was, after passing through the subordinate stations, appointed Captain of one of his Majesty's ships of war, on Jan. 15, 1746-7: and on all occasions, whether under an Admiral, or as Commodore, exerted himself as a vigilant, skilful, and brave officer, as the naval annals of Europe can testify. At the general election in 1761, he was returned one of the members for St. Edmundsbury, to the 12th parliament of Great-Britain; but vacated his seat, in April, 1763, by accepting the Commission of Colonel of the marines in the Plymouth division, in the room of Admiral Sir Piercy Brett. In November following, he was nominated one of the Grooms

of his Majesty's Bedchamber, and was chosen soon after for Saltash in Cornwall, in the room of Mr. Cleveland,

3. Frederic, born on Aug. —, 1730, is one of the Chaplains in ordinary to his Majesty; and also one of the Principal Clerks of the Privy-seal.

4. William Hervey, born on May 13, 1732, was elected member for St. Edmundsbury, in the room of his brother, Augustus-John, in 1763.

John, Lord Hervey, had, by the same Lady, also four daughters; Lady Le Pell, married to Constantine Phips, Esq;

Lady Mary, wife of George Fitz-Gerald, Esq; Merchant in London, who died on May 1, 1762. The said Lady Mary, together with her sisters, Emily-Caroline-Nassau, and Caroline, had, by his Majesty's warrant, dated June 6, 1753, a grant to enjoy respectively the same place, pre-eminency and precedency, in all assemblies and meetings, as daughters of an Earl of Great-Britain; as if their father had lived to enjoy the dignity of an Earl of the kingdom.

His Lordship (who departed this life on Aug. 5, 1753, in the 47th year of his age) was well heard, both in the house of Commons, and in the house of Peers, where he distinguished himself on several debates, and was much esteemed for his learning and oratory.

He was succeeded, in the title of Lord Hervey, of Ickworth, by his eldest son, George-William, who also, on Jan. 20, 1750-1, succeeded his grandfather, as Earl of Bristol. His Lordship, by his grandmother, on the death of Henry, 10th Earl of Suffolk, of the surname of Howard, became, with Elizabeth, 2d wife of John, 1st Earl of Portsmouth, joint heirs to the said Earl of Suffolk's estate, and to the barony of Howard, of Walden: and at the funeral procession of Frederic Prince of Wales, on April 13, 1751, was one of the six supporters of the pall. His Lordship was nominated Ambassador-extraordinary to the court of Spain, on June 17, 1758: and while he resided there in that quality, shewed himself a Minister of great vigilance, capacity, and spirit; particularly with relation to the family-compact, which was concluded on August 15, and ratified on Sept. 8, 1761, between the branches of the Bourbon family, and occasioned his Lordship's departure from Madrid, without taking leave, on Dec. 17 following, and the reciprocal declarations of war between Great-Britain and Spain, on Jan. 4 and 18, 1762.

TITLES.]

Hervey, Earl of Bristol.

TITLES.] George-William Hervey, Earl of Bristol, and Baron Hervey, of Ickworth.

CREATIONS.] Baron Hervey of Ickworth, March 23 (1703) 2 Queen Anne; and Earl of Bristol, Oct. 19, 1 Geo. I.

ARMS.] Gules on a Bend, Argent, three Trefoils flipp'd, proper, or vert.

CREST.] On a Wreath, a Leopard paffant (holding in his dexter Paw, a Trefoil flipp'd, proper) bezantee, and gorged with a ducal Coronet, and chained, Or.

SUPPORTERS.] Two Leopards, fable, bezantee, with ducal Collars, and Chains, Or.

MOTTO.] JE N'OUBLIERAY JAMAIS.

CHIEF-SEAT.] At Ickworth, in Suffolk, 2 miles from St. Edmundfbury, and 75 from London.

CARTERET, *Earl Granville.*

THE surname of this noble family has been variously written in authentic records, as Carteray, Charteray, Carteres, Cartred, Katereck, Caterek, Kerteret, Quarteret, and Carteret; and yet the several persons, so named, appear to be of the same race; it being customary, in those illiterate times, for names to vary, according to the apprehensions of the writers, as is well known to all our antiquaries.

In the annals of Normandy, as also in an old history, written by Lewis de Couis, entitled, Histoire des Croissades; and in the charters of the cathedral of Coutance, and of the abbeys of Fontenelle and Bec, great and honourable mention is made of the Lords of the house of Carteret, of whom the chief, A. D. 1002, took on him sovereign authority in the barony of Carteret. This is evident, from a charter found among the archives of the said church of Coutance, wherein Sir William de Carteret is mentioned, as Co-Lord with the King of France, of the barony of Carteret, in Normandy.

It is also evident that Guy, Lord of Carteret, was living A. D. 1000, and had the name of L'Oiselaer, from being an extraordinary markfman. He was father of Godfrey, who, on his return from a pilgrimage, founded the abbey of Fontenelles, where, at that time, was but a meadow.

This Godfrey had four sons, of whom [a] Aufrey, and Mauger de Cartérays (as the name was then wrote) accompanied William Duke of Normandy, in his victorious expedition into England, A. D. 1066.

In the roll of Battle-abbey, [b] that contains a list of those of the greatest eminency, who came in with the Conqueror, the name is wrote Cateray; and the said Aufrey had issue Reginald, his son and heir.

Du Moulin [c] has transmitted to us the names, and arms, of those Lords of Normandy, and other provinces in France, who were at the conquest of Jerusalem, under Robert Courtheufe, Duke of Normandy, and Godfrey de Bouillon, Duke of Lorrain; and among them Monsieur Reginald de Charteres is said to bear on his banner, Gules, un Fesse Fusilee, Argent, and a Label, Azure. Which label shews he was eldest son, and

[a] Gab. du Moulin's gen. hist. of Normandy, p. 184. [b] Hist. Normanorum, p. 1124. [c] Gen. hist. of Normandy, p. 12.

probably

probably his father living at the time of that expedition [d], which was concluded on in 1096, the 9th year of King William Rufus. Duke Robert, with his followers, behaved with such conduct and courage againſt the infidels, that when the Chriſtians had taken Jeruſalem, [e] it was, by general conſent, offered him to be King of it. But having juſt before heard of his brother William's death, he refuſed it, haſtening home to aſſume his kingdom of England; and arriving in Normandy, was received with general applauſe by his ſubjects there, after being from them three years. How unfortunate he was in all his actions afterwards, is fully related by our hiſtorians; and it may be preſumed, that this Sir Reginald de Charteres (or Carteret) had ſome ſhare in his adventures.

Philip, [f] ſon and heir of the ſaid Sir Reginald, was Lord of Carteret in Normandy, and of St. Owen in the iſle of Jerſey. He had alſo poſſeſſions in Guernſey, and founded the church of Tourteval in that iſland. The time, and occaſion, of that foundation, is preſerved in the regiſters of the ſaid church, whereof the right honourable Sir George Carteret, great-grandfather of John, late Lord Carteret, and Earl Granville, obtained the following certificate [g]:

' Wee underſigned, the Bailly and Deane of the iſland of
' Garnezey, Doe certify unto all whom it may concerne,
' that according to the regiſters which wee have ſeene and
' examined, relating to the building of the churches in the
' ſaid iſland. The honorable Philip de Carteret (as he is there
' ſtyled) of the antient and noble family of the Carterets of the
' iſland of Jerſey. In the yeare of our Lord one thouſand one
' hundred twenty and nine, did build the parochial church of
' the pariſh of Tortevall in the ſaid iſland of Garnezey, at his
' own coſt and charges. Beeing the accompliſhment of a vow
' he had made, when in danger of ſhipwracke. That in
' caſe it was Gods pleaſure to deliver him out of the danger
' he was then in, he would build a church, where he ſhould
' with ſafety land.

' In witneſſe whereof wee have ſet our hands and ſeales to
' this preſent writing, this ſixteenth day of Aprill, in the yeare
' one thouſand ſix hundred ſixtye and nine.

' W. Andros Bailly, Pe. Sauſmares, Decan.

---

[d] Hiſt. of England, vol. 1. p. 116. [e] Ibid. p. 119. [f] Seager's Baron. MS. in hac famil. & al. MS. & lib. not. l. 14. in coll. arm. [g] Ex ſtem. hujus famil. per Hen. St. Georgii Richmond Fecial, in lib, not. l. 14. in coll. arm. eniraia.

Carteret, Earl Granville.

The seal of the Bailly is, a Saltiere voided, on a Chief three Mullets; a Crescent difference: and the Dean's is, on a Cheveron, between three Leopards Faces, as many Castles, impaling three Heads of Arrows.

To the said Sir Philip succeeded [h] Reginald, his son and heir, styled Baron Carteret in Normandy, in 1156, the 3d of Hen. II. He had issue [i] two sons, Reginald, and Richard.

Which Reginald de Cartray (as the name is wrote in the reign of King John) was intrusted with the defence of the island of Gereseye. And King John, at Montfort, on July 24, 1213, the 5th of his reign, sent, by Peter de Praers, [k] his commands to him, to take care that the Lords of the Fees, and others, in the islands of Gerseye and Gernesey, should demand no more of their men, than what was reasonable for the defence of the islands from foreign invaders.

The said King, in the 9th of his reign, from Clarendon, on Dec. 27, signifies [l] to Richard de Chartray, that he sends unto him his nephew Philip de Chartray, as an hostage for his brother Reginald de Chartray; but on what account, the record don't specify.

The said Philip de Chartray [m] succeeded his father Reginald, who lost his barony and lands in Normandy, [n] for his adherence to the crown of England, when that duchy was delivered up to the French, in 1204, the 6th of King John.

Which Philip, [o] being with Hen. III. in his expedition into Britany, in the 15th year of his reign, merited so greatly, that the next year, he, with Amery de St. Amand, [p] were constituted Governors of the islands of Jersey, Guernsey, Alderney, and Sarque, by patent dated at Reading, on Oct. 25, 1232, 16 Hen. III. wherein his name is wrote Philippo de Cartred. In 19 Hen. III. he had two licences to go to the French King, to try if he could regain his lands in Normandy, [q] the one dated on May 30, and the other on June 6, which being remarkable, I shall insert them as copied literatim from the originals in the Tower; as it also verifies the assertion, that names vary according to the apprehension of the writers of the records, being so differently wrote in seven days.

Rex licentiam dedit Philippo de Charteray, quod accedat ad Regem Francie, pro terra sua quam dicit esse jus suum in Normannia, perquirenda si posset. Ita quod postquam terram illam recuperaverit, det illam duabus filiabus suis quas habet ad illas

---

[h] Ex stemmate præd.   [i] Rot. clauf. 9 Joh. m. 7.   [k] Pat. 5 Joh. m. 8.
[l] Rot. clauf. 9 Joh. m. 7.   [m] Ex stem. ut antea.   [n] Cambden's Britannia enlarged by Bp. Gibson, p. 1519, 1520.   [o] Fall's account of Jersey, p. 94.
[p] Pat. 16 Hen. III. m. 1.   [q] Pat. 19 Hen. III. m. 8.

mari-

maritandas, & postea revertatur ad insulas Regis ibidem moraturus sicut antea moratus est. In cujus, &c. teste Rege apud Merewell, xxx° die Maii.

Rex omnibus ad quos presentes littere pervenerint, Salutem. Sciatis quod concessimus & licentiam dedimus Philippo de Cartred, quod accedat ad regem Francie ad impetrandum si potuisset, quod idem Rex reddat ei terras suas in Normannia in quibus idem Philippus. dicet se jus habere. Ita quod postquam recuperaverit, det eas filiabus suis quas habet, & postea revertetur ad insulas regni nostri. In cujus Rei Testimonium, &c. Teste Rege apud Westmonasterium VI° die Junii.

The particulars of his negociation are not on record, but our historians agree, that he rather chose to quit his patrimony in Normandy, than renounce his allegiance to the King of England, or become a subject to the French Monarch.

In 1252, 36 Hen. III. this Philip de Carteret, [r] and Jordan de la Hodge, had the King's command to repair personally to survey the castles in the islands of Gereseye and Guernseye, and to take an account of what condition the arms were in, when Drew de Barentyn, bailiff of the said islands, was discharged from that office ; and in what condition Richard de Grey received them, and to certify the same under their hands and seals. Dated at Westminster, on June 9.

When he died, I don't find ; but in 2 Edw. I. our records mention Philip de Karteret, and John de Karteret. And it is evident, from several authorities, that Philip de Karteret was the eldest son and heir of the last Philip ; and it may be presumed, that John de Karteret was his brother.

On an extent of all belonging to the King in the island of Jersey, in November, 2 Edw. I. Fhilip de Karteret, and John de Karteret, were of the [s] great jury of the said island, who said, that Wynceley's fee owes a full relief to St. Owen's fee ; and that the King ought to have the custody of the Lord, and the heirs, and the rents of such persons, as shall be under age at the death of their fathers.

The said Philip had to wife [t] Margaret, niece to Philip Daubeney, Bailiff of the islands of Jersey, Guernsey, &c. an officer of great dignity there, [u] being the head of justice in civil affairs, holding immediately by patent from the King (whom he represents in court) and his seat is raised above that of the Governor. By which Margaret he had issue Reginald de Carteret, his son and heir ; but before I proceed to treat of the said Reginald, I shall make some mention of John de Carteret, brother of Philip.

---

[r] Rot. clauf. 36 Hen III. m. 14. [s] Esc. 2 Edw. I. No. 53. [t] Inquis. in insul. de Jersey, ann. 2 Edw. I. in tur. Lond. [u] Acc. of Jersey, p. 102.

Which John, in 32 Edw. I. [x] was one of the three specially assigned by the King, to enquire into a certain controversy, about the manour of St. Clement, in the isle of Jersey; which being very remarkable, and brought before the King and parliament, I shall give an extract of the record, as it shews the custom of those times.

Pleas before Henry de Gildeford, and his associates, Justices itinerant in the island of Jersey, Monday after the feast of St. Peter ad Vincula, in the 32d year of King Edward the first [y].

The King by his writ, directed to Henry de Gildeford, commands him to certify immediately under his seal, how it came to pass, that he, together with the other Justices his associates, appointed to hold Common-pleas in the island of Jersey, took into the King's hands the manour of St. Clement in that island, belonging to the Abbot of Mount St. Michael. In pursuance whereof, the said Henry de Gildeford, transmitted the record and proceedings, as follows:

The King, by his Attorney Geffrey de Memgrant, sued the Abbot of Mount St. Michael, and his convent, for the manour of St. Clement, with the lands and tenements to the same belonging, of which the King's grandfather was seized in fee, who gave it to Peter de Peverell for his life. After whose decease, the same Abbot's predecessors took possession thereof, and held the same. The said Abbot and convent, by their substitute, say, that they and their predecessors, time out of mind, viz. from the days of Richard Duke of Normandy, ancestor to William the Conqueror, held the said manour, without disturbance. But they give not this as an answer to the Justices, who are not impowered by their commission, to ask, sue, or call, for what belongs to other persons; neither in their commissions, are any such clauses or powers contained. The aforesaid Geffrey, who sues for the King, says, that the Justices, by their commission in the seat of justice, represent the King's person, and have power to ask, sue for, and call, for what belongs to the King or his ancestors, in what manner soever possessed, or injuriously with-held. Furthermore he says, that King John, grandfather of our Lord the King, being in possession thereof, gave it to Peter de Peverill for his life, as before is said. Wherefore he demands, that the aforesaid Abbot and convent reply to the action of the King, either by assenting or dissenting; which, if they deny, he is ready to prove true, as before is said, and to abide by what the King's Jury, and the court, shall advise, &c. And the aforesaid Abbot and convent said peremptorily, that they will not answer to the King's Judges here, as to the ma-

---

[x] Esc. lib. MS. Pergamen in archiev. tur. Lond.   [y] MS. Ibid.

nour, because they have no power, by their commission, to demand the aforesaid manour of them, in the manner they do, nor to oblige them to reply on that account; but were ready, with submission to the King, extrajudicially, evidently to pursue their right. Whereupon the aforesaid Geffery, who sued for the King, demanded judgment against the aforesaid Abbot and convent, without further defending. Wherefore, upon conference before the King's Jury of Knights, and others, free tenants, they were of opinion, that the Judges had power, according to the custom of the nation, to demand and sue for things in possession, and them to hold: that the King ought to recover the said manour from the Abbot and convent aforesaid, because they contradicted not the seisin of King John, grandfather of our Lord the King, as of fee and right; or did they answer ought to the King's action, or shewed why the said manour should belong to them. Therefore the Sheriff was commanded to take the said manour into the King's hands, the same safely to keep, and to account for the issues thereof, &c. Afterwards the aforesaid manour was valued at eighty-four pounds two shillings, Turon money, and delivered to Philip le Evesque, Laurence de Sevenock, and William Longiner; to answer to the King the value thereof. And now, before the parliament, the said Abbot and convent sued for remedy, &c. To which was answered by the King, that if the said Abbot and convent had right therein, or can shew any deeds or writings of the aforesaid church of St. Michael, to declare the right of the church, they might sue for the King's favour therein, as they shall see opportunity. Afterwards, at the King's parliament at Westminster, in the huitains of the blessed Mary, the year aforesaid, the said Abbot came and demanded Oier, to shew the right of his church aforesaid. Upon which the said Abbot alledged, that the said manour anciently was called the land of Peter the Monk, and the which land, with the appurtenances, Richard, Duke and Prince of Normandy, grandfather to the late Conqueror, William King of England, &c. gave to the place (situate in St. Michael's Mount) called the Tomb, and to the brethren there dwelling, in the isle of Jersey, and produced an old deed without a seal, under the name of the aforesaid Duke, which witnesseth it: also produced a certain deed of our Lord the King of England, Hen. II. by which the same King granted and confirmed, to the Abbot and Monks of Mount St. Michael, all the grants made to them by his ancestors, scilicet Earl Richard the 2d, and the Countess Gunnora his mother, Earl Robert son of the said Richard, and William King of England, brother of the said Robert, and King Henry his son, in lands and churches, tenths and rents, &c. but more

especially

especially in all of which they were seized at that time, as the deeds of grant testify: and by a certain writing under the name of one Philip de Albeyne, late Bailiff of our Lord the King in the islands, for the assises there held in full assise, witnesseth, that he rendered to the aforesaid abbey and convent, surely and quietly, all their estate in Jersey, both by sea and land: and he says, that he and all his predecessors, late Abbots of the aforesaid place, were always seized of the manour aforesaid, with the appurtenances, from the days of the grant. So that the said manour was never after in the hands of King John, nor did that King give the manour aforesaid to any one. And this he is ready to prove by his country, or otherwise, as the court of our Lord shall allow, &c. And afterwards, upon rehearsing the Abbot's reasons aforesaid, before Walter Bishop of Litchfield and Coventry, Henry Earl of Lincoln, Roger le Brabazon, with other justiciaries, and others the King's faithful subjects in council, &c. it seemed to the council, &c. That enquiry should be made on the aforesaid articles, which the aforesaid Abbot pretends to prove, viz. If the aforesaid manour be that same land contained in the aforesaid deed, as afore declared: and if the aforesaid manour was in the seisin of King John aforesaid: and how and which way the said manour came to the said King: and if the said King gave to Peter le Peverill aforesaid the same manour, and the manner of that gift, &c. and if the aforesaid Abbot, and his predecessors, were continually seized of the same, from the time of the grant of the aforesaid Duke of Normandy, &c. as the Abbot affirms. And the Abbot in like manner demands, that enquiry be made, &c. as aforesaid.

Therefore King Edward I. commands the Governor of the island, or his Lieutenant, to cause to come before John de Caterek (as the name was then wrote) Nicholas de Chayne, and John Dutton, assigned to enquire of the aforesaid articles, at such time and place, which they shall make known, as well such, and so many Knights, and good and lawful men of the leet aforesaid, as customary, and who have no affinity to the Abbot: by which the truth of the matter, touching the premises, may be known and enquired into: and that the aforesaid John, Nicholas, and John, on the inquisition there to be made, shall make known to our Lord the King, under their seals, &c. such inquisition.

I now return to Reginald de Carteret, son and heir of Philip. Which Reginald in 2 Edw. I. was possessed of lands in right of his mother Margaret, niece to Philip Daubeney, and his heir (as it should seem by the inquisition then taken) but the original record being torn, and not legible in one part, it cannot so evidently be made to appear, that she was heir to the said Philip. The inquisition sets forth, *z* that all the juries in the 12 parishes in the island of Jersey, viz. of Gronvil, Holy Trinity, St. John, St. Ellery, St. Laurence, St. Mary, St. Clement, St. Martin, St. Saviour, St. Broelard, St. Owen, and St. Peter, certify, That Reginald de Carteret holds lands worth yearly twenty pounds, in the parishes of St. Owen, and St. Peter, late [Here the record is torn, and not legible] Philip Daubeney then Bailiff of the islands, gave to Philip de Carteret, father of the said Reginald, and Margery his niece, mother of the same Reginald. And being called upon to give an account of his right to the said lands, the said Reginald answered, That he and his father held the said lands quietly for forty years, and upwards, by grant from the King of England. But the same lands being taken into the King's hands, a day was assigned in the quindenes of the Purification of the blessed Virgin, to produce the deed of grant; and further, to shew an account of the said lands whilst in their possession, and by what power he put up an Esperkeria in Port-Stoke, and why he took, as his right, a chase, and warren for coneys, in the parish of St. Owen, &c. and why he forced his tenants in his manour of Aftal, held of the King, to do him homage: and why he caused Hamelin de Huga, to be cited before the Bishop of Coutance.

Also the jury of the parish of St. Owen *a* certify, on their oaths, that Reginald de Carteret holds certain lands of our Lord the King, at the will of the Bailiff, paying yearly seven shillings. They also say, that the King receives yearly of Wyncele's fee ten shillings, by the hands of John de Carteret.

The before-mentioned Reginald de Carteret was very serviceable to Edw. I. in his wars, both by sea and land.

In 1296, 25 Edw. I. the King sent his commands *b* to Henry de Cobham, Governor of the isles of Jersey and Guernsey, That in consideration of the good services, which his beloved and faithful Reginald de Carteret had performed in the isle of Jersey, he had granted him seven casks of wine which he took from the enemy: therefore, that he should not demand the sum of thirty-five pounds sterling, due from the said Reginald for those wines, but should pay, without delay, the arrears of wages due to him, whilst he was in the King's service, in the castle of the said isle of Jersey. Dated at St. Edmundsbury, Nov. 23.

In 1304, 32 Edw. I. this *c* Reginald de Carteret, Henry de Guldeford, and John de Mytton, were Justices itinerant; and

---

z Inquisit. in insul. de Gereseye, ann. 2 Edw. I. cor. Joh. Wyg, & Radul de Broughton in tur. Lond.   a Ibid.   b Claus. 25 Edw. I. m. 26.   c Placita assis. apud Guerner, 32 Edw. I.

affizes were held before them, the Monday after the feaſt of the apoſtles Peter and Paul, in the iſland of Guernſey. Our hiſtorians have made no particular mention of his ſervices, tho', without doubt, they were remarkable. For King Edward, in 1306, the 35th year of his reign [d], grants, to his beloved and faithful Reginald de Carteret, thoſe lands and tenements forfeited in the iſland of Jerſey, by Thomas Paignell, and which he held by the death of Robert de Melaces, and the which Otes de Grandiſon holds by grant of the King for life; to have and to hold to the ſaid Reginald, for his life freely, and to his heirs for ever, after his deceaſe, paying yearly ſixty pounds ſmall Turnois, and a pound of cummin-feed. Witneſs the King at Lavertoſt, 4 December. Per petitionem retornatam de conſilio.

This Sir Reginald de Carteret died before the 2d year of Edw. II. and left iſſue three ſons, John, Philip, and Jeffery, as the records and inquiſitions ſhew; though, in ſeveral pedigrees, Philip is made to be the eldeſt ſon, which is not likely, as the other is named firſt in the records.

In 2 Edw. II. the King recites [e], That, upon complaint againſt the ſubſtitutes of Otes de Grandiſon, that the inhabitants of the iſlands of Jerſey and Guernſey had ſuffered great injuries and damages by them, as by their petition appears: and inclining to redreſs their grievances, he had aſſigned Juſtices to enquire into them, &c. Whereupon John de Carteret, Philip de Carteret, and Robert de Carteret, complained againſt the Juſtices levying great fines of themſelves, without a jury, which was not cuſtomary; and that ſeveral other matters ought to be redreſſed; and particularly [f], John de Carteret and Philip de Carteret complain, That they and their anceſtors, time out of mind, had their eſperqueries for fiſh, of which they were deprived; therefore they deſire, that a jury of twelve men, of every pariſh, may be appointed to enquire into their right, that they may have juſtice done them, and have liberty of buying of other perſons, beſides thoſe that belonged to the King. To which anſwer was made, That if they proved their aſſertion, they ſhould have the King's allowance thereof. And Philip de Carteret came before the King's Juſtices at Weſtminſter, with others of the ſaid iſlands, who ſet forth their ſeveral injuries; and the before-mentioned Philip particularly complained of the badneſs of the Turon money. Whereunto anſwer was given, That the money current in the iſles was the ſame in value as it was anciently, and before the laſt war.

[d] Pat. 35 Edw. I. m. 45.   [e] Plac. quer. in inſul. Guerner & Jerſey coram Joh. de Freſingfeld, &c. ann. 2 Edw. II. finiente.   [f] Ibid.

Carteret, Earl Granville.

Likewise in 1309, 2 Edw. II. [g] on the Monday before the feast of St. Barnaby, Philip de Carteret, and Jeffery his brother, having been summoned to shew by what title they claimed wreck of sea in Pagnell's fee; they answered, That King Edward the first gave the premises to Reginald their father, which Robert de Melesches held for life, and were forfeited by Thomas Pagnell, a Norman, &c.

Sir John de Carteret (the eldest son of Reginald) had to wife, Lucia de Winchelais. And in 1320, 13 Edw. II. by indenture in French, bearing date on Friday after the Annunciation of the blessed Virgin, wherein he is wrote Sire Jean de Quarteret, Chevalier, he gives and grants to Sir Nicholas de Cheyne, his heirs and assigns, all his rents, tenements, and possessions, in the island of Guernsey, paying to the said Sir John, for his life, eighty pounds Turnois, with two robes or gowns yearly for himself and Lucy de Winchelais his wife.

In 14 Edw. II. [h] the petition of the inhabitants of Guernsey, Jersey, Serk, and Aurney, to the parliament, setting forth, That whereas the King had appointed John de Carteret and William Bourne, his Justices, to enquire into divers trespasses and misdemeanors done by the servants of Otto de Grandison, Governor of the said isles, they the said Justices had proceeded therein by virtue of the King's commission, till the same was superseded, to the great detriment of the said isles, &c. it was answered, Let a writ be issued out to repeal the supersedeas, and that the Justices proceed according to their commission. This Sir John de Carteret died [i] without issue, and Philip de Carteret, his brother, was his heir.

Which Philip died in or before 1328, the 2d of Edw. III. for in that year the King signified to the Governor of the islands of Jersey and Guernsey [k], That whereas Reginald, son and heir of Philip de Carteret, deceased, cannot leave the island of Jersey to go into England, personally to do homage to the King, for the lands and tenements there belonging to his late father, by reason of his being Governor of the King's castle there, and for certain other causes; therefore the King, of his special favour, respites his homage for a year, provided he performs the accustomed services. Dated at Woodstock, the 8th day of June.

The year after, it appears that he was at Amiens in France [l], and did homage to the King there; who thereupon, from Amiens, on June 8, 3 Edw. III. sent to John de Roche, Gover-

---

[g] Placita in insul. de Guerner, anno 2 Edw. II. coram Joh. de Frefingfeld, &c. [h] Plac. parl. apud Westm. 14 Edw. II. [i] Ex stemmate ut antea. [k] Clauf. 2 Edw. III. m. 24. dorso. [l] Rot. fin. 3 Edw. III. m. 4.

nor of the islands of Jernsey and Geresey, that he had taken the homage of Reginald de Carteret, son and heir of Philip de Carteret, deceased, of all the lands and tenements which the said Philip, his father, held of the King in chief, the day that he died: therefore he commands him to accept security from the said Reginald, for his relief for the said lands of his father, which being in the King's hands by his death, he further requires him to give him full seisin of them.

In 4 Edw. III. on an inquisition concerning the rents of the King, in the isle of Jersey [m], the jury found, that Reginald de Carteret held, in the parish of St. Owen, the manour of St. Owen, with the appurtenances, by homage, suit of court and relief. But in lieu thereof, when the King's service required, in time of war, or for defence of the castle of Gourney, he should serve, at his own expence, forty days, with horse and arms, &c.

In 5 Edw. III. he was [n] summoned to answer to a plea of Quo Warranto, on Wednesday after the feast of St. James the apostle, why he claimed to have free warren in his lordship and lands in the parish of St. Owen, and his dwelling there, and wreck of sea upon all his lands in that parish, & esperkeriam de piscibus per homines suos captis in aquis Domini Regis, &c. And the said Reginald came and said, That he is Lord of the manour of St. Owen, and that he and all his ancestors, time out of mind, were seized of the said manour, and of the demesne lands there, and had free warren, &c. therein, without interruption.

In 12 Edw. III. the French, under their Admiral Bahuchet, having taken the island and castle of Guernsey, and continuing in the possession thereof three years [o], they several times invaded the island of Jersey, burning and destroying the houses, corn, &c. and often attacked the castle of Mont-Orgueil, called Gowry, which was valiantly defended by Dru de Barentin, the Governor, and Sir Reginald de Carteret, till, in one of the attacks, the Governor being slain, Sir Reginald was chosen to succeed him by the inhabitants of the island, and performed many great exploits against the enemy.

In 14 Edw. III. the French, renewing their attacks, made stronger efforts in order to take Mont-Orgueil-castle, which being valiantly defended [p], John Barentin, the Lieutenant-governor, and others of the garrison and commonalty of the

---

m Inquis. 4 Edw. III. cor. Rob. Nortonne, &c. in insul. de Jersey.   n Plac. apud longam villam in insul. Guerner, cor. Rob. de Scardeburgh, &c. anno 5 Edw. III.   o Ex stem. huj. famil. ut antea, in lib. not. l. 14. in col. stem. intrato.   p Ex stemmate præd, and Fall's account of the island of Jersey, p. 61, 62.

Carteret, Earl Granville.

said island, were slain. Whereupon, by the council and consent of the jurors, and others of the commonalty, Sir Reginald Carteret had again the chief command; and on that occasion he was allowed twelve-pence per day for himself; and for twelve men at arms each six-pence per day; twelve other armed men each four-pence per day; fifteen archers each at three-pence per day; and for eighty-seven archers and servants each at two-pence per day.

These attack and insults of the French alarmed the parliament in England, and drew a representation from it to the King [q], To keep the sea, and to purvey for the navy, and to defend the isles of Jersey and Guernsey; which the King promised. And the same year (14 Edw. III.) by advice of his council [r], sent a letter to his beloved and faithful the Bailiff and Jurats, and all others of the island of Jersey, commending their steady loyalty, and endeavours for their preservation, so eminently proved; acknowledging, that he had always found, the greater they were pressed upon, the more warm were their affections, in opposition to his adversaries, and in defence of his rights. It was therefore consonant to his honour, to respect every particular person for such stedfastness, and to reward their services, &c.

The French being still masters of the island of Guernsey; the deliverance of the inhabitants from their servitude was too great an enterprize, for those of Jersey to undertake on their own strength alone. But hearing [s] of a fleet ready to sail from England, with reinforcements the King had sent, and of orders given to the commanders, Reynold de Cobham and Jeffery de Harcourt, to attempt, in their way, the recovery of the said island; the inhabitants of Jersey, under their leaders (whereof it is not to be doubted Sir Reginald de Carteret was the chief) went out and joined the fleet, and chiefly, by their valour, both the island and the castle were retaken; but many of their leaders honourably lost their lives on that occasion, of whom my author mentions (from an old manuscript history of the island) the Sieurs de Winchelais, de Matravers, de Huyfes, de Garis, de la Hougne, Lempriere, and others. It is certain, that this Sir Reginald de Carteret was the Sieur de Winchelais, as Lord of that fee; and I find no further mention of him after. He left issue three sons, as is evident from our records; of which I take Philip to be the eldest, and that he died without issue [t]; for Reginald de Carteret, his second son, was at length heir to

---

[q] Sir Rob. Cotton's abridgm. of the records in the Tower, 14 Edw. III. p. 29.
[r] Rymer's fœdera, tom. 5. p. 186. [s] Fall's account of Jersey, p. 63, 64.
[t] Ex stem. ut antea.

the whole eſtate. Philip and William de Carteret are mentioned in our records, in 23 Edw. III. and were probably brothers to the ſaid Reginald. The ſaid William de Carteret died in March that year [u]; and by inquiſition taken in Jerſey, on July 20, 1349, before John Mautravers, Governor of the iſles, the jury found, That he held of the priory of St. Martin, in the iſland of Guernſey, a manour or fee of the Abbeſs of Caln; and alſo held lands and tenements in fee of the King, paying the uſual fee-farm rent to the King's Provoſt there; and that the ſame was worth, at his death, yearly thirty pounds; that he alſo held lands and tenements in the pariſh of St. Mary, in the ſaid iſle, paying, as an acknowledgment, to the King's Provoſt yearly, five ſhillings and ſix-pence, Turnois money; and that he died the firſt week in March laſt; and that Philip de Carteret was his brother and heir, who was of the age of 35 years, or thereabouts; whereby it is probable he was the eldeſt, and died without iſſue; for from Reginald de Carteret, his brother, the preſent Earl Granville is deſcended. The firſt mention of him, that I find, is in 1353, 27 Edw. III. on a complaint of Julian de Winchelais, the Tueſday after St. Simon and Jude [w]: for that the ſaid Reginald de Carteret had ſeized in the pariſh of St. Saviour, the court and cuſtom of the ſaid Julian, which he held in the fee of Meleſches [x]. To which Reginald replied, That he had good cauſe for the ſame; William de Winchelais, his uncle, and the ſaid Julian, having held two courts at Longville, in the ſaid fee of Meleſches; but that anciently there was but one court; and that the holding the ſaid courts, was to the prejudice of him the ſaid Reginald. Whereunto Julian anſwered, That ſhe and others had, for 40 years laſt paſt, and more, held three or four aſſizes without diſturbance. On which, after ſeveral arguments in court, judgment was given, That the ſaid Reginald ſhould allow the ſaid Julian the court and cuſtom aforeſaid.

To this is appendant a ſeal of green wax, viz. in a Shield, three Lions paſſant gardant, circumſcribed S. BAILIVE. INSULE. DE JERSEY. On the reverſe, within a ſmall Shield, a Tree.

Our hiſtories, about this time, are full of the triumphs and ſucceſſes of Edw. III. ſo that the French were in no condition to give any diſturbance to the iſland of Jerſey, &c. But towards the latter end of that King's reign, the French again greatly retrieved their affairs: Bertrand de Gueſclin, Conſtable of France, famous for his many victories over the Engliſh,

---

[u] 23 Edw. III. p. 2. n. 150.   [w] Ex ſtemmate prediĉt.   [x] Ex eodem ſtem.

passed suddenly from Bretagne into Jersey, with an army of 10,000 men, and therein the Duke of Bourbon, and the flower of the French chivalry. He had observed, says the author of his life [z], that the situation of Jersey and Guernsey very much favoured the descents of the English into Bretagne, where the war had spread, and raged as hot as in France, and where he himself then was warring against the English; for that by laying up their stores and provisions in those islands so near at hand, they were easily and readily supplied from thence when they wanted. D'Argentrè, in like manner, tells us, That Du Guesclin [a] eyed the islands, as la retraite seure des Anglois; i. e. the sure retreat of the English.

It does not appear, that the inhabitants offered to dispute his entrance into the island. They put all their hopes in the strength of the castle, and their resolution to defend it.

This Reginald de Carteret had the chief command, and with him seven of his sons, who, by their prudence and valour, encouraged the rest to hold out to the last extremity. Nothing was omitted on the part of the assailants, in carrying on the siege; some of the out-walls were thrown down by sap, which however did not affect the main body of the place. At last it came to this composition, That if not succoured before Michaelmas day next ensuing, they would surrender, and the Constable should break up his camp and depart. Such compositions were then frequent: and the Constable being returned into Bretagne, soon after heard, that the English fleet had appeared at sea, coming to relieve the castle, which accordingly was performed.

For this great service, in preserving the island of Jersey from falling into the hands of the French, which was solely attributed to the conduct and courage of the said [b] Reginald de Carteret, and his sons, he and they were all knighted in one day; as is observed in an ancient manuscript of this family, wrote in the reign of Queen Elizabeth; as also by Ashmole, and other authorities.

His eldest son Sir Reginald de Carteret, Lord of St. Owen, and Longville, was constituted [c] Bailiff of the island of Jersey, an officer of great dignity, before described. He was famed for his wisdom, and all manly virtues; and died in 1381, the 5th of Rich. II. leaving Philip de Carteret, his son and heir, under age, in ward to the King, [d] who in that year granted the custody of him to Roger de Walden, parson of the church

[z] Lib. 6. sect. 6. p. 242, 243.   [a] Fall's account of Jersey, p. 71.   [b] Ex stem. ut antea, & ex collect. Eli. Ashmole in musæo Oxon. No. 546.   [c] Ex coll. Ashmole ut supra,   [d] Rymer's fœd. tom. 7. p. 349.

of Drayton, in com' Leicester, together with all the lands and tenements of his late father, Sir Reginald de Carteret, Knt. deceased, held in capite in the island of Jersey; paying 10l. per annum into the Exchequer, at the usual feasts of Easter and Michaelmas; for which the said Roger gave security to the King.

Which Philip de Carteret, in 8 Rich. II. was of [f] full age, and the King sent his precept to the Bailiff and jurats of the island of Jersey, that Philip, son and heir of Sir Reginald de Carteret, Knt. deceased, who held in capite of the King, being of full age, they were commanded, on proof of his age, to deliver to the said Philip, without delay, full seisin of all the lands and tenements of his said father.

This Philip signalized himself in many brave [g] actions; and by his conduct and valour, the island of Jersey was again preserved from falling into the hands of the French, during the contentions between Hen. VI. and Edw. IV. Queen Margaret had made over the islands of Jersey, Guernsey, &c. to Peter de Maleurier, a French nobleman, for assisting her against King Edward; and thereupon the French surprized the castle of Mont-Orgueil. Nevertheless Sir Philip de Carteret, by his interest with the [h] inhabitants, kept the castle of Grosnez, and half of the island, in obedience to the crown of England, and maintained frequent skirmishes with the French for six years, till King Edward had quiet possession of the throne; and then Sir Richard Harleston, Knt. Vice-admiral of England, being sent with a squadron of the King's ships to Guernsey, Sir Philip sent to him for succour, and the fleet blocking up Mont-Orgueil by sea, Sir Philip, with the islanders under his command, besieged it by land so effectually, that the French were at length forced to surrender the said castle.

The reverend [i] author, in his account of Jersey, gives us this memorable relation of the taking of the castle, and dispossessing of the French. The Admiral, leaving his ships in Guernsey road, hastened privately to Philip de Carteret, at his manour of St. Owen, and there they two entered into a consultation about the properest means to recover the castle. The result was, to go about it instantly, before the French knew of an English fleet so near them. They then lay confident and secure; but if alarmed with the apprehension of a siege, they would provide against it, compel the country to store and victual them, and give notice to their friends in Normandy, of the danger threatening them. To think of carrying the castle by force, would

---

[f] Rot. Franc. 8 Rich. II. m. 9.   [g] Ashmole, ut antea, ut antea, p. 22.   [i] Ibid. p. 80, 81, 82, 83.   [h] Fall,

be rashness and folly. What only could be done with any probability of success, was, by a close blockade, to reduce those within to such straits and necessities, as would make them even glad to be suffered to depart with their lives; and for effecting this, the utmost speed and secrecy were requisite. Accordingly, never was a design of this nature more prudently and happily conducted. The word, being given by Philip de Carteret, went in a moment through the island, passing from hand to hand; and in the beginning of the appointed night, the people took to their arms, and marched in great silence to invest the castle. At the same time, the fleet weighed anchor and sailed from Guernsey: so that in the morning, the French, to their great surprize and amazement, saw themselves surrounded, and shut in both by sea and land. Although it was judged not proper to make any forcible attack upon the castle, yet there was a great deal of action, and it cost the lives of divers of the inhabitants in defending their lines, and repelling the sallies of the besieged; and the Seigneur de Rosel is, particularly, numbered among the slain on one of those occasions.

In the mean time, the French were contriving how to get aid from Normandy, which they knew would not fail them, so they could but make their condition known there. ‘At length ‘ they imagined, that possibly a boat might pass undiscovered ‘ through the fleet, under favour of the night; and it being the ‘ last and only shift left them, they resolved to put it to the ‘ trial. Though they needed but one boat, they caused two ‘ to be built; one openly upon the rampart in view of the be- ‘ siegers, the other near the former, but hid, and out of sight. ‘ The workmen were ordered so to time their blows, and ‘ strike evenly together upon the two boats, that from the ‘ camp without, no sound might be heard, but what would ‘ be supposed to come from the boat on the rampart. By this ‘ device, that, which lay out of sight, was finished, while ‘ the workmen were seen still busy about the other. Our ‘ people were not ignorant, what use the boat was intended ‘ for; but having no suspicion of any other, besides that which ‘ they had in view, the wile might have succeeded, if an ‘ islander (whom the French had constrained against his will ‘ to take pay with them) had not shot an arrow, with a letter ‘ tied to it, into the leaguer, which laid open the stratagem; ‘ advising withal, that the next night the finished boat would ‘ be let down the walls, and sent to sea. Of this, informa- ‘ tion was immediately given to the fleet, which kept a strict ‘ watch, and the boat was intercepted. And so the French, ‘ seeing all hopes of relief cut off from them, and themselves ‘ in the extremest distress and want of all things, beat a parley

'and surrendered. Which good news, when signified to the
'country, by setting up again the standard of England upon
'the castle, it diffused such an universal joy among the people,
'as is not to be expressed.
    'The islanders gained much honour by this siege, and had
'thereupon a new charter granted them, with special acknow-
'ledgment of their good service. And the same (says Mr.
'Fall) has ever since been inserted and repeated in all our
'charters to this day, in perpetuam rei memoriam. Sir Richard
'Harleston was recompensed with the government of the island.
'But what reward was conferred on Philip de Carteret, who
'had been the very life and soul of the undertaking, I cannot
'find. However, he could not miss that, which always at-
'tends the doing of brave and worthy actions. I mean the
'public esteem, and the inward satisfaction of having faithfully
'and honourably acquitted himself, to his King and to his
'country, following therein the example of his ancestors.'
    Thus far my author, who relates the said circumstantial deliverance of the island from the French, out of an old manuscript chronicle of the isle of Jersey.
    The before-mentioned Philip de Carteret [k] had to wife a daughter of Sir —— Newton, Knt. of Gloucestershire, by whom he had issue a son, after his own name Philip, who died before him, leaving by his wife Penna, daughter of —— Perrine, of Caux, in the county of Tauf, in Normandy, a son named also Philip, heir to his grandfather, at whose death he was under age.
    It is said, out of an ancient manuscript, [l] that this last Philip de Carteret was in ward to the King, for the space of eighteen years; so that when he had performed his homage, elder-trees did grow in the hall, and other places of his manour-house, by the covetousness of those that had the custody thereof, during his nonage. He married [m] Margaret, daughter and sole heir of the before-mentioned Sir Richard Harleston, of the county of Lincoln, Knt. Governor of Jersey; by whom he had issue [n] nineteen sons, and two daughters. The eldest son Philip died unmarried, Edward succeeded his father as Lord of St. Owen, &c. and Helier de Carteret, as Lord of Handois.
    The names of the other sons are not mentioned in the pedigree, so that it is likely most of them died infants, or unmarried.
    Helier, who was Lord of Handois, rendered himself remarkable, by his integrity, honour, and justice; whereof it is observed, that when Sir Hugh Vaughan, Governor of Jersey,

[k] Ex stemmate ut antea, & Ashmole præd.   [l] Ibid.   [m] Ashmole.
[n] Ex stemmate.

by his haughty and arbitrary conduct, had rendered himself obnoxious to the island, and was screened by the noted Cardinal Wolsey, Prime Minister of England [o], ' So great a pa-
' tronage did not deter this Helier de Carteret, Seigneur de
' Handois, from carrying the complaints of the country, with
' his own, up to court, and there, in the very face of the
' Cardinal, called so loud for justice, that at last he obtained
' it, and the insolent Governor was removed.' The same author gives us this further account: ' This Helier de Carteret,
' for love to his country, fortitude, and other laudable accom-
' plishments, shines very bright in our annals. He was bro-
' ther to the Seigneur de St. Owen, and so of a house fruitful
' of patriots.'

He left issue only a daughter, Margaret, married to Helier Carteret, Esq; son to his brother Edward. Which Edward Carteret, Esq; [p] was Carver to Prince Arthur, eldest son of Hen. VII. and departed this life in the 22d of Hen. VIII. leaving Helier, his only son, heir to his estate.

Which Helier Carteret, Esq; was also Bailiff of the isle of Jersey, and very early conformed to the Protestant religion. In 4 Edw. VI. he was [q] commissioned to administer the usual oath to Sir Hugh Poulet, Knt. Governor of Jersey, &c. as also to take an inventory of all the ordnance, artillery, munition, and other habiliments of war, left there under the charge of Henry Cornish, Deputy to Edward Duke of Somerset, Governor of the said isle.

He was also in commission, with [r] the said Sir Hugh Poulet, the Governor, to sell and dispose of all the lands, tenements, &c. appertaining to free chantries, chapels, fraternities, masses, obits, &c. which belonged to the King in the said island, as appears by indenture of sale to Edward Crawford, his heirs and assigns, dated on July 12, 1550.

The French, flattering themselves with hopes of success by King Edward's minority, had [s] seized the island of Sark, having formed a scheme, by making a settlement there, to subdue the islands of Jersey and Guernsey: whereupon they first made an attempt on Guernsey, and being repulsed, they after landed in Boulay-bay in Jersey, but were so well received by this Helier de Carteret, and the inhabitants, that they returned to their ships, and their loss was computed at 1000 men. On their going to St. Malo to refit, no fewer than 60 dead bodies of gentlemen were brought on shore to be buried. And

---

o Fall's account of Jersey, p. 86.   p *Ashmole ut antea.*   q Rymer's foed. tom. 15. p. 261.   r Ex indentura in stemma, præd.   s Fall, ut antea, p. 87, 88.

Henry II. King of France, was so much out of countenance at the disappointment, [t] that he forbad any report to be made, not only of the event, but of the expedition.

In 1552 (6 Edw. VI.) he is the first named in a [u] commission with eleven others of the principal persons of the isle of Jersey, authorizing them, or any six of them (whereof this Helier, and John Clark, Esq; or one of them at the least, to be of the number) to call before them the inhabitants of Jersey, to assess every of them, according to their goods and lands, towards the building of two fortresses, one in the Ilet of St. Helier, and the other in the Ilet of St. Aubyn; as also to settle a yearly pension, to be gathered out of their lands, for the charges of the safe keeping them, and to appoint officers, to make all manner of provisions for the edification of the said fortresses. Which order and cessment, so made, was directed to be put in writing, to remain for ever.

For his good services, Queen Elizabeth, in the 7th year of her reign, in consideration of 50l. (to be paid to Nicholas Carey, Gent. Receiver-general of Jersey) grants to this [w] Helier Carteret, Esq; and his heirs for ever, the isle of Sark, with all members and liberties thereto belonging, and all castles, edifices, buildings, &c. meadows, pastures, woods, waters, &c. with all tythes, advowsons, presentations, rectories, vicarages and chapels; with all goods or chattels of felons, &c. to be held of the crown in capite, paying an annual rent of 50s. Cambden, in his Britannia, mentions Sir Philip de Carteret to have been the first who had this island; but it is evident this Helier, the father of Philip, had the grant of it.

He married Margaret, daughter and heir of his uncle Helier Carteret, Esq; by whom he had issue a son Philip, hereafter mentioned, who succeeded him in his estate of St. Owen; and Amicias, 2d son, who had the lordship of Handois, and in right of his wife Catharine (the heir of the families of Lampriere, and St. Martin) was possessed of the lordship and estate of la Trinite, wherein he was succeeded by Joshua Carteret his eldest son, who, by Jane Herau, his wife (of an ancient family in the island) left issue Sir Edward Carteret, Knt. and Amicias, 2d son, who left an only daughter Mary, Lady of la Trinite, and was married to Sir Charles Carteret, Bart. hereafter mentioned.

Sir Edward Carteret (elder brother of Amicias) knighted on the restoration, was Gentleman-usher of the Black-rod, in the reign of Charles II. and took to wife Elizabeth, daughter

---

[t] Hayward's life of Edw. VI. in hist. of Eng. vol. 2. p. 298.   [u] Strype's memorials, vol. 2. p. 484.   [w] Pat. 7 Eliz. p. 3.

Carteret, Earl Granville.

of Robert Johnson, Esq; Alderman of London, by whom he had issue [x] Edward Carteret, born on March 18, 1664; Charles, baptized on July 24, 1667; and Elizabeth.

Philip Carteret (eldest son of Helier Carteret) was knighted by Queen Elizabeth; and being a Gentleman of worthy principles and public spirit, he undertook to plant such a colony in the island of Sark, as should keep out the French; and accordingly he enlarged the settlement thereon, whereby it was in a condition to oppose any attempt that might be made on it.

This Sir Philip Carteret lived to a great age, and was highly honoured by the inhabitants of Jersey, who had so good an opinion of his wisdom and judgment in affairs, that they generally followed his advice; particularly, in petitioning James I. to grant them the Liturgy, as used in the church of England, which had not been introduced in the reign of Queen Elizabeth. This being assented to, the States of the island specially deputed Sir Philip Carteret, Knt. Joshua Carteret, and Philip Carteret, Esqrs. Jurats and Justices of the isle, to consider of such canons and constitutions in ecclesiastical affairs, as might be fitly accommodated to their circumstances: and accordingly they [y], together with the Dean and ministers of the isle, drew up a body of canons; which, after several corrections and amendments made therein, by Archbishop Abbot, the Lord-keeper Williams, and the learned Dr. Lancelot Andrews, Bishop of Winchester (commissioned thereunto by the King) received the royal assent on June 30, 1623, 21 Jac. I. and were thereupon transmitted to Jersey, to have the force of laws in matters ecclesiastical, as they have to this day.

The said Sir Philip Carteret took to wife [z] Rachael, only daughter and heir of George Paulet, Esq; eldest son of Lord Thomas Paulet, 2d son of William, first Marquis of Winchester, ancestor to the present Duke of Bolton; and by her had issue four sons, and two daughters; Sir Philip; Helier, from whom the present Lord Carteret is descended; Amias, who was a Captain in the wars of the Low Countries, in the reign of James I. and died without issue; as did also Gideon de Carteret, the 4th son. Rachael, the eldest daughter, was first married to ——— Beaver, of the isle of Jersey, and 2dly, to ——— de Vic; and Judith, the youngest daughter, was wife of Sir Brian Johnson, of Olney, in Buckinghamshire, Knt.

Sir Philip de Carteret, the eldest, was Lord of St. Owen, &c. as also Deputy-governor of the isle of Jersey, in the reign of Charles I. He took to wife Anne, daughter of Sir

[x] Ex reg. eccl. paroch. St. Martin, in camp. com' Midd. p. 299, 390. & Append. No. xII. [z] Ex stemmate de Paulet. [y] Fall ut antea,

Francis Dowfe, of Broughton, in com' Southampton, Knt. and by her had iffue five fons, and four daughters; Philip; Peyton, who was Captain of Prince Maurice's guards in Holland, and was drowned with that Prince, leaving no iffue; Francis, who died unmarried; Thomas, a Captain in Ireland, who married ———, daughter of Rockofin, Lord of Nazaret in Flanders, and left no iffue; and Edward, who was knighted by Charles II. and was of the houfhold to James Duke of York, but likewife left no iffue.

The daughters were, Doufe, who died unmarried; Elizabeth, wedded to the right hon. Sir George Carteret; Margaret, to Sir Henry de Vic, Knt. and Bart. and Chancellor of the moft noble order of the Garter; and Anne, wife of Dr. Daniel Brevint, Prebendary of Durham, and Dean of Lincoln, whofe only daughter and heir was firft wife of Sir Edward Huffey, of Welborne in Lincolnfhire, Bart.

Philip Carteret, the eldeft fon, fucceeded to the feigniory of St. Owen, and was High-bailiff of the ifland of Jerfey. He took to wife ———, daughter of ——— Dumarefque, and by her had iffue Philip Carteret, Efq; his only fon and heir, 19 years old in 1669, who fucceeded his father, anno 1662, and was created a Baronet on June 4, 1670, 22 Car. II. He died about the year 1693, leaving his eftate and dignity to Sir Charles Carteret, Bart. who married Mary, daughter and fole heir of Amias de Carteret, Efq; fon and heir of Jofhua de Carteret, Efq; Lord of la Trinite, whereby that eftate accrued to the faid Sir Charles. He was one of the Gentlemen of the Privy-chamber to Queen Anne; as alfo High-bailiff of the ifland of Jerfey; in which office he was continued at the acceffion of King George I. on Aug. 1, 1714, and departing this life foon after, was buried in the north ifle of Weftminfter-abbey, on June 8, 1715, leaving no iffue; fo that the title of Baronet, conferred on his father, became extinct. He left his eftates of St. Owen, la Trinite, Sark, &c. to John, the late Lord Carteret, and Earl Granville, the heir-male of his family.

I now return to Helier Carteret, Efq; 2d fon to Sir Philip Carteret, by Rachael his wife, daughter and heir of George Paulet, Efq; before-mentioned; which Helier Carteret, Efq; [y] was Deputy-governor of the ifland of Jerfey, in the reigns of Queen Elizabeth, and King James I.

King Charles I. on May 2, 1638, the 14th of his reign, conftituted him the King's Proctor in the ifland of Jerfey; and on June 18 following [z], he obtained a grant to himfelf,

[y] Ex ftemm. in offic. arm. præd. [z] Pat. 14 Car. I. p. 43. n. 4.

and George Carteret, Esq; his son and heir, of the office and place of Bailiff of the island of Jersey, during the lives of either of them, or the longer liver of them.

By his wife Elizabeth, daughter and coheir of —— Dumaresque, he had issue three sons, and two daughters; George; Philip, from whom no issue is remaining; and Reginald, who died unmarried.

His eldest son was the right hon. Sir George Carteret, Bart. whose eminent services to the crown, and to his country, were rewarded, by the advancement of his grandson to the dignity of a Peer of this realm, immediately after his decease; Charles II. having designed that honour for the said Sir George, as is declared in the preamble to the patent.

This Sir George Carteret [b] was born in the island of Jersey, in 1599, 41 Eliz. his father, Helier Carteret, Esq; being then Deputy-governor. He went early into the sea-service, and, by his conduct and courage, had acquired the character of an experienced officer, when Charles I. ascended the throne, on March 27, 1625; which recommended him to the favour and esteem of George Villiers, Duke of Buckingham, by whose interest he was made joint Governor of Jersey, with Henry, afterwards Lord Jermyn, in the 2d year of that reign. He afterwards [c] obtained a grant, dated on Dec. 12, 1639, 15 Car. I. of the office and place of Comptroller of all his Majesty's ships.

On the commencement of the civil war, he was in those posts, and of great eminency and reputation in naval command [d], says the Earl of Clarendon; and was in such esteem of men of all persuasions, for true honour, courage, and abilities, that when (as the noble author [e] recites) ' the resolution of the house of
' Commons, and the concurrence of the Lords, was peremptory,
' for sending the Earl of Warwick Admiral of the fleet, it was
' resolved by them, that Captain Carteret, Comptroller of his
' Majesty's navy, should be Vice-admiral; who, thinking it
' became his near relation to his Majesty's service, to receive
' his royal pleasure, before he engaged himself in that employ-
' ment, addressed himself for his directions. But the King
' looking upon the fleet in a manner taken from him, when
' another, whose disaffection to his service was very notorious,
' was, contrary to his express pleasure, put into the command
' of it, would not countenance that fleet, and that Admiral,
' with suffering an officer of his own to command in it, un-
' der the other; and therefore ordered Captain Carteret to de-
' cline the employment, which he prudently, and without

[b] Account of Jersey, p. 96.   [c] Pat. 15 Car. I. p. 22. n. 16.   [d] Hist. of rebell. 8vo. vol. 2. p. 679.   [e] Ibid.

' noise,

' noise, did; and thereupon another officer of the navy, the
' Surveyor-general, Captain Batten [f], an obscure fellow, of
' very different inclinations to his master, and his service, was
' substituted in his place.' ' Whereas (to use the noble histo-
' rian's own words) if Captain Carteret had been suffered to
' have taken that charge, his interest and reputation in the navy
' was so great, and his diligence and dexterity in command so
' eminent; that it was generally believed he would, against
' whatsoever the Earl of Warwick could have done, have pre-
' served the major part of the fleet in their duty to the King;'
and laments this as a most fatal error; ' and [g] which the King
' had shortly after cause to repent, for that Captain Carteret
' hath since sufficiently testified, how advantageously to his
' Majesty, he would have managed that charge.'

As he gave up that command in the fleet, he likewise quitted his place of Comptroller of the Navy; and withdrew himself and his family to the island of Jersey, being well assured of the hearty concurrence of the inhabitants to receive him [h], whom he established and confirmed in their loyalty to the King. After which, his fidelity to his Royal Master, and the ardent courage he had always shewn, induced him to venture himself in the dangers of the field; and to that end he transported himself into Cornwall.

How opportunely he came there, is well expressed by our historian [i], who, after relating the great straits of the Cornish forces, for want of ammunition, against which they had no probable hope, proceeds to say, ' In this instant, as if sent by Pro-
' vidence, they met with an opportunity they had scarce cou-
' rage to hope for. Captain Carteret, the Comptroller of the
' King's navy, having, in the beginning of the troubles, after
' he had refused to have commands in their fleets, without
' noise withdrawn himself and his family out of England to
' Jersey; and being there impatient of lying quiet, whilst his
' Master was in the field, transported himself into Cornwall,
' with a purpose to raise a troop of horse, and to engage in that
' service. When he came thither, he was unanimously im-
' portuned by the commanders, after they had acquainted him
' with their hopeless and desperate want of powder, to assist
' them in that manner; that the many good ports in their
' power might be made of some use to them in the supply of
' powder. Whereupon he shortly returned into France; and
' first upon his own credit, and then upon return of those com-
' modities out of Cornwall, as they could well spare, he supplied

---

[f] Hist. of rebellion, 8vo. vol. 2. p. 482.   [g] Ibid.   [h] Account of Jersey, p. 96.   [i] Lord Clarendon's hist. of rebellion, 8vo. vol. 3. p. 136.

' them

' them with such great proportions of all kinds of ammunitions, that they never found want after.'

This seasonable service, the King graciously acknowledged in the following warrant [i]:

'Charles R.

'TRUSTY and well-beloved, we greet you well. We having received information of the several good and faithful services, which you have performed for us, during the present rebellion, particularly in sending of supplies to our western armyes, and ammunition; in carefully providing for our two castles of Mount-Orgueil, and Elizabeth, during the insurrection in our isle of Jersey; reducing the said isle to our obedience; and often relieving our castle of Cornett, when it was in very great distress for want of victuals: which good services, as we have thought just to testify unto you our gracious acceptance of, and return you our thanks for the same; so do we yet further rely upon your affection to us, in the further providing for, and procuring all fit means to preserve, as well those places under your command, as also our said castle of Cornett, from the further attempts of the rebels, and endeavouring to recover, and thoroughly to reduce our islands of Guernsey, Serke, and Alderney, still detained from us by the said rebels; assuring you, that whatsoever charges you, or your partners, shall be at, in so doing, the same shall be made good unto you, either upon those places, or in such other ways, as may not only be to your content; but likewise remain as a testimony of our favour and bounty towards you. And so we bid you heartily farewel. Given at our court at Oxon, this 21st of January, 1644.

'By his Majesty's command,

'GEORGE DIGBYE.

'To our trusty and well-beloved
'Colonel George de Carteret,
'our Lieutenant-governor, and
'Bailiff of the isle of Jersey.'

Immediately after this, the King conferred on him the honour of Knighthood at Oxford; and before his departure from thence, advanced him to the dignity of a Baronet [k], by letters patent, bearing date on May 9, 1645, 21 Car. I.

i Ex evident. in stem. in offic. arm. præd.   k Pat. 21 Car. I.

On his arrival at Jersey, the same year, he found, that the parliament, by their agents, had, in his absence, seduced some of the inhabitants to espouse their interests; on which he confined some of them; and the members of Westminster were so alarmed at it [1], that on Sept. 11, 1645, they ordered a declaration to be drawn, 'That if for the future he put to death any of the isle, whom he should take prisoners, for every one so slain, the parliament will hang up three of the King's men, their prisoners.' And so great was their indignation against him, for his loyalty to his Sovereign, that afterwards, in their propositions to the King, for a peace [m], he was among those persons of eminence, who were excepted from pardon; which they also renewed in their treaty with the King, in the Isle of Wight.

He continued watching all opportunities of doing the King service, or in succouring or assisting his friends; many whereof, when they were driven out of England, retired to Jersey, and were received by Sir George Carteret, with all the courtesy and kindness, that could possibly be demonstrated. He kept an open table; and his generosity and public spirit to those distressed loyalists, who stood in need of his assistance, is hardly to be paralleled; and plainly shewed, his integrity and honour were superior to any private views.

On March 17, 1645-6, the members at Westminster, being informed that the Prince of Wales was in Scilly, and in some straits for want of provisions, they agreed to send a letter to him, in a loving and tender way (as [n] Whitlock writes) to invite him to come to both houses of parliament, and reside in such place, and have such attendants, &c. as should be approved by both houses: and accordingly the letter [o], from both houses, was sent to him the next day, which, as Lord Clarendon relates, was delivered to him by a trumpeter from Sir Thomas Fairfax, and might be called a summons, rather than an invitation. His Highness, therefore, with the advice of his whole council, embarked for Jersey on Thursday, April 16, 1646, and having a prosperous wind, landed there the next day. There came with him Thomas Howard, Earl of Berkshire, the Lord Capel, the Lord Hopton, the Chancellor of the Exchequer (afterwards Earl of Clarendon) and others; and [p] soon after the Lord Colpeper, the Lord Digby, the Lord Jermyn, the Lord Wentworth, the Lord Wilmot, and others.

l Whitlock's memorials, p. 165.　m Sir Edw. Walker's historical discourses in the treaty of the Isle of Wight, p. 17, 18.　n Memorials, p. 203.
o Ibid.　p Clarendon's hist. 8vo. vol. 5. p. 2, 4, and 15.

Sir Harry Killigrew was also resolved to go to Jersey, and took the first opportunity of transporting himself from Falmouth, with some officers and soldiers, to St. Maloe's, in Britanny; from whence he wrote to the Chancellor in Jersey, to procure a bark to fetch him thither; which q, 'by the kindness of Sir 'George Carteret, was presently sent, with a longing desire to 'receive him into the island, having an extraordinary affection 'for him, as well as the Lords Capel, and Hopton, and the 'Chancellor. Within two days after, on view of the vessel 'at sea (which they well knew) they all made haste to the har-'bour to receive their friend; but to their infinite regret, they 'found his body there in a coffin, he having died at St. Ma-'loe's, the day after he wrote his letter, and desired that his 'dead body might be sent to Jersey, where he was decently 'buried.'

The accession of the Prince of Wales, with so many persons of distinction, into the island, who brought little with them for their subsistence, was of course very expensive to Sir George Carteret; yet he chearfully entertained them; and well knowing it behoved him to take care for supplies r, he equipped about half a score small frigates and privateers, which soon struck a terror all over the channel, and brought in many captures, whereof several are recited in Whitlock's memorials.

The Prince was so well pleased with his entertainment, that, having taken an account of the island s, 'both himself, and 'all the Lords with him, were of opinion, that it was a place 'of the greatest security, benefit, and conveniency, to repose 'in, that could have been desired and wished for; till, upon 'a clear information and observation of the King's condition, 'and the state of England, he (the Prince) should find a fit 'opportunity to act; and the Prince himself seemed to have 'the greatest aversion and resolution against going into France, 'that could be imagined.'

However, the Queen, his mother, very strongly solicited his repair to her; but his council had no inclination to trust the heir of the kingdom of England with those who had shewed so little kindness to the father, and had originally fomented the rebellion; it being an incontrovertible fact, that the troubles in Scotland were, in their rise and progress, fomented by the intrigues of Cardinal Richlieu, as appears by letters from Robert Sidney, Earl of Leicester (then ambassador in France) which I have published in two volumes folio, from the originals at Penshurst-place in Kent, and from his Majesty's office of papers and records of state.

q Clarendon's hist. 8vo, vol. 5. p. 24, 25. r Falle's account of Jersey, p. 98. s Hist. of rebellion, 8vo, vol. 5. p. 4.

Carteret, Earl Granville.

The Lords Capel, and Culpeper, were therefore sent to the Queen his mother at Paris, to diswade her from desiring the Prince's repair into France, and were instructed (among other particulars) to tell her in his name [t], ' That he had great rea-
' son to believe the island of Jersey to be defensible against a
' greater force than he supposed probable to be brought against
' it. That the inhabitants expressed as much chearfulness,
' unanimity, and resolution, for the defence of his person, by
' their whole carriage, and particularly by a protestation volun-
' tarily undertaken by them, as could be desired. And that
' if, contrary to expectation, the rebels should take the island,
' he could, from the castle (a place in itself of very great
' strength) with the least hazard, remove himself to France;
' which, in case of imminent danger, he resolved to do; and
' whether his remove out of the dominions of his royal father,
' (except on such a necessity, or apparent visible conveniency)
' may not have an influence on the affections of the three
' kingdoms, to the disadvantage of his royal father.'

The Queen was deluded by the arts of Cardinal Mazarin, who wanted the Prince in France, to drive the better bargain with England, as conjunctures should fall out; and no promises were spared to decoy him over to them. The Lords Capel, and Culpeper, stayed [u] at Paris with her Majesty full three weeks; during which time they only prevailed with her to suspend the Prince's removal from Jersey; and at last she sent her peremptory commands for his repair to her. It was debated in the Prince's council [w]; but his positive declaration to comply induced all of them (except the Lord Culpeper) to desire his Highness's pardon, if they did not further wait upon him. And it is observed by the Earl of Clarendon [x], ' That if the
' King's fortune had been further to be conducted by any fixed
' rules of policy and discretion, this so sudden remove of the
' Prince from Jersey, might have been looked upon, and cen-
' sured with severity; as an action that swerved from that pru-
' dence, which, by the fundamental rules of policy, had been
' long established.'

When the Prince came into France, he was so slighted and disregarded, that it has often been admired, after he was restored to his kingdoms, that he would ever put any confidence in so faithless a court. This may seem a digression from my account of Sir George Carteret; but as he had the principal share in providing for the Prince and his company, I thought it necessary to recite how he came to leave the island.

t Hist. of rebellion, vol. 5. p. 7, 8.   u Ibid. p. 15.   w Ibid. p. 28.
x Ibid. p. 29.

It is likewise remarkable, that several of the council staid with Sir George, when the Prince was in France; and the Chancellor of the Exchequer (after Earl of Clarendon) resided with him no less than five and-twenty months. And this respite from attendance he employed in writing that incomparable history he has left us, begun before, but often interrupted. The noble author has himself taken notice of the assistance he had from the King in his work, whilst he was in the island [y].

'The Lord Capel hearing of the difference between the par-
'liament and the army, left his friends there, and waited on
'the King at Hampton-court, and gave him a particular ac-
'count of all that passed at Jersey, before the Prince's remove
'from thence, and of the reasons which induced those of the
'council to remain still there, &c. And from thence the King
'writ with his own hand a very gracious and kind letter to
'the Chancellor at Jersey, &c. He thanked him for under-
'taking the work he was upon, and told him he should expect
'speedily to receive some contribution from him towards it.
'And shortly after he sent to him his own memorials of all that
'had passed from the time he left his Majesty at Oxford, to the
'very day the King left Oxford to go to the Scots, &c.'

His residence was in Elizabeth-castle, with his friend Sir George Carteret; and there, saith my author [z], I have seen still standing (and looked on with a sort of veneration) the humble house where that great and good man spent five-and-twenty months on that work; the house, in memory of him, retaining a long while after the name of la Maison du Chancelier.

When Charles I. made his escape from Hampton-court, he seems to have had Jersey in his view; for at his coming to the sea-side, i. e. Southampton river, where embarkations for that island are usually made, he [a] asked Ashburnham (whom he principally trusted) where the ship lay: which made Berkeley and Legge conclude, that the King resolved to transport himself.
'And after they had made some stay in that part next the sea,
'and Ashburnham had been sometime absent, he returned with-
'out any news of the ship, with which the King seemed
'troubled.' It is certain, that Ashburnham was in the secret of his escape; but how the design of the King's transporting himself miscarried, has never yet been brought to light. His Majesty had great reason to repose the most entire confidence in Sir George Carteret, the Chancellor of the Exchequer, being also with him; so that it is very probable his design was to go to them.

[y] Hist of rebellion, vol. 5. p. 70. [z] Falle, in his account of Jersey, p. 102.
[a] Hist of rebellion, vol. 5. p. 78.

When the terrible blow was given, which laid the head of the good King, and with it the Crown and Monarchy, in the dust, on Jan. 30, 1648-9, the Prince was at the Hague in a very destitute condition. Yet Sir George Carteret [b], readily and solemnly, proclaimed him at Jersey, with all his titles. And afterwards when his Majesty was in the greatest perplexity, whither to bend his course (not a court in Europe shewing any regard to his necessities and distress, or willing to receive him) he remembered the loyalty and integrity of Sir George Carteret, who by his interest with the inhabitants of the island had two years before signally relieved him, when he could set his foot no where on English ground with safety. Therefore resolving to visit him again, he made his journey through Normandy, and embarked himself for Jersey, where he arrived the latter end of Sept. 1649.

On Oct. 3, 1649, as Whitlock writes [c], came letters from France, that Prince Charles went from the court towards Caen in Normandy, and from thence intended to go for Jersey; that his train was but sixty horses, and six coaches with six horses apiece, and that many of his servants, and some gentlemen, went on foot; and that he had but 300 pistoles left him to defray the charges of his journey: that afterwards he [d] arrived at Jersey, with 300 persons in his retinue.

He was accompanied by his brother the Duke of York, with several of the nobility; and as the noble historian has observed, they were supplied by Sir George, with all necessaries without any benefit to himself [e]; when the Lord Jermin, who lived in great plenty at Paris, was so wonderfully jealous of the profit he challenged from thence as governor, that he made a demand of some of the money raised on the sale of the King's demesnes in the island; because, as he alledged, his receipt, for the time to come, would not remain so great as it had been formerly.

His Majesty, when Prince, had procured his father's leave, for making Sir George Carteret his Vice Chamberlain [f]; and he now constituted him Treasurer of his navy, which at that time consisted chiefly of the privateers which Sir George had provided, and the men of war with Prince Rupert. By Sir George's interest in the navy, one of the frigates, belonging to the Parliament, went to him at Guernsey, as Whitlock [g] relates, and that after he had got possession of her, he turned off all the mariners. This was in March, 1649-50. The same author recites [h], that in May 1650, Captain Green had

b Account of Jersey, p. 105. c Memorials, p. 412. d Ibid. p. 413.
e Hist. of rebellion, vol. 5. p. 324. f MS. not. L. in Offic. Arm. g Memorials, p. 380. h Ibid. p. 440.

brought

brought into the Isle of Wight, a ship of five guns belonging to Sir George Carteret, governor of Jersey, bound for Virginia, with many passengers, all sorts of goods, and tools for husbandry, in order for planting an island, which the Prince (as he calls him) had given to Sir George.

It was said before, that the King came into the island the latter end of September; and he staid there till the latter end of March following, when on the invitation of the Scots, he embarked for Holland to be nearer to treat with them. During his abode he found the same dutiful people, as they were before to him whilst he was prince [i]. None were denied access to him, neither did he disdain invitations and entertainments from the gentry, at their habitations, as he rode about the island. With all parts of which he grew so well acquainted, that he drew a map of it with his own hand, intending no doubt to keep the same in remembrance of a place, where he had enjoyed more peace and quiet than hitherto any where else, within or without his dominions. Which map is in the Heer Van Alderhelm's cabinet of curiosities at Leipsic in Saxony [k], where it is shewn to travellers.

It is enough to say, that whilst his Majesty was in Scotland, the usurping powers in England were making great preparations for reducing Jersey, enraged at harbouring the King in defiance of them, and alarmed at the taking so many of their traders by the privateers, who continued cruising in the Channel, and even took ships out of the very harbours; whereof Whitlock gives several instances. In October 1651 the armament, fitted out against the island, put to sea under the command of Admiral Blake, and Major General Haines, who had the charge of the forces for the descent.

On October 20, fourscore sail (which were but part of the fleet) came to an anchor in St. Owen's bay [l], which lies open to a westerly wind, that blows at least one half of the year, and when raised to a storm, rolls in such a sea as no ships can stand against, without danger of perishing every moment. But the same unaccountable success, which used to attend the rebels, did also then attend them; for whilst they lay in that bay, they had such smooth water, as the like had not been known in so advanced a season. This somewhat startled the people, but not so much as the dismal report, which on a sudden flew about the island, of the King being prisoner, and at the mercy of his enemies. They had heard of the battle at Worcester, &c. and sorrow and despair might be seen in every face. The most dis-

[i] Account of Jersey, p. 107. [k] Dr. Brown's travels, p. 172. [l] Account of Jersey, p. 110. ex relat. de la prise de l'isle & des chatteaux de Jersey par les rebelles d'Angleterre, MS.

pirited cried out, that it was in vain to contend any longer with powers who like a torrent bore down all before them, and what good would the facrificing themfelves do the King, when perhaps he was no more. For what could be expected from thofe bloody mifcreants into whofe hands he was fallen. Here it was, faith my author [m], ' That Sir George Carteret had need ' of all his authority, and of the great refpect which every ' body paid him, to keep many from laying down their arms. ' Nor peradventure would that have done, had he not pru- ' dently concealed his own fears, and put on an air of uncon- ' cernednefs, as difcredited that report among the troops, who ' watched his looks, and feeing no alteration there, concluded ' that he muft know more than they, and believed nothing at ' all of the ftory. By that means he raifed their fpirits again, ' and brought them on to face the enemy.'

On October 21, early in the morning, their cannon began to play, which was anfwered by that on feveral little forts and redoubts in the bay, and by twenty-four field pieces, always following the militia on a march. Some of the leffer frigates advanced fo near the fhore, as brought both parties within dif- tance to ply their fmall arms, and the iflanders boldly waded into the water to meet their enemies, returning their fire, and calling them aloud, ' Rebels, Traitors, and Murtherers of their ' King.' This lafted four hours, after which the whole fleet drew off, and went to St. Brelade's bay (about a league from that of St. Owen) where being anchored, they fent back a fquadron to St. Owen, and others towards St. Aubin's bay, St. Clement, and Grouville, meaning to tire and diftract them, by making fhew as if they intended to land in all thofe places at once. Accordingly feveral companies were detached to wait on their motion; the main body of the fleet lying ftill at St. Brelade's bay, and the beft part of the camp there likewife to obferve it.

On October 22, a little after midnight, the enemy, at St. Brelade, were perceived to fhip off in feveral flat-bottom'd boats about four thoufand foot (as was conjectured) in order to make a defcent, which they attempted by break of day, under covert of their fhips, which fpared neither powder nor fhot on that occafion. But feeing themfelves repulfed from two fmall forts that had been raifed in the bay, and the iflanders drawn up on the fands to receive them, they retired to their fhips, and re- turned to St. Owen, leaving only nineteen men of war in St. Brelade's bay.

[m] Account of Jerfey, p. 110. ex relat. de la prife de l'ifle & des chateaux de Jerfey par les reballes d'Angleterre, MS.

This obliged Sir George Carteret to follow them again to St. Owen, after he had posted some companies of the militia, his own company of fusileers, and all the dragoons, to oppose those remaining at St. Brelade. The enemy being come to St. Owen, directed their course to the farthest point of that bay, as if they meant to land there, whither they were accordingly followed by the islanders. But it soon appeared their design was only to harrass them; for they suddenly tack'd about, and steered to the opposite point; which motion was likewise attended by the forces on shore; the enemy firing furiously with their cannon all the while.

Night coming on, it was thought necessary to send the troops, which had been three days and two nights under arms, exceedingly fatigued with so many marches and countermarches, and much incommoded by a small rain that had not ceased ever since they were in action, to refresh in the neighbouring villages; the indefatigable Governor, Sir George Carteret, with a small body of horse, not departing all the while from the shore; the enemy were the same day reinforced by a squadron of fresh ships; and that night proving extraordinary dark, under the favour of it, they landed a battalion; which as soon as discovered, was with great bravery and resolution charged by Sir George Carteret the Governor, and the horse he had with him. The enemy [n] confessed, 'They were desperately charged with a body of horse 'for about half an hour; and many were killed and wounded.' But the infantry being dispersed all along the coast for refreshment, had not time to come in to sustain the horse; and the enemy pouring in fresh men, they were forced to retire. On which all further opposition ceasing, there followed a general landing of the rebels; and the next day, October 23, so furious a tempest arose from the west, that if they had not by their landing and lucky reduction of the island gained a retreat for their fleet into the ports, the greatest part of it had perished; for one of their stoutest ships was dashed against the rocks, and not a man saved of three hundred that were in it. Though they were yet only masters of the open country, and not of the castles, the news of that success was received [o] with great joy, by those called the Parliament, who ordered a public thanksgiving thereupon.

The fort of St. Aubin, which commands the harbour of that name, might have proved a hindrance to the fleet's taking shelter there. And though Sir George [p], who knew how important the preservation of it was at that critical hour, had

---

[n] Whitlock's memorials, p. 488.   [o] Ibid. 489.   [p] Account of Jersey, p. 115.

given a most strict charge to the officer and soldiers in it, to hold out to the last extremity, he was ill obeyed, and with grief saw the place yielded up as soon as summoned. The manuscript relation the author quotes, imputes the utter loss of the island to that too precepitate and hasty surrender; reasonably supposing that the enemy's ships, quitting St. Owen's bay to come into St. Aubin's for security against the storm, could never have kept upon their anchors, betwixt the two fires of Elizabeth castle and the fort. Nor did Mount-Orgueil hold out long, being not in that condition it anciently was; very little having been done to support it, since Elizabeth castle was made the residence of the Governor. And no news coming yet of the King, all hearts, but Sir George Carteret's, were so intimidated, that 'tis rather to be wondered at, that any resistance at all was made, when they could not tell for whom they exposed their lives.

It is further related from the said manuscript, 'That Sir
' George, having shut himself up in it, was resolved upon a de-
' fence worthy his courage, and of the goodness of the cause
' in which he was engaged. With him went in sundry prime
' persons of the island, magistrates, clergymen, and others.
' The garrison consisted of three hundred and forty men
' mustered for service, with provisions for eight months in pro-
' portion to that complement. After summons from the com-
' mander of the rebels, and such an answer from the Gover-
' nor as became him to give, the cannon was pointed against
' the castle, which could be brought no nearer than about three
' quarters of a mile; all betwixt St. Helier's hill and the castle,
' being sea or sand, without firm ground whereon to raise bat-
' teries. Firing at such a distance could not much damage the
' walls; all the harm done, for many days, from the continual
' fire of twelve thirty-six pounders, amounted to no more than
' beating down some parapets, which were soon made up with
' turf.' It was now far in November, when the joyful news came of King Charles II's arrival in France; on which Sir George dispatched Mr. Poindextre, to congratulate his Majesty on his miraculous deliverance, and inform him of the state of the garrison.

A poor fellow, brought in by a party sent out for intelligence, gave information, that the enemies, with great labour, were drawing up St. Helier's hill two monstrous guns, the like whereof had never been seen in the country. It was easily understood what they were, viz. two very large mortars, which being fixed, threw shells into the castle, of near thirty inches diameter; one of which, happening to fall on the church, did most dreadful execution. This was the old church of the
abbey

abbey of St. Helier, under which was a magazine of stores and provisions, and twelve barrels of powder for the service of the artillery in the lower ward. The bomb broke through two strong vaults, and setting the powder on fire, scattered ruin and desolation all round, destroyed the provisions, and killed forty of the best soldiers in the garrison, besides armourers, carpenters, and other workmen useful in a siege.

So unexpected a blow caused a great consternation in the place, and gave occasion to some more faint-hearted than the rest, to talk of surrendering. But though Sir George by his prudence quieted all, yet he found it necessary to acquaint the King, with this new incident, and to crave his assistance, if so be his Majesty could prevail with the court of France to grant it. With this message he sent his chaplain the Rev. Mr. Durell (afterwards Dean of Windsor) Mr. Poindextre not being yet returned. The King's answer was to this effect, ' That all his solicitations had been in vain, and would still ' be so though repeated never so often; such a conjunction ' there was of counsels and interests betwixt Cromwell and the ' Prime Minister Cardinal Mazarine: that he relied on his ' known experience and ability, to do what to him should seem ' proper; yet advised him rather to accept of a reasonable com- ' position, than by too obstinate a defence, bring himself, and ' so many loyal gentlemen into danger of being made prisoners ' of war.'

Sir George seems to have had a noble ambition, that this should be the last of the King's garrisons to bend under the power of the rebels; and in fact it was the last. Therefore seeing the castle still tenable, no breach made, no disposition of the enemies for an attack, he resolved to keep them out some time longer, and concealed the King's permission to treat, that the knowledge of it should not renew the cry for a surrender. But at length provisions growing short, the number of defendants lessening daily by death and desertion, and no possibility of supplies or recruits, he concluded to yield to necessity, which the bravest men are forced to do without loss of reputation.

I shall now recite the account which the enemy gave of the siege and surrender. Letters [q] of December 5, 1651, ' That ' the third shot at Elizabeth castle in Jersey, fell upon the old ' church there, killed and wounded thirty persons, and en- ' dangered the Governor Sir George Carteret; and his Lady, ' and the chief of the island. That this made so great an im- ' pression on the Lady Carteret, and the other Ladies, and ' some few men, who were afraid to be taken, that ' the next night they embarked for France. That this shot

[q] Whitlock's memoirs, p. 491.

' spoiled

'spoiled great store of cyder and provisions. That several of
their men made an escape, and some being taken, were forthwith tried and executed.'

Letters ʳ 18 December, 'That the hard duty of the soldiers
in Jersey, had caused much sickness among them, so that
they brought themselves to a fourth night's duty; and that
Elizabeth castle held out obstinately.'

Letters ˢ 27 December, 'That Elizabeth castle was surrendered to the Parliament on articles; and in it 17 brass pieces,
36 iron pieces, 450 muskets, &c.'

Sir George staid in the island to settle his affairs, till about
the middle of January, and then embarked for St. Maloes,
where, as Whitlock writes ᵗ, he had but coarse entertainment;
only himself, and nine more, being suffered to come into that
town, where he staid a short time, and then went to Paris to
the King. In this the Earl of Clarendon agrees, who relates ᵘ,
'That Sir George Carteret having well defended Jersey, his
Majesty sent him orders to make the best conditions he could,
which he shortly after did, and came himself to Paris, to give
the King a larger information in that affair; and afterwards
remained in France under many mortifications, by the power
and prosecution of Cromwell.'

The next mention that I find of him, is in 1652, when
being disposed to travel, he obtained this very honourable and
remarkable certificate ʷ.

Charles the second, by the Grace of God King of Great-
Britain, &c. 'To the most Serene, Famous, Potent, High
and Illustrious Emperors, Kings, Princes, Dukes, Marquises: of the orders of Earls, Barons, Rulers, and their Vice-
gerents, of castles, fleets, rivers, ports, &c. and to all others,
either of civil or military power, &c. to whose loving hands
these shall come, greeting. Whereas our faithful and truely
well-beloved subject and servant Sir George de Carteret, our
Vice-Chamberlain, and Treasurer of our Navy, Knt. and Bart.
hath given so many marks of his steady loyalty, to our most
serene Lord and Father of blessed memory, as well as to us;
deserving highly for his singular behaviour both by sea and
land, not only in many expeditions, when he had the command of our navy, particularly in that of the siege of Salley,
which he reduced to our obedience: but also in the civil
wars, when he took the island of Jersey out of the hands of
our enemies, and defended the same for eight years, till by
our leave (we not being able to send him any supplies) he sur-

---

ʳ Whitlock's memorials, p. 493.   ˢ Ibid. p. 494.   ᵗ Memorials,
p. 495.   ᵘ Hist. of rebellion, vol. 6. p. 455, 456.   ʷ MSS. notat.
14. in Offic. Armor.

'rendered

Carteret, Earl Granville.

'rendered the same upon good conditions; which was the last of our dominions that fell into the hands of the rebels. We, therefore, thinking it necessary to make known the merits of so famous and gallant a man, do recommend him with these our letters, by which we most friendly require all and singular persons of such kingdoms, dominions, territories, jurisdictions, towns or castles, the aforesaid Sir George Carteret shall have occasion to travel through, with his family, company, servants, horses and arms, &c. to permit them free passage both by sea and land, in going, transporting, or returning, or wheresoever his occasions shall call him. And graciously to receive him, with the highest regard, friendship and protection, worthy of such unshaken loyalty and valour, both in council and in war. Which good offices we shall in our turn gratefully acknowledge. Given at Paris, Feb. 8, 1652, in the 4th year of our reign.'

After this, by the power and prosecution of Cromwell, he very narrowly escaped with life, being committed prisoner to the Bastile, and all means used with Cardinal Mazarine, to have him sent in custody to England.

Lockhart, Ambassador in France, to Secretary Thurloe, Aug. 5, 1657, gives him [x] account, 'That orders go to-morrow for arresting Sir George Carteret at Paris, and that Col. Fitz-Maurice, and another Irishman (whom he had cause to suspect as the chief persons employed for debauching the English forces) were made prisoners, and were to be sent to the Bastile, where they may have occasion to see their old friend Carteret.' Likewise in another letter to the said Secretary [y], bearing date Sept. 5, Sti. No. 1657, he thus expresses himself: 'I have several times writ about a charge against Sir George Cartwright. He hath been in prison near this three weeks; and the little Queen hath cried, and made the greatest noise about it imaginable, and sayeth, there is no other quarrel against him, save that he was a faithful servant to her husband.'

In answer to which, Thurloe to Lockhart 19/29 Nov. 1657 [z] writes, 'I have herewith sent the information against Sir George Cartwrite, which will be made good upon oath; and is of so high a nature, that I hope the Cardinal will cause him to be delivered to be proceeded against. If such things be suffered, it will be unsafe for any of our ships to come into the ports of France.' Also in another letter to Lockhart of 14/24 Dec. 1657, he tells him: 'As for Cartwrite, I

[x] Thurloe's state papers, vol. 6, p. 421.   [y] Ibid. p. 482.   [z] Ibid. p. 620.

'doubt

'doubt whether it be better to banish him, or keep him in
'prison. He is a notable instrument of Charles Stuart's; and
'therefore in case the Cardinal will not deliver him unto H. H.
'which would be a very generous action, I think it best that
'he be kept in prison until further consideration be had of
'him.'

However his friends were so industrious in their intercession for him, that he had obtained his liberty, before this last letter from Thurloe was received by Lockhart, who writes to him from Paris, Dec. $\frac{16}{26}$ 1657. [a] 'Sir George Cartwright is ba-
'nished France: he gave out first, he would go into Flanders
'and seek his revenge; but hath since fallen upon calmer
'thoughts, and goes to Savoy, and from thence to Venice, if
'he can meet with any imployment there.'

In 1659, he was [b] at the city of Rheims, from whence he repaired to the King at Brussels, about the end of Dec. that year; and followed him to Breda, where those letters were prepared for the Parliament and General Monk, which brought about the Restoration of the Royal Family, and put an end to the sufferings and banishment he and his faithful subjects had undergone.

His Majesty being restored to his kingdoms, Sir George Carteret rode with him in his triumphant entry through the city of London, on May 29, 1660 [c], and the day after he was pleased to remember his loyal and faithful services, by declaring him Vice-Chamberlain of his Houshold, and of his Privy-Council, being at the same time sworn thereof, with the Marquises of Hertford, Dorchester, Ormond, and other Nobles. He was also constituted Treasurer of the Navy; and at the Coronation of the King, on April 23, 1661 [d], had the honour to be specially appointed, by his Majesty, Almoner for the day, and attended accordingly.

He was elected [e] by the Corporation of Portsmouth to the first Parliament called by Charles II. which met at Westminster on May 8, 1661, and was a leading Member in the House, being the first named in several Committees.

In 1663, 15 Car. II. [f] he had the honour of being Proxy to Christian Prince of Denmark, who had been elected Knight of the Most Noble Order of the Garter; and was installed and took possession of the stall assigned to him.

On the Duke of York's resignation of Lord High Admiral of England, in 1673, he was constituted [g] one of the Commis-

[a] Thurloe, p. 682.   [b] Baker's chronicle, 7th edit. p. 653.   [c] Ibid. p. 713.   [d] Account of the King's coronation in Baker, p. 738.   [e] Ex Collect. Brown Willis, Armig.   [f] Ashmole's Ord. of the Garter, p. 439, 444.   [g] MS. not. L. 14 præd.

sioners of the Admiralty: and in 1676 was one of the Lords of the Committee of Trade. His eldest son, Sir Philip Carteret, being unfortunately slain in the great sea fight with the Dutch, on May 28, 1672, he thought it prudent to provide in his life time to keep up the honour of his name, and family; and there being the greatest friendship between him and the Right Hon. John Granville Earl of Bath (who had been so instrumental in the Restoration of Charles II.) a marriage was agreed on between them, of his eldest grandson the Honourable George Carteret, with the Lady Grace Granville, youngest daughter of the said Earl; which was solemnized [h] on March 9, 1674-5, when they were both very young: it appearing by the entry of the marriage and descent in the college of arms, signed by Sir George Carteret, April 27, 1675, that his grandson was then but eight years of age.

At length this Right Hon. brave, and accomplished man, departed this life in a good old age, in favour with his Sovereign, who designed him [i] the honour of Peerage; and in the highest credit with the most considerable persons of the nation. His actions fully demonstrate his eminent abilities, fortitude and virtues; and the following account of his death was published in the London Gazette, N° 1477: ' Whitehall, 14 Jan. 1679,
' this afternoon died the Right Hon. Sir George Carteret, Vice-
' Chamberlain of his Majesty's Houshold, being near 80 years
' old, of which he had spent 55 in the service of his Majesty
' and his Royal Father.' And the King had so just a sense of his great services, that by his warrant, dated Feb. 11, 1679 (the day before his burial) it is recited [k], ' That whereas he
' died before his Patent for his Barony was sued out, his Ma-
' jesty authorises Elizabeth, his widow, and her youngest chil-
' dren James Carteret, Caroline, wife of Sir Thomas Scot,
' Knt. and Louisa, wife of Sir Robert Atkins, Knt. to enjoy
' their precedency and pre-eminency, as if the said Sir George
' Carteret had actually been created a Baron.'

He was buried at Hawnes [l] in the county of Bedford, on Feb. 12, 1679, Elizabeth his Lady surviving him, who also lived to, a great age, being [m] interred by him, on March 19, 1696. She was his first cousin, and daughter of Sir Philip Carteret of St. Owen, Knt. which estate now centers in the present Earl Granville, as heir male to the said Sir Philip.

Sir George had issue by her three sons [n], 1. Sir Philip; 2. James Carteret, who was Captain and Commander of an East-

[h] Lib. Benefact. in Colleg. Armor. p. 49.   [i] Bill fignat. 23 Car. II.
[k] Ex lib. Comit. Marefcal. in offic. armor,   [l] Ex reg. eccl. paroch de Hawnes.
[m] Ibid.   [n] Ex stemmate intrat. in lib. L. in Colleg. Armor. præd.

India ship, and aftewards of a man of war in the reign of Charles II. but he, as likewise George the third son, died unmarried. He had also five daughters, 1. Anne, married to Sir Nich. Stanning of Marriston, in com. Devon, Knt. of the Bath, and Bart. who died in 1668; Caroline, to Sir Thomas Scot, of Scots-hall in Kent, Knt. Louisa Margareta, to Sir Robert Atkins, of Saperton in com. Gloucester, Knt. son of Sir Robert Atkins, Knt. of the Bath; Rachel, and Elizabeth, who died unmarried.

Philip Carteret, his eldest son, eminently distinguished himself in the civil wars, and was knighted by Charles II. at his arrival in Jersey. He was Governor of Mount-Orgueil castle, when it was besieged by the Parliament forces in the year 1651; o which having been neglected after the fortifying of Elizabeth castle, he could not make any long defence, and it was thought most prudent to capitulate for their lives and fortunes. It is recited by Whitlock, that on Dec. 31, 1651, a petition was presented to the Parliament from Colonel Philip Carteret, and the rest of the late officers of Mount-Orgueil castle, in the isle of Jersey: p That according to the articles upon surrender thereof, an act of oblivion may be passed for the petitioners, which the Parliament ordered accordingly, and approved of the said articles,: and on January 3 following, they ordered Sir Philip Carteret's lands to be restored to him. After the restoration of the King he married Jemima, daughter of Edward Montagu, the first Earl of Sandwich, Vice-Admiral of England; and was with him q in the great sea fight with the Dutch in Solebay, May 28, 1672, wherein his Lordship, in the Royal James, having maintained a fight of five hours, with two Dutch men of war (one of them commanded by Rear-Admiral de Ruyter) and bravely repulsed them with three of their fireships, was at length fired by the fourth, and perished in the flames; and with him Sir Philip Carteret, who would not forsake him, though many had left the ship.

His said lady Jemima died before him r, and was buried at Hawnes, on November 21, 1671. By her he had issue three sons, Sir George Carteret, Bart. created Lord Carteret; Philip, second son, baptized at Hawnes s, on May 20, 1669, who was Captain of the marines, and Lieutenant to Sir Francis Wheeler, Admiral of a squadron of men of war designed for the Mediterranean-sea t, who was foundered in a storm, as he was sailing from Gibraltar towards the Straights, Feb. 17, 1693, his own

---

o Falle's account of Jersey, p. 116.   p Whitlock's memorials, p. 494, 495.   q Burchet's nut. of transactions at sea, p. 402, 403.   r Ex reg. eccl. paroch. de Hawnes prædict.   s Ibid.   t Pointer's chron. hist. vol. 1. p. 400, 401.

Carteret, Earl Granville.

ship the Suffex being loft, and the Admiral, Captain Carteret, and the whole crew, except two Moors, drowned.

Edward Carteret, Efq; third fon [u], baptized at Hawnes, Nov. 28, 1671, was elected [w] to parliament for the borough of Huntingdon, in 10 Will. III. and afterwards ferved [x] for the town of Bedford, in the firft year of Queen Anne. On the acceffion of George I. he was chofen for the borough of Beerealfton, in the county of Devon; and on April 4, 1721, he, with Galfridus Walpole, Efq; were conftituted Poftmafter-general; in which place of joint Poft-mafter-general he continued till his death, which was on April 15, 1739. In 1699, he married Bridget, daughter of Sir Thomas Exton, Dean of the arches court of Canterbury, and Judge of the high court of Admiralty, by whom he had iffue three fons and three daughters; George, who died at Weftminfter fchool in 1718; Edward, who, being appointed in 1731, one of the Council to the Eaft-India factory of Bengal, died there the fame year; and Philip, who died in April, 1727. His three daughters were Bridget, who was one of the Maids of Honour to Queen Caroline, and died unmarried; Anna-Ifabella, wedded to Philip Cavendifh, of Weftbury in the county of Southampton, Efq; Treafurer of Greenwich-hofpital, and one of the Admirals of his Majefty's fleet; and Charlotte, who died unmarried in 1731.

I now return to George Lord Carteret, who, in confideration of his own merits, and the fervices of his anceftors, was raifed to that honour when he was but fifteen years of age.

The preamble to the patent [y] fets forth, ' That his Majefty
' King Charles the fecond, defigning to advance Sir George
' Carteret, late of Hawnes in the county of Bedford, Knight
' and Baronet (he being defcended of an ancient and worthy
' family of that name, which, for many ages paft, had flou-
' rifhed, with much reputation, in the ifland of Jerfey) whom,
' by reafon of his eminent fervices to the late King (of bleffed
' memory) as alfo to himfelf as Vice-chamberlain of his houfe-
' hold, Treafurer of the royal navy, and one of his moft ho-
' nourable Privy-council, he had conftituted Vice-treafurer of
' Ireland, and Treafurer of his military forces there; all which
' employments having managed with fingular prudence, inte-
' grity, and diligence, his Majefty intended to have made him
' a Peer of this realm, had not his death prevented it.'

' Whereas alfo, Sir Philip Carteret, Knight, eldeft fon to
' the faid Sir George, imitating his father's moft loyal example,

. Ex regift. eccl. de Hawnes præd.   w Ex collect. Browne Willis, Ar.
x Ibid.   y Bill fignat. 23 Car. II.

' loft

Carteret, Earl Granville.

'lost his life in his service, in that notable sea-fight with the
'Dutch, which happened on Tuesday the 28th of May, 1672
'(his father then alive) leaving issue Sir George Carteret, now
'also of Hawnes, Baronet, grandson and heir to the above-
'specified Sir George. His Majesty therefore taking into con-
'sideration, the singular merits of the grandfather, and father,
'in testimony of his real sense thereof (by letters-patent, bear-
'ing date the 19th day of October 1681, in the 23d year of
'his reign) advanced him to the degree and dignity of a Baron
'of this realm, by the title of Lord Carteret, of Hawnes, be-
'fore specified, to hold and enjoy to himself, and the heirs-
'male of his body; and for lack of such issue, to Philip Car-
'teret his brother, and the heirs-male of his body; and for
'default of such issue, to Edward Carteret, his other brother,
'and to the heirs-male of his body.'

His Lordship did not take his place in the house of Peers till after the revolution [z], being introduced on January 30, 1688-9, on which day the question was put, ' Whether or no there was 'an original contract between King and people.' In this dispute, ' Whether King James had broke that original contract,' it was carried in the affirmative; and therein the Lord Carteret concurred.

His Lordship departed this life on September 22, 1695, in the 26th year of his age, and was buried [a] near his grandfather at Hawnes, on the 30th of the said month. He had issue, by the Lady Grace, daughter of John Granville Earl of Bath, before-mentioned, three sons and a daughter,

1. George, who was baptized at Hawnes on Feb. 11, 1688, and buried there on June 8, 1689:
2. John Lord Carteret, late Earl Granville:
3. Philip, born at Hawnes on November 6, 1692, distinguished for his great proficiency in learning, who died in the 19th year of his age, on March 19, 1710, and was buried in Westminster-Abbey, where a neat monument is erected to his memory, by the late Earl Granville, with an inscription, wrote by Dr. William Freind, master of Westminster school:
4. Jemima, who died unmarried, and was buried at Hawnes, on May 30, 1733.

The Lady Grace, their mother, had so true a love for her Lord, and honoured his memory so far, that though she was, on his decease, in the bloom of life, she continued a widow to her death, greatly honoured and respected by all her acquaintance. King George I. in consideration of the great services of her father, the Earl of Bath (the only person intrusted

---

[z] Journal dom. Procer. 1688.   [a] Ex regist. de eccl. de Hawnes præd.

Carteret, Earl Granville.

Charles II. and General Monk, in the arduous affair of the reftoration of monarchy and epifcopacy) created her Ladyfhip Vifcountefs Carteret, and Countefs Granville, by letters-patent, bearing date, January 1, 1714-15, in the firft year of his reign, with limitation of thofe honours to her fon John Lord Carteret, late Earl Granville, with remainder of the title of Vifcount Carteret to Edward Carteret, his uncle, and the heirs-male of his body. By the death of her nephew William-Henry, Earl of Bath, in 1711, her Ladyfhip became one of the two coheirs to her father John, Earl of Bath's great eftate in Cornwal and Devonfhire, &c. in which counties her paternal anceftors were poffeffed of Bydeford, Kilkhampton, and other manors, from the time of the conqueft. And, by the noble alliances of her family, fhe derived an illuftrious defcent from the Courtenays, Earls of Devonfhire; from the Bohuns, Earls of Hereford; and fo from King Edward I. Alfo from the Beaumonts, the Lords Bonville, the Gorges, the St. Legers, Butlers, Earls of Ormond, with many other antient and honourable families. And her defcendants have a right to the arms, crefts, and quarterings, of her noble father, the Right Honourable John Earl of Bath. The creft his Lordfhip bore was, on a chapeau gules, turned up ermine, a griffin paffant or. But his anceftors fometimes bore three other crefts, as is evident from their feals, and from the pedigrees and quarterings of the family, in the vifitation of Devonfhire, A. D. 1620, the original whereof is in the Harleian library, and a copy in the College of Arms, marked C. 1.

Her Ladyfhip, departing this life on October 18, 1744, was buried in Weftminfter Abbey; and her only furviving fon, John Lord Carteret, then became Vifcount Carteret and Earl Granville.

Which John Lord Carteret, Vifcount Carteret, and Earl Granville, born on April 22, 1690, was only four years and five months old at his father's deceafe. His Lordfhip was carefully educated at Weftminfter fchool, and afterwards at Chriftchurch College in Oxford.

On May 25, 1711, his Lordfhip was introduced into the Houfe of Peers, where he diftinguifhed himfelf, by his ardent zeal to the fucceffion of King George I, who appointed him [b] one of the Lords of his bedchamber, on his acceffion to the throne: And being appointed, by his Majefty, Bailiff of the ifland of Jerfey, his Lordfhip, July 20, 1715, took the oaths to qualify himfelf for that office, in his Majefty's prefence, at St. James's. Alfo when difcontented people had fomented a

[b] Pointer's chron. hift. p. 785.

rebellion, he was conſtituted, July 6, 1716, Lord-lieutenant and Cuſtos Rotulorum of the county of Devon. Which truſt he held till Auguſt 11, 1721, when, on his Lordſhip's reſignation, Hugh Lord Clinton took the oaths in council, being appointed thereto.

On January 25, 1718-19, he was appointed Ambaſſador Extraordinary, and Miniſter Plenipotentiary, to the Queen of Sweden; but did not ſet out on his embaſſy till June 1 following. His Lordſhip embarked in the river for Gottenburgh, in his way to Stockholm, where he arrived June 30, 1719, after eight days paſſage from Gottenburgh. On July 6 he preſented his memorial to that Queen, and had her Majeſty's anſwer the ſame day. His firſt buſineſs was, to remove the difficulties in the commerce of the Britiſh ſubjects in the Baltick, and to procure ſatisfaction for the loſſes they had ſuſtained; wherein he ſucceeded ſo well, that the Queen ordered an equitable compenſation to the rightful claimants, and that the ſhips belonging to Great Britain ſhould have freedom of commerce and navigation in the Baltick, and not be moleſted, though they were bound to ports taken by the Czar of Muſcovy from her Majeſty. And his Lordſhip, in a private audience, on November 6, 1719 (when he firſt took on him the character of Ambaſſador Extraordinary and Plenipotentiary) offered the King his maſter's mediation to the Queen, to make peace between Sweden and Denmark; alſo his Majeſty's mediation between Sweden and the Czar; and the Queen accepted both mediations.

The peace between Sweden, Pruſſia, and Hanover, concluded by his Lordſhip, was proclaimed at Stockholm, on March 9, 1719-20. Having alſo ſettled a preliminary treaty between Sweden and Denmark; and having been appointed Ambaſſador Extraordinary and Plenipotentiary, with the Lord Polwarth, to the congreſs at Brunſwick, for finally adjuſting all differences in the North, his Lordſhip had audience of leave of the King and Queen of Sweden, on June 9, 1720, at Carlberg, and had the honour to dine the ſame day with their Majeſties, who expreſſed their eſteem for him in the moſt gracious terms. On June 13 he ſet out for Denmark, and on the 19th, at Fredricſburgh, he had his firſt audience of the King of Denmark, by whom he was very favourably received. His Lordſhip brought with him the treaty of peace between Denmark and Sweden, agreed to and ſigned on the part of Sweden; which, after a conference on July 1, and another on the next day, between his Lordſhip and the Daniſh miniſters, was agreed to likewiſe by the King of Denmark, and ſigned by his Miniſter Plenipotentiary on July 3.

The King being then at Hanover, this mention is made of his Lordship in the London Gazette:

'Hanover, August 19. The King has been pleased to ap-
'point the Earl Stanhope, the Lord Carteret, and Sir Robert
'Sutton, to be his Majesty's Ambassadors Extraordinary and
'Plenipotentiaries at the congress at Cambray'

The ratifications of the treaty of peace, between Denmark and Sweden, were exchanged on October 22, 1720, at Copenhagen; which put an end to the war that had so long raged between Sweden, Russia, Denmark, and the King of Prussia. Whereupon his Lordship, taking his leave of his Danish Majesty, proceeded to Hamburgh, which place he left on November 15, 1720, and coming through Hanover in his way to England, arrived at St. James's on December 5, O. S. following.

His Lordship was graciously received by his Majesty, who was so well satisfied with his successful negotiations, that he soon after appointed him his Ambassador Extraordinary to the court of France; but when he had received his instructions, and was preparing to set out for that kingdom, James Craggs, Esq; Principal Secretary of State, departing this life, on February 17, 1720-1, the King was pleased to appoint his Lordship to succeed him in that office on March 4, ensuing; and the next day his Majesty being present in council, at St. James's, he was, by his command, sworn one of the Lords of his most honourable Privy Council; as likewise one of his Majesty's Principal Secretaries of State, and took his place at the board accordingly.

On May 26, 1723, the King declaring to his Privy Council, that some extraordinary affairs called him abroad for the summer, his Lordship thereupon was appointed one of the Lords Justices for the administration of the government. And by his Majesty's command, his Lordship, and the Viscount Townshend, his two Principal Secretaries of State, were appointed to wait on him at Hanover.

The King set out from Hanover, on his return for England, on December 18; but the Lords Carteret and Townshend arrived at the Hague on the 19th, and had several conferences with the chief persons of the government there on affairs of importance. His Majesty was detained at Helvoetsluys, by contrary winds, from the 24th to the 27th of December, O. S. when the wind coming to the S. E. his Majesty embarked, and after a very fine passage landed at Margate, about two on Saturday the 28th, with the Lord Carteret, and the Lord Townshend.

Carteret, Earl Granville.

On April 3, 1724, there being several removes at court, the Duke of Newcastle succeeded the Lord Carteret in his office of Principal Secretary of State; and his Lordship the same day was constituted Lord-lieutenant of Ireland. His Lordship's affairs requiring his continuing in England for some time, it was October 22, 1724, when he embarked on board the Dublin yacht, at Holyhead, about one in the morning, and had so quick a passage, that he landed at Dublin the same day about noon. He immediately proceeded to the Castle with the usual solemnity, and in the council-chamber took the oaths appointed to be taken by his Majesty's Lieutenant and Chief Governor of Ireland. His Lordship was well acquainted with the state of the nation before he went over, and procured Mr. Wood's patent for coining halfpence and farthings, which had been complained of as a great grievance, to be revoked. Whilst his Lordship was in Ireland, his Majesty in council, June 1, 1725, declaring his intention of going out of the kingdom for a short time, was pleased to appoint him one of the Lords Justices during his absence.

On Sept. 21, 1725, his Excellency went with the usual state to the House of Peers, and being attended there by the Commons, delivered his speech to them from the throne: And having given the royal assent to several acts, concluded the session with another speech, on March 3, 1725-6.

His Lordship having constituted Hugh, Archbishop of Armagh, R. West, Lord Chancellor, and William Conolly, Esq; Speaker of the House of Commons, Lords Justices during his absence, embarked for England, and arriving at St. James's in May, 1726, was graciously received by his Majesty.

On May 31, 1727, his Lordship was again declared one of the Lords Justices for the administration of the government during the King's absence, who set out from St. James's on June 3, following, and died on the 11th, at Osnabrug, in his way to Hanover.

Upon advice thereof, the Lords of the Privy Council, assembling at Leicester-House, his Successor George II. caused them to be sworn of his Privy Council, the Lord Carteret being present, who was also at the proclaiming of his Majesty at Leicester-House, and signed the Proclamation on June 14, 1727. And his Majesty in Council at Kensington, July 29, that year, was graciously pleased to declare his Lordship Lord Lieutenant, and Chief Governor of his Majesty's Kingdom of Ireland.

His Lordship went over in November following, on a new Parliament being called; and on Tuesday, the 28th of the same month, went with the usual state to the House of Peers, and

and being seated on the throne, sent for the Commons, and directed them to chuse a Speaker: And they having unanimously elected the Right Honourable William Conolly, Esq; into that office, he was by them presented to his Lordship, and approved of. The same day he opened the session with a speech to both Houses, who unanimously resolved upon humble and dutiful addresses to his Majesty, which were presented to his Excellency on November 30, 1727.

The Parliament continued sitting till May 6, 1728, when his Excellency gave the royal assent to twenty public acts; and then making a speech, expressing his regard for the welfare of that kingdom, the Lord Chancellor, by his command, prorogued the Parliament to Tuesday, June 4. And his Lordship appointing the Archbishop of Armagh, Thomas Windham, Esq; Lord Chancellor, and William Conolly, Esq; Speaker of the House of Commons, Lords Justices, during his absence, embarked for England, and arrived at St. James's about the middle of May, 1728.

In 1729, his Lordship returning to Ireland, and on September 23, the Houses of Parliament meeting, according to prorogation, opened the sessions with a speech; and the Lords and Commons attended him with their respective addresses, both to the King and his Excellency, on the 25th. Several bills having passed, after being approved of by the Council in England, as usual, his Lordship on April 15, 1730, addressing both Houses from the throne, ordered the Parliament to be prorogued to May 14, following: after which, viz. on the 20th of the same month, he embarked for England, and arrived on the 30th at London.

As his Lordship had continued Lord Lieutenant of Ireland the usual time, his Majesty in council at Windsor, on June 19, 1730, was pleased to declare his Grace, Lionel Duke of Dorset, Lieutenant-General and General Governor of his kingdom of Ireland; and the Earl of Chesterfield Lord Steward of his houshold, in the room of the Duke of Dorset. Whereby his Lordship had no public employment from 1730, till February 12, 1741-2, when his Majesty, at St. James's, was pleased to declare him one of his Principal Secretaries of State, and the next day he was sworn in council, and took his place at the board accordingly.

In September, 1742, his Lordship was sent to the States General, to concert measures with them, in that very critical juncture, for the support of their liberties, and the good of the common cause.

In 1743 he waited on his Majesty to Hanover, who, before his leaving St. James's, appointed him one of the Lords Justices,

tices, and his Lordship attended all the campaign that year in Germany.

His Lordship by descent from his grandfather, Sir George Carteret, Vice-chamberlain of the Houshold to King Charles II. and of his Privy-council, being one of the eight Lords proprietors of South and North Carolina [c] : and the other seven Lords proprietors having sold and surrendered their respective rights and titles therein to his Majesty, confirmed by act of parliament, in the second year of his reign, intitled, ' An act for establishing an agreement with seven of ' the Lords proprietors of Carolina, for the surrender of their ' title and interest in that province to his Majesty.' And all his Lordship's rights and titles whatsoever, in the Carolina's, being saved and reserved unto him by the said act, he, by his humble petition to his Majesty in council, in 1742, reciting the several letters patent, made by King Charles II. to Edward, then Earl of Clarendon, George, then Duke of Albemarle, William, then Lord Craven, John, then Lord Berkeley, Anthony, then Lord Ashley, Sir George Carteret, Knt. and Bart. Sir William Berkeley, and Sir Iohn Colleton, Knt. and Bart. all since deceased ; as also the Act of parliament before recited : And that he is still entitled to one undivided eighth part of the said provinces, and of all the premises granted by the said several letters patent, as also of the arrears of quit rents, duties, &c. humbly prayed his Majesty, that his said eighth part of his soil of the said provinces, and territories, might be set out, and allotted to him, as should be agreed on between persons, to be appointed by his Majesty, and the said Lord Carteret. To hold and enjoy the same for ever hereafter in severalty, to the said John Lord Carteret, his heirs and assigns; together with all and every the same royalties, powers, &c. (the government thereof only excepted) as far as concerns such eighth part to be so allotted to the said John Lord Carteret. And thereupon humbly offered and proposed to his Majesty, his heirs and successors, his share and interest of and in the government of the said provinces and territories ; and to convey, release and confirm, to his Majesty, his heirs, &c. the other seven parts of the said provinces.

Whereupon his Majesty referred the said petition to the Lords of the Committee of his most honourable Privy council; which was referred by them to the Lords Commissioners of trade and plantations, who having examined the said petition, reported to the said Lords of the Committee of Privy-council, ' That it would be for his Majesty's service, that the said Lord

---

[c] Grant and release of one eighth part of Carolina from his Majesty to Lord Carteret, 17 Sept. 18 Geo. II. and surrender of seven eighth parts of Carolina from Lord Carteret to his Majesty.

'Carteret's property should be separated from that of his Ma-
'jesty, wherein the said Lord Carteret should enjoy, whatever
'he was entitled to by the charters of Carolina, and the aforesaid
'act of Parliament, and conceived the method, &c. proposed
'by the said Lord Carteret, would be most effectual.' Which
report, the Lords of his Majesty's Privy-council taking into
confideration, did agree in opinion with the said Lords Commiffioners of trade and plantations: And on August 24, 1742,
made their report to his Majesty, that the said Lord Carteret's
property should be separated from that of his Majesty's.

They moreover proposed, that the respective Governors of
South and North Carolina, or either of them, be ordered to
nominate and appoint proper persons, as Commissioners on his
Majesty's behalf, not exceeding five, who, in conjunction with
a like number, appointed by the said Lord Carteret, as Commissioners on his behalf, should be impowered to set out, and
allot to the said Lord Carteret, one full eighth part of the provinces of Carolina, in such part or parts thereof, as should be
agreed on by the said Commissioners, and that they should be
required to make a return of the said proceedings to his Majesty
in council, within eighteen months after the date of his Majesty's order; and also to lay before his Majesty a plan, containing a full and exact description of the said lands, together
with the respective boundaries thereof, in order (in case his
Majesty should approve thereof) for conveying the same to the
said Lord Carteret, in such manner, as should be advised by
his Majesty's Council learned in the law: Provided the said
Lord Carteret made a surrender of all his pretensions to the government of the said provinces of Carolina, &c.

Thereupon his Majesty in council, on Sept. 15, 1742, ap-
proving thereof, and by his order Commissioners being appointed, to allot to the said Lord Carteret one full eighth part
of the provinces of Carolina; they, by their report to his Majesty in council, dated December 6, 1743, certified that in pursuance of his Majesty's said order, they did set out and allot to
the said John Lord Carteret, one full eighth part of the provinces of Carolina, in one entire separate district in the province
of North Carolina, next adjoining, and contiguous to the province of Virginia; which eighth part is bounded on the north
by the line which divides Carolina from Virginia; to the east
by the great Western-ocean, commonly so called, and as far
southerly, as Cedar-stake, set upon the sea side, in the latitude
of 35 degrees and 34 minutes, at north latitude, being six
miles and a half to the southward of Chickinacomack inlet;
from that stake by a west line, which passed twenty-five feet,
to the southward of the house wherein Thomas Wallis liveth;
and

and fo weft, as far as the bounds of the charter, granted to the Lords proprietors of Carolina by King Charles II. which weft line went 1660 poles to the north of the fouth end of Bath-town: And the faid Commiffioners did, purfuant to order, tranfmit to his Majefty a plan, containing a full and exact defcription of the faid one eighth part of the faid provinces and territories, fo fet out and allotted to the faid John Lord Carteret.

And purfuant thereunto, on May 9, 1744, his Majefty was pleafed, with the advice of his Privy-council, to approve of the allotment of land thereby made to the faid Lord Carteret, and to order Mr. Attorney, and Mr. Sollicitor-general, to prepare fuch inftruments or deeds, as are propofed by the faid report, orders, &c. Accordingly, on Sept. 17, 1744, 18 Geo. II. his Majefty by indenture of the one part, and the right honourable John Lord Carteret on the other part, in confideration of the faid Lord Carteret's furrendering, releafing, and confirming to his Majefty, all his eftate, right, title, and intereft, of, in, and to the government of the faid province of Carolina, and of, in, and to the faid feven eighth parts, divided from the faid one eighth part, fo allotted to the faid John Lord Carteret; and alfo the faid Lord Carteret's affigning to his Majefty, all arrears of quit-rents, debts, &c. then due and owing to his Majefty, and to the faid Lord Carteret, from the farmers, tenants, &c. of the faid feven eighth parts of the faid provinces, fituate within any part of the feven eighth parts thereof: Did thereby grant, &c. for himfelf, his heirs and fucceffors, to the faid John Lord Carteret, his executors, adminiftrators, and affigns, all the faid one eighth part of the provinces fo feparated, and allotted to the faid John Lord Carteret, by the faid commiffioners, with all the yearly rents, iffues and profits thereof, &c. together with all rights, privileges, royalties, liberties, immunities, &c. of what kind foever, within the faid one eighth part of the provinces or territories, in as ample manner and form, as the faid John Lord Carteret, &c. held, ufed or enjoyed, by virtue of letters patent, granted by King Charles II. Excepting neverthelefs out of this grant, the powers of making laws, calling or holding of affemblies, erecting courts of juftice, appointing judges or juftices, pardoning criminals, granting titles of honour, making ports or havens, taking cuftoms and duties on goods, &c. executing martial law, exercifing any of the royal rights of a County Palatine, &c. or exercifing any other prerogatives, &c. relating to the adminiftration of the government of the faid one eighth part of the faid provinces: To hold the faid one eighth part, &c. to him, as aforefaid, his heirs, and affigns

Carteret, Earl Granville.

for ever; yielding and paying to his Majesty, his heirs and successors, the annual rent of one pound thirteen shillings and four pence on the feast of All-Saints, for ever: also one fourth part of all gold and silver ore found within the said eighth part of the premises.

On November 24 following, his Lordship having resigned the seals into his Majesty's hands at St. James's, William Earl of Harrington was appointed one of the principal Secretaries of State in his place.

On February 10, 1745-6, his Grace the Duke of Newcastle, and the Earl of Harrington, resigning, at St. James's the seals of their respective offices of principal Secretary of State, his Majesty was pleased the same day to appoint his Lordship to be principal Secretary of State; but on the 14th of the same month, his Lordship resigned the seals again into his Majesty's hands.

On June 22, 1749, at Kensington, his Lordship was elected one of the Knights Companions of the most noble order of the Garter, together with the present King, the Margrave of Anspach, Duke of Leeds, Duke of Bedford, and Earl of Albemarle; and was installed with them at Windsor, on July 12, 1750. In 1751, his Majesty having been pleased to appoint his Lordship President of his most honourable Privy-council, he was sworn at Kensington on June 17, and kept that office till his death. And his Majesty at St. James's declaring in Council, on March 30, 1752, his intention of going out of England for a short time, was pleased to nominate him one of the Lords Justices during his absence. And his Lordship was with the Duke of Cumberland, and other great officers of state, commissioners for opening the session of parliament at Westminster, on May 31, 1754; also in another commission for putting an end to the session on June 5 following, when they prorogued it to Thursday the 8th of August.

His Lordship first took to wife, at Longleat, on October 17, 1710, Frances, born on March 6, 1694, only daughter of Sir Robert Worsley, Bart. by his Lady Frances, only daughter of Thomas first Viscount Weymouth, by Frances, his Lady, eldest daughter of Heneage second Earl of Winchelsea, by the Lady Mary his wife, daughter of William Duke of Somerset, and the Lady Frances his Dutchess, eldest daughter of the famous Robert Devereux, Earl of Essex, the favourite of Queen Elizabeth.

Which Lady, after accompanying his Lordship thrice to Ireland, when he was Lord Lieutenant, also accompanied him to Hanover, where she died on June 9, 1743. Her Ladyship was
brought

Carteret, Earl Granville.

brought over, in November following, and buried in Westminster Abbey.

His Lordship died on January 2, 1763, aged near 73, having had by his said Lady three sons.

1. The Honourable George Carteret, who was born February 14, 1716-17, and died in June, 1721.
2. The Honourable John Carteret, who was born on October 19, 1719, and died young.
3. Robert Viscount Carteret, now Earl Granville.

Likewise five daughters.
1. Frances, who died an infant.
2. Lady Grace, who was married on July 22, 1729, to Lionel, Earl of Dysert, of the kingdom of Scotland, and died on July 23, 1755, leaving issue.
3. Lady Louisa, born September 15, 1714[d], who was married on July 3, 1733, to Thomas, second Viscount Weymouth, and died on December, 25, 1736.
4. Lady Georgina-Carolina[e], born on March 12, 1716, and married Feb. 14, 1733-4, to the honourable John Spencer, Esq; brother to his Grace Charles, Duke of Marlborough, who left issue by her one son, John, now Earl Spencer. And she, secondly, married William Earl Cowper.
5. Lady Frances, born on April 16, 1718[f], and married on May 24, 1743, to John Hay, Marquiss of Tweeddale.

His Lordship, on April 14, 1744, married, secondly, Lady Sophia, daughter of Thomas Earl of Pomfret, and the Lady Henrietta-Louisa his wife, daughter and sole heir to John Lord Jefferies, by his wife the Lady Charlotte Herbert, daughter and heir of Philip Earl of Pembroke and Montgomery. Her Ladyship was delivered of a daughter, Lady Sophia, on August 26, 1745, and died on October 7, following of a fever.

6. Lady Sophia, the said daughter, married on Feb. 3, 1765, to William Lord Wycombe, Earl of Shelburne, &c.

Robert, the present Earl Granville, was born on September 21, 1721; and in 1744 was, on a vacancy, returned member for the borough of Yarmouth, in the isle of Wight, to the ninth parliament of Great Britain. His Lordship, besides his paternal estate, inherits that of his grandfather, Sir Robert Worsley, before-mentioned; but is yet unmarried.

TITLES.] Robert Carteret, Lord Carteret of Hawnes, Viscount Carteret, and Earl Granville.

CREATIONS.] Baron Carteret, of Hawnes, in the county of Bedford, by letters-patent, Oct. 19, 1681, 33 Car. II. Viscount Carteret and Earl Granville, Jan. 1. 1 Geo. I.

d Ex Inscript. sup. ejus Arca. in Eccl. paroch. Deveril Langbridg', sepult.
e Ex regist. præd.   f Ibid.

ARMS.]

Carteret, Earl Granville.

ARMS.] Quarterly, firſt and fourth, Gules, three Clarions or Claricords, Or, for Granville; ſecond and third, Gules, four Fuſils in Feſs, Argent, for Carteret.

CREST.] Above a Wreath, upon a Mount, a Squirrel Sejant, all proper.

SUPPORTEES.] Two wing'd Deer, Gules, attir'd, Or.

MOTTO.] LOYALL DEVOIR.

CHIEF SEAT.] At Hawnes in the county of Bedford, four miles from Bedford.

END of the FOURTH VOLUME.

THE INDEX.

A.

ADAIR, Mr. 137
Adams, Thomas 247
AILESFORD (FINCH) EARL of 340
——— Heneage 340, 341, 342
ALBEMARLE (KEPPEL) EARL of 130
——— Arnold, Jooſt *ibid.*
——— William-Anne 133
——— George 137
Alderſey, John 143
Allen, John 152
—— Sir Chriſtopher 325
Allington, Giles 350
Allot, Anne 303
Ancram, William, Earl of 36
Andover, William, Viſcount 341
Andrews, John 56
Angleſea, Chriſtopher Villiers, Earl of 160
Anneſley, Brian 350
Anſtis, John, Garter 40
Anthony, ——— 302
Ap Harry, Johan 245
Appeſley, Sir Allan 291
Archbold, Sir Henry 312
Archer, Thomas, Lord 97
——— William 274
Argyle, John Campbell, Duke of 299
Arlington, Iſabella, Counteſs of 336
Arthington, Henry 286
Arundel, Henry Fitz-Allan, Earl of 114
——— Sir John 191
——— Francis 292
——— of Trerife, John, Lord *ibid.*

Aſhburnham, John 186
——— William 186
——— John, Lord 223
Aſhley, Solomon 356
Aſhurſt, Sir Henry 329
Aſtely, Thomas 31
Aſtley, Sir John 339
Atherton, John 223
Athlone, Godart de Ginkell, Earl of 127
Atkins, Sir Robert 288, 397
Audre, Walter de 101
Ayleſbury, Robert Bruce, Earl of 280
Aylesford, Heneage, Earl of 312

B.

Babington, Thomas 28
Bacon, Benjamin 337
Bagot, Sir John 155
——— Sir Walter 312, 332
Bangham, Edward 273
Banks, Sir John 341
Barker, Henry 152
Barnes, Captain 31
Barret, Charles 251
Barrymore, James Barry, Earl of 227
Baſſet, William 2
——— Ralph, Lord 276
——— Thomas 277
Baſtard, Polexfen 188
Bathurſt, Peter 281
Bayley, Sir Nicholas 329
Bearcroft, Philip 152
Beauchamp, John 190
Beaufort, Henry, Duke of 151
Beaumont, John 23
——— Richard 158
——— Anthony 159
Beckwith, Sir Leonard 216

Bedford,

INDEX.

Bedford, Wriothesley, Duke of	178
Beeston, Henry de	211
———— Ralph	287
Bellasyse, Sir Henry	32
Bellers, John	156
Bellew, Walter, Lord	292
Belward, Richard de	210
———— William de	ibid.
Benne, ————	190
Bennet, William	334
———— John	334, 335
———— Thomas	334
———— Richard	ibid.
———— Simon	ibid.
———— Ralph	335
———— Sir John	ibid.
———— Sir Thomas	336
———— John, Lord Ossulston	337
———— Charles, ————	ibid.
Benson, Robert	341
Berkeley, Sir Henry	198
———— Henry, Lord	278
Berkshire, Thomas Howard, Earl of	34
Berners, John, Lord	42
Bertie, Peregrine	188
Bertram, Ralph de	5
———— Roger	8
Best, George	33
Bigberry, William	179
Bilson, Thomas	309
Bingley, Robert Benson, Lord	341
Birmingham, Miles, Lord	301
Blacket, Sir William	116, 178
Blague, Thomas	207
Bland, Sir John	341
Blandford, William, Marquis of	208
Bletsoe, Lord St. John of	153
Blount, Sir Walter	73
———— Sir John	301
Blythman, Jasper	287
Bocking, Edmund	350
Bodvile Sir John	224
Bokenham, Thomas	71
Bonithon, Edward	191
Bostock, Sir Warren de	232
Boteler, William	190
Bourchier, William	42
Bays, John de	179
———— John	301
Bradford, Richard Newport, Earl of	221
Brampton, Brian de	237
———— Family of	238
Breadalbin, John, Earl of	176
Breant, Falcase de	39
Brereton, Sir William de	217
———— Sir Randal	219, 221
Brevint, Daniel	380
Brews, John de	276
Bridgwater, Scroop Egerton, Duke of	178, 332
BRISTOL (HERVEY) EARL of	343
———— John	355
———— George-William	358
Brome, Sir Christopher	75
Bromley, John	217
Bromwick, Sir John	244
Brook, John	278
Brown, Thomas	152
———— Francis	157
———— Sir Thomas	187
Brudenel, James	313
Buckingham, Countess of	159
———— George Villiers, Duke of	159, 160, 169
Burley, Sir John	245
Burnel, Acton	33
Burston, ————	194
Burton, Henry	179
———— Robert	ibid.
Butler of Bramfield, John, Lord	159
Butt, Richard	188
Button, Sir William	261

C.

Cæsar, Robert	145
Cale, Adonia	179
Calveley, Sir George	223
Canel, William	191
Capel, Sir Henry	335
Carew, Sir Nicholas	31
———— Sir William	151

Carew,

INDEX.

Carew, Sir George 193
Carey, Sir William 179
Carr, Sir Robert 337, 355
Carrio, William de 41
Carswell, William 180
Carter, Rev. Mr. 127
Carteret, Philip 182, 361, 362, 369, 376, 379, 400
────── Sir William de 360
────── Aufrey de ibid.
────── Reginald de 360, 362, 366, 370
────── John de 363, 364
────── Sir Reginald 368, 373
────── Sir John de 369
────── William de 372
────── Philip de 374
────── Helier de 376
────── Edward 377, 399
────── Apricias 378
────── Joshua ibid.
────── Sir Edward ibid.
────── Sir Charles ibid.
────── Sir Philip 379, 397, 398
────── Amias 379, 380
────── Gideon 379
────── Sir George 380, 381
────── Sir Charles 380
────── Captain James 397
────── Captain Philip 398
────── George, Lord 399
Cary, Sir Edward 326
Castlemain, Roger Palmer, Earl of 174
Castleton, James Saunderson, Earl of 122
Catesby, Thomas 332
Cave, Sir Ambrose 327
Cavendish, Philip 399
Chelmundeleigh, Sir Hugh de 211
Chester, Hugh Kiveliock, Earl of 210
────── Randal ────── ibid.
────── Rennelph de Blundeville, Earl of 212
Chesterfield, Philip Stanhope, Earl of 31

Cheyney, Sir John 217
Chideock, Sir John 103
Chichley, John 345
Chiffinch, William 177
Child, William 140
────── Sir Lacon William 145
Cholmley, Sir Richard 185
CHOLMONDELEY (CHOLMONDELEY) EARL of 210
────────── Hugh, Earl of 225
────────── George, Earl of 226, 228
Cholmondeley, Robert 211, 212, 213, 229
────── Hugh, Lord of 212, 213, 219, 221
────── John, of Chorley 213
────── Sir Richard 214
────── Roger de 215, 216
────── Richard 217, 218, 219
────── Randle 219
────── Thomas, of Vale Royal 223
────── Charles, ────── ibid.
────── Robert, Lord 224
────── General James 227
Clanricarde, William, Earl of 279
Clare, John Holles, Earl of 290
Clarges, Walter 281
────── Sir Walter 282
Clarke, John 156
────── Richard 158
────── Sir Rowland 325
Clavering, Roger 301
Clerk, (or, de Malpas) Hugh le 210
────── Sir Peter de 211
────── David le 212
Clervaux, Sir John 103
Cleveland, Barbara, Duchess of 174
────── and Southampton, Charles, Duke of ibid.
Clifton, Gervase, Lord 31

Cobb,

INDEX.

Cobb, Captain	194	Coventry, Thomas		*ibid.*
Cocket, John	348	——— Sir Thomas, Lord		*ibid.*
Coghlene, Francis	356	——— Sir John		143
Coke, Sir Edward	159	——— Francis		144
Coles, Mr.	152	——— George, Lord		147
Colles, John	143	——— John, ———		148
Collins, ———	350	——— Thomas,—	149,	152
Colthorpe, Sir William	345	——— Walter		151
Colville, Edward	338	——— John Berkeley		152
Compton, Sir Henry	116	Courtenay, Sir William		341
——— Sir Thomas	159	Cowling, John		190
Conolly, William	298	Cowper, William, Earl		410
Constable, Sir Marmaduke	27	Cradock, George		225
——— Sir Robert	215	——— William		334
Conway, Edward, Viscount	252	Crassus, Raimond		41
Conyers, Sir John	23, 108	Craven, Sir William		146
——— John, Lord	32	Crawford, John		312
——— Richard	107	Credye, John		193
——— Sir Christopher	116	Creedy, William		179
——— William, Lord	215	Creighton, Robert, Bp. of Bath		
Cooke, Edward	186			186
Cookes, Sir Thomas	95	Cresset, John		249
Coppleston, Henry	180	Creswell, Robert		108
Coppleston, Christopher	182	Croft, Sir Jasper		232
Corbet, Roger	71	Crofts, Sir Edward		247
——— Sir Roger	219, 244	——— Sir John		336
——— Thomas	241	Crooke, Sir George		334
——— Peter, Lord	242	Cumberland, Henry Clifford,		
——— Sir Andrew	250	Earl of		216
Cornhill, Henry de	41	——— Francis ———		
Cornwall, Sir Edward de	238	Earl of		290
——— John	249			
Cotes, Thomas	244	**D.**		
——— John	281	Dacre, William, Lord		74
Cotton, Richard	116	Dalton, John		33
——— Thomas	278	Danby, Thomas		287
——— Sir Robert	*ibid.*	Darcy of Chich, John, Lord		114
Condray, Peter	74	Dartmouth, William, Lord		309
COVENTRY (COVENTRY) EARL		DARTMOUTH (LEGGE) EARL		
of	139	of		300
——— Thomas	149, 151	——— William 312, 314,		
——— Gilbert	151			341
——— William	151, 152	Dashwood, Sir Francis		96
——— George - William		Daubeney, Philip		363
	152	Davenport, John		218
Coventry, Henry	139, 145, 152	Davys, ———		302
——— William	139, 146	Dawney, Sir Thomas		28
——— John	139, 143	D'Arcy, Michael		2
——— Vincent	140	——— Philip		4
——— Richard	*ibid.*	——— Sir Philip		7, 8
				D'Arcy,

INDEX.

D'Arcy, Robert 7
—— Norman 9
—— Sir John 9, 18, 23
—— John, Lord 10, 18, 22, 28, 287
—— William 18
—— Sir Roger ibid.
—— Thomas, Lord Darcy of Chiche ibid.
—— Philip, Lord 20
—— Thomas, —— 23
—— George, —— 28
—— Sir Arthur 29
—— Sir Henry 31
—— Sir Edward ibid.
—— Sir Robert ibid.
—— Thomas 31, 33
—— Conyers, Lord 32, 33
—— Sir William 32
—— Henry 33
—— Marmaduke ibid.
—— Sir Conyers 35
De Arecy, Norman 1, 3, 5
—— Robert 2, 3
—— Thomas 2, 3, 5
—— Roger 5
D'eincourt, Ralph, Lord 2
D'Jong, Peter 208
De la Bere, Sir John 232
Denbigh, William Fielding, Earl of 159
Deniband, John 179
Derby, James Stanley, Earl of 290
Dethick, George 336
—— Sir William Garter ibid.
Devic, Sir Henry de 380
Digby, John 157
Doddington, Sir William 143
Donkoff, Count 339
Donolan, James 292
Dorman, George 221
Doublet, Sieur 37
Dowse, Sir Francis 380
Dray, Sir Richard de 46
Drew, Thomas 55
Drokensford, John 46
Drury, Henry 347
Du Roy, Frederic-Charles 290
Vol. IV.

Ducket, John 53
Dugdale, Sir William Garter 40, 210
Dumaresque, —— 380, 381
Duncomb, William 334
Dutton, Sir Thomas 211, 218
Dysart, Lionel Talmash, Earl of 221, 413

E.

Edgcumbe, Pierce 150
Edwards, Samuel 194
—— Sir Francis 229
Effingham, Thomas, Lord Howard of 288
Egerton, Philip de 211
—— John, of Oulton 223, 225
Elwes, Gervase 354
—— Sir Gervase ibid.
Essex, Algernon, Earl of 35
—— Robert, Earl of 279
Exeter, John Cecil, Earl of 337
Exton, Sir Thomas 399

F.

Fairfax, Sir William 28
—— Thomas, Lord 173
Fauconberg, Thomas Bellasyse, Viscount 29
Faulkner, Richard 56
Felton, Sir Thomas 355
Fermor, Sir John 31
Ferrers, Edward 75
—— Sir Humphrey 281
—— of Chartley, Elizabeth, Baroness ibid.
FERRERS (SHIRLEY) EARL 275
—— Robert 280
—— Washington 282, 283
—— Henry 282
—— Laurence ibid.
Finch, George 281
—— John 341
—— John Saville ibid.
—— Henry ibid.
Fisher, Sir Clement ibid.
Fitton, Hamon 211
Fitz-gerald, George 358
—— Sir Robert 18
E e Fitz-

INDEX.

Fitz-geralds in Ireland, defcent of	41
——— Robert	39
——— Henry	ibid.
——— Warine	ibid.
——— Gerald	40
——— David, Bifhop of St. David's	ibid.
Fitz-harding, John Berkley, Vifcount	176, 196
Fitz Hugh, Henry, Lord	22
——— John de	344
Fitz-marmaduke, John	100
Fitz-other, Walter	38, 39
——— Sir Other	39
——— Robert	41
——— William	42
Fitz-Reynfrid, Gilbert	45
Fitz-Warrin, William, Lord	42
Fitz-Williams, Sir Richard	286
——— Sir Thomas	348
Fleming, Sir William	285
——— Gilbert Fane	338
Fogg, Jonathan	313
Foley, Thomas	262, 271
——— Philip	329
Fowke, ———	176
Frampton, George	140
Frankland, Frederic	120
Frecheville, Sir Peter	29
——— John, Lord	34
Fulford, Francis	187
Fulthorp, Sir William	101
Furnefe, Sir Robert	281

G.

Gage, Sir George	351
——— Sir Edward	ibid.
Gardiner, John	250
Gargrave, Thomas	288
Gafcoigne-Nightingale, Jofeph	282
Gafcoigne, John	286
——— Sir William	287
Gerard, Gilbert, Lord	211
Gerrards, of Bromley, Bryn, &c.	41
Gifford, Sir John	278
Glanville, Sir John	193

Glinne, John	191
Gloucefter, Thomas of Woodftock, Duke of	42
GODOLPHIN (GODOLPHIN) EARL of	190
——— Sidney	205
——— Francis	207
Godolphin, John de	190
——— Alexander	ibid.
——— David	ibid.
——— Thomas	190, 191
——— John	190
——— William	191, 196
——— Sir William	191, 198
——— Francis	191, 194, 197
——— John, Lord	194
——— Sidney	194, 196
——— Henry, D. D.	194, 198
——— Francis, of Baylis	199
——— Sidney, Lord	203
Goïeth, William	343
Gooderick, Sir Henry	308
Goulbourne, Sir William de	211
Gower, William, Earl	410
Grafton, Henry, Duke of	174
Graham, Richard	150
Grandifon, William Villiers, Vifcount	174
GRANVILLE (CARTERET) EARL	360
——— John	401
——— Robert	410
Granville, John, Earl of Bath	397
——— Grace, Countefs	401
Gravemore, S.	133
Gray, Richard	115
Green, Walter	56
——— John	152
Grendon, Henry	244
Grey, of Wilton, Henry, Lord	22
——— Sir Henry	75
——— of Werke, Ford, Lord	337
Greyftock, John, Lord	23
Griffith, Sir William	221
——— Walter	250
Grofvenor, Sir Richard	223
Gunning,	

INDEX.

Gunning, John	153	Hervey, Count	*ibid.*
Gunter-Nichol, Sir Charles	314	——— De Yuvon	*ibid.*
		——— Henry	*ibid.*
H.		Hervey, Ofbert	344
Hackluit, Sir John	246	——— Adam	*ibid.*
Hallifax, George Montagu, Earl of	120	——— William de	344, 345
		——— John 345, 348, 350,	352
Hampden, Richard	329		
Hanmer, Sir Thomas	352	——— Sir Nicholas	345, 348
Harbottle, Bertram	106	——— Thomas 345, 347, 355	
Harcourt, Sir Simon	327	——— George	346
Hare, Sir John	142	——— Gerard	347
Hartlefton, Sir Richard	376	——— Sir Thomas 348, 354	
Harley, Sir John de	231, 245	——— Sir George	348
——— Sir William de	231	——— William, Lord 349, 354	
——— Nicholas de	232	——— William 350, 356, 358	
——— Sir Richard de	233, 246	——— Francis	350
		——— Sir William	351
——— Henry de	237	——— Carr, Lord	355
——— Malcolm de	*ibid.*	——— Henry Afton	356
——— Sir Brian	244	——— Charles	*ibid.*
——— Sir Walter	245	——— Felton	*ibid.*
——— John, Bifhop of Hereford	247	——— Felton-Lionel	*ibid.*
		——— John, Lord	357
——— Thomas	249	——— Auguftus-John	*ibid.*
——— Sir Robert	250	——— Frederic	358
——— Col. Edward	253	Hewet, Sir Thomas	116
——— Edward, of Eywood	262	——— George, Vifcount	*ibid.*
——— Robert	263	Heydon, Robert	183
——— Rev. John	273	Heyton, Thomas	213
——— William	*ibid.*	Hickes, Sir William	33
——— Thomas, Alderman	*ibid.*	Hicks, Sir William	327
Harman, John	344	Hildeyard, Sir Robert	33
Harper, Thomas	279	Hill, Thomas	221
Harrington, Sir James	106	Hilton, William, Baron	108
——— Sir John	158	Hoblyn, Thomas	194
Harrifon, Sir Thomas	33	Hodfeng, Ralph de	44
——— William	326	Holcombe, Simon	151
Hartopp, Sir William	186	HOLDERNESSE (D'ARCY) EARL	1
Harvelt, Heer	127		
Haftings, Robert de	41	——— Conyers,	
Haward, William	350		34
Henhull, Richard de	217	——— Robert,	
Herbert, Charles, Lord	169		35, 36
Hern, Frederic	178	Holford, Chriftopher	223
Heron, William	18	——— Sir John	*ibid.*
Hervey, Anthony	183	Holland, Henry, Earl of	329
——— Robert Fitz	343	Holt, Sir Lifter	312
——— Bifhop of Bangor	*ibid.*	Hooton, Robert	285

INDEX.

Hooton, Sir Richard	288	Keppel, Barnard Van Pallant, Lord of	130
Hopwood, Roger	246	—— Rabo, Van	ibid.
Horde, Thomas	291	—— Admiral Auguftus	135
Howard, Lord Thomas	29	—— General William	137
—— Thomas	169	—— Frederic, Bifhop of Exeter	ibid.
Howard, James	174		
—— George	298		
Howe, John	337	Keyt, Sir William	145, 151
—— Scroop, Vifcount	ibid.	Kildare, Thomas, Earl of	18
Hunt, Rowland	329	Killigrew, Sir William	125
Huntingdon, Theophilus, Earl of	282	—— John	190, 193
		Kilmurry, Robert, Vifcount	211
Huffey, Sir Edward	380	—— Thomas,	282
Hutchins, Samuel	261	Kinderton, Peter Venables, Earl of	223
Hutton, Matthew	33		
Hyde, Sir John	155	Kingfley, Sir Richard de	212
—— of Hindon, Thomas, Lord	178	Kinnoul, George, Earl of	272
		Kitfon, Sir Thomas	325
		Knevet, Sir Henry	326
J.		Knightley, Sir Edmund	71
Jefferies, John, Lord	410	—— Sir Richard	109
Jeffreys, ——	140	Knollys, Henry	327
Jermyn, Alexander	116	Kurtwick, ——	115
—— Sir Robert	351		
Jersey (Villiers) Earl of	154	**L.**	
		Lacon, Sir Richard	244
—— Edward	176	Lacy, Gilbert de	242
—— William	177, 178	Lambton, John	107
Inchiquin, William Earl of	176	Langden, Robert	191
Ingram, Sir Arthur	334	Langley, Sir William	115
Jocelyn, Thomas	155	Langton, Sir John	23
Johnfon, Thomas	96	Lanfdown, George Grenville, Lord	177
—— Nicholas	194		
—— Sir Henry	298	Lafcelles, Duncan de	44
—— Robert	379	Latimer, Edward Ofborn, Lord	335
—— Sir Brian	ibid.		
Johnfton, Secretary	187	Lea, Thomas	286
Jonas, Sir Henry	119	Lee, Sir Henry	325
Irby, Sir Anthony	327	Leeds, Thomas, Duke of	208
—— Sir Edward	329	—— Peregrine, ——	271
		Lega, Hugh de la	300
K.		—— William de la	ibid.
Kaye, Sir Arthur	313	Legard, Sir John	34
Keckwith, George	193	Legge, Thomas	300
Kellaway, William	180	—— John	301, 303
Ken, Chriftopher	186	—— Dr. Thomas	301
Kenn, Chriftopher	216	—— Simon	ibid.
Keppel, Arnold-jooft, Van	130	—— Robert	301, 303

Legge,

INDEX.

Legge, William 301, 304
—— Edward 302, 313
—— Richard 302
—— Heneage, Baron of the Exchequer 313
—— Henry Bilson ibid.
Leigh, Charles 120
Lempster, William, Lord 187
Le Pell, Nicholas 357
Levinge, Sir Richard 282
Lewis, Thomas 97
Lewisham, George, Viscount 313
Lexington, Robert, Lord 34
Leyes, Robert 344
Ligonier, Sir John 229
Limbury, Sir Philip 9
Lisle, Robert, Baron 39
Litchfield, Henry Lee, Earl of 174
Liulph 99
Lloyd, Humphry 109
—— Dr Robert Lumley ibid.
Lovain, Godfrey de 41
—— John de, Baron of Estains ibid.
Lovett, Thomas 278
Ludlow, George 71
—— Peter, Earl of 122
Lumley, Sir William de 100
—— Sir Roger de 101
—— Sir Robert de ibid.
—— Sir Marmaduke ibid.
—— Robert 102
—— Sir Ralph de ibid.
—— Marmaduke, Bishop of Carlisle 104
—— Thomas de ibid.
—— Sir John ibid.
—— Thomas, Lord 105
—— Bertram 106
—— George, Lord ibid.
—— Thomas 107
—— Richard, Lord 108
—— John, —— 108, 110
—— George 109
—— Lloyd, Dr. Robert 114
—— Anthony 115
—— Roger ibid.

Lumley, Richard, Viscount ibid.
—— Henry, the General 116
—— Henry, Viscount 120
—— Charles ibid.
—— John ibid.
—— James ibid.
—— George-Augustus, Viscount 122
Lymington, John Wallop, Viscount 338
Lyngen, Sir Ralph 245

M.

Macclesfield, Gerrards, Earls of 41
Macklew, Simon 247
Mainwaring, Sir Randle 219
—— Charles 223
Malpas, Hugh, Baron of 210
—— Robert, —— ibid.
—— Sir William de 211
—— George, Viscount 229
Mansel, Bussy 178, 356
—— Thomas, Lord 356
Mapletoft, Rev. Mr. 194
Markham, Geffery 109
Marlborough, John, Duke of 208
Marwood, Sir Henry 34
Master, Sir Streynsham 151
Maur, Lawrence de St. 101
May, Sir Humphry 354
Melton, Sir John 28
Menill, Nicholas, Lord 20
Meredith, Sir Thomas 193
—— Amos 223, 282
—— Sir William ibid.
Mering, William 156
Merrick, Owen 223
Metcalfe, Thomas 33
Meltham, Sir Thomas 28
Middleton, Thomas 223, 272
—— Sir Thomas 225
—— Sir Hugh 272
Milbank, Sir Ralph 35
Milbourne, Charles 273
Milward, Thomas 31
Minors, Roger 249
Minshul,

INDEX.

Minshul, John 223
Muchel, William 252
Molineux, Francis 33
―――― Robert 154
Molyns, James 48
Monington, Richard 246
Monson, Sir William 187
Montacute, Anthony Brown, Viscount 349
Montfort, Christopher 287
―――― Launcelot ibid.
Montjoy, William Blount, Lord 71
Mordaunt, Lewis, Lord 31
More, Francis 116
Morewic, Hugh de 101
Morewood, Gilbert 334
Morgan, John 273
―――― Sir William ibid.
Morleux, Sir William 53
Morley, Nicholas 346
Mortimer, Roger 240
―――― Edward, Lord of Wigmore ibid.
Mountcassel, John Maccarty, Viscount 290
Mulgrave, Peter de Mauley, Baron of 20
―――― Eliz. Countess of 337
Musgrave, Philip 312

N.

Nanfan, Giles 249
Napier, Sir Theophilus 35
Nernuytt, Sir John de 345
Nevil, Hugh de 39
―――― Edward 72
―――― Sir Henry ibid.
―――― of Raby, John, Lord 103
―――― Sir Thomas 350
Newcastle, Thomas Holles Pelham, Duke of 208
―――― John Holles, Duke of 272
Newmarch, Sir Adam de 285
Newport, Sir Francis 252
Newton, Sir Peter 219
―――― Sir John 327
―――― Sir ―――― 376

Nigel, Robert Fitz, Baron of Halton 211
Norreys of Rycot, Henry, Lord 184
North Wales, Rygwallon, ap Convyn, Prince of 40
Northumberland, Aldred, Earl of 99
―――― George, Duke of 174
Norton, Sir Daniel 303

O.

Ogle, Ralph, Lord 108
Okeover, Humphry 208
Opdam, Van Wassenar, Lord of 130
Orange, Henry, Prince of 124
―――― William III. ―――― ibid.
Orkney, George Hamilton, Earl of 122, 176
Ormond, James Butler, Earl of 18
Othoere and Other 38
OXFORD and MORTIMER (HARLEY) EARL of 231
―――― Robert 268
―――― Edward 272, 273, 274
Oxford, John, Earl of 86

P.

Packington, Sir John 143
Paget, Lewis 315
―――― William ibid.
―――― William, Lord 315, 327, 328, 329
―――― Henry, Lord 325
―――― Thomas, Lord 326
―――― Thomas 329
Packenham, Simon 155
Parker, John 188
Paston, William 345
Pauncefoot, Thomas 75
Paulett. See Poulett.
―――― William 179, 338
―――― Sir John 179
―――― John 180
―――― George 379
Pawlet, Sir George 75

Pedwardine,

INDEX

Pedwardine, Sir Roger de 9
Pembroke, Philip, Earl of 187
Pembrugge, ———— 252
Pendaws, Sir William 194
Perrers, Alice 50
Peshale, Robert de 100
———— Sir Hammond de 244
Phillips, Sir Erasmus 31
Phipps, Constantine 358
Pierrepont, Francis 331
Pigot, Thomas 186
Pitt, Thomas 223
Plantagenet, Elizabeth 107
PLYMOUTH (WINDSOR) EARL of 38
———————— Thomas 94
———————— Other 97
———————— Other-Lewis ibid.
Poley, John 350
Pollard, Sir Lewis 181
Pollington, William 285
Pomfret, Thomas, Earl of 410
Poole, Sir Geffery 74
—— Mary 309
Pope, Henry 350
Popham, Alexander 187, 261
Portland, William Bentinck, Earl of 176
————————————— Duke of 273
POULETT (POULETT) EARL 179
——————— John, —— 187, 188
——————— Vere, —— 188
——————— Sir Thomas 179
——————— Sir William ibid.
——————— Sir Amias 179, 182
——————— Sir Hugh 180
——————— George 183
——————— Sir Anthony ibid.
——————— John, Lord 184, 186, 187
Poultney, Sir Thomas 278
Powtrell, Walter ibid.
Prestland, Richard 219
Preston, Henry 325
Prestrop, Ralph 232
Prideaux, Sir Peter 184
——————— Thomas 190

Puissar, Marquis of 176
Pulisdon, Sir Roger 232
Pulteney, Michael 31
Purbeck, John Villiers, Viscount 159

R.

Rayner, Sir William 159
Redman, Sir Matthew 104
———— Sir Richard 286
Redyshe, Alexander 31
Reresby, Sir Thomas 286
Reynolds, James 351
Rhodes, Sir Godfrey 290
Richmond, Charles Lenox, Duke of 134
———— James Stuart, Duke of 169
Ridel, ———— 275
Ridge, Thomas 356
Rinfey, John 190
Rivers, Richard Savage, Earl 127
———— Thomas Darcy, Earl 351
Rivet, Sir Thomas 325
Robinson, Sir Metcalf 33
ROCHFORD (ZULEISTEIN) EARL of 124
————————————— William-Henry 125, 127, 128
————————————— Frederic 127
Rockingham, Edward Watson, Lord 290
Rogers, ———— 140
Rokeby, Sir ———— 31
———— Sir Thomas 34
Rolle, Dennis 186
Roscommon, James Dillon, Earl of 288
Rosseter, John 176
Rotheram, John 35
Rotherfield, Peter de 285
Rouse, Sir Edward 247
Ruish, Sir Francis 288
Russel, Sir Thomas 216
Rutland, Francis, Earl of 169
Ruytenburgh, Heer Van 227
St. John,

INDEX.

S.

St. John, Sir John	173
——— Oliver	187
——— Sir Walter de	223
St. Pierre, Urian de	212
Salisbury, James Cecil, Earl of	335
Saltonshall, Sir Richard	252
Sambourne, William	73
Sanders, William	159
Sandford, ———	329
Sands, Sir John	27
——— William, Lord	ibid.
——— Thomas, Lord	75
Sandwich, Edward Montague, Earl of	398
Sansbury, Thomas de	211
Savage, Thomas	152
Savage de Nassau, Richard	127
Savile, John	287, 341
Saville, Henry	29
——— Sir John	ibid.
——— Sir William	95, 143
——— Sir George	122
——— Sir Gervase	288
——— Thomas	291
Scarborough (Lumley) Earl of	99
——————— Richard, ———	117, 120
——————— Thomas, ———	121
——————— Richard, ———	122
Schonbergh Meinhardt, Duke of	36
Scot, William	75
——— Sir Thomas	397
Scroop, of Upsal, John, Lord	23
——————— Ralph, Lord	72
Scroop, of Bolton, Henry, Lord	109
Scrope, William	33
——— Richard	75
Scudamore, James	335
Seager, Sir William, Garter	40
Sebright, Edward	142
Sewall	275

Shaftsbury, Anthony, Earl of	143
Sheffield, Sir Robert	278
Shelley, Henry	116
Shirley, James	275
——— Sir Ralph	276, 277
——— Sir Thomas	276, 279
——— Francis	278
——— John	ibid.
——— Sir George	ibid.
——— Sir Henry	279
——— Sir Charles	ibid.
——— Sir Robert	280
——— Sir Seymore	ibid.
——— Robert, Lord Ferrers, of Chartley	ibid.
——— Sewallis	281
Shuckburgh, John	116
Sidenham, John	180, 184
Sidney, Thomas	196
Skinner, Edward	291
Slaughter, John	292
Smith, William	158
——— Thomas	186
——— John	336
——— Sir Robert	357
Smithson, Hugh	298
——— Sir Hugh	ibid.
Somerset, William Seymour, Duke of	34
———— Charles ———————	342
Sothill, John	156
South-Wales, Rhese and Griffith, Princes of	40
Southampton, Thomas Wriothesley, Earl of	34
Spencer, Edward	127
——— Hon. John	410
——— John, Earl	ibid.
Spragge, Sir Edward	302
Spurstow, William de	216
Stafford, Robert de	241
Stanhope, John, Lord	224
Stanley, Thomas	219
——— Sir Richard	252
Stanning, Sir Nicholas	398
Stapleton, Sir Brian	28
——— Sir Henry	34
——— Sir Nicholas	47
Stephens,

INDEX.

Stephens, Nathaniel 261
Stillington, John 33
Stote, Sir Richard 96
STRAFFORD (WENTWORTH)
EARL of 285
—————— Thomas 288, 292
—————— William 290, 299
Strangeways, Sir James 22
Streeche, Sir John 48
Suffolk, James Howard, Earl of 174
—————— Theophilus Howard, Earl of 175
Suffex, Thomas Saville, Earl of 160
—————— Thomas Lennard, —— 174
Sufuvalo 275
Swinford, Sir Thomas 22
Sydenham, Sir John 187, 191

T.

Talboys, —————— 301
Talmaſh, Sir Lionel 223
TANKERVILLE (BENNET) EARL of 334
—————————— Charles 337, 338
Taviſtock, Francis, Marquis of 137
Taylor, Robert 334
Tempeſt, Sir Richard 27
Teys, Richard de 285
Thakel, Gilbert ibid.
Thanet, John, Earl of 147
Thimelby, —————— 116
Thirkeld, Sir William 105
Thomas, John 133
—————— James 348
Thompſon, Sir William 116
Thornton, Roger 107
Thweng, Marmaduke de 101
Thynne, Henry-Frederic 143
—————— Thomas 177
Tirwhit, Adam 103
Tiſdale, Thomas 335
Tregour, Sir John de 190
Trenchard, Sir George 351
Treworgan, Roger 190
Trollop, Thomas 107

VOL. IV.

Tryon, Charles 281
Turvey, Thomas 96
Tweddale, John Hay, Marquis of 410
Tylliott, William 106
Tynneſlow, Henry de 285
Tyrrel, Thomas 352
Tyrwhitt, Sir Robert 31

V.

Vavaſour, Sir Peter 71
Vaughan, Sir Thomas 246
Vaux, of Harrowden, Thomas Lord 30
Venables, Peter, Baron of Kinderton 280, 281
Vere, Sir George 71
—— of Tilbury, Sir Horatio, Lord 187
Verney, Sir Robert 191
—————— John 263
Vernon, George Venables 178
—————— Sir Thomas 223
—————— George 280
—————— James 298
Veſey, Henry 350
Vilar Benedict le 155
Villiers, Pagan de 154
—————— Gilbert de ibid.
—————— William ibid.
—————— Sir Nicholas 155
—————— Sir Francis de ibid.
—————— Sir John de 155, 157
—————— John 156
—————— George 158
—————— Sir Edward 159, 173
—————— John, Lord Villiers, of Stoke 159
—————— Sir William 160
—————— Lord Francis 169
—————— Edward 175
—————— Henry 176
—————— Frederic William, Viſcount 179
—————— George-Buſſy, Viſcount ibid.
Vincent, Sir Francis 183
Ulſter, Richard Burgh, Earl of 18

F f UXBRIDGE,

INDEX.

UXBRIDGE (PAGET) EARL of 315
—— Henry 331
—— Thomas-Catesby 332
—— Henry ibid.
Vylers, Alexander de 155

W.

Waldeshoff, Walter de 276
Waldgrave, Sir William 325
Waller, Sir William 328
Walpole, Sir Edward 137
—— Sir Robert 229
Walsh, Thomas 278
Warcop, Peter de 3
Warncomb, Richard 248
Warren, Edward 228
—— Sir George ibid.
Warton, Michael 186
Warwick, Philip 34
—— Thomas Beauchamp, Earl of 300
Washington, Sir William 159, 308
—— Laurence 281
Waterhouse, Sir Edward 158
Watton, Agnes de 275
Weeks, Christopher 336
Wenman, Philip, Viscount 174
Wentworth, Thomas 28, 287
—— William 285, 291, 292
—— Richard de, Bishop of London 285
—— William de ibid.
—— Sir Thomas 286
—— Golden Thomas ibid.
—— Michael ibid.
—— Sir William 288, 291
—— Sir George 288
—— Peter 291
—— Paul 292
—— Allan ibid.
West, William 29, 31
Westby, Wardel George 35
Westmoreland, Francis Fane, Earl of 34
Weverham, Hugh de 211
Weyland, Thomas de 344

Weymouth, Viscount 410
Whitley, Thomas 97
—— Percival 286
Wickham, William 346
Widrington, Sir Thomas 95
Wigmore, Richard 336
Wilbraham, Thomas 221
—— Sir Richard ibid.
Willey, Sir Andrew de 235
Williams, William 109
Willoughby, Sir Hugh 277
—— Thomas 325
Wilmer, William 338
Wilmot, William 186
Wilson, Sir Thomas 350
Wiltshire, Charles, Earl of 148
—— Sir John 348
Winchelais, Lucia de 369
Windsor, William 42
—— Hugh de ibid.
—— Walter de 44
—— William de 44, 45
—— Richard de 46, 48
—— James de 48
—— Sir William de ibid.
—— Alice de 54
—— Sir Miles ibid.
—— Brian de 55
—— Thomas 59, 71
—— Sir Andrews, of Bradenham 62
—— Edmund 71
—— William, Lord 72
—— Edward, —— 80
—— Miles ibid.
—— Frederic, Lord 87
—— Henry, —— 89
—— Thomas, —— 91
—— Thomas Hickman Lord 92
—— Thomas, Viscount Windsor 95
—— Dixey ibid.
—— Andrews 96
Wingat, John 157
Wingfield, Sir Richard 348
Winterwade, Rynold de 285
Wintworde, William ibid.
Wiseman, Sir William 116

Wloukeslow,

INDEX.

Wloukeflow, Hugh de 221
Wodehous, William 285
Wolley, Hugh 245
Woodrove, Sir Richard 286
Woombwell, Nicholas 287
Worcefter, William Somerfet, Earl of 74
——— Edward, Earl of 92
Worfley, Sir Robert 409
Wray, Sir Chriftopher 29
Wroth, Sir Henry 126
Wroughton, Thomas 279
Wyche, Sir Hugh 58
Wycombe, William Lord, Earl of Shelburne 410
Wymondham, Adam de 55
Wyrrall, James 287
Wyvill, Sir Marmaduke 33
——— Sir Chriftopher 34

Y.

Young, Edward 129

Z.

Zuleiftein, Frederic de 124
——— Maurice 126
——— Henry *ibid.*

END of VOL. IV.

Printed in Great Britain by
Amazon.co.uk, Ltd.,
Marston Gate.